The Virgin, the King, and
the Royal Slaves of El Cobre

CULTURAL SITINGS

Elazar Barkan, Editor

CULTURAL SITINGS presents focused discussions of major contemporary and historical cultural issues by prominent and promising scholars, with a special emphasis on multidisciplinary and transnational perspectives. By bridging historical and theoretical concerns, CULTURAL SITINGS develops and examines narratives that probe the spectrum of experiences that continuously reconfigure contemporary cultures. By rethinking chronology, agency, and especially the siting of historical transformation, the books in this series go beyond disciplinary boundaries and notions of what is marginal and what is central to knowledge. By juxtaposing the analytical, the historical, and the visual, the series provides a venue for the development of cultural studies and for the rewriting of the canon.

The Virgin, the King, and the Royal Slaves of El Cobre

Negotiating Freedom in Colonial Cuba, 1670–1780

María Elena Díaz

STANFORD
UNIVERSITY
PRESS

Stanford,
California

Stanford University Press
Stanford, California
© 2000 by the Board of Trustees of the
Leland Stanford Junior University

Printed in the United States of America
on acid-free, archival-quality paper.

Library of Congress Cataloging-in-Publication Data

Díaz, María Elena
    The Virgin, the king, and the royal slaves of El Cobre : negotiating
freedom in colonial Cuba, 1670–1780 / María Elena Díaz.
        p.   cm.—(Cultural sitings)
    Includes bibliographical references and index.
    ISBN 0-8047-3718-5 (cl., alk. paper) : ISBN 0-8047-4713-X (pbk.)
        1. Slavery—Cuba—El Cobre—History. 2. Caridad, Virgen de la.
    3. El Cobre (Cuba)—Social conditions. I. Title. II. Series.
    HT1079.E4 D53 2000
    306.3'62'09729165—dc21   00-032197

Designed by Eleanor Mennick.
Typeset by Robert C. Ehle in 10/13 Electra.
Original printing 2000
Last figure below indicates year of this printing:
09 08 07 06 05 04 03 02

To the cobreros

Acknowledgments

In a way "acknowledgments" constitute a memory about the production process of a project, in this case a book. As I point out frequently in this book, memory has its own designs and is strongly shaped by genre conventions. The "acknowledgments" genre is particularly formulaic and obdurate in its rhetorical ways: it inevitably reads as a bright and seamless story of helping hands and open doors. There are usually neither villains nor ambiguous characters in these narratives. The usual obstacles and frustrations that obstruct the research, writing, and publication process are resolutely silenced. Only occasionally can the alert reader detect a sour note here and there by carefully reading in between the lines—or into the silences. Without substantial contextualization, acknowledgment sections would remain opaque documents for a historian trying to study cultural and intellectual production processes and how they were recalled by contemporaries. For a long time I dreamed of breaking—or at least bending—the genre when my time came, of letting my memory flow and my mind speak freely. In the end, however, I too have submitted to its dictates. Still, I will skirt the inventory-of-names modality of the genre even at the risk of leaving out many people. Individuals who have been left out hereby join in the "collective forces of production" behind this project.

Research on Cuban topics can prove to be a test of endurance and commitment to a project. For a historian, there are not only the increasing funding problems related to traveling to archives abroad, but in the present case, I was also caught up in the middle of the Cold War. Since sagas have no place in the acknowledgments genre, let me simply thank the Tinker Foundation at the University of Texas at Austin for providing the funds to fly me to Cuba and to explore the scant possibilities of carrying out extended research there. The Fulbright-Hays Foundation funded the initial year of dissertation research in Spain (but explicitly forbade the use of its funds to do any research in Cuba). Fortunately, I was able to carry out almost all of my research in metropolitan archives in Seville and Madrid. Hopefully, the time will come when funding will not be subject to politically motivated restrictions. Subsequent research trips to the archives in Spain, to the Leví Marrero files at the Florida International University, and a later brief trip to Cuba were mostly financed with my own hard-earned savings and in two cases by contributions for airline tickets from the Academic Senate at the University of California at Santa Cruz (UCSC).

After research trips are over, the issues of time and labor for the analysis of the material and the writing come to the fore. UCSC funds and services to support faculty research were not exactly bountiful. But this institution's enlightened policy of granting junior faculty "course-relief" quarters and early (pretenure) sabbatical leaves for research and writing is unmatched elsewhere and was invaluable in the successful completion of this long manuscript. The UCSC Academic Senate provided some limited funds as well for student research assistants early on in the project. Production, however, inevitably turned into a cottage industry when I had to turn to members of my family for help in entering baptism records and village family census data into the computer. Both my mother Lilita Balsera-Díaz and my sister Marissa Díaz-Walker donated their skilled labor to the cause. I extend my gratitude to them for the long and tedious hours of work done with precision and accuracy. I thank as well those students who performed some labor in this project.

After research and writing are over, there follows the very mechanical (or perhaps artisanal) process of preparing a manuscript for publication, an extremely meticulous and time-consuming process, which usually constitutes invisible and unacknowledged labor. The Document Publishing Center at this campus helped me prepare an early version of the manuscript to submit for reviews. Unfortunately such aid was not forthcoming in the manuscript's final preparation for Stanford University Press, which resulted in my working many long hours and weeks while juggling many other responsibilities. When my eyes were already too tired, nearly blind to the page, Patricia Sanders at the Merrill Faculty Services came to my aid and did accurate and valuable proofreading work. The new Humanities Research Institute at this campus provided some funds for the preparation of the book's index. I thank the institute for the rare promptness and efficiency with which it processed the small grant. Overall, I have discovered that the actual material production of a book—the publication process itself—is so laborious and cumbersome that I will never again in my life read a book in the same (mystified) way.

Other people have contributed to the production of this book in more intangible ways. There are, of course, the innumerable intellectual debts accumulated through the years. It is always difficult to decide where and when the time count begins, because projects often constitute provisional syntheses of lifetime influences. I will highlight some of the most "recent" and enduring ones. My graduate advisor Richard Graham opened the field of slavery to me and through his notorious seminars introduced me to a vast range of ways of approaching history. His encouragement and support throughout my graduate school days (right up to the day of my defense) are deeply appreciated. A mentor, I guess, always remains a mentor beyond the event of graduation. I am indebted to him for his professional advice in the last stages of copyediting and publication of "the book," and thank him for resuming his advising role when very much needed. My historical demography course with Myron Gutman opened up another side of history to me and taught me the basics of village census records and work in the computer age (depending, of course, on availability of resources). For many years now conversations with Ana María Alonso about history and anthropology, as well as of Latin American and Cuban studies, have been among the most intellectually stimulating in my career. She read at least two versions of the whole manuscript. Her intellectual feedback, and her interventions, down to the editorial level, have left their direct imprint upon this book. Pablo Vila opened the door to the literature on social identity and had the imagination to see the promise of my first written pages. Douglas Foley read an early version of the manuscript with an ethnographer's eye and provided helpful comments. I cannot write stories as well as he does, but I get by. More important were the various and unending conversations about anthropology, texts, popular culture, movies, the ways of academia—and the humor with which these exchanges took place. My sister Viviana Díaz-Balsera refused to read anything (she had heard enough), but conversations ad nauseam with her about literary criticism and textual analysis constituted an important early (and ongoing) form of training exercise for a historian. They were also a good arena for showdowns between the academic disciplines we embodied and for the settling of sisterly matters.

My interest in Cuba laid dormant for many years and then was triggered with a force in 1980. It happened during my return trip as an adult after twenty years of absence from a mythical country I had left as a small child. Thereafter the imagined ties of community were gradually rewoven in absentia. Ultimately the desire to take a more active part in that island's history materialized in the gesture of writing a slice of its history from afar. I discovered the legendary village of El Cobre in the Archive of the Indies in

Seville during the late 1980s. The village first came to life through the voices and notations of seventeenth- and eighteenth-century people. I did not actually "see" the place I had been conjuring in writing until a short visit in 1996. To be sure, a historian can never "see" or visit the place she writes about for it lies buried in the past, so let's just say that I stepped into present-day El Cobre in that year. Village life and its more recent history came alive during that visit through my cicerone and friend Julio Corbea. We compared notes about the village's history, about mining, the Virgin of Charity's and related cults, and other matters. We visited the old mining shafts, the sites where earlier sanctuaries of the Virgin as well as the former parish church stood, and the river that crossed the village (today a mere rivulet). And we corroborated whether old names of sites on an eighteenth-century map were still current. Julio also introduced me to villagers from all walks of life who answered some of my questions and talked to me about their memories. Julio put at my disposition other writings on El Cobre and the Virgin as well as his own pieces all of which have been cited in this work. Caridad opened the doors of her house in El Cobre without knowing me. I thank her for her hospitality. In Santiago de Cuba, Raul and José (I cannot remember their surnames) took me to the September 8 annual festivities honoring the Virgin of El Cobre and helped me take photos for this book during that event. We followed the custom of making an all-night pilgrimage from the city of Santiago de Cuba to El Cobre in the vespers of the celebration. It was a long night of peripatetic storytelling about past and present in that region of Cuba. Casa del Caribe, a vibrant research center in Santiago de Cuba, opened its doors to me during my visit. Olga Portuondo and I shared uncanny moments talking about seventeenth- and eighteenth-century people in El Cobre that we both had met through the same or similar documents. She gracefully facilitated me some documents as well. Even though we do not see eye to eye on some matters, there was a special pleasure in being able to talk casually with someone about the past as if it were a shared present. Trini and her husband took me to El Morro in Santiago de Cuba and again to the Sanctuary in El Cobre. They also put me up in their house in Santiago de Cuba and made me feel at home.

Elsewhere in the world people connected to Cuba in more remote ways also participated in the production of this book. Nora Muntañola put me in touch with José Vega, a Cuban living in San Francisco. José let me use some of his own photographs and memorabilia of Our Lady of Charity and her sanctuary in Cuba. Meanwhile Nora discovered in her parents' house in Barcelona an early-nineteenth-century print of the Virgin of Charity with a fitting family story behind it. After her marriage to a Catalan man around the turn of the century, Nora's Cuban grandmother came to settle in Barcelona. This old print (with its own personal and social meanings behind it) was among the valued possessions the young bride brought into the Old World from her homeland in the Caribbean. She died during childbirth, and her young son José rescued the print of the Virgin of Charity, which to him emblematized the memory of his lost Cuban mother. More than ninety years later it hangs from a wall in a privileged place of the family house. I thank José (Pepe) Muntañola and his daughter Nora for the photograph of this family print. The personal history behind it enhances the larger social and cultural history narrated in this book.

Other debts include people who read parts of the manuscript at some point. In my women's reading group my colleagues Gail Herstatter and Alice Yang Murray read and commented upon it despite the distance of their own periods and regions of scholarly interest. Cindy Polecritti came closer to the topic at hand with her study of popular religion in medieval Europe and Renaissance Italy. We have shared many conversations about shrines, virgins, and saints. Lynn Westercamp also came near with her focus on gender and religion in colonial (North) America. Lynn deserves a special mention for having read the whole manuscript, I believe, more than once. Her ongoing support and interest in my work are truly appreciated. Another special thanks goes as well to Beth Haas, a historian of the Southwest, who was also part of the women's reading group. Her timely advice and encouragement during a receding tide is not forgotten. My colleague Jonathan Beecher also took upon himself the task of reading this manuscript. I thank him for the effort and for his support. Writing a book in a second language is no easy task, and finding a good editor who can correct and polish a text without changing an author's meaning and style is an even more difficult task. David Sweet, another colleague, did fine editing work in a couple of chapters, as did Ana María Alonso. Other readers and editors also chipped in here and there. Ultimately, however, none was able to obliterate the "foreign accent" and Spanish inflections in my text. Perhaps that makes it all the more personal. On another front, Herbert Klein read parts of a draft of Chapter 1 and promptly answered some questions about how to better count people. John Thornton oriented me through some place names in the Congo region. I also wish to thank my anonymous readers for their comments and support. I will keep their identities secret here, even though some have more or less openly identified themselves when I bumped into them at conferences here and there. Last but not least, I thank warmly my editor at Stanford University Press, Muriel Bell, for her encouraging words and her strong support of the manuscript.

Finally, there have been many friends who have bore with me the pangs involved in the laborious process of giving birth to a book. They all know who they are. I thank them for their encouragement or, at the very least, for their forbearance. A special heartfelt thanks goes to Irene Pettit for her wisdom and guidance in helping me face the tasks at hand. Several generations of students have graduated hearing much about a book on royal slaves and a Virgin in Cuba, but without seeing the final product of their professor's travails. I hope they continue to be avid readers of history and bump into this book somewhere on the shelves of a library or bookstore. They need not send back a "response paper" of the reading, however. Romantic partners were not able to seduce me away from the hold of "the book," nor did I manage to enchant them with my storytelling gifts. They came and went while the book remained in the making. My cousins, uncles, and aunts have forever been hearing about a book I was said to be writing. My mother, who initially went out of her way for the cause by diligently pounding census data into the computer, now cannot bear to hear about the book any more. My sister Vivian understands better for she is already into her second book. My sister Marissa might someday try a first one. My maternal grandmother Justina Pérez, who was a lucid and funny oral historian as well as my main link to the (family's) transnational past, quietly slipped away without getting to see it. My father, Vicente Díaz Pendás, did not get to see where his sensible eldest daughter's abstruse ways would lead her. And my dear friend Segundo Portilla (mi Second) also left too soon. For those who are still around and willing to read, this is the story. . . .

M. E. D.
Cafe Roma, Berkeley
November 1999

Contents

Contents

Illustrations

Illustrations

The Virgin, the King, and
the Royal Slaves of El Cobre

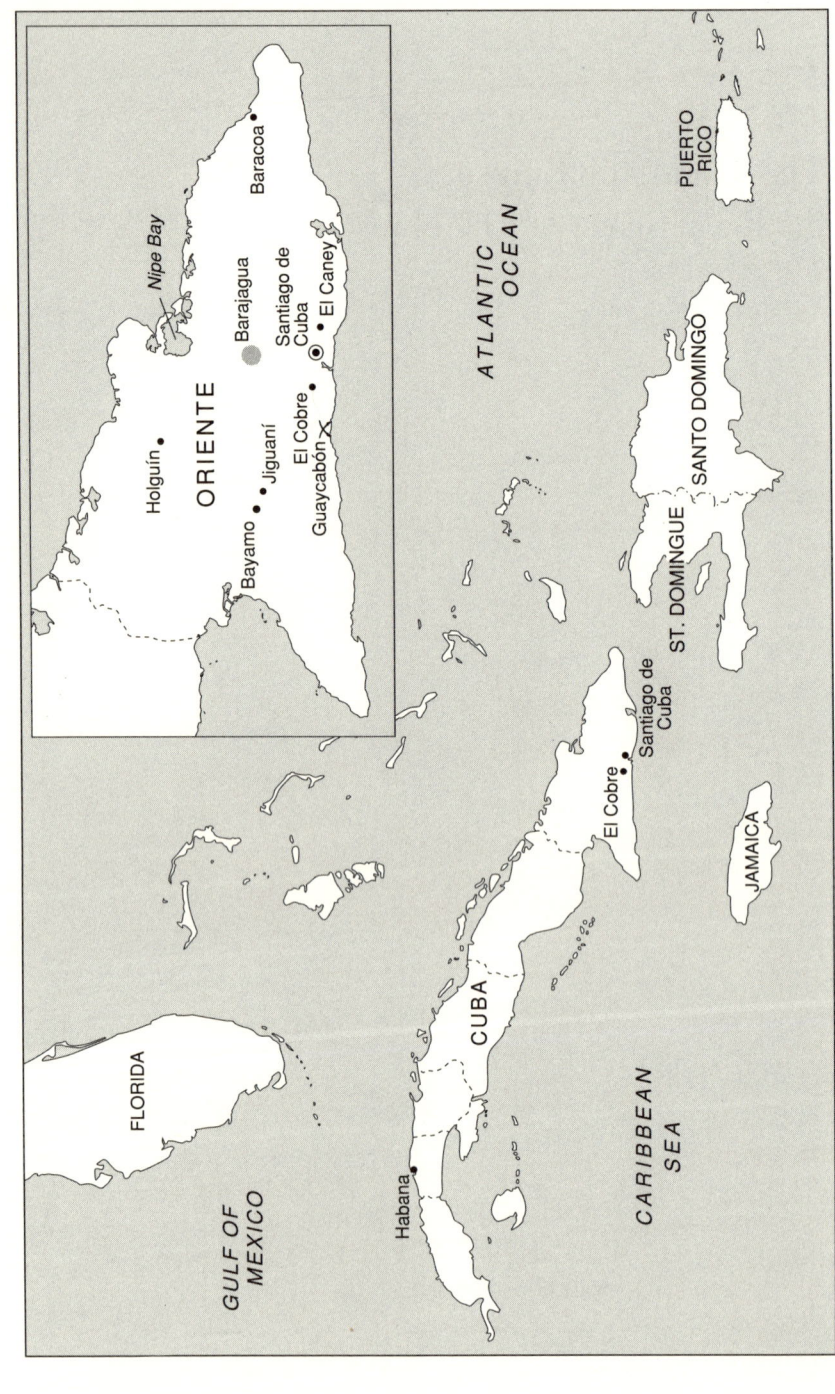

ATLANTIC OCEAN

PUERTO RICO

SANTO DOMINGO

ST. DOMINGUE

Santiago de Cuba

El Cobre

JAMAICA

CUBA

Habana

GULF OF MEXICO

FLORIDA

CARIBBEAN SEA

ORIENTE

Baracoa

Nipe Bay

Barajagua

Santiago de Cuba

El Caney

Holguín

Jiguaní

El Cobre

Bayamo

Guaycabón

Preamble: The Village of El Cobre

El Cobre is a small, deceptively plain village of legendary character for the Cuban people. Black or white, resident or exile, religious or secular, Cubans identify it as the abode of Our Lady of Charity, patroness of the Cuban nation and, for many, a Cuban version of the Yoruban deity Oshun. The story of la Virgen de la Caridad del Cobre is often linked in the island's social imaginary to ideas of the nation, creolization, syncretism, and all sorts of miraculous—and historical—interventions. Oral legend and popular visual iconography have it that the Virgin appeared to three fishermen in the Bay of Nipe: a black or mulatto, an Indian, and a white. These fishermen represent the trinity of races constituting the Cuban nation (excluding the usually excluded Chinese). Throughout the four centuries of the shrine's existence, various sectors of the population have repeatedly invoked, contested, and reinvented this Marian tradition. Many forms of community and social identity, both religious and secular, as well as multiple—and at times conflicting—political agendas have been, and still are, formulated through this powerful story of the past.

El Cobre today is a tranquil copper-mining village with some 17,000 inhabitants living in its urban and rural jurisdiction.[1] The village lies in the mountains of the Sierra del Cobre in the legendary Oriente province, the eastern region of the island, some ten miles from its capital city of Santiago de Cuba (see Map 1). Although oral history in the eighteenth century placed El Cobre's origins in pre-Columbian times, Spanish written sources place the foundation of this mining village in the early sixteenth century, thereby making it one of the oldest colonial settlements on the island. The legendary relation of this place to the miraculous Marian effigy only goes back to the seventeenth century, however.

Facing page : MAP 1. Cuba's Oriente and its Caribbean frontier.

Many people are aware that the basilica towering over the village is a twentieth-century construction now relocated from the original site. But the effigy of Our Lady of Charity that it houses is said to be the very same miraculous Marian icon once recovered from the Bay of Nipe (see Figure 1). Thus, the "authentic" effigy in the sanctuary is literally and metaphorically an image from the past. Other tokens of former—and recent—times hang from some of the walls in the sanctuary's "chamber of miracles." Bunches of tiny silver, gold, and copper body parts, known as ex-votos, as well as crutches, and even insignia of soldiers who fought in the Cuban Revolution and later in Angola, stand today as testimonies of the healing stories, miracles, and desires of thousands of pilgrims throughout the centuries. They are meant to display the fame and power of the effigy across time.

Infrequently visited for many years after the Cuban Revolution, the Marian sanctuary in El Cobre has recently recovered some of its previous popularity. On September 8, 1996, during the annual feast day of the Virgin, unprecedented thousands of people made their way up the hill and the long stairs leading to the sanctuary as pilgrims had done for centuries (see Figure 2). Whether as locals or as *orientales*, as nationalists, as Catholics, as Afro-Cuban religion practitioners, as traditionalists, as supporters, opponents, or would-be reformers of the socialist regime, as tourists, as entrepreneurs, or as scholars, these visitors converged in this historical and mythical space, bringing old and new meanings to the reactivated public celebration.

More recently, on January 24, 1998, the effigy of the Virgin of Charity of El Cobre made a pilgrimage to the nearby city of Santiago de Cuba, where Pope John Paul II officially reenacted the coronation of the effigy as "patroness" and (more anachronistically) "queen" of Cuba (she had been so crowned by proxy before in the 1930s). The ceremony took place in the Plaza Maceo, near the statue of the independence mulatto hero, Antonio de la Caridad Maceo. Referring to her as the "Virgen mambisa" (the legendary name given to the revolutionary insurgents), the pope intentionally linked the Marian tradition to another sacred story of the past: to a collective memory of independence and patriotism. It was a politically symbolic gesture that skirted any reference to the colonial origins of the Marian tradition; indeed, a spectacle meant to unify—and reconcile—all Cubans as a (Christian) community over and above ideological differences—by all counts a feat that may take a veritable miracle from the Virgin/Mother of all Cubans. The presentist subtext and political agenda of the ritual presided over by the pope was also one of religious opening with an ambiguous call

FIGURE 1. The Virgin of Charity standing in her altar niche at the sanctuary of El Cobre. (Courtesy of José Vega)

FIGURE 2. The long stairs leading to the sanctuary full of visitors during the annual Marian festivity of September 1996. (Author's photograph)

for more "freedom." Thus, the Virgin was symbolically (and to many, religiously) invoked to intervene in a new historical moment. The spectacle of the Virgin's coronation in Santiago de Cuba intended ceremoniously to mark (and to foment) new relations between the church, the state, and the Cuban people; new kinds of identity and new forms of "freedom(s)" that were in the process of redefinition and negotiation. Now, just as centuries before, the multisided political, social, cultural, and religious possibilities of this mercurial Marian discourse were invoked by different sectors of society to represent other claims.

Although an important symbolic site to imagine national community throughout the twentieth century, an earlier conception of this powerful Marian tradition was linked to the consolidation of a different kind of community. The tradition of Our Lady of Charity examined in this book was related to the making and legitimation of an unusual community on the island and, more generally, in the Americas: a pueblo—and not a maroon community—of slaves and free people of color within the structures of seventeenth- and eighteenth-century colonial society. In the midst of this extraordinary racially mixed pueblo, which emerged in El Cobre after the

FIGURE 3. A view of the open copper mine quarry in El Cobre. (Author's photograph)

1670s, the cult and tradition of the Virgin of Charity grew to become a major local, regional, and, some two centuries later, national tradition in Cuba. (A second conflicting and diasporic site overseen by a clone of the Virgin of El Cobre emerged after the Cuban Revolution among the exile community in Miami.)

The past and present converge in El Cobre in other ways too. A large open quarry of copper mines provides the material referent for the name of the village: El Cobre (*cobre*, or copper) (see Figure 3). For better or worse, the history of El Cobre has also been connected with copper mining since its early days. For generations, local families have worked in these mines under the aegis of the Spanish Crown, private contractors, foreign companies, the socialist state, or as independent miners. The centuries-long cycle of rises and declines of mining production in El Cobre has constituted yet another important historical horizon for the development of social and political life in this village.

People from all over the globe—Africa, Spain, the Caribbean, China, England, the United States, and elsewhere—have converged in El Cobre at different points in its history to work in the copper-mining industry. Traces of their presence linger in fragments of the town's life and social memory. Although miners today tend to trace their family histories back to grandfathers and great-grandfathers who worked the mines in the nineteenth century, some local surnames, like Cuzata or Cruzata and Quiala, are of African origin. These names were found among the first generations of slaves brought into the Real de Minas at the turn of the seventeenth century. Long-standing local lineages like those of these two families constitute a living record of how far back mining ancestries—and history—go in this village.

More recently, a group of Cuban intellectuals—namely, historians, anthropologists, and artists—from El Cobre and from the neighboring city of Santiago de Cuba have recovered another strand of the past in the present. With the financial backing of an international agency, UNESCO's division of cultural projects, they inaugurated in July 1997 a giant sculpture commemorating the "maroon (runaway) slave" created by the Cuban artist Alberto Lescay. The monument recalls both the village's and the island's history of slavery as much as it celebrates the spirit of rebellion and freedom symbolized by the maroon figure. While the monument to Antonio Maceo in Santiago de Cuba commemorates the struggle for freedom of Cuban Independence rebels, that of the anonymous maroon slave in El Cobre memorializes another, earlier manifestation of the spirit of freedom among "people without history."

This monument may deflect some attention from the almost exclusive association in the Cuban social imaginary of El Cobre with the Virgin's sanctuary and to a lesser extent with the copper mines. Perhaps this giant sculpture will draw out other memories from the past—fresh but hidden associations between the Marian sanctuary's legendary character, copper-mining production, and rebel slaves. Other reinvented traditions that mix the past and present in unexpected ways may eventually emerge out of oral or written stories about these sites.

This brief cartography of El Cobre's landscape interweaves space and time together. It offers the reader some reference points in the present to lead her or him back into the formidable, yet little-known, history that follows. This is not a story about maroon slaves, however. Instead, it is a more complex history of another kind of enslaved people who at times made use of collective flight to further their social and political ends, but who also

---

Facing page : MAP 2. Period map of the Oriente coastline, ca. 1690s. (AGI, Mapas y Planos de Santo Domingo 103)

mobilized in many other ways to negotiate freedom (or forms of freedom) and to make a local homeland in colonial Cuba. In this narrative about the royal slaves of El Cobre, both the Virgin of Charity's tradition and copper-mining production constitute crucial aspects of the story, but so does the colonial military system represented by the garrisons and fortifications of the Santiago de Cuba region that the *cobreros* (the people of El Cobre) were forced to construct and defend in the name of an abstract and distant king. The historical cartography of our story, then, encompasses a wider space that extends beyond the local sites of the village (see Map 2).

Introduction

The Virgin, the King, and the Royal Slaves of El Cobre is not a standard story of slavery. It is a story about some peasants and miners in colonial Cuba who were slaves of the king of Spain and whose patroness was a Virgin who became legendary for her miracle-working powers. More specifically, this is a study about the social imagining and remaking of a particular form of slavery—slavery to a king—and the parallel reconstruction of a most unusual kind of community in the New World: a *pueblo,* or a village community, constituted almost exclusively by royal slaves and free people of color. This study examines primarily the relations that developed among the Virgin, the king, and the royal slaves as the latter imagined and negotiated social identity and forms of freedom in different spheres of life.

In 1670, the Spanish Crown confiscated the copper mines and slaves of Santiago del Prado (more commonly referred to as El Cobre) in eastern Cuba from its private contractor. Earlier in the century these copper mines had constituted the major enterprise of the region; and their exploitation had been fomented by the Crown who viewed them as a means to provide for the needs of its artillery. Years of neglect and failure to comply with the terms of a contract, however, had led to the Spanish Crown's belated intervention and confiscation. At that time, 271 slaves, most of them Creole, became the king's slaves, thus placing them in a category whose practical and ideological meaning would be worked out in subsequent years through practices in everyday life, litigation, and revolt. What would it mean to be slaves of the king? Would it mean having any kind of privileged status? Was slavery to the king to be imagined differently from slavery to anyone else? What kind of arrangements would it entail? How was the relation between distant master and slaves to be mediated?

Although scarcely noticed in the literature, the Spanish state owned and made use of *esclavos del rey* (king's slaves) in Spain as well as in its overseas territories.[1] In the New World, royal slaves were employed in the construction and operation of state projects, particularly when Indian labor was not readily available, but the most sustained use of the king's slaves involved the massive fortification projects of the Caribbean.[2] While these works drew on a variety of sources for their always underfunded labor requirements throughout the seventeenth and eighteenth centuries, fortresses were, to a large extent, built by royal slaves. As early as 1604, for instance, there were 163 royal slaves and 34 Spanish, French, and Dutch *forzados* (penal convicts) assigned to work in the Havana garrison of El Morro.[3] In Cuba alone, one historian found that there were about 2,000 royal slaves and convicts employed in the fortification projects of Havana during the late eighteenth century.[4]

Overall, beyond largely impressionistic references to royal slaves, nothing much is known about the organization of life and work among these bondsmen, about how these slaves were viewed by others, or about how they viewed themselves.[5] Although responses to those questions would depend on particular contextual factors and on the politics of different situations, in the case of the king's slaves of El Cobre, royal slavery came to acquire special and ambiguous ideological and practical meanings.

One of the more remarkable aspects of what royal slavery came to entail in the case of the royal slaves of El Cobre was their reconstitution into a pueblo. By 1730, El Cobre was one of only fourteen duly constituted settlements—that is, cities, towns, and villages—on the island, at least two of which, but perhaps three, were Indian corporate pueblos. By 1773, El Cobre had grown into a sizeable village of 1,320 inhabitants, of whom 64 percent were royal slaves, 2 percent personal slaves, and 34 percent free people of color, mostly manumitted descendants or relatives of royal slaves.[6] The establishment of a pueblo of royal slaves and freed persons with a corporate land grant, a limited *cabildo* (local government), and local militia companies with their own officers strikes the historian as unusual, for, legally, as "outsiders" in the body politic, slaves were not allowed to form such a polity. Even pueblos constituted largely or exclusively by freedmen and *castas* (racially mixed people) were uncommon in the Indies. Yet, more Afro-American villages formally recognized as pueblos than heretofore suspected may have existed in the Spanish colonial world, particularly in the Caribbean and circum-Caribbean region—in places such as Panama, Colombia, and Venezuela—where free people of color outnumbered slaves, or where military considerations may have modified the usual order of things. At least two other Afro-American villages in this area during the seventeenth and eighteenth centuries are known: Gracia Real de Santa Teresa de Mose in Florida, and San Lázaro de los Minas in Santo Domingo. Both, however, were pueblos of freedmen who were the direct beneficiaries of the Spanish Crown's sanctuary policies for the enemy's escaped slaves.[7] In Puerto Rico, oral history has it that the pueblo of Loíza Aldea was once a black village, perhaps a community of slaves. In other parts of the Caribbean, particularly the English Caribbean, Afro-American peasant villages became widespread only after the abolition of slavery in the nineteenth century.[8]

This kind of community is particularly significant, because, given the outsider status attached to African slaves and to a lesser extent to their descendants in the New World, a pueblo would have constituted some form of recognized corporate persona in Spanish civil society. I argue that, in the case of the king's slaves of El Cobre, life in and as a *pueblo* entailed important reformulations of the meaning of slavery that pushed its limits into the realm of freedom. Yet, constituting a pueblo would not only have implied the negotiation of some minimal political concessions, but also it may have represented one way available to people of African descent to reimagine, remap, and root their identities within the societies of the New World in a nondiasporic manner. More than Creole royal slaves, the enslaved people of El Cobre came to identify themselves alongside their fellow freedmen and -women as *cobreros* (people of El Cobre), a term still in use today to identify the locally born people of that village. The cobreros developed a sense of *patria chica* (literally, small homeland) that turned mere place of birth into local homeland. They also developed both a social memory as a community and a collective voice as a people that pushed them to speak and mobilize publicly as a whole, over and above individual status as free or slave.

In its broadest sense, *The Virgin, the King, and the Royal Slaves of El Cobre* is a story about colonization in the New World, but of Spanish colonization as it unfolded in the early modern period and, more specifically, of colonization as approached from "below." Likewise, the study also constitutes a general examination of creolization, particularly of creolization among people of African descent and within the wider structures of colonial society. Moreover, it is also a story about the articulation of a "Creole" identity and of the early shape that this ideology took during the late seventeenth and eighteenth centuries in this community of royal slaves and free people of color. Ultimately, however, this local history is about the making of royal slavery and the negotiation of customary practices associated with that status. More importantly, it is a story about the active and explicit contention of entitlements and de facto freedoms under slavery in a rural settler—and not plantation—society, however military and "frontier" the character of this settler society may have been at the time.

Imagining Social Identity

In this study I emphasize that the practical changes and the redefinitions of social identity—as royal slaves and as members of a pueblo—that emerged among the inhabitants of El Cobre during the years of Crown rule (1670–1780) took shape within the bounds of dominant colonial institutions and ideologies, and not outside their scope. Accounts of subordinate groups cannot be divorced from the wider dominant structures and strictures of society and the state of which they inevitably form a part. Indeed, the figures of the king and Virgin constitute tropes of the wider political and religious discourses or ideology from which the cobreros had to speak at the time, as well as of the institutions and practices of state and church with which they also had to contend politically. Thus, in seeking to redefine their status and identity, these royal slaves were not free to reinvent themselves as they pleased (if indeed, structuralists would claim, people are ever free to invent themselves or their freedom anywhere). Instead, the king's slaves had to reconstitute themselves along the horizon set down by Spanish law and Spanish cultural or social norms and institutions of the time—as I show here, bending, stretching, redefining, and reinterpreting them wherever possible. Close attention to these reformulations of hegemonical premises within an early modern colonial world constitutes one of the main aspects of the cultural approach of this study.[9]

Royal slavery in El Cobre became a highly ambiguous form of slavery that blended into de facto freedom in different nodes of social life. In this study I focus on how social identities were represented, acted out, or contended in a wide range of practices that include provisioning arrangements, living accommodations, litigation and its texts, economic and market activities, naming practices, religious celebrations, property holding, land claims, arms bearing, limited self-government, and the production of social memory and stories of the past. Thus, I examine here a wide array of social, cultural, political, and economic activities that provide a many-sided view of royal slavery—and freedom—in this village. The all-too-frequent exclusive focus on slavery as a form of coerced labor, or as Manuel Moreno Fraginals put it, at least after the arrival of modernity, "as a mere factor of production," seems to have preempted any justification for the study of other social and cultural aspects of the lives of enslaved people, inside or outside the plantation context, in Cuba and elsewhere in the Spanish New World.[10] Indeed, at times, it is as if the very writing of slaves and Afro-Americans into history has unwittingly reproduced the logic of slavery in the past— by representing and bonding people of African descent in the literature exclusively to their laboring context and to questions about the productivity of slavery as a system of labor.[11] However, these gaps are not only found in the more ample historiography of slavery and abolition; there are still few studies about the free population of color in colonial Latin American historiography in general, and even fewer about freedmen and -women in Cuba, where in the eastern region free people of color constituted an important sector of the population. This study straddles both the study of slaves and free people of color in this community both as distinct groups and as they lived in what I would approach as a more fluid continuum between slavery and freedom.[12]

Slavery and freedom constituted a continuum across not only social groups at different stages of formal manumission or under different customary arrangements within slave societies but also, I would add, within a particular person's life, in the different activities outside the space of forced labor through which he or she could imagine and actualize being something other than a slave. If, for instance, one takes as a starting point Orlando Patterson's general definition of slavery as "social death" and "natal alienation," or Stanley Elkins trope of slavery as a "total institution," or Moreno Fraginals's contention that slavery implied complete "deculturation," then every customary practice or established entitlement that constituted an enactment of a social or even territorial tie outside the master-slave bond may be read as a de facto recovered fragment of "human rights" and a piecemeal achievement of freedom in a person's life, even if it coexisted with major aspects of enslavement. In this sense, it may be useful to disaggregate the practices, particularly the customary practices that constituted slavery and freedom in a particular place and time without reifying or essentializing categories. Another spin on this approach is to examine not only the making and negotiation of "custom" in social life or of the meanings of categories, but also if and how some practices came to be understood as "entitlements" or even de facto rights under slavery, at least in particular times and places. It constitutes a more dynamic, processual, or even political approach to aspects of life that have been subsumed under the ample code term of the "slave community," particularly in U.S. historiography.

However exceptional the ways in which royal slavery came to be imagined, negotiated, and lived in El Cobre, I suggest that both the large and, in particular, the smaller processes of the contention of meaning and identity, and notably of freedom and slavery, described throughout this book may be taken to exemplify microdramas and events that occurred to a lesser extent throughout slave societies of the Atlantic world. Rather than enslaving people in the past and in our texts to an overdetermining category of "slavery," it may be useful to see the ways in which their lives overlapped—and to discover how they made them overlap—with those of other sectors of society, particularly other free but subordinate groups of colonial society.

And yet, the general practices of everyday life and the mobilizations of villagers examined in this study could have represented as well important ways in which freed people may have construed their identities and rights after individual manumissions. In this sense, the social history of this local village also straddles the struggles of many freedmen and -women in the colonial world.

The study unfolds in the seventeenth and eighteenth centuries in the eastern region of Cuba, in a time and place that is less historiographically privileged than the nineteenth-century Cuban sugar plantation belt.[13] In the seventeenth and eighteenth centuries this eastern area blended into a wider Caribbean region (see Map 1 in Preamble). It constituted a military frontier with islands such as Jamaica and Saint Domingue in a sea still haunted by corsairs and enemy ships. Cuba's Oriente (eastern region), however, also formed part of a shady zone where official Caribbean enemies engaged in a friendly, albeit dangerous, contraband trade. While the Oriente region lay at the periphery of other Caribbean plantation neighbors that were at the center of the global circuits of sugar, its "hinterland" character was analogous to that of other Spanish Caribbean islands, where the sparse population and small-scale economy consisting of cattle ranching, the production of some sugar, tobacco, and staple crops, alongside military considerations, all shaped the tenor of life. Yet, regardless of its frontier character, the eastern region of Cuba was also very much part of the wider Spanish colonial world. The dominant imperial culture supported by church and state, to some extent in this book emblematized by the figures of the Virgin and the king, had also penetrated these supposedly neglected edges of the New World. What most interests us here, however, is the more popular imagining of this enveloping imperial culture and the room for negotiation that some of the most marginalized sectors of the population, namely, slaves and freedmen, could find in it.

The King

I study how the royal slaves ideologically portrayed their relation to an abstract master who was also the monarch and how that image affected their social identity, their sense of entitlement, and their political practice. The popular image of a just but distant king intrinsic to the royalist political culture of the period was a symbolic figure onto which all manner of benevolent and protective policies could be projected. The figure of the king constituted an ideological "vessel" capable of holding multiple and contradictory meanings. The royal slaves of El Cobre often invoked this imagined powerful figure to legitimize their claims vis-à-vis more immediate figures of authority and to contend policies in everyday life, in the courts, and in other forms of mobilization like flight (*cimarronaje*) and revolt. The confusing, ambiguous, and conflictive character that real and imagined relations between the royal slaves and the master/state/king could often take were noted by a governor who remarked, "A lot of sagacity [is needed] in order to explain to them [the royal slaves] the difference between vassals and slaves."[14]

But the king also represented the power and authority of the Spanish state in its multifarious early modern legal and administrative aspects. Thus, I look at royal policy toward these slaves and, more specifically, at the direct relations between royal officials or the local state and the slaves under their charge. What kind of considerations informed and constrained the state's policy vis-à-vis these slaves? How did royal officials, in turn, envision royal slavery? How were relations between master/state and slaves managed and mediated?

One particularly interesting aspect of these royal slaves' relation to the state was their active engagement of the courts. Although regulated and repressed by the law and the state, the king's slaves, like other subordinate groups in the juridically obsessed Spanish polity, litigated, protested, and filed complaints to demand "good treatment," to claim land, to protest abuses, to denounce improprieties (particularly smuggling) on the part of royal officials and even of ecclesiastics, and eventually to claim freedom for the community. They sought redress at all the appeal levels of the judicial system in the Spanish Empire. They traveled to courts in the immediate regional capital of Santiago de Cuba, to Havana, to the High Court in the neighboring island of Santo Domingo, and across the Atlantic to the Supreme Council of the Indies in Madrid. The results of these practices could be moderately successful, ambiguous, or a failure, and they usually entailed great expenses for the community. But like other indefatigable litigants in the Spanish polity, the royal slaves and freedmen of El Cobre persevered in their use of the courts.

The work of Richard Kagan has shown how widespread was the practice of litigation among even subordinate groups such as the peasants in early modern Spain. Woodrow Borah, William Taylor, and Steve Stern, among others, have shown the pervasive use Native Americans made of litigation to redress injustices. However, scholars are just beginning to learn of the uses black people—free or slave—made of the colonial courts. While slaves had very limited rights that could be protected by law, Christine Hunefeldt has shown that they made good use of the courts in Lima. Rebecca Scott has found them employing the courts in pursuit of emancipation once special legislation leading to gradual abolition was enacted for late-nineteenth-century Cuba. Aline Helg has noted that later in the century and still under Spanish rule the free people of color in Cuba formed islandwide associations and litigated all the way to the Supreme Council of Madrid for racial redress.[15] Their status as slaves to the state and as members of a community may have situated the king's slaves of El Cobre particularly well to use these state mechanisms to their own ends; but they seem also to have been used, albeit to a lesser extent, by other enslaved sectors of colonial society as well as by the freemen and -women of color. Their pervasive use of the courts shows to what extent these Creole enslaved villagers understood the political culture of the colonial world within which they had to operate, regardless of their very limited rights.

Yet, I show in this study that as in the case of their dealings with the church, the practical results of this subordinate group's engagements and accommodations with colonial power were highly ambiguous. It took the freedman Gregorio Cosme Osorio, for instance, sixteen years of litigation in Madrid to finally obtain a collective grant of freedom for the community. But, as I argue in the Epilogue, this was an ambiguous freedom that in many ways did not differ from what royal slavery had entailed in former times. The imagined possibilities of freedom still had to be negotiated within the real constraints of power. Thus, the actual meaning of these enslaved villagers' acquired juridical freedom had once more to be renegotiated in practice.

The king's slaves of El Cobre also formed strategic alliances with and against other sectors of the society beyond their local village. Although their relations with church personnel, who as will be seen were central in this case, were relatively cordial, there was also tension between the two groups.

Furthermore, a state bureaucracy of officials ranging in rank from captain general to governor had to mediate the abstract relation between master/king and royal slaves. In the best of cases, this situation could provide the royal slaves with a wider array of officers to appeal to or report on, none of whom had direct property rights upon the slave. The cobreros protested private citizens' actions against them to the governor, and the governor's actions against them to the captain general, to the judges in the High Court and the Council of the Indies, as well as to church officials ranging from parish priests to bishops. This exposure to and interaction with the state through the law, its administrative hierarchy, and the judicial system speaks to the level of incorporation of these slaves into the broader political structures of colonial society. These local forms of mobilization meant relations to wider and more complex forms of power as well as the development of political maneuvering practices not far removed from those of other subordinate free vassals operating within the same polity—whether in alliance or in opposition to the state. But even if these royal slaves' political mobilization experience is extraordinary as far as the experience of slavery is concerned, their political activity was nonetheless reflective of that of other subordinate free sectors of colonial society, in Oriente and elsewhere in the Indies.[16]

The Virgin

After the Crown's confiscation of the mines, the reputation of El Cobre underwent a significant transformation from a major export mining center to a major center of religious worship in the region. What had until then been but a marginal and modest Marian cult in El Cobre grew into a major religious and cultural tradition in Cuba. By the mid-eighteenth century Bishop Don Pedro Agustín Morell de Santa Cruz wrote, "The sanctuary of El Cobre is the richest, most frequented, and most devout in the Island, and the Lady of Charity the most miraculous image of all those venerated [in Cuba]."[17] Our Lady of Charity of El Cobre would eventually become the island's patroness in the early twentieth century and continue to be an important and plurivocal symbol in the island's social imaginary to this day. How did the early transformation from local to regional shrine take place? Why the spectacular growth of the cult after the Crown's confiscation of the mines?

The Virgin of Charity (or for that matter other Virgins in the Spanish Americas) has not awakened the same academic and intellectual fervor that

Our Lady of Guadalupe has in Mexican studies. Leaving aside the earlier ecclesiastical historical accounts of Our Lady of Charity and her sanctuary in El Cobre, there has nonetheless been a modest but significant secular tradition of studies and reflections about this Marian figure in Cuba during the twentieth century. These writings all have a literary, anthropological (or folklore studies), and historical bent that focuses on the supralocal character and significance of what has become an important symbol of the Cuban nation in the twentieth century. In fact, this small corpus of writings can be said to fall within a line of early (revisionist) nationalist thinking that sought to articulate and reinvent the Cuban nation and that gave shape to important traditions with which to imagine, in Benedict Anderson's sense, that kind of wide and encompassing community.[18] This intellectual production on the Virgin constituted an elaboration of the ethnic symbolism behind the popular image of the three racially marked figures, the three "Juanes" (an Indian, a black or mulatto, and a white), to whom in oral memory the Virgin was said to have appeared in the Bay of Nipe (see Figure 4).

Perhaps the key essay in this line of writing on the Virgin was José Arrom's "La Virgen del Cobre: historia, leyenda y símbolo sincrético" (The Virgin of Charity: history, legend, and syncretic symbol) written in the 1950s. The gist of this essay and of this kind of thinking is succinctly exposed in the title and in the following words that close the piece: "In the canoe [of the three fishermen] goes portentiously the essence of our [Cuban] nationality."[19] More recently, Olga Portuondo Zúñiga in her *La Virgen de la Caridad del Cobre: símbolo de cubanía* has engaged in a similar if more historical overview of the cult from the seventeenth century to the "present" (before and outside the Revolution). Although her study is the most historically informed, her thesis also follows the previous line of Arrom and even that of an unpublished work by Fernando Ortiz.[20] In all of these accounts the Virgin becomes a unifying symbol of Creole syncretism as well as an early and imminent manifestation of the (ontological) essence of the Cuban nation. Even Antonio Benítez Rojo's postmodern reformulation of the Virgin of Charity as a symbol of the Caribbean archipelago—rather than just the Cuban nation—is based on an interpretation similar (if more ironical and poetic) to that of the above-mentioned syncretic tradition.[21]

Overall, the exegesis in these works regarding the Indian tradition is weak and contrived; that of the African one is perhaps anachronistically associated with the more recent cult of the creolized Yoruba deity Ochún in Santería, and that of the supposed ethnically white Spanish Christian tradition is not always placed in a wider context of popular Christianity and reli-

FIGURE 4. Twentieth-century image showing the Virgin of Charity and the three "Juanes" representing the "three races" said to constitute the Cuban nation. Note the Cuban flag as background to the scene. (Courtesy of the Cuban Heritage Collection, Richter Library of the University of Miami)

gion. Nonetheless, the entwining of these ethnic readings does constitute a significant development and phenomenon in the island's cultural history: a twentieth-century rendition and reformulation of the Marian story with a revisionist, more populist, and ethnically inclusive idea of the nation, one which has become widely diffused today.

In contrast, a more orthodox, conventional, and conservative formulation of the nation is depicted, for instance, in the mural behind the cloned effigy of the Virgin of Charity of El Cobre found in the hermitage of Miami. This chapel has come to represent a diasporic space of Cubans in exile, one often charged with strong political meanings regarding the present and the past.[22] In the visual text of this mural, Indians are relegated to the initial screen of colonization and blacks perhaps to the legendary figure in the mythical canoe. Allegedly, forty-four (racially invisible and mostly nineteenth-century) "major figures" in a conventional "great men approach" to Cuban historical tradition spin around the central Christian Marian/mother symbol of the nation.[23]

My study approaches the Virgin's cult from a more explicitly historicist and even local perspective. Rather than use the Virgin to reify a nation that did not yet exist, even in the protonation form that is often confused with a "Creole" consciousness or identity, I approach it in a different historical context to see what it was doing then and not so much now. I find intriguing things occurring in this early colonial rendition of the story and in the process of making or remaking tradition at that point in time. Furthermore, I also approach this widespread Marian phenomenon as an early historical instance of what may be termed the localized appropriation of a "transnational" Catholic popular culture in this corner of the Spanish Empire, by an unusual kind of community.

Going back to the title of this book, of its three figures that of the Virgin may be the most easily understood as "imagined" by the reader. She may seem imagined not only because of her more intangible historical character but also because of the miraculous and portentous powers attributed to her by devotees since the seventeenth century. From the modern scholarly position of this book's narrative, miracles are, literally speaking, imagined events even if these events were viewed as fantastically real among the cultural community of devotees.[24] I do not deal with the ontology of miracles in this study; but I do refer to the Virgin's imagined and real character in other ways.

I examine how the church and royal slaves imagined the figure of Our Lady of Charity and how she became an important site for the construction of social memory and identity in this local community. The official foundational story for this Marian cult was produced by a royal slave elder in El Cobre who claimed as a child to have been witness and protagonist in the miraculous event of the apparition. As the Virgin's fame and power grew in the region, so did the legendary character of the village that she had selected as her abode. The growth and institutionalization of this popular Marian cult, however, also went hand in hand with the material growth of the apparatus sustaining it and with an increasing penetration of the church. I study the ambiguous and mutually dependent relationship between the church and the royal slaves invested in the sustenance of the cult, and in the preservation of the community when under attack by the state or other sectors of colonial society. To what extent were the relations between church and community complicit or exploitative and in what sense? Did the purported protective relation of the Virgin vis-à-vis this local community play any role in the negotiation of identity vis-à-vis the state or other sectors of colonial society? Just what gave the cult a "popular" character in the first place, particularly given its ecclesiastical control?

African Ethnic Identities?

Despite present interest in all kinds of manifestations of ethnic expression in the past, this local history does not—cannot—deal with questions of the cobreros' ethnic identity. Issues of race are addressed here, but they are often subsumed under slavery. There is simply very little in the written historical record that would permit an in-depth interrogation of the topic. Chapter 1 traces the changes in naming practices for two or three generations of slaves in El Cobre, but this is as far as the study can go. That chapter shows how, against the general convention whereby Creole slaves usually shed the "African" second name or "surname" that indicated their Old World origin, as well as their *bozal* (African birth) status, some slaves in the Real de Minas gave their Creole children "African" names. At least two such names (Quiala and Cruzata) became surnames in the community and are still in use. Others, however, tended to disappear soon after the Crown's confiscation of the mines, as Hispanic surnames became prevalent. There is little else in this study about African elements that may have been openly, secretly, or unwittingly preserved among the cobreros. More importantly, there is no indication in the available documentation that any other African practices were intentionally used as identity markers during this population's long process of creolization across generations.

The present identification of Our Lady of Charity with the Cuban Yoruba deity Ochún in the Afro-Cuban religion of Santería and in Cuban folklore in general is a phenomenon of the mid- to late nineteenth century, and in the Oriente region even later (see Figure 5). Indeed, many of the institutionalized Afro-Cuban religious cults of the present are the relatively recent result of the massive forced migration of slaves into the island, particularly its western sugar belt, during the nineteenth century. Thus, it would be anachronistic to look for underlying religious syncretisms between the Virgin of Charity and Ochún in the cobreros' cultural repertoire during the late seventeenth and eighteenth centuries. But that does not mean people in those early centuries did not create their own eclectic and informal beliefs and practices alongside those of a popular Christianity, itself full of miracles and magic and spectacle.

Even though Creole cobreros did not recognize themselves as "Africans" (they did make a point at times to distinguish themselves from African *bozales*) they could very well—like cobreros today who identify themselves as Cubans and socialists or even as Catholics—have also cultivated a hybridized identification with certain creolized African practices. Indeed, African coded memories and practices may have been present in the cobreros' music, dance, prayers, and other details of life. It is not known, for instance, how the cobreros worshipped the Virgin musically during her annual festivities or what kind of music was played in El Cobre during those celebrations in church or in processions. There is an oblique suggestion, however, that creolized African music and dance may have taken place in the secular dances in people's houses during the Virgin's annual festivities. At any rate, given the lack of references in the written record, I have left the ethnicity issues relatively undisturbed in the silence of the past and focused instead on other equally compelling aspects of this story.

Sources and Methods

A local history about peasants, slaves, or peasant slaves, in which not only practices but also voices find their way onto the written page is often difficult, particularly when the period studied is remote from oral memory. The sources enabling such a venture in this case are both rich and limited. This study makes use of documentation in which the voices of those groups have been unusually well represented and inscribed, even though, as every historian knows, good representations and inscriptions of voices are always relative matters. The voices in these records, however, are for the most part public voices, a point to which I will return later. Thus, the sources for this study are also limited insofar as enormous chunks of life, identity, and memory are excluded from the written archive and are impossible to recover except through the reader's own imagination, or through reading in the interstices of the written shreds of the story. But that, generally speaking, has always been the curse of the historian.

FIGURE 5. A modern artistic representation of Ochún in Casa del Caribe, Santiago de Cuba. Note the bare breasts depicting the erotic symbolism of this deity in Santería, which contrasts with the virginal and maternal symbolism of her Christian counterpart. (Author's photograph)

Some royal slaves and freedmen in this community were literate and left behind a few written documents. Thus, in this sense, the record for this case is indeed special. The problems of "authenticity" that may arise regarding the representation of these voices then would be in principle no different from those usually raised or ignored in the regular documentation the historian faces with a literate subject. Is this the "true" frame of mind of the document's "author"? Is it "representative" of others in his or her group? To what extent is this voice mediated by dominant discourses and ideology? Is there "truth" in what is being represented? Is writing, as opposed to speaking, more expressive of the "true" voice of the subject? Whatever questions are raised by literate records of these slaves should, in any case, be also raised of elite literate subjects.

Another kind of documentation that claims to represent the voices of people in the past, in this case, those of these most subordinate groups are the extant texts presented in the state's judicial context. The community was quite active in the courts so that petitions, memorials, and *representaciones* (literally, some court documents were known as "representations") representing its case and claims are available as well. Although these representations are often more illustrative of public, official discourses generally mediated by scribes or professionals, these are complex texts in which "lay" voices are intertwined with official language or discourses, often in revealing ways. At the very least these texts constitute evidence of what must have passed as legitimate proposals and discourses at the time, otherwise they would not have even been raised in official contexts. Yet, they often represent as well the terms in which claims were politically and publicly framed in less official settings. Indeed, a case could be made for the intermingling of languages and voices in different sorts of contexts, that is, for the by now old-fashioned (but still insightful) "heteroglossia" posited by the Bakhtinian theoretical fad of not so long ago.[25]

Although public voices are more privileged in the record, they are often less privileged by the historian. But these public voices constitute a central and indispensable part of everyday life: they constitute the dialogue that subjects carry out with authorities and power in society and thus form an integral part of social and political life in any community. These voices constitute the public identities that people are able to construct and, as such, are no less important than other "privately" imagined identities and desires. In fact, a case could be made that even more "private" (usually considered more "authentic") voices—expressed in letters, autobiographies, or even diaries—are also public voices. People speak and write in relation to purposes and audiences.[26] I will discuss further particular "authorial" issues and the claims I make regarding the main documents along the way.

I also make use of oral depositions such as Juan Moreno's narrative of the miraculous finding of the Virgin's effigy as well as those found in a judicial investigation made in 1737 where fragments of life and voices of people in the community can be directly and obliquely found as related to authorities. Although I have used these more as texts to be ideologically interpreted than to be taken at face value for their social data, I have sometimes worked them carefully at both levels. Ultimately this historical study is strongly based on the story these enslaved villagers constructed vis-à-vis authorities.

Finally, I use other kinds of sources as well: baptismal records of royal slaves, early matrimonial records, and the more conventional and abundant village censuses have been used to research social historical aspects and practices rather than issues of voice and ideology. I have ransacked these texts to generate demographic facts, to draw information on occupation, slave ownership, family and household living arrangements, and naming practices, as well as to reconstruct life histories of individuals and families. Parts of this book are based on intensive, time-consuming "linkages" drawn through different sorts of documents. Weakest of all, by contrast, are the sources with any economic information—systematic quantitative information to be sure. Overall, suffering from the historians' typical anxiety-of-insufficient-sources syndrome, I have milked every possible source to the last drop and then insisted on analyzing and including as much detail of local life as possible in my study, particularly given the usual dearth of such local material for subordinate groups. Furthermore, rather than focus on any single or partial aspect of this community, I also decided that I would try my hand at a multisided (or "total") historical account of social, cultural, political, and to a lesser extent economic, life in this village and settler region. I also try to make use of several kinds of interdisciplinary analytical insights and approaches to the material—from social and political, anthropological/cultural, literary, and gender ones, to those related to the "construction" of identity, community, and social memory—integrating them or bringing them together from a historical perspective. Finally, this study touches on many issues and themes in the ample historiography of the Americas. Yet, this study is also lacking important comparative contexts that need yet to be researched in order to attempt more significant and ample generalizations. This work and some of the questions it poses, then, may serve as a reference point for further studies of subordinate groups in Cuban colonial society and elsewhere.

A short trip to Cuba enabled me to engage in some oral history among present-day cobreros, attend festivities and rituals, do research on some matrimonial records, and collect other sparse material. Most of the research for this work, however, was carried out at the National Historical Archive in Madrid and particularly the Archive of the Indies in Seville. This community's long and protracted litigation in Madrid from 1784–1800 led to the production of a thick dossier made up of several *legajos* (bundles of documents) kept today in the Archive of the Indies. The wide array of material patiently compiled by the cobreros and their legal representatives who were faced with urgent "life-and-death" matters constitute the core of this study. Their enemies, however, also compiled documents, which can be found in the dossier. Finally, I also use documentation that made its way to the archives more slowly throughout the long century in question. From the National Historical Archive in Madrid I have mostly taken documentation for the nineteenth century that I use scatteredly throughout the pages of this book and particularly in the Epilogue.

In structuring the material and chapters of this book I have struggled with ways in which to best integrate topical and chronological issues, deal with synchronic and diachronic perspectives, and work through the available documentation, which was not always of equal value to run through time. The main period covered by the study is the long century under royal jurisdiction that went between 1670 and 1780. A wider span of time extending further back to the turn of the seventeenth century and forward to the turn of the nineteenth, however, frame the outer limits of the study to better situate change and continuity. Chapters are primarily organized in a topical way with some internal diachronic movement, but they are also placed in a rough chronological order in the book.

Chapter 1 steps back to the early seventeenth century to trace demographic and cultural aspects in the creolization process of the mining complex's African slaves throughout most of the century. Chapters 2 and 3 examine the transformations that took place in El Cobre during the transitional decade of the 1670s right after the Crown confiscated the mines and de-privatized the mining jurisdiction. More specifically, these chapters focus on the ideological and practical redefinition of identity that occurred as the former private mining slaves became the king's slaves. Chapters 4 and 5 examine the emergence of a major center of regional worship as the local cult to the Virgin of Charity took center stage in El Cobre. While Chapter 4 focuses on the production of the foundational story of the finding of the miraculous Marian effigy and its appropriation by these royal slaves, Chapter 5 deals with the actual development of the apparatus sustaining such an important popular tradition. Although many of these chapters move forward into the eighteenth century, their main focus is on the new local order taking shape in the last part of the seventeenth century, after the mining settlement came under Crown rule.

The rest of the book—Chapters 6 to 11—is grounded for the most part in the eighteenth century. Despite "flashbacks" into the transitional decades of the late seventeenth century, these chapters deal for the most part with different aspects of local life once the community became consolidated into a pueblo of royal slaves and free people of color. For this second part of the study, I rely mostly on the abundant documentation produced during three major episodes of conflict in the eighteenth century: the first under the administration of Governor Don Joseph Canales (1708–1709); the second under Governor Don Pedro Ignacio Ximénez (1729–1738). The third conflict, the reprivatization of the mines that sent the cobreros to litigate in Madrid, is not covered in this study, except summarily in the Conclusion. Nonetheless, I also make use of the rich documentation about previous decades that the drawn-out litigation of those years generated. In any case, rather than produce a long narrative of the earlier conflicts and events, I have used the documentation produced during those episodes to reconstruct and analyze the structures of everyday life in the community, how they were understood by different parties—and how they were contested. Because the chapters are thematically organized, it is difficult to render the simultaneity of the time frame in which they are based or the events which produced the data under consideration. Nonetheless, the chapters all follow a similar internal sequence and are based on the same episodes. A chronology of events for "quick reference" is provided in Appendix 1.

There is no particular order in which the reader must get through the chapters in the second part of the book. To be sure, the way they stand organized reflects some thematic clustering among particular chapters, but no major chronological requirements dictate their ordering. Since whatever little diachrony is left in this synchronic part of the book is internal to the chapters, several reading routes are possible. Some readers, for instance, may prefer to begin with Chapter 11. Aside from its thematic examination of the royal slaves' use of the courts and the wider regional political scene in which this mobilization unfolded, this chapter provides the most linear account of the above-mentioned conflicts. As such, it may provide a broader—and neater—picture earlier on in the reading process. In contrast, reading it last may better wrap up the different thematic threads of this "total" local history.

A general chapter-by-chapter map of the second part of this book may help the reader choose the route she or he prefers to take. Chapter 6 deals with the significance of land and landholding practices in El Cobre. Chapter 7 focuses on property-holding and inheritance practices via the study of slaveholding patterns in the village. Chapter 8 examines the informal but important local copper-mining industry that the royal slaves of El Cobre took over after the Crown's confiscation of the mines. If agricultural and mining occupational practices were related to the royal slaves' autonomous self-provisioning practices—the internal "slave" economy, so to speak—Chapter 9 deals with the forced labor system to which the king's slaves were subject in the region's fortification projects. Finally, Chapters 10 and 11 are somewhat coupled as they deal with political institutions and practices at the local, regional, and imperial levels. While Chapter 10 examines the unusual institution of the *cabildo* that emerged in this community despite the slave status of its inhabitants, Chapter 11, as mentioned before, focuses on the royal slaves' extensive use of the courts at different levels as well as on the vertical political alliances that they relied on to navigate the judicial system. Overall, the only reading rule that needs be retained in this part of the book is that the Conclusion remain a conclusion and the Epilogue an epilogue.

CHAPTER 1

From African Slaves to Creole Royal Slaves

Demographic and Cultural Transformations

There are no props, nor houses, nor equipment,
tools, cattle or anything but slaves.
— Inventory of the Mines of Santiago del Prado,
May 9, 1677

The Material Context

When the Crown took over the Real de Minas of Santiago del Prado, the once prosperous mining settlement lay practically in ruins. Copper production had been in decline for decades and after the late 1640s had virtually come to a halt. Not discounting the possibility of higher copper production rates unaccounted for due to contraband trade, between 1648 and 1672 the mines of Santiago del Prado only produced a total 1,290 quintals (1 quintal = 100 pounds) of copper—a lower volume than the annual average of metal that the mines had produced at their all-time high early in the century. Indeed, the volume of copper produced during those years of drastic decline meant an annual average of copper production of no more than 52 quintals of metal—a volume that the king's slaves would later be able to surpass while surface mining on their own account.[1]

That decline led to a slowdown in the production rhythms, a breakdown in the coordination of the many ancillary economic activities that sustained large-scale production in the mining-agricultural complex, the deterioration and even destruction of the mining and processing infrastructure, the emigration of free, skilled personnel, the demilitarization of the zone, the early halt in the importation of new slaves, and the underutilization of what at that time constituted a substantial slave labor force. Already by 1665, Don

Antonio Matta y Haro, a contender for the administration of the mines, had written to the Crown, "The mines are in total ruin, the only thing that remains are the slaves."[2] Finally, this dire situation led to the Crown's belated intervention and the decision to confiscate the mining jurisdiction in 1670.

The picture left behind in the inventories of the Real de Minas drawn up in 1670 and especially in 1677, particularly when placed against that recorded in 1620, was a vivid reflection of the social transformation, and material deterioration, of the old mining order, albeit one that from the perspective of the remaining enslaved population could have looked quite bright. Back in the 1620s aside from the contractor's Big House there had been only twelve tiled houses, which housed personnel and their families in the settlement. Yet, other buildings such as a well-adorned and furnished parish church, a small hospital with its own chapel, a slaughterhouse, several storage houses, and smelting, blacksmith, and carpentry workshops were also sturdily tiled structures that reflected the self-contained and dynamic character of Santiago del Prado. In addition, 112 thatched huts that housed some 315 slaves, a few soldiers, and some lower-status free workers completed the earlier social landscape of the Real de Minas.[3]

By the 1670s, there was no trace of the old hospital, or of the slaughterhouse, or of the several tiled houses where the skilled and clerical personnel of the mines had resided. The earlier infrastructure of production reflected even more dramatically the ravages of time and natural catastrophes, as well as the lack of use and maintenance. One of the former smelting workshops was described in 1670 as consisting of "some timber, poles, and stone pillars and some tiles hanging from the roof and others laying around in the ground."[4] Although in 1670 another smelting workshop had some working tools, by 1677 both workshops were simply declared demolished with no materials to be found in them. A locked warehouse behind the Big House contained some working tools, and the blacksmith's shop also contained some working instruments. Even the priest's house, which had never been abandoned, was described as "very battered [muy maltratada]."[5] The parish church, as will be discussed in Chapter 5, had recently been reconstructed by the slaves "on their own account and name," but most of its religious paraphernalia—the alms of formerly more prosperous parishioners—had been removed as the better-off settlers left.[6]

The total assessed value in 1677 of all the remaining property in the settlement—excluding land and slaves—amounted to a meager 500 pesos, the value of one skilled slave at the time. In contrast, the very large (325) slave workforce was valued in its totality at 80,870 pesos, while all the land of the mining jurisdiction was assessed at 10,000 pesos.[7] Those 500 pesos, then, constitute the quantified representation of the material deterioration of the settlement at the time of the Crown's confiscation of the mines. An even more blunt and devastating observation of those conditions in the inventory of 1677 reads: "There are no props, nor houses, nor equipment, tools, cattle, or any other thing but slaves."[8]

Aside from the reconstruction of the parish church, one other fleeting glimpse of change, rather than just of static decay, was that of the Big House, which had served as the contractor and administrator's residence and the former seat of power in the settlement. In 1677, it lay sparsely furnished and neglected: "Its roof and windows and walls are battered [maltratadas]."[9] Foreseeing no immediate use for the vacated and dilapidated house, Governor Don Andrés de Magaña had donated its roof tiles to the hermit Melchor de los Remedios and the slaves. The gift was both material and symbolic. The valued tiles were to be employed in the reconstruction of a thatched hut that for many decades had served as a modest Marian shrine on top of a hill next to the mines.[10] With one emblematic gesture the governor had finished dismantling the old order, flaunted his newly acquired authority over the previously private and autonomous jurisdiction, and heightened the visibility of the church in the new order of the mines of Santiago del Prado. And yet, with this charged gesture Governor Magaña had, wittingly or unwittingly, highlighted and strengthened the less institutionalized and most popular expression of the church in the settlement. Hermits and slaves, formerly the most marginal sectors in the Real de Minas, now played a major role in the reconstruction and transformation of local public space.

The royal slaves would appropriate and reconstitute this depleted space as they became—along with the hermit, the parish priest, perhaps some free people of color and a couple of soldiers—virtually the sole inhabitants of the settlement. The material transformation of space had started with the reconstruction of the parish church. The peripheral shrine to the Virgin of Charity was now given a new, and soon spectacular, prominence in the religious and social horizon of El Cobre. Finally, 80 thatched huts "that the said slaves have built as living quarters for themselves and for their wives and families" stood instead of the 112 former ones. It is unclear how recent these particular bohíos de guano were and whether by then these ephemeral dwellings had already been relocated around the plaza, to each side of the parish church and onto the other side of the river that crossed the settlement.[11] This was the spatial layout that would eventually mirror the transformation of the Real de Minas into a pueblo of king's slaves.

The Population Dimension: Demographic Creolization

From the time of the Real de Minas's recorded prosperity in 1620 to that of the material ruin witnessed by Crown officials in 1677, the number of slaves in the settlement barely changed.[12] A mere increase of 13 bodies—or souls—made the difference between the population count at the peak of Santiago del Prado's most productive years and at the political close and opening of a new period. That new period under Crown rule would not only be associated with social and cultural change but also it coincided with an expansion of the enslaved population of El Cobre through natural growth that would persist at differing rhythms throughout the next century.[13]

Although strictly demographic factors having to do with the gradual creolization of the slave population of El Cobre—including increasingly even sexual ratios—may have been largely responsible for the overall population growth that began to take place in the last decades of the seventeenth century, there seems to have also been a sudden upsurge in fertility (or a local "baby boom") in the immediate years following the Crown's confiscation of the mines in 1670. In effect, it seems as if among the many changes that marked the new local order under Crown rule, transformations in sexual practices, in conditions leading to a higher propensity to procreate or to a greater willingness to embrace parenthood among slaves in El Cobre, had also taken place: as if local history had also had an impact upon this most intimate and bodily of spheres.

In stark and simple terms, the contrast between the population regimes in these two periods is illustrated by the fact that in the fifty-seven years that elapsed between 1620 and 1677 the bonded population of the mining settlement had only increased by 13 slaves (315 to 328), while fifty-seven years later, in 1735, it had more than doubled, growing at least by 364 slaves (328 to 692)—not counting at least 31 others and their descendants who had bought their bodies out of bondage during those decades (see Table 1). Even in a shorter time span, from 1677 to 1709, the enslaved population of the mines grew from 328 to 493 royal slaves (again excluding 21 manumitted ones and their descendants), a minimal increase of 165 people in roughly three decades. Despite a significant increase in manumissions—albeit mostly male manumissions—from the early 1740s on, the trend in the population growth of royal slaves continued throughout the eighteenth century, if at a slower pace. Indeed, almost one hundred years after the Crown's takeover of the mines, in 1775, there were 896 royal slaves in El Cobre. The expansion of the slave population throughout these years was due exclusively to natu-

TABLE 1

Population of El Cobre, 1608–1775

Year	Royal Slaves			Free and Royal Slaves
	Total	Males	Females	Total
1608	212	151	61	
1620	315	205	110	
1647	311	175	136	
1665	280	145	135	
1670	271	135	136	
1677	328	163	165	
1709	493	235	258	606
1735	692	331	361	920
1773				1355
1775	896	363	533	

SOURCES: Inventories of Slaves: 1608, AGI-SD 451; 1620, AGI-SD 1631; 1647, AGI-SD 104; 1665, AGI-SD 104; 1670, AGI-SD 1631; 1677, AGI-SD 1631. Family Censuses of El Cobre: 1709, AGI-ESC 93A; 1735, AGI-SD 451; 1773, AGI-SD 1628. Slave Family Census of 1775, AGI-SD 1628.

ral increase. No new royal slaves were bought by the Crown after it took over the mines in 1670.[14]

Overall, the wider community of El Cobre, including royal slaves and their freed relatives and neighbors, also evinced continuous expansion throughout the eighteenth century, although these more general increases were not exclusively due to natural growth. Altogether, by 1709 El Cobre was a community of 606 free and slave inhabitants. Its population expanded throughout the eighteenth century to 920 people in 1735 and to 1,355 in 1773 (Table 1). All these villagers—except the clergy and perhaps a few other inhabitants at each time—were people of color. Although for the most part they were descendants of the enslaved workers assembled in the Real de Minas of Santiago del Prado during the early decades of the seventeenth century, some were people of color who had in-married and settled in the pueblo.

Readjusting End Points: The Natural Population Growth of the 1670s

Recasting the end points of the first period (1620–1677)—always subject to the limits imposed by the records at hand—the bonded population of the Real de Minas looks less static, but some of the points of greater demographic flux and the forces impelling population expansion become starker.

Moving back in time to the opening of the seventeenth century one finds that in 1608, some eight years after the first major export-mining operations had been mounted in the region, there were 212 slaves in the mining settlement, most of whom were West African males. Twenty-six children under the age of 8, all born in the new land as Creole slaves to some of the 48 adult female slaves in the Real de Minas, reflected in their small number and limited age range the recently arrived and assembled status of the bonded population of El Cobre in 1608.[15] But by 1620, the slaves of the mining complex had seen an expansion in their numbers to 315 souls—a dramatic increase of 103 slaves in twelve years (Table 1).

Despite difficulties in provisioning the slave market in this region, an unspecified amount of this initial increase would have been due to new arrivals. In 1608, Captain Don Francisco Sánchez de Moya reported to be expecting from 100 to 150 new slaves.[16] These were years of intensive mining production—perhaps the most productive of all—when building up a substantive labor force and replenishing its ranks with new slaves was a feasible economic policy, distribution mechanisms permitting.

There had also been, however, some natural growth behind the marked increase in population by 1620. Seventy-five children living in 35 family units were probably second-generation slaves in Santiago del Prado.[17] Yet, one striking image captured in the inventory of 1620 was the high number of childless couples (45) living in the mining complex. It was a baffling, but by no means uncommon, picture of apparent infertility among African-born slaves exhibited elsewhere in the Caribbean more than a century later as well, but one that may also have been related to recent arrival.[18]

After the initial population expansion at the beginning of the seventeenth century, which was partly due to forced migration, not until the 1670s—at least in the recorded population counts available during that interval—did the bonded population of El Cobre cross the 315 limit reached in 1620: 311 in 1647; 280 in 1665; 271 in 1670; and 328 at its peak in 1677 (see Table 1). Despite this continued stagnation (or even slight decline) of the slave population, a rapid spurt in growth can be detected again between 1670 and 1677, immediately after the Crown's confiscation of the mines. Making provision for the possibility of undercounting in the inventory of 1670, the number of royal slaves in El Cobre went up from 271 to 328 people between that year and 1677—a considerable increase of 57 lives in some seven years. It was this last population upsurge that replenished the enslaved population of El Cobre to its 1620 level. More importantly, contrary to the first spurt of growth in the early decades of the century (1608 to 1620), the local population expansion in the 1670s was solely due to natural increase. No new slaves were purchased during those years. Nor had there been any purchases for many decades when mining production had been in steep decline.

That the population increase during the decade of the 1670s was due to natural growth can be further supported by counting small children—and the proportion of these children to childbearing women—registered in the slave inventories through the years. The number of recorded surviving children aged 4 or under born to enslaved women at several points in time during the second half of the seventeenth century had increased with a measured—if undoubtedly coincidental—regularity: 30 in 1647; 35 in 1665; 40 in 1670. But by 1677, the recorded number of surviving children aged 4 or under, that is, born after 1672, shot up to 64—indeed, a "baby boom" that coincided with an important local historical event, namely, the royal takeover of the Real de Minas.

That this sudden increase in newborn (hereafter 0-year-old) to 4-year-old children in the 1670s was not solely related to a higher number of childbearing-age females (ages 15–45) in the population of 1677[19] is illustrated by the ratio of children (ages 0–4) to women of childbearing age at different points in time: 697.6/1,000 in 1647; 673/1,000 in 1665; 666.6/1,000 in 1670; and 790.1/1,000 in 1677. More difficult to determine, of course, were the precise reasons that led to these changes in local fertility. Was it a change in sexual, childbearing, or even perhaps birth control practices that led to this expansion of newborn children in the settlement? Or was it perhaps a more unlikely sudden lowering of the infant mortality rate? Or was the recorded increase in fertility more trivially due to suddenly more accurate counting and inscription practices?

At this point one can only point to the apparent "coincidence" between an immediate change in the local political regime and a local demographic one in the 1670s. Was there any kind of relation between the body and local history and society that these changes reflect? While there are no definitive answers, the questions raised by these historical and demographic transformations are tantalizing.[20]

Other Demographic Dimensions of Creolization: The Sexual Distribution of the Population

Although the enslaved population in Santiago del Prado flourished alongside the consolidation of a new order in the mining jurisdiction, other profound transformations in that population's sexual, generational, ethnic, and racial makeup had been gradually taking place throughout the years of decline in mining production. The changing demographic profile of this bonded social group represented the human ground in which broad and local historical processes left their mark as they interacted with biological ones. That changing demographic profile would, in turn, have an impact on the social life of the community.

By 1677—and even years before—the enslaved population of El Cobre no longer reflected the classic characteristics of early slave plantation populations that it had once exhibited.[21] Uneven sexual ratios had marked this bonded population for years after it had been first assembled in El Cobre at the turn of the century. In 1608, there were 247 males for every 100 females in the mining complex—a rate that roughly approached the Crown's legally prescribed minimum of 1 female slave for every 3 males in the configuration of an enslaved workforce. Only the 26 Creole children born in the settlement by then reflected nature's inclination to produce roughly equal numbers of male and female bodies (13 males and 13 females). In principle these Creole-born generations—if not subjected to further selective human interventions through transfers and sales—would be the main motor behind the eventual balancing out of the sexes in a given closed slave population; however, the process could take decades to unfold. In 1620, the overall sexual ratio was 186/100, and in 1647, 128/100. It was not until 1665 that the effects of the selective policies of the first decade finally abated with 107 males for every 100 females. The decade of the 1670s even witnessed a slight inversion in the ratio in favor of the female sex with 99/100 in 1670, and 98.7 enslaved males per 100 females in the settlement. The sexual balance among royal slaves would keep tipping in favor of females in the following century, particularly after 1740 when local social processes such as mostly male manumission trends dramatically affected sex ratios not so much in the overall community as among the enslaved population itself.[22]

Although even sexual ratios did not necessarily mean that enslaved men and women in El Cobre would choose partners among themselves, it did facilitate social mating, particularly given the restricted mobility of bonded people. For example, in 1620 all but 2 women had settled down with a slave partner from El Cobre—32 of them with children, and another 45 without—while 63 single men lived alone, either by choice or by force of demographic circumstances. By 1665, and to a lesser extent among the younger cohorts in 1647, however, there were—at least numerically speaking—enough men and women in the mining settlement for almost everyone to have a partner. To live or not to live with a partner in El Cobre by that time, then, would have been a matter of choice and not merely of a restrictive demographic scenario. In 1677, for instance, there were some 15 women with children in the settlement apparently living without a partner and 21 single men living by themselves—or at least, in the case of these slaves, living without slave partners from El Cobre.[23]

Perhaps more obviously, more even sexual patterns meant greater numbers of females of all ages populating social space in the settlement, affecting habitat, and providing a different quality to everyday life in the community. Finally, such even ratios tended to translate demographically as well into higher fertility rates in a population and greater possibilities of overall natural population growth.

Age and Generational Distribution

The age and generational makeup of the bonded population of the Real de Minas also changed slowly throughout the decades prior to the confiscation of the mines. The overwhelming male and adult population assembled in the mining settlement for its alleged sheer physical laboring capacity—although some would become skilled workers too—gradually contracted and gave way to a more youthful population with greater proportions of dependents. As mining production declined, so too did the need or capacity to maintain a steady replacement rate of working-age laborers in the complex.

In the early decades of the seventeenth century when the slave population was still mainly composed of African slaves and new arrivals, child-dependency ratios were roughly on the order of 13.9 children (ages 0–15) per 100 working-age adults (ages 16–60) in 1608, or even 32.9 children to adults in 1620. Some twenty-five years later, by 1647, these ratios were already at a high 70.6 children per 100 adults, a proportion not far from that of subsequent decades.

Yet, at midcentury, children still constituted only around 25 percent of the enslaved population in the settlement, while working-age adults only 35.5 percent. The single largest age category of slaves in 1647 were the elderly (age over 60). Indeed, elderly men and women in their 60s, 70s, 80s, and even 90s—in addition to 3 believed to be centenarians—constituted an overwhelming (and improbable?) 40 percent of the bonded population in the complex.[24] Their dependency ratio to working-age adults was an extraordinary 114/100! These were the survivors of the imported workforces brought into the Real de Minas in the first two decades of the century. The contours of a receding past were still palpably present at midcentury in the population's demographic profile.

The extraordinarily high proportion of elderly slaves in relation to the working-age group of midcentury, however, dwindled progressively throughout the following decades. That was perhaps one of the clearest trends that this population underwent as it literally creolized and renewed itself. By the 1670s the elderly slaves had become a small minority at the top of the population pyramid. Their dependency ratios to working-age adults had declined to a mere 11.3/100 in 1677, while that of children to adults had increased to 89.8/100. At that time, the proportion of age groups in the enslaved population of the settlement had undergone further transformations: while the proportion of working-age adults had increased to 51.2 percent and that of children had also increased to 44 percent, the proportion of the elderly had dramatically declined to a mere 5.7 percent of the enslaved population in the settlement.

The growing number and proportion of children in the settlement since the turn of the seventeenth century not only may have given life in the settlement a more familial character, but also it increased the provisioning burden of the working-age sectors of the population and the requisite child-rearing activities. As to the elderly, they acquired a disproportionate presence in the mining settlement by midcentury. After mining production dramatically declined (and with it the possibility of a continuous replacement of the laboring force through the importation of slaves), as the new enslaved Creole generations began to emerge, and as the aged first generations of slaves began to die off, the presence of elderly enslaved people became more subdued, or at least more proportionate to that of other age groups. In effect, by the 1670s, the sex and age distribution of the slave population of El Cobre had attained the profile of a "natural" growing population, one far from the "classic" early plantation slave population profile with which it had started off at the beginning of the seventeenth century. The lobbed "Christmas tree" population profile of earlier decades had finally attained a pyramid shape of early modern "normal" populations, a "normality" that reflected more closely the natural rhythms of life and death in a population.[25]

Racial Composition

With the years, the racial composition of the slave population of El Cobre also underwent changes. In 1620, all but 2 enslaved women were registered with a partner, and the latter were all slaves. It seems that until then not much miscegenation had taken place in this slave community of mostly African slaves. Mulatto children did not begin to be born in significant numbers in El Cobre until the late 1630s.

TABLE 2

Racial Composition by Age Groups, 1647 and 1670

	1647			1670		
Ages	Mulattos	Percent of Mulattos	Total Slaves	Mulattos	Percent of Mulattos	Total Slaves
0-9	29	48.3	60	31	40.7	76
10-19	1	3.1	32	26	41.9	62
20-29	6	12.7	47	8	19.0	42
30-39	4	16.6	24	9	32.1	28
40-49	0	0	13	3	10.7	28
50-59	0	0	10	0	0	18
60-69	2	4.8	41	0	0	10
70-79	0	0	35	0	0	0
80-89	2	4.5	44	0	0	2
90-	0	0	5	0	0	5
Total	44	14.1	311	77	28.4	271

SOURCES: Inventories of Slaves: 1647, AGI-SD 104; 1670, AGI-SD 1631.

The total proportion of mulatto slaves in El Cobre in 1647 was only 14.1 percent, but the overwhelming majority of these racially mixed slaves (65.9 percent) were children under age 10. As many as 29 children under 10 years old were recorded as mulattos in the inventory of 1647—a figure that meant a significant 48.3 percent of all children in that age group. In contrast to this figure, only 15 mulattos could be found among the rest of the enslaved population in El Cobre in that same inventory—most of them in their 20s and 30s. Among the latter age groups, mulattos constituted 12.7 percent and 16.6 percent, respectively, of their cohorts (see Table 2).

Thus, relatively little racial intermixture can be said to have taken place in Santiago del Prado during the first three decades of slave life in the settlement—perhaps the more telling given the fact that there were a considerable number of Spanish male soldiers stationed in the settlement, particularly before the 1620s during the period of the most intensive mining production.[26] By 1670, the overall proportion of racially mixed slaves in the settlement had gone up to 28.4 percent (Table 2). Although the highest proportions of mulatto slaves registered in the inventory of 1670 were concentrated in the age groups under 20, the proportions of mulattos in age groups under 40 also remained high, thereby reinforcing the fact that it had been in the decades of the 1630s and 1640s that a miscegenation trend became significant.

These racial mixtures in the population, particularly among recent Creole generations, often meant sexual practices among unequal partners and in "illicit" terms. Such sexual patterns may not have taken hold during the early decades of the century in the Real de Minas, when the slave population was for the most part African. It may have been with the sexual maturation of first-generation Creole slaves that sexual encounters between different racial groups became more prevalent. In any case, whether borne by African or Creole slave women, it was not until the 1630s and 1640s that significant numbers of mixed-race children began to be born and raised in the mining settlement.

The racial composition of this royal slave population continued changing throughout the following century so that in 1773—precisely almost a century from 1670—the proportions had been inverted: 19.3 percent of the royal slaves were recorded as black, while the overwhelming majority (80.7 percent) was racially mixed. The racially mixed population included mulattos and *chinos* (a racial label that emphasized some mixture of black and Indian blood). In the village census of 1773, 61.8 percent of royal slaves were labeled as mulatto and 18.8 percent *chino*. Thus, by the 1770s, El Cobre had become an overwhelmingly racially mixed community.[27]

It is difficult to assess the local significance of race in El Cobre. In 1677, of 12 skilled slaves in the mining settlement, all but 3 were black. Of these 3 mixed-race skilled workers, 2 were the most highly valued slaves in the Real de Minas. They were assessed at the enormous amount of 1,000 pesos in 1677—almost twice the amount of any skilled slave worker in the settlement at the time.[28] These highly valued mulatto slaves, whom I will introduce in the next chapter, seem to have had literacy skills.

A century later, when racial mixture had become widespread in El Cobre—and when more detailed data about the village's population became available—it seems clearer to us that race did play a role as a social marker internally in the community. While, for instance, enslaved people predominated in all racial categories, their presence was more strongly marked among blacks (71.3 percent), and even among *chinos* (79.5 percent), than among mulattos (56.7 percent). Even if one combined the two racially mixed groups, enslaved people were still more predominant among blacks (71.3 percent) than among the others (60.8 percent). Although in El Cobre access to land could be more important than a skilled occupation, only 1 black in 1773 had a skilled job (as a smelter), while the other 14 skilled occupations were held by 12 mulattos and 2 *chinos*. Furthermore, all the best housing in the village—all 5 tiled houses and 11 of the 16 *caídizos* (housing also made of masonry)—in 1773 were occupied by mulattos, while only a free black, an enslaved *chino*, and 3 whites occupied the other 5 *caídizos*.

The Enslaved Population's Ethnic Makeup

The Meaning of Naming Practices in El Cobre: From African to Creole

While in 1608 most of the enslaved workforce recently assembled in Santiago del Prado had been African-born, by the time the Crown confiscated the mines in 1670 virtually all slaves in the settlement were first- and second-, even third-, generation Creoles. The outlines of that population's changing composition, and particularly what that change may have entailed before the 1670s, can only be obliquely surmised from the classifications and slave inscriptions found in inventories of that period. Just as a brief archaeology of material culture and the organization of space traced through the inventories of the mines reflected social and economic transformations in the settlement, so can traces of wider demographic, social, and cultural patterns be found in the names and naming practices left behind in slave inventories.

Among the most widespread cultural naming practices of Spanish slave societies was that of attaching an "ethnic" appellative to the baptism names of African-born slaves, thereby indicating bondmen and -women's Old World regional origin. This naming convention—mapping territory on the orbit of the slave trade into New World identities and marking distinctions between "outsiders" and "insiders," even among slaves, the most peripheral or marginal elements of the social body—still serves historians in the present as a guide to "origins" in the past. More basically, this and other naming conventions also serve as parameters of Spanish colonial society's differing ways of thinking about identity.

The term "Creole," meaning "born in the New World," or rather "of the New World, but originally from elsewhere," was another such appellative, if a more generic one, sometimes attached to the Christian names of slaves.[29] This simple classificatory scheme—a wide range of African "ethnic" names versus a simple generic Creole identification term, was often the manifestation of the underlying *bozal* (African-born) versus *criollo* (Creole) opposition.[30] Although strictly speaking this binary scheme applied to place of origin, it seems to have carried cultural connotations in Spanish slave societies—*bozales* as first-generation outsiders were still culturally distant subjects, while Creoles, born and bred in the New World, were supposedly more adapted and integrated into the ways of the Spanish colonial world. What social distinctions—or prerogatives—the category of "Creole," for instance, actually entailed in practical terms, as well as what both categories meant to enslaved populations (or to the free of color) in terms of identity issues is not really well understood yet; nor is it known whether at any point a Creole identity carried any political weight however slight, as it would eventually do in the case of many "ethnic" Spanish Creoles. Such close ethnography of social life remains to be done.[31]

Naming conventions in the Spanish colonial world also tended to make distinctions between slaves and free through the use of family surnames, usually Hispanic surnames. Slave social alienation was thus reflected in the lack of need to publicly mark blood ties and familial origins through naming practices. At times, the master's surname could be given to a slave, but this convention tended to reflect "property" rather than "blood" ties (albeit the possibility of other connotations should not be dismissed). Thus, a transition into freedom would generally include the acquisition of a surname that could be independently passed down to descendants, thereby reflecting a new identity and in principle a new kind of insertion into the social body. In short, the only naming convention (and common pool) uniting all sectors in colonial society, regardless of origin or status (but not of gender), was the baptismal first name, which usually had some Christian historical or biblical reference. Although evangelized (free) Africans would also partake of this naming convention in their own homelands when initiated to Christian religion through baptism, a Christian name was a new identification convention imposed on all African enslaved people and thus actually an element or sign of forced acculturation.[32] Keeping in mind these simple naming conventions, what can be surmised from the names of the enslaved population of Santiago del Prado?

In the Beginning Most Were Africans

In 1608, 123 of the 186 adults (66.1 percent)—and as many as 103 of the 138 (74.6 percent) males among these adult slaves—were explicitly identified as of African origin through an "ethnic" last name, while only 2 adults were labeled with the more generic term *criollo*.[33] With the exception of the 26 young children labeled as "negritos criollos," no other slaves were identified by territorial origin. A few merely had an epithet referring to a physical trait or an occupation ("Antonio fat", "Bartolomé smelter"). Still others, particularly females, were inscribed merely with their Spanish baptismal name; or again, in an early Spanish gendered gesture projected onto slaves, some 5 females—and only females—had attached to their names in the inventory a reference to their spouse as, for example, in the case of "Lucía mujer de

Alejandro" (Lucia, wife of Alejandro). The 26 children listed separately and distinctly recognized as locally born were, in a way, jointly acknowledged as a new local generation. They were the tip of the creolization wave that would slowly transform this population from below throughout the following decades.

Most of the first West African slaves in the settlement came from the region of Angola. Of the 138 adult male slaves found in the settlement by 1608, 57 (41.3 percent) were explicitly labeled as "Angola" or "Engola"; and among the whole adult female population, 10 out of 48 female slaves (20.8 percent) were identified as of that same origin. If only the explicitly African ethnically marked groups are taken into account, then 55.3 percent of the African males and 50 percent of the females came from Angola, while the rest came from other scattered regions.[34] Larger historical forces having to do with the provisioning contracts that the Spanish Crown had with the Portuguese—particularly during the decades that the Braganza house was subsumed under Hapsburg rule—and intense Portuguese political and military engagements in Angola during the late sixteenth and early seventeenth centuries undoubtedly had an impact on the number of captive slaves shipped from this region and that were available in the legal slave market of the Spanish territories at the time. The second largest West African representation in the Real de Minas early in the century was from the neighboring Congo region, also heavily under the orbit of the Portuguese slave trade in those years. People from the Congo were represented with 10 male slaves (9.7 percent of the explicitly identified African males), and 4 additional female ones (20 percent of African women). Other groups had a less marked presence—2 Viojos (or Biohos), 2 Enchicos, 2 Gaitas, 2 Gongas, 4 Masongos, and 2 Nambos. Finally, 20 other African last names were represented only once.[35]

It is impossible to determine if any memories of tribal conflicts or alliances from the Old World had a bearing in the new and confined world of the settlement. It is, however, more plausible to assert that with so many slaves from a given—even if widely encompassing—region who may have more or less understood each other and who may have shared various constellations of religious beliefs and other cultural practices, people from the Angolan region may have been able to reconstitute themselves as a group to a greater extent than any other "ethnic" group that may have been represented in the range of 28 or so different "African" names in the mining settlement. That neighboring presence may have in fact grounded life in the settlement in some kind of wide "Angolan"—or neo-Angolan—cultural matrix.

It is not clear, however, if Angolans continued to be the majority in the settlement with subsequent arrivals of enslaved people. Subsequent inventories record a significant expansion in the range of "African" names among the enslaved workforce in the settlement. While in 1608 there were 122 men and women bearing 32 different African names of which the two most frequent—Angolans and Congos—represented extensive regional areas with the scope of a kingdom, by 1620, the range of African inscriptions included 65 names borne by 91 slaves, mostly males, of which 17 to perhaps 22 represented carryovers from 1608. These figures indicate that in only twelve years 43 new African names had appeared in the slave lists of the Real de Minas (and 14 had been dropped) and that basically there was a greater dispersion of names—and perhaps African origin—among the workforce of the settlement in 1620. More importantly, while 67 Angolans (57 males) were recorded in the inventory of 1608, twelve years later, in 1620, there were only 6 males thus inscribed.[36] Although undoubtedly this expansion in the range of names indicated that the slave population of Santiago del Prado must have become more "ethnically" heterogeneous with new arrivals, yet another phenomenon reflected in 1620 may have veiled the relatively strong cultural homogeneity of 1608. Indeed, it is unlikely that 89.4 percent of the male Angolans and all of the females could have disappeared in twelve years, or, particularly in the case of males (for it did happen in that of females), that the African identification of so many of them could have been obliterated in the inscriptions of the inventory of 1620.

In effect, what the decline of an Angolan identification may have also indicated was a more prevalent use of somewhat different naming or identification conventions. The widening range of "African" names, the smaller count of slaves bearing any given "African" name, and more particularly the marked decline of an appellative as regionally encompassing as that of "Angola" all suggest that the use of more concrete identifications—such as tribal or "ethnic" ones within a kingdom—may have accounted for the apparent reduction of Angolans, as well as for the general expansion of names. Furthermore, slaves may have also changed their assigned "African" names to more significant collective identities or perhaps to individual names. The case of Manuel Catungue may illustrate this name-shifting process. In 1620 there were 2 Catungues—both with the same Christian name Manuel—listed in the inventory of the mines. Twenty-seven years later, one of them was inscribed as Manuel Catungue Rey (King) in the slave listing of 1647, and eighteen years later undoubtedly the same man, now older by a purported "thirteen" years, bore the name Manuel Angola

Rey in the inventory of 1665. Thus, Manuel was identified—or identified himself—not only as someone from Angola but also as a Catungue. That the Catungue name may have stood for more than an individual name is indicated by the fact that there were two men bearing the same name. And finally, although there were no Catungues listed in the inventory of 1608, there were 6 Manuel Angolas, any 2 who may, or may not, have been the Manuel Catungues of 1620, the King Catungue of 1647, and the King Angola of 1665, thereby illustrating the process of naming and renaming, inscription and reinscription, or the coexistence of different names.

The Angolan presence may have indeed been stronger than the minimal 60 Angolan identifications indicated in 1608, for other African names in the inventory of 1608 also indicated Angolan prominence: Andala may have referred to Ndalu Kisuva, a district in the region; or Moxongo from Songo; Mondonguero or Mondongo from the Ndongo; or an Enchico from a particular people around the Malebo Pool. Similarly in the 1620 inventory, there appeared either two new people from Matamba, a kingdom in East Angola, and two Malembas from the Lemba area, or four Angolas from 1608 now calling themselves Matamba and Malemba.[37]

That African names borne by these slaves did not always reflect regional or "ethnic" names but perhaps also individual names is suggested by a few cases such as that of a María Enbote in 1608 whose name or nickname simply meant "good," or Antón Emputto whose name meant in Kikongo "Portugal" or "Europe," possibly alluding to the Portuguese presence in Angola. Others such as Juan de Sossa Cabra—Sossa being a Portuguese surname—may have reflected baptism in Angola even before enslavement or conversely enslavement to a Portuguese man by the same surname before ending up in this corner of the Spanish Caribbean.

The same process of flux in the range of African names continued until 1647, years after any significant new inflow of slaves had taken place and when those with African names were overwhelmingly the aged survivors of the first generations in the settlement.[38] Although in the twenty-seven years from 1620 to 1647, the range of African names had only expanded slightly from 65 to 69 names (now borne by 107 slaves), 20 names had been retained, 45 had disappeared, and 49 new ones had made their appearance in the slave inventory of 1647. Of those, a variety of 11 to 15 last names constituted retentions from 1608. Although their names may have changed, the actual use of African names among the older generation in 1647 bore witness to the fact that African-born slaves had retained their new or old (or simply creolized) names throughout many decades (and different inventory takers), rather than dropping that African-based identification after years of residence in the New World. Significantly, individual identity among male slaves was more marked by the range of African names than by that of Christian names in the settlement in 1608, 1620, and (at least among older slaves) in 1647.[39] Perhaps because females were less likely than males to carry a second name, their Christian first names became the most significant marker and the range of Christian names exhibited among females was wider than among males.[40]

Even though by midcentury the overall proportion of African slaves or slaves with "African" names in the population had decreased, the sheer number of these early groups—and their apparent longevity—ensured that traces of the African pasts that they embodied were still visible and alive in the settlement. Although African captives were forced to acculturate rapidly into the confined new world of slavery, and more slowly perhaps into the wider sphere of colonial society, like first-generation immigrants anywhere they would not have completely shaken off former identities deeply engrained in the body and in their memories. The parental and elderly status of this sizeable group of first-generation African men and women may have strengthened their authority and helped to perpetuate some of their ways among the slave community of the mining settlement.

Manuel Catungue Rey is again a case in point. In fact, he may reflect the prevailing importance of Angolans in the settlement, despite their apparent reduction by the 1620s and 1640s.[41] This enslaved Angolan had arrived in the settlement some time before 1620. Like so many enslaved people of that generation in El Cobre, Manuel Catungue either had a very long life or records distorted his age (or both). He was not only inscribed, already as a 60-year-old man, in the slave roll of 1647 but as a 73-year-old one in that of 1665 as well. Although his name had appeared without any royal title in earlier inventories—that of 1620, and perhaps that of 1608—at least fully forty-five years after his arrival, in the later decades of his life, the old Angolan man was being recorded as Manuel Catungue Rey (1647) and Manuel Rey Angola (1665). That is, decades after his possible defeat, capture, and enslavement somewhere in Angola, Catungue was still constructing himself in Old World terms. Indeed, that status may have been sufficiently well established in the settlement as to be acknowledged in two official lists. His Angolan royal status, however, did not achieve Manuel Catungue any position of equivalent, if defiled, rank in the New World settlement's shallow slave hierarchy as for instance a *mayoral* (overseer). The operating sphere of Manuel Catungue King of Angola, if any, may have been different. In short, although most of these African-born men and women had spent more than half of their lives in bonded exile, they could still recognize—at least in title—Old World rankings and status. Indeed, Manuel Catungue may have been able to find a small constituency among the local diaspora of fellow enslaved Angolans willing to recognize his rank.

Yet, King Manuel Catungue, as well as the other elderly African-born men and women of 1647 and even 1665, were to be the last direct mediators of yonder worlds, or fragments thereof, in Santiago del Prado. For the falling curve of mining production after the 1620s meant a halt to any demographic—and cultural—replenishment of the population from the ranks of newly arrived working-age groups with Old World bodies and fresh memories and words, ways, and gods from elsewhere. The more immediate contact that the enslaved and freed creolized people of El Cobre would have with African slaves in the next century would be through a few personal African-born slaves of their own.[42]

Forms of Creolization: Creolization of African-Born Slaves

Although there is no direct evidence of the presence of any Afro-Cuban *cabildos* (African ethnic-based associations) in the mining settlement, such associations could have very well existed in El Cobre as they did in many urban settings in Cuban colonial society.[43] Again invoking the suggestive case of Manuel Catungue King of Angola, there was another possibility within the colonial world for his title of "King," namely, head of one such *cabildo* with a mainly Angolan constituency. In that case, his title of "King" suggests a more creolized African, or more specifically, "Angolan" identity and rank. Indeed, the African *cabildo* and its practices can be approached either as the Africanization of a New World imaginary or conversely as the creolization of an African imaginary in the Spanish Indies.

The process of creolization took different shapes for slaves in the New World. One form of creolization was the more elementary one that African-born generations underwent during their lifetime. The retention, reenactment, or even reinvention of Old World identities—or shreds of identity—in memories and practices by African-born generations in particular did not mean that there was absolutely no acculturation among these people, however coerced this cultural "creolization" may have been. Practices and memories of the past would integrate, clash, or coexist with new practices and customs encountered in the New World—even though changes resulting from the "encounters" with "Europe" and the "New World" may have begun to take place in some cases back in enslaved people's Old World homelands. In the New World there was coerced acculturation into the rituals and meaning of slavery as well as into new work routines. There was also for many—including for people from the Congo and Angola who had long practiced copper mining in parts of their homeland—the familiarization with the mining, working, uses, and value of copper in this New World setting.[44] Although the consumption of cassave, tobacco, sugar, and rum was also spreading in regions of West Africa at the time, these goods constituted aspects of creolization for many of the African-born slaves in Santiago del Prado.[45] So did relatively abundant dietary consumption of meat in the cattle-rich island of Cuba. Of course, creolization also meant changes in habitat including new attachments to small provision grounds and to new huts or dwellings built with local materials and resources.

Then there was forced baptism and evangelization leading to a coerced or chosen Christian identity that coexisted and merged with many former gods, beliefs, and practices. The first sustained evangelizing efforts into the world of Christianity—that major aspect of what acculturation into the Spanish world was all about—were carried out in this mining settlement by a singular figure: a hermit caretaker of a very modest Marian shrine next to the mines.[46] The figure of a hermit, exotic as it sounds to a modern reader, was not particularly unfamiliar to Spanish Christians at the time. Hermits were found throughout shrines and hermitages in Spain and later found their way to the Spanish Americas, including Cuba.[47] That solitary lay religious figure may not have seemed particularly odd to many African-born slaves either; they could have associated hermits with shamans or mentors of the occult and the sacred back in their homelands too. Yet, the hermits in the mining settlement may still have faced a daunting job of evangelization among these forced migrants from Africa. That in the early mining days supernatural practices of African origin were still quite alive in this mining complex is attested to by the actual deportation of two slaves from Santiago del Prado to Cartagena for practicing what in Spanish discourse went by the name of "witchcraft" (hechicería).[48]

Creolization of African-born slaves would also have meant some new language acquisition inflected by the cadences and sounds of mother tongues. As pointed out before, creolization also meant coexistence, exchange, and intermarriage first with enslaved people of other African groups living in the same corner of the Indies, and later with Spaniards, Creoles, and even some neighboring Native Americans and mestizos. It meant familiarity with the new profane music to be heard in the celebrations of the Spanish colonial world, as well as with new music in the world of the Christian sacred (church music performed by African and Creole musicians, *atambores* and *chirimía* [wind instrument] players in the mining complex). Such music produced with new instruments and according to new aesthetic rules would presumably have resonated, as elsewhere in the island, alongside other kinds of music based on different sets of sounds and rhythms and instruments from various West African worlds.[49]

As suggested before, even when bearing the trace—or memory—of African origin, the very names of African-born slaves in the mining complex were often emblematic of forced and assumed colonial practices that modulated and modified Old World identities. Spanish Christian names or for that matter "African" names marking either point of enslavement, or even kingdom, tribal, or regional origin may have been far from the naming practices in use among different African groups where naming conventions may have construed identity in different ways.[50] The possibility, however, that some African-derived names may have been chosen by slaves has already been suggested, too.

"Africanizing" Creole Slaves

Besides the extended practice among African-born generations of retaining an alleged "African" name—or a creolized version thereof—throughout their lives in forced exile, there was yet another naming trend, however secondary or idiosyncratic, operating among slaves in the mining complex of Santiago del Prado. This trend became a customary practice that broke with the colonial convention of "African" names as marking slave trade orbit identification and African territorial origin, and it became particularly clear in the inscriptions of slave names in 1647, 1665, and 1670, but to a lesser extent in 1677 and thereafter. It was the Creole practice of giving an American-born slave child an "African" second name—either through direct parental transmission or more arbitrarily at times. In 1608 there were already a few traces of this cultural practice, as three of the first 26 Creole children born in the settlement were named Francisco Gurubayo, María Cayaya, and Barbola. There were, at least in the record, no adults at that time bearing those African derived names, however. The Creole slave Francisco Gurubayo still had his "African" name in 1647.

Similarly, although by 1647, virtually all slaves belonging to the older generations retained "African" names, there were a few "African-named" males and females among the younger Creole generations, too: María

Bioho (age 20), María Lunguengue (age 30), Pedro de Cusata (age 12), Domingo de Matamba (age 12), Thomás Matamba (age 26), Juan and Salvador Longuengue (ages 14 and 20), Miguel Catondo (age 25), Pedro Bioho (age 30). Likewise, in 1670 there were Creole slaves in Santiago del Prado still bearing "African" names: there were again, the by-then usual, Matambas (3 of them; 1 as young as 6 years old), Lunguengues (5 of them), Quialas (3), Cuzatas (4) in addition to 2 Mayalas (ages 36 and 11), 2 young Calafates (ages 11 and 8), a 24-year-old Antón Mofongo and a 6-year-old Pedro Molumba. Among Creole females there were just 2 Quialas (ages 16 and 9), but again a female's identification through a second name was never as full as in the case of males. The repetition of some of these (creolized) "African" names among young Creole slaves suggests the possibility of their having acquired the role of a family name—or a surname—by midcentury. What these names reflect is that while indeed some of these "African" names were functioning as family surnames marking kinship relations among slaves, others may have been individually chosen names as in the cases of solos like the Creoles Antón Mofongo or Pedro Molumba. Thus, the "African" names that in fact marked *bozal* (African-born) slave status in colonial society may have been assumed and turned into individuated names, or even more significantly, into surnames in the case of a few families. This latter form of creolization of "African" names was more radical in that it marked and recognized independent kinship identities among slaves—a phenomenon that had become extended by the 1670s, but more commonly through Hispanic surnames. At least two of those surnames deriving from African names turned into lineages that survive to the present in El Cobre: the Cruzatas (Cussatas, Cuzatas) and the Quialas. They can be found in slave inventories as early as 1647.

Creolization as "Hispanization"

Another form of creolization found among American-born slaves constituted a firmer grounding in the colonial Hispanic cultural matrix: the practice of using Hispanic surnames. It is not clear how these Spanish surnames—names such as Cosme, Moreno, Ortiz, de los Reyes, Salas, González, Vicente—were originally adopted by the Creole slaves of El Cobre, but by 1647 some had made their appearances in slave inventories, and by the 1670s they were relatively well in place.[51] These naming practices were more conventional markers of Creole status, but they were also equally radical in the public enhancing of kinship identities, particularly in the case of slaves.[52] While in the 1670s parentage and genealogy can only be traced in documents with difficulty, by the eighteenth century it is possible to trace genealogies of a good number of people in El Cobre through village family censuses and baptism records. During the eighteenth century the use of surnames had become widely spread in El Cobre—including in official inscription practices—and they seemed to have been used for the most part as patronymics.[53]

Although, as mentioned before, some African names had been transformed and creolized into surnames by 1670, Hispanic names had become most prevalent as surnames. After the 1670s, the process of creolization as manifested in the practice of acquisition of surnames and in their Hispanization moved even more quickly. By 1677, almost all the males heading a family (and some single ones) were recorded with a surname. By this time, some Matambas, Longuengues, Quialas, Cuzatas, and Viojos remained as family names. Few traces of these African second names remain in the baptism records after 1680, however. The Longuengues seem to have changed their names, and their children were not inscribed with that African name thereafter. And while two Matamba sisters were occasionally registered in the baptism records with that African surname, they were at times inscribed instead with the Christian second name of "Asención."[54] By 1720, only the Biojos, Quialas, and Cuzatas had become lineages.

Conclusion

At the time of the Crown's confiscation of the mines in 1670, El Cobre had a more or less static population of 271 slaves—by no means an inconsiderable concentration of slaves in any African slave-driven enterprise in the New World, not to speak in Cuba, at the time. In fact, at about this time it began to become a fast-growing population, one expanding through natural reproduction and not through importation. The material ruin of the mining settlement contrasted with its rich and thriving human component. This human component had itself undergone profound transformations throughout a long drawn-out process during the seventeenth century: a demographic and cultural creolization with important implications for its emerging character as an imagined community in the New World.

While gradual creolization had transformed the sex and age profile of this population and provided the ground for self-sustained growth, the historical event of the royal takeover of the mines seems to have been significant in unleashing an increase in fertility in El Cobre that continued into the eighteenth century. In any case, by the time the Crown took over the mines of Santiago del Prado, the enslaved population living and working in the settlement was mostly Creole and already exhibited the "pyramidal" structure of other "normal" (or "natural") populations in the early modern world.

Creolization in El Cobre also entailed a change in the racial profile of this enslaved population. The appearance of racially mixed enslaved people, however, did not begin to become an important trend until the late 1630s—some three decades after the first African slaves had arrived at the mining settlement and two decades after the first Creole slaves had been born in Santiago del Prado. Indeed, it may have been among this first generation of Creole slaves that miscegenation became a more widespread practice and not among their African parents. The racially mixed population of the mining jurisdiction would continue expanding throughout the eighteenth century until it would become the overwhelming dominant sector of the population in El Cobre. Mixed racial origin may have even become a significant status marker in this community, particularly during the eighteenth century.

Finally, slave naming practices in the mining settlement throughout the seventeenth century reflected not only the changing "ethnic" composition of the enslaved population but also they provide an oblique glimpse of other kinds of cultural creolization processes at play throughout the decades. Baptismal names reflected the initial (forced) acculturation to enslavement and a Christian world, if later there may have been some parental choice in naming within the range of available Christian names. Actually, rather than a mechanical repetition of a narrow set of names, Christian names in the settlement constituted a relatively wide range of names conferring some individuality to their bearers, particularly in the case of females. In the case of African-born males, "African" second names had a broader range than Christian first names suggesting that they were more significant markers of distinction and individuality. Furthermore, African-born slaves seem to have retained throughout their life in forced exile their "African" names, although there seem to have been changes and shifting usages in these names. Finally, there is also evidence in the records of Creole slaves who received "African" names (from their parents?) and moreover that some of these names marked some kind of filiation or familial relation. By midcentury there seemed to be last names among many slaves that were already functioning as "surnames." Although by the 1670s, most of these familial identifying names (or "surnames") were Hispanic, a handful of them were

"African" names. By the eighteenth century most enslaved people in El Cobre carried Hispanic family names or surnames that seemed to have constituted for the most part patronymics.

The changing naming processes exhibited by the slave population of El Cobre illustrate some autonomy in the choice and use of names by these slaves and reflect some cultural creolization processes under way among this enslaved population. These creolization processes had to do not only with the acquisition of Hispanic names, but moreover with the adoption of Hispanic naming conventions related to the importance of marking and identifying familial origin in colonial society through the bearing of an ascriptive surname. The adoption of this kind of naming convention, however, also had a more radical signification in the context of a slave society for it meant the public bearing of an identity based on natal ties independent from the master-slave relation; indeed, it meant the adoption or appropriation of a practice (even an honor) that was in principle associated with free people rather than with slaves. One may even say that it meant some kind of reformulation of what it meant to be a slave.

CHAPTER 2

Slavery to the King

Shaping Social Identity

These slaves are not like the others, they are the King's.
— Governor Don Andrés de Magaña, ca. 1672

The Crown's confiscation of the ruined mines of Santiago del Prado did not bring back the prosperity of the earlier mining-based economy. Instead, the takeover heralded a new local order that would last for more than a century: a corporate pueblo of royal slaves and free people of color. This kind of imagined community emerged from novel turns on standard colonial ideology, old precedents combined with fresh opportunities, and new junctures through which overlapping and conflicting interests among groups were reshuffled. Generally speaking, the unusual community that took shape upon the ruins of the mining settlement resulted from an intricate negotiating process among several sectors of colonial society, including the state, the church, and the king's newly acquired slaves. Put in more symbolic terms, the kind of colonial community that El Cobre became after the Crown's confiscation of the mines was to a large extent produced by the relations among the king, the Virgin, and the royal slaves.

This chapter deals with the transformations that began to take place in the mining settlement during the initial years of Crown rule. These changes were not only related to the local reshaping of political authority and social custom but also to the ideological and practical making of a social identity, slavery to the king. What shape did royal slavery begin to take in this corner of empire? What kinds of practices—and forms of freedom—began to be associated with it? Did the identity take any special imagined character? How contended was the meaning of slavery to the king in those early days?

The words, practices, and incidents examined in this chapter reflected the public contours that royal slavery began to take in the first years of the 1670s. During these early years social identity took new public forms, and the limits of freedom and slavery were tested in different spheres of local life. Social identity was reinvented in small events and large incidents, imagined through social practices and interactions, carved out of improvised solutions and concessions, and asserted politically and disputed in unexpected exchanges as well as in particular claims and concerted action. As it is by now commonplace to state, history is not only embodied, or imagined in "big" or "great" events but it is often wittingly or unwittingly produced, enacted, or recognized in the simplicity of ordinary and quotidian events too. I write from that premise. At times I purposefully, and not naively, stretch what may be considered customary historiographical limits to the type of events that are accepted as constitutive of "history."

For the most part, the practical changes associated with the making of social identity examined in this chapter were chronicled by three local participant observers—a member of the private contractor's family, a parish priest, and a slave—in private correspondence and in a letter to the Crown. Their texts often constitute a collection of short, at times pointillistic, vignettes of life in the settlement in the early 1670s. I term these vignettes *microevents* because of their apparent insignificance as historical detail, their often incidental, anecdotal, and even impressionistic quality, or their personal and local character. A "thick description," reading and contextualization of these at-first-sight-dismissible microevents however may elucidate wider trends of local social change, or at least illuminate different spheres of local life at the time.

The three chroniclers selected current incidents in El Cobre that they found significant, problematic, and emblematic of the transformations taking place under the new royal administration of the mines. Overall, they portrayed these events as a regrettable rupture between the past and the present. Although they proceeded from different local sectors in the social order of the mining settlement, the three chroniclers spoke from the same political position, namely, one supporting the old private order of the mines. Implicit in the point of view from which they chronicled events were standard principles and conventional understandings about slavery, social relations, and private property. Their (always critical) texts about current life in El Cobre constituted narratives of dislocated order, anomie, misguided change, and misrule.

The documents these men left behind provide different layers of information to the historian: brief glimpses of actual life during the transition years into Crown rule; indication that the related microevents were seen by contemporaries as part of a transformative process, that is, that they were regarded or construed as a major "change" from the previous mining order; and testimony of the contended character of these changes. The three major chroniclers whose texts I refer to were: Don Antonio Matta y Haro, a family member of the former private contractor who was vying for the administration of the mines; Father Don Pedro de Cerquera, the former parish priest who stayed on for a few years in the settlement; and Nicholás Montenegro, a royal slave who had been a favorite of the contractor's Eguiluz family. Not all the discussion of this chapter is grounded in the microevents depicted in these local chronicles, however. There are also reconstructions and contextualizations based on other sources.

A Royal Slave Chronicler

Perhaps the most direct account of the major practical and ideological changes occurring among the king's slaves themselves was provided by a member of the community, the royal slave Nicholás Montenegro. In a letter to his former private mistress, Doña Paula Eguiluz y Montenegro, who was then living in Havana, Montenegro reported and criticized the latest and most appalling local events taking place in El Cobre under Governor Magaña's rule. Who was this allegedly literate—and politically conservative—Nicholás Montenegro?

The fifty-two-year-old Montenegro was "a mulatto slave, son of a [female] slave of the accountant Juan de Eguiluz."[1] That genealogical-cum-property identification purportedly set him apart from other slaves whom Eguiluz had received upon taking over the administration of the mines in 1620, ostensibly constituting him as a private slave not subject to confiscation by the Crown. More specifically, Montenegro had been the loyal slave of Doña Paula de Eguiluz y Montenegro, daughter of Don Juan de Eguiluz and wife of Don Antonio Matta y Haro (one of the three chroniclers). At a time when the royal slaves of El Cobre were developing independent familial and kinship identities through their own sets of surnames, Montenegro and fifty-five-year-old María de Eguiluz were perhaps the only slaves in the settlement bearing their masters' family name. Whether his surname indicated a mere property relation to the master or a close, and perhaps illicit, kinship relation to that branch of the family is difficult to determine. However, Montenegro himself sustained an apparently unreformed identity as his former mistress's private slave even after she had been evicted from the settlement. Although Montenegro, along with other royal slaves, had been appointed *mandador* or *alcalde* (official or bailiff) to oversee order in the mining settlement for the state, he also (secretly?) acted—or pretended to act—on behalf of the old private contractor's family.

Montenegro was among the 28.4 percent mulatto slaves living in the Real de Minas in 1670.[2] One of the most skilled artisans in the mines, he had the prestige of holding the title of "master" welder. Although during this period there seemed to exist no significant racial distinctions among holders of skilled occupations in the mining settlement, Montenegro's racial identification as a mulatto and his highly skilled position may have played a role in the relatively high status he attained as an appointed slave officer.

More importantly, Montenegro seems to have been literate. The court dossier in which Montenegro's letter to his former mistress was included (and thanks to which it was preserved) explicitly noted that it was written "in his own hand and signature" [*escrita de su letra y firma*].[3] However surprising or exceptional it may seem to a modern reader that a slave in El Cobre was literate, Montenegro may not have been the only one. There seems to have been at least one other literate royal slave in the settlement at the time, Juan de Santiago Vicente. Like Montenegro, Santiago Vicente also held the title of "master," in this case master smelter, and he, too, was mulatto. Moreover, the latter held another official slave position in the 1680s, "captain of the people of the mines."[4] Both enslaved men were appraised at the astonishing amount of 1,000 pesos in 1677—twice the value of any other skilled slave regardless of race in El Cobre at the time.[5] This may have reflected not only their skilled training, or even their lighter race, but also the high value placed on their literacy. In fact, although far from common, throughout the following century too, literacy was by no means nonexistent among the enslaved and freed people in El Cobre.[6] And one hundred years later, by the 1770s, there was even a resident teacher in the village.[7]

Transferring Authority

After the state's takeover of the mining jurisdiction, the authority and property claims of the former contractor's family were suspended—provisionally in 1670, particularly after 1677, and indefinitely from 1700 to 1780. Indeed, the descendants and heirs of private contractor Don Juan de Eguiluz were physically removed from Santiago del Prado. Captain Don Francisco Salazar y Acuña, Eguiluz's eldest daughter's husband, who had been granted his father-in-law's mining contract in 1648, was imprisoned pending an investigation of the case; and Matta y Haro, husband of another of the Eguiluz daughters and himself a contender for a new contract of the mines, returned to Havana hoping to see a favorable resolution of his case. Thus, after 1670, a rapidly growing population of 271 slaves was left behind in the settlement without any direct administration. A few freemen and -women, some married to royal slaves, may have remained in El Cobre as well. The aged and frail caretaker of the local Marian shrine, the hermit Melchor de los Remedios stayed until his death in 1681. In addition, the governor probably stationed a small regiment of soldiers in the settlement, but there is little evidence recorded of their presence in the mines at this time.

One remaining figure of authority in El Cobre was the parish priest. In former days, the parish priest had been employed by the private contractor, although many of his fees for sacraments and religious services had been paid by free and prosperous parishioners living and working in the settlement. The administration of the sacraments to the slaves and their evangelization, however, had also been tasks accruing to his ministry in Santiago del Prado. After the confiscation of the mines, Father Cerquera stayed on to administer spiritually to his enslaved parishioners and to supervise everyday life for about two years, after which he was replaced by a new priest. Although Father Cerquera began to receive his salary from the state, he remained an ally of his former employers and a critic of the governor. His two early letters strongly reflected those loyalties; his language, opinions, asides, judgments of the governor's policies, and attitudes toward the slaves evince an attachment to the old mining regime in which proper order had prevailed. Future parish priests, however, would often be more supportive of their enslaved parishioners. Indeed, they would become supporters of the new local order of El Cobre where, after all, they worked, served God, and lived quite well for decades.

Given the power vacuum in the abandoned mining complex, provisional solutions to the problem of the administration of the slaves had to be devised. The improvised character of the governor's policies toward the former mining slaves under his authority, or at times his failure to control everyday events in the mines, marked some of the first important changes in El Cobre. Although the new slaves of the king often benefited from some of the governor's expedient policies or from his benign neglect, this was not always the case. Indeed, while the interests of governor and slaves may have at times converged, they often clashed as well.

Conferring a Special Character to Royal Slavery

A Scandalous Microevent

Little is known of how royal slavery was construed elsewhere in the Spanish Empire, particularly in the fortification works of the New World where the greatest concentration of *esclavos del rey* could be found. Little has been written—or even been wondered—about this form of slavery or what it entailed. To be sure there was some ambiguity to the category itself, one that could at times be invoked to make special claims: slavery to the king could either be considered a form of slavery like any other, or it could be regarded as a distinctive form of servitude by virtue of the master's royal status. Yet another possibility, of course, was that various sectors of colonial society imagined the category differently, contending any alleged special character to it. In any case, these were matters that were often settled by custom. Yet, custom and tradition are forged historically, often in the flux of everyday life and particular incidents.

That royal slavery came to be imagined by some, including the governor, as different from regular slavery becomes especially clear from a microevent recounted by the parish priest, Cerquera, in one of his letter/chronicles to his former employer, then residing in Havana. The episode illustrates particularly well how the meaning of royal slavery was produced through the social exchanges and simple incidents of everyday life. In the following episode, which took place sometime between 1670 and 1672, the governor articulated, and to a certain extent publicly acknowledged, a conception of royal slavery as a separate and special category of bonded people.

The reported microevent took place during an audience with the governor regarding the latter's contended rental of the *hato* (pasture lands) of Barajagua (part of the mining jurisdiction) to Father Francisco Ramos of Santiago de Cuba. Cerquera recalled:

The day when some slaves that had been called by [Governor] Señor Don Andrés made their appearance in [Santiago de] Cuba to answer if the cattle in the *hato* was wild or if it belonged to Father Ramos, they took great liberties with the said Father in his [the governor's] presence for it [the exchange] reached a breaking point [*rompimiento*].[8]

Losing his temper, Ramos did not feel compelled to mince words with slaves. According to Cerquera's letter, Ramos told the slave Salvador Lunguengue that "he would buy him, dishonoring him with words."[9] To the dismay of Cerquera (and almost certainly of others present as well, particularly Ramos), the governor intervened on behalf of the royal slaves. According to Cerquera, directing himself to Ramos, the governor remarked: "Father, these slaves are not like the others, they are the king's. They have a regard for words."[10] The parish priest, Cerquera, closed his narration by commenting ironically on the importance of those words and the governor's handling of the matter: "Indeed, Señor, they [the slaves] who are bad, are sure to get better hearing such things."[11]

The implications of this episode, then, were not lost on its chronicler, Cerquera, nor as he noted, on the royal slaves. The governor made an explicit distinction between regular and royal slaves—a distinction that Cerquera and Ramos did not favor. Indeed, it was as if the governor ascribed honor to these slaves by virtue of their master and endowed them with the right to a respectful verbal treatment that acknowledged their special status. Thus, in the priest's story, not only did the royal slaves speak against a white person—an ecclesiastic and the son of an elite family—but also "they took great liberties with him." Interestingly, despite Cerquera's criticism of the governor's intervention in the exchange, the priest utilized the term "dishonoring him [the slave] with words," unwittingly attributing some honor to the slaves as well.

Echoes of the governor's construction of royal slavery in this incident were heard many years later in the king's slaves' public representation of their identity. The reader will repeatedly recognize instances of that special conception throughout the pages of this book. Suffice it to point out here one such invocation of their identity as the king's slaves evident in a collective representation directed to the island's captain general. In it the royal slaves made some claims to expected "good treatment"—in this case in relation to contested land and labor requisitions. In the 1730s, the king's slaves recalled, "The experience of our ancestors was that they were attended to when they went to the said work [in the fortification projects]. . . . Under other governors they [our ancestors] were heeded like slaves of whom we are slaves."[12] (See Appendix 6.)

The Claim to the Means of Production: Land

After the confiscation of the mines a transformation in land tenure took place in El Cobre. No longer would Santiago del Prado constitute a self-sufficient private estate on which large- or medium-scale agricultural production took place alongside (or instead of) copper-mining production, and in the midst of which slaves could work in provision grounds (conucos) set aside "so that they can be better sustained and contented."[13] Amidst the general confusion of the initial years—even before any final judicial determination as to the status of the mining territory had been made—different sectors of colonial society, including the royal slaves, began to consider the territory encompassed in the mining jurisdiction as newly opened *realenga* land (vacant royal or public lands) to be appropriated for their uses.

However, the land of the mining complex was *realenga* only superficially, that is, only in the sense that it had reverted to the Crown. In fact, the mines constituted part of a separate jurisdiction whose integrity presumably had to be preserved, given the possibility of recontracting or reactivating mining at some point in the future. Yet, Governor Magaña allowed the *cabildo* (local government) of Santiago de Cuba to grant parts of the mining jurisdiction's land to citizens of that city as if it were public land and to dispose of other pieces for the city's own use. Land distributions were easily carried out because of the extraordinary facility with which *cabildos* could allocate land, a prerogative local bodies retained in Cuba until 1729. By adjudicating to itself the right to grant "public" land from the adjacent mining territory, the *cabildo* of Santiago de Cuba not only extended its control and power over the neighboring jurisdiction but also it actually dismantled the integrity of the mining complex. Indeed, Cerquera denounced such land-grabbing in a letter to Matta y Haro as early as 1672. Wrote the priest with some irony: "This [territory] seems to be *realengo* as all try to take control over it. . . . Tamayo got Angolosongo from the *cabildo* where he breeds pigs and he also got Cauto Arriba, [and] the mulatto canon got Yarayabo. . . . I will ask for the Hatillo for myself to see if at least I can get something out of these mines."[14] In addition, former private contractor Salazar appealed the confiscation through legal channels, strongly protesting in 1677, "The *cabildo* of the city of Santiago de Cuba has given out without citation or consent some lands within the limits pertaining to the said mines."[15] Salazar kept his original titles to lands he claimed the *cabildo* despoiled him of through improper grants.

Competing claims over land in the mining jurisdiction were based, at least initially, on a convenient ambiguity regarding the status of the territory. Such claims revolved around confusing questions: Was land legally still the private property of the former private contractor, Salazar? Or did it constitute a separate and distinct corporate jurisdiction under royal control due to the confiscation? Had this territory become (*realenga*) public vacant land that the *cabildo* of Santiago de Cuba could rightfully distribute? Or, to add the royal slaves' own take on the new situation, was the territory of the royal mining jurisdiction theirs in view of their status as the king's slaves?

Land became a focus of political struggle for the royal slaves of El Cobre from the early years of transition into Crown rule and throughout the eighteenth century. The land issue that first, and perhaps most saliently, came to represent these enslaved people's understanding of their prerogatives and special entitlements as the king's slaves was that of the *hato* of Barajagua. This extensive *hato*, some 16 leagues from the core of the mining settlement, had played a key role in the provisioning of meat for mine personnel.[16] Plentiful wild game, particularly pigs, roamed the forests of Barajagua. For the slaves of El Cobre, that *hato* constituted, above all, an important common hunting territory, and for those more inclined to breed animals, an open ground on which to establish their modest corrals. As an ample source of meat and hides for their internal economy, Barajagua, however distant from El Cobre, complemented the farming land in the settlement.

As early as 1672, Magaña used his authority over the newly acquired Crown jurisdiction to rent Barajagua to Ramos, whom I already introduced dishonoring the royal slaves with words. The rental immediately became a burning issue in the settlement, because, according to the parish priest, the royal slaves "complained to the governor how taking away Barajagua meant they could not subsist themselves."[17] The royal slaves based their entitlement to the usufruct of this pasture land partly upon a right to provision themselves on royal land.

Montenegro provided an inside glimpse of the ideological changes taking place among royal slaves in Santiago del Prado when he, like the parish priest, informed his mistress of the governor's controversial rental of Barajagua:

Father Ramos rented the *hato* of Barajagua for 200 pesos but only [rented] the grass leaving free the *monterías* [hunting grounds] for the people of these mines [*gente de estas minas*]. And they [the enslaved people of these mines] did not like it because they say that Barajagua and the *monterías* are all theirs, that the King gave it to them.[18]

According to this account, the claim of the "people of these mines" (note how Montenegro refers to his fellow slaves) to this valuable pasture land—indeed, their exclusive entitlement to it—was also based on their belief in a royal land grant to the community. Although Montenegro disapproved of the fragmentation of what he still considered his former master's private territory, he also opposed the royal slaves' claim that the *hato* "belonged" to them because the king had made them the grant of it, just as he disapproved of the king's slaves' appropriation of other resources.

Decades later the enslaved inhabitants of El Cobre were still making similar claims to Barajagua and other land as king's slaves. While the royal slaves retained access to Barajagua for the rest of the seventeenth century, somewhere between 1711 and 1713 the *hato* was rented again.[19] Although thereafter royal slaves would never again recover the prized *hato*, Barajagua remained a conflictive issue and a vivid memory in their accounts of the community's identity throughout the eighteenth century.

Other Enactments of Royal Slavery According to Montenegro

In another illustration of how royal slavery began to be shaped in practice during the first years of Crown rule, Montenegro related the following microevent to his mistress:

Since my Lady left these mines, Miguel Congolo planted himself in the *covacha* and has taken advantage of all the cacao produced in both harvests of this last year and when I told him how he could do that, that those cacaos belonged to my Lady Doña Paula, he responded to me that they belong to the King and so [did] he.[20]

Miguel Congolo, then, explicitly assumed an identity as the king's slave and implicitly defined his royal status broadly as an entitlement to the freed property that became part of the Crown's mining jurisdiction, in this case the cacao harvests he had been appropriating. Montenegro, in contrast, contested the meaning of that identity by harking back to established assumptions about private property and master-slave relations. Two ways of imagining identity and rightful order in El Cobre—one based on the past and the other on a new present—clashed in the dialogue between the two enslaved men.

The king's slaves of El Cobre also believed they were entitled to the copper tailings left in the mines from former mining days. Once more, the old regime and entitlements that emanated from a jurisdiction organized around claims to private property were openly questioned and dismissed in favor of a new set of principles. An apparently concerned Montenegro wrote to Doña Paula: "As I tried to prevent Pedro Viojo from taking copper, he said to me that he did not recognize these mines as belonging to my Lady Doña Paula, but that they are the king's. All the others said the same."[21] The new principles implicit in this microevent suggest again that slaves considered these mineral resources as public, that they were entitled to the property of their new master the king, as well as to a means of production to make a living—a concise and practical reference to a change in the social and labor relations of the mining settlement.

Some of these formulations and their related practices met with the governor's approval—or, more probably, his indifference. Montenegro, for example, reported having informed the governor that royal slaves mined copper on their own, without even paying taxes for it:

> I told the Señor governor [that they were extracting copper] and he asked me what kind of copper it was and I said that the tailings [*pedacitos*], and he hasn't responded a word to me yet. That is bound to be the situation of an estate without its owner [*en este estado está al fin, hacienda sin su dueño*].[22]

Thus, according to Montenegro, the governor, too, ignored his appointed *mandador*'s repeated efforts to preserve older mining principles and strictures as well as his former (private) master's interests. Extracting copper from light surface mining (albeit not directly from deep mining) became an important informal industry in El Cobre in subsequent decades. Royal slaves' right to this copper, and their exemption from taxation, reappeared as a contended issue in future years as well.[23]

In addition, the king's slaves shaped their identity publicly through another everyday social practice. Montenegro's critical eye for meaningful local change provides a cameo about changes reflected in the dressing practices of El Cobre. He linked such practices to new attitudes among the slaves, to their new sense of identity, and to new market-oriented activities made possible by informal copper mining:

> There is no other occupation today in these mines nor other aspirations than to obtain more copper and to embellish their bodies. . . . They no longer take pride in adorning their skirts with [simple] laces, now they use silver ones. Before there was too much arrogance among these señores and señoras, as my Lady well knows, but today it is too much for they say publicly that they are free [*horros*].[24]

According to Montenegro, royal slaves associated their release from private slavery and the new (dis)order in the mining settlement under Crown rule with freedom, or at least with greater freedom than in former times. Not only did royal slaves freely appropriate the copper tailings of what they regarded as their mines but also they gained access to purchasing power in the market. This concrete and practical freedom made possible the concomitant freedom of choosing clothing with which to publicly construct their social image. In other words, access to the market enabled slaves' expressions of individuality and control over their social body, so to speak. Montenegro's remarks also imply that participation in the market led slaves (and presumably other subordinate groups) to transcend their fixed place in the established social order. In this case, such dislocations were evidenced in breaches of sumptuary laws and dress codes such as the use of silver lace among enslaved women and even free females of color; in manifestations of "wealth" and empowerment that the conservative Montenegro considered "arrogant" and out of place in the case of slaves; and in provocatively explicit statements that articulated these changes as forms of freedom.[25] Even if there was bias and exaggeration in Montenegro's account of a new local prosperity, intensification of laboring activity among the enslaved people of El Cobre, and of the "luxuries" they were now able to afford, his understanding of the significance of these apparently minor expressions of social identity and status through dressing practices was to the point.[26]

The king's slaves also made use of dress as a way of testing the limits of social place in colonial society. Montenegro pointed specifically to the defiant garb of at least one slave, Germán: "Their audacity and impudence has led them to do in Santiago [de Cuba] what they had never dared before, to wear hats and cloaks."[27] Although Montenegro uses the plural, he was specifically referring to the case of the slave Germán who had "the boldness of taking away Captain Ignacio Ramos's hat and go around walking with it. . . . " Germán's behavior was considered so transgressive that it led to orders for his arrest. That the governor sent orders to Montenegro to arrest this royal slave points to yet another set of striking political and social events taking place in El Cobre.

Transferring Authority and Redefining Political Relations

The first official royal orders regarding the new administration of the mines and their slaves arrived in September 1670. Upon receiving the royal edict charging him with the administration of the mining jurisdiction, Magaña called an audience with the affected parties. He summoned the parish priest Cerquera; Matta y Haro, who stood for the heirs of the private contractor; and some slave *alcaldes*. That slaves were summoned to an audience with whom colonial society regarded as people of honor and that bondmen were represented by slaves bearing the title of *alcaldes* must have constituted an unusual event or a breach of protocol, suggesting rather unconventional practices in the making. Two years later Matta y Haro related the microevent to the Crown with some indignation:

Having gone [to the governor] and having read extraofficially the Royal Edict of Your Majesty, he told the *alcalde* slaves, you have already heard, now you don't have anything to do with the Captain General, nor with Don Francisco Salazar [then under arrest], nor with Don Antonio [Matta y Haro], only with me.[28]

With these words the governor had drawn a political line between past and present. Indeed, he had publicly—if "extraofficially"—divested the two rival brothers-in-law and the captain general, who dealt with the initial transactions regarding the case from Havana, of all authority over the slaves. This act established Governor Magaña's authority as the Crown's representative over the mining jurisdiction and its 271 royal slaves. Slave *alcaldes* would act thereafter as liaisons between the royal slaves and Magaña.

What, then, were the slave officials' duties in the mining settlement? Were these altogether new positions and practices in El Cobre, or did they have a precedent in the old mining order? Can duties related to these positions be considered reformulations, at times radical reformulations, of slavery?

That slave *alcaldes* had existed before the 1670s is clear from the fact that Magaña was able to summon these officers to his closed "investiture" meeting in 1670. At that time, Magaña had not so much created these positions, but rather made already existing *alcalde* officials directly responsible to him. Furthermore, Matta y Haro, who had lived in the settlement in the 1650s and 1660s, seemed familiar with those positions although he "did not know with what foundation they [some of the slaves] were given this name [of *alcaldes*]." Matta y Haro thought that the title *alcalde* had been given to those "in charge of making sure that others went to the Church and to Mass to pray."[29] The very need to clarify why some slaves in El Cobre held the title of *alcaldes* spoke to the unconventionality of the practice. According to Matta y Haro's description, in former years the office of *alcalde* had corresponded to that of *mandones*, *capitanes*, and *alguaciles de la iglesia*, lower-level ranks of Indian officialdom used by the church elsewhere in the New World to enforce religious duties in their newly evangelized congregations.[30] However, the position of *alcalde* in the Real de Minas, and perhaps those of *mandadores* and *capitanes* (whose titles resembled those of the church *mandones* and *capitanes* elsewhere), may have been derived from religiously related appointments.

The role of the church in the mining settlement—especially in the evangelization of the first-generation African slaves—may have given rise to such offices among slaves years before. As early as 1608, a slave named Domingo had been trained as sacristan of the church in the mining complex—a role often played by clergy.[31] Moreover, at least since 1647, the church made use of the slaves of the Real de Minas to perform its liturgical music.[32] Although these occupations had little direct bearing on the enslaved congregation in comparison with the role of *alcalde*, for example, they reflected the local church's long-standing tradition of incorporating slaves into religious activities.

Yet, while the office of *alcaldes*—and those of *mandadores* and *capitanes*—entailed primarily religious disciplining functions during an earlier period, by the 1670s the *alcades'* jurisdiction had certainly expanded to encompass secular responsibilities as well. In summoning the slave *alcaldes* to the meeting in 1670 and placing them under his direct orders, the governor may have begun to redefine their links to former masters and to the church (as well as perhaps to some more recently established liaison to the colonial state through the captain general in Havana). Slave officers would now constitute the political link between local authorities and the royal slave community. In fact, royal slaves took on unusual duties regarding slaves' authority to implement local law and order, implying a reformulation of political authority in everyday life in El Cobre as well. In subsequent years, the relation between the king and his slaves would in some ways approximate that of Crown and vassals, subordinate vassals, to be sure, like the Crown's Indian wards, but in any case an ambiguous relation to a distant and symbolic master mediated at different levels by the state apparatus.

Although several royal slaves acted as officials in El Cobre during the 1670s, very few of their names survive in the historical record. One that has reached us is, of course, that of the *mandador* Montenegro. His case, however, is somewhat paradoxical. As already mentioned before, while his position as a slave official entailed expanded duties granted by the governor, Montenegro himself defined his position in his chronicle letter not so much as royal slave serving the Crown, but rather as private slave overseeing the interests of his former masters—a position not acknowledged by most slaves in the mining settlement, or, for that matter, by the governor. Montenegro's case suggests how the conflictive loyalties the governor attempted to address in his "investiture" meeting still plagued the settlement not only with respect to the parish priest but even perhaps with respect to some slaves like Montenegro.

Some of the most striking duties that slave official positions took on in the early 1670s, particularly under Magaña's administration, are evidenced in microevents narrated by our local chroniclers. As *mandador*, for instance, Montenegro received orders from the governor to arrest royal slaves—a local police duty traditionally performed by free *alcaldes* in the Spanish world, and not by slaves. Montenegro's primary allegiance to the authority of his former master and his attachment to the old private mining order, however, could at times lead him to resist the governor's orders and his duties as *mandador*. To his mistress Eguiluz, Montenegro related, "The governor sent me an order to apprehend [the defying slave Germán who had worn a hat and cloak in Santiago de Cuba] and I, remembering that he had grown up in my Lady's own house, let him go, he has run away."[33] Instead of following orders from the governor, Montenegro thought to please his mistress by letting her former house slave go. Although one should not dismiss Montenegro's possible friendship with Germán in the decision to shirk his duty, he told his former mistress that he had overstepped the governor's authority in deference to her.

The extent to which the duties of *alcaldes* were redefined under Magaña's administration is more starkly illustrated in a personal story recounted by Matta y Haro in his own chronicle of scandalous microevents in the mines:

On December 27th of last year, 1670, [Magaña] sent a written order to the *alcaldes* of the Mines, who are slaves there, that I still have in my power . . . where he ordered that a little fourteen-year-old [female] slave, who was serving me and my wife and who, having proceeded from forty-six [slave] pieces that my father-in-law bought for the mines, was our slave . . . , be returned to her mother, and he made our own slaves the executors of his injustice, . . . [thereby] affronting and insulting us [as] . . . people of honor.[34]

Aside from a concern with property rights over the slave girl, the narrative strongly decried the governor's ways of proceeding. Not only were there now slave *alcaldes* in El Cobre, but also the governor assigned them law enforcement duties normally reserved for free members of the body politic. Furthermore, to Matta y Haro, this policy was untenable and especially humiliating, for it had been extended to his own person. Indeed, in this case the policy marked a complete inversion of the social order: slaves had been endowed with authority over masters, and blacks and mulattos over whites. Specifically, in the truly extreme situation depicted by Matta y Haro, royal slave *alcaldes* were to act as law enforcement agents over a white man, a Spaniard, an alleged *hidalgo* (a nobleman), and a former master. Matta y Haro spoke for the hierarchy and honor that structured social life at the time, particularly for those aspiring to a high social or class position. From that vantage point, the governor's policies were indeed acts of political and cultural aggression—political in their radical displacement of power and authority, and cultural in their dismissal of the ritualized social conventions of colonial society.

This microevent also points to the charged politics of humiliation and encoded aggression in this corner of the colonial world and illustrates the early incorporation of the king's slaves of El Cobre into the political circuits of colonial society. Although, as will be seen in later chapters, the king's slaves would sometimes operate as pawns of well-placed citizens and royal officials in the political chessboard of Santiago de Cuba, they stood to benefit from the personal vendettas, factional conflicts, and institutional interests played out in the city's political theater.[35] In the midst of the conflict between the governor and claimant, the slaves benefited not only by the return of the girl to her mother in the community but also from the deployment of power by royal slave officials.

The incident denounced by Matta y Haro, however, exemplified more than just the new role of royal slave officials or of the politics of symbolic aggression in which the king's slaves became implicated. It also represented another sort of transformation of social relations in the mines. The change in authority over the mines severed former relations between private master and slaves. Moreover, the story obliquely suggests that the governor, as representative of the Crown, acknowledged family bonds and prerogatives among the new royal slaves, or, more tellingly, opened up a process in which the principle of *patria potestad* (parental rights) would constitute a more important part of the new local order and of the king's slaves' social identity. In effect, royal slavery, in practice, would mean greater autonomy and more power to the community and to the family.

In a series of statements taken by the courts in the 1780s and 1790s, statements intended legally to determine who was free and who was enslaved, several people distinguished slavery to the king from personal slavery. In effect, respondents linked slavery to the king to certain prerogatives and practices associated with freedom. Some responses even hinted at the significance of familial ties and obliquely of *patria potestad*. Francisco Xavier de Quiala, a freedman from El Cobre, testified that "everyone lived in his [or her] own house, serving their own parents without any known master except the king."[36] Pedro Antonio Moreno, another freedman from El Cobre, declared that he had known a woman named Teresa Coba "living in her house without a private master, [that] she did not know any other master but God and the King. . . ."[37] Similarly, José Basilio Maestre, a mason of Santiago de Cuba who knew Rafaela Sánchez "from the said pueblo, [observed] that she enjoyed freedom without subjection to any person except to [her] said mother."[38]

Slaves with the Rank of "Captain"

Finally, the position of *capitán* (captain) may have overlapped, or have been conflated with that of *alcalde* or *mandador* in El Cobre, but this particular title could be traced at least to the 1620s in the settlement. It is unclear, however, what that official position entailed in earlier days, or how it may have been transformed in the 1670s. From at least 1620 to 1665, the title of *capitán* was held by the same man, a slave named Francisco.[39] A title used in different contexts, *capitán* could have referred to the clergy's attendants in evangelizing activities among slaves or presumably to the captain of a working brigade (although in this case that of *mayoral* [overseer] seems to have been preferred). Moreover, the term captain could have applied to the leaders of African *cabildos* or associations as well. More conventionally, however, that title may have referred to military rank, too. Indeed, a thirty-four-year-old slave, Alejo, was registered in the inventory of 1647 with the title of *alférez* (ensign or lieutenant),[40] one that suggested that some military hierarchy may have existed among the slaves of the Real de Minas since the very early days, or perhaps again of an African *cabildo* with titles corresponding to a military hierarchy.[41] These slaves had in fact been called upon at least by a previous governor in emergencies such as enemy attack. The fact that advanced age and physical impairment had not disqualified Francisco from holding a position requiring physical exertion suggests that his may not have been primarily a military role. At any rate, the existence of a *capitán*, of an *alférez*, and of several *mayorales* at different points from 1608 to 1647 points to a rudimentary slave hierarchy in the early mining settlement, too.

By 1677, once Captain Francisco died, the rank of *capitán* passed to seventy-seven-year-old Juan Moreno, a Creole slave who had been a *mayoral* in the 1640s. Contrary to slave inventories in 1608, 1620, and 1647, no slave *mayorales* were registered in the inventory of 1677. Of the former *mayoral*, now *capitán*, Moreno, more is known than of former Captain Francisco. Captain Moreno was known as one of three "seers" who as a child brought to El Cobre the miraculous effigy of the Virgin Mary, found at sea, and with it a new Marian cult.[42] Such an honor may have made him the right person to succeed Captain Francisco, particularly if the position entailed religious duties. Whatever the rank of *capitán* may have once entailed, by 1677 Captain Moreno's responsibilities and authority extended beyond matters strictly religious and military.

When the king's slaves of El Cobre, for instance, protested a Crown policy that sought to transfer many of the male royal slaves to work in Havana, the elder Captain Moreno apparently had the authority to represent the royal slaves and make a collective petition on their behalf. In addition, when in an act of political defiance, the royal slaves fled to the surrounding mountains to strengthen their petition, Captain Moreno again negotiated with authorities in the name of his fellow slaves. In both instances, Moreno assumed the role of official representative and advocate for the royal slaves. Indeed, he functioned as a mediator between the slave community and the state.[43] At any rate, Captain Moreno's involvement in the community's political protests—both in the legal and illegal ones—shows that royal slave officials were not merely local agents of the master state. They could also act fairly independently from authorities on behalf of the community, thereby making their political liaison to the state work both ways. Although in future decades, many royal slave *alcaldes* and officials felt compelled to put their loyalty to the colonial state over that to their fellow villagers—and sometimes kin—others would, despite risks, take the community's side, or a side in a factionalized community. Yet, in cases where local slave officials could not—or did not—officiate as advocates of the community, the royal slaves of El Cobre selected their own *apoderado* (legal spokesman or proxy) among their ranks to act on their behalf as Captain Juan Moreno did in the present case.[44]

By 1687, Juan Moreno's successor to the ranked position of *capitán* was a man from a younger generation, Juan de Santiago Vicente, a fifty-seven-year-old man whom I introduced as the counterpart of Montenegro in skills, race, literacy, and highest assessed value (1,000 pesos). Santiago Vicente's views and identification, however, may have differed from those of Montenegro for he had been among those whom the latter had denounced for taking and smelting copper on his own account.[45] Repeatedly a widower, the three marriages into which Santiago Vicente entered as a royal slave by 1688 had been to freewomen, a sign perhaps of his high standing despite juridical slavery.[46] And, by 1709, when he had finally become free, Santiago Vicente had already married the fourth freewoman in his life.[47] Captain Santiago Vicente's position and authority—like that of Montenegro as *mandador* in the 1670s—may have been based on criteria having to do with his skills, his economic means, perhaps his mixed race, and his general high social standing in the community.

The vague position of *capitán*, like that of the *alcaldes* and *mandadores*, would become institutionalized sometime before 1709. In this case, it came to denote the highest officer position in the hierarchy of a properly constituted local militia company. It may be noted by way of closure that by 1709, however, the then-seventy-nine-year-old freedman Santiago Vicente had lost his title of captain. Instead he had become lieutenant (*teniente*) in the village militia company.[48] The title *capitán* was now held by the freedman Thomás Rodríguez and had acquired a clearly military character. And yet, Captain Rodríguez and Lieutenant Santiago Vicente, symbolizing two generations and types of captains in El Cobre, had become related to each other through marriage. Rodríguez had married the former captain's daughter and, as was customary in El Cobre at the time, even lived in his father-in-law's household for some years.[49] Indeed, however changed, specialized, and institutionalized the position of *capitán* may have become with the years, the high rank remained in the same family for many decades, thus providing an interesting kinship continuity between past and present as well as a glimpse of how families in El Cobre could consolidate social status and position across generations.

In short, although with the decline of mining production many years before the former private slaves may have already begun to enjoy greater autonomy in their lives, royal administration for them came to entail a more distant and mediated subjection to a master, in this case "the king" or the state. More concretely at this time, it became subjection to the governor of the island's eastern region. One of the most controversial of the governor's practices came to be the use of slave officials with the title of *alcaldes, mandadores,* or *capitanes* to maintain order in the mining jurisdiction. Although precedent seems to have existed in El Cobre for some of these slaves' official positions, the governor conveniently expanded or transformed the functions of these offices as the situation required. Regardless of their initial expedient character, these positions and the practices they entailed became precedents for the development of related community institutions. In fact, they would ambiguously blend into (political) forms of freedom in coming years.

Conclusion

The chronicles of the *mandador* Montenegro, the parish priest Cerquera, and Matta y Haro provide pithy glimpses of the social dislocations and transformations in the mining settlement after the Crown took over the jurisdiction. Their texts also register their opposition to these changes whose implications they all too well were beginning to discern.

It was above all the dismantling of a formerly privately held jurisdiction that opened up the space for quite radical and long-standing transformations in El Cobre.[50] The transference of the mines and its slaves from "private" to "royal" hands first came to entail the actual "freeing up" of the means of production in the jurisdiction (i.e., land, mines, resources, and labor) to the usufruct claims of several sectors of colonial society, including the royal slaves. As the Crown's intermittent efforts to find a new private contractor in subsequent years had little success, the mining jurisdiction remained for the most part free of any private form of administration or ownership at least until late in the eighteenth century.[51] What became consolidated during this long hiatus of more than one hundred years was an unusual local order, one based on social relations and political practices only beginning to take shape in the early 1670s. Much had yet to be worked out and negotiated.

Overall, the disarray of the early years of Crown rule did not merely translate into more autonomy (and freedom) for the slaves. Above all, it evinced more significant cultural and political transformations in the royal slaves' reformulation of claims, entitlements, and social identity in the colonial order of things.

CHAPTER 3

An Unusual Proposal

The love for our *patria* [homeland] and our work
move us to ask . . . the mercy of being allowed to
stay in our pueblo, paying tribute, in whatever
manner it is arranged for us while we find [a way to
pay] for our freedom. . . .

Most of the Creole, blacks and mulattos of the said
mines are married and we have our families whom
we have always had to support. . . .

[We manifest our] desire for greater opportunities in
the royal service [to] carry out great [military]
actions, and even if they go unrewarded, we will
remain content to have achieved them. . . .
                              —Captain Juan Moreno, July 13, 1677

In 1677, a political clash over the future of the king's slaves took place mainly, but not exclusively, between royal slaves and the state. Royal orders to
transfer the best and most able male royal slaves to work in the fortification
projects of Havana threatened the dissolution of the enslaved community in
El Cobre. The royal slaves revolted by fleeing collectively to the surrounding mountains. But more than *cimarronaje* (flight) to the margins of society
in search of—an often romanticized—"freedom," the king's slaves made use
of this act to negotiate some "freedoms" and prerogatives as a "people" within the boundaries of colonial society.
     Of the event itself little is known, but the confrontation left behind a
petition and a letter from the king's slaves with some unconventional proposals slipped under the veneer of a mild legal framework and language.
This chapter focuses on how the enslaved people of El Cobre imagined and
contested social identity within the discursive parameters of early modern
colonial ideology. It uncovers key aspects of the royal slaves' imagined iden-

tity only seven years into Crown rule, at what I take to be a decisive moment in the community's local history. The chapter examines carefully the ideological formulations (or reformulations) informing what I argue are relatively bold proposals in the petition. But rather than distilling the social and political boldness of some acts, statements, or events through the critical remarks and observations of contemporaries as I mostly did in the previous chapter, here I operate more from the "omniscient" position of the historian. It is in the tension between conventional and unconventional notions articulated in the petition that the significance of the king's slaves' proposals must be sought in this case.

The King's Early Policy Regarding His Royal Slaves

Initially, the Crown's conception of royal slavery regarding a master's legal prerogative to sell or transfer his or her slaves seemed no different from that of a private master. But law and custom in the Spanish Empire set some restrictions on the master's rights of disposal over his or her slaves, so the Crown made provisions accordingly. In 1673 a royal edict ordered the sale of the newly acquired slaves of El Cobre in the island or abroad.[1] In proper Christian and legal fashion, however, the Crown called upon the executors of its policy—royal officials of the treasury and the bishop of Cuba—to sell slave families together. Furthermore, in accordance with an already established custom on the island, the Crown also extended its slaves the option of *coartación*, that is, the possibility of buying their own freedom in installments after an initial down payment of usually 25 percent of the slave's assessed value. *Coartación* was an important avenue of mobility out of slavery, particularly for urban slaves in the Iberian world, but it could take a slave long years to finance this investment.[2] Honoring the traditional practice of *coartación* without going as far as offering a full Christian manumission, or even a royal grant of freedom for defense services to the Crown, His Majesty recommended assessments of "modest" prices for the freedom of his slaves. Those who could not be sold, either to other citizens or to themselves, could be remitted to work in the ongoing walling of Havana alongside other royal and privately rented slaves. That same year and a year later in 1674, other edicts followed overturning the initial orders to sell the slaves (although not the concession of *coartación*) and giving priority to the policy of transferring the royal slaves to the fortification projects of the capital, first calling for fifty of the youngest and ablest slaves in the mines, then raising the number to one hundred and fifty or more. The only condition specified in one of the edicts was that the royal slaves' transfer to Havana should not interfere with the defensive needs of Santiago de Cuba itself.[3] That proviso offered a key loophole through which conflict over the destination of the slaves could be negotiated if need be.

When the transfer orders arrived in Santiago de Cuba some time in 1674, Governor Don Andrés de Magaña proceeded in well-known "I obey but do not comply" fashion. The governor did not enforce the orders claiming the slaves would resist the attempt to send them to Havana by fleeing to the mountains. Understandably, he would prefer to avoid responsibility for such a disaster that could carry heavy penalties during his *residencia* (tenure) review. Thus, slave resistance through *cimarronaje* was perceived early on as a possible political limitation on the local state's ability to enforce Crown policy. As for the original option of *coartación*, the royal slaves seemed to have made no immediate attempt to initiate the process of self-manumission through the advance of any down payment. Either the new royal slaves may have felt too secure and complacent given the initial confusion, improvised character, and general looseness of the new royal administration, or they may have simply lacked the means to initiate *coartación* at the time, despite the appropriation of resources that, as may be recalled from Chapter 2, had been taking place in the settlement. In any case, policy toward the slaves was also blocked by the fact that the former private contractors had appealed the Crown's confiscation of their property. The Crown appointed a judge to adjudicate the civil case, but pending formal judicial process, matters remained suspended and tied to local considerations under Magaña's rule.

The arrival in 1677 of Judge Don Antonio Ortiz de Matienzo to carry out his judicial investigation and to give official closure to the civil case triggered anxieties among the royal slaves. It was the kind of anxiety common to the experience of slavery where masters had the prerogative to move and sell their slaves. In a petition drawn up two months after the judge had arrived to make his official inspection of the mining settlement and take inventory of the existing property, the royal slaves expressed their fears to the judge: "We have heard that you will remove [from Santiago del Prado] those [slaves] selected in the [judicial] settlement that you will oversee regarding the many slaves it is said our King and Master will receive from Don Francisco, [and they will] send us to the city of Havana."[4] Such a realization may have shattered not only aspects of a longer-standing sense of identity but also the ideas that had been projected onto a newly emerging community of king's slaves.

The royal slaves expressed their fears and their reluctance to move in writing. On July 13, 1677, a petition from Captain Juan Moreno, pleading that his fellow bondmen be allowed to remain in El Cobre, reached Judge Ortiz de Matienzo.[5] Four months after the petition was presented, seeing that no response was forthcoming, the royal slaves fled to the mountains. From the mountains they negotiated their return back to El Cobre with the judge.

Who Speaks? Whose Words?

The petition was allegedly authored by Captain Moreno: a "Creole *negro* [black slave] and native of the mines of Santiago del Prado of this city of [Santiago de] Cuba, in his name and on behalf of the other Creole slave natives of the said mines, we the slaves of His Majesty. . . ." Whatever the rank of captain of slaves may have represented then—and as discussed in Chapter 2 it may well have had a combination of military and religious significance—Moreno's title gave him some legitimate authority as leader and in this case as representative of a constituency. The very same title and authority that colonial officials conferred upon Moreno, he invoked on this particular occasion to authorize himself to speak publicly, albeit guardedly, against the master/king/state's orders and prerogatives.

The political act of drawing up a collective petition was itself significant. Although slaves made official petitions and filed claims in the courts, collective petitions or letters claiming to represent the will of a group tended to be more rare, mostly because slaves had few opportunities to form corporate groups or associations and to mobilize in those terms.[6] Moreover, the voice in this document referred to a collective identity that was construed not only in terms of royal slave status (in terms of a common master) but more remarkably in terms of place of birth as well (the Creole natives of the mines). Origin, particularly local territorial ties, became a central notion in these royal slaves' public construction of identity and in their reformulation of slavery.

And yet, although Moreno took official responsibility for the petition, he was not literate. If the document represented the collective voice of the king's slaves of Santiago del Prado, who inscribed their oral voice as a public text since Moreno could not write? Did that written voice represent Moreno's and the royal slaves' words? To what extent can authorship be attributed to them? Did that textual voice really articulate the royal slaves' imagined identity?

As pointed out in Chapter 2, literacy seems not to have been completely absent from this royal slave community. If Moreno was illiterate, other royal slaves were not; someone else could well have acted as amanuensis for him. How such texts on behalf of the community could be produced by a member of the community is illustrated by a later case of which record exists. In the 1730s during a conflict with the local colonial state that led to another political act of flight to the mountains, the royal slaves wrote notes or letters to different authorities. Although these letters allegedly were not authored by an official of the community as in the case of Moreno—they were more anonymously authored by "el pueblo" or the "royal slaves"—they came from a villager in El Cobre. Antonio Salazar charged his fellow slaves two pesos (roughly five days of work for a free-wage worker at the time) for his highly valued writing services.[7] Situations like this may have been common in the history of the community, including in the case of Moreno's petition of 1677 and a subsequent letter four months later.

There was also the possibility of a clergyman, a parish priest, or a chaplain of the Virgin's hermitage, who may have been willing to write on behalf of the slaves. There is direct evidence of at least one such case in which the priest actually identified himself in the text as writing on behalf of his enslaved parishioners.[8] Moreno's petition, and his subsequent letter, could have been written by one such clergyman. At other times, illiterate groups could make use of the services provided by more professional writers, but these formal and informal scribes had to be provided with the information and the details to be addressed in any given document. This information would have to be provided by the client. There are official representations on behalf of the royal slaves that, although their texts may not have actually been written by them, spoke so closely of local issues and history that the voice of the members of the community is loud and clear in them. Some of these documents—and their voices—will be discussed throughout the pages of this book. Moreno's petition may have been one such case, too.

The style of Moreno's petition was not polished. Although the text exhibited awareness of some simple rules of written protocol (witness, for example, Moreno's presentation), there were also passages that read almost like a transcription of oral speech. (The reader may consult the original Spanish text, set forth in Appendix 3.) Ultimately, the identity of Moreno's amanuensis remains unknown.

Problems of authorship (and "authenticity"), however, are more complex than issues of actual literacy. They are also often more complex than issues of individual voice. In any case, letters and documents to authorities provide the historian with access to the discourse with which subordinate groups have to transact publicly claims with other sectors of colonial society—an important and integral aspect of how these sectors of society also lived within the system and acted historically. Moreno's voice in the text can also be seen as representing an accommodation between his constituency's claims and the dominant ideology that formed the basis of public discourse, particularly in dealing with interlocutors such as colonial authorities. Ultimately, then, the claims I make for Moreno's (and the royal slaves') voice(s) in this text are not so much how they spoke "privately" to each other, or among themselves, but rather how far they could dare to represent and imagine themselves publicly in colonial society. The extent to which dominant colonial assumptions could be bent even in these cases can be surprising.

At any rate, regardless of whether the petition was directly written by a royal slave, dictated to a letter writer, or redacted by someone such as a low-educated clergyman, the public discourse it inscribed would find its way into practice and into scattered documents in subsequent decades. In this sense it is possible to corroborate whether there were any echoes of it in other spheres of local life. In part, what leads me to engage this document in such a close fashion is that it constitutes the earliest available integrated articulation of several aspects of the identity and discourse that not only came to be associated with royal slavery in this region of Cuba but also that the enslaved people of El Cobre often invoked throughout the next century, as will become clear in Part 2 of this book. Furthermore, as indicated before, the particular situation in which this text was produced and the political mobilization that followed meant that both its claims and also presumably the formulations on which they were based were up for negotiation during this event. That is, the text also constituted a performative act.

The Petition's Text and Its Subtexts: Some Unusual Proposals

Defining Home and Identity

The petition was ostensibly a formal plea for *coartación*, a right which, as already mentioned, the Crown had officially recognized in one of its earlier edicts. But behind the normalcy of legal conventions, the deferential language, and the restrained pleas, a bolder ordinary language with more dramatic proposals could be heard also. What were the proposals found in this petition? Why were they so remarkable? What kinds of imagined identity were asserted in it?

The royal slaves asked, "The love for our *patria* [homeland] and our work move us to ask . . . the mercy of being allowed to stay in our pueblo, paying tribute, in whatever manner it is arranged for us while we find [a way to pay] for our freedom. . . ." The petition closed by stating, "We ask and plead that you deem us presented [for *coartación*] ordering, that we be considered thus, which will be justice and mercy that we ask for and which is most necessary."[9]

The text suggests that no steps had been taken in the direction of *coartación* because no down payments had apparently been made.[10] Moreno, however, was not just formally demanding the acknowledgment of slaves' customary entitlement to a *coartación* already recognized by the Crown. Nor was he even asking for the special mercy of being recognized as *coartados* (in process of *coartación*) without having yet set down the required first installment.[11] Beyond these claims, Moreno was pleading that his fellow royal slaves be allowed to remain in El Cobre. Indeed, underlying the explicit claim for *coartado* status was also Moreno's most culturally and politically loaded formulation: that El Cobre was "our *patria*" and "our *pueblo*," or that the king's slaves wished to remain in El Cobre, their homeland, as a "pueblo."

The actual reference to El Cobre as a pueblo—one then constituted mostly by slaves, a few free people of color, a parish priest, and a hermit living in the midst of worn-down structures—may seem like a bold linguistic, cultural, and political gesture, particularly as slaves lay outside the body politic and could themselves not constitute corporate entities or pueblos, properly speaking.[12] The ruined settlement was by then not even a village of freemen to which slaves could at least claim a peripheral residential status. Indeed, most references to Santiago del Prado at the time were to "the mines" as Moreno's own introductory statement attests. Although the slaves of El Cobre may have constituted a slave community for decades, community takes many shapes. To publicly constitute and think of oneself as a pueblo in the Spanish colonial world, however, had some particular connotations.[13]

The process of construing themselves as members of a pueblo, however, may have begun to unfold in the 1670s, as the former privately held territory came under royal jurisdiction and as the royal slaves appropriated resources and land. Furthermore, as I noted in Chapter 1, during the 1670s the royal slaves had reconstructed the parish church "at their own cost," thus materially and symbolically reclaiming that structure for themselves.[14] Nonetheless, although a parish church was in the Spanish Empire a sine qua non in the establishment of a pueblo, by itself it did not constitute one. A pueblo had a corporate status and identity, rights to land, and minimal political representation in the form of a *cabildo*. Recall, however, that civil positions such as *alcaldes* with some policing and representative functions had begun to emerge in this community under Magaña's administration. Such forms of managing the slave force in El Cobre may have constituted ambiguous practices interpreted as signs of some political legitimacy. Finally, as I point out in Chapters 4 and 5, the reconstruction of the hermitage to the Virgin and her cult as the centerpiece of community also took on the meaning of supernatural representation and patronage. These were all practices that gave shape to a new sort of imagined local community, a form of community that would eventually be regarded and recognized as a pueblo by different sectors of colonial society, and not just by its enslaved inhabitants.

The distinction in everyday life and parlance between a slave community in a mining settlement, a parish, and a pueblo, then, may have become blurred at some point in time—for the royal slaves perhaps long before 1677, for other sectors of colonial society not until years later. Indeed, where most men who left written words behind them had seen "mines" or a mining settlement with slaves until about the 1690s, Moreno, and his amanuensis, had seen a pueblo since at least 1677. While it was not until the 1690s that colonial authorities seem to have begun to systematically refer to this slave community as a pueblo, the first document to reach us that formally inscribed the royal slaves as such was a village census drawn up in 1709.[15] Pueblo status would have been more or less formally acknowledged as a fait accompli around the turn of the eighteenth century, when the High Court of Santo Domingo allegedly granted 1-surrounding league of territory to the community to sustain itself.[16] Such a grant constituted the minimal territory prescribed by law to constitute a village entity, an issue to which I will return in Chapter 6.

Moreno's text linked the royal slaves' collective identity with ties to a local territory, thereby invoking one of the most significant identities of free people in the Iberian world—that of the "patria chica."[17] Captain Moreno declared that he and the people he represented wished to remain in El Cobre because of the "love for our *patria*." What was striking about the petition's discourse was not so much the identification of the slaves as Creoles, or as *naturales* (natives) of a particular locality (in this case they were formally natives to the mines of Santiago del Prado), but the affective attachment to local territory and community that was thereby explicitly invoked and what that tie presumably entailed.

Moreno opened the petition introducing himself and his fellow royal slaves as "Creoles," or slaves born and reared in the Indies.[18] A Creole identification in colonial society implied a generic New World natal origin that often meant some cultural assimilation into Hispanic colonial society as well. More is known, however, about what a Creole identity may have meant in the case of people of Spanish descent than for slaves. Little is known, for instance, about what situations impelled American-born slaves to invoke a Creole identity, or how far those claims could take an enslaved person in colonial society.[19] Yet, a Creole identification was still a vague identity that did not entail belonging to a concrete community or a polity. It was also an identification that fell well within the scope of slave discourse. The term *patria*, like that of *pueblo*, would have been a more loaded expression, particularly when the enunciators were slaves, even if they were Creole slaves.

Patria was a term that turned mere place of origin into a homeland: a different cultural, social, and political entity altogether. The ideology of *patria* referred to an inclusive bond of community that implied an enduring solidarity constructed through a common history or tradition, and perhaps some common rights and institutions that were linked to territoriality as well. The term *patria* in the seventeenth and eighteenth centuries still referred for the most part to a local community, in effect to a *patria chica*.[20] This local homeland was no less "imagined" in its creation or "invention" of tradition and a collective identity than the larger community of the nation-state that would emerge decades later in the nineteenth century.[21] These local homelands were part of politically bounded units, such as pueblos, town, and cities representing the smallest constituent units in the body politic.

Moreno's invocation of a patriotic tie may have been among the first such invocations among people of color to reach us from the past. Here were slaves, the ultimate outsiders in society, turning themselves into natives of the New World, making claims on their Creole status and, moreover, binding that Creole identity concretely to a pueblo and a local territory. Moreno's invocation of a patriotic tie to a territory in effect rooted his fellow slaves in a bounded locality in a way that effectively negated the supposed "natal alienation" inherent to the condition of slavery.

In principle, the "social death" that enslavement represented deprived the slave of all "rights" or claims of birth and thus excluded him or her from any legitimate social order.[22] In actual practice slaves were able to reinsert themselves into different kinds of social relations outside the forced legal master/slave bond and to claim some customary, if restricted, rights that suggest that they did have some "social life," so to speak.[23] Yet, any recovered "social life" should be considered politically as a reclamation of human rights, a reconstitution of custom, and a reconfiguration of imagined identities. The claim to a public identity as a pueblo or as a people with *patria*, however, was a particularly bold political act in the case of slaves. Perhaps the most fascinating aspect of the discourse found in Moreno's petition was the extent to which it ignored or refused to acknowledge the "social alienation" entailed in the condition of enslavement and the ways in which it subtly inserted these royal slaves into the legitimate civil polity despite their slavery.

Perhaps the most radical political claim implicitly made in the petition not only when invoking a Creole identity, but specifically an identity based on *patria* and pueblo, was a sort of birthright that entitled a subject to live in his or her locality of origin or official residence, a right recognized in the case of freemen but not really in the case of slaves. Indeed, in a free person's case, the negation of that birthright would have constituted "exile" or banishment: a suspension of political rights as a form of criminal or civic punishment. In principle, no such political rights held in the condition of slavery.

Subsequent Manifestations of Pueblo Identity

The ways of speaking, imagining, and enacting community found in Moreno's petition were not confined to that early document. They reflected as well modes of speaking and acting in social life evinced in many other kinds of subsequent sources. Indeed, they echoed the royal slaves' articulation of collective identity throughout the following century. An identity based on the local *patria* and the pueblo recurred in these royal slaves' and freedmen's informal or spontaneous statements. It continued surfacing in more official representations as well thereby suggesting that, despite its controversial character (and some opposing voices), such a manifestation of social identity came to hold a certain degree of legitimacy, or at least that the formulations on which it rested had become tolerated among a good part of colonial society.

In the 1730s, for instance, the *alcaldes* of El Cobre sent an informal note to the governor of Santiago de Cuba referring to El Cobre as "este *país*" (this [local] country) where Francisco Salazar—an alleged outsider who, ironically, carried the same name as the mines' former private contractor some six decades ago—"was residing in the company of our brother Bernardino . . . and wanting to disturb our beloved Pueblo."[24] The conception of El Cobre as a "país," a bounded locality, made its native members "sons" of the territory and "brothers" to each other as in the case of local homeland. The language of kinship evoked the affective and "natural" character of the bonds of community and territory. Similarly, in the correspondence of some freedmen with Gregorio Cosme Osorio who officially represented the pueblo in Madrid at the end of the eighteenth century, the villagers often addressed him as "our brother" (albeit also as "our friend").[25] In this metaphorical kinship system the *alcaldes*, and even the elders, of the village were regarded as "fathers." In a letter to Governor Don Pedro Ignacio Ximénez at about that time the *alcaldes* manifested that they were trying "to fulfill our obligations as *alcaldes* and fathers of Our pueblo."[26] In other informal letters and notes to the governor (possibly written by Antonio Salazar), sublevated cobreros referred to El Cobre as "nuestro lugar" (our place), and in most written documents they signed themselves as "vecinos [citizens] of Santiago del Prado," as "natives of Santiago del Prado," as "we the pueblo," or even as the "slaves of His Majesty," or "this pueblo of His Majesty," which made them all synonymous or complementary identities.[27] In a representation to the Crown in 1798, the freedman Justo Cruzata identified a fellow villager who had been harassed by a bailiff in Santiago de Cuba as "one of my compatriots."[28]

Although the term *cobreros* (people of El Cobre) became prevalent, at least in the records, some time toward the 1760s, some documented references can be found as early as the 1730s.[29] More than royal slaves the enslaved people of El Cobre had become cobreros alongside their fellow freemen, over and above their legal status as slaves or free people. Deriving from the village's also informal name of El Cobre (and that name, in turn, reflecting the place's firm association with its copper mines) the term cobreros framed this people primarily as natives (and compatriots) of a bounded locality in the island's map, very much in the way that the natives of the capital city of Santiago de Cuba were known as *cubanos*, those of Bayamo as *bayameses*, and those of Habana as *habaneros*. The cobrero Martín de Salazar, for instance, wrote to his compatriot Gregorio Cosme Osorio in 1792, "They are going to finish with all the cobreros, so many enemies are persecuting us [these days]."[30] The term was still in use in the nine-teenth century as opposed to settlers (*colonos*) in El Cobre, and today the people of El Cobre call themselves cobreros.

Furthermore, the cobreros' bounded local identity became grounded as well in deep-seated linguistic practices. Although references to the sound of words are rare in the written record, a witness from Santiago de Cuba, Don Lorenzo de Vegueyferos declared in 1737 that he "did not see any of [the men] who were in the *monte* . . . but that by the metal of the speech [the witness] recognized that they were from El Cobre."[31] Likewise, Juan, a Creole private slave of Captain Don Gaspar de Arrate, stated in that same investigation that "it was about midnight . . . when entering the *Monte* four men came up to him [and] that he recognized they were blacks from El Cobre by their speech [*por el habla*]. . . ."[32] Thus, the cobreros seem to have developed their own locally distinct Spanish accent—a sign of a profoundly internalized sense of local collective identity unreflectively enacted in everyday speech.[33] In this sense, their speech behavior—or their linguistic "tradition"—reflected not only their socialization to the world of the Indies as Spanish-speaking Creoles but also their own particular inflection of that language in their local *patria*.

One of the most lucid observations of the kinds of bonds and identities that came to effectively structure social life among the cobreros, as well as of the political connotation of these ties, was made in the late eighteenth cen-tury precisely by one of the main enemies of the pueblo. More than one hundred years after Captain Moreno enunciated in his petition quite unconventional, and yet acceptable, notions regarding the imagined identi-ty of his fellow slaves in their local *patria*, the basis and validity of that iden-tity became seriously challenged by the alleged heirs of Salazar y Acuña, the contractor of the mining jurisdiction at the time of its confiscation in 1670. In 1780 the heirs pretended a return of things in their so-called territory to the status quo before the confiscation of the mines in 1670. That meant in effect the undoing of a century of established local tradition in El Cobre, a problem addressed in the Epilogue. Suffice it to point out here how the heirs—negatively but accurately—described the bonds among cobreros at that time. Don Francisco Mancebo y Quiroga protested to the Crown:

Last year [the free cobreros initiated] another [legal] process where they . . . claimed infinitely for the freedom of their *slave compatriots* calling us unjust usurpers of the royal property. . . . Lately the cobreros free and slaves, since they constitute a small population, are all relatives within the fourth degree, or at least

> they are godfathers and godmothers, godchildren, friends *and forcefully compatriots that make a common cause* in this matter . . . in view of the bonds among them of kinship, friendship, and *patriotism,* how can they be trusted? [emphasis added][34]

Mancebo disgruntledly acknowledged the overlapping ties among the cobreros—including those of local *patria.* Indeed, he indicated (and decried) that kinship, friendship, and fellow patriotism were the primary forms of identity that oriented social and political praxis among the cobreros—over and above their individual juridical status as free or slave. Mancebo y Quiroga was objecting to the legitimacy of those social bonds among slaves from his strictly legalistic and culturally rigid construction of slavery as a form of total "social alienation." He protested the complicity of authorities in the recognition of those ties as both free and slave cobreros were allowed not only to make common political cause but also to mobilize legitimately through judicial channels as if they all had civil rights.[35] Mancebo y Quiroga's text is significant because it chronicled both the continuity in this community of the very identities that Moreno had first articulated in 1677 and the force of these social bonds in activating social and political practices among the cobreros. Furthermore, it obliquely reflected the (to be sure, contended) recognition that their corporate identity still retained in the region and that enabled them to carry on their litigation with the support of some sectors of colonial society.

The Bonds of Family, Pueblo, and Patria

Captain Moreno's petition also intertwined the social bonds of family with those of pueblo and *patria* to formulate the cobreros' plea to remain in El Cobre. Although claims based on family "rights" were decidedly more conventional in the case of slaves than those based on a corporate identity rooted in local territory, there were yet more radical turns to such familial entitlements. Moreno openly declared in the petition that the slaves of His Majesty did not wish to be removed from El Cobre "because most of the Creole blacks and mulattoes of the said mines are married and we have our families whom we have always had to support." Moreno was thereby laying out two different claims: one mostly based on the law, the other on custom. Concretely, the petition set forth its claims as a right to preserve the bonds of marriage to which even slaves (as Christians) were entitled by Spanish law, and then pushed them further by appealing to the force of "established custom." In doing so, it also proposed the preservation of self-provisioning arrangements structured around the family unit, including the conservation of the cobreros' gender roles as heads of family and provisioners.

By invoking the bond of marriage, Moreno appealed to conventional cultural understandings in the Catholic world regarding the sacramental character of marriage and the indivisibility of that bond—one that given its degree of holiness was also recognized by Spanish law.[36] Marriage in particular constituted an instance whereby Christian identity and dicta could supposedly outweigh slave status in Iberian society, or at least could provide the ideological ammunition with which to frame conflictive situations. In this sense, there was nothing particularly unconventional in the memorial's argument about the need to preserve the slaves' marital status or even the integrity of the whole family. The plan to remove the ablest and strongest male slaves from El Cobre, the petition implicitly claimed, threatened the dissolution of the family. The Crown certainly would not want to be accused of separating married couples, breaking up Christian families, and violating godly (and legal) precepts.

The prescription to respect the marriage bond, and to a lesser extent the parental one, among His Majesty's slaves seems to have been taken relatively seriously by royal officials throughout most of the eighteenth century. It was enforced, albeit in a perverse way, when the sixty-year-old Pedro Viojo, his wife Florencia, and this couple's three young children, aged four to ten, were sold as a unit in 1677 to cover some litigation costs to conserve Barajagua as part of the mining jurisdiction.[37] Likewise, in 1700, the governor of Santiago de Cuba refused to send twelve slave miners requested by the governor of Cartagena to work on mines in that province in exchange for twelve African slaves. Don Joseph Correoso incorrectly stated that there were none left who knew how to smelt "but even if there were some, there would be many inconveniences since they are married and have children and since they have grown up as if they were free."[38] Thus, by this time the removal from El Cobre seemed particularly problematic, not only because of legal considerations regarding the marital status of slaves but also because of their quasi-free status as members of a pueblo. In the 1730s the dictum to respect the marriage bond (but not necessarily the parental one) was strong enough to be recognized as binding even in the case of judicial punishment for alleged sedition. Approving Governor Ximénez and Captain General Güemes y Horcacitas's suggestion for punishing the cobreros implicated in leading a small uprising in the village, the Crown's attorney wrote:

It is convenient to impose on them the penalty of separating them from the pueblo [and] distributing them around this City [Havana], that one [indicating Santiago de Cuba] (if there is no inconvenience in leaving them so near), Trinidad, and the town of Puerto Príncipe, for being the places of most formality. . . . If among the women or men that shall be distributed there are some who are married, it is important to attend to their matrimony and that you send them to the same place.[39]

Note as well that removal from El Cobre was here portrayed quite matter-of-factly by royal authorities as banishment and used as a form of punishment for a legal transgression, in this case the supposed crime of sedition (just as exile or banishment to the presidios was in the case of freemen). Underlying such a policy may have been the by then established understanding that, at least in the case of cobreros, forced separation from the pueblo (or the *patria*) was only legitimate as a form of punishment for criminal transgressions, as a way of exacting justice, and not as a master's prerogative. But even in such cases the law supposedly had to make space to accommodate the (divine and legal) precepts regarding the sacramental matrimonial bond.

The radical formulation in Moreno's petition, therefore, was not the demand for the preservation of the marriage bond or of the integrity of the family in the case of Christian slaves. After all, wives, maybe even children, of the king's slaves could have been transferred to Havana alongside family heads. Moreno's more radical formulation consisted in the wish to preserve familial bonds in situ, as part of a wider community that he termed a pueblo and a *patria*.

Furthermore, Moreno's appeal to the integrity of the family in their locality was linked to his claim that they "had always had to support their families." That "always" was certainly questionable. Moreno was more specific in a letter to the judge when he clarified that "it has been twenty years since we have been sustaining ourselves without any help from an administrator."[40] As far back as 1608 slaves in the mines had been granted *conucos* (slave provisioning grounds), but according to Captain Don Francisco Sánchez de Moya, manioc production in these had complemented and not substituted for slave rations. It had been mostly since the 1660s that the slaves had been forced to rely more on their efforts to subsist. By the 1670s the slaves had *estancias* (subsistence family farms), instead of the smaller *conucos*.[41] But in suggesting the timeless character of the practice of sustaining families Moreno was transforming it into tradition. In doing so, he appealed to the binding force of custom and implicitly portrayed it as an immemorial prerogative relatively independent from the master's arbitrary will, one with the added moral (and legal) force of preserving the bonds of family. Thus, in this case Moreno was emphasizing a continuity with a past based in the late years of the former private order of the mines rather than rooting his claims in the new order under Crown rule, a more recent and still brittle order in the making.

Finally, the petition of 1677 also framed the issue of self-subsistence in terms of standard Iberian ideology about the role of the *pater familias*. This ideology presupposed a gendered organization of production based on family groups constituted by a father and his dependents. The role of family head and provider signified fully the socialized status of men in colonial society—a role not always expected from master-dependent slaves. Indeed, the role of *pater familias* constituted an inversion of the regular dependent status of slaves. The removal of the most able men from the settlement, Moreno seemed to argue, would leave many wives and children without a male head of household responsible for their subsistence. Although such a situation could presumably call for a different set of provisioning arrangements for the slaves, Moreno held to the dominant cultural ideal among free people of a *pater familias*-centered organization of production. Implicit in his reference to the families "they always had to subsist" was the affirmation of loyalties and responsibilities to them over and above those owed to their master/king. But by reminding the Crown of their preeminent provisioning role, the memorial of 1677 also alerted the state to the new burdens it would have to face in supporting the slaves once the most able *patres familias* were sent away to work in Havana. The argument would be a recurring one throughout the eighteenth century, set out for differing claims— notably, land, or greater extensions of time off from forced labor, as will be shown in Part 2 of this book.

King's Slaves and Soldiers

Finally, a major aspect of the identity of the royal slaves of El Cobre was linked to military service. Flaunting the obedience of the slaves by listing the various occupations in which they had been traditionally employed (working in the mines, building the Holy Church, hunting fugitive slaves of citizens in Santiago de Cuba), and to their loyalty to the Crown in having responded promptly on the occasions of enemy attack, Moreno rhetorically expressed their continuous "desire for [even] greater opportunities in the royal service [in order to] carry out great actions which even if they go unre-warded we will remain content to have achieved them."[42] More concretely, the petition offered the slaves' services "to defend the garrison of Cuba or any other place," noting that "whenever the opportunity has arisen with some [unexpected] event the governors have remembered to call on us even though we are humble black slaves of Our King and Lord. . . ."[43] In the pro-tocol of the time, supplicants listed services—particularly military servic-es—to obtain a favor, even when declaring a disinterested motivation.

In a follow-up letter to the judge, Moreno reiterated the point of their for-mer military service, defending his fellow slaves from the accusation of dis-obedience for having fled to the mountains. Moreno wrote, "When the occasion comes up we never fail [to obey] with ardent zeal what our superi-ors have ordered us and in this occasion when the enemy came to that city it was not necessary [to order us,] it is well known that their ships were in [the port of] Guaycabón and that that Post was guarded with seventy-three slaves of His Majesty [*sic*], *vecinos* [residents or neighbors] of this place. . . ."[44] It is not clear to what event Moreno was referring, but it was probably to the English invasion of Santiago de Cuba in 1662.[45] At that time, the royal slaves were still private slaves, however.

References to military service as an act of service to the Crown could presumably have won them freedom according to a generous reading of the law.[46] The petition suggested that at least it could have won them a special right to remain in El Cobre and not to be treated as regular slaves. Moreno called the concession to remain in El Cobre "the prize of [His] Majesty [for our services] that God save, we await on this point as his humble slaves. . ."[47] Regardless of services in the past, Moreno also offered the Crown the serv-ices of its royal slaves in the future, not only for routine slave work but also for "the great actions" of military defense of the Crown's colonial outposts in the region, virtually offering to turn the king's slaves into soldiers of the king.[48]

With a vast territory to defend in the Indies and sparse Spanish popula-tion settlements, the Crown had turned early in the seventeenth century to the enlistment of freemen of color into militias for the defense of various regions in the empire. In Havana, for example, the first militia company of mulattos was organized in 1600, and thereafter the recruitment of men of color was expanded so that companies of black men were created alongside those of mulattos. Indeed, Cuba became the one territory in the Spanish Empire where militias of color became most prevalent in the defense network of the Crown.[49] Although Native Americans were rarely used in the defense system of the Spanish Empire, in Cuba the Indians of the village of El Caney and later of Jiguaní belonged to their own militia companies during the eighteenth century, and probably before.[50] The militias of El Caney had also been entrusted with the watch and defense of the coastal post of Juraguá in the seventeenth century (see Map 2 in Preamble).[51] While slaves were the one male sector of colonial society hardly tapped for military duties except perhaps in the most extreme of emergencies, Moreno's petition proposed to break that proscription by suggesting the incorporation of the king's slaves of El Cobre into the defense system of the region as well. Moreno hinted at the unconventional character of the practice, by pointing to the cobreros' capacity for such responsibilities *despite* their humble status as "black slaves of His Majesty."

Indeed, Moreno's reference to the mining settlement of Santiago del Prado as a pueblo may have performed further work in this regard. The reference to a village may well have pointed to its potential function as a buffer population center to the south of Santiago de Cuba. The transference of the ablest men to work in Havana would depopulate and dismantle the budding pueblo, even though only a slave pueblo, and thus destroy its defensive and military potential in the Santiago de Cuba region, and this only to privilege the labor needs of the competing region of Havana. To preserve His Majesty's slaves in El Cobre as a pueblo would be in the Crown's interest. The Crown would acknowledge that much in coming years. In 1732, for example, the Crown attorney made a categorical statement of policy in that regard when it emphasized

the convenience of the conservation and maintenance of that pueblo with slaves and other free citizens because that garrison is frontier with an enemy colony like the Island of Jamaica and during times of attack the said slaves move to guard the port of Guaycabón, 5 leagues from that settlement where the enemies can disembark so that there is no doubt that they serve for the defense of the Island.[52]

The cobreros themselves recognized the importance of their defensive role and emphasized it at times in their writing to colonial authorities. To Dean Pedro Agustín Morell de Santa Cruz the natives of El Cobre wrote in 1735 through the pen of the cobrero Antonio Salazar: "You should be aware that we are slaves of the king [and] our Master has given us a post of so much risk as that of the port of Guaycabón to defend it from the infidel enemies of the faith . . . all of which should be worthy of your greatest attention."[53] The potential military role of the king's slaves, however, was not portrayed in the petition so much as a responsibility to protect the local *patria*, as to defend the central colonial garrison of Santiago de Cuba and, therefore, primarily, as an expression of loyalty to the Crown. Indeed, in the above statement to the dean, as well as in the petition of 1677, the cobreros depicted such service as an honor and at the same time as a duty to the Crown that could ambiguously rest either in their enslaved relation to their master and their special status as the king's slaves, or in their quasi-free character as vassals of the Crown.

The Mobilization's Outcome

On hearing the news of the royal slaves' flight, Judge Ortiz de Matienzo reacted swiftly and ordered that a *bando* be publicly cried out, calling on the royal slaves "to present themselves in the said mines assuring them in the name of His Majesty that no one will be removed from them against his will. . . ."[54] The judge was, in effect, conceding the royal slaves some control over their own destination, perhaps even a de facto *fuero de domicilio* (right of residence) in "the said mines."[55] That decision would mark a first step in the process of recognizing the royal slaves of Santiago del Prado as a pueblo.

In true legalistic fashion, the judge proceeded to ground his concession on the royal edicts at hand. Thus, the Crown's orders were suddenly interpreted in a different light. Ortiz de Matienzo argued within the space granted in the cited royal edict of April 18, 1673, that the defense needs of the city of Santiago de Cuba should have priority over those of Havana, and thus the slaves need not be remitted to that city. The judge was accepting the petition's argument regarding the utility of His Majesty's slaves for defensive purposes and perhaps accepting Moreno's offer to be placed "in the royal service to carry out great actions." Ortiz de Matienzo also invoked the orders of "another edict" that granted permission to facilitate the terms of *coartación* to the slaves.[56]

It is impossible to say whether without their act of flight the royal slaves of El Cobre would have obtained the concession to remain living in El Cobre and eventually be recognized as a pueblo. The colonial state at the time was not able to control a force of 328 slaves hiding in the mountains around the settlement, or at least could only do so at the risk of losing a good part of the "human capital" through bloody confrontations. The slaves' flight into the *monte*, however, would not only represent a possible loss of capital; this massive flight threatened to occur in a frontier region that faced an enemy across the sea and arose during a particularly conflictive period of Caribbean history. Armed royal slaves and the possibility of an enemy attack constituted a threat to security and public order that always lurked in the background of local royal officials' dealings with the community.[57] In general, that kind of threat constituted one of the restraining forces on the colonial state's demands on its royal slaves and provided the latter with a relatively important negotiating space throughout the rest of the seventeenth and eighteenth centuries.

Conclusion

The royal slaves were able to stay in El Cobre throughout subsequent decades. Moreno's petition reflected the ideology and discursive limits within which the political aspirations of this subordinate group of enslaved people could be articulated in the early modern Spanish colonial world. The alchemy of the petition consisted in wielding an imagined identity based on *patria*, pueblo, family, and military status that curbed, even overrode, the master's quasi-absolute power and authority over his slave property. Somewhat disguised underneath the normality of dominant languages and cultural presuppositions about proper life in the body politic, some unusual (and radical) proposals were found. The unconventionality of these proposals resided more in the kind of subjects claiming to speak publicly in those dominant voices—in effect claiming such discourses and the identities they sustained for themselves—than in any apparent innovation in the ideology itself. In this sense, the radicalness of the petition's more submerged voice lay in claiming for slaves certain bonds of birth and origin that were constitutive of a free status and identity in colonial society: to wit, the bonds and identities that construed a (free) person as part of a family, a land, a community, and to some extent a polity. These claims obliterated to a considerable extent the "socially alienated" status and deracinated character of the slave in colonial society. Without going as far as claiming juridical freedom, the royal slaves of El Cobre anticipated freedom in a forthcoming *coartación*; in the meanwhile, while still in the space of slavery, they redefined their status as slaves, renegotiated their place in colonial society, and reinvented their public identities in words and practices.

The following years witnessed the emergence and recognition of a new sort of imagined community in the island and with it new and more ambiguous ways of living between slavery and freedom. Perhaps the most radical entitlement that the royal slaves of El Cobre were able to negotiate with the king was becoming a corporate community; indeed, the one and only Afro-Cuban pueblo in the island's history. The making and legitimation of this controversial community concretely evinces as well some of the cultural and political processes involved in the construction of (local) *patria* and its related forms of Creole identity in Cuba at this early point in time.

The Virgin in Local History

The said slaves attempted to take the Virgin of
Charity [from the sanctuary] because they said she
was theirs and that she was their remedy.
  —Don Joseph de Losada, Santiago de Cuba, 1731

Brother, the divine Lady of Charity and Remedies
has made the most patent miracle that can be
imagined, for we have been able to obtain through
some gentlemen in this city [Santiago de Cuba] . . .
an edict very favorable to our pueblo.
                    —Salvador Quiala, El Cobre, 1784

The consolidation of the royal slaves of El Cobre as a pueblo went hand in
hand with the institutionalization and expansion of a local Marian tradition
during the late seventeenth century. The conversion of this local site into a
major center of religious popular culture in the Oriente region transformed
the village's regional profile. Where El Cobre had once been famed for its
thriving export mining industry, it would hereafter be especially known for
its prodigious Marian effigy and her miracles.

Although the production and expansion of this local Marian cult was a
complex process involving the participation of different sectors of colonial
society, the royal slaves played a central role in shaping the contours of this
tradition, particularly as they claimed this Virgin patroness and protectress
of their budding community. Indeed, the Virgen de la Caridad del Cobre,
who more than two centuries later would become a quintessential symbol of
the Cuban nation, was at this key moment in the production of her tradition
conjured by a group of Creole royal slaves to ground another kind of imagined community—that of their own *patria chica* (local homeland).

In 1687, a full decade after the king's slaves had obtained the concession to remain in their *pueblo*, Juan Moreno, who, as readers may recall from Chapter 3, had represented the royal slaves as their captain in 1677, addressed colonial authorities once again. This time, however, Moreno spoke to ecclesiastical authorities, and not to state officials. Furthermore, he no longer spoke as captain, but instead as a privileged witness, as a protagonist in a portentous story about the past, as a divinely chosen instrument in the Christian order of things, and as oral historian of his community. Moreno recounted several miracles he recalled, including how he and two Indian brothers had found a prodigious Marian effigy in the sea.[1]

A small notarization ceremony spoke to the still modest character of the emerging pueblo's local Marian cult. That notarization, however, constituted not only a legitimating ritual act of the Marian shrine but also of a Creole royal slave's own version of the shrine's foundational story—and by extension, of the unusual community that claimed the shrine as part of its tradition. The apparition story that Moreno narrated and the popular cult it grounded became a major discursive site for the articulation of the community's identity and for many of its political aspirations throughout the late seventeenth and eighteenth centuries. Such traditions were important religious and cultural expressions of local community as well as politicized statements cast in the hegemonic language of Christianity. They formed part of an overarching Catholic culture of saints, heroes, holy figures, stories, and plots, all vying for "universality," or, in more modern terms, for "global" expansion, malleable to multiple local permutations and appropriations.

"Global" Expansion and Transformations of the Marian Cult and Its Stories

The cult of Mary, with its own genre of stories of miracles and apparitions, began to attain popular dissemination in Western Christendom in the twelfth and thirteenth centuries when Marian shrines began to colonize the Spanish (and Western European) rural landscapes, displacing the popular cults of saints and their relics that had in their turn colonized pagan sites. By the end of the fifteenth century, for example, a wide network of Marian shrines was firmly in place throughout Spain.[2] With the colonization of the Indies, the wave of Marian devotions that was then swaying the Iberian world—particularly as part of the Counter-Reformation—was transplanted to the New World. There, it took time to expand, and acquired new signification in the politics of conquest and evangelization.[3] Some of the major shrines in the Indies, such as that to the Virgin of Guadalupe in Mexico and the Virgin of Copacabana in the Andes, were built literally atop important pre-Columbian sacred sites—thus pointing to the import of this cult in the evangelization and colonization process. Although underlying plots were retained, New World miracle stories of Mary were adapted to new audiences and historical situations. Indians, for instance, came to play a major part in such stories.

But if Indians became ubiquitous protagonists in New World Marian stories about the global expansion of Christianity or about the emergence of a distinct New World church (or later about the birth of independent nations), it is significant that slaves and blacks hardly ever appeared in stories associated with major New World images and shrines.[4] Even in the circum-Caribbean region, where the black population was larger, the absence of blacks from this religious genre is conspicuous. The patent exclusion of this sector of colonial society is not easy to explain in light of the fact that other subordinate groups were incorporated into major roles in such narratives. Could this be due to a lingering "outsider" status of blacks, even Creole blacks, because their arrival to this New World was associated with slavery? Could their absence from these widespread stories be due to the fact that they could not constitute legitimate symbols of New World societies, at least in what became officially recognized stories and shrines?

Although the apparition story of Our Lady of Charity of El Cobre related by Moreno constitutes a significant innovation in this Christian Marian genre (particularly in its New World incarnations), it does not change all the conventions of the New World genre, for even in Moreno's narrative Indians still played leading roles. Rather, the change in the genre consisted in the addition of a black—in fact, a slave—protagonist to the story line. In practice, too, the change may have consisted in the official recognition of a slave's voice as main witness/authority/author of a foundational memory and story. It is as if in the case of the Virgin of El Cobre, slaves wrote themselves—and were allowed to write themselves—into a mainstream story, altering a genre from which they tended to be excluded regardless of their evangelization, creolization, and incorporation into the New World. Indeed, it was a white figure that had to make its way into this Marian narrative sometime between the late nineteenth and early twentieth centuries as Our Lady of Charity became the paradigmatic symbol of the Cuban nation. Overall, the inclusion of slaves in this story, the role of a royal slave as main witness and living repository of this memory, and the development of the island's major eighteenth-century shrine in an Afro-Cuban pueblo constituted significant modifications of mainstream religious and cultural conventions at the time that merit further research in Latin American colonial studies, however.

Although Marian miracle narratives in general were part of a story genre with its own set of conventions, there was also room in them for improvisation, for the incorporation and accommodation of real events from local history (particularly in the earlier and more direct versions of the alleged events), and for the embodiment of local meanings. So if the basic plot and structure of the stories themselves had a generic character, the details that fleshed out the "master story" provided particular spins to these tales and to their messages. Moreover, there were often tensions between versions of the stories produced and circulated among different sectors of society particularly in terms of their narrative emphasis, meanings, and implications.

Social Memory and (Marian) Stories: Juan Moreno's Version of the Apparition

The communication act involved in the notarization ritual constituted a double transaction between the witness who gave the account and sought its legitimation (the royal slave Moreno) and his official interlocutors (church authorities). First, the actual version narrated by Moreno must have been influenced by the presence of such authorities, especially given the power relations between the parties involved in the exchange. Second, the recording process itself may have included subtle glosses or alterations on the part of the church's scribe. Hence, the story that emerged from the notarization act represented a negotiation of the agendas of both parties. In a sense, it reflected a "holy" alliance, so to speak, between royal slaves and some sectors of the church against other groups in colonial society intent on reestablishing the cobreros' former status as ordinary slaves. Thus, although the story and its notarization may be read as an act of resistance (of cobreros and sectors of the church) to the status quo ante, undoubtedly it also reflected domination: the recorded construction of the tale was literally subject to the church's approval and ratification (not to speak of the more loose process in which these stories are composed in social life). Thus, the story that Moreno told remained within the bounds of orthodoxy, even when it may have broken the general trend on slave and black participation. Moreno's story about the finding of a miraculous statue was based on a Marian master code whereby the Mother of God appeared to the wretched, lowest, and most disempowered all over the world: to children and women, to shepherds and peasants, to Indians, and, more rarely in the colonial world, to blacks and slaves. This genre of stories and legends codifies an important ideological tenet of Christianity, namely, the value of all men and women in the eyes of God, where, in fact, the underprivileged can become overprivileged through divine favor. Making use of this dominant narrative, the royal slaves of El Cobre articulated an account of their past that expressed their present concerns in a manner relatively acceptable to the church and to different sectors of colonial society, high as well as low.

Moreno's story of the apparition not only recalled real or supposed events in the past but also immediately referred to the royal slaves' actual situation in the 1680s. While manifestly speaking to the origins of the shrine in the distant past, the subtext also spoke to the social identity and ensuing claims that the king's slaves were still struggling to consolidate at that moment. I take the production of social memory to be a fundamental practice in the process of imagining and legitimating identity. Stories about the past ground identities in the present. They also provide the foundations for concurrent claims related to those identities. Occasionally, another dimension that points to the future by disclosing glimpses of imagined, yet suppressed, possibilities is latent in social memory as well. Beyond a mere expressive and reflexive activity, then, the invocation of the past constitutes an important discursive practice that actively configures the present and imagines the future.[5]

According to Moreno, the Virgin had appeared to him and two native Indian brothers when he was a boy of about ten, around 1604.[6] (The original Spanish text of Moreno's testimony appears in Appendix 4.) On their way to some salt mines in the Bay of Nipe, he and the Joyos brothers saw from their canoe what at first looked like a bird amidst the foam of the sea. As they drew nearer, however, they realized that there was an image of the Virgin with an engraved sign that read "I am the Virgin of Charity." Rescuing the effigy from the sea they noticed that her clothes were dry and, according to the logic of Marian stories, immediately detected a miracle in such an unlikely occurrence. They took her back to the overseer of the cattle ranch of Barajagua, who in turn informed Captain Don Francisco Sánchez de Moya, administrator of the mines at the time, about the event. Sánchez de Moya ordered that an altar be built in the pasture lands of Barajagua and that a lamp be kept lit at all times in honor of the Virgin. Moreno's emphasis on the Virgin's initial sojourn in Barajagua could well serve to sanctify the king's slaves' claims to that disputed pasture land in the mining jurisdiction that only a decade before Governor Don Andrés de Magaña had tried to strip from them.[7]

In Barajagua, still the periphery of the mines, the Virgin continued performing miracles (and thus pressuring the powers that be) to make her way into the center of the Spanish colonial order represented by the village. Under the care of one of the Indian brothers she began to disappear at night from the altar and to reappear the next morning with her clothes wet—a perfect inversion of the initial miracle. If then she had appeared, now she disappeared; and if before her clothes were dry when in the sea, now they were wet when on the land. This common Marian theme of the Virgin's power to invert the normal order of things could well stand in the story as a metaphor of her power to also transform the colonial social hierarchy in which the cobreros had the status of ordinary slaves.

When the administrator Sánchez de Moya was informed of the new miracles performed, he ordered the local priest and infantry troops stationed in the mines to escort her into the parish church in a ritual procession attended by all the *vecinos* (residents) of the place. Once it was decided that the Virgin merited a hermitage, the top of the Loma de la Cantera (Quarry Hill) became the chosen site for it. But for the following three nights the Virgin again protested the selected site by sending off puzzling lights into the sky. It did not take much for everyone to figure out that the Virgin was dissatisfied and that she wanted her sanctuary built right next to the mines, in the Cerro de la Mina (Mine Hill). In this sense, she made her way through supernatural signs to the exact place where she wanted to stay—another central motif in the genre of Virgin stories. Through this metonymical association with the mines she became, at least in Moreno's implicit text, the protector of the mines and the slaves, their representative in the supernatural sphere. (See Figure 6; note the highlighted episodes depicted in the medallions of this nineteenth-century print.)

The position of the cobreros as slaves in the social organization of the mines in the past was well represented in Moreno's recollection of the apparition. While the Virgin appeared to him and the Indians outside or beyond the colonial social order—in nature—they took her back into "culture" or "civilization" through the prescribed sociopolitical channels, which at the same time she subverted.[8] The three men first had to present her to the *mayoral* overseeing them. He, in turn, passed the news on to the royal administrator, because it was Sánchez de Moya whose prerogative it was to legitimize and recognize the validity of the miracles taking place among his slaves and workers and on his lands. His jurisdiction, then, extended over spiritual affairs as well. Once Sánchez de Moya had been convinced of the Virgin's miraculous faculties, he gave orders to the ecclesiastical and mili-

FIGURE 6. Nineteenth-century popular print portraying the Virgin of Charity over the village of El Cobre (not yet over the Cuban nation). Highlights of the "Apparition" story are depicted in the medallions. (Courtesy of Nora Muntañola)

tary sectors stationed in the old mining settlement to bring her into the center of the colonial order over which he ruled. Thus, according to Moreno's story, the whole social order of the mining settlement had been activated by the miraculous finding of the Marian effigy. But in his story the Virgin defied Sánchez de Moya's authority at each point until she made her way to the mines and became the representative of its miners. In this way the Virgin came full circle from the Indians' and slaves' hands to the center of the community and back again into the slaves' domain in the mines.

In this account, then, the old social order of the mines and the colonial system in which the cobreros were slaves was represented by Captain Sánchez de Moya, the white and free *vecinos* of the place, the overseer, the military, and the parish priest. It was precisely this old local order that the former mining slaves had been trying to obliterate in the years after the Crown's confiscation of the mines, since it prevented their own consolidation into a pueblo. In this story the introduction of the Virgin into the mines symbolized a new imagined order brought about by the Creole slaves and the Indians. This new local order represented the royal slaves' own appropriation of the space of El Cobre to found a community of their own, one where the Virgin's cult could become the focus of religious worship and the Virgin their patroness.

There was yet another potentially more radical, if also ambiguous, flash of the past in this account. This element—what I will call the story's utopian implication—was in fact embedded in the genre of Marian stories itself. This utopian dimension was implicit in the episode of the apparition of the Virgin in the sea. Significantly, this is perhaps the most forceful image of the myth—its "headline," so to speak—and has become the most frequently reproduced theme in the iconography of the Virgin, at least in the twentieth century. (In Figure 6 above, three of the six medallions deal with this episode at sea. See also Figure 4 in the Introduction.) As mentioned before, the Virgin appeared to the Indian brothers and the Creole slave outside the sociocultural system, in "nature." Although this episode could represent the triumph of evangelization, as it did to many, and ultimately, even the colonization of the imagination, it may also be read as an expression of radical appropriation. For it was in this natural sphere, away from the fetters of the colonial system, including the institutionalized church, where both slaves and Indians shared a common destiny by establishing an unmediated connection to a supernatural order represented by the Virgin. In this supposedly natural, uncolonized space of the sea Indians and Creole slaves were empowered by the miracle of the apparition, and it was there where the vision of an imagined order in which they were the sole actors unfolded.

The latent radicalism of this episode was toned down by subsequent episodes in which the Virgin was introduced into the social order of the colonial world. The resolution of the narrative, then—the return of the Virgin to the slaves' sphere within the colonial order of the mines—constituted a pragmatically acceptable vision announcing a new and better order, but one which unfolded within the parameters of the colonial world. (See the last three medallions in Figure 6.)

The subtext of the apparition tale delineated the cobreros' social identity and claims in other ways, too. According to Moreno, the Virgin had appeared to him, a Creole slave, and to two Indian brothers. Indians were the original "natives" of the land, a point stressed in Moreno's testimony (his companions were "native Indians"). While slaves and Indians were constituted as distinct groups in the story, they were, nonetheless, placed in a structurally equal relationship to the Virgin—a comment on the standing of both groups in the social order as well. Witness, for example, the fact that they were out together for the same reasons, and all reported equally to the same overseer. However, the kinship tie between the Indian brothers reinforced the idea of their being "one people" and in that sense distinct from the slave boy Juan Moreno. It is also possible to read age as a significant element in the story. Thus, while the Indians were adults, the Creole slave was a boy, just as the Indians as a people had preceded African slaves and their descendants in Cuba and, more specifically, in El Cobre. The Virgin's chosen people were the cobreros and the Indians; her selected, and therefore hallowed, place was the land they inhabited. The story of the apparition legitimized through divine favor the royal slaves' unusual claim to the land and community of El Cobre. And by juxtaposing black men and Indians it turned, so to speak, the former into natives of the place. The myth thus encoded several ideas and tenets about the origins of the cult and the place of both groups in colonial society. In fact, as the royal slaves' community consolidated, they were in many ways organized like an Indian corporate community.

My symbolic analysis of Moreno's account of the apparition as legitimized by the church does not mean that his story was "fictive" (although allusions to supernatural interventions no less than the rigid generic conventions generating a set pattern of motifs may reinforce that impression among modern readers or those who do not share the discursive premises of his religious system). Nor is his story less "symbolic" if it is shown to reflect or recount "real" events (i.e., that there were in fact two Indian brothers by that name, that Captain Sánchez de Moya existed, that there was a hermitage in the hill of the mine and an abandoned tiny altar in Barajagua, even that there may have been some cures that people interpreted to have been miraculous, and so on). The point is that in any account the choice of details, their emplotment, what is highlighted and commented upon is rhetorically significant and constitutes the basis for a cultural reading.

The symbolic possibilities and flexibility of this narrative as a story of origin and its close relation to contextual issues can be better grasped if one follows some subsequent transformations in the episode of the apparition. Less than a century after Moreno's testimony, and once the sanctuary and cult were well rooted in El Cobre, Bishop Don Pedro Agustín Morell de Santa Cruz wrote after his official visit to the village that Our Lady of Charity had appeared to "three blacks of the slaves of El Cobre."[9] To some outsiders, then, even to those quite familiar with the community and the cult, as Bishop Morell de Santa Cruz had been for some thirty-five years, the origins of the shrine seem to have been exclusively associated by that time with the cobreros. Similarly, centuries later when Our Lady of Charity of El Cobre had become the patroness of all Cuba (and El Cobre a metonym for the island), the three figures of the apparition turned into a black, an Indian, and a white: the three alleged "races" at the "origins" of the Cuban "nation." The specificities of the contexts in which these transformations of the story occurred are unknown, but clearly a process of intentional or unintentional symbolic rewriting had taken place.

A Later Version

Some of the same master themes of the Marian story genre, including their local modification in Moreno's account, resonated in a simpler tale produced almost one hundred years later, in another moment of crisis. Not only were the most salient narrative motifs of the "original" apparition-miracle story reiterated in this later account but also some of the implicit rhetorical strategies in Moreno's subtext resurfaced in this tale. In fact, at times these strategies were made transparent by the explicit glosses that accompanied some of the passages in the later text. The two narratives clearly mirror each other. While the passage of time between the two stories, the mostly oral (and visual) character of the transmission process, and the death of firsthand witnesses to the alleged events had by then obliterated most of the historical details of Moreno's more nuanced narrative, the rhetorical processes and the politics informing the production of both accounts of this social memory were quite similar.

The later account was produced or written down in the context of a conflict that unfolded after 1780, one that seriously threatened the survival of the community.[10] In a way, the reenslavement and dispersal of the cobreros taking place in the 1780s was precisely what the former mining slaves had struggled to avoid shortly after the Crown confiscated the mines in the 1670s. In this sense, despite distance in time, the contexts for the production of both stories were roughly similar. Thus, the previously suggested connection between the community's local presentist concerns and the political role of the Marian story related to the cult of the Virgin of Charity was evinced once again, and perhaps more starkly, in the later, eighteenth-century version.

In one of the first representations drawn on behalf of the community in the judicial battle that followed the 1780 attempt to reprivatize the mining jurisdiction, the cobreros' claims to the land of El Cobre, to their de facto free status, and to life as a pueblo were partly embedded in this new rendition of the Marian legend. The text produced in 1783—a representation to the Crown protesting the reenslavement and dismantling of the community and a petition that its members be heard in court—may have been somewhat unusual in its unabashed and heavy-handed use of religious discourse.[11] While not totally oblivious to the legalities of the case, the document may have revealed a considerable naivete regarding what constituted proper discourse in a juridical context, particularly at the end of the eighteenth century. However, it was precisely the candor of some of these representations intended for legal purposes that allowed them to reflect "lay" persons' languages and ideologies, too.

The document was signed by two cobreros and a Spanish merchant. While it is impossible to know who actually drew the formal petition, the document, or a draft of it, must have been written by a cobrero or by someone familiar with the community, perhaps one of the ecclesiastics living in the pueblo. The details of past and present life in El Cobre must have been provided by a resident of the village, probably the pueblo's representative, Gregorio Cosme Osorio, himself literate and a cosigner of the representation.[12] Regardless of the actual authorship of the document, its account was firmly grounded in the religious discourse associated to this Marian cult. More importantly, it embodied the community's position and echoed previous themes related to the cobreros' social identity and their political aspirations. If it did not constitute the direct voice of a single member of the community, then the account at least demonstrated how the cobreros' association with this Marian cult may have granted their aspirations some legitimacy among other sectors of colonial society.

In this story the statue of the Virgin was found "in the Bay of Nipe . . . by some of the natives . . . two of whom were slaves and [the other] two Indians."[13] While the connection between black and Indian had been represented through different narrative motifs, in this passage both ethnic groups were explicitly portrayed as "natives" of the land and of El Cobre. But instead of the two Joyos Indian brothers and the slave child Juan Moreno of the earlier story, this version spoke of two Indians and two slave men.

What is most interesting about the changes in the later account is how they encoded old as well as new issues. One such issue was the claim to "nativeness" to the land, and, more specifically, to El Cobre, established through analogy to the Indians and through divine favor. In this version, however, the role of the cobreros' ancestors was foregrounded even more than in Moreno's account—a change exemplified by the reshuffling of names. Both Indians in the later account had shed the names Moreno had given them—names that had historical accuracy, since they appeared in the list of the personnel working in the mines in 1608[14]—and instead bore names and surnames found in the community at some point during the eighteenth century. In this sense, Indian figures of the past were renamed as cobreros in the present and subsumed into the community. While the memory of Juan—a key actor in the original story, the official witness of the apparition story recorded in 1687, and a cobrero slave himself—was retained, the names of the other players in the drama had been changed. And although Juan Moreno's surname had been forgotten or suppressed, his first name had not been altered. Indeed, "Juan" had acquired symbolic dimensions, as the name was extended to the two Indians as well. Curiously, the play on names even served to mark off the three "original" actors in the apparition drama (all named Juan now) from the additional one who was called Félix. The symbolic significance of this modification in the social memory of the apparition is shown as well by the fact that more than two centuries later—when the motif of three men who encounter Mary at sea had undergone yet another transformation in popular lore (at some point they had become a white, a black, and an Indian, or some version thereof)—the three men had become widely known as "the three Juans" (los tres Juanes) (see Figure 4 in the Introduction).

The significance of changing names was also thematized in another passage of the representation. After listing the names of the two black (i.e., slaves) and Indian natives who had found the miraculous statue, the text immediately remarked that all four men "were later called by the name or surname of *de la Caridad* [of Charity]." The renaming of the four natives after Our Lady of Charity turned all of them into kin by virtue of their relation to the Virgin Mother. Furthermore, it symbolically merged the three main figures even more obviously into a single "Juan de la Caridad."

Finally, the addition of another slave to the original trio and the closure of the generation gap between the men rendered more symmetrical the symbolic presence of blacks and Indians in the story and perhaps further served to make the cobreros' own ancestors more preponderant. The account then skipped many other details in Moreno's narrative and dwelled on the key episode about the selection of the shrine's location by combining old motifs—the appearance and disappearance of the effigy and the beautiful lights on the hill—with current issues:

The individuals of the city of [Santiago de] Cuba wanted to take the Divine Image to their county (giving the pretext that those people [the cobreros] were incapable of paying proper cult to Our Lady) and resolved to carry her in a procession to the city of [Santiago de] Cuba. But once on the way, Oh marvels of the All Powerful! she returned through the faith of those to whom she had had the pleasure of manifesting herself. The procession had not advanced more than a league when she disappeared *giving to understand that it was the will of God that she remain in the said pueblo of Santiago del Prado to console those to whom she had wished to manifest herself.* . . . That night she manifested herself on the top of the hill in the midst of four beautiful lights. She was immediately housed in a hut while a temple *paid by the natives* was built. And even with all these proofs the residents of [Santiago de] Cuba kept wanting to take her away [emphasis added].[15]

Clearly this rendition of the story also hinged on the theme of the Virgin as the protectress of the natives of El Cobre. But the dramatis personae after the apparition episode were reduced to the pueblo as a whole and the citizens of Santiago de Cuba—an allusion not only to the ongoing conflict between the cobreros and their enemies residing in the neighboring city, but also to the struggle between the local community and that city, the capital of the eastern provinces of Cuba and seat of the colonial authorities of the region. The narrative also explicitly portrayed the conflict over the appropriation of the image (or the Marian discourse) between the officials in the city of Santiago de Cuba and the subordinate cobreros (who, it was said, were incapable of rendering her "proper cult").

Further Politicization of the Virgin's Miracle Stories:
The Power of Divine Intervention

The representation of 1783 added its own politically motivated miracles to the earlier apparition narrative. In a gesture of explicit political linkages between discourse and context, Cosme Osorio and his cosigners related:

> In the past year of 1781 Don Andrés Duany [one of the claimants to the mines who had in fact taken part in the assault] had the courage to profess the following words in the midst of the sack and reenslavement of the natives saying that [the cobreros] should not be allowed to pray or perform ceremonies to the Virgin because she would free them from becoming slaves, and that if they angered him he would take the Virgin away and place her in his sugar mill. . . . But this miserable man paid his due some days or some minutes later with a sudden acute pain that took away his life leaving his family in terror.[16]

The Virgin's usual individual healing miracles were strongly politicized in this and other stories by ascribing divine causality to disease or accident and turning it into retribution. The narrative spoke as well of the fear that Mary's power could provoke and of her effective disciplining actions (actions in this case projected onto the community's enemies and even onto colonial authorities). And finally, the episode alluded to her power to intervene in the world, preventing the cobreros' reenslavement and insuring their continuity as a pueblo—a theme that I argued was implicit in Moreno's account as well.

Another story recounted in the same document may offer a glimpse of how popular belief and religious piety may have spurred actual political support for the cobreros' community among some sectors of colonial society. The narrative recalled the events following the reprivatization orders of 1780.

> Some days later the Governor [Don Vicente Manuel de Céspedes] was forced [by royal orders] to hand over the natives of El Cobre to their pretended owners called the heirs of Eguiluz; but as he was arriving at the pueblo, fearing what he was about to do, it suddenly happened that a daughter of the said Governor accidentally fell ill without giving any sign of life. In this conflict, [the governor] turned to the Sanctuary of Our Lady in whose presence they made the corresponding exclamations and promises, and putting a mantle of the Divine Lady over the sick girl she found herself instantly free of her illness. This created so much fear in the Governor that it did not allow him to proceed with the surrender [of the slaves] and he retired [from El Cobre]. At this time began their [the heirs'] implacable hatred of their Governor.[17]

For a modern historian, the story's interest as a "nonspurious" piece of evidence lies at several levels. On one level, the strongest perhaps, the story deploys and reflects the discourse of a religious believer and Marian devotee who was a contemporary of the political events. From that position, the Virgin was perceived as the protectress of the community, one displeased with the prospect of the cobreros' reenslavement and with the alteration of the status quo in El Cobre. Moreover, she was seen as capable of wielding her great powers against those who dared act against her will—certainly a consideration that at least fervent believers may have wanted to take into account when dealing with the community. Furthermore, in invoking this Marian discourse, its producer made use of what he rightly or wrongly considered to be a legitimating and widely shared discourse that could elicit support for the cobreros' cause among the recipients of the document. Thus, both the story and its political uses illustrate how, by virtue of the cobreros' association with the Marian cult, their claims to community may have been legitimized in the eyes of many believers.

However, a riskier reading of this story may be ventured as well. The episode could be granted a more conventional form of historical facticity if its religious ground (with its encompassing space for the portentous and miraculous) remains suspended. What if beyond constituting a historical "fact" about the discourse and perceptions of the author of the representation and other believers, this story/account also reflected accurately some of the narrated events (that Governor Céspedes's daughter was sick, that they went to the sanctuary, that the governor had second thoughts about the reenslavement of the cobreros, and so on) as well as Céspedes's motivations and construction of those events in terms of Marian religious discourse? A representation from the heirs, who indeed became Céspedes's enemies, had this to say about the governor's political support of the cobreros:

In the year 1780, after having handed over to us the mines, slaves, and lands according to Royal Executory Order, the free cobreros sponsored by the Governor Don Vicente Céspedes and other subjects, fulminated against us a terrible [judicial] process that resulted in the said gentleman's despoiling us of what he had handed over with so much solemnity.[18]

While the motivations for this support ultimately remain uncertain, it would not be too far-fetched to suppose, as indeed the miracle story suggests, that Céspedes was or became a Marian devotee and that his conversion may have informed his backing of the cobreros. Although admittedly problematic at this level, the story, at least symbolically, illustrates beautifully how the perceived power of the Virgin of Charity may have generated support for the cobreros—perhaps even among individuals in positions of power.

Other Strategic Invocations of Our Lady of Charity by the Cobreros

The Virgin of Charity's power embodied in these stories and her role as protectress of the community was often invoked by the cobreros in other sociopolitical situations as well. Extant documents provide some glimpses of what may have been regular appropriations in the community. In a representation drawn in the early 1730s that referred to an episode in 1709, the cobreros pointed out that Governor Don Joseph Canales had tried to despoil the pueblo of its lands and means of self-subsistence. According to the cobreros, "had it not been for Our Lady of Charity we would all have died of hunger."[19]

Similarly, in other moments of crisis when cobreros had to deal with authorities, they invoked the Virgin's power. In a letter to the then-imprisoned Governor Don Carlos Sucre, cobreros complained about the oppressive policies of his successor, explained why they had revolted, and sought his advice, seemingly invoking their privileged status vis-a-vis their patroness: they assured Sucre, "We have been asking Our Lady of Charity in our prayers that she give good success [to your plight]."[20] To Governor Don Pedro Ignacio Ximénez the cobreros sent another letter mediating their request for leniency in the following terms: "In the name of Our Lady of Charity we ask you to look at us with charitable eyes."[21]

More radical and less ingratiating toward authorities was another act of appropriation and empowerment that took place during a revolt in 1731. Before taking to the surrounding mountains in protest of Ximénez's policies toward the community, the cobreros went to the Virgin's sanctuary with the intention of taking the image with them. Finding it closed, they fired some shots into the air from atop the hill of the mine and left for the mountains.[22] A report of the incident noted, "The said slaves had made movements attempting to take the Virgin of Charity because they said it was theirs and that she was their remedy."[23] Similarly, the parish priest wrote, "They have determined among themselves to remove the Image of Our Lady to take it away with them."[24] Thus, in these cases, the cobreros' sense that the Virgin represented them and that the effigy was theirs came to light. Furthermore, on that same occasion, the cobreros did take to the mountains the "king's banner" belonging to the village's militias in a display of their loyalty to the Crown and their trust in royal protection.[25] This incident of manifest political appropriation was informed by some of the very same discursive premises that undergirded the apparition story and a royalist ideology. It emblematizes as well the alliance that in the community's imaginary existed between the Virgin, the king, and the royal slaves.

The cobreros also framed events in Marian religious terms among themselves. During their litigation process, some cobreros saw the Virgin's protective hand intervening on behalf of the community. In a letter to their own cobrero representative in Madrid that recounted the latest business transactions related to their case, an important member of the community wrote, "Brother, the divine Lady of Charity and Remedies has made the most patent miracle that can be imagined for we have been able to obtain through some gentlemen in this city . . . [list of documents] and an edict very favorable to our pueblo."[26] In this case, Salvador Quiala explicitly expanded the conventional sphere of miracles—from healing prodigies and delivery from natural catastrophes—to the political realm of the human: the Virgin offered access to the legal documents that would save their pueblo. Quiala also advised Cosme Osorio not to "remove from your memory my Lady of Charity or the little bald [*calvito*] Saint Anthony for I trust they will get you through successfully."[27]

Eleven years later, however, Cosme Osorio indeed seemed to have removed the Virgin of Charity from his memory. He had not, however, given up the popular belief in Marian miracles and intervention that he also shared with other people throughout the Spanish Empire. In 1795 after learning that the cobreros had received some important correspondence he had sent through "a bishop or a canon of Madrid," Cosme Osorio wrote along the same lines that Quiala had: "[The dignitary's favor] has been a miracle of Our Lady of Solitude of La Paloma street who is venerated in this Royal Court and to whom I have recommended you all for [our] general good."[28] Cosme Osorio's distance from El Cobre and his long stay in Madrid; his greater confidence in metropolitan legal channels and his distrust of local ones (which even Our Lady of Charity may not have been able to affect); the direct links of Our Lady of Solitude's shrine to the royal court and presumably to litigants from all over Spain and its overseas empire (a floating group of which Cosme Osorio was then part of); and the desire to access supernatural protection through the concrete materiality of an effigy (a central aspect of Catholic popular devotion), may have motivated Cosme Osorio's shift in Marian loyalties, if not his continued participation in a wider (or more "global") Marian popular culture.

African Inflections of the Marian Cult?

The importance of the Marian cult that emerged in El Cobre raises other questions. I suggested earlier that the story related by Moreno was filtered through the orthodoxy of the church, not only in terms of the generic structures that shaped the story but also more concretely in the actual recording situation of the notarization ritual. Moreno's foundational narrative was a proper Christian Marian miracle story even if the protagonist role of the slave was innovative, its encoded proposals bold, and its political aims local. The notarization ritual too may have been unusual insofar as the testimony of a slave became the main account and insofar as other slaves testified about miracle stories they had witnessed or heard as well.

It is impossible to know what other versions less "supervised" by the church coexisted with this particular foundational story. There is evidence of a slightly different version—not narrated by Moreno but allegedly recovered from oral history by the first official chaplain of the sanctuary sometime between the late 1680s and 1703. In Father Don Onofre Fonseca de la Caridad's account, a slave girl named Apolonia witnessed the lights at the top of the hill that indicated where the Virgin wanted her hermitage built. This episode was also represented in a nineteenth-century print of the Virgin of Charity's apparition story (see Figure 6; this episode is portrayed in the third medallion down to the left). Although there were no "Apolonias" in the inventories of the mining settlement at the alleged time of the events—and in this sense no historical figures around 1608 like those cited by Moreno—there was one "Polonia" in 1620 and two of them in 1647 (aged eighty and twenty).[29] This episode or detail, then, may have been a contested element of the story with unknown local significances. In any case, a female intervention would not be unusual in a genre in which girls—although not usually slave girls—often became "seers." Thus, the Apolonia version still represents an orthodox Christian version of the story, despite the unorthodoxy of the race and slave status of the girl.

Local (or regional) Marian stories transversed with African deities, powers, and motifs from the seventeenth and eighteenth centuries, however, have not reached us. Except for an act of what may have constituted a more widespread popular culture of "witchcraft," no such accusations were raised against the cobreros, even by the most virulent enemies of the community who looked for any excuse to indict them.[30] The better-known, and more radical, appropriations of Our Lady of Charity in Afro-Cuban popular religious tradition—in Santería or the even more eclectic *espiritismo*—are more recent (see Figure 5 in the Introduction and Figure 7 below).[31] That, however, does not mean that Africanized hybrid versions of this Marian legend and other figures did not exist, or had not existed from the beginning of the cult. After all, slaves who had allegedly witnessed and lived through the apparition events—whatever these may have actually been—were for the most part Central West African (mainly Angolan) people.[32] As I already mentioned, the boy Juan Moreno belonged to the first generation of Creole slaves in the settlement. If more unorthodox stories shot through with African—and perhaps Native American—meanings were generated and circulated at the time, they remained part of an oral popular culture that would have coexisted with the more "orthodox" (if also popular, politicized, and in many ways "unorthodox") trend discussed in this chapter. But such aspects of this Marian cult are difficult to recover today.[33] It may be valid to point to the present existence of syncretisms—or hybridized beliefs and practices—in order to imagine and suggest similar dynamics and possibilities in the past not to be found anywhere in the written record. However, the forms of such contemporary syncretisms should not be automatically and ahistorically projected into the past. The creolized African cult to Ochún/Virgen de la Caridad, at least in its more institutionalized forms, seems not to have been "planted" in the island until the last century, and in the Oriente it arrived from the western side of Cuba in the twentieth century.[34] In fact, the great Yoruba influence that in Cuba is known as Lucumí concentrated in the western region of the island. Oriente primarily experienced the influence of the Congo (Bantu) region, as was also the case in Santiago del Prado in the early seventeenth century.[35] In any case, the information is too scant to allow for even informed speculation at this point. What I suggest here is that hybrid practices probably abounded and perhaps had even coalesced into traditions, but one can only reach them through the historical imagination. At any rate, coexisting with them, or as part of a fluid cultural continuum there were Creole popular Christian traditions in which Afro-Cubans and *castas* (racially mixed groups) also partook, such as the worship of la Virgen de la Caridad.

The focus of this study has been then, perforce, on the Christian version of the religious phenomenon: the story and cult produced under the aegis of the church. Although it may not seem as exotic, autonomous, or coun-

FIGURE 7. An altar in an Afro-Cuban *espiritista* house-temple in El Cobre. Note that the Virgin of Charity is just one among many saints in this eclectic private altar. (Author's photograph)

terhegemonic as more Africanized renditions of Our Lady of Charity, this chapter has shown the political and subversive possibilities that a more mainstream Christian popular cult could also have in colonial society. Should this Christian version be dismissed as "inauthentic" because it does not reflect any particular African memory? What if it constituted a dominant (colonial) discourse whereby an unusual form of community could be legitimized and bold claims for Creoleness and nativeness to the New

World could be advanced? Could it not reflect as well authentic Christian religious piety? The popular culture of the fantastic and of the "real maravilloso" full of stories of prodigies, cures, and transactions with the saints and deities of the other world, often full of spectacle in its processions and festivities, and at times full of profound devotion too, could easily coexist or merge with other expressions of popular culture and religion. In fact, it is precisely these more fantastic (some would claim quasi-"pagan") aspects of the Christian tradition that would have fit quite well with other creolized religious traditions.

CHAPTER 5

Remaking a Marian Tradition

On the top of the Mine there is a hermitage to Our
Lady where a hermit lives with license from the
Bishop of the Island.
—Inventory of the Mines, November 30, 1608

The sanctuary of El Cobre is the richest, most
frequented, and most devout in the Island, and the
Lady of Charity the most miraculous statue of all
those venerated [in Cuba].
—Bishop Don Pedro Agustín Morell
de Santa Cruz,
December 8, 1756

In the 1670s, the king's slaves began to reconstruct a small *ermita* (hermitage) to Our Lady of Charity in El Cobre—the same shrine around
whose origins Juan Moreno spun his tale of miracles. By the mid-eighteenth
century at the latest, the humble local hermitage of former times had
become the richest sanctuary in the island, and the alleged popularity of the
image had traveled far beyond its local confines. The reconstruction of this
hermitage, however, was metonymical of broader material, social, and cultural processes involved in the creation of any major Marian tradition not
only in the past but in the present too.[1] Traditions do not just emerge: they
are historically made and remade. A probing into how that of the Virgin of
Charity of El Cobre was made illustrates the wider processes involved in the
production, institutionalization, and sustenance of this kind of tradition and
its related apparatus.

To be sure, there are some intractable factors involved in the creation of
a major Marian tradition, particularly when linked to a shrine. The success
and popularity of an effigy and its shrine require a reputation for miraculous
powers. An active shrine usually requires ongoing "proof" of the effigy's
powers to enable it to sustain its fame (after all, some effigies can fall from

popular grace and cease being recognized as miraculous too). Admittedly, it is difficult to explain the religious phenomena of faith whereby people claim to witness miracles or confer miraculous powers on a particular effigy. But there is a more tangible, yet often overlooked process that also plays an important role in sustaining an image's popularity: the promotion of the alleged miracles. The process of promoting the fame and reputation of an effigy and of creating the concomitant apparatus to sustain it as a powerful tradition is the subject of this chapter. It is the most historically concrete part of a more complex story.

The study of the remaking of the Virgin of Charity's cult from a local modest devotion into a major local and regional tradition also has other political dimensions directly linked to the cobreros' history. The timing of the transformation, or the transformation itself, was not fortuitous. Rather, it took place precisely as the former mining settlement became a pueblo of royal slaves. Given the vacuum of power in El Cobre after the Crown's takeover of the mines, and particularly the new quasi-"public" character of the territory no longer under private control, conditions became extremely favorable for ecclesiastic and lay devotees from outside the settlement to penetrate, sponsor, promote, and help transform a formerly marginal cult. Although the cobreros played a major role in the construction of the Virgin of Charity's tradition, the production of that tradition was not only a local effort.

If the last chapter focused almost exclusively on the cobreros' own appropriation(s) of a dominant Marian Christian discourse, this chapter expands that local story by adding new dimensions to the picture. It sheds light not only on the relation that the church and other sectors of society had to the Marian cult but also on their bearing on the community that was its seat. Moreover, the wider picture delineated in this chapter provides a glimpse of the kind of popular Christianity prevalent in this Caribbean corner of the Americas and more widely in early modern Spain and its colonial world.

The broader story recounted in this chapter also raises questions regarding the ambiguous sense on which a tradition such as that of El Cobre can be considered "popular," particularly given its strong ecclesiastical control. It may be appropriate to acknowledge the often shifting meanings and references of the term "popular" in the literature, since some of the implicit issues raised by these uses will emerge at several points in this chapter.

The term "popular" does not—cannot—denote actual lay "autonomy" from ecclesiastical influence, supervision, or even control, particularly in post-Trentian Catholicism.[2] In this sense, ecclesiastic penetration and promotion of the cult in El Cobre need not disqualify it as a "popular" phenomenon. Aside from the question of lay autonomy, the term "popular" has been used to contrast educated and ecclesiastic renderings of the faith from more simple (or simplistic) versions of it—a distinction that, as will be seen, is only to a certain extent apposite in the case of this Marian tradition, as well as in other cases. Yet another use of the term "popular" sometimes refers to social distinctions within the laity itself: between the religious beliefs and practices of the elites and those prevalent among the lower, that is, "popular," sectors of society. In these cases, the term "popular" is often implicitly counterposed to a presumably exclusive "high" religious culture among elite sectors of society, a misguided notion as the Marian cult of El Cobre suggests. Although given such a thematic amalgamation, the term "popular" may seem unwieldy, and perhaps misleading, to be of much use, I still find the term helpful in this case. Ironically, I use it purposefully to blur the lines of another kind of commonly assumed distinction: one usually drawn between Afro-Cuban and Catholic religious expressions, as one being "popular" and the other almost necessarily "elite."

A Modest Tradition of the Past: Before the 1670s

Besides Moreno's own memories, all that remain about the early years of Our Lady of Charity's shrine are a few laconic references to a Marian hermitage and its hermit custodian. These scant references themselves constitute eloquent reflections of the modest and rather lusterless character of the cult in the midst of the mining boom years. The earliest evidence of an *ermita* dedicated to the Virgin in El Cobre is found in a report on the state of the mines of Santiago del Prado made in 1608. At the very end of an inventory sketching the economic and social activity of life in the mining settlement—and perhaps reflecting its peripheral and unimportant standing at the time—is the following reference: "On the top of the Mine there is a hermitage to Our Lady where a hermit lives with license from the Bishop of the Island."[3] In his report of expenses, the administrator of the Real de Minas, Captain Don Francisco Sánchez de Moya expanded a bit further on the scant reference:

. . . a hermit of exemplary life, Matías de Olivera, to whom the King, at my request and supplication, designated a hill of the Mine where he made a hermitage dedicated to Our Lady of Guidance, Mother of God of Illescas, [he] is given an alms of 1 real each day for the oil of the lamp, so that he continues with the good custom of the slaves saying their prayers every night in the Church of these mines, as he does, . . . [he receives] a ration of cassava and fish, when available, for he does not eat meat.[4]

Twelve years later, an inventory of the mining settlement echoed similar observations: ". . . a hermitage that is in the hill of the mine, dedicated to Our Lady of Guidance, Mother of God, of Illescas, open and covered with tiles and on wooden pillars, with an altar and a small statue of Our Lady, and other images in prints, and a house where a hermit lives."[5]

The budget assigned to the hermitage and its hermit reflects the austerity, not to say marginality, of the budding cult. The per diem ration given out to the vegetarian hermit was no different from that distributed to the slaves except for the substitution of fish for meat. The allowance of one real daily for the expenses of the hermitage was also minimal and probably sufficient only for the oil of the lamp. The simplicity and modesty of the hermitage was attested to by an altar made up of the small image itself, a lamp radiating the permanent light considered indispensable for any "decent" religious cult, and the surrounding picture prints—perhaps the only donations affordable by what may still have been a fringe of humble devotees.

Yet, the most important center of religious worship in the settlement was the parish church. In contrast to the austere hermitage, the paraphernalia of this temple abounded in silver objects and silk and embroidered cloth upon which devotees had poured their alms for a cult that would not only reflect their piety but also their own station in life.[6] The patron saint of Santiago del Prado was the apostle Santiago (Saint James). An effigy of this saint "brought from Spain" presided over the main altar in the church and the settlement itself bore his name. In addition, two cofradías (lay brotherhoods)—one dedicated to Saint Barbara, patroness of artillerymen, and the other to Our Lady of the Rosary—were housed in two of the church's three main altars and constituted the focus of religious devotion and sociability in El Cobre.[7] It is possible that the lay brotherhood of the Rosary was a cofradía of people of color as was the case elsewhere in the New World, but there is no explicit indication of that in the record.[8] Both of these lay brotherhoods' altars, however, were better furnished than the ermita to the Virgin on the hill. These altars were still found in Santiago del Prado's parish church in the late 1640s.[9]

Aside from signs of the modesty and marginality of this Marian shrine in the past, references in the early accounts of the mining settlement point to the image's Spanish advocacy as "Our Lady of Guidance of Illescas." Retroactively and with many decades of hindsight, Moreno recalled in 1687 that the advocacy of the effigy had been of Our Lady of Charity from the very moment of the miraculous finding. Indeed, this "origin" motif was particularly emphasized in Moreno's foundational story when he stated that the effigy found in the sea was standing on a wooden plank that bore a sign reading "I am the Virgin of Charity." But if in 1620 the effigy in the hermitage standing on the Hill of the Mine was Our Lady of Guidance of Illescas, by the mid-seventeenth century there were three effigies in the settlement's *ermita*—and all were named Our Lady of Charity![10] By this time, then, new images had arrived to the hermitage or former ones had been renamed. It was also sometime during the 1640s that a new caretaker of the shrine, the hermit Melchor de los Remedios, changed one of the effigies' name into "Our Lady of Charity and Remedies."[11] At some point that advocacy was also creolized and rooted locally as the image took on the name of "Our Lady of Charity [and Remedies] of El Cobre." Varying references of this sort suggest a flexibility in the advocacies or the facility with which effigies moved in and out of the hermitage in a period when the devotion would have still been in the making.

It is unclear if from the beginning the effigy of the Virgin (whichever one it may have been) was considered miraculous as Moreno stated in his story, or if that reputation was created much later. It is impossible to establish with the documentation at hand just when the view about the fantastic character of these foundational events began to emerge. At this point all that can be done is to counterpose Moreno's narrative with the routine and fragmented accounts of Captain Sánchez de Moya, the inventory takers, and an ecclesiastical account written in 1703. This exercise raises suggestive questions about social memory and the making of tradition, but it provides no definitive conclusions.[12]

In 1608, Captain Sánchez de Moya dealt with the foundation of the hermitage in a routinely official manner: as administrator he had the power to allow the construction of the *ermita* in his jurisdiction and obtained the formal royal approval for it. The bishop also had to grant his own license, or a patent so to speak, for the construction of a chapel and for the accreditation of a particular hermit as caretaker. The main decisions, however, were in the administrator's hands. Moreno's own narrative about the foundation of the hermitage emphasized the authority of Sánchez de Moya to make decisions about the fate of the effigy and the cult. But in Moreno's account, the Virgin also subverted Sánchez de Moya's authority at every point of the story—perhaps a later embellishment following generic conventions in Marian apparition and miraculous stories.

According to Sánchez de Moya's report of 1608, the mining administration sustained the hermit in payment for his evangelization efforts among a still mostly African slave force in the settlement. Thus, in these early fleeting references, the fringe figure of a hermit is linked to a liminal Marian cult as well as to the also marginal figures of slaves, particularly African slaves, in the mining jurisdiction. Was it Matías de Olivera who taught African and Creole slaves like the boy Juan Moreno the meaning of miracles, of vows, of promises and deals with the saints, of the power of effigies and relics, of the healing power of the oil in the Virgin's lamp? Was it he who taught them how to cast events in a miraculous light, that is, in the world view of a popular Catholic Christianity and in its genre of Marian stories? Indeed, was it Olivera who in the early decades of the seventeenth century or many years after turned a prosaic story about an effigy into a miracle story, a story that Moreno and the cobreros then inflected in their own ways?[13]

Olivera—an old soldier (and possibly a deserter) from Santo Domingo—had been found living in a cave on a hill near the mining settlement, today still known as the Loma del Ermitaño, or the Hill of the Hermit. Moreno recalled him in relation to a few miracles.[14] He remembered, for instance, listening to the hermit from the mines next to the chapel scolding the Marian effigy when she miraculously disappeared from her altar and reappeared with her clothes wet.[15] Moreno associated the first healing miracles with the oil of the lamp (also a motif and practice in healing shrines elsewhere) with Olivera. At any rate, if in Moreno's acute or fading memory, portentous events occurred in that humble and austere chapel overseen by this Spanish hermit, these recalled miracles did not seem to lead at the time to any major material expansion of the hermitage. Nor of its wealth or its shrine. In the 1670s the royal slaves were found rebuilding a still humble chapel overseen by Melchor de los Remedios, its last hermit custodian.[16]

Hermits and Popular Religion

It is almost surprising to find hermits as late as the seventeenth century, not to say the eighteenth century, and to find them not only in the New World but also in the supposedly religiously barren landscapes of the more "hinterland" areas, like Cuba. Although Bishop Morell de Santa Cruz did not report them elsewhere during his pastoral visit throughout the island in 1756–1757, he also found them at another major shrine in Cuba—the sanctuary to Our Lady of Regla in the bay of Havana.[17] The tradition of hermitage, and specifically of hermits taking up the custody of chapels, was a particularly extended one in early modern Spain.[18] Few of these more modern hermits, however, would live in complete isolation as the early desert hermits did. Their retirement, instead, would consist of solitude in the shelter of a chapel, often while wearing the habit of a third order and begging for alms. At least in El Cobre, hermits were always *españoles* (Spaniards or whites).[19] To be sure, Moreno referred to the first caretaker of the Virgin as one of the Indian brothers who had found the image, but ecclesiastical accounts do not regard him as a hermit but as "a sort of sacristan."[20] At least one slave child in the late seventeenth century, Domingo Quiala, lived with Melchor de los Remedios and helped him attend to the hermitage,[21] but there is no evidence in the village censuses of black hermits around the sanctuary. There were no female hermits either; instead, pious lay women could live in private houses as *beatas* (lay holy women). Indeed, it seems that a *beata* lived in El Cobre during the 1730s; she was a free mulatta from outside the village. Sister Flores may have settled in El Cobre to live near the sanctuary. The sixty-seven-year-old woman, however, does not seem to have made any vows of poverty, for she had four personal slaves—two adult females and two girls—serving in her house in 1735.[22]

Because of the lay or semilay status of hermits, and their marginal character, their custody of chapels and shrines reflected the less institutionalized and usually more spontaneous nature of popular devotions. Yet, some control of the church over the degree of orthodoxy of these popular village cults was insured by the bishop's required approval of their guardians.[23] In the case of El Cobre, as I have noted, this approval had to come from the royal administrator of the mines as well. But, hermits could exert a strong hold over a cult by controlling access to the effigy, and when said to be miraculous, to its relics or to the source of its powers. Olivera distributed the oil of the lamp at his discretion to devotees who came to the shrine in search of a cure. According to a history of the sanctuary, the hermit Melchor de los Remedios—who entered the service of the hermitage in the late 1640s and stayed as caretaker until his death in the late 1670s—seemed to have had decision-making power over whether or not the Virgin's statue should be removed from her shrine in a public prayer for rain.[24] In fact, these lay guardians could even exert strong influence over the direction and shape of a cult. As already mentioned, Melchor de los Remedios was remembered as having modified the title of the Virgin of El Cobre to that of Our Lady of Charity *and* Remedies.[25] At another time the bishop clashed with this same hermit over the latter's unauthorized decision to repair the Virgin's statue.[26]

In this sense, although hermit custodians may have represented a less official and more popular presence in local lay devotions than ecclesiastic figures, they themselves often promoted, mediated, and controlled popular access to a venerated image. Moreover, hermits were also subject to supervision and control from an ever-watchful church, particularly after the Council of Trent. Thus, in the case of Catholicism—especially after the Counter-Reformation—the popular character of religion, or of a particular devotion, was never devoid of hierarchical control.[27] That did not mean, however, that these devotions were not often permeated by ancient or more recent pagan meanings and practices. Although historians often see the retained popular character of such devotions in their deviation from ecclesiastical orthodoxy, these devotional deviations were often also shared by ecclesiastics, and even highly educated clergy. Indeed, they constituted aspects of a widespread popular culture in which lay and ecclesiastics, educated and illiterate people, high and low sectors of society all partook—a point to which I shall return later.[28]

After the Crown's confiscation of the mines, and after the hermit Melchor de los Remedios died in the late 1670s or early 1680s, ordained clergy became the caretakers of the hermitage. While the number of hermits dedicated to the cult of Our Lady of Charity expanded in the eighteenth century, they played a subordinate role to the chaplain of the sanctuary. An important role for hermits then was to travel throughout towns collecting alms for the sanctuary and spreading word of the effigy as a miracle worker.

Local Shrines in Cuba

The first Marian hermitage in El Cobre seems to have been a modest local cult, not much different from others reported in the island during the seventeenth and eighteenth centuries. Shrines, chapels, stories of miracles, and traditions such as the one in El Cobre were common throughout Spain and the New World. In Cuba, for instance, there were other special effigies and local shrines that never acquired the fame and power of that of Our Lady of Charity of El Cobre, but they nevertheless indicated how diffused these forms of religious culture were even in the backwaters of the empire. Bishop Morell de Santa Cruz mentioned several in the mid-eighteenth century during his extensive pastoral visit throughout the island.[29] In the Indian pueblo of El Caney, for example, there was no hermitage, but there was a shrine in an altar of the parish church to a miraculous image of Our Lady of Guadalupe.[30] In the city of Bayamo there was what the bishop considered a "moderately decent" hermitage to a miraculous image named Nuestra Señora de la Candelaria del Dátil. In the isolated town of Baracoa, religious culture in general seemed to have been on the wane. The bishop reported that the parish church had fallen down and the only church in use was a hermitage to a miraculous cross called the Santa Cruz de la Parra. Bishop Morell de Santa Cruz saw this local hermitage as very poorly ornamented, indeed as "indecent." Local people told the bishop that it was (literally) a miracle that the small hermitage was still standing. In Puerto Príncipe the *cabildo* (local government) had sworn vows to the effigy of María de los Santos Dolores found in the Serafizo Convent as patroness of snakes because of epidemics of these creatures that occurred in the city for many years. The practice reflected the widespread custom in Spain of making collective vows to an image so that it would deliver the community from a particular misfortune.[31]

A larger city such as Santiago de Cuba could simultaneously have several particular devotions to miraculous effigies and even several patron saints. In 1782, for instance, the official patron saints of this city included Saint James (Santiago), Saint John Chrysostom, Saint Francis of Assisi, and Ecce Homo.[32] A painting of the latter in the cathedral was considered to be miraculous since at least the seventeenth century.[33] The trajectories of some of these devotions had their ups and downs, however. In 1744 a complaint was registered in the books of the city's *cabildo* regarding the neglect in which the annual festivity to the Archangel Saint Michael had fallen.[34] In 1771, another complaint was inscribed in the *cabildo* records to the effect that the festivity of the patron Saint James "has for some years now been celebrated with little decency and solemnity."[35] Cases such as this reflect the decline in popular favor of a saint and his or her cult despite official recognition.

Marian effigies also had some devotions in the city of Santiago de Cuba. The Virgin of Carmen had festivities celebrated in her honor in 1672 as well as processions and rogations to deliver the city from a great drought in 1673, but thereafter disappeared from the *cabildo*'s records.[36] Almost a century later, however, a cult to a new Marian effigy, the Virgin of Dolores, seemed to be on the rise. The records of the *cabildo* note that in 1769 alms were collected from devotees "so that with her protection this community may be redeemed from the dreaded ruins brought about by the earthquake."[37] A crown for the effigy was received from Rome in 1771 and scapulars were sold or distributed to devotees as the Virgin had been declared local patroness of earthquakes. Five years later festivities and rogations to this Virgin were organized to obtain protection from an epidemic of smallpox ravaging Santiago de Cuba in 1776.[38] As these cases show, even the city's official *cabildo* became involved in the promotional strategies that contributed to the making of popular devotions and traditions associated with particular effigies.

In the late eighteenth century there may have also been a special devotion, or perhaps a vow, to Saint Anthony in El Cobre. In 1783, for instance, the cobrero Salvador Quiala commended Gregorio Cosme Osorio in Spain to Our Lady of Charity and to "the little bald [*calvito*] San Antonio whom I trust will get you out well."[39] But rather than a local devotion, perhaps Quiala's invocation reflected a wider regional one particularly active in those years, albeit one ostensibly related to a different sphere of crises. Indeed, "given the repeated droughts and periods of sterility that this city suffers" the *cabildo* of Santiago de Cuba elected and swore Saint Anthony of Padua patron saint of the fields and garden plots in 1782, just a year before Quiala invoked the protection of this saint in his letter.[40]

In short, local shrines and devotions were found in many of the island's villages, towns, and cities. The very modest hermitage to Our Lady of Charity found in the mining settlement in the first part of the seventeenth century seems to have been no more than one such local shrine. What became significant in the case of El Cobre was that local shrine's path to fame after the Crown's takeover of the mines and in tandem with the emergence of a most singular pueblo of royal slaves. Only one other shrine seems to have rivaled the popularity and wealth of El Cobre since the eighteenth century: the shrine to the dark Virgin of Regla in Havana.[41]

Expansion of the Cult after the Crown's Confiscation of the Mines

The Material Reconstruction

In 1738, Bishop Don Juan Lasso de la Vega placed the "origin of the hermitage, or chapel, where the Miraculous Image of Our Lady of Charity is venerated [today] some sixty or seventy years ago" (thus in 1670 or 1680) and added, "I have been told that [at first] it was a very small hut and [that] later a small stone masonry church with a sacristy and a room for the chaplain was built with alms from devotees."[42] Years later, in 1756, Morell de Santa Cruz reported, "At the beginning the [effigy] was placed in a very poor and humble church but some fifty years ago [1706] a new one [made] of tiles and masonry was erected."[43] Whether these accounts referred to a single long construction process or to two different stages of reconstruction is hard to say; however, the bigger and richer sanctuary that stood in place throughout the eighteenth century was built after the Crown's confiscation of the mines.

Whether the royal slaves' reconstruction of the parish church and of the hermitage in these years represented an act of devotion, of appropriation of space, or perhaps even an act of labor coercion by the church, it would in any case have also been an important political statement. Parish churches were a sine qua non of any duly constituted pueblo and usually the first public structure erected in them. In reconstructing the parish church "at their own expense," the royal slaves were not only taking over the temple but also making some claims to communal status and perhaps even to pueblo. One detail illustrates well the social transformation of space that took place in El Cobre's parish church. In the 1620s there was a wooden rail that separated the chorus from the main body of the church "so that behind it the black slaves [could] listen to mass separated from the whites."[44] Once they became the main parishioners in the settlement, the enslaved cobreros did not have to stand behind the rail—they could take over the main chapel.[45] Thereafter it would be up to the emerging pueblo of royal slaves and free people of color to replenish their newly appropriated and reconstructed parish church.[46] All the images and paraphernalia that had previously populated and adorned the church had been removed as the settlement became depopulated.[47] Eventually the cobreros would sustain the parish through regular fees and contributions.[48]

The royal slaves not only reconstructed their parish church in the 1670s but they also rebuilt the Virgin's hermitage. The first glimpse of the cobreros' reconstruction of the Virgin's hermitage was provided in an inventory of the mines drawn up in 1677. The notary pointed out that Governor Don Andrés de Magaña had given the tiles of the Big House to the hermit Melchor de los Remedios for the reconstruction of the small hermitage.[49] The reconstruction of the hermitage, however, became a longer, major project that went beyond the 1670s and into the early 1680s.[50] By the early 1690s, a hostel for visiting pilgrims had been built next to the hermitage, which added to the shrine's already established regional character.[51] In subsequent years a long paved road to the sanctuary was constructed. Indeed, by the 1730s at the latest, the Marian shrine in El Cobre was no longer a hermitage, but instead a sanctuary. The temple was a relatively large chapel (116 feet long, 40 feet wide, and 24 feet high)—a structure even longer than the village's parish church. It now had three altars with abundant ornaments and "jewels" "very estimable because of their value and beauty" instead of the cheaper picture prints (*estampas*) that adorned the walls of the early hermitage. In addition, the sanctuary had a pulpit, two organs, a clock, and a portico with three bells.[52] A sacristy stood in the back and next to it the dwellings of the chaplain, his servants, slaves, and the hermits who still came to reside in the sanctuary, albeit now in a subsidiary role. Furthermore, already by 1735, the sanctuary must have been so well endowed that it owned nine private slaves—called "slaves of the Virgin"— and the chaplain had five more of his own—a far cry from the situation of earlier hermits.[53] By midcentury, but probably much earlier, the sanctuary of El Cobre had become "the richest, most frequented, and most devout [sanctuary] in the Island."[54]

Sponsoring and Financing the Material Expansion of the Cult

The expansion of the Marian cult's material infrastructure had not been merely a local effort as sometimes portrayed in the cobreros' representations. Individual devotees from outside the village donated labor and skills in exchange or as an expression of gratitude for some healing favor too. Wealthier devotees also helped finance the cult with their alms and donations, and their reasons were similar to those of poorer ones. Lay people as well as clergy were among the individual donors. The *chantre* of the Cathedral of Santiago, Don Diego Franco, donated the silver lamp on the Virgin's altar together with a fine table scarf and other gifts after he was able to miraculously expel three stones from his bladder. A master carpenter from Santiago donated his labor in the 1680s after recovering his sight, and another carpenter from Santiago, Juan Cabes, promised four months of work to the Virgin if she cured him from *gálico*. Lieutenant Antonio Espinoza from Bayamo himself made the organ that he donated to the sanctuary. At least once when the instrument broke he also donated his labor to fix it, for which Our Lady of Charity rewarded him with another cure.[55] These stories of miracles and of quasi-contractual exchanges between mortals and the Virgin reveal similar customs shared among different sectors of society with respect to a miracle-making effigy. The wealth of a shrine displayed the public fame and sacred power of the image as it was directly related to her alleged miracles. The pomp of the cult fed the effigy's reputation, and that reputation in turn attracted more prospective donors and devotees in search of cures.

The cobreros themselves contributed materially to the growth of the sanctuary with their labor services, voluntary or exacted by the clergy, and perhaps with monetary donations as well.[56] Representations on behalf of the community drawn many years later recalled those services and took full credit for the construction of the sanctuary. One claimed with exaggeration, although with political sagacity:

The first effect of their prosperous situation [after the confiscation of the mines] was to construct a beautiful temple to their patroness Our Lady of Charity [who had] miraculously appeared to the primitive natives [of El Cobre], adorning it with jewels of so much value that all the altar of Our Lady was made of silver . . . and they constructed a road of masonry that is about a fourth of a league from the base to the top of the hill where the sanctuary is located.[57]

Another representation drawn up in 1793 stated that the cobreros "erected a beautiful temple that still exists . . . [it was] reedified by the natives themselves."[58] The text explained that in addition to their labor services, the cobreros made monetary disbursements "of 100 pesos per freedman and 50 per slave [head of household?]" to construct the paved road to the sanctuary—a far-fetched claim for a peasant village but one that nonetheless may have contained some truth even if in terms of lower expenditures and a century-long span of time.[59] At any rate, regardless of the actual way in which the cobreros contributed to the construction of the village's new Marian sanctuary, in their accounts to the courts these exactions or donations were portrayed exclusively as an act of local patronage. No acknowledgment was made in these texts of the copious alms that grateful devotees from outside the village also contributed. Indeed, in these representations to the courts, the construction and adornment of the sanctuary took on a political role, one deployed to buttress the cobreros' claims to communal life as a pueblo, to give testimony to their Christian commitments, to flaunt the alleged economic power of the community, and to emphasize the cobreros' role in the development of the colony. The latent political significance of the erection of such a temple in El Cobre—and of its wealth—then, did not escape the authors of these representations. If outsiders had partly appropriated this cult, and if their gifts and donations became material expressions of blurred local boundaries, then the cobreros in turn politically invoked the wealth and fame of the temple for their own purposes, too.

Yet, regardless of who may have actually financed the material expansion of the sanctuary, the cult to the Virgin of Charity of El Cobre could neither have survived nor developed as it did without a community to ground it.

Indeed, the growth, legitimation, and preservation of an important shrine, if not always its establishment, goes hand in hand with a primary population settlement or a community, however small, that can provide the fundamental and continuous social backdrop to keep the cult alive. Shrines are usually associated with local communities from which they partly derive their names and identities and to which they are said to confer protection and special favors. Conversely, local communities often derive their collective identities, at least their religious ones, from shrines in their jurisdiction.[60] The relationship between shrine and community becomes particularly strong when members of that community have been directly involved in the foundational (and miraculous) events leading to the formation of the shrine. In this sense, the growth of the cult to the Virgin of Charity of El Cobre was linked to the consolidation of a pueblo in El Cobre after the Crown confiscated the mines. Not only did the members of this pueblo—royal slaves, for the most part—provide much needed support to the shrine through labor services and monetary contributions or the exactions obtained from them, but they also sustained the regular cult by participating in the daily rosaries and, especially, by the women's singing in the chorus of the sanctuary.[61] Indeed, the success of the Marian shrine of El Cobre was directly related to the preservation of the cobreros' community.

Social and Political Transformations: Ecclesiastical Personnel Takeover

Beyond major transformations in the cult's material infrastructure, important social and political changes also occurred in the local Marian tradition of this village. After the 1670s, El Cobre became a kind of no-man's-land that facilitated the penetration of private ecclesiastics and the organized church. The rise of the Marian cult in particular attracted more than the usual share of clergymen to this village.

In 1683, only five years after the cobreros had obtained the concession to remain in El Cobre, and shortly after the hermit custodian Melchor de los Remedios died, Chaplain Don Onofre Fonseca de la Caridad, an ordained priest and devotee of the Virgin, retired to the hermitage with no official position or salary. Fonseca de la Caridad's decision was a step in the direction of a greater ecclesiastical penetration of the settlement. Lay hermits would never again recover their former place as the main, or sole, custodians of the hermitage.[62] Fonseca de la Caridad had the support of some ecclesiastics from Santiago de Cuba—possibly exiles and friends from

Jamaica—also interested in the promotion of the Marian cult.[63] This small group of ecclesiastical devotees took the initiative to notarize Moreno's account in 1687 to officialize the cult.

Fonseca de la Caridad stayed on as chaplain for twenty-eight years (1683–1711) and was a key force behind the institutionalization of the cult. He was able to assure the continuity of the sanctuary's personnel (and perhaps his own salary) by obtaining a chaplaincy that would thereafter provide an autonomous and steady income for the sanctuary's chaplains. Two ecclesiastical devotees ordered the imposition of a chaplaincy on their sugar mill, suggestively named "Our Lady of Charity," in 1705. In return, weekly (sung and recited) masses for their souls were to be performed in the Virgin's sanctuary forever. The price for their souls' assured rest was 250 annual pesos (the interest on the 5,000 pesos value of the property's mortgage), which constituted approximately the ongoing salary for a chaplain at the time. While the fund was private, conditions set down by the donors stipulated that the chaplain's appointment was to be made by the church, free of royal patronage or of the jurisdiction of the state.[64] With that proviso, the sanctuary's independence was assured—a measure that may have been more difficult had the mines still been in private hands. It should be noted that although appointments were to fall under the purview of the church, private individuals—in this case almost all ecclesiastics—had provided the capital to sustain it.[65]

By 1738, however, the governor and bishop in Santiago de Cuba were fighting over rights to appoint their favorites—and over the jurisdictional control that pertained to each. Worldly interests may have made coveted posts of positions in enterprises of popular culture such as major shrines. In stressing the Marian cult's autonomy (at least from royal patronage) the bishop noted, "[The chaplain] has sustained himself only with the alms of the masses offered by devotees, not having concurred Your Majesty, nor your Royal Patronage with any alms for the said church, lamp, nor sustenance of the chaplain, having been always been there only with the license of his bishop."[66] In fact, the church was claiming authority over a sector of a jurisdiction that supposedly belonged to the Crown. In this sense, the church, too, negotiated its imagined prerogatives with the state. The matter was referred to Madrid where the king resolved that both appointees share the chaplaincy until one of them died. The number of ecclesiastics in the pueblo was thereby increased to three, including the parish priest who was under royal patronage.

The number of personnel of the church in El Cobre grew concurrently with its fame—and the possibilities of sustenance, work, and perhaps enrichment—of the sanctuary. In 1750, there were funds in the sanctuary to finance the position of organist. By that same year there were five ordained priests living in El Cobre: two in the parish church, two in the sanctuary, and a fifth probably associated with the latter.[67] In 1756 Bishop Morell de Santa Cruz decided to augment the capital rent (*censo*) for the organist's salary. In that same year the bishop toyed with the idea of assigning yet another clergyman to attend to a hospital he intended to sponsor in the village, perhaps to complement the healing shrine.[68] By midcentury the presence of the church had indeed become overwhelming for a village of that size. Most villages of about El Cobre's size in the region during the 1750s had one or at most two clergymen.[69]

It was not only the number of clergy in the village but also the extent of their tenures—often for life—that speaks to the strong ecclesiastical presence in El Cobre, too. As mentioned before, Chaplain Fonseca de la Caridad spent almost the last three decades of his life in El Cobre's sanctuary. His successor, Chaplain Don Thomás Bravo, became chaplain in 1712 and remained in the sanctuary for twenty-two years until his death in 1734. Both Chaplain Don Francisco Suárez Calderín and Chaplain Don Julián Joseph Bravo succeeded Thomás Bravo in 1734, sharing the chaplaincy of the sanctuary for some years. Suárez Calderín retained his post for only nine years (he died in 1743), but Bravo was chaplain for twenty-seven years, until his retirement in 1761.[70] The sanctuary's chaplains, however, were not the only lasting ecclesiastical presence in the village. Some parish priests also lived for a long time in El Cobre. Father Don Juan Jacintho de Silva took his position in 1724 and was still the village's parish priest thirty-two years later in 1756. The beloved Father Don Alejandro Paz y Ascanio, a Canarian priest, arrived in the 1790s and did not retire until the early 1830s.[71]

The possibilities for individual profit and enrichment open to ecclesiastics in El Cobre were reflected in the property holdings they acquired. In the 1730s and 1750s, resident clergymen in the village had each a few personal slaves of their own, although their number was small.[72] In addition, the acquisition of village land and the development of some agricultural enterprises may have constituted additional sources of income for the local clergy as it often did elsewhere. In the 1760s the community accused the sanctuary's chaplain, Father Julián Joseph Bravo, not only of appropriating village land but also of trying to sell it as private property.[73] Similarly, by 1773 a younger brother of the former parish priest Silva owned a small sugar mill within the village's jurisdiction that he may have inherited from his brother.[74] The parish priest Paz y Ascanio, who had also seen to the first publication of a history of the sanctuary in 1829, had built a considerable estate in the environs of El Cobre by the time of his death in the early 1830s. Paz y Ascanio willed parts of his legacy to the sanctuary, to the cathedral in Santiago de Cuba, and to his nephew.[75]

It is not clear, however, if clergymen in El Cobre made use—personal or official—of the labor of the king's slaves. Although the human "estates" of the Crown and the church seem to have been kept distinct, there were a few cases that suggest some kind of servitude of royal slaves to the clergy. Overall, however, the cases are so few and the circumstances so unclear as to render them extremely ambiguous. Resident clergymen had their own kind of households where several sorts of people resided: relatives, personal slaves, some unrelated free persons, one or more (free) hermits, and a few cobreros, usually young, or if adult, female. In 1739, for example, the parish priest Silva had two royal slave brothers aged twelve and fourteen in his care (perhaps in training or service as "mass boys"). The children had lived with their families until at least 1735 when suddenly they appeared in the census as in the charge of the priest. Sixteen years later two other royal slave brothers aged twelve and fifteen were also residing in Father Silva's household, along with seven relatives of the priest, a free woman aged eighteen, and seven personal slaves.[76]

Similarly, in 1739 one of the chaplains of the sanctuary, Father Suárez Calderín, had four royal slaves under his care: a twenty-two-year-old single mother and her one-year-old child; and another single mother, the thirty-four-year-old named Ana María de Salas and her six-year-old son, Odoardo. Ana María was the wife of one of the "Virgin's slaves" and Odoardo was their son; the latter following his mother's status, was legally a king's slave. Likewise, in 1750 three of the sanctuary's other eight slaves were also married to other royal slave women who were recorded as part of Father Bravo's household—perhaps they had become as well the clergyman's domestic servants.[77]

More generally, the relationship of the royal slaves to clergymen in the village seems to have mirrored that of parishioners, but there was plenty of room for ambiguity in these relations, too. The exactions clergy obtained from the cobreros seem to have been collected as tithes, and as fees for sacraments and other services.[78] These were, however, the usual fees paid by free parishioners elsewhere in the Spanish Empire. In this sense, whatever exploitation of royal slaves the church may have engaged in, it was the kind of abuse against which parishioners—especially peasant parishioners—all over the empire, including Spain, continuously protested.[79] Yet, the cobreros' status as royal slaves may at times have given a particular inflection to the parish priests' hold over his parishioners. The parish priest Silva, for instance, complained to the Crown in the 1750s that many women in El Cobre were disappearing in order to baptize their children as "free" in Santiago de Cuba and elsewhere, a practice that deprived him of his income in baptism fees and deprived His Majesty of future slaves.[80] Incidents such as this denunciation reflect conflictive relations between clergy and cobreros. In addition, the church also benefited from the community's labor for construction and maintenance purposes, but again these services may be more clearly understood as a widespread internal levy throughout the Spanish Empire than any particular imposition upon these royal slaves.[81]

Despite conflictive relations with the community—and at times exploitative ones—clergymen also constituted political allies and supporters of the cobreros. When not functioning as spokesmen for the community, they could, as often was the case of parish priests in the Spanish Empire, function as scribes, serve as witnesses, give counsel, provide contacts and references, and act as intermediaries to higher colonial authorities. In 1708, for instance, Father Don Juan Antonio Pérez wrote to the Crown a denunciatory letter against the abuses of Governor Don Joseph Canales on behalf of his parishioners and declared in the cobreros' favor during the High Court judge's investigation.[82] Other former parish priests gave testimonies on the community's behalf too. Despite his denunciations in the 1750s of cobrera women who left the village to baptize their children as free elsewhere, at other moments of crisis that priest gave favorable reports about his parishioners and gave witness of the abuses of at least one governor. The letter Father Silva submitted to the Crown during the revolt of the early 1730s was crucial in absolving the cobreros from the charge of sedition.[83] When two royal slaves tried to cross to Santo Domingo in 1728 to present their grievances to the High Court, it was through regional clerical networks that the priest of Baracoa helped them embark from that port.[84] Similarly, Father Paz y Ascanio was almost removed from his post by orders of the regional governor in the mid-1790s for his active support of the embattled cobreros.[85] During those years too, the church provided the channels for secret correspondence between cobrero village *apoderados* (legal spokesmen or proxies) in Spain and El Cobre.[86]

Even high dignitaries of the church, such as the Dean and later Bishop

Morell de Santa Cruz (1720s–1760s), Bishop Lazzo de la Vega in the early 1730s, and Bishop Don Joaquín Osés y Alzúa in the 1790s became tactical allies and at times important protectors of the community in the wider politics of colonial society.[87] In these conflicts, governor and bishop or state and church often clashed over issues in the village. Overall, the involvement of high-ranking ecclesiastical officials in local politics was most probably linked to their investment in the preservation of a community that anchored such a successful Marian cult. In this sense, church and cobreros' overlapping agendas and working alliance can be seen as a colonial pact. This is not to deny, however, that there may have been other more altruistic and Christian considerations informing ecclesiastic support for the community, too.

Promotion of the Marian Cult: Writing History, Making Tradition

In order to receive official recognition, a cult also had to be grounded in a proper historical account that demonstrated the extraordinary nature of the shrine since its origins. The notarization process of 1687 where Moreno had recounted his allegedly firsthand account of the apparition events was a first step in that direction. The ritual of inscribing what had previously been an informal oral account also meant fixing its meaning and memory in the official archives of the church. While the legend of the "apparition" continued to be transmitted generation after generation through oral accounts and iconic representations that obliterated and modified the various details of the story, subsequent written tradition would be irrevocably tied to the version recorded in that notarization process. Both traditions, oral and written, however, interacted and influenced each other at different points in time.

The process of generating a proper (written) "history" out of an oral social memory became the task of several chaplains of the sanctuary. Once more, the resolute Fonseca de la Caridad was the first and most important of a local line of ecclesiastical historians. His manuscript (1703), like that of other ecclesiastics thereafter (as well as Chapter 4 of this book), was based on Moreno's notarized narrative.[88] The treatise, which aimed to give a greater legitimacy and recognition to the cult through the written word, was not published. One may suppose, however, that as elsewhere in the Spanish peninsula and Mexico, miracle books and histories of shrines circulated in manuscript form among elite educated groups who could read (and hopefully provide alms).[89] Six decades later, in 1766, Chaplain Julián Joseph Bravo wrote another history of the sanctuary with his own spin on Fonseca de la Caridad's manuscript.[90] Bravo's manuscript was not published either.

In 1782, another chaplain of the sanctuary, Father Don Bernardo Ramírez, edited Fonseca de la Caridad's first manuscript, but again, this text was not published either.[91] Not until 1829 did the parish priest Paz y Ascanio revise Ramírez's edition of Fonseca de la Caridad's original text.[92] This nineteenth-century manuscript became the first publication of the history of the cult, but soon after others followed in 1830 and 1840.[93] Yet another edition was republished in 1853.[94] Aside from Moreno's notarized oral account examined in the last chapter, the only histories to have reached us are Julián Joseph Bravo's and Paz y Ascanio's. Fonseca de la Caridad's first manuscript (1703) has been lost.[95]

These treatises and manuscripts were also forms of seeking official legitimation from the church for a popular cult. To receive official approval, these texts needed to be explicitly grounded in correct exegetical commentary and an erudite theological referential apparatus (not completely different from the modern scholarly referential framework and the review apparatuses of academia). Publication, which may have happened only in the cases of the most important cults, would be a mark of great symbolic distinction (particularly in the island's early days when manuscripts would have been sent abroad for publication because there were no presses in Cuba).[96] At times these treatises constituted a good contrast between learned and popular expressions of religion. In the more learned ecclesiastical context, for example, local events and miracles became reenactments of biblical episodes and proper dogma. But surprisingly, at other times these treatises could focus the formal exegesis on certain parts of the text only (which could be skipped over by less-devoted readers) while concentrating in a more interesting, popular, and readable way on the miracle stories.

Foregrounded Meanings in the Ecclesiastical Historical Tradition

Irrespective of their engagement in exercises at theological scaffolding (a remarkable challenge, one imagines, for provincial clergy), the texts produced by local ecclesiastics also contained simpler plotlines and encoded messages, albeit often somewhat different from local renditions like those examined in Chapter 4. A brief comparison of the extant ecclesiastical histories of Our Lady of Charity demonstrates the meanings given to Marian stories in the written tradition at the time (or perhaps particularly by clergy and other sectors of colonial society). These ecclesiastical accounts are structured around some major themes, but they also put their own more or less successful spins on the narrative tradition.

Paz y Ascanio's published text (1853) based on Fonseca de la Caridad's 1703 manuscript (hereafter the Paz y Ascanio / Fonseca text), for instance, does not open its history of the apparition with the miraculous finding of the effigy by the three inhabitants of El Cobre as Moreno's story did. Instead, the ecclesiastics who authored (or edited) the treatise inserted into the narrative a previous episode harking back to the ("heroic") historical period of the conquest and the early evangelization of the Indies. The episode was a well-known story about the conversion of an Indian cacique that had the added legitimacy of forming part of the written tradition of the chronicles. In this version, the effigy of Our Lady of Charity that Moreno and the two Indian brothers found floating in the Bay of Nipe was allegedly the same miraculous effigy lost or hidden by the Christian Indian cacique a century before.[97] The main actors in this Conquest episode were Spaniards and Indians, thereby excluding the slaves from this earlier moment in the story. In this sense, the general account of Paz y Ascanio / Fonseca's formal treatise was closer to the more common plot of New World Marian stories where Indians tended to play the foundational roles. Although Chaplain Julián Joseph Bravo's manuscript (1766) dispensed with the superimposed Conquest episode, it does nod to the New World Marian genre by renaming one of the two Indians who found the effigy of the Virgin of Charity in Cuba like the Indian seer of Our Lady of Guadalupe in Mexico: Juan Diego.[98]

Overall, the written ecclesiastical tradition stressed the Virgin's supralocal character more than her local links to the community of royal slaves. Bravo, for example, rhetorically highlighted this overarching and supralocal element by explicitly organizing testimonies belonging to different sectors of colonial society in a hierarchy mirroring social structure: miracle stories of ecclesiastics first, then those of the military, followed by those of elite sectors, the poor, blacks, and slaves. The clergymen's narratives also tried to show as widespread a geographical sphere of the Virgin's miracles and fame as possible. One of the miracles in Paz y Ascanio / Fonseca's text took place in Mexico, and three others narrated by Bravo occurred in Jamaica. However, the Virgin's sphere covered the eastern region of El Cobre, Santiago de Cuba, and Bayamo.

Yet another inflection of Our Lady of Charity's story within the written ecclesiastical tradition can be found once more in Bravo's manuscript of 1766. Father Bravo's rendition of the sanctuary's history illustrates once more the turns and significations that a narrative could take in different hands. His manuscript, for instance, has more than its share of miracles related to the precariousness of life in this military frontier zone of the Caribbean, thereby reflecting the fears and anxieties of life in Oriente in the eighteenth century. In fact, Bravos's narrative thematized the historical and military role of the Virgin of Charity in the preservation of the Spanish Empire and "true" religion against British enemy attacks. Another particular spin found in Bravo's text, one related to the latter theme, was the saintly status and foundational role conferred to the hermit Melchor de los Remedios (1640s–1670s). According to Bravo, the seventeenth-century hermit had prophesied the major historical role that Our Lady of Charity was to play in the region as protectress from the British enemy, particularly during Admiral Vernon's invasion of Oriente in 1741.[99]

In short, the Virgin of Charity in this ecclesiastic written tradition takes on a strong political role by intervening in the events of history. But rather than Marian interventions of a local character such as those found in the cobreros' narratives (i.e., the political and military attacks on the pueblo and the attempted reenslavement of the royal slaves), the Virgin of the ecclesiastical texts intervenes on behalf of imperial Spain and the "true faith" in the "larger" events of the Conquest or in those related to British enemy attacks.

Whether or not these ecclesiastical texts also manifest an early Creole identity is open to discussion.[100] It is indisputable, however, that their narratives follow the conventions of what I have termed a *New World Marian genre*. These include, for instance, the use of New World characters as seers or as the beneficiaries of miracles (Indians, and in this case slaves, but also castes and Spanish Creoles); or concrete references to New World historical settings, situations, and events (such as the Conquest, or pirate attacks, or British invasions); or the addition of American locations to the title of the Virgin's advocacy (i.e., Virgen de la Caridad del Cobre). But by themselves these conventions do not necessarily constitute signifiers of a "Creole" identity. They could as well thematize, for instance, the expansive (or even "global") claims of Christianity, of an orthodox Catholicism, or even of a colonial project. Other rhetorical analytical considerations having to do with plot sequences, relations between episodes, and types of miracles as well as pragmatic ones dealing with actual contextual issues, significations, and uses must be brought to bear upon assessing these narratives' manifestation of a Creole identity. The matter, thus, remains unsettled and pending a separate study.

Popular Inflections of Ecclesiastical Texts

Oral popular culture left its strong imprint in the ecclesiastic Marian written tradition too, thereby evidencing the wide diffusion of similar beliefs, stories, and traditions among different sectors of colonial society, high and low. One of the miracle stories about the Virgin's historical interventions in Bravo's text reflects the influence of popular accounts about, or even by, slaves. Father Bravo wrote that during Admiral Vernon's attempt to take Santiago in 1741, a Spaniard who had been taken prisoner heard:

> The people of Cuba were *hechiceros* [sorcerers] because they had displayed [to the English] an army so copious as [a forest of] trees . . . and how once General [*sic*] Vernon returned to the port of Jamaica with his army and had given back the slaves he had taken to their masters, the latter recounted to their companions in the Haciendas that they had not taken [Santiago de] Cuba because of a Virgin that made prodigies. . . .[101]

The basis for this account is provided by the rumors heard by a Spanish prisoner among Jamaican slaves (and perhaps soldiers) in Admiral Vernon's expedition. Bravo's narrative is ambiguous, but suggestive. It merges voices and conflates points of view in confusing yet provocative ways. It is not clear if in the story Admiral Vernon refrained from attacking Santiago de Cuba because he feared a formidable Spanish army or what he recognized to be a formidable vision. Just who in the account takes the display of a mighty Spanish military force to be a special "effect," a vision, or a marvel produced by the Virgin? The Spanish prisoner who allegedly gave the account, the Jamaican slaves that he overheard, the admiral who retreated, or Bravo who wrote it all down? Who believed what in Bravo's narrative? And how did some witnesses come to know that it was all a prodigious vision and not "the real thing"?

Moreover, the line between sorcery and miracles seems confused in the voices, or in Bravo's account of these voices. The British slaves (and perhaps the soldiers) had apparently conceived of this vision as a feat of sorcery or of a Virgin (sorceress) who "made prodigies," or perhaps both. Yet curiously, in recognizing the "prodigy" as a miracle, that line becomes blurred in the clergyman's voice as well.[102] Furthermore, that Bravo attributed so much authority to the slaves' rumors, account, and comments in the validation of the "miracle" is itself significant. No rigidly exclusionary tendencies toward oral popular accounts fraught with pagan notions are exhibited in the chaplain's choice of this episode for his written treatise. And the relatively smooth recasting of the portentous event from an act of "sorcery" to a "miracle" may itself be suggestive of the dynamics of cultural and religious syncretisms at the time.

Finally, Bravo ended the account of this episode by adding that some days later, after the return of the English to Jamaica, three slaves who had either witnessed or heard from other slaves about the portentous power of the Virgin fled Jamaica with their wives in a canoe. Lost at sea, they saw a dove with a white ribbon and followed it to safety in Santiago de Cuba. Governor Don Francisco Antonio Cagigal de la Vega received the runaways (or gave them sanctuary) and, significantly, sent them to El Cobre to thank the Virgin rather than to any other shrine in the city. In his narrative Bravo connected the two miracles allegedly witnessed by Jamaican slaves and saw in them manifestations of the rising fame of Our Lady of Charity that was beginning to circulate even among the enemy—or perhaps especially among its slaves.

The Tradition of Ex-votos: A Popular Form of Social Memory

The claim to an effigy's miraculous powers is a sine qua non of a successful shrine. While ecclesiastical histories publicized miracles through the written word, miracles were also made public through the iconic popular tradition of ex-votos left behind by grateful devotees.[103] This is not the place to deconstruct discourses about the "miraculous," or even less to question their claims to "truth." Suffice it to say that the incorporation of a miracle story into an ecclesiastical treatise presupposed the author's (usually the sanctuary's chaplain) validation of an event as a miracle. (And in turn, the publication of such a treatise meant even higher official validation—and regulation—of the type of event that constituted a miracle.) But the hundreds of ex-votos kept in a shrine constitute more spontaneous and less-mediated popular constructions of what constitutes miraculous events. The "miracle rooms" in which they were, and still are, exhibited constitute archives (or museums) of the popular imagination—not just with regard to people's constructions of the miraculous but also in terms of the forms and tokens they make use of to signify these miraculous events. To be sure, a chaplain's discretion of what will be on display still constitutes a form of selective regulation. The ex-votos themselves often follow particular formats, but the spectrum of "miraculous events" may be wider and the regulation looser.

The tradition of ex-votos was alive in El Cobre at least since the late seventeenth century.[104] In the 1680s, Isabel de Lagos, a native of Santiago de Cuba, left her mole in the sanctuary as testimony of her healing and a man named Juan left behind his crutches after he began walking.[105] Although moles are nowhere in sight in the sanctuary today, one can still see sets of crutches hanging from the ceiling of the "miracle room." One particularly popular tradition of ex-votos in El Cobre was that of tiny silver, and sometimes gold or copper, charms in the form of body parts. Bunches of these small icons of miracles—anonymous popular testimonies from the past through which people of all walks of life approached events in their lives through the notion of "miracles"—hang from panels in the sanctuary's "miracle room" today. In the 1770s—and perhaps long before—there was a silversmith, a free man of color, residing in El Cobre who probably engaged in this kind of work. The village census at that time also registered a painter who rather than working miracles into silver may have recorded them in pictures.[106]

Today ex-votos in El Cobre no longer take the form of these tiny silver body parts; and older pictures, if ever any there were, are no longer around. Modern ex-votos now include photographs with hand- or typewritten testimonies, iconic artifacts such as a toy car, paintings (one about a miracle in a present-day "raft" crossing to Florida), a fragment of an early Cuban flag, and even uniform batches from 26th of July Movement combatants in the 1950s and from Cuban soldiers who later fought in Angola (see Figures 8 to 10). These ex-votos point to devotees' political construction of miracles too. Although early ex-votos in the Virgin's "chamber of miracles" seem to refer exclusively to healing miracles, in Chapter 4 I discussed the cobreros' construction of miracles in politicized ways too. The miracle books written by the clergy also reflected some politically inflected miracles, such as when the Virgin intervened to save devotees from the English enemy's hands, or in Father Bravo's account of the prodigious vision that scared Admiral Vernon away from the attack of Santiago de Cuba.

A story about an unconventional ex-voto recounted by a present-day cobrero is suggestive of how popular renderings of miraculous events may have also been received in the past by chaplains and lower clergy. A man in El Cobre who many years ago was miraculously saved from a falling rock, decided to turn the rock itself into his ex-voto.[107] The transportation of the rock to the top of the hill where the sanctuary stands constituted a feat in itself, but apparently that was also part of the devotee's vow to the Virgin. While the sanctuary's chaplain allowed the large rock to stand as an ex-voto near the entrance to the miracle room for some days, he was apparently unwilling to incorporate such an unseemly artifact into the collection for good. The rock soon disappeared from the sanctuary's grounds. The story constitutes a contemporary reenactment of some of the themes suggested above: ex-votos in the popular imagination may take a wide range of forms;

FIGURE 8. An ex-voto from a late-nineteenth-century Cuban soldier displayed in the sanctuary's "chamber of miracles." (Author's photograph)

FIGURE 9. More recent ex-votos from defenders of the Cuban Revolution and from soldiers returned from Angola on display in the sanctuary's "chamber of miracles." (Author's photograph)

FIGURE 10. Ex-voto painting of present-day rafters caught up in a storm and miraculously saved during their flight into exile. Note the evocation of the three-"Juanes"-in-the-canoe motif in the painting, which is on display in the sanctuary's "chamber of miracles." (Author's photograph)

lay devotees have some autonomy on how they construe their miracles and how they represent them; the chaplain, however, selects and ultimately regulates what constitutes a proper representation. Although the chaplain in this story eventually discarded this "popular expression" of gratitude to the Virgin, at least the devotee had his way in making the offering in his own terms. One can only wonder at how many ex-votos may have not crossed the threshold into the "room of miracles" in the sanctuary's history—and what forms they may have taken.[108]

Festivities

The annual festivities to the Virgin of Charity were also an important part of the making of tradition. The major feast day took place on September 8.[109] While that day and its vesper may have been the central focus of the celebration, the festivities—probably the Sunday holidays— allegedly lasted until the end of the month. Some of these feast days were endowed by pilgrims who had been recipients of miracles during one such celebration. A devotee endowed one such holiday "perpetually" after he was able to walk following Mary in a procession on her feast day. The cobreros themselves sponsored the *octava* (the eighth day). Several endowments and sponsorships throughout the years could indeed add up to several weeks of celebrations.[110]

Pilgrims came to the sanctuary particularly during these festivities, which were sometimes occasions for miracles. At times they came en masse after particular crises. For instance, Bravo wrote, perhaps with some exaggeration, that after the earthquake of 1766 more than one thousand pilgrims had come to the annual festivities of the Virgin that year (that figure would have been almost the equivalent of the whole population of the village at that time).[111] Presumably these festivities would have been occasions for business in the village, as they would be in the nineteenth and twentieth centuries,[112] and as they began to be more recently after a hiatus of some three decades during the Revolution.[113] During the first decade of the eighteenth century, these festivities had already acquired great importance, as evidenced by the fact that high dignitaries from the nearby city of Santiago de Cuba, including governors, prelates, and *cabildo* members often attended both the religious celebrations as well as the social ones.

Contemporaries did not leave behind effusive descriptions of these celebrations in the record, particularly regarding their more social and performative aspects. Some oblique references for this early period, however, can be found. In a wider investigation regarding Governor Canales's administration (1708–1709), the latter was accused among other things of "not having attended properly to the authority and luster of his position . . . " when during the "festivities to the Virgin of Charity that are celebrated in El Cobre he congregated at the door of his [*sic*] house men and women whom he forced to dance dishonest and censured dances which [he] executed himself."[114] "Dishonest" and "censured" dances can be read as code terms of the time for popularized Afro-American styles of dancing apparently diffused throughout different sectors of society, including the white population as well.[115] It is not clear, however, if such dances were censured for their purported "lasciviousness" or for any African ethnic marking (or for both). Canales's response to these charges addressed the point of "decency," acknowledging the censor's eye:

He said that some of the principal families of this city [Santiago de Cuba] met together in the houses where he was visiting [and] out of honest entertainment they danced . . . with the decency that corresponds, [he] just as the others did, and that the Provisor and Vicar General of this city was present in the celebration and was staying in the same house and that in his sight something prohibited would not be executed.[116]

Other eighteenth-century observers elsewhere in the Caribbean have pointed out that such "lascivious" dances were popular among all sectors of the population and tolerated in churches and processions as well, so that the presence of the provisor and vicar general of Santiago de Cuba may not have constituted a deterrent to these practices, once they had acquired the force of custom.[117] Nonetheless, Canales's account also gives us a glimpse of the private celebrations that punctuated social spaces in the village during these festivities, but that were perhaps also pervaded by music and other practices of popular culture.

On a different note, Governor Céspedes was accused by his enemies of excessive friendliness with the cobreros because he was seen dancing with them during the festivities of the Virgin in the 1780s and even "putting his hat on women's heads."[118] On this occasion dignitaries were seen mingling more freely with the common people, and although the accusation did not involve the propriety of the sociability between high and low sectors of society, it was raised to signify political sponsorship outside the social realm. No mention is made in this case of the kind of music Céspedes was dancing to with the cobreros or if their bodies were knowingly or unknowingly moving to creolized African patterns of rhythm and sound. In any case, the cobreros—as well as other sectors of colonial society, even Spanish ones— would have probably participated in these expressions of a creolized popular culture.

Finally, there were also more ritualized and official aspects to these celebrations in which colonial authorities participated alongside cobreros—and which the latter also contended. At least in the 1720s, for instance, a conflict over protocol broke out between a *cabildo* official from Santiago de Cuba and one from El Cobre when the first tried to take precedence over the latter in the seating arrangements in the church.[119] Thus the cobreros participated in these celebrations in more official capacities, too.

Conclusion

Traditions cement social identities and imagined communities. But the production, institutionalization, and sustenance of a tradition and its related apparatus entails several related processes. The production of the Virgin of Charity's tradition entailed, among other things: the imposition of a private chaplaincy, the individual initiative and promotional efforts of particularly dynamic chaplains, the continuity of ecclesiastical personnel and their ongoing religious services, the active financial backing of the sanctuary by a coterie of ecclesiastics and by the alms and labor of hundreds of private devotees, the expansion of the material infrastructure, the official (or notarized) reconstruction of a special, and, if possible, marvelous past, the production of a written (and preferably published) history, the financial sponsorship of as many days of annual festivities as possible, and of course, the existence of a community.

The institutionalization and expansion of the Virgin of Charity's tradition played an important role in legitimizing the cobreros' claim to community, or at least in garnering the support and protection of an ecclesiastic sector who was invested in the preservation of the cult. Without a local community in El Cobre there could be no major shrine. The preservation of one went hand in hand with the preservation of the other. Therein lay a strategic yet fundamental aspect of the "holy alliance," or "colonial pact," between church and pueblo; between the Virgin and the royal slaves. Ultimately, the cobreros did not control a cult that became heavily administered by an ecclesiastic sector. Nonetheless they participated in it as laymen and women, in fact, as the corporate community whose patroness and special protectress this powerful effigy became.

The case of the Virgin of Charity's cult in El Cobre shows how widely these Marian beliefs, practices, and devotions circulated among different sectors of colonial society: ecclesiastical and lay, elite and popular, Spanish and Creole, colonial and colonized. The more significant distinctions in this extended popular culture of Christianity may be found in the actual ways in which different sectors of colonial society appropriated its discourses. Thus, partaking of this encompassing dominant culture, the cobreros helped produce this major Marian tradition in their *patria chica* (local homeland). Yet, in doing so, they also conferred their own locally distinctive political and social significations to "their" tradition.

A Mainly Farming Village

[El Cobre's] first beginning and foundation had
been three Indian cacique brothers: one had his
home in Baracoa and his name was Coa, the other
was named Cuba and lived there [in Santiago de
Cuba], and the third lived in the village of El
Cobre and his name was Cobe. He had sold
himself with the greatest humility during the
Conquest without it being even necessary to fire a
shot. He [the speaker] mentioned the lands that the
Cacique Cobe had owned at the time and [said]
that His Majesty had given them as a mercy to the
Pueblo of El Cobre and its natives [the cobreros].
— Francisco Sánchez, April 8, 1790

[The witness declared that] the land where he, his
father, and his brothers had their *estancia* [farm] is
the King's.
—Testimony of Cipriano Rodríguez, 1737

Profound transformations in the mode and relations of production took place
in the Real de Minas after the Crown took over its jurisdiction in 1670.
Although the transition to the full subsistence agricultural regime that came
to characterize economic life in El Cobre was probably a more gradual
process than suggested by the political change in its administration, the de-
privatization of the territory was a cornerstone in the consolidation of a new
economic, social, and cultural order in the mines. Key aspects of social identity, both collective and individual, were intrinsically linked to the way
land—or more specifically landholding patterns and entitlements—came to
be understood in this community throughout most of the eighteenth century.

To be sure, the territory of the mining jurisdiction was dramatically
reduced after the 1670s. During the first early years of the transition into
Crown rule, the *cabildo* (local government) of Santiago de Cuba stepped in

to allocate lands to citizens of that city as if the territory of the Real de Minas had become *realengo* (royal or public land).[1] While the original jurisdiction of Santiago del Prado once comprised 6 leagues north to south and 5 leagues east to west,[2] by the turn of the eighteenth century the royal slaves were only able to retain 1-surrounding league from the core of the settlement (or 2 leagues in each direction) through an alleged allocation of land by the High Court of Santo Domingo.[3]

Although a 1-league radius around the village constituted a dramatic reduction in the scale of the previous mining jurisdiction, it also represented the minimum land legally allocated in the foundation of pueblos. In this sense, the territory assigned to the community represented, or had the potential to be regarded, as a public validation (if not an official creation) of a corporate persona. The allocation could also be imagined as the sanctioning of a right to land. These landholding formulations constituted a radical stretching, if not altogether a transposition, of conventional meanings (and rights) attached to slavery. In other words, at stake in the grant of land—and symbolically in the land itself—were colonial formulations of identity and entitlement that blurred the lines between slavery and freedom, at least in this particular sphere of life. To be sure, there was unresolved ambiguity and tension underlying the imagined significance of collectively held land in the cobreros' case, between a right to land by virtue of slavery to the king or by sheer corporate pueblo status (granted by the king), but these distinctions were conveniently slippery and shifting.

Despite the overall reduction of the territory, the de-privatization of the mining jurisdiction initially gave the royal slaves access to more land, particularly as the new royal slaves appropriated abandoned resources and occupied vacated spaces in the jurisdiction. One may visualize a whole remapping of the former mining territory as royal slaves and religious personnel became the main inhabitants of the place. The dwellings of the king's slaves began to take center stage around the parish church to form the nucleus of the new pueblo, the larger fields disappeared, the slaves' provisioning grounds expanded into small *estancias* (farms) and some perhaps into larger ones, and these farms moved forward from the periphery to take over the land lying closer to the village. In the *estancias* that now covered the settlement's main grounds, the cobreros continued cultivating cassava and other staple crops. Subsequent decades would also see the sprouting of a number of *vegas* (tobacco farms) in the local landscape, as well as a few larger sugar and livestock estates.

Particularly significant in the case of El Cobre was the fact that royal slaves came to hold *estancias* instead of *conucos*—the term referring to the garden plots and provision grounds granted to slaves in colonial Cuba. In effect, at some point before 1677, if not long before, the *conucos* of the old mining days gave way to the *estancias* and *vegas* of better days.[4] Although the difference in extension of land that these types of landholding entailed was substantial, the social distinctions that they evoked were even more significant. *Estancias* were standard landholdings associated with freeholders in Cuba, and *conucos* referred to very small land units—so small that they were not even recognized in the official land tenure system. More importantly, *conucos* were land plots associated with enslaved and part-time cultivators, and not with full-time farming. Whether through actual ownership, usufruct, or rental, *estancias* and *vegas* were the mark of peasant and yeoman status in colonial Cuba. Furthermore, these individual landholdings also activated important familial and gender-based identities in El Cobre.

Little to nothing is known of rural life in colonial Cuba outside the ubiquitous sugar plantation complex in the island's western region. Although the cobreros' local economy is here placed in a broader regional context, it is impossible to compare it with that of other small rural producers in the island. All one can do at this point is to uncover the social and material rural world the cobreros made as they became a "reconstituted peasantry."[5] The first part of this chapter examines the broader collective issues related to landholding and agricultural production in El Cobre and the cobreros' mobilization around those issues; the second part disaggregates local land tenure patterns and related occupational practices at an individual or microlevel, focusing on their sociocultural significance.

Social Meaning in Local Precolonial and Conquest Lore

Some of the identity issues and themes related to corporatization of the territory were encoded in the short but valuable piece of local legend about three cacique brothers (see the epigraph at the opening of this chapter). The legend encapsulates well the colonial imaginary of land, community, king, Indians, "origins," and "history"—or more precisely, the cobreros' popular and local rendition of that social imaginary. I approach that narrative of the past from the same cultural and political angle that I employed with the "Virgin apparition" stories.

In 1790, a royal official interviewed Francisco Sánchez, an eighty-five-year-old cobrero, to make a report requested by Madrid. As was often the case in this genre of reports on "el modo en que corrían las cosas" ("the way things used to be"), local custom, and tradition—or more often than not a contended version thereof—was supposed to reside in the memory of the oldest men in the community who acted as oral historians. In this case, the royal official trying to recover the cobreros' account of the past asked Sánchez what he knew about "the origins and foundation of El Cobre." While the official had in mind the usual story of the contractor Eguiluz's administration of the mines and the Crown's confiscation of the jurisdiction—a story Sánchez also knew—the old man took his interlocutor further back into a legendary foundational time in local history that skipped the episode of the early export-mining days. Although the royal official dismissed as "nonsense" the story Sánchez claimed he had heard from his own elders, for some fortunate reason he or his scribe wrote down at least the excerpt cited at the opening of this chapter.[6]

The legend is, above all, a royalist story about king-granted rights to land and to recognition as a corporate community, particularly in the politicized backdrop in which the tale was related and recorded. The immediate context for Sánchez's "narrative event" was an official investigation carried out in the midst of the dramatic conflict that took place after the (re)privatization of the mines in 1780. This charged context, then, gave the story a particularly strong political edge. Indeed, the narrative event itself constitutes an instance of the contended character of some of the issues encoded in the story.

Like the "Virgin apparition" narratives, the "three cacique brothers'" story constituted another instance of a local remaking of social memory. Although grounded in different discourses (one religious and Christian, the other secular and royalist), embedded in different genres (one Marian, the other one loosely colonial pre-Columbian lore and social memory), and bolstered by varying degrees of historical detail and accuracy, these two kinds of narratives of the past constitute foundational stories sharing many motifs and issues. While in the Virgin's story the cobreros' special link to the land and territory of El Cobre was sanctioned by divine—or Marian—will, in the more secular story of the three caciques the imagined source of legitimation was instead—or also—the king. Indeed, after subjugating the cacique Cobe and taking his lands by right of conquest, the king granted that bounded territory to his royal slaves, thereby turning them into the new holders of the land and the first settlers of what became the colonial village of El Cobre. More generally, the figure of the king in the story implicitly had the absolute power to take and give land, to alter the social order, to favor his own slaves, to allow and legitimize an "anomalous" situation such as that of slaves constituting a corporate community, and to turn them, like Native Americans previously, into full natives of their new local territory (presumably with landholding and residential rights).

Furthermore, by tracing the name of "El Cobre" to the cacique Cobe, the story obliterated the pueblo's foundation as a Spanish copper-mining settlement (*cobre* means copper in Spanish) where the cobreros had been regular mining slaves. Instead, the narrative grounded the origins and boundaries of the cobreros' imagined community in the ancient past of precolonial and Conquest history. One can hear in the story, however, an officially sanctioned colonial narrative about the imposition of the Spanish order over and above a defeated Native American one and the latter's almost voluntary submission to the Spanish Crown. In fact, stretching the reading of this legend further, one could also find some anachronistic echoes in it regarding the military role of the cobreros as defenders of the Spanish Crown, whereby the king rewarded them with land (as in the case of conquerors).

And yet, in the social imaginary of some Creole sectors of colonial society, the precolonial order also seemed to hold an ancient and noble aura that could confer symbolic legitimacy and pedigree to colonial communities: indeed, that could equip them with what may have been a valued "New World tradition," so to speak.[7] The story of the three caciques, for instance, related how the cobreros became the inhabitants, natives, and preservers of ancient land, even if by conquest and royal intervention. Furthermore, the stature of the modest pueblo of El Cobre was enhanced in a show of local pride by its kinship to what had allegedly been two important regional *cacicazgos* (caciques' jurisdictions) and its juxtaposition to two major centers in colonial times: Baracoa (the first colonial settlement and capital of the island) and the city of Santiago de Cuba (the island's second capital). From yet another perspective, the diachronic continuity of El Cobre from its days as an Indian *cacicazgo* to a colonial community of king's slaves also suggested a synchronic analogy between these two groups in the eighteenth-century colonial present. Not only were there two Indian communities in the environs of this village of royal slaves at the time (Jiguaní and El Caney) (see Map 1 in the Preamble), but El Cobre had in common many organizational features with them.[8]

This foundational story of El Cobre seems to have been borrowed and adapted from the oral (and written) archive of precolonial and Conquest popular lore in Oriente at the time. Foundational stories of other population centers in the region were also based on a similar structure of Indian caciques recalled in their names. The story of the foundation of the city of Bayamo (see Map 1 in the Preamble), for instance, involved a cacique named Bayamo who ruled over the whole province during precolonial times and particularly over a triangle of villages in that province. This was a popular origin story that according to Bishop Don Pedro Agustín Morell de Santa Cruz circulated in the mid-eighteenth century throughout the region.[9] In this sense, rather than inventing the "three cacique brothers" origin story, the cobreros were more probably appropriating and rewriting regional lore. In doing so, they were also inserting their tradition as a local community in the oral social memory of Oriente.

In short, the story of the three caciques constitutes a particularly eloquent (and poetic) manifestation of this community's local imaginary. The precolonial legend encodes the cobreros' understanding of their rights to land, territory, and corporate identity. Although this story of the past constitutes a popular rendition of royalist political discourse and rights of conquest, that dominant discourse is appropriated to legitimize an unconventional and unusual form of community and land rights.

Conflicts over Land Rights and Collective Political Mobilization

Although at the turn of the eighteenth century the cobreros' community had managed to retain from the previous mining jurisdiction 1-surrounding square league of land and the *hato* (pasture lands) of Barajagua, that territory would be substantially reduced during the following decades.[10] As peasants elsewhere, the cobreros mobilized extraofficially through the usual strategies of harassment of invaders but also as free subjects in the Spanish Empire's courts. The case of the pasture lands of Barajagua notwithstanding, throughout most of the eighteenth century, conflict over land—specifically arable land—revolved around issues of boundaries and encroachment. It was really not until after the (re)privatization of the mines in 1780 that the cobreros' corporate right to arable land was brought radically into question.

Barajagua Yet Again

Until the 1730s, the cobreros' most urgent and insistent protestations were against the loss of Barajagua, a livestock provisioning ground, not arable land. Indeed, while the royal slaves managed to retain Barajagua some decades after Governor Don Andrés de Magaña attempted to rent (and even sell) it in the 1670s, the *hato* was once more rented to a citizen of Santiago de Cuba some time between 1711 and 1713.[11] The cobreros' letters and representations, written in the midst of the final conflicts over Barajagua in the 1730s, illustrate well how public identity and the prerogatives of royal slavery with regard to land were imagined and contested during these years. Although these statements and accounts of how things were in the past echoed some of the major claims encoded in the "three cacique brothers" story, the discourse was less "legendary," and the "time" alluded to as precedent was located in a more recent past. The formulations related to landholding entitlements also took some further turns.

In a letter to Dean Morell de Santa Cruz, a clergyman often friendly to the community, the royal slaves wrote "all together [in one voice]" how they understood their entitlement to land:

Having enjoyed for a long time the many mercies with which Our Lord and Master has honored us—for he ordered that all the *realenga* lands and the *hato* of Barajagua where we bred our animals for our well-being and that of our children be given to us for our sustenance—we find ourselves without them ever since [the administration of] Governor Luis Sañudi y Analla [1711–1713].[12]

To the captain general in Havana they also wrote:

Your Highness will realize [through a royal edict previously alluded to] the way in which His Majesty favors us and orders that we be attended to in that [land] and other matters. . . . For even though [our ancestors] were not given more than 1 real for the food [they received while working in the fortification projects], *they had as their own all the land that our Lord and Master has*, where they planted their crops and bred their cattle and hogs with which they could cover the shortness of the said ration [emphasis added].[13] (See Appendix 6.)

Several issues were conflated in these passages. First of all, royal slaves reasserted their traditional claim to all the royal lands and to Barajagua as provision grounds, that is, to the entire territory under the original mining jurisdiction: a decidedly bold claim indeed. The royal slaves based their right on their privileged status (they were favored with these "mercies" by their Lord and Master); and on the principle that what belonged to their master they had usufruct rights upon (they had *as their own* all the land of their master, or all the land under royal jurisdiction). Moreover, like in the "three cacique brothers" story, they also based their right to land on royal "orders," on the king's will, and in a more legalistic turn, on the legality represented by the alleged royal edict.

A more general standard principle, however, also undergirded these statements, namely, the master's obligation to sustain his or her slaves. In effect, this was one of the few protections extended to slaves (at least formally) by Spanish law and which in the royal slaves' own formulation of rights took the force of legal and moral entitlement.[14] Of course, a moral economy lay behind the notion of what adequate subsistence entailed, or, rather, what adequate sustenance meant for a slave—a practical meaning that may have been the object of subtle or open conflict between masters and slaves elsewhere in the Americas as well.[15] In Cuban colonial society, proper subsistence for the ordinary citizen—or even for royal slaves—entailed a diet based on cassava bread and meat.[16] Therefore, short of being provided a direct ration, the king's slaves were to be allotted adequate land with which to produce these staples for themselves and their families.

More importantly, the above formulations indicate a further conceptual jump in the cobreros' articulation of a slave's right to be provided for. In a reformulation of standard slaveholding ideology, the master's obligation could as easily become the slave's right; moreover, the slave's right to subsistence could be equated with the right to the *means* of self-subsistence. In this case, the means of subsistence meant land, and according to the royal slaves' understanding of the moral economy, specifically arable land for the production of cassava as well as common land for animal husbandry or hunting (namely, Barajagua). The king's slaves' allusion to the well-being of their children in other statements also connoted a self-recognition of their roles as heads of households and family provisioners. In this reformulation of slaveholding ideology, the master-slave relation was also cast as a reciprocal or quasi-contractual relation centered on land.

Although in 1728 the pueblo sent representatives to the High Court of Santo Domingo to demand Barajagua and protest other abuses, and in 1731 revolted for similar reasons, the cobreros were unable to recover the prized *hato*.[17] Given the continuous meat supply problems of Santiago de Cuba throughout the eighteenth century, it was not surprising that Barajagua was such a coveted landholding and that it led to repeated attempts by the *cabildo* of Santiago de Cuba to appropriate it.[18] The renting of Barajagua for commercial cattle ranching (with the ensuing supply quotas imposed on these grants) constituted a potential source of direct supply for the city and a steady annual rent for the always-depleted royal treasury. It was the interests of a village against those of a powerful city, of a subsistence economy for enslaved peasants against a commercial one that would have fulfilled provisioning needs for the city of Santiago de Cuba—undoubtedly a familiar losing battle.[19]

But curtailed access to hunting and pasturing grounds and in general the reduction of available land to the pueblo went beyond the loss of Barajagua. A broader trend toward privatization affected the cobreros negatively in their access to other *realenga* land as well. It resulted in the loss of the *realenga* they had used as substitute for Barajagua: the land of Guarinao and El Ramón, some 9 leagues away from the pueblo. The cobreros had expanded into this *realenga* land where they had established *estancias*; but their main use was as pasture land to hunt wild game. Although the *cabildo* of Santiago de Cuba attempted to sell some of this land to two *vecinos* (residents) of that city—Don Sebastián de Herresuelos and his brother Don Pedro—the cobreros were able to block the sale. According to a *cabildo* report, after Herresuelos received private title to his land, "they [the brothers] abandoned it because he was persecuted and provoked by the slaves of the said mines [and] demanded back the money they had placed in the Royal Treasury [which] was returned. . . . [Thus] the slaves remained in the use of the said lands for their pueblo."[20] It is not clear if the harassment of the new owners was physical (as was at times the fate of encroaching settlers at the cobreros' hands), or if the cobreros fought it in the courts. During the conflict of 1731 over Barajagua, the cobreros also claimed the territories of El Ramón and Guarinao, and apparently they were conceded to them. By the 1750s, however, the *realenga* territory of El Ramón was demarcated, sold, and privatized through the process of *composición de tierras* (land title verification), to be examined below.[21] Thereafter, whatever access the royal slaves may have had to this land would have been through the payment of rent to a private owner.

The Privatization Process and the Problem of Shrinking Community Arable Land

After the 1730s, the cobreros saw themselves in a struggle to retain their surrounding corporate league of territory against increasing privatization and in some areas commercialization of land. This invasion of community territory was often carried out and legitimized through the process of *composición de tierras*, a royal policy that ordered the privatization or sale of *realenga* land to the highest bidder and the proper validation of land property through royal titles to be obtained through the payment of a fee.[22] This land reform process was belatedly pushed in Cuba throughout the eighteenth century, particularly in midcentury.[23]

Although by the turn of the eighteenth century, the territory of the island was still sparsely populated, there remained little "free" land to appropriate. There was, however, much imprecision and confusion as to the boundaries of properties; and furthermore, much of this already "privatized" land had no proper title of possession. The *cabildos* on the island were able to retain their early powers to grant land until 1729, but this power extended to the grant of usufruct to land prior to royal confirmation of possession—a process that was often not seen to its end.[24] Although this unfinished process had not precluded the de facto sale and disposal of land as private property (with the restrictions that defined private property at the time), the Bourbon Crown had first sought to juridically legitimize and "rationalize" the situation through the orders of *composición* in 1713 and the appointment of a *juez de tierras* (land judge) in 1720. In 1735, the Crown made obligatory the royal confirmation of the possession of any *realenga* land. It went one step further in 1746 by requiring the revalidation of any land titles obtained after 1618, by authorizing denunciations against usurped land, and by ordering that ecclesiastics who held land be subject to the same requirements of *composición*, that is, that no special privileges would accrue to them as clergymen. In 1754 the Crown issued new orders simplifying and facilitating the process of *composición* throughout its American territories.[25]

In the 1730s the cobreros still held to their surrounding square league of arable land; however, they complained that it was not sufficient for their subsistence. While 1-surrounding league may have been plenty for a population of 605 in 1709, the shrinkage of surrounding arable land and the growth of the village's population meant considerable pressure upon land resources. Referring back to the past thirty years, one cobrero recalled in 1734: "We have represented our necessities to the Justices of that city [Santiago de Cuba] with the cited petitions that have been continuous since your Excellencies have been taking those lands away from us until we have been left with 1 league around where you can see if it is possible for so many families of His Majesty to be able to maintain themselves. . . . "[26] (See Appendix 6.)

Despite the fact that the privatization process also threatened public access to *monterías*—the common right of pueblos to hunting ground and access to timber—it was above all the community's arable land that was affected by the process. The surrounding league was still more or less in place in the 1730s, but it would be chipped at further in subsequent decades. One case that illustrates the process in action and that was strongly resisted by the community was that of Don Baltasar Díaz de Priego's claims and attempt to privatize community territory. The case led to the measurement of the community's boundaries and to a wave of litigation against other encroachments.

In 1757, Díaz de Priego, a citizen of Santiago de Cuba, claimed a *realengo* near El Cobre through the process of *composición*. Accordingly, the land was measured and Díaz de Priego obtained formal title of it. In 1760, the courts issued an eviction order to the cobrero Gregorio Puente whose farm lay within the privatized territory. Protesting the order, "the slaves of El Cobre presented themselves to the tribunal claiming that they did not have terrain where to set their farms and asking that a measurement and survey of the land that corresponded to them be carried out."[27] The governor then issued orders for an investigation. The old parish priest Don Juan Jacintho de Silva testified on behalf of the community that throughout the more than forty years that he had lived in El Cobre, the pueblo's rights to 1 league in each direction had been in force. In 1766, the Crown's attorney declared null the procedure of *composición de tierras* made on Díaz de Prieto's behalf and ordered a measurement of the village's territory as well as a formal demarcation of its boundaries.[28]

The mapping of the territory made in 1780 revealed that natural obtrusions (such as mountainous and useless territory in the Sierra del Cobre to the south) undercut the theoretical 1 league of land available to the village for farming purposes. The assayer of land himself read the territory of El Cobre as follows: he appraised 20 *caballerías* of very poor land in the mountainous south side of the village at 10 pesos the *caballería*; and "as to the rest of the terrain . . . which is arable, although partly difficult to work, in which there are 158 *caballerías* I appraise them at 60 pesos."[29] These 158 *caballerías* of partly usable land were the actual limits of the pueblo. They constituted 37.5 percent of the ideal 1-league radius. Together with the 20 *caballerías* of very poor land, they constituted 42 percent of the land supposedly available to the village.[30] Indeed, in addition to the natural obstructions in the south, human intrusions had further undercut the community's territory from the remaining directions. According to the findings diagrammed in Map 3, about one-third of the territory within the 1-league-radius circle of the pueblo had been invaded. Map 3 shows the area of land available to the pueblo during the 1770s in the context of the theoretical surrounding league (see map caption as well).

A wave of conflict and litigation between cobreros and neighbors followed in subsequent years.[31] Among the denunciations that the cobreros carried out in the aftermath of the measurement of community land, for instance, was one made in 1775 against Señor Pedro Valiente and Captain

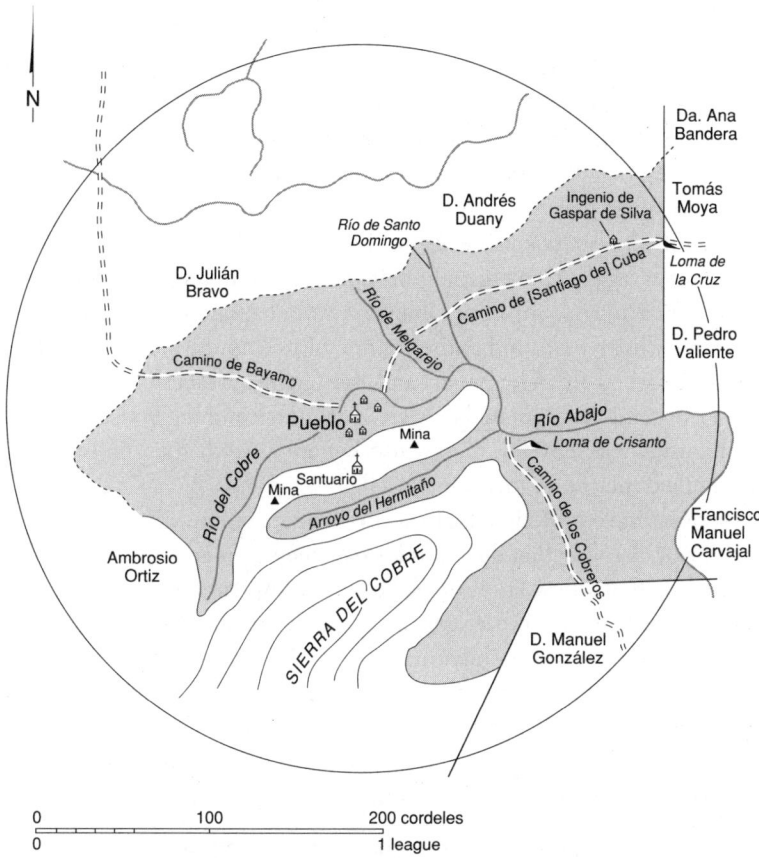

MAP 3. Farmland available to the pueblo of El Cobre between 1773 and 1780, in the context of the theoretical one-league radius. (Sources: José de Zayas, "Plano de las Tierras Delineadas al Cobre," ca. 1780, AGI, Mapas y Planos de Santo Domingo 468; José de Zayas, "Mapa del Real de Minas del Cobre," Aug. 7, 1780, AGI, Mapas y Planos de Santo Domingo 467)

Thomás de Moya, captain of the *pardo* (mulatto) militia regiment in Santiago de Cuba. "The commissioners of the Pueblo of El Cobre and the slaves of His Majesty" protested that Valiente "has sold a portion [of land] belonging to our domain, given the boundaries up to the Loma de la Cruz that were adjudicated [in our favor] by the demarcation."[32] Captain Moya had at some point bought a piece of land from Valiente and, in turn, rented part of it to a freedman named Hilario. The latter had been ordered by Moya to prevent the cobreros any access to the timber on his property. It is not clear what the result of the denunciation was, but Moya was ordered to present proof of the notarized transaction and his land title; Hilario was called in to give testimony of the terms of his rental deal; the cobreros' representative was ordered to submit the village's demarcation map; and further information regarding the community's ongoing litigation with other encroaching neighbors was ordered submitted as well.[33]

The conflict over land, however, was not just with "outsiders" to the community. It also took place against longtime residents of the pueblo, and in particular, against a clergyman, Chaplain Don Julián Joseph Bravo, who as the reader may recall from Chapter 5 was chaplain of the sanctuary for more than thirty years and author of one of its unpublished histories. The dispute between this clergyman and the pueblo evinces the tension that could exist and accumulate between local clergy and the community. The mechanisms whereby the clergy also benefited from the community are succinctly displayed in this case as well.

In 1766, Bravo protested the measurement of community land previously carried out claiming that the cobreros had been granted too much land and demanding that a new land survey be made.[34] Apparently land that he had appropriated fell within the village's officially declared boundaries. A second measurement was then carried out, but it confirmed the results of the first. The community then took Bravo to the courts. The cobreros' representation described their conflicts with the clergyman and accused him of extortion. Their narrative reflects both the process of whittling away at the community's land and the general tenor of local conflict over land:

> The *Beneficiado* [clergyman] made in this territory a *labranate* [sic] [cultivation] and has claimed that the land where he made the *labranante* is his, not having bought it from anyone who could sell it to him, . . . the *Beneficiado* took away the *argollas* [iron rings] set by His Majesty [and] has sold two possessions and more *labranzas* that we had in the land that he appropriates, leaving us only two-fourths of 1 league as territory. . . . He continues to press us so that we pay him rent and we have not wanted to pay without order of His Majesty, [and] he oppresses us violently taking away from us for the rent some horses, from others silver, from others chickens from others hogs. . . . He does not let us cut the timber in the said *monte* with which we sustained ourselves. . . .[35]

The conflict in this case was one over the character of rights to land. The cobreros accused Bravo of privatizing corporate land that could only provide usufruct rights by selling it, charging community members rents for it, and even proscribing their traditional free access to *monterías* in the village's surrounding territory. The scenario may have run something like this: having usufructed the territory as an alternate source of income to his chaplain's salary—perhaps even with the consent of the community as was the case with many parish priests—Bravo may have overextended his customary rights by eventually claiming private possession of the land in question. It is not clear if Bravo had obtained any title to the land through *composición* or through any fraudulent means, or rather, if invoking ecclesiastical privilege he had excused himself from the need for the royal validation of title despite Crown orders to the contrary in 1746.[36] In any case, the result of the litigation between the community and Chaplain Bravo is not known, but the process seems to have been interrupted by the (re)privatization of the mines in 1780. At that point the conflict over land took a dramatically different turn as the community's more fundamental right to corporate land, and not just to contended territorial boundaries, was challenged.[37]

The struggle over land during the eighteenth century was not exclusive to the peasant-slaves of El Cobre, however. Increasing litigation took place among individuals in other sectors of society also caught in the "rationalization" and privatization processes underway. In 1752, the governor of Santiago de Cuba pointed to the frauds and conflicts in his jurisdiction that the process of *composición* was giving rise to. He wrote to the Crown about the "many quarrels and disputes that the commissioners find themselves full of, and families due to [these disputes] are full of hatreds and the [appointed] subdelegates having no fixed salaries have to live from the frauds in the [land] denunciations presented to them, because they are poor."[38]

Finally, it was not only private *vecinos* in the region or the cobreros who were disputing boundaries and demarcations at the time. The Indian peasant village of Jiguaní litigated over land throughout the eighteenth century.[39] Its location in the more economically dynamic district of Bayamo would seem to have placed it in a particularly precarious position. Similarly, by the 1730s, the other Indian pueblo in the region, El Caney, even closer to the capital of Santiago de Cuba than El Cobre, also protested encroachments into its jurisdiction.[40] Thus, the cobreros were one among other sectors in the Oriente region—and the island in general—resisting the changes in land tenure under way by the middle years of the eighteenth century.

Material Considerations: El Cobre and the Wider Region in the Eighteenth Century

A bird's-eye view of the regional context may provide the general background in which the daily life of this village unfolded. The importance of

TABLE 3

Land Tenure Patterns, Eastern Region, 1756

	Estancias *and* Vegas	Sugar	Hatos *and* Corrales	Houses	Population
Santiago	219 and 205	56	82	1,418	11,793
El Cobre	104 [14]*	[6]*	[9]*	140	1,183
El Caney	75	8	1	83	500
Jiguaní**				102	588
Bayamo	908	63	297	1,810	12,653
Baracoa	60	[60]*	[60]*	158	1,169
Holguín	36 and 42		56		1,751

SOURCE: César García del Pino, ed., *La visita eclesiástica* (Havana, 1985). Table 3 is an adaptation of García del Pino's own table (1985, XXXII).
* Bracketed data indicate that Bishop Morell de Santa Cruz counted them as *estancias* (farms) but specified that tobacco, sugar, or livestock was also produced in some of them (the number of which appears in brackets).
** The bishop provided no land tenure data for this Indian village.

cattle ranching in the regional economy of Oriente during the eighteenth century is attested to by the number of *hatos* under the jurisdiction of Bayamo and Santiago de Cuba (see Tables 3 and 4). But the contrasting economies of the two major cities of the island's eastern region are reflected in the sheer diversity of enterprises in the first city—the high number of *hatos*, sugar mills, and even *estancias* and *vegas*—that were indexes of an economic vitality not found around the capital city of Santiago de Cuba. Much of the economic dynamism of Bayamo was based on its well-known and prevalent contraband trade with the British and the French. While Santiago de Cuba also engaged in illicit trade, the city may have had less to exchange. Santiago de Cuba had in its hinterland fewer sugar mills, *hatos*, and tobacco farms. By contrast, the city of Baracoa in the northeastern region of the island was a world apart. It was sealed off from the region by surrounding mountains, which turned it into a self-enclosed economy with few links to the rest of the Oriente region. Whatever commerce was carried out in that first colonial city in the island, it went out into the Caribbean Sea.

Besides tobacco, cattle ranching, and some sugar production, Santiago de Cuba also had an agricultural sector of independent producers servicing the urban areas, but it was a small one. In 1756, Bishop Morell de Santa Cruz registered only some 219 *estancias* in Santiago de Cuba's rural district producing agricultural staples to supply a population of 11,793, of which some 3,693 were slaves. He also registered the considerable number of 205 tobacco farms. By contrast, the bishop registered 908 *estancias* (and *vegas*) in the district of Bayamo supplying a similar population of 12,653 inhabitants. But if Santiago de Cuba counted on only 219 *estancias* to supply its inhabitants, the much smaller settlement of El Cobre, with only one-tenth of the population of that city, had almost half the number of *estancias* of its neighbor (see Table 3). Similarly, a regional census for 1780 again recorded 200 farms in the environs of the city of Santiago de Cuba to feed an exclusively urban population of 11,014 inhabitants, while El Cobre had some 167 *estancias* for a total population of 1,370 at that time (see Table 4).[41] The other population center with more or less a major focus on farming production was El Caney, and later Jiguaní, Indian villages that may have played a similar regional role in supplying larger cities.

El Cobre's Economy and Regional Role

By the mid-eighteenth century there were 104 family farms in El Cobre, among which, due to their small size, Bishop Morell de Santa Cruz barely distinguished 6 *trapiches de miel* (small sugar mills), 9 farms with hogs (quasi cattle ranches), and 14 *vegas* (see Table 3).[42] By 1780, the recorded number of *estancias* had increased to 167, while the number of sugar mills remained more or less steady at 5 (see Table 4). That increased number of *estancias* may have pointed more to a greater subdivision of farms than to any real expansion of farming, however. Besides suggesting some internal differentiation in the village, what these figures mostly show is the diffusion of small ownership in El Cobre and of peasant production in the village.

The main staple cultivated in the *estancias* was manioc or yucca, the basis of the cassava bread consumed by the popular sectors of the popula-

TABLE 4

Land Tenure Patterns, Eastern Region, 1780

	Estancias	Sugar	Corrales	Hatos	Houses	Population	Urban Population
Santiago	200	43	29	82	1,513	12,884	11,014
El Cobre	167	5	0	0	513[?]	1,370	1,360
El Caney	45	0	0	0	119	778	531
Jiguaní	200	1	3	16	334 [?]	1,883	—
Holguín	97	14	106	76	323	3,459	2,414
Baracoa*	—	—	—	—	417	1,972	—

SOURCE: Census of the City of Santiago de Cuba and Its Jurisdiction, Feb. 24, 1780, AGI-Cuba 1272.
*No data on land tenure is provided for Baracoa.

tion. Other crops such as plantains and vegetables (*menestras*), however, were also grown in these family farms.[43] Manioc is an easily grown and resistant crop with a high yield of seed to fruit—in fact, it has the highest productivity in weight of food produced per unit of land of any other tropical plant. Manioc has the capacity to grow well in nearly any kind of soil, even marginal land—a consideration important to the cobreros given the far-from-excellent quality of arable land in El Cobre. Furthermore, manioc is a crop that does not require intensive or meticulous labor for its cultivation. Based on a conservative estimate for the northeast of Brazil, where it also constituted a staple crop among slaves and free peasantry, it would have taken a cultivator one month to produce a yearly supply of cassava for two persons, two months for a family of four, and so on. Manioc was an ideal crop insofar as it was not subject to seasonal constraints (in fact it could be harvested more than once a year), it could be stored for long periods in the ground, and its cultivation did not require much attention.[44] These were all important factors that gave flexibility to an agricultural regime that could otherwise be seriously disrupted by the requirements of the king's slaves' corvée labor. Thus, the flexibility of the agricultural regime involved in manioc production also allowed males to retain control over this most important work domain, the land resources related to it, and their occupational identity as farmers and, more fundamentally, as family providers.

El Cobre's *estancias* contributed to supplying the city of Santiago de Cuba with their main staple, manioc. But even though the cobreros may have operated within a regional market, cassava may not have been the most lucrative product to offer. The low value of yucca and of the cobreros' *estancias* is reflected in the price fetched by some farms confiscated and appraised by the government in 1737 after a riot in the village. In this case it was not so much the land itself that was appraised as the cobreros could not properly "own" it, but rather the unharvested produce still stored in the ground. The prices for these farms ranged from a very low 2 pesos to a more substantial 20 pesos—with a general average of 10.4 pesos for each of the nine confiscated *estancias*.[45] Interested local buyers were given two months to pay for their newly acquired unharvested farms—a schedule that may have reflected the time required to accumulate such capital in this village. Ten and one-half pesos, however, was a little more than what a horse would fetch in this locality (6 to 10 pesos—a mule was even appraised at 18 pesos), the equivalent to forty-two days of work for an unskilled (free) laborer in Santiago de Cuba at the time and twice as much as the annual rent of farmland in the region.[46]

The first quarter of the eighteenth century was the Golden Age of tobacco production in the island. So valued had this product become in the Spanish imperial economic order, that the Bourbon Crown imposed a monopoly on its trade in 1717.[47] Tobacco also became a major export crop in the Oriente region, in the areas of Santiago de Cuba, Bayamo, and particularly in the northeastern zone of Mayarí. Despite the preponderance of manioc farming in El Cobre, some cobreros turned to the cultivation of tobacco too. In 1756, for instance, there were 14 tobacco farms (out of 104 *estancias*) within the local jurisdiction of El Cobre (see Table 3). That is, 13 percent of the farmers in this community had turned to the production of tobacco. Although by 1773, twenty-eight households in El Cobre (or 18 percent) had a member who was a tobacco farmer, only eighteen of these farmers (11.6 percent) were heads of households who probably owned a farm.[48]

A "counterpoint" of tobacco and manioc here lies beyond my limited talents as an essayist. Suffice it to point out that in El Cobre, and in Cuba in general, both crops were cultivated in small plots. Although one was a cash crop cultivated mostly by yeomen farmers, the other was mostly a subsistence crop produced by peasants. Contrary to manioc, tobacco production requires intensive cultivation, skillful selection, and attention to detail. In fact, as Fernando Ortiz puts it in his illustrious counterpoint with sugar, tobacco requires not only attention, but "solicitous, pampering care" at each point of its cultivation.[49] Such fastidiousness is virtually unknown to manioc, whose greatest virtue perhaps lies in its sturdiness and self-sufficiency, so to speak. Ortiz goes as far as claiming, "Tobacco is one of the most difficult crops in the world to cultivate and its technique is the most highly developed in the whole field of Cuban agriculture."[50] Given these requirements, it is hardly surprising that royal slaves would have the necessary time to engage in its production. Thus, tobacco farms in El Cobre were in the hands of a selected few. They were, with some exceptions, free men who could fully dedicate themselves to the intensive cultivation of this crop.

In 1776, the Tobacco Factory of Santiago de Cuba—which bought tobacco for the royal monopoly—had under its jurisdiction four large *partidos* (divisions) in Oriente: (Santiago de) Cuba, Cauto, Guaninicum, and Guantánamo.[51] This large area included a total of 514 *vegas* of which 369 (or 71.8 percent) were individually owned and as many as 145 (28 percent) were worked by the peons or slaves of the individual farms on their own account and presumably in some kind of sharecropping arrangement (see Table 5).[52] The cobreros' tobacco farms fell for the most part within the *partido* of Cauto, the jurisdiction with the greatest number of *vegas* as well as farmers in the region. Overall, the cobreros owned a minimum of twelve *vegas* in the *partido* of Cauto or 7.6 percent of the small-holding tobacco farms in that *partido*.[53] These, in turn, constituted 3 percent of the individual *vegas* in the total jurisdiction of Santiago de Cuba's Tobacco Factory, a small but by no means inconsequential production in broader regional terms.

In Cauto itself, there were eighteen smaller *subpartidos* (subdivisions). Cobreros with *vegas* could be found in the *subpartidos* of El Cobre, as well as in El Ramón. The *subpartido* of El Cobre was relatively large; it included seventeen individual *vegas*, not counting five others sharecropped by peons or slaves.[54] Of the seventeen individually owned *vegas* in this *subpartido*, a minimum of seven (41 percent) could be clearly identified as belonging to cobreros, but the number was probably much greater. In El Ramón, there were nine listed *vegas*, of which at least five (56 percent) clearly belonged to cobrero farmers. Other tobacco farms belonging to cobreros may have been found scattered in other areas farther from El Cobre.[55]

The small character of tobacco farming in general is illustrated by the average number of hands working in the region's *vegas*: the overwhelming majority of them were worked directly either by the owner, or by one or two additional peons who may or may not have been slaves.[56] The individually held tobacco farms in the *partido* of Cauto were overall the smallest ones, since they had the lowest average number of workers per *vega*. Indeed, almost one-third of these farms were worked directly by the owner, while another one-third were operated by the owner and a peon. Overall, a grand 93 percent of the individually held *vegas* in Cauto were operated by an owner and three or less workers. The cobreros' *vegas* fell fully within this range. Of the twelve tobacco farms identified as owned by cobreros, four were operated just by the owner; five had an additional peon (or slave) working alongside the owner; two had two additional peons; and only one had three workers in addition to the owner.

Among tobacco growers (*vegueros*) in El Cobre there were several members of the slaveholding Cosme family. While the wealthy Captain Joseph Cosme, who in 1767 owned twelve slaves, had died by 1773, his two sons Francisco and Ventura were among the twelve tobacco farmers selling to the Tobacco Factory of Santiago de Cuba in 1776.[57] Both Francisco and Ventura Cosme had two peons each (probably slaves) working in their *vegas*.[58] These two brothers alongside Joaquín González (who had three peons or slaves) were the largest tobacco producers in the village and their farms were above the average for the region as a whole (see Table 5). Other

TABLE 5

Tobacco Farms (Vegas) and Workers, Jurisdiction of Santiago de Cuba, 1776

	Vegas	Workers*	Average Workers per Vega
Santiago de Cuba	52 [12]**	130	2.5
Cauto	213[56]	386	1.8
Guaninicum	147 [47]	285	1.9
Guantánamo	102 [30]	207	2.0
Total	514 [145]		1.96

* Operators include owners and peons in the individually owned *vegas*.
** Bracketed data specifies number of *vegas* held or sharecropped by workers (*operarios*).
SOURCE: "Jazmia de los tabacos sembrados en los partidos de esta factoría de Santiago de Cuba," May 17, 1776, expte. 270, AGI-Cuba 1184.

tobacco farms owned by cobreros were smaller, but as will be discussed below, most of these cobrero tobacco farmers were free people.

Although cattle farming was another major economic activity in the Oriente region, it was not a significant one in El Cobre. While Bishop Morell de Santa Cruz observed some small corrals in the cobreros' *estancias*, the census of 1780 recorded no *hatos* or corrals in that village's jurisdiction (see Tables 3 and 4). The 1775 family census of El Cobre (limited only to royal slaves), however, recorded eight related to three widows; one married man and his wife; and three young boys (ages nine to fifteen) who probably worked for someone else. In fact, going by their surnames, it is possible to cluster these eight listed people into three cobrero families that may have owned small cattle ranches in the area.[59] Furthermore, by the 1790s there are references to an *hato* called "La Ceiba" belonging, once again, "to the Cosmes" (the same powerful Cosmes who also owned the largest tobacco farms in the village).[60] The free cobrero Justo Cruzata was recorded in 1782 as having just established a cattle ranch in Angolosongo;[61] it is not clear, however, if this location lay within the immediate jurisdiction of the pueblo, although it had once been within the mining jurisdiction.

Finally, of the five sugar mills in the jurisdiction of El Cobre listed in the 1780 census (see Table 4) at least one belonged to the former parish priest's brother Don Gaspar de Silva. The sugar mill may have been very small for in 1773 Silva owned only five personal slaves.[62] Other even smaller sugar mills, however, may have also been owned by cobrero villagers. The free cobrero Simón González had an old *ingenio* (small sugar mill) in the 1730s and his son Francisco González had an *ingenio* in the 1790s, perhaps the same one inherited from his father.[63] Yet, other sugar mills included in the jurisdiction's count may have referred to estates encroaching on the village's territory, like the sugar mill of the Duany family of Santiago de Cuba; and two others 2 to 5 leagues away from the pueblo (see Map 3). While the latter may not have actually encroached within the village's surrounding league, they lay within the former mining jurisdiction's territory.

Overall, the principal agricultural activities in the village were manioc farming, some tobacco production, and to a much lesser extent cattle ranching and sugar. Despite the general homogenous character of El Cobre as a modest farming village, by the mid- to late eighteenth century at the latest there was some internal economic differentiation in the pueblo, as well as some estates that belonged to people who were not cobreros by birth. The available data does not allow for a more detailed breakdown of land tenure in the village or any further reconstruction of the economy at a regional, local, or household level.

Internal Aspects of Social Identity Grounded in Land: Gender, Kinship, and Freedom

It is difficult to reconstruct the transformations at the microlevel of production that took place in El Cobre after the Crown's confiscation of the mines. Little is known of the regime of *conucos* in El Cobre, or for that matter in the island in general, to determine just what kind of changes, if any, took place in the cobreros' landholding system as they became reconstituted peasants and king's slaves.[64] All one may aspire to delineate—without much regard to the cobreros' past as private slaves—are some aspects of the local rural world constructed in El Cobre by the 1730s.

Beyond material considerations, this section discusses the kind of social meanings that may have been attached to land and work among this early Caribbean "reconstituted peasantry." For it was in the cobreros' relation to land that important aspects of gender- and kinship-based identities, and not only corporate pueblo or *patria* ones, were actualized and lived. Piecemeal aspects of this social imaginary have been extracted, reconstructed, and interpreted out of microevents and "speech acts," fragments of recorded life, as well as out of censuses and numbers.

Farming Identities

There were few households in El Cobre where there was not at least one person engaged in the direct cultivation of the land. Of the 222 households in the village in 1773, only 17 (7.6 percent) had no person identified either as a land cultivator in general (*labrador*) or more specifically as a *veguero*.[65] Of male heads of household with a registered occupation in the local family census of 1773, 74.3 percent were identified as *labradores*, and 10.9 percent as tobacco farmers, giving a total of 85.2 percent engaged in agriculture.[66] Except for the tailor's household in 1773, even in the houses of artisans in the village there was always a son, a son-in-law, at times a wife, or more rarely a young daughter who was involved in agriculture.[67] The wife and nineteen-year-old son of the tile-maker Ambrosio Suárez were land cultivators. Likewise the son of the silversmith Antonio Campos was, at age twelve, the only *labrador* in his family. At that early age Joseph Campos probably cultivated the land with his father when the latter took time off from his artisanal tasks. Or Joseph may have worked in a relative's, probably an uncle's, farm. Full specialization may not have always been a viable option in a modest rural village such as El Cobre so that even artisans would have had to work the land at least on a part-time basis. The royal slave Alejo Sánchez, for instance, was one of the few smelters in the village in 1773, but he—along with other members of his family—was also engaged in tobacco production, an activity demanding meticulous care and a considerable investment of time.[68]

The *labradores* of this eighteenth-century agricultural (and mining) pueblo were for the most part *labradores de estancia* or *estancieros* (farmers).[69] While 75 percent of male royal slaves in the village were identified as *estancieros* in 1775, only 11 percent were recorded as *vegueros*. Most of the heads of household growing tobacco in this village were freemen (78 percent), although many of these freemen (43 percent) were married to a royal slave woman and had enslaved families. Only four (22 percent) heads of household among the recorded tobacco farmers were themselves royal slaves. This profile may indicate that either local tobacco farmers were able to accumulate greater wealth and manumit themselves; or, as suggested before, free men had more time than royal slaves to dedicate themselves to the intense cultivation of tobacco.

Gender and Farming

In eighteenth-century El Cobre, farming was strongly—but not exclusively—associated with male work. It may have been to a lesser extent in former days.[70] In the early mining slavery days of Santiago del Prado, as elsewhere in the Caribbean, gender distinctions, at least with regard to the division of labor in the master's sphere of work, may have been more blurred. An inventory of the mines and slaves made in 1647 recorded most slave women, even old slave women, as being in possession of tools such as machetes, *calabozos*, and hoes, for working in the mines' extensive agricultural fields and also in their *conucos*.[71] Although it is generally held that whole slave families worked in provision grounds when available, one unresolved aspect in the general historiography of the "slave economy" (not to speak of Cuba) is the basis of the land distribution. Were *conucos* given out to individual slaves, both male and female, or predominantly to males, particularly on a head-of-household basis? How were customary ownership or even usufruct rights to these provision grounds imagined?

Whatever the case in the cobreros' slave (or even African) past, by the time they became a "reconstituted peasant" community, the agricultural sphere may have acquired a different gendered character, perhaps one closer to the lines of a colonial social imaginary regarding free people. I suggest that freedom and slavery were imagined as differently gendered statuses or identities (although, of course, these social meanings may have been a common object of negotiation and contention in everyday life), just as other social categories, such as class and ethnicity, for instance, tended to be. Reconfigurations of identity or social mobility often involved reshuffling of roles whether at collective or more individual levels. In the case of El Cobre, the situation became particularly interesting and complex in that males took on gender attributions of free men despite the fact that they carried the strongest burden of forced labor, or slavery in the community.

By the early 1770s, the overwhelming majority (85.3 percent) of males with a registered occupation were engaged in agricultural activities, while the remaining ones were either day workers (*jornaleros*) or artisans such as carpenters, smelters, blacksmiths, and the like who may have also turned to agriculture on a part-time basis. Even boys in this rural village began to learn how to cultivate the land and to forge their occupational identities as farmers from the early age of ten, an age at which the majority of boys in the pueblo were already listed as *labradores* or *estancieros*. Although females were also listed as *estancieras* in the 1770s, they were to a considerably lesser degree. Contrary to the case of males, females' association to agriculture was strongly related to life cycle considerations.

The gendered assumptions underlying the design of the village census cited above, however, were notable in that only the occupations of males—whether free or slave—were recorded, much as if they were the only economically active members in the household and the community. In this official depiction of the laboring sphere in El Cobre, males were portrayed as skilled workers, and they were largely the ones involved in the agricultural activities that sustained life in the pueblo. This implicit construction of males in the census reflected socially imagined assumptions about gender current in the wider society, at least with regard to (free) members of the body politic. Indeed, it was part of the dominant Spanish ideology that male heads of household were the fundamental providers of the family—precisely the ideology repeatedly invoked by the cobreros in their labor and agrarian confrontations with the state when claiming the means to provide for their "wives and children."[72] More specifically, by controlling and engaging the land, males, and particularly in their role of *patres familias*, had the symbolic power to directly produce the "daily bread" emblematic of subsistence and to activate a gendered social identity that made them into proper subjects in colonial society, thereby effacing their dependent and degraded status as slaves.

If the family census of 1773 was narrow in its depiction of males as the sole economically active members in this village, that of 1775—more limited in that it excluded free people in the community—offered a more richly textured picture of working life in El Cobre. In this census, females—or at least enslaved females—were also portrayed as the economically active members of the household and of the community and their occupations were recorded along with those of male royal slaves.[73] Although farming was not the dominant occupation among these females, many adult women in the pueblo and even some girls were engaged in agricultural activities—in fact at times they held or headed these farms themselves. Perhaps the most extreme case was that of the thirty-nine-year-old widow Francisca Antonia González who headed a virtually all-female household in the pueblo, consisting of her two young daughters (aged twelve and seven, the elder one already a seamstress), a four-year-old son, and her twenty-nine-year-old sister who was a lamp maker. González's farm was found in the Turquino district, perhaps one of the more retired of all the territorial zones in El Cobre. Although she may have summoned the help of relatives on occasions, it was she who seemed to carry the burden of farming as the family had no retainers. A family division of labor in this case may have developed primarily among two sisters who shared a residence (probably their late parents' house): one engaged in farming in the mountains of the Turquino region; the other in making lamps in the family's village house where her young niece also had also taken up sewing. Sister and niece in the village house may have shared other domestic chores and looked after the younger children.[74] A typical and probable denouement to this family's life cycle situation would have been that although the widow González would not remarry, her single sister (and later her own daughters) would; these women would bring their husbands to reside in their village house—and possibly to take over the farm—at least until they in turn became widows.

The majority (60 percent) of royal slave females with an occupation were primarily identified with nonagricultural occupations considered more "proper to their sex" such as sewing, hat making, or weaving. These aggregated figures, however, do tend to overplay the occupational role and identity of women as cultivators of land, for a developmental cycle seems to have structured their occupational careers more strongly than in the case of males. An important stage in women's occupational trajectory was reached at about age twenty-six, only a few years after the average age of marriage for females in this community (twenty-three years). At age twenty-six, there was a dramatic increase in the proportion of women engaged in agriculture that suggests a greater engagement in agricultural activity roughly at the time they began to form their own families. But it was really not until they reached their forties that women became firmly associated with farming or perhaps in many cases only with the ownership of farms, as in the above related case of the widow Juana Francisca González. Unfortunately, these censuses do not distinguish between "ownership" rights and work or occupation, so that, for instance, the "estancia" entry in a census could refer to either situation, or again, to both.

Farming seems to have become increasingly important in female lives not only with age but also with changes in marital status. While only 24 percent of single slave females with a registered occupation were *estancieras* in this community (and as many as 62 percent among them were seamstresses), 50 percent of married slave women had turned to agriculture as they became wives and mothers. But the highest proportion of *estancieras* among females in El Cobre was found among women who had become widows. As many as 75 percent of this sector of the female population was identified as *estancieras* in the census of 1775. Moreover, although only a few women worked in tobacco farms, if those who did so are included with those working in cassava-producing farms, then 57 percent of married royal slave women were agriculturalists and 85 percent of widows were identified with land-related activities. That proportion of *estancieras* among widows was roughly equivalent to that of *labradores* among the total male population of El Cobre, as if with the late years in the female life cycle, gender boundaries became more fluid. Few of these widows were engaged in what seemed like the more youthful, sedentary, and gender-specific occupation of sewing. But, in the cases of widowhood, the occupational identity of *estancieras* may have been more associated with the inheritance and head-ship of these family farms and may not have necessarily indicated the full engagement in farming. That may have depended on considerations such as the number and age of sons in the household and the more remote possibility of owning slaves.

Despite the showing of these women in the agricultural sector, however, more informal and occasional glimpses of everyday life and work in the cobreros' farms indeed find mostly males working, even owning, and interacting with each other in the village's farming spaces, although access to those farms seemed to have been at times obtained via females. Some spontaneous moments in rural life can be culled from the accounts that some cobreros (albeit male cobreros) made during the course of an official interrogation carried out in 1737, after a local tumult; by linking people and households through village hearth listings; and by reference to a royal official's reported confiscation acts after that same tumult. These flickering images also capture the family-based character of agricultural production or even of property-holding rights in these farms, as well as the more distant kinship ties that were also often operative in this sphere of work.

Gender but also Kinship-Based Spaces

Claudio Alcántara, a sixty-two-year-old royal slave who identified himself as a *labrador*, recalled during an interrogation in 1737 that some years before he was repairing the house in his *estancia* "with the help of his two muchachos [adolescent boys]" when the village *alcaldes* (local government officials) inconveniently summoned one of them to do his labor stint in the fortification projects of Santiago de Cuba. Likewise, Alcántara also declared to authorities during the interrogation that "he has his *estancia* in Río Abajo . . . and that a son of his named Joseph who is already a man, [and] two nephews of his named Pedro Regalado [age twenty-nine] and Joseph Miguel who is twelve years old work in it [with him]."[75] In Alcántara's accounts only males were found working in the farm—young, adolescent, and adult males related through kinship ties. His twenty-one-year-old daughter, a nineteen-year-old niece living with the family, and his wife, however, were not mentioned. The family (and gender) character of production in these *estancias* could also extend across households in the pueblo: while Alcántara's son Joseph and his nephew Joseph Miguel lived with him and his wife, his twenty-nine-year-old nephew Pedro Regalado lived with his young family in his wife's parental house.[76] Thus the recently married Pedro seems to have had no property of his own—at least not yet—as he depended on his side of the family for farmland and on his wife's side for a village dwelling. Or perhaps Pedro had joint usufruct rights over part of his uncle's land but did not have his own separate farm. It is not known how harvested produce would be divided in cases where consumption took place in different households.

Likewise, when authorities asked the twenty-five-year-old royal slave, Cipriano Rodríguez, whether his *estancia* was on royal land, this *labrador* responded that indeed "the land where he, his father, and his [older] brothers had their *estancia* is the King's."[77] Rodríguez made reference to a shared familial ownership of the farm, but this, again, was a co-ownership among the family's males, for Rodríguez did not include his five sisters as partaking in the ownership of the family farm. And while one of Rodríguez's brothers was, like him, single and living in the parental house, his oldest brother retained rights to "ownership" or use of his natal family's farm even though he lived in a separate house with his own young family. Thus, joint rights to *estancias* among both single and married males in the family also extended across households in the village as in the case of Alcántara and his nephew, Pedro Regalado.

That *estancias* were considered (at least by men in the village and by colonial authorities) for the most part, but not always, to belong to males, and that individual kin worked in and held contiguous or nearby land plots is evinced by some (male) cobreros' mapping of one of the village's rural districts during an interrogation: Río Abajo (see Map 3, above). When asked to indicate "how many *estancias* belonging to slaves of His Majesty *vecinos* of El Cobre are there in Río Abajo," several cobreros listed some eighteen owners.[78] Of these, all were males except the seventy-nine-year-old widow María Micaela del Agua. The latter, however, was not just a regular *estanciera*. With "eleven or twelve slaves, females and males," Agua happened to be the largest slaveholder in the village throughout the 1730s and probably the largest farm owner, too. Thus, although most *estancieros* were male, María Micaela del Agua fits well the village profile whereby older females, particularly widows, were overwhelmingly identified as *estancieras* (however, at her age, and with eleven or twelve slaves at her disposition, she was undoubtedly more an owner than a direct producer). It is not clear if her sons-in-law Joseph Francisco Rodríguez and Gregorio Vicente labored on the widow's own land or if they owned farms (and land) that were contiguous to their mother-in-law's *estancia*. While the latter could be suggestive of a division of Agua's farmland, both scenarios point to these men's access to land through their wives, the widow's youngest daughters (or granddaughters). And although the twenty-two-year-old Gregorio Vicente lived with his own young family in his own parental household while working in or near his mother-in-law's *estancia*, thirty-three-year-old Joseph Francisco resided with his family in Agua's house in the common uxorilocal (wife-centered) residential arrangement of this community.

And yet, it was not only Agua's sons-in-law who either worked in her farm or by then had acquired their own farms near hers; five other sons of the widow—the Lieutenant Félix de los Reyes, Juan Antonio, Bernardo, Lorenzo, and Juan de los Reyes—each had his *estancia* near his mother's in Río Abajo. They were also neighbors of hers in the village. The rest of Agua's family in 1735 lived in neighboring households in the pueblo, but their farms must have been located elsewhere—particularly that of her eldest son, the prominent Captain Ignacio de los Reyes—because they were not listed as part of this district. All in all, however, there were five to seven farms belonging to kin of María Micaela del Agua concentrated in the same district, and together they constituted from 33 to 44 percent of the farms in the district of Río Abajo. Thus, Agua's land was surrounded by or had been divided into the farms of several descendants—sons, daughters, and grandchildren—suggesting a frozen moment in the process of transmission, and perhaps division, of family land in this community. Agua retained owner- and headship of her farm and slaves amid seventeen other male-held *estancias*, regardless of her advanced age; nevertheless, it seems that male kin (including sons-in-law) were succeeding her in the control over what may have been a large piece of family farmland. Control or ownership of farms appears to have fallen back into the hands of females only when the wives of these men themselves became widows. Indeed, in 1775 Juana Bautista Quiala, the widow of one of Agua's sons, Bernardo, headed the family farm in Río Abajo as well as a large extended family household of more than eighteen people, including the families of four of her married adult children.[79]

Lest it be thought that the case of the Reyes's family was exceptional, in the district of Río Abajo there were at least four other closely located farms belonging to members of another family, the Quialas: Xavier Quiala, Juan Ravelo Quiala, Juan Ravelo's brother Juan Manuel Quiala, and the latter's son-in-law Periquillo (who also repeated the uxorilocal residence blueprint by living in Juan Manuel's village house in 1735).[80] This pattern provides further evidence that family land was distributed, inherited, or worked among different family members, either through joint usufruct rights or separate ones related to a division of land. The cases of Periquillo and of Agua's sons-in-law hint at a possible pattern of land transmission in this pueblo, namely, the incorporation of a son-in-law not only into the village family house but in some cases also into the family farm or the eventual grant of part of that land to sustain the new family. But the previous cases of Claudio Alcántara, Cipriano Rodríguez, and other sons of María Micaela del Agua also point to the pattern of males gaining access to farms, or joint rights to farms, through their own natal family's legacy. In general these cases suggest a bilateral system of land transmission; however, actual usufruct may have been more gender segregated, favoring males.[81]

To be sure, property rights in this village were not absolute rights to property. In the case of farms, the cobreros only had usufruct rights over the land and could only have inherited and held jointly or separately those rights, not the land itself. However, these farmers actually owned the produce and the houses on the land; and it was the produce that was valued in the appraisals, not the land or the farmhouse. This is attested to by the fact that Alejandro Moreno's *estancia* had no value after its yucca was harvested by Lieutenant Nicholás Velasco Calderín's troops "and it was left with nothing."[82] In the case of Jacintho Rodríguez's confiscated *estancia*, the lieutenant again reported: "The produce of this one was taken out and it was not sold."[83] Although most of these confiscated farms—or their unharvested produce—found buyers in the pueblo, the confiscated village houses were not sold or appraised. As Velasco Calderín reported, no one was willing to buy them. Perhaps it was more difficult to view village family houses as commodities than *estancias* given the commercial value placed upon agricultural produce and animals.

In general, although women may have had rights to land, and often worked it alongside their male kin, the interviews and the mapping of a village's rural district suggest that the males were regarded by cobreros (and, as I will discuss further, by authorities) as the "owners" of these farms. Yet, María Micaela del Agua exemplified the possibility that control of farmland could be attained by widowed and older women, in particular. Her case also indicates the highest level of internal economic differentiation to be found in this pueblo. Furthermore, although most of the family heads in the Río Abajo district were related to each other, they also seem to have held their own separate *estancias* as enumerated by the cobrero witnesses. Given the kin-based landholding patterns in the district, these individual family heads may have held small parcels of land in a larger family holding. Regardless of the manner of land division and of actual "ownership rights," these cases also suggest the existence of family legacies in the form of land transference. Thus, they point to the ability of these corporate villagers—whether free or royal slaves—to hold and transmit "rights"—whether property or use rights—by virtue of their own kinship bonds.

Gendered Familial Spaces: Farms and Village Houses

In El Cobre, families had access to a house in the village and to a farm in the surrounding territory. In 1773, for example, only about 16 percent of the village population had no village house that they could claim as theirs or their family's, where they could reside during their Sunday visits or longer stays in the pueblo. Whereas estancias were regarded as belonging mostly to males, village houses were construed more as female space.

This pattern is attested to by the fact that during the conflict of the 1730s that led to the already-referred-to interrogations, property was confiscated from several of the implicated cobreros. The property confiscated from males consisted of estancias and animals, while village houses, or parts of them shared with other siblings or husbands, were taken from women[84]—a material expression of the culturally construed gender spheres in this community, but also of females' right to property with perhaps some hints of separate conjugal property rights. Of the thirteen men from whom property was confiscated, estancias were taken from ten and horses from eight. In the case of the thirty-seven-year-old single woman, Francisca de los Reyes, on the other hand, only "one part of the [village] house shared among five siblings" was taken by the state, which suggests joint ownership of unpartitioned familial property in the case of some of these houses. Among the other eight women allegedly implicated in the tumult, none had an estancia and only one "had no house" to take over, and another lived with her mother whose house was confiscated. The rest had houses seized.[85]

Finally, possible gendered conventions on property holding in this rural village are once more suggested in a land distribution that took place in 1843 to overturn the corporate structure of land tenure earlier decreed by the Crown.[86] The de-corporatization policy behind this land-distribution effort followed customary landholding patterns in the village in the distribution of the newly privatized land. At this time, not only were individual titles to estancias given out but also the cobreros received titles to house plots in the village. In general, males received 57 percent of the grants to land, while women received a still very high 43 percent of all individual titles. Such a distribution points to the widespread role of women as "owners"—now full property owners—of land in this village; indeed, this role may have been unusually high in relation to other Spanish ethnic communities. Of these grants, however, 132 consisted of farmland or *estancias* while 220 were house plots (*solares*) in the village's nucleus. Males received the overwhelming majority (76.5 percent, or 101 grants) of the farmland, while females obtained title to a majority (120 grants, or 54.5 percent) of the house plots, which echoes the gendered social imaginary suggested earlier as prevalent in eighteenth-century El Cobre. I suggest that the fact that such a high number of titles were given out to females—and that they distinctly held most of the housing property—may reflect perhaps not so much the high number of female-headed households as a long-standing trend in this village of separate conjugal property rights as well as of gendered spaces and family legacies. The (still high) 23 percent of *estancias* granted to females may have indeed reflected female-headed households, particularly those of widows.[87]

Explicit Female Occupational Identities

While the voices of some male villagers who owned *estancias* in the Río Abajo district can be heard in the record of the interrogations, female voices are curt and faint. All one can hear today are the voices of eight allegedly disorderly women who were also arrested for interrogation. But these women only answered a few preliminary identification questions, otherwise declining to speak or relate anything to authorities.[88] One question they did answer regarded their occupation. From their short and simple answers can be gathered what they considered to be their own primary occupational identity. Of the eight women interrogated in 1737 only three declared themselves to be engaged in the cultivation of land in some way; the other five identified themselves to authorities as involved in nonagricultural occupations: one stated she was a spinner, another a seamstress, and three others copper gatherers.[89]

Of the three women who based their occupational identity in agriculturally based activities, María de la Rosa (sixty years old) whose husband, a freeman, was away in Santiago de Cuba, declared that she dedicated herself to work in her small *conuco*—a kitchen garden, not a farm.[90] And yet, while she confined herself to her own garden, at least one of her sons, the twenty-eight-year-old and recently married *alcalde* Hilario Norate, who also lived in his wife's house, had two *estancias* of his own confiscated.[91] Thus, there were at least two farms in the family held by a male child, while María de la Rosa only held a *conuco* and a village house. Although another married woman, Simona Vicente (forty years old), identified herself fully as an *estanciera*, the thirty-five-year-old María Magdalena Quiala construed her relation to farming in a more complementary way: she was an "*estanciera* with her husband."[92] Almost all the male witnesses interrogated—and there were more than twenty—identified themselves as *estancieros*; only two stated they were *vegueros*; and those few who held local *alcalde* positions used that official identity as their response.

Conclusion

The cobreros founded their claims to land on a series of formulations that ranged anywhere from a slave's basic right to subsistence, to special entitlements as the king's slaves, to the corporate rights of a pueblo under colonial law. In fact, they often combined these formulations or stretched them to their limits as, for instance, when they turned a slave's legal entitlement to be properly provided for by a master into a claim to the means of self- and family subsistence. Or when they extended the claim to land for the provisioning of their families to both pasture and arable land. Or yet again, when they made collective claims to land and called for anything from (a minimal) 1-surrounding league of land to (ideally) the whole territory of the mining jurisdiction. Indeed, the land question in El Cobre went beyond mere material or economic considerations. At issue were also definitions of social identity and ways of life. Particularly striking in the case of these royal slaves was the corporate dimension of social identity grounded in communal rights to land and the strong sense of entitlement that led to persistent mobilization in colonial courts. Ultimately, the cobreros' natal ties to village land—and to *patria chica* (local homeland)—subverted their socially "dead" status as slaves, or even as royal slaves.

At the microlevel, landholding and working practices in this community activated other kinds of social identities and natal ties among the cobreros too. Farmland in El Cobre was not just worked by individuals, or by members of the nuclear family, of even by kin living in the same household. Farmland was often worked by family or relatives dispersed through different households in the pueblo—a sign perhaps of land shortage in the village, but also of the extended familial networks that found expression in the agricultural productive sphere. Farming and landholding practices may have even marked and symbolized terrain associated with particular clusters of families in the village as the case of the Reyes's and the Quialas's control over large parts of the Río Abajo rural district suggested. These land tenure patterns may have also reflected intergenerational land transmission practices among the enslaved villagers.

Finally, farming activities and landholding practices also seemed to ground gender identities to a considerable degree, at least throughout the eighteenth century and part of the following century. Despite forced absences from the village to work in the Crown's fortification projects, male royal slaves remained entrenched in the agricultural sector of the local economy, and farming spaces remained to a large extent under their control. These particular aspects of rural life and local production in El Cobre may have partaken of wider dominant concepts about properly male and female spheres in Spanish colonial society. Farming activities and spaces, however, were not completely closed to females in this village, at least not to the degree that other occupations such as hunting and most forms of artisanal labor were. Although females may not have been fully associated with agricultural activities or identified as "farmers" or "estancieras" since childhood as males were, many became engaged in these farming activities and identified as such with age and position in the life cycle. Yet, as Chapter 8 will show, women in El Cobre may have relied more on other "female" activities such as mining for their contribution to the household economy and for access to the market.

Paradoxically, few cobreros today would consider themselves campesinos, *labradores* (farmers), or *agricultores* (agriculturalists). Men in El Cobre these days are mostly miners (even though some miners or retired miners also have *conucos*, or minuscule gardens where they grow some crops).[93] But the importance of a farming identity was still strongly alive in the village during the first decades of the nineteenth century. In fact, when around the 1830s El Cobre turned once more to large-scale mining production, the cobreros resisted being incorporated into a new mining order that may have resonated with memories of slavery or that may have threatened to obliterate long established forms of male-gendered identity in this village. In 1838, a royal official reported, "The women occupy themselves in the separation of the minerals *but the men say that they are farmers* [agricultores] [emphasis added]."[94] It is not clear, however, until how late in the nineteenth century the cobreros were able to sustain that agricultural identity.

CHAPTER 7

Owning Personal Slaves

An Extreme Instance of the Right to Property and to Familial Legacies

Most cobreros were royal slaves. A few were masters of slaves, too. In 1735, Juan Capistrano and his wife Juana Josepha were both slaves of His Majesty, yet they owned a twenty-two-year-old personal slave named Antonio. At that time, the royal slave Albina Cosme and the freeman Juan Ravelo owned a forty-seven-year-old bondwoman named Manuela, a slave that Cosme probably inherited from her family. The orphaned royal slave María Dorotea de Ojeda, possibly along with her siblings, became owner of the slave Gervasio, most likely at the death of her parents. The royal slave widow Manuela Matamba had inherited, perhaps from her deceased husband (or parents), two slaves by 1735; she and her husband had been owners of slaves as far back as 1709. Free cobreros, particularly free male cobreros, however, were more prone to own slaves than were royal slaves, probably because of greater resources to purchase them, but perhaps as well because of more clear-cut rights to property. The free couple Fernando de Rosas and his wife Beatriz González held two slaves in 1735, Antonio, age twenty, and Nicholás, age ten. They acquired a third slave, Victoria (age seventeen), some time during the ensuing four years. The couple had also been owners of slaves since at least 1709. The seventy-seven-year-old freed widow, María Micaela del Agua, whom I discussed in Chapter 6, was mistress to eight slaves in 1735 and to ten in 1739. Indeed, the widow turned out to be one of the two largest slaveholders in the cobreros' history as a pueblo of king's slaves.[1]

A ghastly microevent provides a pithy view of several aspects of slaveholding and "rights to property" in this village of Oriente. In 1737 royal troops persecuted and killed freeman Bernardino Bernal for leading a local riot in El Cobre. The military official sent by Governor Don Pedro Ignacio Ximénez to reestablish "law and order" in the village, Lieutenant Don Nicholás Velasco Calderín, proceeded to confiscate Bernal's property as

well as that of other alleged participants in the event. Velasco Calderín confiscated Bernal's *estancia*, its produce, and a horse, but he stopped short of
taking a male slave because, as the lieutenant reported to the governor, "I
understand that he [the slave] certainly belonged to the first wife of the
deceased [Bernardino Bernal]."[2] The lieutenant then reported having
returned the slave to the *alcalde* Joseph Cosme—himself soon to become a
freedman and, alongside María Micaela del Agua, the village's largest eighteenth-century slaveholder. The *alcalde* (local official), in turn, returned the
slave to Bernal's children, the legitimate heirs of their mother's property.
The heirs of Clara Matamba were represented by the eldest daughter, a
twenty-six-year-old single woman named Eusebia who, like her late mother,
was a royal slave. Eusebia then became head of the household, which consisted of her four younger siblings and a niece.[3]

Most striking about this episode is the sense of "normalcy" with which
Velasco Calderín wrote about the property claims and testamentary capacity of unfree people and his explicit articulation of the inheritance rule
regarding female property and bequeathal rights. It is unclear if the possibility of owning (and inheriting) slaves constituted a prerogative conferred
upon these royal slaves in recognition of their special identity, or whether it
constituted some kind of customary entitlement that they were able to gradually appropriate, perhaps through some kind of stretched reading of a right
to the *peculium*.[4] It is not clear either if, in the case of royal slaves, only the
rights to inherit and own personal slaves, or also a "right" to buy slaves
"freely" in the market were at stake here.

In contrast to other parts of this book, there are, unfortunately, few voices to listen to in this chapter. Aside from one confiscation report by Velasco
Calderín, there are no texts, statements, or memories from whence to weave
socially imagined meanings about slaveholding practices in El Cobre. I rely
in this chapter almost exclusively on several eighteenth-century local family
censuses to count slaveholders and slaves as well as to spin family histories.[5]
Here, one is almost exclusively in the silent realm of social history, gazing at
fragments of local life from the outside. It is impossible to establish if a right
to own property—and particularly this form of human "property"—or even
to have servants had ever been contested issues between cobreros and colonial authorities, and if so, on what terms. To be sure, it is even impossible to
know if the cobreros, or some cobreros, may have imagined personal slavery
any differently than other sectors of colonial society, or, for that matter, if it
may have been at any point an issue in the community as well. Similarly,
given the paucity of references other than hearth listings, one cannot exam-

ine questions such as the character of slavery in a rural community where most people—even some slaveholders—were enslaved to the king or the kind of cultural, social, and human relations that were established between the creolized inhabitants of El Cobre and the new, small, locally owned generation of African slaves.

What an examination of bare slaveholding practices among the cobreros can do is provide an oblique glimpse of another significant slice of life in this eighteenth-century rural village. Indeed, where slaveholders can be concretely traced through their slaves across several decades of family censuses, a study of these masters and their slaves reveals not only some local patterns related to the (to be sure, not generalized) practice of possessing and transmitting slaves in this community and the role of kinship in these processes, but also to some of the broader principles that may have undergirded other customary property-holding practices and "traditions" in this village. Although the material does not always allow for the precise delineation of the rules and customs regulating local slaveholding, or more generally property rights and transmission processes (these tend to be messy and contradictory even for a contemporary anthropologist who can witness them or ask directly about them), it does reveal some general trends already operating among these reconstituted peasants by the early eighteenth century, if not before. This mapping of slaveholders as property holders may also suggest, if in only a sketchy—and perhaps perverse—way the more general process of reformulating and reshaping local custom and "traditions" within the dominant legal framework of colonial society, or perhaps out of a wider bricolage of legacies. The available material (in this community, elsewhere in Cuba, or abroad in the Caribbean, Africa, Latin America, or even throughout different regions of Spain) is too fragmentary to firmly ground more serious comparative efforts at the present stage of research, however. Ultimately, if nothing else, the study of slaveholding practices in El Cobre shows the degree to which authorities took for granted or tolerated the applicability of what in principle were regarded as proprietary entitlements among free people to the enslaved inhabitants, or some inhabitants, of this community.

Slaveholding in El Cobre: A General View

Only a small proportion of households owned slaves in El Cobre. That proportion fluctuated between 4.5 percent (1773) and 12 percent of all households in the pueblo (1739) during most of the eighteenth century. The low incidence of personal slavery is more markedly reflected in other population measures: personal slaves comprised between 1 and 3 percent of the village's total population throughout the century (5 percent if the clergy's slaves are included)—an extremely low figure in comparison to the island's average of 22.8 percent in 1774.[6] Only the nearby Indian peasant pueblos of Jiguaní and El Caney had a comparably low incidence of personal slavery: just 2 and 1.9 percent of their respective populations were comprised of slaves in 1780. Thus, legal disabilities regarding the slave status of most of the pueblo's population do not seem to have been the main factor motivating the low incidence of personal slaves in the case of El Cobre for legally free Native Americans also had similar proportions of personal slaves in their own communities. Moreover, racial and ethnic factors may not have by themselves exclusively accounted for low levels of slave ownership in these three peasant villages either. As of 1780 there were still other larger population centers in Cuba's eastern region that did not have high levels of personal slavery. Slaves, for instance, constituted only 7 percent of the highly mixed population in the agriculturally diversified city of Baracoa (population 1,972) and only 8 percent of the mostly white cattle-ranching district of Holguín (population 3,479). In comparison, only in Santiago de Cuba (population 12,884) did slaves number as much as 28.8 percent of the population in 1780. At any rate, whether due to factors particular to El Cobre, to class, to race and ethnicity, to productive regimes, or to more general circumstances affecting the whole region, at no point in the eighteenth century was personal slavery extensive in El Cobre.[7]

Generally speaking, slaveholders in El Cobre were a small, tightly knit, modest group of peasants or small producers who belonged to the poorest strata of the island's slave-owning classes. With the exception of two cases, no cobrero slaveholder in the eighteenth century ever held more than four slaves. In fact, the overwhelming majority owned only one or two slaves. The few who owned four slaves actually had only two adult slaves, the rest were children. Even the two slave owners with the most slaves in El Cobre were not large slave owners. María Micaela del Agua and Joseph Cosme held between eight and twelve slaves each at some point during the 1730s and 1750s–1760s, respectively. Overall, the mean number of slaves locally held by cobrero slaveholders fluctuated between 1.5 (1709) and 2.4 (1773). Slaveholders in El Cobre were particularly poor as compared to, for example, slaveholding peasants in an analogous region in late-eighteenth-century (1788) Brazil, namely, the manioc-producing region of Jaguaripe where peasant slaveholders held a mean of 4.5 slaves.[8] However, slaveholders among free people of color in Brazil, as in El Cobre, for the most part held only one or two slaves. No one, however, was ever a large slaveholder in El Cobre during the eighteenth century; even the white clergy held between one and seven slaves each. Moreover, the total number of personal slaves owned by the three clergymen together never amounted to more than eleven (1750), although the Marian sanctuary owned between eight and ten slaves, called the "Virgin's slaves," during the 1730s and 1750s.[9]

As in the case of classic Caribbean slave population profiles, including that of the cobreros' ancestors in the early mining days, most (79 percent) private slaves in El Cobre were adults, and males constituted 72 percent of the total adult slave population.[10] A reconstruction of the economic activities of cobrero slaveholders shows that most masters in the 1770s were associated with some kind of small-scale commercial production, usually of sugar, tobacco, or livestock. None of the village's fifteen skilled artisans, however, held a slave in 1773, even though earlier in the century Sergeant Juan de Ojeda, a coppersmith, may have bequeathed to his children the male slave whom they held in the 1730s. Most likely, slaves in this rural village were not only employed in commodity production but also in the production of manioc and other foodstuffs for household consumption or sale, as well as in other areas of the subsistence economy. Bernardino Bernal, for example, owned an *estancia* with manioc produce where he probably employed his deceased wife's slave, but he also sent this slave to the *monte* to hunt wild pigs for the family's meat consumption needs.[11]

Many of the slaveholders in El Cobre were related to one another; slaveholding among these rural villagers seems to have been mainly a family affair. In 1773, for example, the Cosmes alone comprised four of the ten slaveholding households in the village (40 percent); members of this family held ten of the cobreros' twenty-four slaves (42 percent). At that time, the González family had two slave-owning households, together owning five additional slaves. Both families constituted 60 percent of the village's slaveholders in 1773 and held 62.5 percent of the cobreros' slaves during that year. Furthermore, these two families had a long tradition of owning slaves that went back at least to the first decade of the century. Such continuity is reflected in the fact that of the six slave-owning households in 1709, five still had family members owning slaves thirty years later. Such long-standing family traditions seem to make slaveholding an even less generalized and less open practice among the villagers of El Cobre. The small and kinship-related character of slavery in El Cobre provides a window to the slave and property transmission practices among these small agricultural producers and to the familial identities such practices may have activated.

A Family Portrait

The reconstruction of the Cosme family's slaveholding history suggests the existence of family "legacies" in the form of slaves, as well as royal slave and free, male and female cobreros' entitlement to this kind of "property." Moreover, this case study also reflects the internal social mobility attained by some cobreros in this village. This notable local family can be traced for several generations across one century, back to 1670 when the former mining slaves became the king's slaves. The slaveholders in the Cosme family descended from Manuel Cosme and his wife Hilaria de Villavicencio.[12] The couple (or each separately) must have met with some economic success early on, for they accumulated enough surplus to manumit family members and obtain slaves. Indeed, in 1689, Hilaria was the first royal slave in El Cobre to purchase her freedom. At that time, she also invested in the freedom of her fourth child, the baby María, spending 190 pesos on both manumissions. Her husband, Manuel, had to save an additional 150 pesos during the next seven years before he, too, could purchase his own freedom, thereby releasing himself from forced state labor requisitions.[13] While at this point in the family history it may not have been unusual for females to manumit themselves before male spouses, the practice became less common in the eighteenth century, particularly after the late 1730s.[14]

The economic activities of this family in the late seventeenth and early eighteenth centuries are unknown, but whatever these were, they enabled the couple to accumulate sufficient wealth to invest in manumissions *and* in slaves. By 1709, when Hilaria de Villavicencio had become a widow, she already owned two adult male slaves who would help support her large household of eight children and three grandchildren. This household also included Hilaria's son Cristóbal Cosme, his wife, and their child. Next door, in what may have been an extension of the main house, lived Hilaria's eldest son, Juan Luis Cosme, with his wife, the royal slave Manuela Matamba, and the couple's children. Juan Luis manumitted himself in 1708, and he and his wife Manuela also owned a slave. Whether the couple acquired the African Antonio Arará by purchase, gift, or inheritance is unclear, but, by then, the second-generation Cosmes had accumulated wealth in the form of a slave and had been able to purchase another manumission—a male manumission in this case.

Juan Luis Cosme and Manuela Matamba headed another large and complex household composed of two other Cosme kin: a brother and a cousin of Juan Luis, and their families. Large joint and extended households like those of the Cosmes were not uncommon in El Cobre, although they were rare elsewhere on the island. Moreover, by 1709 several Cosme families not only constituted joint and extended households but also they formed a residential bloc, one that entailed the sharing of living space in the village and perhaps, but not necessarily, the economic cooperation of household members in productive enterprise.[15] What was particularly salient in the profile of this family was the frequency of residential arrangements whereby female spouses lived in their Cosme husbands' kindred space. More common among families in El Cobre was the converse residential pattern whereby a husband went to live, if only for a few years, in his wife's parental household. This widespread wife-centered pattern also occurred among the Cosmes in the next generation, however.

But the Cosme family's slaveholding "story plot" thickens: twenty-six years later, after the widow Hilaria Villavicencio died, personal slaves were scattered throughout the households of three of her oldest daughters and the families of two deceased sons. In 1735, Manuela Matamba owned two male slaves, and the two married sisters, Albina (a freedwoman) and Paulina Cosme (a royal slave), each also owned an adult male slave. These two sisters shared the same house (probably the sisters' parental house) with their own families, thereby evincing a wife-centered (uxorilocal) residential arrangement. Moreover, an adult female slave was found in the household of another of the late Hilaria de Villavicencio's daughters, Juana Chrisostoma Cosme, a royal slave and unwed mother living alone. Finally a slave family of four lived with Villavicencio's unmarried granddaughters, twenty-two-year-old Rosa Cosme, a freewoman, and nineteen-year-old Gregoria, also a freewoman. Both, like their aunts Paulina and Albina, probably shared their late parents' family house.

It is not far-fetched to suppose that, as in the case of Bernardino Bernal and Clara Matamba's slave, some of the Cosmes' personal slaves may have been passed down through inheritance, particularly as they all belonged to the same line of the family, and other Cosme branches did not own slaves. Interestingly, most of the second- and third-generation slave-owning Cosmes were females (widows, married, and single women, and unwed mothers), a fact that shows there was no bias against females owning or inheriting property as widows or daughters. For some unknown reason, however, most of these second- or third-generation daughters, whether free or royal slaves, did not pass slaves on to their own children. They were able, however, to retain their slave "family legacy" for many decades, in some cases at least until the 1750s. Although most of the Cosmes' slaveholding relatives manumitted themselves or were born free, some females—like Manuela Matamba, Juana Chrisostoma, and Albina—remained royal slaves all their lives. Either their royal slave status did not keep them from owning and inheriting slaves, or if it did, such a prohibition was overridden by family rights to inheritance. The case of these women also may suggest that the manumission of females was less a priority than that of males.[16]

One line of the family became especially prominent in the patrimonial consolidation and transmission of slaves. In 1735, Manuela Matamba (Clara Matamba's sister), by then the widow of Juan Luis Cosme, owned two slaves whom she may have inherited from her husband or perhaps from her own natal family. The career of her son Joseph Manuel Cosme, who had recently married Graciana Ojeda, a woman from another slaveholding household, was beginning to take off at the time for he also was *alcalde* of the village in those years. Joseph Cosme started his slave patrimony with Francisco, whom he received in vivo from his mother some time between 1735 and 1739.[17] Joseph's five sisters and the husband and child of one of them lived in their mother's household, again exemplifying an uxorilocal residential arrangement. These women all shared the remaining family slave.

By 1750, Joseph Cosme had increased his wealth and status considerably; by then he owned as many as eight slaves. Moreover, at that point, his whole family had been manumitted, and Cosme had crowned his career with the rank of captain in the village militia where his eldest son served as lieutenant. In effect, Joseph Cosme reached the pinnacle of success in the pueblo, while some of his relatives still made up a good portion of the small slaveholding group in El Cobre. By 1750, Joseph Cosme himself; his brother Rafael; his aunts Paulina, Juana Chrisostoma, María, and Eugenia; and his cousin Rosa—all of whom were Manuel Cosme and Hilaria de Villavicencio's descendants—had control over two-thirds (fourteen) of the cobreros' twenty-one slaves. Joseph Cosme himself owned more than one-third (eight) of those.

After Captain Cosme died in the late 1760s, his two sons, who until then had lived in the parental house with their own families, split from the main family house, settling in separate but contiguous households. Both sons and Cosme's widow inherited three young slaves each. The two brothers had no sisters with whom to share the parental fortune, which by this time was partly based on tobacco and livestock production. Thus, almost a whole century and four generations had gone by in this family of royal slaves and freedmen and -women during which slaves or the means to acquire them seems to have passed from one generation to the next. Although the male line con-

tinued the slave-owning tradition most forthrightly through several generations of the Cosme family, both males and females transmitted and inherited slaves just as in other families in El Cobre. The joint family living
arrangements among many of these Cosmes also suggest the transmission of
familial houses, as the case of Captain Cosme's two inheriting sons and
widow shows.

In short, several general trends can be culled from the Cosme family's
history: slaveholders included both royal slaves and free members in the
family; masters were linked together in a kinship network in one branch of
the Cosme family; there was a continuity of slave-owning families throughout the century and personal slaves seemed to be transmitted from one generation to the next; both males and females owned, inherited, and in some
cases may have bequeathed personal slaves; and finally there was a pro-
nounced presence of females and widows among slave owners, as well as of
royal slaves among females. Furthermore, women of various statuses — widows, married and single women, and unwed mothers — were slaveholders in
this family.

Inheritance Patterns

Inheritance practices among juridically enslaved people constituted a
customary adaptation of Hispanic law that, as mentioned before, seemed to
have received some official recognition in El Cobre, at least in the first half
of the eighteenth century. That Lieutenant Velasco Calderín did not confiscate the royal slave Clara Matamba's personal slave in 1737 and that he
made a formal report to Governor Ximénez (an archenemy of the
cobreros), invoking inheritance rules as the logic justifying his procedure,
attest to the force and legitimacy of this custom by then. Furthermore, royal
slaves, especially female royal slaves, were routinely recorded as slaveholders in village family censuses at least as far back as 1709, a comment on the
"normalcy" with which slaveholding practices among royal slaves were
regarded by colonial authorities. It is unclear why the number of royal
slaves, including the more common female royal slaves, among slaveholders
in the village virtually disappeared by the 1770s. It may have been due to
harsher restrictions on royal slaves' customary entitlement to own slaves, or
perhaps to a greater propensity of the cobreros to invest in self-manumissions rather than in slaves as the higher rates of manumissions beginning in
the 1740s may suggest.[18]

Bilateral inheritance practices like those found in the Cosme family were sanctioned by Spanish law. Whether such a bilateral inheritance rule represented a local instantiation of the general colonial law (de jure or also of the land), or whether it constituted a local development proceeding from other circumstances or traditions is impossible to determine at this point.[19] Bilateral customary inheritance rights, for instance, also occurred, at least until recently and among rural lower-class sectors, in other Caribbean societies such as Guyana and Jamaica, especially with regard to the institution of "family land." While in the former case it has been noted that such a pattern may have developed from the Dutch-Roman colonial tradition, it has also been suggested that the pattern is attributable to an African legacy. In any case, these Caribbean customary patterns contrast with British tradition where inheritance is patrilineal and primogeniture rules.[20]

Other slaveholding practices in El Cobre could have constituted local inflections of Hispanic property and inheritance law that may or may not have reflected broader regional or islandwide slave-owning customs. No studies exist for other places in Cuba, so it is impossible to contextualize customary slave transmission practices further here. In any case, official legal systems usually provide a grid that coexists (and sometimes interacts) with locally developed customs. Moreover, these systems can be altered in social practice or even manipulated to accommodate social actors' sense of their family interests, social and economic circumstances, or their own conceptions of the proper disposal of patrimony.[21] While in principle Spanish law called for the partitioning of the patrimony equally among all children regardless of sex, it also made some allowance for joint ownership.[22] In El Cobre, there exists strong evidence of unpartitioned familial property, particularly in the form of village houses shared by siblings, especially female siblings, but in some cases in the form of slaves too. As pointed out in Chapter 6, although there may also be a similar general principle underlying the use of farmland in El Cobre, the evidence in that case is even more sketchy. Finally, whereas Spanish law tended to favor the conjugal community even when making allowance for the protection of a wife's endowment and inheritance, the cobreros may have shown a more marked local tendency toward maintaining separate conjugal property rights, whereby blood kinship ties became highlighted.[23] This local custom may have also interacted with joint ownership practices to produce this community's own local inflections of Hispanic law, if not an altogether parallel customary law.

The case of the freeman Bernardino Bernal and the royal slave Clara Matamba once more is particularly telling in relation to some of these aspects of property-holding and transmission practices. It is not clear how

Clara Matamba acquired the slave Thomás, but her "property" rights to him were kept distinct from her husband's, at least as far as formal inheritance rights went. Although, Bernal did have "use" rights over the slave,[24] the couple's children inherited their rights to the slave from their mother. Bernal, for his part, seemed to hold separate property or usufruct rights over the family farm and its produce, for Lieutenant Velasco Calderín had no qualms about confiscating it and a horse, valued at 20 and 7 pesos, respectively.[25] Similarly, although Eusebia, as eldest sibling, may have become the head of her household in 1739, the slave Thomás seems to have been bequeathed as familial property to all the children, or at least to the coresident children, not to a single heir.

The case of the González sisters illustrates even more clearly some of the joint inheritance and property-owning customs with regard to slaves in this village. The royal slave Jacintha González became a head of household and inherited, with her siblings, the nineteen-year-old slave Manuel Antonio when her father, the free widower Simón González, died some time between 1731 and 1735. Although Jacintha was married, her husband, the royal slave Salvador Nicola, did not live in the village, so Jacintha took charge of her two young children and her four sisters, aged fifteen to twenty-five. In fact, not only Jacintha's husband but also her four brothers all worked outside the village in 1735, making Manuel Antonio the only male helping the household with everyday subsistence chores pertaining to male labor.

Yet, Jacintha did not become the sole heir to the slave in her family. Fifteen years later, in 1750, a census taker referred to Manuel Antonio, who then lived separately with his own family, as the "slave of the González [sisters] [*esclavo de las González*]."[26] By this time, those González sisters who were still alive had their own families, and, although they no longer shared a residence in the same family house, they still shared ownership—or usufruct—rights to the slave they had inherited in the 1730s. That Manuel Antonio was recognized as belonging jointly to the González sisters also shows that their "property" was distinct from that of their husbands—indeed perhaps as the private funds that daughters could inherit from their family of origin, share with their own siblings, and hold apart from conjugal property.[27] Such joint familial property patterns would seem to reinforce blood-based kinship identities—in this case, particularly among females. It is also telling that, at least by 1750, the personal slave Manuel Antonio headed his own household in the village—a point to which I return in another part of this chapter.

The recognition of females' rights to hold separate property in the nuclear family unit, their acquisition of property rights through parental inheritance, and the frequently unpartitioned character of familial legacy that has been discussed in relation to local slaveholding practices also show up in another of Lieutenant Velasco Calderín's confiscation attempts, one that did not involve personal slaves but rather a village house. Not only had Velasco Calderín been unable to confiscate Bernardino Bernal's wife's slave, but also he was unable to confiscate the royal slave Hilario Norate's house. As Velasco Calderín reported to Governor Ximénez, people in the village had informed him that "[The house] belonged to his [Hilario Norate's] wife and a sister-in-law of his."[28] Thus, as in Bernal's wife's case, Velasco Calderín recognized Norate's wife's separate property rights, this time in relation to the village house where the family resided, but he confiscated two *estancias* that belonged to Norate.[29] Furthermore, that María de la Trinidad Espinoza, Norate's wife, shared her house with her maternal aunt suggests that the women (both of whom were royal slaves) inherited the real estate from Espinoza's maternal grandparents and that, indeed, these rights did not pass to husbands as joint conjugal property. Instead, they were kept distinct, understood as the woman's own property acquired through her natal family line. This case, in which female maternal kin shared an unpartitioned familial house, also shows that, contrary to Hispanic law, legitimate and illegitimate children may have had equal inheritance rights in El Cobre, for María de la Trinidad was the daughter of an unwed mother.[30] In yet another case, Velasco Calderín expropriated "one fifth of a house" belonging to Francisca de los Reyes, one of the women actually involved in the tumult. How her share of family property was taken over by the state remains a mystery, but the event points again to the joint ownership of village houses by siblings (in this case, both male and female ones).[31]

Indeed, as the Cosme family's residential patterns illustrate, complex households were quite common in El Cobre and may well have reflected the custom of passing down village houses as unpartitioned familial property.[32] As many as 48 of the 116 households (41 percent) in El Cobre in 1735 were complex households. Furthermore, the overwhelming majority of these joint households were uxorilocal (more generational analysis is needed to determine whether they were matrilocal as well).[33] For instance, in 77 percent (37 of 48) of the village's joint households, kinship ties between members of the different resident families were identified; of these, in 27 households (73 percent), additional household residents came from married daughters' or female siblings' families. In one case, as many as four daughters (or siblings) and their families lived in the same household. Only in seven cases (19 percent) did sons bring their wives to reside in their parental house, and in only three cases (8 percent) did the complex household consist of both sons' and daughters' families. Thus, village houses may have been mostly shared—and perhaps inherited—by females who may have acted as the gatekeepers of their family's living space in the village center, but males may have also retained rights to return to the natal house, perhaps later in life. Nonetheless, as suggested by Velasco Calderín's confiscations of local property, males may have been more likely to own—and acquire—rights to family farms (mainly *estancias*). Thus, a general bilateral inheritance system may have been locally inflected by particular gender-based modalities as males may have been more prone to inherit and "own" farmland and females the house plots in the village.

Inheritance of slaves, however, did not seem to follow such strongly marked gender patterns.[34] In fact, partly because inheritance customs did not discriminate against females, women became prominent as slaveholders in this village. Not only did there exist cases of slaveholding households headed by widows and single daughters, but even some married women acted as de facto heads of household when their husbands spent years away from the village. Although actual "ownership" is not always clear in these cases, these women at least held usufruct rights over the slaves in question. Altogether, females constituted roughly from one-third to more than one-half of the slaveholders in the village at different periods. Moreover, if cases of identifiable married female slaveholders in male-headed households—like Paulina and Albina Cosme—are also taken into consideration, the proportion of female slaveholders in this village is even greater, making them at some points clearly the dominant sex among the pueblo's slaveholding members.

From Masters to Slaves

Shifting perspectives from the cobrero masters to their private slaves, one finds that by 1709, there were six slaves in the village who were from the Old World. By that time, however, there were no more first-generation African royal slaves in El Cobre. In their forced exile to this distant village in the New World, these African personal slaves were in some ways repeating the experience of their Creole masters' parents, grandparents, or great-grandparents. Any direct local link to the African continent came now through the cobreros', the resident clergymen's, and the Virgin's private slaves. One wonders what influence, if any, the memories, stories, and practices—religious and otherwise—of this new local wave of Africans, however small, had in Creole families, among individual cobreros, or in the village in general. Similarly, one can only speculate with regard to the kind of relations that may have been established between masters and slaves.

In 1709, most personal slaves in El Cobre were African slaves. Pedro Arará and Juan Mina, slaves of Bernardino Bernal and Clara Matamba, were not totally isolated in their new local environment in the Indies, for instance. Even in this small rural village they could find some company among others from their African home region who like them had become servants to Creole masters. A Mina woman and three other Ararás (two women and another man), all roughly the same age, were dispersed throughout four households in the pueblo. Assuming that old social and political cleavages in their respective African homelands did not separate them in the New World, these two Minas and four Ararás could at least find someone else in their immediate foreign habitat with whom they could communicate in their own language or share common memories of the past or even experiences of social and cultural "adjustment" in the present.

To complete the slave profile of El Cobre in this early period, there were also two Creole slave men similar in age to their African counterparts. While Ararás and Minas made up the majority of private bondmen and -women in El Cobre at this point in time, in subsequent decades slaves from other regions in Africa would also make their way into the village. Creole slaves were in the minority at the turn of the century, but they became more prevalent among the private slave ranks in the village by the 1730s.[35] Finally, there was also a five-year-old girl in 1709 named María, probably Lucrecia Arará's daughter. Because of the usual conventions of local censuses throughout the Spanish (and Iberian) colonial world where kinship relations among slaves were hardly ever specified, the census taker, almost certainly the parish priest, did not explicitly indicate the kinship relation between Lucrecia and María, nor did he identify who the girl's father was. Although by then official inscription practices representing the cobreros as free subjects were used in this kind of record (as family units in households constituting a pueblo), personal slaves in El Cobre were portrayed in the same conventional terms in which regular slaves were usually recorded elsewhere. Lucrecia Arará's little girl María may have been born in El Cobre; thus, at least by virtue of birth, she may have constituted a first-generation cobrera female, an identity one cannot be sure applied to María as a personal slave in this village.

With the passing of time, personal slaves in El Cobre may have been more commonly Creole slaves, but evidence is confusing on this issue. In the 1767, for instance, Captain Joseph Cosme remained indisputably the largest slaveholder in the village, with six or seven of his previous slaves still with him and two new African and three new Creole slaves in his household at the time. Of Cosme's twelve slaves only three were females (aged sixteen, eleven, and one) and all three were Creoles. Although Creole slaves were in the majority in his household, the *bozales* (African born) were all adult working-age men, while the seven Creole slaves were all under twenty-two years of age, with four children aged one to eleven included among them. Cosme very likely bought some of the children, because there was no woman of sufficient age among his slaves to have borne them. Although the census taker specified who were *criollos* and who were *bozales*, the African ethnic name of the *bozales* was not specified in the census of 1767. Thus, for instance, Rafael Cosme's slave, who a decade before had been recorded as Pedro Congo, had become Pedro Cosme in the census of 1767. Similarly in the village census of 1773 private slaves were inscribed with their master's family name; only their position as last on the household census list and their identification as a "personal slave" explicitly indicated their status. What did the change in naming convention indicate in this case? Could it strictly mark ownership, or could it connote in this case some creolization, or even a more ambiguous integration into the household, the family, and perhaps even the community?

Finally, although very little else was revealed about personal slaves in these hearth calls, the parish priest, who officiated as census taker in 1767, indicated that all of Captain Joseph Cosme's slaves were "confessed and confirmed," so at least posterity may rest knowing that they were up-to-date in their Christian sacraments. That record of sacramental status was kept equally for free people, royal slaves, and personal slaves. That the same inscription conventions were used for all illustrates the purported lack of earthly social distinctions in the Christian community. It also shows the close supervision and regulation that participation in that Christian community often entailed. Just as the former mining slaves had been turned into Christian subjects—a first step in a longer creolization process—and taught the meaning of miracles, Virgins, saints, and other religious figures and artifacts, the new generation of African slaves entering the pueblo would also be subject to the same learning and rituals, even if they may have left a mark in the community in other ways.

The Market for Slaves

It is not clear how slaves were bought and accessed in El Cobre. They may have come directly, for instance, from newly arrived cargoes, perhaps even from the much extended contraband trade in slaves taking place from areas such as Puerto Príncipe and Bayamo. Or they may have been obtained in the domestic market instead. Adult slaves introduced through contraband could be bought for as little as 100 pesos in the 1730s.[36] Although this may have been a relatively accessible price that could have facilitated slave ownership to lower sectors of the population, it would also evince authorities' toleration of (and involvement with) contraband slaves even in this community. Was there a lively domestic trade in slaves so that even royal slaves could participate in this market? Was the market so open, even when the slave trade restrictions were rigorous, that a slave could buy a slave in eighteenth-century Cuba? Particularly in the early years of the century, there were a good number of local slaves who were of African origin and were probably obtained from the slave trade. By the 1730s, however, the majority, but by no means all, of the personal slaves in El Cobre seemed to have been Creoles.

Although personal slaves may well have been born in the village, as the presence of enslaved children may suggest, a few cases show that the cobreros (at least those who were free) replenished or augmented their slaves through purchases. At the turn of the century, at least by 1709, thirty-two-year-old Fernando de Rosas and his wife Beatriz González owned thirty-year-old Francisco Criollo, a Creole slave roughly of the same age as his free masters. Twenty years later, however, the masters were still around, but Francisco was nowhere to be found in the local record. He may have died, fled, been sold, or perhaps even manumitted. Despite their relatively grown-up children—a nineteen-year-old daughter and a fifteen-year-old son—by 1731 the free couple had replaced their former slave Francisco with the sixteen-year-old *bozal*, Antonio Congo. Four years later, in 1735, Rosas and González had acquired the ten-year-old Nicholás and again four years later, in 1739, they had added to their household a third slave named Victoria (age seventeen). The origin of these last two slaves is unknown. Regardless of the origin and purpose of these "investments" (one in a still small child), Rosas and his wife had been able to periodically supply themselves with new slaves.

Similarly, in 1731, the royal slave Albina Cosme and her free husband Francisco Ravelo had three slaves: Pedro Joseph (age thirty-eight), Manuela (forty-three), and Joseph Egidio (six). Four years later, in 1735, they only retained Manuela, having perhaps sold or lost by death or flight the other two. Fifteen years later, by 1750, the by-then-aged Albina (seventy-seven) and Francisco (seventy-five) had replaced Manuela with the twenty-seven-year-old José Congo. Yet, not all was turnover and change regarding enslaved servants: Albina's unmarried sister, the royal slave Juana Chrisostoma, retained from 1735 to 1750 the same slave, Catharina.

The Character of Private Slavery in El Cobre

The small-scale character of slave ownership in El Cobre, and perhaps the slave status of many owners, and of most of the village itself, may have shaped the character of slavery in this pueblo in particular ways. As this book demonstrates, the cobreros, as king's slaves, had considered themselves above regular slaves and had come to link a series of customary entitlements with their status as royal slaves. How lines between "freedom" and "slavery" may have been blurred with personal slaves in this community is difficult to say.

The royal slaves of El Cobre sometimes married personal slaves of citizens in neighboring cities, but this does not seem to have been a common practice. In 1709, for instance, only three female royal slaves were married to personal slaves (two in Bayamo, one in Santiago de Cuba). In that same year, however, there was one royal slave woman in the village married to a white man, but as many as eighteen were married to free men of color (while some thirty-eight to royal slave men). By 1735, the number of royal slave women married to personal slaves had gone up to at least seven females in the village (five resided with their families in Santiago de Cuba; at least one other was able to live with her slave husband and their children in El Cobre; and the remaining one also remained in El Cobre, but it is not clear if her husband did so too). Significantly, three of these seven women married to personal slaves came from the same family or household (and at least one was a daughter of one of the three royal slave women married to personal slaves in 1709, thereby repeating the maternal pattern).[37] In 1735, on the other hand, there were as many as forty-nine royal slave females married to free men of color (and one hundred fifteen to royal slave men).

Yet, despite the relatively rigid status boundaries between royal and personal slaves evinced in these marriage patterns, at least one identifiable case shows that dramatic mobility could also take place in this village and that sometimes these personal slaves could be incorporated into the community. In 1735, Teodoro del Puente was registered in El Cobre's hearth listing as a "slave from [Santiago de] Cuba" who had recently married the royal slave Juana Cruzata. The couple lived in the widow Margarita Adamés's household along with Cruzata's nineteen-year-old son from a previous marriage and with their new children aged one and four. Teodoro del Puente's situation must have represented one of the possible arrangements whereby slaves lived on their own and paid an agreed-upon fee to their master. Or perhaps he was far along in the process of *coartación* (self-manumission), because he was able to reside with his family in El Cobre. Fifteen years later, in 1750, both Puente and Cruzata had manumitted themselves (although not their children) and the couple headed their own complex household of eighteen people, including married and unmarried children, grandchildren, and other relatives. In addition the couple owned two personal slaves: thirty-seven-year-old José Antonio, and twenty-one-year-old Nazaria Magaña, probably José Antonio's wife. Thus, Puente had acquired sufficient mobility since his arrival in the 1730s as a slave not only to head his own household and become free along with his wife but also to become one of only ten slaveholders in the village in 1750. Indeed, Puente's case reveals a former private slave's successful incorporation into the pueblo.

But did the cobreros' personal slaves marry into the community too? During the 1750s and 1760s a few cases can be identified of personal slaves in the village who married royal slaves and set up their own households separate from their masters. Such slaves may have become part of the community by virtue of marriage and residence in a separate household, or even through residence in their spouse's family's household. Antonio José, a slave of the freeman Luis del Río, was married to the twenty-five-year-old royal slave Juana Manuela. The couple had a six-year-old child. The family lived in one of the multifamily households in the village, perhaps in the bride's parental household, alongside the family of one of the daughters of the house. Antonio José's own master, Luis del Río, lived with his own family and his brother's family, perhaps as renters, in another multifamily female-headed household in El Cobre, but no kinship relation between household head or her family and that of Ríos can be identified. Indeed, it is not even clear if the Ríos family were freed cobreros, or if they were newcomers to El Cobre. In any case, one of their personal slaves married into the community and lived separately with his family.

Similarly, by 1767 Juan Vanegas, a "slave of Captain Cosme," had been married to his wife, the royal slave María Eugenia (forty-two), for many years, and the couple had two adolescent sons both of whom carried their enslaved father's surname (interestingly, Vanegas, not Cosme). They too lived in a large multifamily household, separate from their master. Likewise, Nicholás Medina, "slave of Francisca de Luna," had recently married the fifty-three-year-old widow María de los Remedios González and headed a household with the children of her previous marriage and their own five-month-old child. And then also, Lorenzo de la Caridad, "a slave of the Virgin" (or the sanctuary) headed his own household with his royal slave wife Ana Francisca Sales.

Most interesting of all, however, was the case of Manuel Antonio, "esclavo de las González" (slave of the González [sisters]) who in 1750 was married not to a royal slave, but to a free cobrera named Juana Quiala. By then, Manuel Antonio also headed his own family's household. Because of their mother's status, the couple's twelve children were all free: they ranged in age from ten months to twenty-one years of age. The Gonzálezes who "owned" Manuel Antonio were Jacintha González and her sisters who had inherited the slave (then nineteen years old) in 1735 from their own father Simón González. Ironically, Manuel Antonio eventually married a freewoman (or she manumitted herself) and his children were free, while his own masters, the González sisters, remained royal slaves.

Thus the line between cobreros and personal slaves may have sometimes become blurred and transformed into that of neighbor and neighbor in this pueblo where personal slaves sometimes married community members and became part of their spouses' families. Although it is not clear how common these cases were, at least those cases where intermarriage took place suggests that the social lines between personal slaves and some cobreros may not have been too rigid.

Conclusion

Although slaveholding was not a widespread social institution in the village of El Cobre, the few cases found point to the existence of family legacies passed down through both male and female lines among these peasant miners. Within the most powerful family in the pueblo, the Cosmes, this type of legacy was transmitted through four generations. Slaveholding families exhibited a remarkable degree of continuity that may have extended to other kinds of property such as farms, houses, and other movable property. These rural villagers shared inherited familial property especially in the form of village houses, and in some cases of slaves, but as noted in Chapter

6, it is more unclear how they did so with land. Spouses sometimes kept distinct ownership rights over inherited property that may have strengthened cognate kinship ties. How distinct conjugal rights over property may have translated into actual household power relations and control over that property is not clear, however.

Although the inheritance patterns generally fell within the framework of Spanish law, local (and perhaps regional, islandwide, or sectoral) adaptations of that law not only allowed royal slaves to own and bequeath slaves and property, but may have also stressed distinct conjugal rights between spouses and given particular gender inflections to the type of property transmitted across generations. Whether these local emphases in transmission practices constituted simple adaptations of Spanish law or an altogether different shift into an alternate system cannot be ascertained from the available material. Comparison with other landholding and inheritance traditions in other villages in Cuba and among other ethnic groups would be extremely helpful in determining the pan-Caribbean (or other) character of El Cobre's customary traditions. In short, the bricolage that may have gone into the making and shaping of these hybrid local traditions requires further research into wider island and ethnic patterns, heterogeneous African, Caribbean, and Spanish American commonalities and differences.

Perhaps the best way to approach the material at this point is on its own terms, for what it can suggest about this reconstituted rural community of king's slaves: the de facto recognition of an extreme right to hold, own, and inherit property even in the form of slaves, the existence of kin legacies and rights, as well as of transmission traditions. The main point is that such property rights and familial traditions were tolerated by authorities and operated in this community at least since the turn of the eighteenth century, if not before. Unfortunately, there is no trace in the record of the extent to which these slaveholding practices, particularly among royal slaves, may have been a contested issue or an entitlement claim at any point in local history. Finally, there is no real trace in the written record of how masters and slaves in this community may have imagined their places in the local social order. Some evidence suggests social boundaries that were fluid; however, at least in terms of the possibility of marrying into the community, not enough can be culled to understand the character of personal slavery in this local community. Silences in the record foreclose those interrogations.

Copper Mining

A Small, Independent, and
Predominately Female Local Industry

To the present, the greatest amount of copper that is
gathered comes from the river that crosses the
middle of the pueblo, some in grains, other in rock
(which is the one that is smelted), . . . to this only
the women are dedicated and are the ones who
search in the deeper pools of the said river.
 — Don Joseph Palacios de Saldustum, July 31, 1739

The elder cobrero miners do not have any
inclination toward the profession of their fathers,
and it should be noted that the women occupy
themselves in the separation of the minerals but the
men say that they are farmers [*agricultores*].
 — Don José de Aguilés, August 31, 1838

Intendant Don José de Aguilés's expression of regret that elder cobrero miners no longer manifested any inclination toward the occupation of their
fathers was an anachronistic misconception. Although their distant enslaved
ancestors had indeed been miners, for more than a century and a half most
cobreros — particularly male cobreros — had worked and identified themselves as farmers. Indeed, after the confiscation of the mines, it was the
women and youths of the community, and not the men, who with or without inclination, had become the (surface) copper miners of El Cobre. This
feminized occupational tradition, as the Intendant noted, continued into the
nineteenth century, albeit under a different set of conditions. With the
exception of some skilled workers and petty merchants who were men,
women (cobreras) and their children mainly sustained the informal, but sig-

nificant, local mining industry that emerged in this rural village and that gave El Cobre its dual character as both a peasant and a mining community.

As the former private slaves of Santiago del Prado began to reconstitute themselves as a peasant pueblo of king's slaves, they also began to reshape the formerly large mining industry by feminizing it, turning to surface mining, working informally on their own account, and producing mostly for a domestic market. Despite the more pivotal role of agriculture in the village's internal subsistence economy, and its ideological preeminence in confrontations with the state, the copper-mining activities of the community may have been more significant in the regional economy at the time. Throughout the late seventeenth and eighteenth centuries, the cobreros became not only the main, but with the exception of some minor interruptions, the sole producers of copper in Cuba, mining, smelting, working, and selling the metal on their own account. The petty character of mining production in their village did not prevent these royal slaves from supplying a considerable regional market; in fact, their sales extended islandwide and, at times, throughout the Caribbean. While in eighteenth-century Jamaica slaves working on their own account controlled the islandwide market in agricultural staples,[1] the royal slaves of El Cobre came to control the market in copper in Cuba.

Reshaping Copper Mining and Recasting Identities

As the reader may recall from Chapter 2, the *mandador* Nicholás Montenegro had been one of the primary (and most biting) local chroniclers of El Cobre in the early 1670s. With his critical eye toward the rapidly changing world of the mining settlement, Montenegro (or his amanuensis) had occasion to hint at—and satirize—the newly emerging local mining order. He remarked sardonically, "They sit in the thrones with their cushions while their children engage in gathering copper and they give them tasks by pounds of copper as if they were their own slaves."[2] Montenegro ironically distorted the taxing labor of collecting rocks, tailings, and nuggets by portraying the cobreros as comfortably laid-back royalty assigning production quotas to their slaves. His parody, however distorted, was revealing in yet another way. In his real or assumed bewilderment regarding the transformations of private slaves into king's slaves he painted the world as having turned upside down. The appropriation of the mines (or their ore) and the independent mining activity taking place among the cobreros symbolically put the former slaves in the owner's or master's place. Parental authority over their children, which slaves had generally been deprived of due to the preeminence of the master's rights, was now reestablished by the early incorporation of children into the family economy, here portrayed as the cobreros' reenactment of a master-slave tie. Apart from the negative significations with which Montenegro depicted the slaves mining on their own account, he succeeded in delineating succinctly the major contours of this mining activity: the daily small-scale production measured by the pound; the active part of muchachos in the informal economy; the family-based character of this activity; and the independent basis of the production process once there was no master, overseer, or employer to supervise, afflict, or oppress the royal slaves engaged in this activity.[3] Indeed, Montenegro dramatized what he perceived to be the significant (and, to him, negative) social implications of the reorganization of mining production in El Cobre. He unwittingly pointed to the social and cultural effects of the dual "peasant-miner breach" that the transformation into royal slaves and the appropriation of mining resources was producing among his fellow slaves. He may also have been alarmed at the pace of change and at how that "breach" rapidly became custom and gave way to a sense of entitlement.

The parish priest Don Pedro de Cerquera, another chronicler critical of changes at that time, also reported to his former private employers what was happening with *their* copper in the settlement:

Today there is the best fair [business] from the river's copper and from the tailings which are sold in exchange for the molasses, tobacco, clothes, soap, and other things that those who wish to buy want. A lot of [copper] has been extracted and until now it keeps on being smelted and it will be so until it is finished. For I promise you that there is no one, old and young, who has not been able to put on shoes in exchange for copper.[4]

Cerquera's observations focused on the exchange value of copper that enabled the cobreros to insert themselves in a market economy and allowed them to buy what they could not directly produce themselves. These were supplementary goods to what were considered fundamental staples—cassava and meat—which in a subsistence economy were directly produced by household members. Montenegro concurred with the priest's observations regarding the royal slaves' connection to the market through their newly acquired access to the copper ore, and the metal's marketable possibilities, concluding: "Indeed, my Lady, copper is the currency that nowadays moves around in the mines."[5]

But Cerquera's ironic remark about the cobreros' (real or exaggerated) consumption of shoes also succinctly symbolized the cultural and social changes taking place in the settlement and hinted at some of the implications of commodity production and insertion in a market economy.[6] His comment suggested that whereas before the mining slaves of El Cobre normally went barefoot, it had now become a widespread (status-enhancing) custom among the royal slaves to wear shoes. Cerquera also used the trope of the shoes to signify (and protest) the current prosperity in the settlement, one that hinged on the slaves' recent appropriation of his former employers' property under the tacit approval of the governor. Whether or not he was aware of the significance of his words, however, Cerquera's remark pointed as well to the cobreros' industry and intense productivity when laboring on their own account and to the transforming possibilities of their labor power when not constricted by the usual impediments of slavery.

Yet the new, expanded possibilities of commodity exchange also presupposed a laborious productive process not apparent in Cerquera's and Montenegro's accounts. In 1709, parish priest Don Juan Antonio Pérez described that productive process, but he did not convey a sense of any mining-related prosperity in the village as the previous chroniclers had done. On the contrary, where Montenegro and Cerquera painted a picture of abundance, of almost hectic production and self-indulgent consumption, Pérez observed an arduous production process barely sufficient to meet subsistence needs. Pérez wrote to the Crown:

To subsist, some of them ingeniously search for copper grains among the tailings that remain from the time of the mines; and they also extract it industriously from the rocks that had been thrown away during the searches leading to the discovery of [new] veins of copper [during the high days of mining activity, and these rocks] near the veins had some degree of metal, but since at that time the main thing was to follow the vein of metal, the surrounding rock was not valued by the administrator, and in that way, with a lot of sweat and work they have reduced some arrobas [1 arroba = 25 pounds] of copper to feed and clothe themselves.[7]

The discrepancies between the two clergymen's accounts lay partly in the agendas of the writers and partly in the realities of the different periods in which they wrote. I will return to the "prosperity" issue and to the political subtexts running through these accounts. At this point, suffice it to say that, despite implicit agendas, Pérez's account also has referential value for the fairly detailed description it provides of the cobreros' mining practices and the sources of the ore they worked.

The cobreros' petty mining activities consisted, then, in extracting value from the slag-heaps left over from the more prosperous export-mining days. In those former years when deep mining had concentrated on working the veins, the metal content of the ore must have been very high, for even the tailings that the cobreros still collected and recycled in the mid-1730s had about a 20 to 30 percent copper content.[8] Of these (finite) tailings there had been in the 1670s "great piles that looked like mountains and they were made when the mines were being worked."[9] Through the years these mounds were leveled off so that roughly a century later an observer could state, "The terrain [is now] flat."[10] In effect, the depletion of precisely those mounds of discarded ore—the ones Father Cerquera was referring to when he reported that "a lot of copper has been extracted and keeps being smelted and will be so until it is finished"—may have affected any "prosperity" based on copper mining that was sustaining the community at the time Cerquera and Montenegro wrote. In that sense, the somewhat contrasting representations drawn up by the participant observers of the early 1670s and of 1709 may not have been completely the result of underlying constructs and political agendas.

Aside from this discarded ore, the cobreros also drew copper from small deposits left on the bank of the shallow river that traversed the village. By the 1730s the river, and not so much the tailings, seems to have been the most important source of copper in the village. Years later a royal official making a report on copper mining in El Cobre stated:

The copper that is gathered in the pueblo . . . proceeds from the River that passes through the middle [of the village] and when the river rises, it brings grains; and the experienced women (because the men do not dedicate themselves [to this]) probe and find in the deposits that it leaves the small pieces of vein that they collect and when they have a portion of about 8 or 10 arrobas they smelt it. . . . They do the same probing the old terrain and a stream that runs behind the Sanctuary of Our Lady of Charity. . . .[11]

After collecting the small rocks from the river and the tailings surrounding the mines the women and youths had to grill, wash, and crush their booty into pieces the size of a hazelnut in order to separate as much mineral from the rocks as possible. Sometimes they even made homemade kilns in holes on their patios to process their harvest.[12] The copper nuggets found by the river and the copper separated from the rocks were the commodities sold or exchanged by the pound in El Cobre. The preliminary mining process dominated by women and young people came to an end at this point. The more skilled and remunerative stages of the local industry, as well as some of its distribution aspects, then passed into men's hands.

The Female Aspects of Copper Mining

Although it is not clear whether in the earlier decades of the cobreros' takeover of petty mining production the activity was already a strongly gendered one, by 1711 there were clear observations regarding the gender and age-specific character of the labor force. Montenegro's and Cerquera's accounts leave us with the impression of a gender-blind copper-mining "rush" within the settlement during its early years. But these writers may have been aggregating all mining-related activities, without any nuanced observation of the division of labor. In 1711, however, a former parish priest testified that "he had seen that women and muchachos occupied themselves in opening holes in the parts where there had been ancient copper smeltings, and washed the sand of the river, and broke tailings from where they obtained copper grains which they extracted to sell."[13] He had been parish priest in El Cobre from 1693–1694 and had continued visiting the pueblo frequently afterward; therefore, his memory of women and children as surface miners would place that division of labor even further back into the 1690s. Similarly, in 1731, Alonzo Vicente, a cobrero familiar with everyday life in the village, explicitly stated, "Everyday the women and muchachos are around with sticks choosing the heaviest rocks . . . and they have the same occupation in the stream known as of the Mines and with the tailings remaining from the old foundries."[14] Vicente's account still made reference to old tailings as a source of ore, making it clear that in the early 1730s they had not yet completely disappeared; but most reports emphasized the riverbank itself as the most constant source of copper.[15]

It is difficult to determine whether the labor-intensive aspects of this informal local mining industry had been regarded as work for women and minors from the very beginning, or if the sexual division of labor reported in 1711 was the result of a more gradual feminization of this work. A slave inventory of 1647 shows that a good proportion of slave women in the settlement possessed hammers used to crush ore.[16] This they continued doing once they had expanded their activities into surface mining on their own account; and they would do it anew when employed by a foreign mining company in the nineteenth century. Perhaps female domination of surface mining activities, particularly at the riverbank, had its origin further back in time, back to practices brought from West Africa by the cobreros' ancestors. In many places on the African continent, including the Congo region, men worked in deep mining, but women and children did the surface gathering as well as the washing and sorting of the ore.[17]

Although the traditional sexual division of labor in the mining settlement may have facilitated women's movement into the labor-intensive collection of tailings after the confiscation of the mines and to the immediate feminization of the entire pre-smelting process, nevertheless it may be true that during the early years when royal slaves first obtained access to the tailings, the "copper rush" involved both males and females, maybe whole families—at least on a part-time basis. But, according to one possible scenario, as the initial "prosperity" diminished along with the mounds of tailings, as the population grew, and as the cultural spheres of work in the pueblo became more sharply defined, men turned their energies almost exclusively to farming and to traditional activities of breeding and hunting animals. Furthermore, as the labor draft system for the royal fortification projects became a reality in the 1690s, and males in particular were systematically removed from the community for extended periods of time, they may have found less time to engage in activities other than farming and hunting. As males entrenched themselves as peasants within this labor sphere, the females and their children may have moved on to control the mining sector of the internal economy more firmly.

Copper gathering may have been particularly attractive to women because it was an activity performed in the vicinity of village houses—in the material and cultural space most strongly associated with females—and it did not require long-distance displacements to outlying *estancias* (farms). Women and children residing in the village could set themselves to work whenever they needed or wanted income or had time off from other obligations. They could thereby control and regulate their work rhythms. In addition, surface copper mining may have been attractive insofar as it constituted a "no-risk" economic activity not particularly subject to seasonal constraints, to the vagaries of the climate, to the ravages of epidemics, or to the dangers of deep mining. Furthermore, copper provided guaranteed access to the market in the village, and in Santiago de Cuba as well—and thus to products that may have otherwise been difficult for women to obtain.

Whether the sexual division of labor within the mining sector of the local economy took shape immediately after the confiscation of the mines or more gradually through the years, by the 1730s contemporaries could construe the cobreros' claims to copper deposits in the village precisely in terms of females' self-provisioning needs, while men, particularly *patres familias*, worked for the state. It was as if while the males as providers had usufruct rights over the land resources of the community, the females as providers had claims over the copper. In 1731, for instance, when the cobreros fled to the mountains to protest Governor Don Pedro Ignacio Ximénez's labor requisitions, as well as the shortage of land and the rental of Barajagua, they also decried the governor's attempt to tax "a fifth of the copper that their wives and children washed from the leftovers of the river for their food and necessities . . . to sustain themselves while their husbands worked in the royal construction projects."[18] Indeed, this constituted an explicit formulation of females' provisioning role, if only a provisional one while the *pater familias* was working outside the village. Additionally, this was a relatively acceptable gendered provisioning role that did not threaten males' control of land, spheres of work, and social identity.

Particularly in the case of the few women who headed households where there were no adult sons, sons-in-law, or attached males, copper mining could provide them with the currency to buy subsistence goods that they or their dependents could not directly produce. Women married to royal slaves whose husbands and sons had to leave the village for two weeks each month to work in the fortification projects, were in a similar situation. Although, as mentioned before, manioc farming and production was considered a male occupation, women often functioned as *estancieras* (farmers) producing the agricultural staples after they married and when they became widows. What females could not, or would not, do was hunt (*montear*), the most important way of procuring meat in the village. Given the centrality of meat in the island's diet during the eighteenth century and its importance in the subsistence household economy, the fact that the sexual division of labor proscribed females from procuring this staple directly was a problem. Men sometimes hunted wild hogs in the *monte* (hills) before departing for work in the fortification projects of Santiago de Cuba so that they could leave their large "families of wife and many children . . . something to eat."[19] But when that was not possible or sufficient, women and youths could provision themselves with meat through the market in Santiago de Cuba, or in the village itself, by producing and trading copper as a commodity. With the copper obtained in a day's work by the riverbank, women and adolescents could buy for themselves and their families 5 to 6 pounds of red meat in Santiago de Cuba, or 2 to 4 pounds in periods of drought and scarcity;[20] and they could produce the other foodstuffs such as manioc for cassava, onions, squashes, and plantains in the family farms and eggs and milk in their backyards.

The liquidity of copper as a scarce commodity in the regional market, then, must have given it an important place in the household economy. When not exchanged for basic subsistence goods, this locally produced metal could also play a supplementary role in the household economy by bringing in commodities such as soap, unrefined sugar, tobacco, clothes, or even the shoes described by an earlier priest. And despite the portrayals of this economic activity as a woman's way of supporting her family or contributing to her household, for many women (and youths) copper mining would have constituted an important independent source of income with which to buy clothing, hair ribbons, handkerchiefs, rosaries, small pieces of jewelry, ceramics, petty commodities of the sort females in the village owned, and perhaps even, in some cases, the silver laces for Sunday-best skirts that Nicholás Montenegro decried.[21] Nonetheless, copper mining seems to have provided women and adolescents with only a small income — one from which it was difficult to accumulate enough savings to procure that most valued and expensive "commodity" of all: freedom.

Copper mining was sufficiently important to elicit from three out of eight women a self-identification as a "copper gatherer" when interrogated by the authorities in 1737.[22] It did not, however, seem to have been a full-time economic activity for the women and youths of the pueblo, at least not by the 1770s. Although copper production was as high as ever in the 1770s, none of the females (or youths) for whom an occupation was registered in the village census of 1775 was identified as a "copper gatherer."[23] Instead, the overwhelming majority of females with a nonagricultural occupation were poorly paid seamstresses.[24] Whether sewing constituted an encompassing symbolic occupational category connoting domestic activities in general, or whether it referred here to another extended, market-oriented female industry in the village is impossible to say. It is not clear why copper gathering was no longer included as an occupational category in the 1775 census, but one may suppose that it was because by then the women in this village combined several occupational activities at the same time, of which part-time copper mining was only one. Indeed, this informal, almost casual aspect is what lent the small-scale industry its truly autonomous character with no overseers, masters, or employers to afflict cobreros with production schedules. It may well have also been a reflection of the low income-generating power of the activity.

Political Subtexts: Their Social and Material Implications (A Parenthesis)

As mentioned previously, there were some representational discrepancies in the accounts of local chroniclers in 1677 and 1709 that were related to the way the role and effects of copper mining among the cobreros was depicted, particularly regarding the alleged "prosperity." Coloring and politicizing these chroniclers' representations was a significant issue—a dispute over the cobreros' right to mine the ore versus the state's right to tax the latter's mining activities or to prohibit them altogether. To be sure, the conflict over mining rights and taxation never acquired the force or intensity that confrontations over land and labor requisitions did in this village. Instead, on the occasions in which the right to mine freely became an explicitly contested issue, it seems to have been as part of a larger cluster of grievances.

As early as 1672, the *mandador* Nicholás Montenegro complained to Governor Don Andrés de Magaña that the royal slaves claimed the tailings of the mines were the king's and refused to acknowledge them as his mistress's private property. According to Montenegro, the governor ignored these protestations. This official indifference and neglect had itself constituted a precedent that petty surface mining activities among the royal slaves in the settlement ought not to be taxed. In this context, then, Montenegro's and Father Cerquera's texts acquired a new political meaning. Indeed, these early participant observers emphasized the profitability of copper mining in order to call attention to the alleged benefits of which the rightful owners of the mines were being despoiled without even the possibility of taxing production. As the reader may recall from Chapter 2, Montenegro and Cerquera had also been critical of the alleged "disorder" that the new mining order under Governor Magaña brought about. Thus, implicit in the *mandador*'s report of the governor's failure to heed his complaint was also a critical depiction of Magaña as a royal representative incapable even of looking after the interests of the Crown through a taxation order. In this sense, Cerquera and Montenegro were evoking a picture of the slaves as usurping and stealing the bounty of the mines. The political implication of their accounts was a call for the prohibition of independent slave mining on the master's property account, or at least a proper taxation of their "profits."

Pérez's account, by contrast, constituted a reaction (and protest) against Governor Don Joseph Canales's harsh policies toward the community in 1708–1709. The governor had criminalized the cobreros' extraction and sale of copper, prohibited these activities under confiscation of property and death penalties, and proceeded to despoil them of all their working tools and to burn down the smelting workshop in the village. In defense of his parishioners, Pérez stressed the bare subsistence surface character of the cobreros' mining activity, thereby legally and morally delegitimizing the governor's prohibition. The parish priest's detailed description of the surface mining aspect of the activities aimed to emphasize that there was neither deep mining taking place in the village, nor the opening of new mines that would mean defrauding the royal treasury. Gathering tailings and taking what the river brought them were not transgressive mining activities; furthermore, it was arguable whether they could properly be considered mining, where that work had once required the extraction of copper from the subsoil.[25]

Finally, Pérez also laid out in his account another basis for the cobreros' legitimate right to mine copper, or at least to extract it from the tailings and the riverbanks. His was an argument similar to that often invoked by the cobreros to stake out their claims on the land, particularly when they defended their corporate right to the territory of Barajagua. According to Pérez, since it was the master's legal duty to provide for his slaves but the Crown was not provisioning them, the king's slaves in effect had a right to the use of these resources as their only lawful means of subsistence. Years later, during a struggle over taxation, this time with Ximénez, the cobreros would articulate this right in their own words by protesting that "the Governor wants to deprive us of the *desperdicios* [wastes] that our Master has given us for our maintenance."[26]

As already pointed out, these resources were construed in particular as the female slaves' means of subsistence, especially when their spouses were away working for the Crown. Thus, from this perspective, the cobreros were not thieves and usurpers of the master's property and of the bounties of the mines as Montenegro had suggested. On the contrary, they were the victims of those governors who, by taxing their copper-mining activities—or worse, prohibiting them—became usurpers of the slaves' bare means of subsistence. The over- or underplaying of the effects of the cobreros' copper-mining activities in these accounts indeed had concrete political and material implications. They also had a bearing on the representation of slaves as dangerously affluent or as dangerously indigent (as when Pérez portrayed them as obliged to eat "wild fruit"). Yet, despite their different political orientations and assumptions of what constituted "prosperity," these accounts may well have relied on a similar assumption: slave status was incompatible with "affluence"; slaves might have a right to subsistence, but they had no right to produce surplus wealth for themselves. While the sight of slaves running a small informal mining industry may have been unconventional in colonial times, the grounds upon which it was publicly attacked or defended seem to have been conventional.

These early texts, and the interpretive problems they present, are emblematic not only of the complexity of the issues behind their production but also of the difficulties historians face in making sense of the past and producing our own historical pictures. It is not an easy matter, for instance, to determine how much "prosperity" the cobreros' mining activities produced in the village's internal economy or, for that matter, to determine what prosperity represented, and for whom.

The Male-Controlled Aspects of the Industry: Who Benefited from Cheap Labor?

While women and adolescents dedicated themselves to the labor-intensive activities of gathering the small and scattered mineral deposits and then separating them from the ore, it was the men who were the smelters, metal smiths, and retailers of this local copper industry. More specifically, the productive and marketing processes became concentrated in the hands of a few men in El Cobre—free and slave.[27] It is difficult to know the relationship between village retailers and the outside market. But if anyone in the pueblo seems to have been able to accumulate some wealth or achieve some "prosperity" from copper mining, it was these few artisans and petty merchants. Furthermore, not only were these male occupations in the local mining industry controlled by officers of the village militias, but they seem to have been dominated to a considerable extent by members of a particular family, the Vicentes.[28] Even in this small corner of the Spanish Empire, military rank seems to have walked hand in hand with socioeconomic advantage, and these masculine ties were often reinforced through kinship bonds.[29]

The concentration of the final processes of the mining industry in the hands of a few individuals in the village, men who also seem to have been able to obtain higher returns and accumulate some savings, represents one form of a sexual division of labor that clearly dated to the early years after the confiscation of the mines. In 1672, slave chronicler Montenegro noted that Juan de Santiago Vicente "was the major smelter [in El Cobre], . . . he has in his house a smelting workshop."[30] Montenegro estimated that Santiago Vicente had smelted more than 40 quintals (1 quintal = 100 pounds) of copper. In addition, the blacksmith Pedro Viojo had also accumulated more than 40 quintals of copper either to sell as metal or as finished products. Thus in only one or two years these two men by themselves had obtained from 40 to 80 quintals. Montenegro also wrote that Viojo had become so "wealthy and arrogant" that he had undertaken the task of sustaining the families of some royal slaves who had gone to litigate for land in

Havana in 1672.[31] The master smelter Santiago Vicente also seems to have been able to accumulate a small "fortune" (it is not clear if the "wealth" came only from smelting) for, although appraised along with Montenegro at the astonishing price of 1,000 pesos in 1677, he had succeeded in manumitting himself by 1709. As noted in Chapter 2, in 1687, Santiago Vicente held the title of captain of the royal slaves of El Cobre, and by 1709 he held the military rank of lieutenant in the already organized militia companies of El Cobre.[32] One wonders if Montenegro himself was ever tempted to become involved in the emerging industry, given that he was a master coppersmith himself.[33]

The forty-six-year-old royal slave (and village alderman) Roque Sánchez, one of the smelters in the village in 1709, also controlled a small capital in the form of property. Like Santiago Vicente before him, Sánchez owned the only smelting workshop with a furnace in El Cobre, one that the village's attorney appraised at 217 pesos and 4 reales (8 reales = 1 peso)—a considerable investment in this poor community.[34] Sánchez was part of the Vicente family through his marriage to Isabel María Vicente—daughter of Lieutenant Santiago Vicente.[35] It would not be far-fetched to think that Santiago Vicente had started his son-in-law up in the smelting business and even passed down his former workshop to Sánchez, who now lived next door to him. Sánchez and Santiago Vicente were not the only members of the Vicente family involved in the mining industry. A generation later, Silvestre Vicente, a free cobrero who named one of his own sons after Juan de Santiago, was one of the few smelters in the village in the 1730s.[36] And another of Silvestre Vicente's sons, Venancio, although apparently not as well off as the others since he remained a royal slave all of his life, was in turn one of the three smelters in the village in 1773.[37] These and other male members of the Vicente family, by blood or marriage, controlled a good part of the skilled work related to the copper-mining industry; and the know-how of the business seems to have been transmitted generationally within their family. Similarly, the copper smelter Alejo Sánchez in 1773 bore the same surname of the smelter Roque Sánchez and may well have been the latter's descendant. This generational continuity within the smelting trade suggests a family- and community-based training and trade transmission process that was independent of the state.[38]

The possibility for some specialized artisans to accumulate savings through the village's small-scale mining industry is more clearly suggested by a parish priest's narration of the unfortunate story of Sergeant Juan de Ojeda. His case shows that the copper industry in El Cobre was not limited to the production and sale of the metal but also included the manufacture and sale of finished products. In 1709, Father Pérez protested to the Crown that the governor's troops had sacked the village, "taking from the blacksmith all his tools, from the coppersmith his smelting instruments [as well as] a copper vat of more than 200 pesos [that he had made] with the intention of selling it to free himself."[39] The sympathetic parish priest was referring to Ojeda's 17.5 arroba copper vat, a piece of work that the village's *apoderado* (legal spokesman or proxy) later appraised at the considerable amount of 218 pesos.[40] It is not clear how Ojeda supplied himself with the necessary ore to smelt and produce this enormous artifact, or how long it had taken him to accumulate it. What is clear, however, is that a considerable amount of copper and money was indeed involved in the project, and this type of skilled work could produce a surplus that could be invested in self-manumission. It is not known if, after the governor's troops took his vat, the sergeant was able to recover it, or even if he was ever able to buy his freedom.[41] By 1731, however, his own slave children had inherited a personal slave named Gervasio—a fact that placed the Ojeda family among the 11 percent of cobrero households in El Cobre that owned one or more slaves at the time.[42] In 1734, at the age of twenty-eight, the sergeant's eldest daughter, María Dorotea Ojeda, was able to buy her freedom for 140 pesos.[43] Despite the loss of his valuable property and with it his freedom in 1709, the coppersmith Sergeant Ojeda was able to accumulate a "small fortune" sufficient to buy a slave and perhaps bequeath some savings to his children. Ojeda had no apparent relation to the Vicente family, but like Lieutenant Santiago Vicente, and Captain Thomás Rodríguez (yet another son-in-law of Santiago Vicente), he was one of the three highest-ranking officers in the village's militia company in 1709.[44]

The retail aspects of the industry were also controlled by a few men in the village. In 1731, the *cabildo* of Santiago de Cuba determined that those "who smelt copper [in El Cobre] pay the *quinto* [the royal fifth tax] since generally these are some private persons who in the said pueblo sell some articles of food as well as clothing."[45] In that same year, for instance, Francisco Farán was one of these copper dealers. He had a shop in the village where he bought by the pound copper brought in by his (female) clients. During a period of thirteen to eighteen years, the considerable sum of 812 pesos and 4 reales had passed through his hands.[46] Another local retailer, who may either have been a more powerful intermediary than Farán, or who may himself (with his family) have been directly involved in different phases of the mining industry was Captain Thomás Rodríguez—another high-ranking officer of the village militia, and a member of the Vicente family by marriage. After buying his freedom in 1705, and marrying another of Lieutenant Santiago Vicente's daughters, Rodríguez spent some years living with his wife at his in-laws' house.[47] By the 1730s, Rodríguez had become an important dealer in the pueblo, capable of controlling different aspects of its trade. In 1737, the cobrero Andrés González reported, "Captain Thomás Rodríguez sends sugar vats to sell in Bayamo in exchange for clothes; and before Holy Week he sent five vats with his sons and Sergeant Patricio Vicente which they took through the forest."[48]

González described here an act of contraband trade carried out by one of the captains of the village militia, his sons, and a military subordinate who was also part of the Vicente family. This smuggling was probably an attempt to evade payment of the royal *quinto* imposed in 1731.[49] That the smugglers traded in Bayamo is not surprising: that city was the most prosperous in the eastern region at the time. Besides the versatility of its agricultural production (including a growing number of sugar mills), Bayamo derived prosperity from a vigorous contraband trade with Jamaica, Saint Domingue, and Curazao. Indeed, Rodríguez may have been shipping off to Bayamo a good portion of the annual copper production of the village, because five copper vats represented a considerable cargo. He may have controlled (or monopolized) the smelting, crafting, and marketing of finished copper products outside the village. The prosperity of his business is suggested too by the fact that he could afford to make such a relatively high investment in clothing as merchandise (probably from contraband trade in Bayamo) for which he presumably had a clientele in the village.

Copper smelting, like other skilled occupations in El Cobre, was never a full-time job. Alejo Sánchez, for instance, was a smelter and a tobacco farmer in the 1770s.[50] Small producers like Sánchez needed to devote just a few days a month to smelting. Larger operations could process more ore in a single smelting, reducing the number of monthly operations required to produce the same yield.[51] But for each one-day smelting operation some eight men were required, a number regarded as excessive by one royal official. According to that official, cobreros at the time were not able to

smelt the metal properly if it is not by force of an imponderable labor and fatigue because [they] only [have] a scarce and remote knowledge that [they] managed to retain from [their] ancestors . . . [and because] there is not among those slaves anyone who can pay for the instruments and tools that are required for the task.[52]

The lack of adequate technology and capital, however, did not just apply to the cobreros' small-scale mining production. It was the scourge of the entire copper-mining industry of Cuba until the nineteenth century.

The Wider Context of Copper Mining

For many years after its takeover of the mining settlement, the Crown tried to find a contractor willing to reactivate the mines, but it could not find anyone willing to take up the challenge. The Crown commissioned a number of feasibility studies, and officials repeatedly pointed to the chronic problems of inadequate technology and lack of capital for investment. Between 1721 and 1732, the Crown undertook a sustained, but short-lived, attempt to exploit the copper mines of Rosario and Bajurayabo, both in the jurisdiction of Havana. Their efforts failed.[53] Personnel to work the mines was imported from across the world: slaves from Africa and free miners and operators from Spain and New Spain. The miners, however, were eventually fired "because of their limited know-how and the excessive costs of their salaries."[54] The Bajurayabo mines produced only 923 arrobas of copper between 1730 and 1732, an average of 77 quintals per year, a figure comparable to the cobreros' own more rudimentary annual production (see Table 6). Although the price paid in Havana for this copper was comparatively high (see Table 7 below), the mines of Rosario and Bajurayabo operated at a loss and soon were closed down due to their "lack of utility."[55] The failed venture seemed to confirm that large-scale copper mining was not cost effective in Cuba.[56] An experiment with a trial smelt carried out as late as 1779 in El Cobre led the royal official in charge to conclude, "It is evident that there is [abundant] copper, but it does not cover the costs [of producing it]."[57]

While the Crown dreamed of larger mining projects, the cobreros continued their unstinting production of copper without the costs of instruments and infrastructure, of imported "experts," of a full-time labor force, or of any kind of management. Considering the simple character of their mining activities — already described through the eyes of contemporaries — the annual production of copper in the village seems surprisingly high. While it is impossible to gauge the exact volume of production, a conservative range of base figures can be established. Table 6 shows the reported range culled from different sources. These figures should be regarded only as approximations that give a general sense of the significance of this mining activity in El Cobre. Overall, they may tend to underrepresent actual production, partic-

TABLE 6

Reported Annual Production of Copper in El Cobre, 1672–1780

	Annual Range
1672	>40-80 quintals*
1713–1731	42-58 quintals
1739	42.5 quintals [425 quintals?]
1732–1755	>31 quintals
1748	175 quintals [?]
1779	75-90 quintals
*1 quintal = 100 pounds	

SOURCES:

1672: Nicholás Montenegro to Doña Paula de Eguiluz y Montenegro, Santiago del Prado, July 7, 1672, AGI-SD 104.

1713–1731: Testimony of Francisco Farán, Santiago de Cuba, [ca. Aug.-Dec. 1731], [untitled cuaderno that came with letter of Governor Ximénez, Dec. 6, 1731], fol. 37, AGI-SD 493.

1739: Report of Don Nicholás Velasco Calderín, Santiago de Cuba, July 31, 1739, AGI-SD 385. Velasco's text reads 1,700 arrobas or 424 quintals annual production which sounds excessive. The figure may be due to a transcription error and the real figure may have been closer to 170 arrobas or 42.5 quintals.

1732–1755: Declared taxed copper figures, Marrero vol. 7:33. The total copper declared for taxation purposes that Marrero estimates for the period 1732–1752 does not coincide with the distributional breakdown that he makes. I have used the higher figure to estimate an annual copper production of 31 quintals.

1748: Barrett 1987, 50. In her brief discussion on copper production in Cuba, Barrett cites an annual production in 1748 of 175 quintals but provides no clear source for the figure. Such a volume of production seems too high, but perhaps it is suggestive of higher production rates than those cited in the documents I have found.

1779: Report of Don Isidro Limonta to Captain General Diego J. Navarro, Santiago de Cuba, Oct. 4, 1779, AGI-Cuba 1231.

ularly after 1730s, when tax evasion and smuggling, such as that carried out by Captain Rodríguez in Bayamo, must have distorted the figures.

Although once the copper produced in El Cobre had ended up in the Crown's artillery foundries in Havana and in Spain, the metal produced in the village was now used to make locally useful products such as kitchen utensils and bells for churches. In 1741, the metal from El Cobre was even used to mint copper coins as a war emergency for a few months.[58] Above all, a steady supply of copper was vital for manufacturing the vats and utensils required for the growing Cuban sugar industry. Copper left the village in ingots weighing one arroba (= 25 pounds) or as finished products to supply the eastern region of the island—particularly the district of Santiago de Cuba and Bayamo, but also Havana.[59]

The cobreros' level of production may have managed to supply a good part of the regional demand for copper—a metal always in short supply in the Spanish Empire—but it was not sufficient to keep up with the increasing needs of the sugar industry of the late eighteenth century. Between 1782 and 1785, Cuba requested and received some 2,300 quintals (an annual average of 575 quintals) of copper from New Spain, which barely met its needs.[60] During the prosperous 1790s, the island imported an annual average of 600 quintals of copper from New Spain.[61] Although production in El Cobre had almost come to a halt in 1781, when most of the royal slave population was removed from the village, a continuation of the annual production of 90 quintals cited for 1778 would have allowed it to supply between 13 and 16 percent of the island's requirement for the 1782–1785 period. After the mid-1790s, when the demand for copper reached its highest point in the eighteenth century, the cobreros would have still been able to provision from 11 to 13 percent of the island's market. During most of the seventeenth century, when the demand for copper was more restrained, the cobreros could have supplied an even greater proportion of the island's total needs. And if the regional market is our point of reference, then the cobreros' production would have supplied most of the demand in Cuba's eastern region.[62] In effect, a royal official in 1739 reported that *this city* [Santiago de Cuba] has supplied itself (and still supplies itself) with the many small portions [of copper] that [the cobreros] collect and smelt to satisfy its needs for vats in the sugar mills and of other necessary works for the service of its houses."[63] The copper also satisfied a wider market, for he added that "[buyers] also come for it from many places in this island as far as Havana and many other parts outside the island."[64] One such external market was the busy port of Cartagena de Indias. As early as 1672, Montenegro reported that 30 quintals of copper ingots had been shipped to that port.[65] Sixty years later, in 1732, the bishop of Cartagena de Indias imported 102 arrobas (25 1/2 quintals) of copper from Santiago de Cuba for church bells in his diocese.[66] Some copper also ended up in Jamaica through the contraband trade.[67]

Prices of Copper: Who Profited from the Local Industry?

The price paid for the copper produced in El Cobre, even during its early days, was (for inexplicable reasons) the lowest in the Spanish Empire, a fact that must have contributed to the further depressing of the industry. Table 7 summarizes the prices of copper in Cuba and elsewhere.

If the prices for the copper produced in El Cobre (or sold in Santiago de

TABLE 7

Official Prices of Copper in Spanish America and
Unofficial Ones in El Cobre (per quintal),** 1610–1780*

	Cuba	New Spain	Peru	El Cobre
1610s	12 pesos and 3 reales	24 pesos		
1710s	16 pesos (Santiago de Cuba)	16 pesos		1.6 pesos
1720s–1730s	25 pesos (Havana)		35 pesos	2 pesos to 2 pesos and 4 reales
	12 pesos (Santiago de Cuba)			5 pesos (Gov. Sucre's proposal)
1779	12 pesos (Santiago de Cuba)			12 pesos [?]
1780		18 pesos		

* Prices paid by the Crown for contracted copper.
** 1 quintal = 100 pounds.

SOURCES: Marrero vol. 3:272, 7:33, and 8:71; Barrett 1987, 28–29; "Tazación," Santiago de Cuba, Jan. 5, 1712, "Demanda," C23, fols. 168–68v, AGI-ESC 93A; Testimony of Francisco Farán, Santiago de Cuba, [ca. Aug.-Dec. 1731] [untitled cuaderno that came with letter of Governor Ximénez, Dec. 6, 1731] fol. 37, AGI-SD 493; Report of Don Diego Peñalver Angulo, Havana, Apr. 15, 1734, fols. 1471–74, AGI-SD 1630; Report of Don Isidro Limonta to Captain General Diego J. Navarro, Santiago de Cuba, Oct. 4, 1779, fols. 1111–13, AGI-Cuba 1231.

Cuba) seem low in relation to prices paid for the metal in Havana, Mexico City, and Lima at different points in time; those paid in El Cobre seem to have been infinitesimal. In 1731, the retailer Farán who traded copper in the village estimated that 812 pesos and 4 reales had been paid for 3,000 arrobas (750 quintals) of copper in El Cobre in the last eight to thirteen years.[68] That meant a price of 1 peso and 6 reales per quintal, compared to 12 to 16 pesos in Santiago de Cuba, and 25 pesos in Havana! Lest it be thought that Farán was mistaken, in 1733 the Royal Council was shocked to learn that the price of copper produced in El Cobre was 18 to 20 reales per quintal (2 1/2 pesos per quintal). Thinking that there may have been a transcription error in the report because the cited price of copper "was too low and it could not be so cheap, for only the costs of excavating, extracting, and smelting should be three or four times greater than the value of 18 silver reales . . . the quintal," the council asked for reconfirmation of the reported price.[69] The source in Cuba, former Governor Matheo López Cangas (1713–1718), explained that such a low price was due to the fact that the copper was produced by the king's slaves who supported themselves with it.[70] Was there a hint here at a taken-for-granted assumption that slaves produced on their own account only for subsistence purposes and at subsistence rates with little or no room for the accumulation of surplus or profit?

Such a low price for copper in El Cobre was possible because of the surface mining character of the small-scale industry that required no costs for excavation and upkeep of the mine. It was also due to the relatively low capital investments in tools and the rudimentary equipment with which the cobreros smelted their copper. In effect, virtually the only costs of production were those of the labor expended in the mining activities—that is, the cobreros' return on their own labor. But given the low price of copper in El Cobre, the cost of labor that went to produce the metal may not even have been based on the ongoing market value of unskilled free labor, but rather on the subsistence cost of the laboring population. Indeed, one royal official estimated in 1739 that for the collected copper nuggets and ore the women "get 1 real of profit a day [or] 2 more or less to eat without having any other cost but their personal labor."[71] One real was considered the equivalent of a day's ration, while 3 reales was the ongoing wage for an unskilled male peon. During most of the eighteenth century, 1 real (by the 1770s, 2 reales) per day was the "payment" that royal slaves received to cover their daily food ration during their two-week draft labor rotations on the fortification projects.[72] Roughly speaking, then, the women miners were earning the equivalent of (or slightly more than) what was officially regarded as the "bare subsistence" income to reproduce the labor force. Thus, although working as free, independent producers, the cobreros, or at least the female and young surface miners, were nonetheless materially earning as slaves.

It is not clear, however, whether the low price of copper cited for El Cobre (as opposed to prices in Santiago de Cuba, for instance) were the prices at which just women and young people in the village sold their product to village retailers (as the retailer Farán suggested); or if those were the prices at which all cobreros—male and female, free and slave, old and young, military or civilian—involved in the copper industry traded. It is difficult to determine just who were the intermediaries pocketing the considerable margins of profit found in the difference between village and city prices (see Table 7 above).

Although cobreros were involved in the retail aspects of the local mining industry, at least in the late 1730s, and perhaps at other points in time, the real leeches of the community were the royal officials assigned there. The cobreros accused Lieutenant Velasco Calderín, stationed in the pueblo after a local uprising, of confabulation with the royal treasury's accountant in Santiago de Cuba, and of exacting copper from them in ways that resembled the infamous *repartimiento de mercancías* or forced distribution of merchandise imposed on Native American subjects elsewhere in the Spanish Indies.[73] The cobreros described this illegal business:

Don Francisco Delgado has put in the power of the said lieutenant many clothes and goods of the kind that they bring from the French [islands] and from Jamaica, and of *aguardiente* that he buys in Cuba and sends to this village; and he forces us to buy them for very high prices in exchange for the copper that we gather. He makes us give him the copper at the prices that he wants, and he impedes us from taking [the copper] to Cuba and selling it to other people to have the advantage. The said accountant sells it over [the price] at which he buys it from us to the English commercial agent.[74]

The accusations were serious: they not only involved extortion of the cobreros but also the involvement of two royal officials in contraband trade with the Jamaicans and the French (a fact that vouches in passing for the underreporting of the figures for copper production in the village). But if the complaint described correctly the operation of outside middlemen in pushing down the local price of copper, it also suggested that this practice constituted a recent breach in custom and that indeed the cobreros, or a few retailers in the community, were used to selling their copper directly and at higher prices to different people in Santiago de Cuba. It may indeed have been the presence of Velasco Calderín in the village that had led Captain Rodríguez at about this same time to send his copper vats to Bayamo through the forest surreptitiously. The cobreros' complaint presumably rested as well upon a claim to a right to operate and trade freely in the market, at least in the regional market outside the village.

Years later, by 1779, in his official report and feasibility study, Limonta stated that the price at which the cobreros sold copper was "3 pesos the arroba [12 pesos per quintal] and sometimes the price goes up to 28 to 30 reales, for it is never expensive, even at 4 pesos the arroba [16 pesos per quintal]."[75] It is not clear just who was selling at those prices, but 12 pesos per quintal would have meant direct access to the market of Santiago de Cuba without the interposition of middlemen, so it may be that by this time the cobreros were selling their copper freely and directly at current prices in that city. What the information does not reveal, either, is whether it was the copper producers themselves, the women and youths of the village, or the local middlemen such as Captain Rodríguez a generation before, who were the beneficiaries of the high market prices in Santiago de Cuba.

An Enlightened Proposal

At least one royal official in the 1720s saw the advantage of low village prices and sought to capitalize on them. Perhaps the most sensible, but also the most radical, proposal was that made by Governor Don Carlos Sucre (1723–1728) in 1724. It reflected what could have been an alternative and more profitable productive mining enterprise, if particular interests and conventional notions had been set aside. Sucre, whom the cobreros considered a friendly governor, informed Cuba's captain general in Havana that he was in the process of making an *asiento* (a provisioning contract or agreement) with the cobreros: it required that they sell all the copper produced to the Crown at 10 reales per arroba (or 5 pesos per quintal). He suggested the Crown give them assistance for mining tools and implements and seek funds with which to make the initial purchases of the metal promptly, "so that moved by interest they would feel stimulated [to produce]."[76] Significantly, the governor was not coercing the Crown's own slaves to produce for their master, but instead sought to motivate them as independent producers through the free-market logic of "self interest." Moreover, by referring to the deal he had cut with the royal slaves as an *asiento*, the governor marked this as a most unconventional formal transaction between master and slave, or for that matter between free persons and slaves anywhere. By providing them with mining tools—perhaps with a shift back into deep mining in mind—and by offering the cobreros a higher price for their copper (as well as their labor), Governor Sucre sought to expand production. In fact, wittingly or unwittingly, this scheme constituted an attempt to ease the degree of "exploitation" of the cobreros' labor by intermediaries, and to become himself (or to make the state) the main intermediary—thereby benefiting the surface miners against those private retailers who controlled the market. If, despite low returns on their labor—or specifically on the labor of women and youths—and a very rudimentary technology, the cobreros had been able to sustain a small but significant production level for so many years, it was reasonable to suppose that higher prices for their products and capital for their tools might reactivate production. Indeed, Governor Sucre's proposal was a sensible attempt to support and stimulate

El Cobre's small-scale mining industry. His was a modest effort that may have reaped much benefit for the Crown (and perhaps for himself too).

The governor was also seeking, of course, to monopolize the supply of copper for the Crown at an extremely beneficial price. If the Crown bought copper at the ongoing prices in Santiago de Cuba, it would have had to pay 12 pesos per quintal. Thus, the royal interest was better served by dealing directly with the cobreros. If the price of copper in El Cobre was 1 peso and 6 reales to 2 pesos and 5 reales per quintal at the time (Table 7), then the governor's rate would have increased the cobreros' earnings from copper by about 100 percent while still saving the Crown a great deal of money. Furthermore, given the production rates and copper prices at the Rosario and Bajurayabo mines near Havana about this time (Table 7), the governor's scheme made even more sense, at least in principle since the opportunities for graft were also multiple. Just at the time when the island's captain general was showing interest in the proposal, however, Governor Sucre's administration term came to an end.[77] His successor and enemy, the feared Governor Ximénez followed no such "enlightened" policies. Instead, Ximénez sought to benefit the Crown by prohibiting the royal slaves from extracting copper freely while taxing them the royal *quinto*, and later collecting taxes on the smelted copper from its buyers.[78]

Indeed, though it made no sense for Governor Ximénez to prohibit the production of that valuable commodity as he first intended, he persisted in handicapping production by taxing the smelting and sale of the metal. Policies aimed at extracting surplus for the Crown through taxes where there was little surplus to be found in the first place tended to discourage further production, or to drive much of it underground. Although the local mining industry survived this period, legally reported production does seem to have declined (see Table 6). It is difficult to say what Governor Sucre's more unconventional proposal would have yielded; but it was quickly forgotten as the former governor, himself a victim of his successor, wasted away incommunicado in a cell at the El Morro garrison.[79]

Conclusion

For several decades before the Crown's takeover of the Real de Minas, mining production had already undergone a precipitous decline as an export industry in Santiago del Prado. Although after the confiscation of the mines El Cobre became a predominantly peasant village, the king's slaves continued producing the metal on their own account. Copper production in El Cobre supplied domestic markets mainly in the Oriente region, but it was also sold abroad through the circuits of the Caribbean contraband trade. In this sense, the cobreros' local economy was articulated into that of a wider region. The main beneficiaries of this industry included merchants and royal officials who profited from cheap local costs and much higher market prices. Consumers, particularly those in the sugar industry, also benefited by providing themselves with a relatively scarce metal for the vans in their sugar mills at relatively low prices. The cobreros' local mining industry did not benefit the Crown directly because it never developed the mechanisms to buy or market the copper itself. Only after the taxation of the royal fifth was imposed after the 1730s did the Crown derive some minimal benefits, but production was never high enough to amount to much profit for the royal coffers.

Aside from its economic significance, mostly at a regional level, this informal copper industry had an even greater sociocultural significance at the local level. I have suggested that mining production did not generate much local "prosperity," particularly as far as the female primary producers went, but it may have created a greater "affluence" (relatively speaking) for the smaller group of men who controlled the processing, manufacturing, and retail selling of the metal. Although in general this economic activity may not have permitted an escape from material poverty for most of these villagers, it had other important sociocultural, even political, implications that could and were construed as forms of freedom. At the most basic level, the royal slaves' mining practices entailed the opportunity—and the decision—to produce a particular commodity, a prerogative not usually available to other slaves. Furthermore, the cobreros defended their (often contended) right to appropriate resources freely from the royal mining jurisdiction. Moreover, the royal slaves were free to organize production on their own terms, and to control it at their own rhythms of work without any external direct pressure or supervision. Finally, the cobreros were free to operate within the market sphere. They sold their own produce (here the ideal of selling wherever they wanted and to the highest bidder was often curtailed, but some cobreros articulated that ideal as a prerogative of which they were being deprived), and bought as "consumers" in the market more or less what they could and chose within their restricted economic means. In short, the cobreros' informal copper-mining activities blurred rigid lines between slavery and freedom in yet another sphere of practical life in this corner of the Caribbean.

Copper mining was another strongly gendered sphere of working life in El Cobre. Surface-mining activities were women's (and children's) work, or rather they were labor and business activities that fell within the female domain. The relatively easy access to the market that these mining activities offered gave cobrera women a greater autonomy, for these productive activities enabled them to provide themselves and their families with commodities that were otherwise difficult for them to produce directly. Ultimately, it was this feminized sector of the cobreros' internal economy that was most fully articulated into the wider economy of the region.

CHAPTER 9

The Unbreachable Burdens of Bondage

Laboring as the King's Slaves

What motivates us to stop working is the great
necessity and the rigor with which you treat us and
by that [requested] edict you will see how the King
Our Master accommodates us [*nos hace
conveniencia*] and gives us rest and [orders] that we
be given good treatment which you haven't given
us . . . because other Governors before you haven't
treated us like this and as long as you don't give us
what our master has given us . . . we will maintain
the stoppage.

—Royal Slaves to Governor Don Pedro
Ignacio Ximénez, ca. 1731

Numerous generations of cobrero families left their imprint upon the sev-
enteenth- and eighteenth-century fortification structures still standing in the
environs of Santiago de Cuba. Year in and year out, throughout most of
their laboring history, the king's slaves left their village for short periods of
time to build and repair the city's garrisons (see Map 2 in the Preamble). At
the construction projects, royal slaves toiled alongside penal convicts, some
free laborers, rented or donated slaves, and sometimes also neighboring
Indians, alleged vagabonds, and other conscripted workers.[1] As slaves to the
king, the cobreros extracted and transported stone from lime furnaces,
denuded the surrounding forests, broke ground for buildings, and built
defensive structures.[2] These towers, castles, and garrisons stand today as
enduring spectacles of a colonial Hispanic past that is representative of "tradition"—at times also of "action and adventure"—for many Cubans (see
Figures 11 and 12 as well as Map 4). Local people regard these fortifications
as the Spanish Caribbean's "pharaonic" constructions; for them the struc-

FIGURE 11. Colonial fortification system in a Caribbean military frontier. El Morro (San Pedro de la Roca) garrison protected the entrance to the Bay in Santiago de Cuba. Early-twentieth-century postcard. (Courtesy of the Cuban Heritage Collection, Richter Library of the University of Miami)

tures evoke the island's preplantation role as the "llave del Nuevo Mundo," the key to the New World. (Garrisons and castles of the colonial past also constitute an intrinsic part of the safe and respectable images sold in the "family" tourism industry of the present.) Contrary to the case with sugar, and despite years of Marxist culture in Cuba, next to nothing exists in the oral (or written) narratives of these formidable structures—now considered monuments—that speaks to the labor process and modes of production which went into their making.[3] There are few histories, stories, or even interrogations about who actually built these garrisons in the Oriente region. For one thing, there is little association in the regional imaginary between old families of El Cobre and the workforce of El Morro (San Pedro de la Roca), La Estrella, or other defensive structures of the region.

It was for the most part the forced labor the cobreros performed in these massive fortification works that defined them as slaves, yet the arrangements under which they toiled during most of the eighteenth century were unusually flexible as compared to bonded labor regimes elsewhere or even to more abstract Spanish slave codes.[4] Although the forced labor regime under which the king's slaves of El Cobre lived echoed the spirit of the most "benevolent" Spanish slave codes, in some important ways that customary

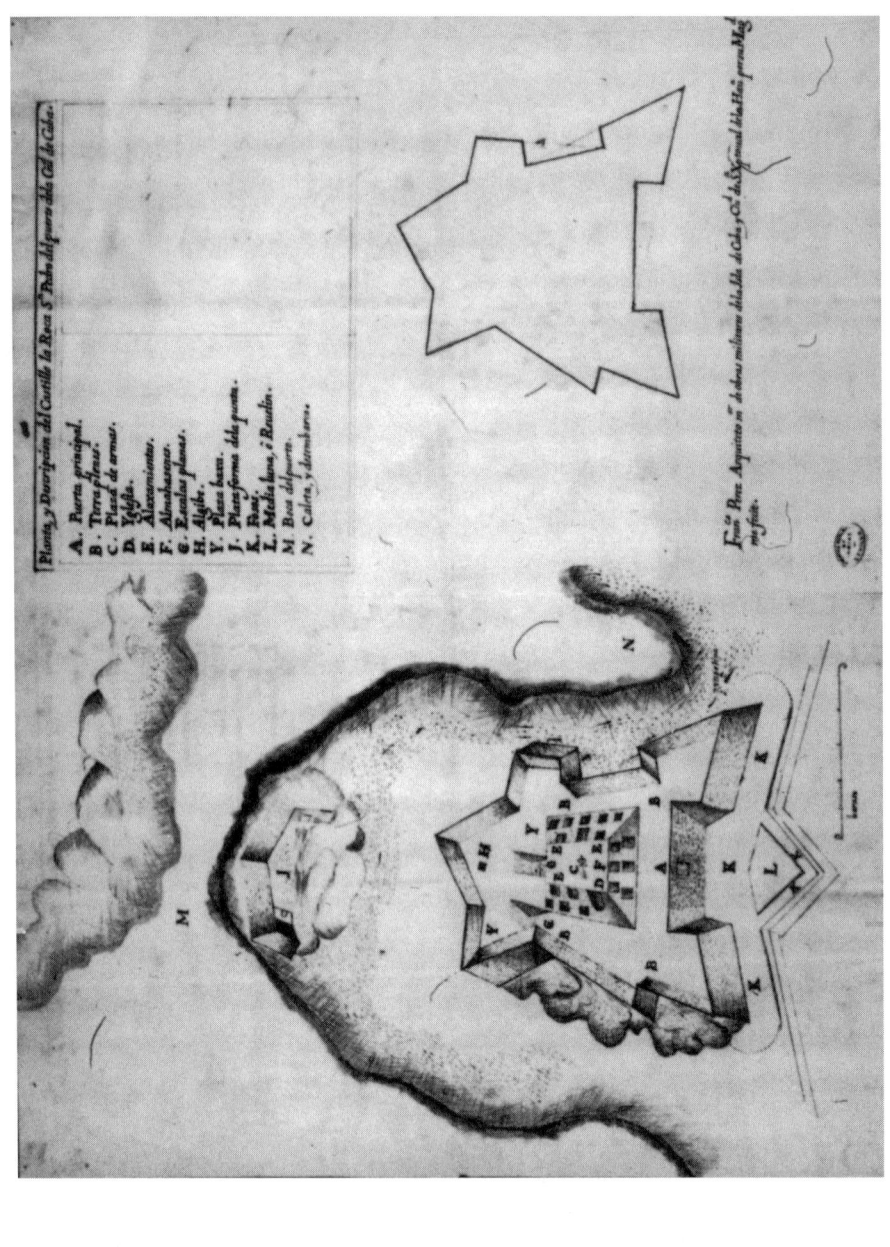

Planta, y Descripcion del Castillo la Roca S. Pedro del puerto dela Cd. de Cuba.

A. Puerta principal.
B. Terraplen.
C. Plaza de armas.
D. Yglesia.
E. Alaxamientos.
F. Almohenage.
G. Escalera pimer.
H. Algibe.
Y. Plaza baxa.
J. Plataforma del puerto.
K. Rari.
L. Muralla baxa, i Revelin.
M. Boca del puerto.
N. Colina, y alentadores.

FIGURE 12. The cobreros toiled in the construction of El Morro garrison's walls. (Author's photograph)

Facing page : MAP 4. Ground plan of El Morro (San Pedro de la Roca) garrison, 1692. (AGI, Mapas y Planos de Santo Domingo 98)

labor regime went beyond the letter of these codes to develop a system closer in practice to Indian corvées, *repartimientos, mitas,* or other kinds of
semibonded labor than to "full-time" slavery. Indeed, even the forced labor
practices to which the king's slaves were subjected reflected the special and
ambiguous status that these enslaved farmers and miners had attained in
colonial society.

The relatively "liberal" labor regime under which the royal slaves of El
Cobre worked during most of the eighteenth century, however, was not
imposed "ready-made." Regardless of how paradoxical it may seem to speak
of "negotiation" when referring to forced labor, the protracted struggle
between His Majesty's slaves and the local state to define "good treatment"
and customary labor practices constituted de facto negotiations, not only
over "bread and butter" (or, more appropriately here, "cassava and meat")
issues such as rations and work schedules, but also over the control of labor
power, entitlements, and, more generally, ways of life and wider principles
grounding social identities. It took years of protests, conflict, court action,
uprisings, and even work stoppages—not just "everyday forms of passive
resistance"—to work out the terms of a labor system that could accommodate the king's slaves' ambiguous and special position in colonial society.[5]
What resulted from this negotiated process can be best described as a dual
labor system, one in which these king's slaves worked part of the time for the
state and part of the time for themselves—and where the time dedicated to
produce on their own account was greater than that dedicated to His
Majesty.

Harnessing a Workforce of Royal Slaves

The slaves of the mining settlement of Santiago del Prado had worked as
rented private slaves in the fortification projects of Santiago de Cuba years
before becoming the king's slaves. After the British destruction of El Morro
of Santiago de Cuba in 1662, a new wave of construction of fortifications
took place.[6] The private slaves of El Cobre were rented out to work in the
reconstruction projects. In the 1660s, for instance, the private contractor of
the mines, Don Francisco Salazar y Acuña, billed the royal treasury the substantial amount of 12,000 pesos for the rental of an unspecified number of
slaves employed in the construction of the Estrella Fort for twenty-six
months and two days.[7] With this contract, Salazar y Acuña put his mostly
idle miners to productive use through a profitable but apparently shady deal
since he had not even complied with his contracted annual copper produc-

tion quota in the first place. Although the cobreros worked in the fortification projects of Santiago de Cuba as rented private slaves before the Crown's confiscation of the mines, they did not labor as king's slaves until about 1690 when Governor Don Juan de Villalobos (1690–1693) began systematically to mobilize them for that purpose.[8] At that point, the terms under which these slaves were to labor directly for the Crown had yet to be negotiated.

Before being definitively assigned to Santiago de Cuba's fortification projects in the 1690s, the royal slaves of El Cobre had been assigned to work at the governor's discretion in an array of public utility projects. Building and repairing roads, driving cattle to Santiago de Cuba from outlying areas, setting and cleaning up after the city's annual religious festivities, and persecuting runaway slaves were among the services they were called upon to perform.[9] The interests served by such labor requisitions, however, were not so much those of the Crown as those of the Santiago de Cuba municipality. To these obligations, one may add the unfailing personal service to royal officials that was standard in Spanish colonial societies.[10] These legal and illegal labor exactions evidenced an ad hoc character that reflected the as yet unsettled status of the king's slaves as well as the lack of a clear policy regarding their destination. Indeed, no institutionalized labor regime was implemented during the early years.

Regardless of the array of labor exactions imposed upon the formidable labor force of El Cobre, such requisitions represented an underutilization of slave labor power. Don Antonio Matta y Haro criticized Governor Don Andrés de Magaña in the early 1670s for not having profitably hired out the slaves of the settlement, "which is what is customary with the slaves in these parts [of the world]."[11] He also proposed a good reason why such employment may have been difficult: "They cannot work for a wage comfortably because they do not live in the city."[12] The uncertainty and laxity of those early years may have also precluded longer-term arrangements. Overall, the improvised nature of these early forced labor exactions may have set the tone for the cobreros' later expectations, eventually perhaps acquiring the force of custom.

In effect, in 1690, when Governor Villalobos took up the Crown's long-delayed orders to reinitiate (the always underfunded) construction projects in Santiago de Cuba, he immediately clashed with His Majesty's slaves. To be sure, in his drive to be recognized as having efficiently advanced construction, the governor not only ignited a conflict with the king's slaves but also alienated many other citizens in the region, including the Indians of the nearby village of El Caney (see Map 1 in Preamble). To meet budgetary constraints in the face of what he regarded as urgent defensive requirements, the governor requisitioned donations of slave labor from the wealthy; from those without means he demanded voluntary contributions of their own labor. In addition, Villalobos demanded one slave from each sugar mill in the jurisdiction; he forced the Indians in El Caney to work on the fortification projects; and he conscripted so-called vagrants "that he found in the city and kept them in fetters in the construction works."[13] Villalobos also realized the enormous potential of El Cobre's underutilized labor force. Much as he pressed slave owners to contribute to the defense effort through the labor of their slaves (never, of course, with their own manual labor), he struck a deal with the heirs of the former contractor Salazar y Acuña, one that gave the state unrestricted use of El Cobre's slaves for construction projects. This deal provisionally lifted some of the remaining restrictions which had previously blocked the Crown's access to the full labor of these slaves. Remaining restrictions were fully removed in 1700.[14]

Conflict broke out as soon as Villalobos began to harness the new labor force for the construction projects. During the governor's two years in office, the royal slaves consistently resisted these labor impositions. In one case, the king's slaves revolted alongside other groups who also refused to note the urgency of the defensive enterprise and to submit to the governor's requisitions. The *cabildo* (local government) acts of Santiago de Cuba memorialized Villalobos as an odious official because "of his arbitrary actions, his tyranny and bad government."[15] Clearly, the overzealous governor had crossed the customary boundaries of tolerable requisitions, for even the elite were irritated by his demands. As had become commonplace, accusations against his requisition practices and matters such as involvement in contraband trade were secretly filed in the High Court of Santo Domingo by citizens of Santiago de Cuba.[16]

When Havana's lieutenant general and auditor, Don Francisco Manuel de Roa, arrived in Santiago de Cuba with orders from the High Court to investigate the reports against Villalobos, he immediately immersed himself in the city's divisive politics. Within the vast Spanish Empire, astounding episodes such as the following were not uncommon. Santiago de Cuba became divided between supporters and opponents of the governor; the factions took the names of the two royal officials competing for legitimate authority, Roistas and Villalobistas. The conflict reached a climax in 1692 when the governor tried to arrest the troublesome Roa. Santiago de Cuba's *cabildo* acts registered that Roa arrived from El Cobre with some three hundred men, invaded the city, and deposed the governor. Moreover, they stated that the men accompanying his expedition, "in addition to some vecinos, were blacks and mulattos and Indians from El Caney."[17] According to the governor, Roa

> went to the mines, making himself strong in the hostel of the Church of Our Lady of Charity, convoking as a caudillo all the black and mulatto slaves there . . . [and the slaves] arming themselves with . . . machetes and knives as well as with some artillery pieces found in the said church. . . . [Roa] gave orders to the gang of slaves working in the construction of the Castle of la Roca de San Pedro [El Morro] to retire to the Mines.[18]

Villalobos later tried to implicate the priest as well by remarking that everything had happened "in the sight . . . of the *Provisor* [Don Roque de Castro Machado] whom Roa frequented, and with whom he ate together in banquets and [other] merrymakings."[19]

Sixty years later, Bishop Don Pedro Agustín Morell de Santa Cruz would inscribe this striking episode of local history, one still alive in popular memory, in the report of his pastoral visit. According to his account,

> [El Cobre] was the most appropriate [place] for [Roa's] designs because the *vecinos* and residents would submit blindly to his orders . . . in order to shake off the yoke of work in El Morro and take vengeance against he who oppressed them to comply with it.[20]

Thus, despite the fact they were slaves, the cobreros were not isolated from the capital city's politics. In effect, they had become, along with the Indians of El Caney, Roistas. In this highly volatile environment, royal slaves, Indians, and ethnically Spanish citizens (including clergy and highly placed citizens) could establish tactical alliances with and against each other in order to advance their interests, a practice that I discuss in more detail in Chapter 11. As exhibited in this case, subordinate groups could join other sectors of society through disturbances of the public order or, more often than not, through the endless accusatory reports that flowed through the empire's judicial conduits—the very kinds of complaints that had brought Roa's investigation to Santiago de Cuba in the first place.

The end of this episode did not bring an end to the conflict.[21] According to a court relator's summary of those fin de siècle years, successive governors who tried to turn the king's slaves into a tractable labor force faced an insurmountable problem: the slaves of El Cobre "did not have the docility that was necessary to reduce them to work, and carried by their vices and idleness they would rebel."[22] Similarly, another attorney's report on a different incident stated in almost verbatim terms:

> The slaves lived possessed of such vices and idleness that it would require great activity and cunning, as well as great rigor to obtain utility from them because it was well known that the governors of that province who had wanted to subject them and bring them to reason had met with great unrest.[23]

Troops were sent to El Cobre in order to bring the cobreros "to reason," repress their alleged "affronts," and curb their "idleness." Military force was used not only by Governor Villalobos but also by Governor Don Diego Oviedo y Baños (1691), his successor Governor Don Sebastián de Arancibia (1692), and later Governor Don Joseph Canales (1708–1709).[24]

The particular details of these conflicts, however, can only be surmised obliquely. It is not altogether clear whether an absolute refusal to work on the fortification projects was at issue or, more likely, whether the particular terms of work in these projects provoked conflict. Notably, Villalobos claimed that Roa had agitated the cobreros and the Indians of El Caney, leading them to believe "that there were royal edicts that stated they were free."[25] At any rate, regardless of the more radical claims for total exemption from forced labor that may have surfaced at different points, other material and pragmatic issues concerning the provisioning of the labor force and its time schedules—or what the king's slaves in general termed "good treatment"—more commonly sparked clashes between cobreros and governors.

Labor Regime and Imagined Identity

A closer reading of accounts born of conflict shows that even when contesting practical labor matters, larger questions of imagined identity and ways of life were also at issue. In 1709, during a new round of conflict, this time against the abuses of Governor Don Joseph Canales, the parish priest of El Cobre assumed the role of spokesman for his parishioners. Father Don Juan Antonio Pérez's letter to the Crown hints at the disputed labor practices that characterized these enslaved villagers and reflects assumptions that were often at issue. In Pérez's portrayal, the labor problems of previous years had been caused not so much by the slaves' lack of docility or their vices and idleness, but rather by the governor's improper treatment. "Bad treatment," the priest implied, constituted not only a legal transgression but also a moral one because it obstructed the cobreros' ability to perform certain fundamental social roles within their families and in the community:

> In the eight years that I have been priest [of this village] I have been edified many times seeing their fervor and devotion to the things of God, Our Lord. And not only by this but also by how their children have been sustained and reared honestly without having had from Your Majesty [any support] for their sustenance . . . for it is correlative that the master feed his slaves. . . .
>
> Since the year [16]91 when the Governor of the city of [Santiago de] Cuba, Don Juan de Villalobos, began construction of the castle of El Morro they [the royal slaves] have been working day by day in [two] squadrons . . . of thirty men and . . . while at the service of Your Majesty they only receive their badly disposed food [and] during the month that they are in El Morro their women and children have to sustain themselves with wild fruits because the ration they receive in El Morro is not sufficient to provide for their households.[26]

As this account indicates, from the 1690s the royal slaves had been organized into rotating squadrons—placed in a corvée labor system that, with some important alterations, would prevail throughout most of the following century. In the earlier work system, the royal slaves labored for month-long periods in the state's fortification projects, alternating with month-long intervals during which they could labor in their own farms to support their families. Royal officials operating under traditional notions of slavery—the natal or social alienation of the slave, complete subjugation to the master's will, and the master's right to the slaves' full-time labor—could either in good or bad faith easily construe month-long respites from forced labor as a manifestation of idleness. The discourse of these royal officials was based both on strict dicta about slavery and on moral strictures related to vice and virtuous labor discipline. Thus, given that full-time work legally entailed only Sundays and holidays off, proponents of a "standard slavery," so to speak, could discern in demands for longer intervals away from forced labor the blooming vices of sloth and indolence, and detect in these expectations the folly of legally bonded people who did not understand what it meant to be slaves.[27] One governor unwittingly suggested as much when he critically observed that "since they have been reared in idleness and in liberty the yoke of slavery became too heavy to bear."[28]

The parish priest's account, however, articulated a different understanding of the roles and circumstances of the royal slaves of El Cobre. From Pérez's perspective, the cobreros were dependable and obedient (indeed, virtuous) workers who, given the unreasonable terms of work set by the state, found themselves unable to provide for their families. In his understanding, royal slaves had social ties other than those to the master; they had a *pater familias* role to play in their community, and this role clashed with the labor requisitions to which they were subject as slaves. According to the parish priest, royal slaves were entitled to the means to provide for their families, hence to a labor system that would either allow the sufficient time, provisions, or income to do so.

In general terms, that view had also been the position argued in Captain Juan Moreno's petition of 1677, as the reader may recall from Chapter 2 (see also Appendix 3). In that early document, Captain Moreno had articulated the slaves' opposition to transfer by claiming that "most of the Creole blacks and mulattos of the said mines are married, and we have our families whom we have always had to support."[29] More than thirty years later, Pérez utilized the same discourse, claiming that the forced labor system imposed on the king's slaves constituted a threat to the slaves' traditional role as *patres familias*.

Instead of claiming the fundamental Christian role of *pater familias* as a prerogative of the royal slaves, however, Pérez was careful to officially present the *pater familias* role as one thrust upon his parishioners by the master/state's unwillingness to provide for its slaves as it was legally bound to do. That neglect, he suggested, morally and legally justified the royal slaves' appropriation of a proper masculine identity that ensured the conservation and reproduction of family and of Christian community. The parish priest represented a sector of colonial society that accepted, recognized, and perhaps even fomented the reconstituted identities of these royal slaves as differing from those of regular slaves. His role as spokesperson for his parishioners in this case reflected a Christian alliance, so to speak, between cobreros and the church.

Governor Ximénez's Attack on Labor Tradition or Custom: 1730s

By the late 1720s at the latest some changes had been negotiated regarding the forced labor regime to which the royal slaves were subjected. The following episode of conflict illustrates not only the kind of customary arrangements that were by then firmly in place but also the force of tradition these arrangements had acquired. Governor Ximénez's transgressions against these traditional arrangements brought about strong resistance from the cobreros. Those transgressions were enumerated in the royal attorney's summation of those conflict-laden years. The labor practices that had become customary by then represented a dramatic reduction in workload—almost by half—from the full-month's labor originally exacted from the 1690s to 1709. Not only had the number of men in each labor squadron decreased, but also the number of squadrons had doubled thereby increasing the intervals of time off work. As if echoing the patriarchal ideology and protestations of the parish priest in 1709, the attorney's review (probably paraphrasing Father Don Juan Jacintho de Silva and Dean Morell de Santa Cruz's own letters in defense of the community) also saw in the governor's intrusive policies an obstruction of the cobreros' ability to perform their role as *patres familias*—a role by now supposedly accommodated into the royal slaves' forced labor regime. The attorney condemned

the vexations, rigor, and bad treatment with which the Governor has treated them, changing the practices of his government . . . [that] being the custom to call squadrons of sixteen men every fifteen days he changed the order bringing to work as many as he wanted, even if free, making them work night and day, even without exception of holidays, so that their families lay abandoned without [the cobreros] being able to attend to them, giving them only 1 real a day for their work, and he exacted 3 or more pesos from the handicapped who were unable to work.[30]

According to this report the only two customary agreements the governor left intact were that of issuing 1 real to slaves at work as a ration and exempting women from forced labor. Ximénez altered the labor system's rotational mechanism, the length of its required laboring periods, and ignored the traditional exemptions of the free, the sick, and the handicapped from the work squadrons. In this sense, Ximénez followed the policy of "rigor" recommended by royal officials in the 1690s "to obtain utility from [the royal slaves]"—in effect, to try to subject them as full slaves. Like earlier royal officials, the governor justified his break with prevailing customs through a standard discourse on slavery, refusing to acknowledge the king's slaves' special status in colonial society. For example, Ximénez deplored that "they are slaves in name only" and claimed that "not withstanding the fact that they are [really and legally] slaves . . . they live without any subjection whatsoever, executing all the infamies and crimes dictated to them by their evil nature."[31] It is unclear what Ximénez imagined as infamies, but he may have been referring either to the "vices" denounced by royal officials in the 1690s, or to the cobreros' history of resistance to the full regime of forced labor. Although the cobreros had made gains in redefining slavery and garnering public recognition of their imagined identity as a pueblo of royal slaves, their anomalous position made them vulnerable to attacks from colonial officials who refused to endow them with any special status as the king's slaves.

That other royal officers did seem to think that royal slavery—at least in the cobreros' case—entailed some special status and that in some official circles a looser forced labor system attained some legitimacy were points obliquely suggested by Ximénez's criticisms of his predecessors' policies. Ximénez protested to the Crown that "previous Governors had overindulged [the royal slaves] . . . [and] had tolerated all the infamies they have committed, which are many and great, telling us it was because they were the slaves of His Majesty."[32] The workload attained by the 1720s had indeed acquired the binding force of tradition, as evidenced by the fact that Ximénez was found guilty of the charges of altering the royal slaves' laboring system. A royal edict stated that the king had "resolved to disapprove what the Governor had executed against the slaves," ordering that the latter be treated "with the greatest moderation and benevolence that is possible and their misery necessitates."[33] The edict further decreed that labor practices be restored to the status quo, finding the cobreros' demands "just . . . for being the same as before."[34] Customary practice was the criteria of justice in this decision, although no explicit acknowledgment of any special status as the king's slaves was officially made. A condemnation of an even wider scope was also registered in the books of Santiago de Cuba's *cabildo*. The *cabildo* acts of 1738 mentioned that Ximénez had forced "*vecinos* and residents [of Santiago de Cuba] to do *faginas* [task work or requisitions] and constructions, making use of violence, with the purpose of proving his zeal to the royal service, without due royal order, and a royal edict has been received prohibiting governors to do such a thing and that the edict be communicated to the entire city so as to avoid such harm [in the future]."[35] This was the type of royal edict that the royal slaves could interpret—and with some reason—as sanctioning their "good treatment."

Finally, the vague allusions to the cobreros' "well-being," to their "desire," or to their "good treatment" were not simply references to labor issues. They were allusions to the land question of Barajagua discussed earlier in Chapter 6. Although the Crown supported the royal slaves' laboring demands by ordering a return to customary practice, it stopped short of conceding the cobreros' demands regarding the return of the land of Barajagua. To the captain general the cobreros recounted that they had responded to a royal official who had demanded that they return to work on the usual 1 real ration: "We were ready to go back to work when a new governor [Ximénez's successor] came in, and when we were given a piece of land to breed animals with which to sustain our children while they grow up and begin to employ themselves in the services of His Majesty. . . ."[36] There was in this statement an implicit claim to a work-for-land, or a quasi-tenancy arrangement grounded in the moral economy of the *pater familias*'s provisioning duties. The claim, moreover, was negotiated through an actual work stoppage.

In the end, the forms of labor mobilization of the cobreros during the 1730s included court denunciations, *cimarronaje* (flight), and de facto labor standoffs. To be sure, the royal slaves envisioned freedom from all labor requisitions, but short of this ideal possibility their negotiating tactics led to the reinstatement of the labor regime that had become customary by the 1720s (if not to the resolution of the land issue).[37] By the 1770s, the forced labor system was still operating roughly along the same lines.

The King's Slaves' Labor Regime

A Mostly Male-Based Slavery

A military ideology permeated the corvée system under which the royal slaves of El Cobre labored: work gangs or brigades, known as squadrons (*escuadras*), were not directed by an overseer (*mayoral*) but by a corporal (*cabo*).[38] Although linguistic terms often acquire regional connotations, the fact that a military principle of organization was used for the slave labor system is significant. Military analogies represented the royal slaves as the king's soldiers, construed their labor obligations in the fortification projects as a service in defense of the king, and served to masculinize slave labor and perhaps the very institution of royal slavery. The labor squadron system seems to have been independent from other free and slave militia companies in the village. However, these groups may have been indistinct at an earlier time, so that after their boundaries became more clearly demarcated, forced labor groups may have retained an earlier military profile.

Only eligible males were organized into the four labor squadrons that, by the 1720s, rotated through work periods of fifteen days at a time.[39] Such squadrons built and repaired military structures in "the service of this garrison." As already mentioned, some men were also employed in the salt mines of Guantánamo, in logging operations, and in capturing runaway slaves, among other less "military services."[40] Muchachos under the age of fifteen and men over sixty were exempted from laboring for the state.[41] By 1735, 48.5 percent of all the male royal slaves in El Cobre were eligible for draft labor, a total labor force of some one hundred sixty male slaves at the state's disposition.[42] The Crown used one or two labor squadrons of fifteen to twenty slaves each during any given two-week period. At most, 9 to 12 percent of all male royal slaves in the village (or only 19 to 25 percent of all male royal slaves) actively labored at any one time. By the early 1770s, the state organized about one hundred eighty eligible males into eight labor squadrons,[43] twice the number of *escuadras* reported in 1730 and four times the number of those organized by the 1690s when the system was set in place.

An Underregulated Labor Force

There exists some discrepancy between the number of squadrons reported for the turn of the seventeenth century (two) and to a lesser extent for the 1720s and 1730s (four) relative to the number of royal slaves eligible for the labor draft. Only for the 1770s, when records become more accurate, does the registered total of eight squadrons approximate the number of units that could accommodate most of the eligible male population. Early in the century, El Cobre provided a total labor force of 60 active royal slaves organized into two labor squadrons while from ninety-two to one hundred ten eligible villagers could have constituted more than three squadrons.[44] By 1735 there were from one hundred sixteen to one hundred sixty eligible royal slaves distributed in four squadrons.[45] If one considers that squadrons by that time were composed of fifteen to twenty men, at most twenty-five, the gap between eligible men and those organized into the two squadrons of 1709 and the four of 1735 is more apparent.[46]

One manifestation of an apparent underutilization of eligible draftees and of the general looseness of the labor system is that of *ausentes* (absentees). *Ausentes* were mostly adult freedmen and royal slaves, a significant number of whom left the pueblo, either temporarily or permanently. In 1709, for example, the local census registered as many as 18 male royal slaves of working age and only three females as "ausentes."[47] In 1735, of the seventy-seven royal slave *ausentes* in the village, forty-four were eligible males of working age and only sixteen were females (most of whom had also married outside the village).[48] This meant that in 1709, 16.4 percent of eligible draftees were away from El Cobre, while in 1735, as many as 27.5 percent of the eligible male workforce was absent.[49]

A major state ritual in El Cobre, performed by the governor and his coterie of royal treasury officials, was the annual mandatory inspection of royal slaves. Commissioners were often sent out to summon royal slaves residing elsewhere for the governor's review. Along with the routine roll calls of His Majesty's slaves, new lists of male and female slaves were drawn up and compared to those of the previous year in order to determine deaths, mistakes, repetition of names, and absences. The raw data compiled was then corroborated with village censuses usually drawn up by the parish priest—all in a more or less successful effort to manage and control the Crown's estate through the best record keeping available at the time. The reviews themselves must have been one of the most humiliating public reminders of the cobreros' slavery. When an inquiry as to the status of one cobrera woman was made, some neighbors reported that Juana Bayesteros, who lived in Santiago de Cuba, was a royal slave only because they knew she attended the reviews every year.[50]

One such surviving inspection report (*revista*) takes several pages to list and account for that year's *ausentes*. This document is also useful because it provides a picture of the distribution and allocation of active royal slaves in service during the review.[51] (In an ironic show of efficiency, these slaves were apparently not required to absent themselves from work to attend the inspection.) According to the report of 1758, at least twenty-six royal slaves were in Havana, nine in Bayamo, eleven in Puerto Príncipe, five in Trinidad, and a few others scattered throughout other towns. These numbers and locations represented a considerable geographical dispersion of cobrero "migrants." Neither the occupations of these *ausentes* nor the reasons for their absence were recorded, perhaps because many had moved away on their own account. The fact that officials only learned of absentees' whereabouts through other relatives in El Cobre suggests that the state had lost control over many of these migrants (or runaways). Annotations such as "Paulino Fonseca married in El Príncipe, brother of Juan Fonseca," "Santiago Sánchez married with a free woman from El Bayamo, brother of Estefanía Sánchez, with family, he is in Sancti Espíritu," or "Domingo Norate, son of Juana Cusata, they say that she has family in Havana" abound in the report and provide an idea of the wider kinship networks linking the cobreros to other parts of the island. Other even more vague references to the whereabouts of absent slaves read as follows: "Silvestre Pico, brother of Francisco Pico, slave of a particular [owner], and of María Ortiz, deceased, he is said to be in Havana"; and Ambrosio Vicente, whose whereabouts were also determined by rumor, was "said to be in Trinidad." The whereabouts of other *ausentes* were simply "unknown." Often next to a name the official admitted blankly, "Se ignora su paradero" (his/her whereabouts are ignored).

All in all the state tried to keep an appearance of control over its absentee royal slaves through genealogical identification in the record, inscription in a relative's household, or some reference to their location. In some eight cases the state lost track of absent royal slaves, in particular those whose parents were deceased. Although for all practical purposes, many of the absent royal slaves could be regarded as runaways (*cimarrones*), neither this official report nor local censuses branded them as such; rather, they were categorized only as *ausentes*. At any rate, *ausentes* in this report added to fifty-one cases of mostly eligible men who evaded the local squadron system. Although licenses would have presumably been required for slaves to leave the village, at least for considerable periods of time (and there were royal officials amenable to this possibility), these cases suggest that the state did not have a strong grip on its labor force.

The Forced Labor Regime at Work

The 1758 report not only tried to account for absentees but also recorded the destination of those royal slaves in active service to the Crown. The document offers an invaluable picture of how the state used its slaves within and outside the squadron system.[52] Three royal slaves, for instance, were "with the Alcaldes de la Hermandad" probably chasing down runaways or fulfilling their policing functions in rural districts. Four additional king's slaves had been allocated to the major overseer of the fortification projects, perhaps for personal service. Another, Juan Lorenzo Calderón, reportedly worked "in the governor's house," undoubtedly in personal service. These cases show that individual royal slaves were also employed outside the squadron system and the fortification projects.

In addition, employed "in the various destinies of the fortress" were nine men who could have constituted a small *escuadra* and four who had been allocated to the *Piragua*, a coast guard boat that patrolled the region's coastal area in search of contraband trade activities. These thirteen royal slaves, then, were employed in defense-related services, and they could have belonged either to one of the work squadrons in the village or to one of the slave militia companies.[53] In addition, twelve other king's slaves duly served in "the royal construction works." Overall, thirty-three royal slaves were laboring at the time of the annual review. The twenty-five in defense-related roles represented a labor force equivalent to two small squadrons, but only one such unit was directly employed in the fortification projects.[54]

Finally, the state had assigned five young royal slaves listed in the 1758 report to several master artisans for training as carpenters and blacksmiths. Four other cases that were likely personal service assignments, but who were recorded as "muchachos also sent to learn a trade," were: Pedro Antonio, whom "the Señor Treasurer took"; two others, who "were taken by Brother Perfecto de León," probably to work at the nearby Franciscan convent or at the hospital; and Ignacio de Loyola, who "returned to El Cobre" from no specific assignment. Significantly, all nine muchachos deserted, preferring to give up their bright futures as skilled workers in order to return to their families and probably become farmers like almost everyone else in the pueblo. The royal official who authored the 1758 report wrote:

The corporal of the detachment in the pueblo of El Cobre will dispose that the appointed muchachos slaves of His Majesty . . . (who before had been placed to learn a trade and deserted), shall be conducted to this City, guarded for their security, so that through my intervention they will be restituted and destined [to work] as agreed.[55]

One wonders who or what these young men had to be guarded from—their parents and relatives, other cobrero neighbors, bandits, or perhaps their own youthful impulses to run away?

The episode shows that the state had decision-making power over which royal slaves would be apprenticed. Yet, the nine desertions roughly during the same period raise other questions. Although these desertions show that the governor's orders were opposed, they displayed a different kind of resistance, suggesting a concerted opposition possibly related to a breach of tradition. Indeed, a petition submitted more than three decades later—the fruit of a negotiation between an *apoderado* (legal spokesman or proxy) of the cobreros with local authorities and the mining heirs who claimed private ownership of the slaves—included a pertinent clause. It clearly stated:

The *púberes* [adolescents] not begin to contribute their wage pension [to purchase their manumission] until the age of twelve for females and the age of fourteen for males, and that after puberty they can be applied to work without extracting them from the protection of their parents who can freely give them the trade [to which] they feel inclined.[56]

All in all, the thirty-three royal slaves reported at work during the 1758 review—forty-two if the disgruntled young apprentices are also included—constituted approximately 22 percent of the male royal slaves eligible for forced labor requisitions and 5 percent of all the royal slaves in El Cobre in the 1750s.[57] These proportions represent a low productivity of the state's slave labor force in El Cobre. Even the number of *ausentes* (at least fifty-one) over whom the state had lost control was greater than the more or less set number of slaves in active service to the Crown at any given point.

Moreover, the implications of this kind of rotational setup, a proportion based on forty-five active slaves against a reserve labor force of an additional one hundred eighteen male slaves suggest a crude estimate of 27.6 percent of the year for each shift (one hundred one days), or three months and eleven days of forced labor for the state each year. A calculation based on a conventional working year that excluded Sundays and holidays (unlikely in defense services) would reduce the time of bonded labor to seventy-eight days per year. The observations made by contemporaries reinforce these numbers.

Laboring for the State

The two-week labor rotating schedule to which royal slaves had to submit after the 1720s meant that in principle each adult male slave in the squadron worked a total of three months per year—somewhat above the time requirements of *mita* and *repartimiento* schedules elsewhere,[58] but way under the two hundred eighty-three laboring days (75.5 percent) of the year required from slaves by Spanish law or the time off granted to slaves for subsistence elsewhere in the Americas.[59] One royal official who may have been intent on minimizing the forced labor duties of the royal slaves said each cobrero had "two months of work per year, and he had ten left to work in his farm . . . and when there is no construction they have the whole year for themselves as their children and wives have it."[60] A later statement by a cobrero claimed that royal slaves worked even less: "They occupied them only 1 month conducting water for the detachments including the black dock workers, the rest of the time they remained free."[61] The extent of compulsory labor exacted from the king's slaves— whether two, three, or even four months of work—represented one-sixth to one-third of their yearly working time.

Provisioning Arrangements at Minimal Cost

The state's expense in the provisioning of His Majesty's slaves was minimal. Basically, it only provided for royal slaves in active service. When working in the *escuadras*, royal slaves received the standard "payment" of 1 real per day,[62] the equivalent of a daily ration of salted meat and a cassava cake.[63] Official wage rates for nonskilled free laborers ran to 3 reales per day in 1735 (4 reales in state accounts in 1777)—2 reales over the basic subsistence rate.[64] The king's slaves did not voice—or at least did not record—many complaints about the adequacy of their own daily rations; however, they repeatedly protested that 1 real per day was not enough to provide for their families. Thus, these "payments" represented the daily provisions that masters owed to individual slaves. These did not constitute remuneration for labor, nor did they allow for the subsistence rations of other family members. Indeed, 1 real (later 2) was the mark of forced labor, for penal convicts working in the fortification projects also received 1 real (later 2) for their daily rations.[65] While the stipend of 1 or 2 reales in principle constituted a fundamental difference between this type of forced labor and the Indian *repartimiento* or *mita* system that called for payment of a minimum wage, in practice *repartimiento* payments also ran below current wages for free labor and may not have differed from the royal slaves' stipend.[66] The case of the Indians of El Caney reflected some variation of that system insofar as they received a minimum wage of 2 reales in 1730 for their *fagina* requisitions, a payment that constituted a step above the basic subsistence rate of 1 real, but that was still below the ongoing market wages of 3 reales.[67]

It is unclear to what extent Indians in El Caney, Jiguaní, or, for that matter, Guanabacoa (at the other extreme of the island) were subject to labor exactions similar to those of Native Americans in the mainland. In the eastern region of Santiago de Cuba, they were known to perform some services such as delivering mail, maintaining roads, and, above all, guarding the coasts. Moreover, at the end of the seventeenth century, the Indians of El Caney had been also called upon to perform construction work in the fortification projects of El Morro—a labor imposition they had refused, eventually becoming rebel Roistas alongside the royal slaves of El Cobre. Similarly, "men from El Caney" appeared in the records of the royal treasury doing "*faginas* in the fortification projects, for which they received 2 reales a day ration"—an indication of the possible semiforced character of that labor.[68] But these are all vague references, for the story of long-standing Indian communities in Cuba such as El Caney, Jiguaní, or even Guanabacoa remains to be told. Nonetheless, even if the type of labor requisitions exacted from the Indian survivors of the "great dying" in this island were different from those of Native Americans in the Spanish mainland, or for that matter, from those of royal slaves, the compulsory labor system to which cobreros were subject had points in common with the corvée labor regimes under which many Native American groups labored elsewhere in the Americas.[69]

Control, Flexibility, and Abuse in the Labor System

The slave corvée system, like the Indian *repartimiento*, was, to a certain extent, a community-administered regime, or one administered by local officials. When the *cabildo* operated in the community, it was responsible for the management of the *escuadra* labor system. The *alcaldes* (local officials or bailiffs) responsible for running the labor system assigned cobreros to each *escuadra*, appointed the *cabos* heading each labor squadron, delivered these units to work, kept track of attendance, and collected fees from those royal slaves wishing to skip a turn so that hired slaves or peons could substitute for them.[70]

By the 1770s, appointed commissioners (also royal slaves) were in charge of running the system. Each of the eight commissioners was responsible for a certain number of households or families (total of approximately sixty males), and they oversaw the recruitment of those males coming of age for their squadrons. Slave females were listed by households separately, coming under the same commissioner for annual reporting purposes and for other internal labor requisitions.[71]

Other aspects of the labor system imposed upon the king's slaves of El Cobre reflected the slaves' additional—if expensive—control over their own labor power. For instance, the king's slaves worked out an informal arrangement with royal authorities whereby a royal slave who did not wish to work in the *escuadras* could skip his turn by making a payment of 3 pesos (or 24 reales) to cover the two weeks, paying a daily 2-real surplus over the state's subsistence ration of 1 real. This fee was supposedly used to hire a slave or peon at regular wages to fill in during the two weeks of *escuadra* duty.[72] The payment arrangement allegedly functioned on a voluntary basis. Royal slaves too sick to work were not required to pay; instead they were shifted to another *escuadra* turn.[73] The free cobrero Captain Fernando de Rosas stated, "The relief of giving money has been [granted] because they [the royal slaves] themselves had asked for it, since it was to their convenience to be able to stay in their farms and in other occupations from which they obtain more profit."[74] Back in 1709, that option was given to free cobreros—not royal slaves—who were occasionally called in to do (forced) "volunteer" labor for the Crown.[75] The arrangement may have been common; in 1731 royal slaves claimed they had paid more than 1,000 pesos in wages during an unspecified period of time—some 333 work turns.[76] This time, the cobreros depicted the arrangement as an extortion, rather than a convenience.

These payment arrangements may have provided royal slaves some flexibility, particularly during harvest time, but they were costly. Through these arrangements royal slaves could buy the labor power of other workers to relieve themselves, if only temporarily, from the labor obligations that defined them as slaves; but they were only able to do so at rates triple the value of their own labor power when working for the state. Many cobreros took advantage of this arrangement only occasionally; others did so on a recurrent basis, thus evincing some economic differentiation among those still enslaved.[77] Whether other cobreros were hired as replacement *jornaleros* (daily workers) and rented slaves worked as substitutes, or whether royal officials pocketed the fees and hired no replacements is left to the readers' imagination.

The cobreros' complaints during the uprising of 1731 suggest the opportunities for graft in a system that allowed for some flexibility. They claimed that during the administration of Governor Ximénez, the sick and handicapped had been forced to pay an exemption fee that was against customary practice. Oftentimes, captains of the militias in charge of the squadrons were responsible for the payment of a fee to royal authorities if their brigades were understaffed. At other times, royal officials protested that squadrons were smaller because of sick or absent slaves. Royal officials declared they had to retain the payment of royal slaves' rations for a few days in order to prevent them from leaving in midweek due to illness. Lieutenant Don Pedro Arando, overseer of the fortification projects, claimed (probably with much exaggeration) that the labor squadrons "were never complete," that sometimes only six or eight men, at the most ten, came from El Cobre in each squadron.[78] He did not indicate whether absentees had paid their exemption fees for substitutes, whether the retained payments were ever given out, or whether some royal slaves left midweek because their daily rations were delayed. In any case, clashes over payments and resistance to work through real or alleged sickness must have been among the commonplace issues entailed in the conflicts in everyday working life.

Borderline Forms of Male Forced Labor: Personal Service and Coartación

There was another aspect of the labor arrangements to which royal slaves were subjected that constituted a borderline form of forced labor. It consisted of personal service to royal authorities and other citizens in Santiago de Cuba. The customary agreement was that after several years in service as a personal servant, a master or employer would provide the royal slave in his or her charge the money to pay for manumission. The illicit character of such deals resided in the practice of framing the manumission as a case of *coartación* (self-manumission), and consequently in the lower prices paid to the royal treasury for the freedom of the royal slave (50 to 100 pesos) in question.[79] Thus, a citizen of Santiago de Cuba could acquire the services of a slave at relatively low prices; the slave would be sustained by the master or employer and paid for his or her labor through the money granted for the *coartación*; and the governor could engage in and benefit from clientelistic practices with the Crown's "property." Governors usually assigned royal slaves to serve royal officials, but sometimes slaves were assigned to the governor's friends as well. That such practices were regarded as established custom in Santiago de Cuba is evidenced by a "vengeance" story that Don Miguel de Mueses related to the island's captain general in 1768. Describing his own assigned royal slave Antonio Rodríguez (a possible *ausente* in that year's annual slave reviews), Mueses described how these "normal" deals operated and how they formed part of Santiago de Cuba's politics:

By orders of the previous Governor Don Lorenzo de Madariaga, the royal officer Lieutenant Don Pedro Sánchez Griñán handed over to me a young cobrero slave of His Majesty to rear and educate him as has been the practice with many of them, and the same Governor took them over for his own service for this motive. Upon my return from the town of Bayamo this year . . . an *alcalde* from El Cobre came to my house with a piece of paper signed by Governor Marqués de Casa Cagigal whereby he ordered the corporal of the squadron to take away the said youngster. I was surprised by this [order] given the channels it came from and that I had not received any notice . . . and I went to see the Governor to see if he would allow me to keep [the slave] for a few days while I found another one to buy, for this one served me in everything and my short means did not allow me to have many slaves. . . . [the governor got angry and refused] and I immediately handed over the said cobrero with sadness and pain. . . . The tears of the slave, the love I had developed for him, and the shame I had to go through stimulated me to facilitate this individual the money that he needed to free himself convinced that it would be at [the same price] as for all cobreros, which by general rule is 100 pesos, under the condition that the individual also undertake the process [of *coartación*] without giving out my name for anything; and given the decrees of the Governor, knowing that it was me who was giving the money [the governor] did not agree to free [the slave] for an amount less than 225 pesos, which is the highest seen to this day for cobreros, but for the already mentioned reasons I had to pay the quantity to the royal treasury the youngster being obliged to serve me as a servant for a certain time to compensate for this benefit.[80]

TABLE 8

Price Range of Self-manumitted (Coartado) Royal Slaves by Sex, 1740–1775

	Males	Females
240–290 pesos	4	—
200 pesos	3	2
150–199 pesos	17	1
101–149 pesos	17	2
100 pesos	45	12
50–99 pesos	37	12
<49 pesos	2	3
Total	125	32

SOURCE: "Corte y Libertades," Dec. 1740 to Oct. 26, 1742, in "Testimonio de autos que varios naturales del Cobre siguieron en Cuba sobre su libertad," 1780, C 29/37, fols. 34–35, AGI-SD 1628. "Certificación corte y libertades," 1743 to Dec. 1775, fols. 63–68v, AGI-SD 1627.

The details illustrating customary practices with respect to personal service and manumission are starkly depicted in this narrative. The complaint also provides a good view of the dynamics of colonial politics and how the royal slaves could be implicated in it. The account speaks for itself: Mueses denounced the governor's motives for taking the slave away and making him pay dearly for the customary or agreed manumission as an act of vengeance for having followed royal orders and imprisoned a relative or *favorecido* (friend) of Casa Cagigal. The aggrieved governor insulted and shamed Mueses not only by depriving him of the slave but also by charging a cobrero *alcalde* with orders to take over the slave—an echo of the personal humiliation story narrated by Matta y Haro almost a century before in the early 1670s.[81] The governor, of course, did not stop at taking away the slave, but further made his subaltern, Mueses, pay a high price for the slave's services. These petty vendettas could be taken to unexpected degrees. Mueses himself made use of another common recourse in colonial society in his account, namely, turning to a higher official—in this case the captain general in Havana—for protection.[82]

Overall, the customary prices for manumissions cited by Mueses and the inflated price demanded by the governor for the *coartación* of Mueses's royal slave fit well with those found in the royal treasury's records. Table 8 summarizes the prices paid to the royal treasury for *coartaciones* of male and female royal slaves after the 1740s. Although not all these manumissions were obtained by way of these deals, the practice may have been an important source of mobility into freedom in the community; one, however, that seemed to favor males over females.

Gender and Work

Gender played a key role in the formation of social identity in El Cobre and in the shaping of the royal slaves' forced labor regime. Not only were the king's slaves associated mainly with the Crown's defense system, a strongly masculine sphere in the Spanish order of things, but the alleged dependent status of females and children constituted a main ideological basis legitimating the rotating character of this corvée labor system. Royal slave females were also subject to labor exactions from the state, but their role in the general forced labor regime imposed on the community was peripheral. Wider gender assumptions regarding proper feminine spheres — not always deemed applicable to regular slaves — also structured the division of forced labor among the king's slaves.

Married slave women were allegedly exempted from working for the state, although "single women and maidens" were sometimes required to work in the hospital of Santiago de Cuba or "in other occupations proper to their sex . . . (for they were always exempted from all fatiguing labor despite their slavery)."[83] Several contemporary cultural assumptions are disclosed in this simple statement: that slavery, in general, entailed "fatiguing" hard labor; that proper female occupations consisted of non-"fatiguing" work; that male occupations entailed hard work; and that slavery made few concessions to any gender considerations. In fact, in most slave societies of the Americas, female as well as male slaves were subject to demanding hard work (the most extreme enactment of this last principle would have probably been the spectacle of female slaves working in the fields of sugar plantations). Although during the earlier mining days female slaves in Santiago del Prado had not toiled in deep mining, they had been employed in other kinds of "fatiguing" occupations such as agricultural production, the heavy labor of transporting extracted ore from the quarry, and other more gender-specific activities in mineral processing. Females had also worked in the construction of public structures such as the parish church and probably continued doing so years later.[84]

The above statement seemed to suggest, however, that female royal slaves in El Cobre were only required to work "sometimes" and that their occupations followed the stricter gender codes of other (free) sectors of society. The occupations "proper to their sex" entailed labor related to the domestic sphere: most enslaved young women were called upon to work in hospitals, as domestic personal servants, or even as wet nurses. Clearly, gender was significant in the way royal slavery was imagined, playing a key role in what became the customary definition of "good" and special treatment as the king's slaves.

At work in the royal hospital, the enslaved cobreras, like lower-class women in Spain and female slaves elsewhere, cleaned, washed, and may have tended to the sick.[85] Such care may have involved more than physical tasks such as feeding, washing, and nursing patients; it may also have incorporated spiritual care. Given the Marian cult alive in their home village, female royal slaves may have urged patients to have faith in the miraculous healing powers attributed to the Virgin of Charity and to the holy oil of her lamp. Some may have encouraged the sick and dying to make vows in exchange for their health. At the very least, some had plenty of healing and inspirational stories to tell and comfort patients with — the kind of narratives that, then and now, are often part and parcel of the subculture of illness.

Although single females were required to perform compulsory labor for the state, their exactions were far lower than those of males. Since the average age of marriage for these women was twenty-three and since adolescents began to work for the state at the age of sixteen, in principle, royal slave females may have owed the state several months of work for about eight years of their lives. In addition, not all these women were employed by royal authorities at a given time. Single women between sixteen and sixty years old constituted a significant proportion of the labor force in El Cobre — particularly by the 1770s. Indeed, at any given point, their numbers could have constituted several work squadrons. Yet, the Royal Hospital of Santiago de Cuba, like hospitals in other colonial towns, was a small institution with only a few beds for soldiers and seamen as well as for the poor; it was hardly a place where large contingents of slave women could be employed at any one time.[86] Thus, labor dues to the hospital would have been organized so as to distribute work among the large number of eligible women, and turns or shifts spaced out accordingly.

The only extended reference to female requisitions in the hospital is a late-eighteenth-century remark in relation to a proof of slave status inquiry.[87] The cobrera in question, however, did not live in El Cobre; she was not single but married, and was either free or passing as such. Neighbors testified that whenever the commissioner called Juana María Bayesteros to work in the hospital, she always paid 2 reales to have another enslaved cobrera substitute for her. This (detested) call exemplified Bayesteros's royal slave status, and her case shows that the exemption fee arrangement applicable to the male squadrons in El Cobre also operated among women, even late into the eighteenth century. Significantly, the episode also indicates that relief from work through the payment of a fee could blur the line between freedom and royal slavery for women, as discussed previously in the case of male cobreros.

Furthermore, the account exemplifies the local apparatus used by the state to control its labor force and exact its requisitions. Commissioners in the 1770s had under their command groups of sixty male royal slaves, and they oversaw the *fagina* system (to be discussed below), the labor squadron system, and the individual females assigned to the hospital as well. A separate commissioner may have kept track of royal slaves residing in other localities, summoning them to the governor's annual inspections and to yearly labor duties.

Perhaps the most interesting aspect of Bayesteros's case is that it suggests that not only single women were requisitioned to work for the state; married women were often also subject to these labor exactions. Even if the testimonies about Bayesteros were false (and there were accusations that they were), the fact that married women were supposedly excused from labor requisitions was not brought up by the defenders of Bayesteros's free status as a sign of the implausibility of the accusations.

Other accounts also indicate that single women were not the only ones called upon to perform compulsory labor in Santiago de Cuba. In some judicial inquiries carried out between the late 1780s and early 1790s to determine the status of individual cobreros, interviewees were asked whether they, their siblings, or their parents were among those cobreros who performed services in Santiago de Cuba. Regardless of whether they realized the intent behind the question, various cobreros responded that their mothers and sisters were indeed called upon to work in Santiago de Cuba and that these women performed personal services for a royal official, particularly the governor. The eighteen-year-old Manuela Borrero, for example, declared that "her father was a soldier and he served the King, that her brothers also served the King carrying water, and that she and her mother went to serve the Governor a few days every month."[88] Manuela must have traveled to Santiago de Cuba with her mother as a girl, for these memories described practices taking place in El Cobre at least six or seven years earlier. The few days at the governor's house every month could have amounted to a considerable labor burden of one or two months of work every year. By contrast, the fourteen-year-old Manuel de Jesús candidly testified that "neither he nor his mother ever went to serve in Cuba but that he had heard that his mother was a slave."[89] Thus, in this case, Jesús's mother, as a married royal slave with perhaps a small child, seems to have been exempted from labor requisitions away from home. The testimony of Antonio Vicente Norate further showed that personal services were not only required from women but also that these could be sporadic. The forty-year-old Norate stated that "his father and [he] went several times to serve the Governor but not his mother and sisters, who were always free and reputed as such."[90]

Finally, a representation drawn up by the cobreros in 1738 points not only to the regular forced labor practices to which females in the community were subject to but also to the abuses to which these customary arrangements were open to. The cobreros denounced the new governor, Don Francisco Antonio Cagigal de la Vega, for ordering that

each day one of our wives and sisters be appointed to go and serve [in Santiago de Cuba] and whoever cannot go pay 1 real; and with this capacity to get many reales, the said *alférez* [Lieutenant Velasco Calderín stationed in the village] appoints up to ten or twelve of those that he knows are sick or have just given birth and after having collected several reales he appoints one who is well and he does this very often so that we are continuously working for him.[91]

The representation points not only to the obligation of female royal slaves to do forced personal service in Santiago de Cuba but also to the assignment of married women, mothers of newborn babies, and the sick to work away from the village. The construction of this practice as a "tyranny" and its denunciation to the king, however, suggest that these constituted transgressive practices that broke with established principle and customary arrangements. The passage also points to the arrangement of paying a fee to skip a labor requisition turn among females, in their case 1 real instead of 3 as in the case of males. The denunciation shows the opportunities for graft built into an otherwise flexible arrangement that was also denounced by male cobreros subject to the labor squadrons. The complaint was filed after a tumult in the village that had led to strong repression of the cobreros around that time and that may have exacerbated tensions and hostility between the state and the local community.[92] The fact that the cobreros filed this denunciation through judicial channels despite the precedent of repression is indicative of how ingrained their sense of entitlement was and how strongly they were willing to mobilize in the defense of their limited labor "rights."

Female Exemptions: A Pronatalist Policy?

Despite the evidence pointing to the exactions of service from married female slaves in El Cobre, several cobreros and royal officials reiterated through the years that a married royal slave woman was exempt from compulsory labor. A 1735 report stated, "Women and children were not occupied in anything."[93] In any case, the relatively high number of women in the pueblo and the lack of large-scale institutions (comparable to the military projects) that could absorb the labor of the formidable local female force may go a long way in accounting for the low profile of the requisitions, if not for the full exemption of married females from labor. Furthermore, the largely defense-related functions of royal slaves and the strongly gendered character of this military realm privileged (in a perverse way) males' productive labor for the state and (fortunately for women) led to the relative neglect of females' productive potential. Under these circumstances female slaves' reproductive role may have become more prominent. That the state followed a calculating pronatalist policy with royal slaves is doubtful, but concerns about population growth did exist.

There are no explicit statements of policy regarding the organization of the king's slaves, particularly for the early years. A 1761 report, however, made some recommendations that reveal the logic behind some of these organizational practices. It suggested that one big company of one hundred royal slaves work "as servants of the artillery of this garrison and the women [be used] for their marriages."[94] The report went on to suggest that "the other [royal slaves] selected for work could be applied to work in the fortification projects," and that muchachos age ten and older "also be brought to apply them in the trades of craftsmanship of the artillery."[95] It added that "married women or those of an advanced age stay in their pueblo so that they can augment it and be available for whatever can present itself."[96] Thus, the report recommended a reorganization of production, directing the labor more toward artillery services than toward construction works and even suggesting the lowering of the age at which boys could be summoned to work or assigned to apprenticeships. No further mention regarding work periods or other kinds of traditional working arrangements was made, nor was any mention of single women made either. However, the report explicitly articulated the role of women in general as that of wives ("for their marriages") who could stay behind to care for everyday affairs in the pueblo. The reproductive function of wives was openly asserted in the statement that "they could augment [the population of the pueblo]." Thus, even in this policy-oriented proposal of more intensified productivity among His Majesty's slaves, married women and older people were exempted from work, becoming virtually the only permanent residents of the village. Indeed, in this harsh work scenario, one that may have found some antecedents in Governor Villalobos's designs in 1691 or in Governor Ximénez's in the 1730s, women's productive role for the state was minimized or neglected in favor of their reproductive role. Whether this proposed (and to a certain degree implemented) sexual organization of production had from early on constituted pronatalist state policy is difficult to say.

The vague pronatalist policy of exempting married women from forced labor proposed in the report of 1761, however, would have been unusually liberal for its time. Gendered policies that privileged female slaves' procreative role over their economically productive one would have been rather unusual in Caribbean slave societies. In fact, a policy that exempted married women from forced labor in the pursuit of reproduction was remarkable, even within the more tolerant tradition of Spanish law. Contrary to pronatalist slaveholders in the U.S. South, slaveholders in the Caribbean, particularly during the seventeenth and eighteenth centuries (and the nineteenth-century in Cuba), placed greater value on slave women's field and domestic labor.[97] Female slaves in the Caribbean and elsewhere in Spanish America were not exempted from forced labor obligations by virtue of childbearing and child rearing.[98] Nor were they exempted in a private copper-mining proposal for El Cobre made to the Crown during the eighteenth century.[99] Even at the turn of the nineteenth century—when the abolition of the slave trade became imminent in the British colonies and ameliorative legislation and practices called for the material reform of slave conditions— slave women were still subject to hard labor between pregnancies and to lighter work around the peak moments of the reproductive cycle.[100] In this sense, the exemption policy toward married royal slave women in El Cobre—whether calculating and rationally pronatalist or only indirectly so—seems unusually liberal in comparison to the ideal and practical standards among contemporary slaveholders.

Although earlier records lack specific pronatalist statements, it can be assumed that once the possibility of a pueblo of royal slaves had been accepted by royal authorities (at least as a fait accompli), the state would have exhibited an interest in seeing its population grow.[101] What may have been at stake was then not so much a slave pronatalist policy per se, but rather a more general concern with augmenting the population of the settlement for colonization and defensive purposes in a still sparsely populated frontier region.

Finally, even if one concedes that from the calculating point of view of the state, royal slave women's "work" may have been producing royal slaves for the Crown, or in other words reproducing the state's enslaved labor force; or from another statist perspective, augmenting the population of settlers in a frontier region; from a local native point of view women's reproductive labor may also be seen as a contribution to the growth and importance of their own corporate community. Indeed, the reproductive role of most cobreras can also be understood from below as a means of generating and consolidating their family identities, their kinship lines through time, and, more generally, the strong natal ties that obliterated the "social death" entailed in slavery.

Borderline Forms of Female Forced Labor: Opportunities for Coartación

Slave women in El Cobre performed another kind of occupation, one exclusively tied to their gender: wet nursing. There are indications that often this occupation, and perhaps other kinds of personal services, received some form of compensation. A representation made by the alleged mining heirs of El Cobre in 1784 protested — probably with some exaggeration — that "nursing cobrera women were paid a wage by day, by week, by month, or for a year . . . or by a deal of freedom . . . in that way many cobreras have freed themselves serving the Governors and Treasurers etc. or particulars . . . that not having finished nursing their children they came out as free."[102] Don Francisco Mancebo y Quiroga accused royal officials of fraud for appraising female cobrera slaves at minimal prices—50 or 60 pesos—when their real "value tended to be 350 pesos."[103] That such deals existed, regardless of gender, was clear from the revenge story regarding the royal slave muchacho whom Casa Cagigal removed from the service of Mueses. Indeed, the prices generally paid for the manumission of female cobreras ranged from a very low 50 to 250 pesos, with an overwhelming majority in the 50 to 100 pesos bracket (see Table 8 above). Extralegal arrangements such as these, when they occurred, may have constituted borderline cases of forced labor. They cannot be properly considered forced labor, for cobreras seemed to have been compensated for wet nursing either through some wages or through manumission.

Internal Services: A Form of Forced Labor?

Finally, by the 1770s, there existed in El Cobre a set of local labor exactions independent from compulsory labor to the state or from the *escuadra* system. This internal labor system was called *fagina*, which may have included free persons as well as slaves. Both males and females were required to participate. *Faginas* were geared toward matters of local public utility, but as usual these practices were also open to graft and abuse by royal officials. In this local system, boys over twelve and under fifteen (an age when they passed over to the squadron system) were subject to work two days every month (or roughly a month per year).[104] It is not clear if adult males in the squadron system were also required to perform labor for the community—a possibility that would have increased male slaves' annual obligations by another month.

Despite their compulsory character, *faginas* were designed to work on local village projects. For instance, in 1772 there were plans to construct or reconstruct a bridge over the river that separated two neighborhoods of El Cobre. At that time, *faginas* had been employed as well in local draining projects, particularly as the river was prone to overflowing. Workers in the *faginas* were also employed in the reconstruction of houses destroyed by fire, flooding, and earthquakes, particularly those owned by "helpless widows."[105] Thus, most *faginas* constituted some form of labor tax for village improvement projects and could not be properly considered direct slave labor for the state.

The *fagina* system was almost certainly used as well in the construction of the parish church and its Marian sanctuary—institutions controlled by the church and symbolic of the local community's corporate identity. However forced these exactions may have been, some leading villagers wrote with pride to the cobrero Gregorio Cosme Osorio, in the 1790s, that "after many years that the [parish] church has laid in shambles . . . [its reconstruction] is on its way; the second day of Easter the first stone was set down on the church, [and] there was a celebration, [that] many people attended."[106] Similarly, the construction of the Virgin's sanctuary at the turn of the century was attributed to the cobreros' efforts in a representation to the Crown on behalf of the community: "They erected a beautiful temple that still exists reconstructed by the natives themselves."[107]

Slave women were also linked to this local labor system. At least in the 1770s, all adult slave females were required to provide for the construction projects' monthly quotas of branches and reeds from tropical trees and wild plants (*bejucos* and *majagua*) growing in the surrounding forests. For females, then, this local labor regime was organized as a task system: each household was to deliver to the commissioners in charge (the same person who oversaw the labor squadrons) a specified amount of reeds proportionate to the number of adult women in the household. Some of this material was destined for the construction of the local bridge while another part was set aside for other community projects.[108] In this sense, these quotas can also be seen as a form of internal tax that resulted in some direct benefits for the community; however compulsory the task system may have been, it cannot, strictly speaking, be considered bond labor for the state.

This said, however, there were ways in which royal officials could make use of the system for their own ends. In 1772, for example, the governor made some changes in policy.[109] He called for the creation of a (communal) fund from part of the sale of the collected reeds and branches. The fund would be used to pay 1-real-and-a-half daily allowance to those royal slaves employed in the relay of official mail or in the transportation of prisoners to the garrison of Santiago de Cuba. Although it could be argued that the proceeds from the local labor exactions were in fact returned to the community or even that the fund was communal (the equivalent to the usually mandated *caja de comunidad* in Native American villages), these funds were being used to finance state activities, or, more precisely, the costs of provisioning royal slaves at work for the state. In addition, part of the fund would be employed to buy paper for the commissioners' record-keeping needs as well as for the modest salary of the overseer of construction projects. Thus, whereas the economic burden of the material for record keeping had previously fallen on individual village officials (who were most likely illiterate and memorized records),[110] now the labor of the communal funds was allegedly used to pay those costs. In addition, the governor ordered that one of the two days of male *fagina* duty was to be dedicated to the collection of *bejucos* and *majagua* for the fund. It is not unthinkable that such a fund was misused by royal officials for their own construction needs elsewhere or more probably for graft.

Gender and Manumission

One result of the defense-related and gender-based forced labor system of the royal slaves of El Cobre was the shape that manumission or, more specifically, *coartación* trends took in this community. Contrary to the more general tendency in the island and elsewhere in Spanish slave societies,[111] males in El Cobre were not only more likely to be free than females but also more likely to manumit themselves, at least after the 1740s. Until that decade, manumissions had proceeded at a slow rate (Table 9). After the 1730s—possibly as a result of the uprising that left the cobreros with the realization that they were no longer entitled to Barajagua as the king's slaves—

TABLE 9

Self-manumissions (Coartaciones), *by Sex and Decade, 1689–1775*

	Males	Females	Total
1689–1699	5	10	15
1700–1709	7	4	11
1710s	0	2	2
1720s	0	3	3
1730s	7	4	11
1740s	32	9	41
1750s	32	7	39
1760s	51	9	60
1770–1775	10	7	17
Total	144 (72.4%)	55 (27.6%)	199

SOURCES: "Certificación libros de contaduría: corte y libertades," Aug. 20, 1689 to Sept. 28, 1734, "Autos Año de 1735," fols. 755–58, AGI-SD 451; "Corte y libertades," Dec. 1740 to Oct. 26, 1742, in "Testimonio de autos que varios naturales del Cobre siguieron en Cuba sobre su libertad," 1780, C 29/37, fols. 34–35, AGI-SD 1628; "Certificación corte y libertades," 1743 to Dec. 1775, fols. 63–68v, AGI-SD 1627.

they made a formal petition for *coartación* once more and began individually to buy their freedom.[112] From 1740 to 1775, the rate of manumission increased radically. More conspicuously, once this tide of *coartaciones* began, females fell behind in their ability or willingness to purchase their freedom. During the few annual manumissions of the first period, females were as likely to manumit themselves as males (particularly given the number of children involved in these early cases). From the 1740s to the 1760s, males constituted from 78 to 85 percent of each decade's manumissions.

The exact reasons for the male bias in *coartaciones* are difficult to ascertain. It is not clear, for instance, whether the cobreros made use of household strategies to accumulate savings for the freedom of heads of household and *patres familias* or whether males had greater control of resources and opportunities outside the village that could allow them to save for their own manumissions. The number of male *ausentes* recorded in the family censuses does point to cases of cobreros who spent years working away from the village, and many of these *ausentes* may have been working to save for their *coartación*. Some, like Rafael Cosme in the 1730s, even came from well-to-do families and were often the older male children of the more prestigious families in the village. Although many of these recorded absentees were cases of cobreros who had simply fled the control of the state and settled elsewhere, many may have been royal slaves employed in the houses of citizens of Santiago de Cuba in the kind of veiled work-for-manumission deals described before. Male cobreros may have been preferred or may have been more willing to engage in deals that took them away from their community for long periods of time.

Overall, however, the fact that males carried the burden of forced labor in the community made it very likely that they were given priority by their families in the liberation process. After all, in terms of forced labor requisitions, married females lived more freely than males. Once free of their bonded labor to the state, males could become true *patres familias* occupying themselves fully with the provisioning of family, particularly since any association between alleged land entitlement and royal slave status had been broken by the events of the 1730s and the definitive loss of Barajagua. Males also had greater mobility than females, as the number of absentees reflects, and probably greater access to income-earning possibilities outside the community. Finally, males' greater opportunities for manumission, or in this case *coartación*, may have also derived from their military service, particularly after Admiral Vernon's invasion of Oriente in 1741 and again after the British invasion of Havana in 1762.[113]

Conclusion

The so-called peasant breach opened by the labor arrangements under which the cobreros worked as the king's slaves throughout most of the eighteenth century was not chimerical. A "reconstituted peasantry" had established itself in El Cobre by the end of the seventeenth century, making instead the forced labor arrangements a "slave breach" in an already reconstituted peasant community fighting to preserve itself as such. More than a "liberal" slave labor regime where holidays were respected and time was granted to tend provisioning grounds, the labor system that became customary among the royal slaves of El Cobre was similar to the semibonded corvée system to which Native Americans were subjected throughout the Americas.

The basic set of working arrangements that became "customary" throughout most of the eighteenth century was negotiated between the 1690s and the 1710s. Although the cobreros did not achieve full exemption from forced labor requisitions as they desired (or as they imagined the Crown may have sanctioned on their behalf), their mobilizations did allow them to negotiate some favorable arrangements. Those labor terms, however, were periodically renegotiated when they were threatened and challenged by the policies of unusually stringent governors who attempted to break with what had become established custom.

The "labor negotiation" processes referred to in this chapter more often than not involved the working out of some kind of agreement over what the ambiguous notion of "good treatment" entailed. "Good treatment," of course, not only referred to legal labor prescriptions (or slave codes), but more importantly to the understandings and customary practices that emerged in relation to an implicit moral economy or to particular constructions of social identity. The cobreros often invoked the king's will to negotiate and legitimize their practical meaning of this abstract term. At other times, however, they mobilized claiming a royal grant of freedom.

Two major aspects of the labor regime negotiated by the royal slaves of El Cobre were its rotating and largely gendered character. The rotational system allowed the king's slaves to alternate between laboring for the master/state in Santiago de Cuba and laboring for themselves in their village; in fact, it meant that they could alternate between "slave" and "free" labor practices. During most of the year, the cobreros occupied themselves as autonomous peasants or farmers, not as slaves. The rest of the year was left for harsh forced labor in the fortification projects and other defense-oriented activities, a strongly masculine sphere from which female royal slaves were excluded.

Paradoxically, although male royal slaves carried the greatest burden of forced labor in the community, the principle that allowed them time "off" stemmed not only from the requirement that individual slaves support themselves but from the patriarchal dictum that conferred upon (free) males, particularly *patres familias*, the responsibility for the provisioning of their dependent families. In this sense, a dominant gender ideology and understanding of the division of labor that structured social life among free sectors of colonial society played a strong role in the extensive concessions that the royal slaves were able to negotiate. The same dominant gender ideology that allocated the main productive and provisioning role to males also privileged females' reproductive role leading to the exemption, at least in principle, of married royal slave women from systematic bonded labor for the master/state. Although single female royal slaves—and often married ones too—were subject to labor exactions (albeit in occupations "proper to their sex"), overall, female royal slaves in El Cobre were far less encumbered with forced labor requisitions to the state than were their fathers, brothers, husbands, and sons.

Finally, the forms of political pressure that these peasant slaves utilized to negotiate their claims to "good treatment" ranged from the usual everyday forms of resistance to more collective and coordinated forms of political mobilization that included flight to the mountains, uprisings, withholding of labor power, and filing complaints in the courts.

Although the Crown ultimately retained command over its alleged slaves, the colonial state was relatively weak, unable—or unwilling—to control completely or manage efficiently an extensive, recalcitrant, and armed labor force. Yet, despite the flexibility of the forced labor terms negotiated, these labor requisitions were also inordinate and excessive. Considering the military defense role that the cobreros also played in the village's organized militia companies, a role proper to free men in the colony, the king's slaves should not, properly speaking, have had the added burden of laboring for the state. Of course, neither should they have had the burden of having to finance their own manumission. Despite active resistance and mobilization, the royal slaves of El Cobre were never able to free themselves completely of forced labor to the colonial state. They were only able to negotiate the extent of the labor burdens that the state imposed on them.

CHAPTER 10

Local Government and Politics

Once in his presence his Highness ordered that
they [the king's slaves] take a seat in the benches of
the *cabildo* [local government] of the said city [of
Santiago de Cuba] with the title of *regidores*
[aldermen] given [to them] in the name of both
Majesties.   —Petition of Cobreros, ca. 1734

The bishop should have kept in mind that the
vecinos [residents] of the said village [of El Cobre],
blacks as well as mulattos, are slaves of His
Majesty . . . since they are slaves they cannot
administer ordinary justice, because it has been a
very irregular thing to have allowed them to appoint
alcaldes [bailiffs].
     —Governor Don Pedro Ignacio Ximénez, 1732

Many royal officials felt at ease with the idea of a *cabildo* of king's slaves in
El Cobre. Others viewed such a local institution as a political and social
anomaly and denied it any legitimacy or recognition. Governor Don Juan
Hoyos y Solórzano for one, had reportedly abolished the *cabildo* at some
point during his administration in 1728–1729 because "it was contrary to the
laws of His Majesty to have *alcaldes ordinarios* [bailiffs] who were slaves."[1]
Other governors kept the conflict alive throughout the eighteenth century
by either reinstating or suppressing the *cabildo* of royal slaves during their
tenures.[2] The cobreros' municipal government retained its controversial
character long after the community had formally obtained its collective
freedom at the turn of the nineteenth century. Repeating the policy of some
governors in the previous century, the captain general abolished the *ayuntamiento* (municipal government) of El Cobre in 1841 and again made an
issue of its irregularity. Wrote Captain General Don Gerónimo de Valdés:
"Lately some occurrences have given me the opportunity to disband an

Ayuntamiento of people of color [in El Cobre], unique in its kind and the scandal of this island. . . ."[3] By this time, however, the anomaly had become exclusively racial. Once the community was formally free the problem had become not so much a *cabildo* constituted by slaves—even if royal slaves— but one made up by people of color.

A *cabildo* was established in El Cobre some time at the turn of the eighteenth century, under the administration of Governor Don Juan Barón de Chávez (1700–1708).[4] The acknowledgment of this local body constituted an institutionalization of a longer process: the reconfiguration of royal slave official positions that had been taking place since the early years of transition into local Crown rule, if not before. However limited the political authority of this local body, what made this institution particularly unusual and controversial in the case of the king's slaves was that in Spanish political culture and jurisprudence only free persons were entitled to access and representation in a *cabildo*. Moreover, the constitution of a *cabildo* was the political expression of a corporate entity and a sine qua non of a duly constituted settlement (*población*) within the body polity. At least in principle, such corporate expression represented a higher form of freedom than even individual freedom.[5] Few communities of free people of color (not to speak of enslaved people) attained corporate status and collective representation in the New World.

In communities of subordinate groups such as Native American villages in the Spanish Indies—or in this case in El Cobre—the *cabildo* could play an ambiguous role, however. On the one hand, it constituted a public enactment of a corporate identity and of limited sovereignty within an absolutist colonial polity, a particularly suggestive, even transgressive, role in the case of an enslaved community. On the other hand, the local *cabildo* was an important mechanism for the imposition of colonial state policy at the local level. *Cabildo* positions could also serve the personal interests and local ambitions of members of the community.

To be sure, the political power and autonomy that *cabildos* held after the first decades of colonization even in the Spanish *repúblicas* of the Indies was highly questionable.[6] As royal power became consolidated in the New World, it penetrated and contended with the jurisdiction of these local bodies. Royal authority interfered with local governments' control of previously important municipal affairs, such as the power to grant land, and compromised the representative character of its officers when *regidores* became perpetual royal appointments obtained through purchase of office. Although in

Cuba sale of these offices became the rule by the end of the sixteenth century, *cabildos* retained the authority to grant vacant land to *vecinos* until 1729, when the Crown belatedly revoked that power.[7] Aside from the significant power it lost, the *cabildo* of Santiago de Cuba had a limited authority; it had power to grant house plots, to administer justice in the first instance, to tax and administer the *propios* (municipal taxes) for public works (roads, ports, slaughterhouses) and rogations or other religious and state festivities, and to regulate the provisioning of meat and foodstuffs, among other things.[8] Perhaps nowhere is the limited political authority of this body more poignantly expressed than in a Franciscan friar's insult directed at some *cabildo* officials of Santiago de Cuba in 1771. When some *alcaldes* entered the convent to intervene in a fight between the friar and a superior, Fray Jerónimo sent them back to what he regarded as their proper jurisdiction, shouting, "Go back to the bones of your slaughterhouse."[9]

While their powers were even more restricted than those of local *cabildos* in the Spanish republics, such local political bodies were also established in the Indian *repúblicas* of the New World.[10] Although the Indian *cabildos* were closely regulated by Spanish authorities through the supervision of the *corregidor de indios* and the parish priests, these local bodies did have some margin of autonomy in running the internal affairs of the community (including the distribution of family plots and the adjudication of local justice). The vigor of this institution among Native Americans has long been a debated issue among historians. Regardless of the ebb and flow of Indian *cabildos'* actual powers throughout the vast territory of the Indies during more than three centuries of colonial rule, this local institution at least conferred symbolic corporate representation and some civil personality to Indians in the colonial body polity. The significance of this institution should be sought not only in the political control that it may have conferred to local *vecinos*—ultimately quite limited in an absolutist colonial regime such as the Spanish one, particularly among subordinate groups—but also in the social and symbolic roles that were locally imagined and enacted through it. Moreover, the *cabildo* should be examined within a wider and more dynamic political arena as other kinds of local authority and leadership could emerge in tandem, and sometimes against, local *cabildo* rule.

In the case of El Cobre, the *cabildo's* legitimacy was periodically questioned by colonial authorities, but it was sometimes also denied authority by the pueblo, or at least by some sectors of the community. Aside from the more radical option of revolt—or at least the effective specter of revolt—

there was another mechanism through which subordinate groups in Spanish colonial society could operate: the more autonomous and directly representative position of a village's *apoderado* (legal spokesman and proxy)—a political position within the colonial polity that will be discussed below. Finally, although public office and representation, whether as *cabildo* officers or as *apoderados*, was exclusively a male prerogative throughout the Spanish Empire, free and enslaved women in El Cobre were active— even portrayed by some males as menacingly active—in local politics in other ways, too.

Social Memory and the *Cabildo*'s Local Significance

Memories and stories about the past often speak about issues of significance in the present. Once more I turn to the cobreros' social memory to uncover their construction of identity and entitlement, as well as the significance they attributed to the institution of the *cabildo*. This time the invoked memory is a "microevent" evoked in vivid detail twenty-five years after its occurrence. The inclusion of this memory in a public representation to the captain general demonstrates the cobreros' own politicization of the microevent and its historical significance to them.

The narrative refers to a conflict between the colonial state and the community that took place during Governor Don Joseph Canales's administration. At that time the cobreros sent their own representative to Madrid to denounce the abuses of the governor.[11] Those accusations led to an official investigation in 1709 by a visiting judge of the High Court of Santo Domingo, Don Nicholás Chirino. The cobreros rendered those events of the past in this account from their own local perspective, but they did so making use of an officially "politically correct" master narrative too.

The memory was structured as a folk story. Among the issues it thematized were: the royal legitimacy of the *cabildo* offices; their corporate representative character; their symbolic prerogatives; and some of the social and political implications of constituting such a local body. As was often the case with the cobreros' public discourse, this story of the past was also cast along the Christian and royalist principles of dominant colonial ideology. The cobreros related:

> . . . seeing the great harm done to us [by Governor Canales] we made the decision to inform our Lord and Master about what was happening to us. And Diego de Rosas, a native son of this said pueblo, [was chosen] for this task, a person who, with Divine Providence, was able to inform our Lord and Master as we learned

from Don Nicholás Chirino, who came to investigate those claims. And having arrived [from the High Court of Santo Domingo] the said Don Nicholás Chirino to the city of Santiago de Cuba, he called the *regidores* who were serving . . . and seeing his order and message we [*sic*] went without any delay, and, once in his presence, His Highness ordered that they take a seat in the benches of the *cabildo* of the said city with the title of *regidores* given [to them] in the name of both Majesties. And in view of such honors they thanked the said gentleman while excusing themselves from taking the said seats that he offered to them because they were poor and of broken color [*de color quebrado*]. And His Highness told them to occupy the seats that it was an order of Our Lord and Master.[12] (See Appendix 6)

In this historical story, the figure of Rosas plays the role of a local emissary to the king of Spain. With the aid of Providence, the emissary was able to reach and inform the cobreros' just but distant Lord and Master of their oppression. The narrative aligns royal and divine justice with local claims. In this classic plot of royalist folklore sprinkled with historical events the cobreros were not opposed to the king or to the law, but rather to the local embodiment of authority in Governor Canales. Judge Chirino came in the name of the king to protect the community and save it from the injustices of the governor. Indeed, the God-and-king-sent judge intended to restore things to their purported harmonious order.

The narrative also dramatizes several other important issues and reflects political practices that the cobreros—and other subordinate groups— engaged in. It alludes to the community's collective recourse to the courts, in this case directly in Madrid, in search of redress against the unjust policies of a local royal official. The story also calls attention to Rosas's role as the cobreros' *apoderado*: as liaison between the local community and higher levels of the Spanish state; and as a legal spokesman and proxy who was a royal slave, not a freeman.[13] Rosas, moreover, was portrayed as a "native son of the pueblo." Overall he embodied not only the cobreros' standing as royal slaves but also their social identity as a corporate body and as a territorially bounded people or family. The story depicts in a flat and unequivocal way the *apoderado* Rosas's alignment with the village's *cabildo* officers against the colonial state in Santiago de Cuba. Relations between community, *apoderados*, and *cabildo* officials, however, could often be more complex, problematical, even conflictive.

Most importantly, the recalled microevent made some important points about the social and political implications of Chirino's recognition of the cobreros' *cabildo*. In one of the most explicit articulations of social class and race in the record of this community, the narrative referred to the cobreros' social taints and therefore to their debased status in colonial society. At issue here was not so much the cobrero officials' slave status as their racial and class status: *nuestra pobreza y color quebrado*, or our poverty and broken color. The king's own emissary, however, overrode these considerations by conferring upon the officials the symbolic prerogatives that their offices required. Furthermore, not only did the judge acknowledge the cobreros' right to office despite their (legal) status, race, and class, but by ordering them in the name of His Majesty to sit on the very benches of the capital city's *cabildo*, he acknowledged the equality in status between the officers in El Cobre and those in Santiago de Cuba. Thus, not only had Chirino legitimized the community's *cabildo* in the name of the king, thereby overriding the possible "anomaly" that such offices among royal slaves or blacks may have constituted, but also, in honoring its officers properly, he raised them to the status of fellow officeholders in Santiago de Cuba. This was, by any measure, a radical memory. The episode and its details constituted a dramatized (if in this case still utopian) rendition of the imagined status that a *cabildo* body granted upon its officials and, by extension, upon the community it represented.

The idea of parity with *cabildo* officers in the city of Santiago de Cuba was at least once ritually contended during the festivities dedicated to the Virgin of Charity in the village. These public celebrations were ideal contexts to symbolically reconstruct social identity and relations among groups, particularly given the enormous amount of energy and attention that protocol matters received at the time.[14] As the Virgin's festivities in September were also attended by *vecinos* of other places in the region, including *cabildo* officials from the capital city of Santiago de Cuba and at times even by the governor, the public horizon of ritual interactions became truly wide on those occasions. Thus, when an *alcalde* of Santiago de Cuba attempted to occupy the front benches reserved for *cabildo* officers in the village's church, the *alcaldes* of El Cobre allegedly intercepted him. As the *alcalde* of Santiago de Cuba protested, claiming precedence in the seating arrangements, a *cabildo* officer from the pueblo reportedly snapped, "They [the royal slave *cabildo* officers] had as much jurisdiction to hang [criminals] as he had."[15] What the *alcalde* of El Cobre meant to establish in his own ghastly way was the equality of both offices, if not of both men, by virtue of their jurisdiction over criminal matters, indeed by the great power they both allegedly shared over life and death. (To be sure, capital punishment would have been out of bounds for a judge of the first instance such as an *alcalde*, but as a rhetorical expression it made its point.)

The Bishop, the Governor, and the *Cabildo* of
Royal Slaves: Contested Prerogatives

Nowhere perhaps was the conflict over the existence, prerogatives, and political significance of a *cabildo* in El Cobre more tersely depicted than in a microhistorical event involving a governor, a bishop, and the cobreros. The irascible Governor Ximénez, narrator and protagonist in the controversial incident, provided an insightful (if critical) reading of the politics of an apparently innocent and simple protocol matter. When newly appointed Bishop Don Juan Lasso de la Vega made a pastoral visit to El Cobre in 1732, he ordered the parish priest to set benches inside the church to honor properly the village's *cabildo* officers. Fearing the implications of such an act of honor (and perhaps sensing a provocation on the bishop's part), Ximénez revoked the bishop's order, asserting his authority over the community as well as his jurisdiction over and above the church's. Ximénez defended his decision to the king by explaining:

The bishop should have kept in mind that the *vecinos* of the said village [of El Cobre], blacks as well as mulattos, are slaves of His Majesty . . . since they are slaves they cannot administer ordinary justice because it has been a very irregular thing to have allowed them to appoint *alcaldes*, that is some *mayorales* [overseers] to subject the others because since they are many, it is necessary to have someone to order them, and particularly to be in charge of appointing the [labor] squadrons of those who come to the construction works . . . and they are not *mayorales* either because they have not been appointed by their master but by their own will.[16]

The governor articulated lucidly the social and political distinction between *alcaldes* and *mayorales*, and decried that custom had illegitimately transformed the latter into the former. To Ximénez the only title, position, and treatment that they, as slaves, could properly aspire to, was that of overseers.

By ordering the benches into the church the bishop (as had Chirino some twenty years before) symbolically legitimized the regular character of the *cabildo* through proper religious protocol. In doing so, he had conferred upon the cobreros the same respectful treatment and status that *cabildo* officials received elsewhere in Cuba and the Spanish Empire. The political implication of acknowledging the legitimacy of that kind of local institution in the village was allegedly openly voiced by the bishop too. Cobrero witnesses told the governor that the bishop publicly said to the parish priest and to the Marian sanctuary's chaplain in the presence of most villagers that "they [cobreros] were free, that they had no other master than the Holy

Virgin, and that their duties were [only] to serve her and attend to her Rosary."[17] Thus, in a way, the bishop was ambiguously recognizing the cobreros' status as free, but also as members of a community irrevocably tied to the sustenance of the Virgin's cult.

By ordering the benches out of the church, Ximénez intended to delegitimize the local significance that these official civil positions that the church was confirming via the bishop's orders. Both governor and bishop understood the politically charged character of ceremony. Ultimately both state and church were disputing the meaning of the cobreros' *cabildo*, and perhaps even their power and jurisdiction over the community's affairs too, a note on the conflicts between church and state in which the cobreros could become part.

The *Cabildo* of El Cobre

In 1709, there were three *alcaldes* and two *regidores* in El Cobre, but by midcentury that political body had grown to four *alcaldes* (two *ordinarios* and two *de la Hermandad*) and four *regidores*—not an inconsequential group of officials for a body whose legitimacy was often in question.[18] Indian villages such as El Caney and Jiguaní in midcentury had similar numbers of officials if in somewhat different combinations. Like El Cobre, the village of El Caney also had four *alcaldes* (two *ordinarios* and two *de la Hermandad*) and five *regidores*. Jiguaní just had two *alcaldes ordinarios* and one *regidor*, but it had an *alférez mayor* and an *alguacil mayor* in addition to two other officials more common to cities. Even the town of Baracoa had a similarly constituted municipal government.[19]

Despite the number of freemen in El Cobre, the members of the *cabildo* were almost exclusively royal slaves, at least in the 1730s, the decade for which the longest list of officials is available.[20] The sheer variety and number of men (twenty-eight different names) in the 1730s suggests that a rotation of the office of *alcaldes*, as well as *regidores* did take place. Although *regidores* were supposedly perpetual as elsewhere in the Spanish Empire, at least in the 1730s some ten (and perhaps as many as fifteen) men were recorded as having held this title, thereby suggesting that these positions in El Cobre may have also rotated. In fact, some three or four cobreros played both roles, and at least one, Ignacio de los Reyes, was also a captain of the militias.[21]

The process of selection of *alcaldes* in El Cobre is clearer than that of *regidores*: they were elected. Governor Ximénez suggested (and criticized) the elective character of the cobreros' *cabildo* when he stated that the *alcaldes* of El Cobre "are not *mayorales* either because they have not been appointed by their master but by their [the cobreros'] own will."[22] In a rare glimpse provided during the early 1730s when the cobreros' *cabildo* was reinstated after an interruption of several years, five *regidores* "were appointed" who in turn "elected the four *alcaldes*" of the village for the incoming year.[23] After the customary swearing in, *alcaldes* received the official staffs symbolizing their positions. Elections and meetings, however, were overseen by the parish priest, and selected candidates were subject to the governor's confirmation.[24] Thus, although there was some limited representational and elective character to the local system, it was also one controlled and regulated by the supervision of the priest and the veto power of the colonial state.

The cobreros were occasionally allowed to meet independently to reach decisions; at other times they met surreptitiously. The royal official sent to the village in the early 1730s to pacify the cobreros and mediate their claims with the colonial state reported:

> . . . about eleven [A.M.] the *alcaldes* stood up [in the meeting at the priest's house] and asked me to give them the whole day to call the pueblo to a meeting to see what they determined and having given them until three in the afternoon . . . they went down to the village and played the *caja* [instrument] and they assembled in the house of one of the said *alcaldes* and from that time until three [P.M.] they remained in the meeting where they had a harmony of noise but I could not make out what they were saying neither did I ask and at the said time I asked them what they had resolved . . . they responded that they were ready to send in eight or nine days one squadron of sixteen men and would continue doing so thereafter . . . [which they did not do later]."[25]

Thus, on occasion general assemblies were called in the village where the *alcaldes* could press the state's case, but ultimately, they had to submit to decisions reached by the pueblo. On other occasions, the cobreros, or a faction thereof, would meet independently and extraofficially in the houses of other villagers, outside the framework of the *cabildo* and the state.[26] The *cabildo* of El Cobre did not have an official building; officers assembled either in the priest's house or, when larger meetings were called, in front of the parish church, or less frequently in an *alcalde's* house.

Duties and Responsibilities: Whose Purposes Did the *Cabildo* Serve?

Although the *cabildo* conferred social honor to the community and to its individual holders, its sovereignty was strongly compromised. In effect, this local political body often—though not always or fully—served the purposes of the colonial state at the local level.

Above all, the *alcaldes* of El Cobre had to make sure that state requisitions were met locally. Despite his criticism of a *cabildo* constituted by royal slaves, Governor Ximénez had admitted its utility to the state. He pointed out that the cobreros had been allowed at some point in the past to appoint their own *alcaldes* "to subject the others because since they are many it is necessary to have someone to order them and particularly to be in charge of appointing the [labor] squadrons. . . ."[27] Thus, the governor (and admittedly the state) viewed the role of these offices primarily as facilitating the management of the slave labor force. In effect, Ximénez saw these *alcaldes* as no more than enhanced overseers, and yet, as he recognized, they were not overseers either, because "they were not appointed by their master but by their own will."[28] Indeed, the royal slave officials were not overseers because of their representative character, their minor judicial functions, and even more simply because of their lack of use of the whip.

Like Indian *cabildos* managing the *mita* and *repartimiento* (corvée) labor systems elsewhere in the Spanish Empire, the *cabildo* of El Cobre was responsible for overseeing the labor draft system, at least until the 1730s. *Alcaldes* were exempted from forced labor themselves, but they had the authority to appoint *cabos*, foremen or corporals, to head the different forced labor squadrons, and were accountable to royal officers for seeing that the full squadrons were delivered to Santiago de Cuba.[29] A dynamic glimpse of an *alcalde*'s role and of that position's clear utility to the colonial state comes from the written orders left behind by Governor Canales and a royal slave *alcalde*, Félix Cosme, precisely at the time when Rosas went to Spain to denounce that same governor's procedures. In this case it is also particularly interesting to observe not only the language used but also the communication channels employed and the role of the written word in the transmission of orders from state to local level and in the village itself.

A note from Canales in 1708 ordered the *alcalde* to select some men in El Cobre to be sent to work in Santiago de Cuba: "After the *Alcalde* of the Village of El Cobre sees this my order he shall find the best four men to work in that village and will send them without delay to this City to work in this Royal House in a construction in process there."[30] And a few weeks later the governor signed another written order stating:

After the *Alcalde* of El Cobre receives this [order] he shall find without any delay eight men to work; and they shall be in this city on Monday at dawn and he should take care to keep track of those who have come to work so that they go as their turn comes; and he should also make them bring a load of *Majagua* [a tropical reed for construction] when they come down.[31]

The notes are indicative of the *alcaldes'* role in selecting laborers for the state and of their duty to manage the labor system on a rotational basis. The governor also exacted other requisitions from the community such as the collection and transportation of material (reeds) for the works via the *alcaldes*. Yet, this correspondence was included in a legal file as evidence of the governor's excesses against the community.

At times, governors tried to make labor compulsory as well for freemen in the community (these requisitions were particularly considered to be abuses and a motive for unrest). In these cases, royal slave *alcaldes* also oversaw requisitions among free cobreros, having the power to fine violations of the governor's orders from this sector of the community too. In this particular instance, the *alcalde* Cosme transmitted the governor's orders to the community in his own voice, and perhaps his writing:

And I order that as far as the construction of the jail of the king my master goes all should know that it is obligatory work and the free [are called voluntarily] as a favor that the king my lord expects from his vassals and for which he thanks them and if they act contrarily they will be fined by 2 *ducados* applied to the same construction works. . . .[32]

The line between enslavement and vassalage to the Crown was blurred in the case of these labor exactions given that labor was declared compulsory for all, at least in the form of a corvée system. The fine constituted a way "out" of forced labor for those freemen who could afford it to pay for a labor replacement in the construction works.[33]

Although orders to *cabildo* officers were officially addressed in the third person (perhaps acknowledging that they would have to be read, probably by the parish priest), Canales also addressed notes more directly and personally to Cosme who seems to have been the governor's right-hand man in the village: "Félix Cosme, accompanying this [correspondence] is the order that you ask me for, although I don't think it is necessary . . . ; also those in the construction works are worse than ever these days. And I thought that you [*tú*] had brought them to reason . . . it seems everything will have a bad end."[34] (It did, for the governor eventually disarmed the cobreros, the latter fled to the mountains and sent Rosas to Madrid to denounce the governor's actions.) As the note shows, the governor relied on the *alcaldes* of El Cobre to mediate labor unrest. This liaison role could often compromise the village officials' loyalties to their community. But the governor's comment also suggests that *alcaldes* were not always successful in mediating the colonial state's orders, or local officials could lose legitimacy in the community if they were perceived as too aligned with the state. Cosme's situation illustrates the predicament in which *cabildo* officers could often find themselves in their official liaison role.[35] In fact, his case shows how *cabildo* officials were sometimes complicit—or at times had no choice but to be complicit—with the local colonial state against the interests of the constituency they allegedly represented.

Either the *alcaldes* of the pueblo did not always comply with their duties, or at times the cobreros themselves would not comply with the bailiffs' orders. In the conflictive 1730s, another *alcalde*, Félix Gerónimo Hernández, declared that he and his companion

have worked as much as possible to assemble some people to come in the second squadron that was to be appointed and that they were looking for them [the royal slaves] in the fields where they have their farms and that they were only able to get eight of the said slaves . . . of which he only knows that three showed up and he does not know where the others are.[36]

Similarly, the *alcalde* Marcelo González stated that "having ordered them not to fail to comply with their obligation they responded that they could not go to anything [the fortifications] until those who had gone to [work and litigate in] the city of Havana come back to that pueblo."[37]

The predicament of *cabildo* officials in the community was perhaps nowhere better illustrated than in the following episode. It took place in the 1730s, again under the conflictive administration of Governor Ximénez. A disgruntled faction in the village had extraofficially commissioned and paid the literate cobrero Antonio Salazar to write a letter on the community's behalf to the Dean Morell de Santa Cruz explaining why they refused to attend work in the fortification projects. The *alcalde* Vicente sent Salazar a message invoking the ties that bound them and saying that "as his brother-in-law and compadre he beseeched him not to write the letter."[38] When Salazar cynically responded that he would desist if the *alcalde* sent him 2 pesos with which to refund the payment that the cobreros had made for his writing services, the *alcalde* responded (or at least the governor was told that he had responded) that "he [as *alcalde*] would execute any order given to him by His *Señoría* [the governor] or from the Señor Dean even if it was against him [his kin]."[39] Thus, in this case, orders from superiors and the *alcalde*'s loyalties as an official would take priority over any other bonds, even those of kinship or of community (patriotic) ties.

Cabildo officials cooperated with the colonial state sometimes against the interests of the community, or sectors thereof, out of intimidation. In the 1790s, the *alcaldes* of El Cobre suggested that the governor forced them to inform against some cobreros and the parish priest by threatening them with imprisonment.[40] The *alcalde* Matías Quiala, who had given some evidence of supporting the parish priest and his own fellow villagers in the community's claims for collective freedom in Madrid,[41] declared to Governor Don Juan Nepomuceno de Quintana:

Señor Brigadier Don Juan Bautista Vaillant [previous governor of Santiago de Cuba] had never threatened him with the underground vaults of El Morro so that he declare or inform about the events in El Cobre regarding its slaves and against the parish priest, that the reports and declarations he had made over the matter were spontaneous and voluntary . . . that the threats [with imprisonment in El Morro] had been if he did not carry out his commission and orders [as *alcalde*] but not to force him to declare or report against the said priest.[42]

That testimony had probably been forced as well. Trying to excuse the previous Governor Vaillant, Governor Nepomuceno de Quintana concluded:

If indeed there had been threats . . . [they had been] due to the [governor's] accusation of [the *alcaldes*'] neglectful and careless compliance with their duties; since they voluntarily avoided the apprehension of the fugitive [slaves] he [the governor] erupted telling them that if they did not proceed with the purity and honor that corresponded to the King's service he would put them in the said vaults of the Castle of El Morro.[43]

From the governor's perspective, then, village *alcaldes* could oppose the local colonial state through passive resistance; but in principle *cabildo* officials were obliged to cooperate with and to represent colonial authorities at the local level.

That *alcaldes* betrayed the pueblo's interests not only out of fear and intimidation but also sometimes out of convenience was made clear at the same time by some sectors of the community who wrote to a friendly bishop:

. . . we have come to understand and to hear from the [free] *Alcaldes* of this Pueblo, the Sublieutenant Fulgencio Ojeda and Nicholás Ojeda, both brothers in hatred and resentment, that our priest . . . obstructed the fraud from which they lived and with which they were living well since they took away our *paysanos* [fellow villagers] the runaway [cobrero] slaves in the *montes* [hills] and made them work in their farms . . . to the point of the said *alcaldes* Ojeda saying publicly that they have been ruined this year for not having those means [the labor of the captured runaway cobrero slaves] and they would not stop until they brought down our priest. . . .[44]

Although Joseph Cosme's rapid rise to the peak of success in the village in terms of ability to manumit his immediate family, to attain the title and rank of captain in the pueblo's militia companies (as well as his son's rank as lieutenant), to acquire slaves, and to construct a tiled house in the village, may have been due to sheer merit or family backing, it could have also been due to friendliness with colonial authorities. Yet, years later the patriarch Joseph Cosme's descendants and relatives were also key to the defense of the pueblo against local authorities as well as in the financial backing of the freedman Gregorio Cosme Osorio, a more distant member of the Cosme family, in the royal court in Madrid.[45]

As is clear from some of these examples, *alcaldes* in El Cobre also had policing duties, notably, functions that did not generally accrue to slaves. Moreover, despite their royal slave status, *alcaldes* had jurisdiction over free and slave cobreros. Félix Cosme wrote in 1709 in a language that reflects the authority, honor, and respect commanded by local officials in the village: "I the *señor alcalde ordinario* of the mines of Santiago del Prado distribute by command of the señor governor this my order of the king, my master to all the *vecinos* and residents of these mines of Santiago del Prado, free and slaves. . . ."[46] Similarly, in another document, Cosme commanded again in a rhetoric of political authority not commonly heard from slaves:

I order that no person [free or slave] can leave this place and go further away than a league [the village's jurisdiction] without my license; that it is against the will of the Señor Governor with the warning that whoever incurs against the order will be fined 4 *ducados* and if the person does not have them, they will be taken from their property, and, moreover, [they] will be condemned to four months in El Morro.[47]

Furthermore, sometimes governors also gave *alcaldes de la Hermandad* and *ordinarios* in El Cobre authority to arrest free or white suspects from outside the pueblo. Governor Canales, for example, sent an order to the *alcaldes ordinarios* of El Cobre to send off the village's *alcaldes de la Hermandad*:

. . . to the roads to [the city of] Bayamo and others to other places, each *alcalde* with five armed men; and any kind of Spanish man [*hombre español*] that looks like a sailor and all the others that they may find on their way to Bayamo, Trinidad, Sancti Espiritu, or Havana, unless he is with license from me, should be apprehended and brought to me; and they should execute this order without delay or otherwise I will make use of the rigor that they merit; and the free who do not want to go to this task will be enslaved forever . . . ;and the slaves that they find on the roads, if they were from this city, shall [also] be apprehended.[48]

Of course, *alcaldes* also had police and judicial functions over cobreros in the pueblo. Sometimes *alcaldes* acted under orders from the governor in Santiago de Cuba for the arrest of villagers in El Cobre. However, they also had authority to arrest cobreros for minor disorders internal to the community at their own discretion. In either case, the arrested person would be put in a stock in the backyard of an *alcalde's* house until either a guard from the city of Santiago de Cuba would come to escort the prisoner to the governor, or the *alcaldes* would select a group to take him down to the city. These jailings, however, were occasions for much conflict in the village. At least twice in the 1730s, relatives and friends assaulted an *alcalde's* house to rescue a prisoner or planned to ambush them as these prisoners were led to the city.[49] Thus, cobreros sometimes opposed their *alcaldes'* judgment regarding the implementation of "law and order."

The Legitimacy of the *Cabildo* in the Community

What legitimacy then did a local institution forming part of the colonial state apparatus have among subordinate people in El Cobre? Were there other alternatives to this political body? Although usually respected, the legitimacy of the *cabildo* officers eroded when the community, or a faction thereof, perceived them to be working too closely with royal authorities or compromising the interests of the village too much. Factionalism in a village and the delegitimation of *cabildo* officers, however, was a widespread phenomenon in the Spanish world, among Indian peasant communities and in the Spanish towns too.

In El Cobre, again during the conflict- and action-ridden decade of the 1730s—a time for which records are also more abundant—a faction of the village attacked the houses of some *cabildo* officers. The *alcalde* Patricio Cosme (yet another member of the village's Cosme clan) reported that thirty rioting men took two prisoners from his house and later

went to the house of the *regidor* Félix Hernández and with their lances they destroyed his door, and from there they went to the house of the *Regidor* Juan Manuel Quiala, they wanted to burn his house.[50]

Cosme also reported that when the tumultuous cobreros freed the prisoners one had called the *alcalde* "un perro vendepueblos" [a village-sellout dog].[51] It is difficult to untangle the actual factional politics in the village at the time, but it was related to a conflict between a radical sector who wanted to pursue litigation in Havana, and others who were more willing to cooperate with the governor and not defy orders directly.

Likewise, in the 1780s and 1790s when the cobreros litigated for their collective freedom in Madrid, many villagers opposed the local *alcaldes* whom they saw as cooperating with the governor and the alleged heirs of the mines. The local *apoderado* Justo Cruzata wrote from El Cobre to the cobreros' *apoderado* Gregorio Cosme Osorio in Madrid:

> *María de la Charidad* has made one of her miracles in that we have found out that the confabulated [denouncers] are certainly the Ojeda [*alcalde* brothers] for it seems to me that from that generation nor from the one that descends from them, nothing good can come forth for a bitter orange tree cannot produce sweet fruit; their great-grandfather was the one who sold the pueblo. . . .[52]

Cruzata connected local past and present by invoking social memory. He linked the *alcaldes'* betrayal of the community to one of their ancestors, who had similarly betrayed the pueblo years ago, perhaps during the events of the 1730s. In the letter to the cobrero Cosme Osorio, the literate Cruzata was more specific about his accusation against the *alcaldes*:

> Friend, I cannot do less than inform you of the events and problems in which I find myself . . . and if not see that they [the Ojeda brothers] have been *Alcaldes* for three years because they are to the liking of the heirs [of the mines] and of the Señor Governor because there is no letter that you send that they do not give to the Governor and the heirs so that we cannot do anything without them penetrating it, so you can consider how we are. I would appreciate it if you [would] inform His Majesty that it is certain that it is they who are the traitors against His treasury. . . .[53]

The *apoderado* Cruzata, a freedman, was condemning the village *alcaldes'* loyalties to the colonial state and to the alleged heirs of the mines rather than to their own (free and enslaved) community.

The *Apoderado* Alternative

Although in the modest *cabildo* of El Cobre there was no official place for a *Procurador General* (attorney general), the cobreros selected their own *apoderados* and emissaries to the courts as events dictated. In 1709 Diego de Rosas had played such a role. Years later, in 1728, the royal slave Matías Moreno took the pueblo's case to the High Court of Santo Domingo and also led a delegation to Havana to petition and file judicial complaints against colonial authorities in Santiago de Cuba. An *alcalde* of El Cobre denounced him to Governor Ximénez, pointing to the cleavages that could take place within the community over the loyalties and legitimacy owed *cabildo* officials:

Matías Moreno was the principal cause of the seditions and disobediences [in the village] . . . ; on several occasions he has criticized the operations of the one who declares for having been obedient to what Your Highness has ordered him to do and for having carried out orders emanating from his Superior; and that the said Matías Moreno has always shown himself displeased for not having been named *regidor* of the said pueblo nor *alcalde* in it.[54]

Indeed, Moreno had clearly been excluded for political reasons when the *cabildo* was reinstated and elections were overseen by church and state. Despite the fact that he was not officially part of the *cabildo*, Moreno became the pueblo's main opposition leader regarding the contested issue of Barajagua during the 1730s. Even while away in Havana, his supporters in El Cobre secretly met in his wife's house to discuss political matters in the village. Moreno here played an ambiguous role as *apoderado* in the courts and as extraofficial leader of a faction in the village.

The political power some men in the village, like Moreno, could exert outside the formal framework of the *cabildo* was evinced in the testimonies of some younger cobreros, who, when arrested, were asked why they had refused to attend work in the labor squadrons, thus "denying the obedience that they owed as King's slaves." The cobrero Lorenzo González responded that he and others "would have shown up for work had it not been for the impediment raised by the said Matías Moreno, Crisanto de Lugo [and a list of others] . . . , who are the Fathers who govern the pueblo."[55] None of the five cobreros González referred to as the "Fathers who govern the pueblo" held or had held a *cabildo* position in the 1730s. Yet, extraofficially they had authority among members of the community.

It is significant that the extraofficial authority of these opponents was construed in terms of a father metaphor. The cobreros imagined the community as a patriarchal family with the symbol of the father as the dispenser of internal law and order. If royal officials in Santiago de Cuba considered the cobreros to be slaves owing obedience to the master, the king, or the governor, the cobreros countered this representation with their own patriarchal one, where they as sons—and not slaves—owed obedience to the fathers of the pueblo first.

Like Rosas in 1709, and Moreno in the 1730s, the cobreros Justo Cruzata and Gregorio Cosme Osorio became *apoderados* during the conflicts of the

1780s and 1790s. While Gregorio Cosme Osorio was selected to represent the cobreros in Madrid, Justo Cruzata became the main local *apoderado* of El Cobre. Both were freedmen and mulattos who possessed strong literacy skills. Thus the community—or rather *the principales* and "fathers" of the village—could also select their own representatives and leaders outside the framework of the *cabildo* and the state. In this sense, the *apoderados* represented a more autonomous alternative in the corporate representation of community within the colonial body politic. Ultimately, however, there was also the better-known option of flight to the mountains and even revolt, which, despite its high risks, could be effective in exerting political pressure on the state. Other leaders would emerge informally in these more transgressive forms of political mobilization. More often than not, different political strategies worked in tandem with different leaders in each sphere.

Administration of Village Funds

While elsewhere in the Spanish Empire *cabildos* oversaw the town treasury (*caja de comunidad*), it is not clear if any official collective fund existed in El Cobre. Community expenses such as litigation were collected on an ad hoc basis. In the 1730s, for instance, Moreno sent word to the village—or at least to the faction behind him in El Cobre—that he needed 100 pesos for the judicial process in Havana. A resident in El Cobre declared to authorities:

Fifteen days ago, the slave Cándido Timoteo from the village of the Mines told [the witness], and with much daring, to contribute 6 pesos to aid that poor pueblo . . . that the help was to feed the men who were going to Havana [to litigate]; and telling him that [the witness] did not have 6 reales . . . he [Timoteo] said with great emotion [*desahogo*] that [the witness] was forsaking the pueblo . . . and [the witness] has heard that some have collected some pesos among them to go to Havana and to Spain . . . and that among those who are going is Felipe Vicente. . . .[56]

Similarly in the 1790s, it was the freedman Justo Cruzata "to whose protection they were also subject (as he was the one who collected the money in the Pueblo to send to the *apoderado* [in Madrid] and other expenses). . . ."[57] Again this money was collected for actions intended to challenge the colonial state. Thus, fees were collected as the need to finance litigation came up and were representative of the cobreros' horizontal network and forms of mobilization outside an official *caja de comunidad*.

Funds for religious festivities, at least those for the Virgin, consisted of obligatory contributions collected by the *regidor* or by the priest. Juan Ravelo "had some [angry] words with Félix Gerónimo, *Regidor*, in the priest's house on New Year's day regarding if he would pay or not what was obligatory for the feast that the pueblo makes to Our Lady of Charity in her *octava* [the eight-day-long festivity]; and for that he was told that the Señor Governor wanted to arrest him."[58] Community projects, such as the construction of a bridge or the repair of the church, were carried out in the 1770s through the internal labor system of *faginas* but perhaps also through the payment of other kinds of fees and contributions.[59]

The *alcaldes* of El Cobre also had limited authority to rent village lands for communal funds. In 1737, for example, they rented plots to two free blacks from outside the village at the customary annual rate of 5 pesos to cover the expenses of the oil for the Holy Sacrament's lamp.[60] Furthermore, the *alcaldes* were reported to have demanded rent payment from a free black, another outsider who had settled upon what he regarded as private land but what the *alcaldes* considered to be village's territory.[61] In this case, *cabildo* officials used their authority to look out for the corporate community's interests against an outsider. It is not clear if, as in Santiago de Cuba or elsewhere in the Indies, *alcaldes* had the authority to distribute land plots among the cobreros or how the land-grabbing process was handled in the village. During the conflictive years of the 1790s, the village's parish priest, Father Don Alejandro Paz y Ascanio, was reported to be distributing (without authorization) plots in the pueblo. It is not clear if the priest's distributions were considered transgressive because of his lack of authority to grant land or because he was giving plots to alleged runaway cobreros who were returning to the village.[62]

Although the cobreros often litigated locally for land as a corporate community, it is not clear if *cabildo* officials represented the community in these instances, or as in the cases of *apoderados* sent to Havana, Santo Domingo, or even to Madrid, community members were especially selected for the job. At least in one case reference is made to "the commissioners of El Cobre" submitting a representation with a land claim to the courts.[63] In another case earlier in the century, the *cabildo* officials of El Cobre had the legal power to confer proxy powers on their selected attorney to represent them in court.[64]

Gender and Political Life in El Cobre

Political life in the village, whether within the official bounds of the *cabildo* institution, or through *apoderados*, was a highly gendered drama whose protagonists were men often in the role of fathers or sons of the pueblo. Did females enter the arena of village politics? If so, how? In times of conflict, as in the 1730s, women became more visible (even though their voices were not much more audible) in the records. In the factionalism of those days, they were not spared from accusations by opponents—particularly *cabildo* officials. Such accusations throw light both on the role of women in village politics and on how those roles were perceived as threatening. To what extent some of the charges raised against them were actually "true" is difficult to say since all the women interrogated refused to answer any questions, instead either feigning ignorance or denying charges. But the fact that charges were brought against them (and the property of some confiscated) indicates that they constituted a threat to certain ways of imagining public order, including a dominant gendered order of things. Particularly significant about these accusations was the kind of actions that some cobreros and authorities construed as "political" and "subversive" at that time.

Colonial authorities detained eight women, some of them related to each other in 1737. The *alcalde* Patricio Cosme asked that they be remitted to the governor in Santiago de Cuba because "they are the ones who instigate [*inquietan los ánimos*] and who incite men to make trouble, for in some of the disturbances that occur at any moment some of them concur and have put on a machete in their belts. . . ."[65] The *regidor* Félix Gerónimo Hernández said that the women in question were "bad and rebellious . . . and María de la Rosa carries a machete in her belt and blaphemes like a man."[66] Joseph Cosme declared that he did not know anything about the detained women, but that he had heard it said "that the most unruly was the *vieja* [old hag] María de la Rosa [and] that she tells men to put on her skirts and let her put on their pants."[67] Tiburcio de Rosas added that Simona [Vicente] "is extremely bad and disturbs the pueblo, that even with the priest she has been impudent for she has raised her skirt to give him her back ['mooned' him]."[68]

All these accusations concurred that the women were present in village riots or played roles as instigators.[69] María de la Rosa (age sixty) was said to use gender metaphors to provoke men and insult their virility. Indeed, a recurring theme in these declarations by male villagers was the implicit double-laden transgression for which females were accountable: for their participation in public disorders and for the gender transgressions that some of their acts allegedly constituted. Yet, other gender-based accusations against these women were even more striking in the context of "disruption of the public order": aside from her shameless transgression against the priest, Simona Vicente (age forty) was accused of dominating her husband Gaspar González by threatening not to sleep with him until he executed or performed what she wanted.[70] The accusation could not have been a more eloquent statement of the linkage between the private and the public, and a truly historically precocious acknowledgment of a "politics of sexuality." Magdalena Quiala's (age thirty-five) political transgressions also constituted articulations between the domestic and local public realms. Lieutenant Velasco Calderín, in charge of pacifying the village, informed Governor Ximénez that Magdalena "is a very small woman but I gather she dominates her husband [Andrés Vicente]."[71] In ruling the house these dangerous women ruled the village—or so the power of these women was construed. Regardless of the true character of the occurrences these women were accused of, it is significant that these charges could be considered "legitimate" denunciations.

Francisca de los Reyes (age thirty-seven) was described as "a resolute woman who did not allow any soldier to enter her house to make embargoes. . . . she has attended all the tumults with her brothers [Juanico and Lorenzo de los Reyes]. . . . she is arrogant and has a talkative style."[72] Magdalena Quiala's mother Isabel de Lugo (age sixty) and her sister Andrea (age twenty-six) were also involved in the public disturbances. But since one was a widow and the other was single there were no domestic politics at issue. These two women were accused instead of turning their house into a meeting place for insurgents.[73]

Juana Chrisostoma (age fifty) was a more singular and complex case: although there were no gender transgressions on her part, as the wife of Matías Moreno she was presumably the main liaison between him and the pueblo. She may even have taken his place while he litigated on behalf of the pueblo in Havana. Lieutenant Velasco Calderín described her as "a virtuous woman, very devoted to the Sanctuary, but with the defect that her husband Matías Moreno apparently left her powers or orders to govern this pueblo [in his absence]."[74] She was reported to be "one with voice and vote in the meetings and reunions that were held during the disturbances of the pueblo."[75] Thus, her political role was a powerful one—with voice and vote—in the public realm. It is not clear how unusual this role was for a female in unofficial political arenas in the pueblo outside the rigid gendered strictures of the Spanish state. In any case, the lieutenant viewed her mainly as playing a proxy role for her husband; perhaps he detained her as a way of harassing or punishing Moreno.

Women could also play de facto, if secondary, leadership roles, particularly among females in the village. In the 1790s, a royal official seeking to penetrate the political affairs in the pueblo reported his meeting with a female cobrera to the governor:

> . . . another cobrera, quite shrewd, young and a slave . . . with whom I had similar conversations given that she is one of those who has preference among them and could propagate the insinuated things . . . [told me] that she would willingly go back to serve her masters, and others [females] would do so too [provisionally, so that the governor would be pleased and testify on their favor], if I took the trouble to make the priest understand . . . all that I had told her and of which she was convinced . . . and that she would try as far as she was capable of to explain to Justo Cruzata [what I had told her] to whose protection they were also subject. . . .[76]

The treacherous royal official who infiltrated the village by "pretending he had come to fulfill a vow to the Sanctuary"[77] seemed to know who some of the most respected and influential members of the community were in the absence of the official *apoderado*. Although the cobrera located by the governor's secretary was young, she was popular in the village, had leadership qualities, and was influential, particularly among women, but perhaps also among powerful men like Cruzata. While the royal official tried to co-opt her to the governor's side, ultimately she recognized the authority of the priest and of Cruzata in local politics and acknowledged them as the designated representatives of the community's collective will over and above her own views, interests, and perhaps gender role.

Finally, although women did not litigate on behalf of the community, they signed petitions in the pueblo. In the petition that the free cobreros sent to the bishop in 1795 on behalf of their parish priest, there were thirteen female names among the thirty-six signatories.[78] Women also made use of the courts on an individual basis for manumission disputes. In her quest for freedom after the privatization of the mines in the 1780s and 1790s, a young widow named Marcelina Antonia de los Reyes went to the courts at several places in the island: Puerto Príncipe, Sancti Espíritu, Trinidad, and Havana. Her alleged master complained to the court that "a *parda* [mulatta], my slave, Marcelina Antonia de los Reyes, supposing herself free has harassed me, taking me to different tribunals in the interior of the Island . . . [and she] has run away from my power in pursuit of the rights that she considers hers. . . ."[79] Her alleged mistress, Doña Ana de Rocha, noted "the temerity with which my slave attempted to [carry out] this [judicial] process and the tenacity with which she follows it." She added, "The intrepid and conflictive [*bullicioso*] character of this mulatta is evinced in the [judicial] process itself."[80] The "intrepid" Marcelina Antonia de los Reyes appeared in courts throughout the island either with her brother or by herself. By contrast, the cobrera Juana María Bayesteros perhaps played a more conventional gender role by allowing her husband, a freeman, to take charge of the litigation in Santiago de Cuba on her behalf.[81]

In short, although excluded from the official *cabildo* or representation in collective litigation—an all-male political realm—women apparently participated in public disturbances, turned working tools such as machetes into weapons, made their voices heard, used their influence, held political opinions, agitated in public and in private, provided alternative meeting spaces in their homes, at times enjoyed the right to vote at public assemblies, stood up to soldiers and agents of the state, insulted priests, and litigated on their own behalf. Indeed, while helping redefine the *patria chica*'s politics, they may have also reformulated local gender roles.

Conclusion

Perhaps more saliently than elsewhere in Spanish colonial society, the local *cabildo* of El Cobre played an ambiguously dual role. On the one hand, it constituted a colonial state mechanism for the regulation of forced labor as well as for the control and governance of local community; on the other hand, the possibility of recognized self-governance, even if limited self-governance, for an enslaved community of people of African descent had particularly strong symbolic, social, and political implications in the context of colonial slave society. In fact, the establishment of such an institution in this particular community constitutes one of the most unexpected and contradictory aspects of El Cobre's local history. Indeed, many contemporaries protested and challenged the existence of such an institution in El Cobre precisely on the grounds of the peculiar legal status of the pueblo's inhabitants. By the nineteenth century, once royal slavery was no longer an issue in El Cobre, that contradiction became articulated solely in racial terms.

Challenges had been voiced during the transitional years of the 1670s, when a *cabildo* had not yet been established among the royal slaves, but when appointed enslaved officials with the titles of *alcaldes* and *mandadores* had begun to incorporate some mediating and policing functions into those roles. These early official positions and the uncommon responsibilities attached to them out of expediency had in effect begun to stretch the practical meaning of slavery. Indeed, their very existence and operation had effectively constituted a redefinition of enslavement in the early years of

Crown rule. The actual organization of a local *cabildo*, however, did not come until the turn of the eighteenth century.

Whether a *cabildo* was allowed to operate in El Cobre by virtue of the cobreros' ambiguous and distinctive status as royal slaves; or because of expedient considerations that eventually became accepted as customary practice and tradition, this local institution conferred upon the native inhabitants of this pueblo a public persona that belied their "social" and, more significantly, their "political death" as slaves. A local *cabildo* political-ly embodied the cobreros' social ties as a community and their natal ties to a *patria chica*. Moreover, its existence turned mere inhabitants of a locality into community and inserted them as such within the broader body politic of the Spanish Empire. It provided some (limited) local sovereignty and conferred upon cobreros some capacity to represent, mediate, and govern as in the case of Indian pueblos. Furthermore, a local *cabildo* entailed the extension of a patriarchal identity beyond the familial and household sphere so that cobrero *patres familias* could also become "fathers of the pueblo." As in Spanish colonial society in general, the political sphere in this subordi-nate local community was a highly gendered domain strongly inflected by patriarchal discourse. Yet, females in El Cobre were also politically active in community affairs. As a result of that political participation, colonial author-ities, local officials, and even fellow villagers sometimes accused cobrera women of transgressing proper gender roles.

Despite the elective character of the *alcalde* positions, the institution's representative aspects, its local policing and administrative functions, and some decision-making capacity, the *cabildo* of royal slaves in El Cobre was too directly subjected to the colonial state, and specifically to the governor of the Oriente region, to wage more than a modicum of effective local autonomous power. Yet, in the cases where *cabildo* officers were perceived to be too aligned with the interests of the colonial state (when and if these went crassly against those of the pueblo), the community, or sectors thereof, could deny the institution's legitimacy and contest its representative claims. In these cases, villagers tapped parallel mechanisms available within the framework of colonial society to defend the community and its perceived interests. Indeed, a cobrero *apoderado* could be chosen by concerned "fathers of the village" to represent the pueblo in the judicial apparatus of the colonial state, thereby, for instance, sidestepping the *cabildo*'s direct ties to governors and other colonial authorities.

CHAPTER 11

Reaching the King

Colonial Courts and Politics

The malice and enmity that [Governor Don Juan
Barón de Chávez] had against me can be inferred
from . . . [his] instigation [of the cobreros] to inform
against me. . . . With the idea of deposing me [Don
Juan Barón de Chávez, Don Joseph Lozada, and
Diego García de Amoco] had the idea that Diego
de Rosas, one of the slaves, go, as he went, to the
Royal Council of the Indies, conniving to portray
me as an infidel in the memorial [the royal slave]
gave with the pretext that I had disarmed some of
the said slaves. . . .
        —Governor Don Joseph Canales, ca. January 1711

If you do not put a remedy to this we will go to
inform the King our master.
                    —Cobreros to Governor Don Pedro
                        Ignacio Ximénez, ca. July 1731

Governor Canales's acrimonious testimony provides a rare glimpse into a
convoluted colonial world in which governors and their allies acted in con-
nivance with subordinate groups against other governors and officials. It was
a world in which slaves could denounce governors in royal courts and
where accusations could include deceptively simple crimes such as the disarmament of fellow (royal) slaves or major ones such as treason. It was a
world, moreover, in which slaves—or at least the king's slaves—were able to
send fellow slaves as representatives to the courts and to travel as far as
Madrid to seek justice from the king.

These—to some extent—extraordinary practices belie once again the
depiction of enslaved subjects like these royal slaves as socially and politically dead or, for that matter, even marginal subjects in Spanish colonial

society. The extent to which this subordinate group employed imperial state mechanisms and appropriated hegemonical discourses to mobilize politically was truly remarkable, particularly in terms of the use they made of colonial courts. The cobreros tapped the Crown's judicial system at *all* levels of appeal: from the Audiencia, or High Court, level to its pinnacle at the Supreme Royal Council of the Indies. Their direct circulation through these courts embraced a vast geographical area that included Santiago de Cuba, Havana, Santo Domingo, and Madrid. Perhaps no other known subordinate group—at least in the colonial historiography of the Spanish Americas—has made collective use of imperial judicial channels in such a consistent, exhaustive, and far-reaching way.[1] Mobilizing at these multiple judicial levels, however, required a wide network of patronage and support. The cobreros' tactical "alliances"—as well as their enmities—also involved figures at the highest secular and ecclesiastical echelons of colonial society, including governors, captain generals, bishops, and cathedral deans.

Mobilization through judicial state mechanisms constitutes perhaps the most surprising aspect of these enslaved subjects' political practice. However, it does not mean that the royal slaves did not also make use of other forms of collective mobilization such as flight (*cimarronaje*) to the hills (*montes*), which was a recurring and alarming nightmare for colonial authorities, particularly in a frontier region such as Oriente. Yet, for the most part, the cobreros did not take up such collective flight as an end in itself. Flight was used as a strategy for negotiating forms of freedom—even freedom itself—within the parameters of a colonial frontier society, and not as an escape.[2] In fact, throughout the history of this community, episodes of flight or sublevations were concurrent with (and not necessarily contraposed to) some kind of political mobilization through the courts. The cobreros' acts of so-called *cimarronaje* have been examined elsewhere and will only form a backdrop here for less-examined forms of political mobilization and negotiation within the body polity.[3]

A study of a subordinate group's use of the Crown's judicial channels requires an examination of the context that enabled their access to those mechanisms in the first place. A mere glance at the political scene throughout a few decades between the late seventeenth and early eighteenth centuries reveals that colonial politics in Oriente was not a placid affair.[4] Although protracted bitter conflicts and factional virulence were not extraneous to regional politics elsewhere in the Spanish Empire, the turbid, turbulent, and at times violent character of the political scene in this corner of the Caribbean may have been exacerbated by its frontier location. The lucrative possibilities of contraband trade and military defense considerations produced considerable tension between Crown and colony, different levels of the state, and rival elite settler sectors in the region. The king's slaves played an active political role in these colonial frontier dramas, too. A good part of these conflicts were played out through judicial channels.

While this community's "holy alliance" with the church—or metaphorically with "the Virgin"—has been discussed earlier, this chapter foregrounds the cobreros' discursive and political relations to the emblematic figure of "the king," or the state. Put succinctly, the king here functions as a larger-than-life figure embodying both a political, legal, and social ideology about the proper order of things in Spain's early modern world and also the Crown's administrative and judicial ruling apparatus, including institutions and personnel and their practices and technologies of power.

Significance of *Derecho* or Law: Rethinking the Judicial Sphere

The royal slaves' use of judicial mechanisms in many ways constituted a practice more fitting of free subjects in the body politic than of enslaved ones. Yet, in Spain's Roman-based slave codes, enslaved persons, despite their inherently social and political "dead" status, were granted some limited legal protections and "rights" that, at least in principle, shielded them from a master's absolute power over their lives and bodies. At the individual level, for instance, slaves had access to the courts to denounce some forms of bad or improper treatment and to claim manumission or freedom under certain circumstances.[5] In addition, Spanish legal codes explicitly distinguished royal slaves by prescribing special rights that allowed them to initiate suits and to appeal in defense of their master's property and (presumably by extension) of his or her own person.[6] This distinction granted the king's slaves an ambiguous legal persona that gave them the possibility to make wider use of royal courts than was normally possible for other slaves. The royal slaves of El Cobre made this special provision a reality.

Much has been made in colonial historiography of the dead letter of the law, particularly in reference to slave codes, and of its misleading representation of "real life on the ground." Naive and idealistic conceptions of the law in early studies of slavery were challenged and displaced by more materialist-oriented analyses firmly grounded in the political economy of the plantation system.[7] In fact, this new genre of studies of slavery virtually eradicated legal systems and judicial issues from its pages. This neglect or dismissal of the judicial sphere unwittingly resulted in the denial of any agency whatsoever to enslaved subordinate groups—or at least to those with some possibility of accessing the courts.[8] Rather than approaching the judicial system narrowly as a static, disembodied, and prescriptive *reflection* of the "real" world as early studies tended to do, it may be productive at this point to approach it from below, in more dynamic terms: as a series of legal, social, and political practices *in* the world that subordinate groups sometimes engaged in too. Along those lines, Lockhart and Schwartz have noted:

Politics [in Spanish colonial society] became the art of fomenting directions in one's favor. . . . Law and litigation were very much in the minds of a wide range of people, most of all among the wealthy and highly placed, but also, when the courts administration was within reach, among the humble, the rural and even Indians, both individuals and corporations.[9]

The statement emphasizes the political significance of the judiciary in the Spanish Americas. Indeed, in absolutist regimes such as the Spanish one, the judicial system may have constituted not only a mechanism to seek justice and redress, but also the only official site in which disenfranchised vassals could battle opponents and contend policy. The above-cited statement further suggests the widespread use of the courts that both elite and popular sectors of colonial society made. The question then becomes to what extent and under what conditions were subordinate groups—including enslaved people—able to make political use of colonial judicial mechanisms and to what effect.

That at least some enslaved sectors of colonial society, especially in urban settings, engaged the state's judicial system has been shown by Hunefeldt in the case of nineteenth-century Lima and, to a lesser extent, by others in Cuba.[10] Although the royal slaves of El Cobre also utilized the courts as individuals, more striking was their access to the courts collectively: as a community, as a special category of slaves (that is, the king's slaves), or as some hybridized version of these categories. For instance, although the cobreros' representatives in the courts were usually royal slaves, the claims presented were often those of a pueblo, or of a pueblo of royal slaves, as in the cobreros' case for land.[11] Similarly, one of this community's most important legal struggles took place after the Crown's attempt to reprivatize the mines in 1780. Even then, the cobreros' use of the judicial system was noteworthy in that they were able to adopt a corporate legal persona to litigate collectively for freedom. Thus, in 1781, Governor Vicente Manuel de Céspedes asserted in a reserved letter to Don Diego J. Navarro that the slaves had expressed "a *'mancomunidad'* [corporativeness] directed to rid themselves of the new [reprivatized] slavery."[12]

Another way enslaved subjects could appeal to the law and be heard in the courts was to perform "acts of service" to the Crown. These included the denunciation of crimes against the state: anything from the uncovering of treason to the identification of counterfeits and the desertion of guards and soldiers.[13] In fact, Spanish legal codes practically invited enslaved subjects to provide these "services"—and thus to participate in the preservation of royal order—by the promise of manumission. These rarely invoked (or rarely studied) Roman-based medieval statutes were activated on several occasions by the royal slaves of El Cobre. In a charged military and economic frontier location such as that of Cuba's Oriente region, these statutes acquired a particularly strong currency and provided some political maneuvering possibilities to subordinate subjects.[14]

Two particular local historical episodes allow us to examine closely the political dynamics behind the cobreros' persistent mobilization through the judicial system: the community's struggle against Governor Canales (1708–1709) and two decades later against Governor Ximénez (1729–1738). Regional conflicts, when approached from below, constitute an intrinsic part of the story about this subordinate group's use of the courts, and not just background to judiciary processes. Thus, paradoxically, the story narrated in this chapter is not cast as a court drama; indeed, most of the action in this story unfolds outside the tribunals. In addressing this aspect of the royal slaves' history the present chapter takes a more direct narrative approach than previous ones in this book. To be sure, attention to voices, especially the cobreros' voices, remains a central pursuit of the study here too; but in this case those voices lead directly to more conventional narrative and referential considerations.

Governor Canales and the Cobreros: First Trip to Madrid

In 1709, the king's slaves sent a representative of their community to the Council of the Indies in Madrid for the first time in the century. Seven decades later, in 1784, they were able to send another fellow cobrero to litigate in Spain, that time on behalf of the community's freedom. Although the first overseas pilgrimage to Madrid was brief, the second one drew out for more than sixteen years. Engagement of the colonial judicial system at its pinnacle not just once, but twice in a century may seem striking for a disempowered group living in a remote corner of the empire. Yet, the cobreros' ability to repeat the feat suggests that the remoteness may be only a mirage and that hegemonical discourses and institutions of the imperial center strongly imprinted life in these frontier locations too.

The selected *apoderado* (legal spokesman or proxy) for the community in 1709 was the forty-one-year-old royal slave Diego de Rosas, whom the reader may remember from Chapter 10's quasi-fictionalized folk account about a "son of the pueblo" who went to see the king. Unfortunately, rich information does not exist to document Rosas's actual trip to Spain or the logistics behind this remarkable use of the judicial system. More prolific are the sources documenting the cobrero Gregorio Cosme Osorio's trip in 1784.[15] From that later case one can surmise that a trip to Madrid was a complicated and expensive undertaking and that vertical networks of sponsorship were crucial to open sea lanes and roads to the courts abroad. Although these networks were generally surreptitious, and therefore more often than not hidden from the record, they can at times be glimpsed and inferred from available sources. Indeed, there are clear suggestions in the record that Rosas was not on his own when he went to Spain.

The above epigraph quoting Canales suggests that the idea of sending Rosas to Madrid had been concocted by his antecessor and two other gentlemen in Santiago de Cuba. Rosas's own representation stated that his denunciation could be corroborated by the testimonies of former Governor Barón de Chávez (then in San Sebastián in Spain) and the *alférez* of Santiago de Cuba, Don Urtado de Mendoza, who happened to be in the court at the time (perhaps filing related complaints).[16] Indeed, it is highly probable that the *alférez*—if not the governor himself—had served as guide to Rosas through the transatlantic trip and later through the labyrinths of the tribunals in Madrid.[17] Like the more educated cobreros Cosme Osorio and Carlos Ramos seven decades later, Rosas may have traveled as a personal servant of the *alférez* or of the governor who had just left his post in Santiago de Cuba in 1708.[18]

Aside from the support of a royal official and some citizens of Santiago de Cuba, Rosas also had some backing from the local church. The parish priest of El Cobre, Father Don José Antonio Pérez, wrote the letter that Rosas first presented to the Council in Madrid.[19] In that letter, Pérez, writing on behalf of his parishioners, denounced the abuses of Canales. In doing so, he acted as scribe and authorized witness of the events in question. It is not known if Rosas, like Cosme Osorio many decades later, also took with him introduction letters to ecclesiastic personnel in Madrid who could have opened other doors for him in that foreign city. Nor is it known if the church played any other support role as it did in the 1790s when, for instance, it served as conduit for secret correspondence between cobrero *apoderados* at the local level and Cosme Osorio in Madrid.[20]

The support of powerful sponsors, however, did not mean that Rosas was at their total mercy. Cosme Osorio operated quite autonomously in the court keeping the village back home abreast of the events. In one of his letters he mentioned to his compatriots, "You'll see how much I have worked by myself only with the help of the attorney [*abogado*], the solicitor [*procurador*], and the moneylender [*prestamista*]."[21] To be sure, Cosme Osorio was literate and relatively well educated, was a freedman, and had spent many years in the court in Spain, but from early on, he took the reins of the case and even removed the proxy power of his sponsor once in Spain. Rosas, by contrast, was an illiterate royal slave who may have been more dependent on his patrons—and for that very reason such a trip entailed many risks and unknowns for the *apoderado* who undertook it. Whatever the case may have been, Rosas was able to communicate his local agenda in the memorial presented to the Council of the Indies.

Bridging Issues: From Local to Imperial Worlds

The immediate event that Rosas and the parish priest denounced in their memorials was the disarmament of the village militias and the burning down of some of the cobreros' houses.[22] In addition, Governor Canales was accused of breaking other legal and customary entitlements of the king's slaves, transgressions that would have been subsumed under the category of "bad treatment," or excessive "rigor." Contested entitlements included in this case certain labor and self-provisioning practices, in particular the extraction and sale of copper; the holding of property such as working tools; and, at least in the case of a confiscated costly copper pan, the means to buy self-manumission.[23] Particularly noteworthy, especially in the case of slaves, was the denunciation of their disarmament and, conversely, the allusion to their customary practice of bearing arms, a practice that was infused with social meaning and with overtones of entitlement.[24] In his memorial to the Council of the Indies, Rosas testified that Canales had ordered a military official of Santiago de Cuba and some mounted soldiers to

disarm the [militia] company that there is in the said place [of El Cobre] with its own Captain and other officers and composed of all those who can bear arms; [the attack] was executed with the greatest ignominy: when formed in the presence of the priest of the pueblo [the governor's soldiers] went to sack all the houses and to set fire on most of them without [the cobreros] having made the least motion of resistance since [the governor] had insinuated that it had all been done in the name of His Majesty. . . .[25]

As if to explain why slaves were bearing arms, the memorial explicitly noted that His Majesty's slaves were "principally dedicated to the armed defense of the Port of [Santiago de] Cuba and its coasts [so that] at any order they were ready to prevent the enemy from infesting [the region] given their punctuality and valor and their knowledge of the [surrounding] *montes*."[26] That "principally" implied other obligations, such as their role as forced laborers and conventional slaves in the fortification projects—obligations, however, that the royal slaves disputed and sought to abolish.

The above words also echo those of Captain Juan Moreno's memorial in 1677. As the reader may recall from Chapter 3, Moreno had invoked the cobreros' military duties as a service that should be rewarded by allowing them to stay in El Cobre and not be transferred to work in the fortification projects of Havana. For Moreno, military service was linked to the prerogatives of living as a pueblo and as *patres familias*.[27] Indeed, for the king's slaves, bearing arms constituted a masculine and honorable traditional practice that (symbolically) protected them from the debasement of slavery and that, in effect, blurred rigid lines between freedom and slavery. In this sense, significant identity-related issues were implicitly violated in the act of disarmament.

Rosas also alluded to the practical defensive role that arms could play in protecting the king's slaves from forceful reenslavement and illegal sale to the British enemy. In so doing, the memorial was not only implicitly invoking the legal right of the royal slaves to protect their master's property in their own persons, but more radically, it also claimed for the royal slaves an entitlement to defend with arms their social prerogatives, including their right to live as a pueblo, their identity (including their Catholic identity against infidels), and their special status in Spanish colonial society.

But Rosas's accusations were not limited to identity-related significations and community issues. His memorial grafted local grievances and entitlements into an even broader imperial scenario. To make a local case compelling to the Council of the Indies, there had to be more serious charges, denunciations of greater import to the Crown's imperial interests. Canales went to the heart of the matter when he declared that his opponents had been "conniving to portray me as an infidel."[28] Indeed, Rosas's deposition in Madrid deftly placed the governor's transgressions in a wider context by virtually accusing him of treason to advance his own illicit trade-related interests. Rosas's representation made the case obliquely in the following terms:

... having the petitioners given no motive for such enormous proceedings against them [and] trying to discover what motives the said Governor may have had, they suspect these may have been directed at leaving the said port [of Guaycabón] defenseless so that the enemies can attack it . . . [for] there are none left to mount guard. And that having disarmed them [the petitioners suspected the governor] would sell and turn them over to the English enemies of this Crown. This can be inferred from the friendship that [Governor Canales] has with the Governor of the Island of Jamaica, only 20 leagues away from that of Cuba, to whom he publicly made the gift of sending a boat [*balandra*] that came back full of merchandise on his account. . . . And to inform Your Majesty of this the petitioners asked one among them to come to this court bringing a letter that the priest of the said place presents giving an account of the abuses of the said Governor. . . .[29]

In stating that the ulterior motive of disarming the village militias had been to clear the way for an enemy invasion through the port of their charge, Rosas insinuated the grave crime of treason. The denunciation bore a special sting given the charged context of Spain's war of succession and the ongoing international hostilities with Britain.[30] The cobrero also accused the governor of involvement in contraband trade particularly in nearby Jamaica, so that Canales's clearing out the coast of royal slave militias was also connected to the landing of illicit trade. In accusing Canales of these crimes, Rosas was effectively making use of the legal precept that invited slaves to denounce acts against the Crown, a service that presumably would lead him to expect manumission in return.

Rosas's memorial, however, did not close without alluding, almost in passing, to a thorny issue: the cobreros' flight to the mountains to resist Canales's abuses. That was an act that had to be accounted for in order to preempt inevitable counteraccusations of sedition from the governor. Although Rosas and the parish priest both stressed that the royal slaves had not resisted the disarmament out of loyalty to the king, the cobrero *apoderado* mentioned that the cobreros fled from their village for fear of further repression and sale to the enemy. That is, self-defense, and not insubordination, had characterized their collective action. Although acts of flight, and particularly of sublevation, had to be played down or framed carefully to avoid serious charges of sedition, it is significant that at this time they could still be justified as a defense against the excesses of a high-standing royal official. At any rate, as this case suggests, resistance through collective flight did not preclude political mobilization through the colonial judicial system, locally or abroad. Despite the risks involved, they could function as concurrent forms of political mobilization.

The royal slave's denunciations in Madrid had immediate results. The accusations sounded serious enough to the Council of the Indies to merit an extraordinary investigation of Canales's activities. Instead of the routine *residencia* (administration review), the council immediately appointed a judge from the High Court of Santo Domingo to carry out a special investigation (*pesquisa*), thereby setting in motion the well-known check-and-balance mechanism operative among overlapping branches of the Spanish state.[31]

Judge Don Nicholás Chiriño arrived in Cuba no later than November 1710. His investigation led to the interrogation of many people in the Santiago de Cuba jurisdiction, including El Cobre's parish priest and the village's *cabildo* (local government) officials. (Recall again the cobreros' memorialized event, examined in Chapter 10, in which the king's emissary had honored the royal slave *regidores* by inviting them to sit in the *cabildo* benches of Santiago de Cuba.) The *pesquisa* in effect provided a local forum wherein the cobreros and other disaffected vassals could testify against the governor and protest his "bad government." Perhaps it even constituted an opportunity to topple him and restore the "king's law" to the land.

The Investigation: Weak Frontiers in the Wider Caribbean

Chirino's local *pesquisa* confirmed some of Rosas's previous accusations, if not altogether his suggestion of treason. The final report points to some of the shady dealings in contraband trade of royal officials and their clients in this frontier region of the Caribbean.[32] The activities glimpsed through this investigation also provide a good sense of what was at the heart of the charged character of politics in this eastern zone. These were in fact the kind of covert activities that provided precious opportunities to subordinate groups to enter into alliances with other groups in the denunciation of common enemies. Indeed, these were activities that gave them recurrent occasions to perform "acts of service" to the Crown and to expect to be rewarded for them, ideally in this case perhaps with freedom.

During Chirino's investigation, Canales was accused of engaging in a wide network of illicit trade involving an international cast of smugglers. Canales had engaged in trade with the French, the English, and with Spaniards too. Ports of illegal trade in the Caribbean network included Saint Domingue, Martinique, Jamaica, Cartagena, and Campeche in the Mexican Yucatan. Canales, for instance, had allowed two French ships to enter the port in Santiago de Cuba to sell their goods, charging an interest of 10 percent for the sales. He had even allowed a Frenchman to publicly and openly sell merchandise worth up to 3–4,000 pesos, including barrels of flour. In another instance, Canales bought 1,000 pesos of cacao from a captain from Martinique and in turn shipped the cacao off to sell at the port of Campeche at a profit. Canales allowed a Basque man who brought commodities from the French colony of Saint Domingue to engage in commerce in Santiago de Cuba. On his own account he also sent hides to sell in Saint Domingue in exchange for gunpowder that he sold to the officials of His Majesty's garrison and storage in Santiago de Cuba. Canales traded in domestic goods too. He sent to other ports in the Indies, like Cartagena, boxes of sugar and tobacco.[33]

Furthermore, Canales had gone as far as making political exchanges with the English, perhaps the source of the accusation of complicity in a possible coastal attack. In the context of hostilities related to the war in Spain, those friendly exchanges could have dangerous political implications. Canales was accused of sending a boat to Jamaica with some English prisoners and gifts to the governor of that island and receiving a gift in turn from his counterpart. More suspiciously, Canales had moved against the Spanish corsair, Captain Lorenzo Martel, after he returned from expelling Englishmen from the Providence Keys (Cayos de Providencia). The governor was accused of confiscating the Spanish corsair's property and his two slaves and of falsely accusing Martel of raping a mulatta woman.[34] Although such charges may seem inflated for a special investigation, they had become politically sensitive given the succession conflicts in Spain and the colonies. Only a decade before, Canales's predecessor and enemy, Governor Barón de Chávez, had led a military expedition against the British in those neighboring islands, a feat that had prompted Philip V to grant Santiago de Cuba the title "Most Noble and Loyal City."[35]

In all these illicit commercial transactions—and in the more political ones too—the governor must have threatened the interests of different people. Although many would have benefited from the contraband trade— including consumers buying coveted foreign goods at lower prices—those not involved due to competing interests or those with personal enmities against the governor could denounce him for it. To be sure, some of these deals were normal, personal commercial operations of governors, customary perquisites of office that compensated them for their otherwise low salaries. In fact, royal officials sometimes made a case for the utility of this trade in provisioning needed goods (such as flour) when scarcities occurred at home or emergencies came up due to delays in the normal trading system or to war.[36] Nonetheless, from the Crown's perspective such deals usually constituted lost sources of revenue and a threat to its mercantilist policies.

Eventually, Canales was deposed, condemned to prison, and his property was confiscated.[37] He was then forced to return to Spain to appeal the Audiencia judge's sentence. The Council of the Indies seemed to follow a lenient policy in acquitting Canales of the most serious charges.[38] Perhaps the terrible ordeals that these inquiries could turn into and the "pain and suffering" to which Crown officials could be subjected by deposition, even before they could appeal for retrial in Spain, may have been considered a sufficient form of disciplining and punishing administrators, at least where contraband transgressions did not exceed tolerable levels, where cases were ambiguous, or where political considerations were not in question or had been satisfactorily clarified.[39] Canales died soon afterward in Spain without the opportunity to recover his post or his honor in Cuba.[40]

The Political Outcome According to the Cobreros

Many years later, the cobreros remembered Chirino's investigation of Canales as a disappointing and frustrating event. While their expectations had been raised by their meeting with the Audiencia judge, their hopes for full redress, change of policy, and reward were soon shattered due to what they saw as locally based obstructions of royal justice. In a representation drawn twenty-five years later, the cobreros vividly recalled their illusions, delusions, and disillusions:

[Chirino said] that he had come for two reasons and that the first was to return to them [sic] what had been taken away [arms and tools?], that our iniquities would end now, that he would show us *how our Lord and Master had us only for the defense of this garrison and His royal Crown.* [He asked us] To give him time to establish himself and he would solve everything.

Everything was left as his highness disposed and we waited for him to call on us again. He did not do so. And having heard *how the officials of the said city were making many efforts so that he would not give and show us what he had promised,* we went to his house and asked him what our situation was. And he responded that it was not too late yet, that we should be patient. With his response we went back to our village while his highness disposed what was more convenient. . . . More than four months went by, and around the time he was due to make his trip, we went to his house a second time, asking him in what situation he was leaving us. And he responded that our well-being was in the Treasury of the said city [*en contaduría quedaba nuestro bien*]; that it was all he had been able to do for us. He went on in his voyage leaving us as we were before, if not with greater needs [emphasis added].[41] (See Appendix 6)

As the memory of the *pesquisa* days suggested, the royal slaves had expected not only a return to the status quo ante, which included rearmament and the restitution of their dispossessed goods, but also exemption from forced labor services to the state ("Our Lord and Master had us *only* for the defense of this garrison and his royal Crown . . ."). Ultimately, lurking beneath this formulation was an even more ambitious claim based on the not too far-fetched presupposition that military service for the Crown ideally entailed full legal freedom in the Spanish order of things. Moreover, in reaching the king to make accusations as serious as that of treason, the royal slaves may have made a further bid for freedom, expecting manumission as their reward for their act of service to the state/Crown and not only for their long-standing military service.

The cobreros backed their expectations of freedom from labor requisitions—or of complete judicial freedom—with the authority and word of Chirino as the direct representative of the king. The recalled episode established that Chirino had left a document in the royal treasury. (But the actual provisions made in this document were not revealed and were left open to speculation.) The cobreros assumed that it contained what the judge had allegedly promised them in their personal meeting. Suffice it to say here that according to the cobreros' narrative of past events, what had prevented the implementation of the king's law and the restitution of the proper order of things—as embodied in the judge's royal provision—were royal officials' vested interests; that is, bad government at the regional level. Thus, the king's orders were literally submerged in the city's archives along with the cobreros' hopes for justice: a hidden but latent force that would sustain their causes long after this major setback.

Independently from the cobreros' dark memory of these years and their disenchantment with what may have been high expectations for their military service and their denunciations, a concurrent assessment may be made of the short-term outcome of this round of mobilization through the courts. The hated Governor Canales was investigated, sentenced, and removed from office; and the cobreros played an important role in the process of bringing him down. The sweetness of retaliation, of seeing a powerful colonial official pay for his transgressions against the community, should not be underestimated. Neither should the witnessing of the humiliation and dishonor that such a *pesquisa*, regardless of the sentence, entailed be overlooked. As far as battling an enemy went, the cobreros had helped vanquish the governor.

There were also other minor positive outcomes, perhaps better seen as reinstitutions of the status quo ante. The royal slaves, for instance, were not sold or removed from their village as they had feared (or claimed they feared). Nor is there any mention in the record of retribution for their flight to the mountains. Nor did the cobreros lose their right to bear arms; indeed, the village militias expanded in subsequent years (by the 1730s there were four companies with their own officers). It is not known, however, if the cobreros received compensation or a reimbursement for the lost property (including weapons) that they claimed in local courts, but orders were issued that arms be returned. Although despite their military service the royal slaves remained subject to forced labor in the fortification projects, the labor requisitions were lowered during the next few years as the number of labor squadrons doubled and the stints at worked were reduced. The cobreros also continued with their copper-mining activities, a new conflict over which did not emerge again until the 1730s. More dismal, however, were the results regarding land claims, for soon afterward the cobreros finally lost access to the coveted pasture lands of Barajagua.[42]

Despite their setbacks regarding the possibility of attaining freedom, full exemption from forced labor requisitions, and the protection of community land (particularly Barajagua), the cobreros did not completely lose faith in the Crown's judicial mechanisms or in the discourse of the king as fountainhead of justice. Two decades later they were back in the courts appealing for royal justice. The cobreros had not forgotten Chirino's visit, or his hidden edict. At least not for another generation.

Cleavages in the State: The Conflict Among Governors in the late 1720s

In 1728, the cobreros undertook another major endeavor through the colonial judicial system. They traveled to the High Court of Santo Domingo asking for the restitution of the pasture lands of Barajagua. Beneath this renewed effort to change policy and seek redress at high levels of the judiciary there continued to lurk political unrest related to contraband trade. This time, the juncture of conflict coincided with the succession of not two, but three governors in Santiago de Cuba: Governor Don Carlos Sucre (1723–1728); Governor Don Juan Hoyos Solórzano (1718, 1728); and Governor Ximénez (1729–1738).

Rampant conflict, partisan politics, and vested interests were perhaps nowhere better evinced than in the warped events that marked the transition between these administrations. In 1718, Hoyos y Solórzano was recalled to Madrid to respond to charges filed against him. When ten years later Hoyos y Solórzano returned to claim back his post, he forced his successor, Governor Sucre, out of office and imprisoned him as a result of the *residencia* review. Hoyos y Solórzano had not been in power more than a few months when he was brought down by citizens in the town of Puerto Príncipe and "sent to Havana in chains," this time to be succeeded by Ximénez (1729–1738).[43] The incoming Governor Ximénez kept former Governor Sucre "in the most hidden cell [of El Morro] not allowing him any communication or defense."[44]

Like Canales two decades before, Sucre attributed the denunciations against him to the machinations of his predecessor and also to those of his successor. The Crown's attorney, for instance, reported that Sucre denounced:

The hate and enmity that [Governor] Juan de Hoyo and his faction had for him, and later too the current Governor [Ximénez] and the *chantre* Don Thorivio de la Bandera who with his restless and troublemaking character is the one who directs and advises [all] including [Governor Ximénez]. [Bandera is] well known for his involvement in deals of illicit commerce; and he used his influence to get [the Governor] involved with the many [illicit] trading ships that had entered that port . . . [and he also] led [Governor Ximénez] to imprison and insult [Governor Sucre's] person and his honor without attending to his character and merit.[45]

The ability to hold a high-ranking official such as a governor, a man with important connections in Havana, in the vaults of El Morro garrison for four years shows that indeed not even elites or high officials in this frontier corner of empire were immune to the ravages of vested interests, safe from the ferocity of factional politics, or completely free from abuses of power.

Regional factionalism spilled over into the island's wider political arena when the island's captain general was also drawn into this conflict. Aside from the personal stakes this official may have had in seeing former Governor Sucre freed, his defense of Sucre was cast as a jurisdictional and regional conflict. Writing on behalf of Sucre's release, the captain general also warned the Crown that

pernicious consequences may follow from not giving a solution to the disorders in [Santiago de] Cuba, being these disorders (as indeed they are) greater each day; for the Governor of [Santiago de] Cuba, and by his example other individuals and places under his jurisdiction, pay little attention to the orders from the General

Captaincy [in Havana] and continue in the old deals of illicit commerce in which they are [all] vitiated, finding no obstruction in their way to continue with it.[46]

Subordinate groups capitalized on the tensions and cleavages at different jurisdictional levels of the state.[47] The possibility of finding in the captain general a sponsor against a governor and other regional enemies did not go unnoticed by subordinate groups such as the king's slaves. But enmities with some governors and royal officials did not preclude alliances with other ones at the local level either. That the cobreros saw Sucre as a friendly governor, that this governor (as Governor Barón de Chávez two decades before) may have supported a trip to Santo Domingo, and that once there the cobreros in turn may have acted on Sucre's behalf is suggested by events described below.

Appealing to the High Court of Santo Domingo

Although appeal to the High Court of Santo Domingo did not constitute the same kind of feat as presentation at the Council of the Indies in Spain, it was not an inconsequential matter either. Appeals at this judicial level required personal presentation in court.[48] For a subordinate group such a trip could entail difficulties, especially when that meant boarding a ship and leaving the island—a regulated matter particularly given the nearness of enemy territory and its threat at sea. Nonetheless, despite difficulties, subordinate groups did have recourse to this Audiencia and visited it as is also suggested by the fact that the nearby Indian community of Jiguaní in the Oriente region sent representatives to Santo Domingo at least three times during the eighteenth century: in 1702, in 1727, and again in 1782 or 1783.[49]

The documentation on the cobreros' trip to Hispaniola in 1728 is not as sparse as that for Diego de Rosas's voyage to Spain in 1709. The royal slave Matías Moreno—perhaps a descendant of Juan Moreno—traveled in the company of another cobrero.[50] Although the two men made the trip on their own, a larger network of sponsorship was required to enable them to leave the island and perhaps to find their way around in Santo Domingo. Among other things, for instance, boarding or travel licenses had to be obtained.

The two cobreros first traveled by land to Baracoa in the northeastern part of Oriente (see Map 1 in Preamble). To do so, they had to traverse 80 leagues of ". . . chains of mountains [which] the abundance of high and dangerous peaks turns into intransitable deserts . . . ," and walk through what Bishop Don Pedro Agustín Morell de Santa Cruz called ". . . the most arduous and feared paths in the whole island. . . ."[51] Despite the travails involved, the cobreros knew the territory sufficiently well to travel on their own. Once in Baracoa, however, things became more difficult. According to the declaration of Captain Simón Mascarreñas who served as lieutenant and confiscation judge in that port, Sucre had sent him a letter "urging him to allow Matías Moreno and a *fulano* [someone named] Ortíz to travel to Hispaniola Island for they were going in search of appeal to the High Court of Santo Domingo."[52] Mascarreñas, however, later declared that he had not let them go "because they were slaves of the King and they did not carry a license or a passport from this Government [Hoyos y Solórzano] and he had received orders not to allow any ship to pass on to the French colony in the Hispaniola Island."[53] Thus the cobreros had undertaken their trip precisely in the midst of incoming Hoyos y Solórzano's succession conflict with Sucre.

Mascarreñas said he thought the royal slaves had returned to Santiago de Cuba, but later "he found out that they made the transit in a boat that the then priest [of Baracoa] had in that port, that he doesn't know if Sucre had interceded with the priest, that he supposes that he had."[54] Whether or not Captain Mascarreñas knew that the cobreros had been able to leave, or whether he was even complicit in the transit, is impossible to say, but that former Governor Sucre and an ecclesiastic had sponsored Moreno and Ortiz was plausible.

What took place during the sea crossing through these multinational waters or how the two royal slaves moved once they arrived in Santo Domingo is not known. Moreno and Ortiz would have had to find their way in the city and appear in court during one of the two weekdays in which the Audiencia was open to hear aggrieved litigants from all districts in its jurisdiction. In the patio of the court, where *apoderados* waited their turn for an audience, the cobreros may have even run into the representatives of Cuba's Indian village of Jiguaní who had traveled to Santo Domingo in 1727 and may have still been awaiting a decision on their case. Besides their own local grievances, Moreno and Ortiz may have taken word to the High Court of the events taking place in Santiago de Cuba. Indeed, at some point during the cobreros' trip, the High Court intervened, annulled Hoyos y Solórzano's claims to the governorship of Santiago de Cuba, and ordered him detained in prison after he was deposed.[55] Yet another governor of Oriente had been deposed, imprisoned, and sent off to Madrid for trial.

Sometime in 1729, the two representatives of El Cobre returned to Cuba with what they considered to be a favorable provision for the return of their land. Upon their arrival in Santiago de Cuba, they found Sucre in prison and a new governor in power. When the cobreros took their provision to Governor Ximénez, they began to face new frustrations. In a note to the governor they protested, "[You] first told us to find a person to whom to give the Royal Provision [presumably an attorney] to make the transaction of what was to be distributed to us and now you say that there is nothing to give us, to give notice to our master."[56] Indeed, making good use of the general ambiguity of jurisdictions in Spanish colonial society and of the related labyrinth-like processes of judicial appeal, the governor refused to recognize the High Court's jurisdiction over the royal slaves' land claims and the official writ it had issued in favor of the community. Once again, while the cobreros had the High Court on their side, they were confronted by a hostile governor. Trying to overturn the High Court's decision—or at least to protract the implementation of the writ—Ximénez suggested that the cobreros appeal directly to the Royal Council in Madrid, thereby engaging in a jurisdiction game characteristic of colonial politics. Success at one level of the state's judiciary apparatus, thus, did not ensure victory. At its best, the colonial state's structure of overlapping jurisdictions could provide subordinate groups with some maneuvering possibilities, but there was the ever-present danger of falling into its loops.

Ximénez not only refused to abide by the High Court's provision; he also engaged in a series of abuses against the community.[57] These intertwined issues led to armed flight—in fact, to rebellion—in 1731 and to protracted conflict throughout the decade. Ximénez's transgressions, addressed throughout the pages of this book, were directed at eliminating the royal slaves' customary prerogatives and at reducing the cobreros to simple slavery. Notwithstanding the long list of abuses, what is of interest for the purposes of this chapter is, once more, the tenacity the royal slaves exhibited in their pursuit of justice through the courts and the (fluctuating) vertical tactical alliances they established during this critical episode of their history.

Approaching Possible Sponsors

In strongly hierarchical societies and authoritarian polities (alas, in more "egalitarian" ones too), patronage and sponsorship constitute crucial forms of power relations and brokerage that allow subordinates at all levels of the hierarchy to maneuver within the system. These patron-client relations may also be understood as "tactical alliances" that the disempowered—but not only them—need in order to promote their causes, negotiate their claims, or seek redress through available state mechanisms such as the court sys-

tem.[58] The cobreros approached several prominent figures of colonial society who, for their own reasons, seemed friendly to the community and perhaps willing to give counsel and support, if at times only covertly for fear of
reprisals. Some of these potential patrons were presumably the governor's
foes. The cobreros left behind some notes and letters addressed to these possible protectors, intercessors, mediators, and allies. Through this documen-
tary material a glimpse can be obtained of the networks they tried to build,
the kind of aid they sought, the concerns troubling them, and the obstacles
they faced. The discourse that permeated these texts also reveals the dominant royalist (and legalist) ideology that subordinate groups often invoked—
and were well advised to invoke—for their own purposes.

To the imprisoned Governor Sucre, for instance, the cobreros sent a letter asking for advice. The letter illustrates particularly well some of the political practices explored in this chapter. The cobreros wrote to Sucre:

> Señor Governor, forgive us for not having visited you in your prison; our desires
> have been to comply with our duty . . . but in our prayers to Our Lady of Charity
> we have been asking her to give a good end to everything. Sir, we would like to tell
> you what is happening to us . . . fearing that Governor Ximénez may imprison us,
> we decided to inform the Captain General [in Havana] about all this and of the
> Governor's bad treatment, so we want to ask you if it is useful to go . . . we are in the
> mountains and we have abandoned the pueblo because we ask them for the Royal
> Provision and they tell us that we are deceived. We also ask them for the two edicts
> of the King Our Lord, the one that Don Nicholás Chirino brought and the other is
> that of Don Francisco Delgado. And they tell us that the King does not protect us in
> anything . . . and that Chirino did not bring an edict but a piece of paper. . . .[59]

The opening passages of the letter are suggestive of the visitation obligations that previous friendly or clientelistic relations between cobreros and
former governor/patron entailed. In this case, the visitation duties may have
also entailed the presentation of gifts in the form of provisions and food.[60]
The cobreros excused themselves by alluding to the political turmoil in
which they found themselves under the rule of Ximénez. As if to compensate for their apparent neglect, they reassured Sucre that they had been
actively praying to their patroness and interceding on his behalf (perhaps
implying that their proximity to the miraculous effigy of the Virgin of
Charity could actually benefit him more than their visits and gifts).

In a royalist discursive context, edicts—as embodiments of royal will and
of the law—took on a particularly powerful symbolic, even fetishistic, role,
if not always an effectual one. This fixation with royal edicts and with a
legalistic conception of king-given rights led the cobreros to repeatedly

demand from authorities that they let them have royal edicts. At times the cobreros protested that these documents had been unjustly hidden from them. It was within this context of conflict that the memory of Chirino's visit some two decades before and the writ he had presumably left behind surfaced once more. The cobreros demanded to see Chirino's lost or, in their eyes, purposefully hidden provision, as well as another edict allegedly issued in the early 1720s.[61] Contestation over the significance and content of these legal texts is evinced in the cobreros' narrative: while they trusted—and perhaps naively inflated—the legal value of the (hidden) texts as royal edicts, colonial authorities opposing them deflated their value and even wrested away the legality of Judge Chirino's provision by terming it nothing but "a piece of paper."

Concretely, the cobreros sought former Governor Sucre's counsel regarding whether they should seek the sponsorship of the captain general—also Sucre's sponsor vis-à-vis the Crown—to appeal to the Royal Council and to denounce their common enemy, Ximénez. The cobreros also made clear the politically dangerous situation in which they found themselves for they had once more fled to the mountains, an act they well knew could be turned—as it was—into a serious accusation of sedition.[62] The royal slaves, however, articulated their collective claims and legitimated their motives for flight within the framework of a royalist discourse.

That armed flight to the *montes* unfolded within the parameters of a royalist discourse, and more specifically, to the cry of "Long live the King and down with bad government," is evinced by some of the actions that punctuated the event. By failing to appear at the governor's annual review of troops on the city's feast day of Saint James the Apostle, the cobreros denied obedience to Ximénez, the highest representative of colonial government at the regional level. But by taking with them to the mountains the village militias' banner and other paraphernalia, the escaped villagers signaled their political and military loyalty to the king. Moreover, at this time, they made an unsuccessful attempt to take the Virgin's miraculous effigy with them too. Thus, the cobreros appropriated the symbols of the king and the Virgin to legitimate their act of resistance and their cause. In so doing, they were also representing themselves as righteous Christian, royal soldiers, and civilized members of the body polity, not as outcasts, rebels, or possible traitors in this frontier zone of the empire. Once more, the excesses and "rigor" of Ximénez—confirmed by letters to the Crown from Dean Morell de Santa Cruz and the parish priest—were initially accepted by the Crown's attorney as sufficient justification for the cobreros' act of insubordination and no

penalties followed, at least not in this round of conflict.[63] After the initial
pacification in which amnesty was negotiated, the cobreros awaited the final
royal resolution to their demands. The edict of 1733 ordered a reinstitution
of things to the status quo ante and reprimanded Ximénez for altering the
customary order of things, but it granted the cobreros neither Barajagua nor
freedom. Still, the cobreros did not lose their faith in the king as fountainhead of justice. Instead, they suspected that local authorities were trying to
swindle them. A new round of conflict and mobilization ensued.

The cobreros not only sought the patronage and advice of state officials
like former Governor Sucre. They also requested intercession and counsel
from highly placed ecclesiastics. During the second round of the conflict
they wrote to Dean Morell de Santa Cruz: "We implore that with your pastoral position and dignity . . . order from the city of Havana to send the
[royal edicts] that are there and that we have asked for . . . and [we want] to
receive the Royal edict with which His Majesty has favored us, and it has to
be the original that came from there [Madrid]."[64] The cobreros had even
come to understand the value of "originals." That demand reflected, however, their deep distrust of officials and politics in Santiago de Cuba, and
their deep trust in a royal will favorably disposed to them. The cobreros' dis-
content with the governor led to threats of denunciation at higher levels of
the state. In a note to Ximénez they boldly wrote, "If you do not put a remedy to this we will go to inform the King our master."[65]

Asking for guidance and support did not necessarily entail compliance
with the received counsel, however. The cobreros also acted independently,
particularly as they came to distrust the advice and judgment of presumed
allies. Trust was a fragile bond that had to be constantly renegotiated.
Although Dean Morell de Santa Cruz counseled the representatives of El
Cobre to be patient, not to resist Ximénez since his tenure as governor was
almost over, the cobreros decided not to heed his advice.[66] Instead, they
refused to return to work in the labor squadrons as ordered and sent a delegation of some twenty to thirty men (Ximénez even mentioned an improbable sixty-eight men) to Havana some time between 1734 and 1735, perhaps
even later. The delegation of cobreros, led by Matías Moreno, planned to
seek new sponsors to help them appeal their case. They sought to approach
the new bishop, Don Juan Lasso de la Vega.[67] The cobreros believed the
bishop to be their friend, as evidenced in 1732 when he had visited the community and confronted Ximénez over the issue of placing benches for *cabildo* members inside the parish church. The bishop, the cobreros reasoned,
would protect them against Ximénez and intercede for them to the captain

general. Thus, by seeking the sponsorship of an even higher ecclesiastic authority in Havana, the royal slaves sidestepped not only their parish priest but also Dean Morell de Santa Cruz.

Most importantly, the cobreros (or a faction among them) sought to denounce Ximénez to the captain general and to appeal to the Council of the Indies. In fact, around this time, they considered sending a representative to Madrid once more, an initiative that for unknown reasons they did not eventually pursue.[68] Instead, they represented to the Royal Council from Havana where some cobreros stayed on for several months, if not years. Litigation in Havana, not to speak of in Spain, entailed high expenses to the community. Mobilization through the judicial system had to be financed by the pueblo. It entailed a considerable investment of resources not only in the litigation process itself but also in the sustenance of its *apoderados* while away from the village and of the families they left behind. The cobreros in Havana, for instance, sent word back to the village asking for the considerable amount of 100 pesos for litigation expenses.[69]

By sending a delegation to Havana, the cobreros sought to sidestep local justice and regional networks of power. But the strategy could entail reprisals. In one of their representations to Captain General Don Juan Francisco Güemes y Horcacitas, the cobreros emphasized the risks involved in denouncing a highly placed figure such as a governor and of litigating or appealing a decision in the courts. The document stated that the cobreros had great fear of Governor Ximénez because "we had complained of His Highness [Ximénez] in the Royal Council of His Majesty and in San Xristóbal of Havana and because His Highness had promised that he would take vengeance on us even if it were to be on the last day of his administration."[70] Among other things, the royal slaves claimed that the governor had intimidated them by "making accusations against them as had been made on different occasions in which the Royal Council of His Majesty has been informed."[71] Engaging the judicial system and filing denunciations against highly placed royal officials were not only costly affairs, they were risky ones too. Indeed, Ximénez would not leave office without taking revenge on the community. And if initially the Crown censured the governor's treatment of the royal slaves (and of former Governor Sucre) and considered deposing him, as conflict escalated locally the Crown changed its position and eventually condoned the repression of the cobreros.[72]

Political Outcome

Internal divisions in the community over how far to go with their claims in the courts and over the return to work in the fortification projects as Ximénez ordered eventually gave way to bitter local factionalism.[73] Conflict escalated and some time in 1737 a group of Matías Moreno's supporters marched through the streets of the pueblo chanting "long live the King" ("viva el rey"). As if denouncing bad government in the village too, they stopped at the doors of local *cabildo* officials in a threatening manner protesting their compliance with colonial authorities and calling one official "perro vendepueblos" ("village-sellout dog").[74] Ximénez took this opportunity to send troops to quell the local tumult, repress opposition in the village, and take his vengeance on the faction that, besides litigating in Havana, had been denouncing him in the courts. Spanish troops killed the main local cobrero leader, Bernardino Bernal, and as exemplary punishment exhibited his head at the village's entrance.[75] Some thirty-six cobreros were arrested, had their property confiscated, and were banished from the village to different cities in Cuba and even abroad to Cartagena and Mexico.[76]

Don Francisco Antonio Cagigal de la Vega (1738–1746) followed Ximénez into office. Despite the vindictive harassment and repression many royal slaves experienced under Ximénez, despite even Bernardino Bernal's "exemplary punishment," or the arrest of the thirty-six villagers, the cobreros resumed their practice of denouncing royal officials and filing grievances in the courts soon after the new governor took office. In this regard, the resilience of this subordinate community was nothing short of formidable.

A representation that the cobreros filed as early as 1738, soon after Cagigal de la Vega had taken power, was unusually straightforward, even candid, in its incriminations. Despite the usual sprinkling of formulaic phrases, the informal voice and tone of everyday life seems to come forth with particular force in this denunciatory narrative. The cobreros protested to the captain general:

We have represented all of these damages and tyrannies to Governor Cagigales [*sic*] and he has paid no attention . . . because of the great friendship that his son-in-law has with the said [royal] accountant and with the said Second Lieutenant who takes part in all of these affairs. And it has made no difference to have gone to the Señor Dean [Morell de Santa Cruz], who used to protect us when Señor Ximénez was governor, so that with his friendship with the said Governor [Cagigal de la

Vega] he would free us from this tyranny; and what he did was to get angry at our request and throw us out without hearing us, whereby we have understood that the said Dean used to favor us when Governor Ximénez was his enemy and now that he is a friend of Señor Cagigales [sic] not only does he not [protect us], but he even gets angry, whereas before he himself would call us to tell us what to do.[77]

Concretely the "damages and tyrannies" denounced this time had to do with Crown officials' monopolization of commerce in the pueblo (specifically, with the forced exchange of locally produced copper at deflated values for goods controlled by the officials, as discussed in Chapter 8), and with inordinate labor requisitions from women in the village.[78] Although the charges in question would have constituted a relatively "minor" denunciation of what was often tolerated by the Crown as "customary" prerequisites of power, the cobreros nonetheless considered it a violation they could not ignore.

Above all, however, the representation points to the shifting, even ephemeral, character of the tactical, oftentimes secret, vertical alliances of a subordinate group. Whereas as an enemy of Governor Ximénez, Dean Morell de Santa Cruz could covertly advise the cobreros—even support or sponsor them before the Crown—as a friend of the succeeding governor, the dean eventually shifted his loyalties. Indeed, in covering up for his new friend Cagigal de la Vega, Dean Morell de Santa Cruz had turned his back on the community, at least with regard to these issues. The cobreros reacted to this realignment of forces by breaking their own loyalties to the dean and denouncing him and his friends to higher colonial authorities. It is not inconceivable that these villagers had sought the sponsorship of other highly placed individuals who supported them in their new round of denunciations, this time against Dean Morell de Santa Cruz and the new governor. The cobreros had already distrusted and sidestepped Dean Morell de Santa Cruz when they had traveled to Havana to seek Bishop Lasso de la Vega's patronage; now they had gone farther by denouncing him as complicit in the shady deals of his allies.

The royal slaves again linked their local grievances to broader imperial concerns and performed an "act of service" to the Crown by denouncing networks of contraband trade in which royal officials were complicit. The cobreros stated in the same representation: "Don Francisco Delgado [royal treasury official] has put in the power of the said lieutenant many clothes and goods of the kind that they bring from the French and from Jamaica [which is what they forcibly trade for copper]."[79] The passage complements the picture of contraband trade networks crisscrossing the Caribbean by illuminating their linkages at the local level: from high-ranking to lower-level Crown officials in Santiago de Cuba, down to the village level. But the denunciation may have taken a particularly sharp edge given the escalating hostilities between the British and the Spaniards that would give way to the war of "Jenkins' Ear" in less than a year.

Ultimately, litigation did not get the cobreros the major concessions they had set out to demand. Although the Crown ordered a return to the status quo ante regarding labor requisitions and other transgressions, it denied the royal slaves a grant of freedom and the community never got the pasture lands of Barajagua back. The issue of freedom, however, was not completely foreclosed; instead, it was settled in a most conservative and conventional way through a reiterated grant of individual *coartación* (self-manumission) at low prices and easy terms.[80] Indeed, perhaps as a result of failed expectations, but as well for military service performed during the British invasion by Admiral Vernon in 1741, the rate of self-manumissions in the village increased sharply in the 1740s.[81] In any event, the cobreros' litigation activities and their denunciations of Ximénez may be said to have exacted a high cost because the community—or a faction thereof—met with strong repression. Although the repression was legitimized as an alleged punishment for this faction's provocation of a local tumult, just as the cobreros suspected, it was probably also brought about by their extensive use of the courts and by their denunciation of Ximénez's transgressions. The immediate fate of the arrested cobreros or those condemned to deportation remains unknown. The trial took place during the last months of Ximénez's administration. However, his successor, Cagigal de la Vega, later reported, "The unrest has been totally extinguished with the banished [cobreros]; those who are [litigating] in Havana and the ones who have run away . . . two years after the last revolution no novelties have been experienced."[82] Yet, many of the cobreros that had been condemned to exile in 1738 were found living with their families in the village in 1750.[83] Thus, many cobreros may have never been exiled, or if they were, then some may have been eventually pardoned and returned to their village.[84]

Denunciations and contestations through judicial channels continued to be a major form of political mobilization throughout subsequent decades. The next known major round of litigation took place in local courts during the 1760s and 1770s. As examined in Chapter 6, litigation in these decades revolved around claims for arable land (and no longer for Barajagua). This episode was immediately followed in the 1780s and 1790s by a second round of long and very complex litigation for collective freedom, both at the local level and in Madrid. While the specifics of all these cases varied, the underlying political dynamics of accessing the courts were in many ways analogous. Similarly, while old figures passed away, new governors, new bishops and parish priests, as well as new representatives of the community stepped in to form new tactical alliances and to mobilize politically through the Crown's judicial apparatus.

Conclusion

At its most general, the law constituted a major hegemonical discourse that delineated the horizon for all kinds of relations in Spain's early modern world. Most obviously in our case, Spanish law defined fundamental categories such as freedom and slavery or relations such as those between master and slave, Crown and vassal, colonial and colonized, or *pater familias* and dependents. Legal formulations and prescriptions, however, were in practice ignored, negotiated, or reformulated by social actors depending on contextual factors and political situations. Concretely in the case of slaves, the limited protections and "rights" that Spanish legal codes extended to them were completely disregarded in the case of highly exploitative plantation locations, or at best they were activated, and even stretched, in the case of military frontier locations such as that of eighteenth-century Oriente. The multiple practical and discursive reformulations of Spanish legal strictures regarding slavery that the royal slaves of El Cobre more or less successfully negotiated, and in fact the ample range of situations into which they grafted their very limited set of "rights," have been examined throughout the pages of this book. Although this chapter has specifically focused on the cobreros' use of colonial courts to contest restrictions and expand the scope of their legal entitlements, this in fact constituted only one among many forms of political mobilization that ranged from micropractices in everyday life which got turned into customary prerogatives, to the more high-sounding ones of collective flight and rebellion.

Overall, the cobreros' exhaustive use of the royal courts as a form of mobilization constitutes yet another remarkable aspect of this unusual community's history. Few subordinate—not to speak of enslaved—groups in the Spanish Americas were able to go as far in the courts and in their efforts to reach the king as these royal slaves. The cobreros' success in accessing royal courts, however, did not imply a successful resolution of their contested claims; but it did not constitute abject failure either. To be sure, at no point were the royal slaves able to obtain the freedom and land that they cherished and imagined the king had granted them. But their mobilization allowed them to defend some customary prerogatives and previously negotiated forms of freedom, as well as to engage opponents in battle with varying results. Above all, the cobreros' far-reaching use of the Crown's judicial system illustrates the resolve and tenacity of this subordinate group despite the costs and risks involved in seeking justice through the courts.

In the absolutist polity of early modern Spain, the discourse of the law was inextricably linked to a royalist ideology that construed the king as a sovereign figure and as the fountainhead of justice. The cobreros did not contest this dominant ideology, but instead, as with the case of the Christian Marian discourse, incorporated it into their political imaginary to formulate and legitimize their claims and their causes. Although the cobreros often personalized the figure of the king as an all-powerful and benevolent master and protector, they also understood the mediation of legal discourse as suggested by their own recurrent invocations of royal edicts and provisions to support disputed claims, and, of course, by their persistent use of the courts.

Just as other subordinate groups did, the cobreros often projected onto the figure of the king an ideal (legal) order of things that they counterposed to the reality of "bad government" by local officials. Paradoxically, the imagined figure of the king often inspired sustained political resistance, as well as strong denunciations against the transgressions of authorities at the regional level. In effect, the royal slaves' invocation of this royalist ideology is in itself significant for the critique of the (local) state that it often entailed. Such a discourse, in principle, did not fall within the recognized discursive repertoire of ("politically dead") slaves subjected to the narrow, private jurisdiction of their masters. Thus, in the very act of publicly speaking this language, the cobreros cast themselves into politically "active" subjects in colonial society.

To be sure, the cobreros' status as royal slaves placed them in direct relation—or subjection—to the state. Yet, rather than interact with a handful of specialized minor functionaries (or quasi-overseers) at the local state level, the king's slaves of El Cobre engaged a wide range of officials in a multileveled state. They also tried to capitalize politically on cleavages within the state and more generally within colonial society. In this strategy they were also helped by special legal provisions that enabled royal slaves to initiate suit and appeal in royal courts on behalf of their master's property, a provision the king's slaves reformulated to accommodate the community's local agenda above the king's interests. Once more, however, the activation of this (and other) legal provisions depended on political considerations and contextual factors.

The frontier location of Oriente provided a fluid and volatile situation in which subordinate groups like the cobreros could have better opportunities to mobilize through the courts. One way to be heard was to perform "acts of service" for the Crown by denouncing widespread contraband activities and possible political betrayals, particularly in the context of international conflicts, and then linking them to local grievances. Above all, however, accessing the courts in colonial society required patronage. Indeed, it presupposed maneuvering within the highly contentious and factional politics of the region in search of tactical "allies" and protectors. Thus, it would be inappropriate, not to say misguided, to portray the cobreros' politics exclusively in internal, closed, and parochial terms under the pretense of some purported local "authenticity" or autonomy that was not possible in the colonial and hierarchical society in which they lived.

Perhaps it is only proper to close with the words of the freedman Gregorio Cosme Osorio who spent more than fifteen years litigating on behalf of the cobreros' freedom in Madrid. Although this local "organic" intellectual was politically active in a period that lies outside the chronological boundaries of this study, a couple of short excerpts from his letters written in the mid-1790s provide a cogent summary of some of the main issues covered in this chapter. Cosme Osorio's words suggest how close to the pinnacle of power he had come and how he thought of his long litigation services in Madrid. Cosme Osorio wrote to his cobrero compatriots in Cuba:

The King has deigned to hear me in court of justice and he gave me to kiss his hand for the sign of zeal and my loyalty in his Royal name. . . . Many people court me for having justified the manly honesty [*la hombría de bien*] of so many unfortunate innocents. The Archbishop of Toledo tells me that I have won the door to heaven in life for the great work I am doing.[85]

If for many decades the cobreros had sought the protection of captain generals and bishops, now Cosme Osorio reassured the community that they had the support of the two most powerful figures in the empire: the king and the archbishop of Toledo. Moreover, Cosme Osorio portrayed his litigation activities in royalist and Christian terms. His was not only a noble, even heroic, political struggle, but also a holy crusade.

Finally, on the verge of a positive judicial outcome to their protracted case, Cosme Osorio remarked on the motivations that drove him to the courts despite enormous costs: "I let you all know that you are free and that it has cost me great amounts [of money], but that means nothing, for just so that they [the contraries, the alleged owners of the mines and slaves] do not get what they want, I would even give my life."[86]

Conclusion

In the social imaginary of the Cuban people today the story of El Cobre is a legendary account of the apparition of the Virgin of Charity, one that is often linked to ideas of the nation, of creolization, and of miraculous interventions in the world. But the social history of El Cobre, particularly that of the period covered by this study, is also the story of another side of Cuba—and of the Caribbean and the Americas in general—that has not yet been sufficiently narrated. Most historical reflection and discourse about colonial Cuba and the Caribbean focuses on sugar and the plantation world. It is as if other dimensions of human experience on the island were buried under the weight of this ubiquitous discourse. The sugar "revolution" in the late eighteenth century represents not only the beginning of plantation society but also of "modernity," "prosperity," and "progress." Indeed, in his classic essay *Contrapunteo cubano del tabaco y del azúcar* (Cuban Counterpoint: Tobacco and Sugar) Fernando Ortiz tried to draw attention to another side of Cuba, that of the yeoman settler devoted to the cultivation of tobacco. But that fine, baroque counterpoint has been, for the most part, drowned out in the literature by an abrasive nineteenth-century concerto for sugar.

The world of sugar takes just a peripheral—but not invisible—role in the local and regional history narrated in this book. El Cobre's is not a tobacco story either; but it has more social elements in common with the rural world of the small settler than with the world of the plantation. Although its social history combines elements from the world of slavery in the island's story of sugar with those of peasants in its story of tobacco, it is also more complex. El Cobre's is a paradoxical story of peasant slave producers and enslaved independent petty miners—miners of copper, rather than gold, silver, or diamonds. It is a story of miners who were females and of males who were mostly subsistence farmers; of farmers who were also forced laborers on the island's fortification projects; of militia soldiers who were slaves, and slaves who were village officials, legal representatives, and, in some cases, also slaveholders. Above all, however, the story of El Cobre told in this book is an account of a particularly ambiguous form of slavery, one to the distant king, and of an apparently unusual kind of rural community, one more commonly associated with Indians in the historiography of colonial Spanish America than with slaves or with free people of color. In short, the history of El Cobre is a "hybrid" historical account of Cuba, the Caribbean, and Spanish America; it suggests that our historiographical genres need to be opened up further to better grasp the mercurial character, paradoxical aspects, and overlapping dimensions of social experience in this New World region.

To be sure, *The Virgin, the King, and the Royal Slaves of El Cobre* is also a story about the tradition of the Virgin of Charity and about imagined community. But it is not yet a story about the making of the Cuban nation, nor is it mainly a story about this important Marian cult. The tale narrated here is part of a wider account of the making and workings of a singular kind of local community among subordinate people in early modern colonial Cuba. Yet, it is also the story of the making of a Creole identity closely linked to the construction of a local homeland and legitimized by the appropriation of this Marian symbol. In some ways this story of El Cobre can also be regarded as a "total history" covering different cultural, social, political, and, to a lesser extent, economic aspects of local life. Finally, although this study stresses differing and often clashing perspectives and ways of imagining social identities—even within the bounds of a common colonial discourse—its major emphasis is on a perspective from below, one oftentimes located and detected in the small events, practices, and details of everyday life.

Slavery and Freedom(s) in El Cobre

I have emplotted the story of El Cobre primarily as being about the making of royal slavery and the negotiation of social meaning and customary practice. Rather than reconstructing structures and describing practices in the different spheres of the cobreros' local life, or even tracing the transformation of these structures and practices, I have attempted to deal with these topics in a more dynamic and, literally, meaningful way. Although I have often referred in this book to the conceptions, principles, and codes of slavery found in Spanish law, I have for the most part approached these phenomena as they were engaged by contemporaries in their social and political imaginary. Furthermore, I portray the negotiation and contention over social meaning and custom as one that is also over entitlements, even *free-*

doms (or forms of freedom) in the different spheres of life within the framework of a slave society. In the specific case of El Cobre, royal slavery became a particularly ambiguous form of slavery in which de facto forms of freedom may have in some cases reached an extent unprecedented in the colonial societies of the New World. But the extreme situation represented by this case, and the long span of time covered in the record, may serve to illustrate starkly the variations and transformations in custom that were possible elsewhere within slave regimes. It also shows the dynamics underlying the making of precedent and custom, and the political contention that was sometimes possible within—if not yet completely against—these slave regimes.

Moreover, given the relative abundance of records depicting voices, I am also able to show that part of these negotiated forms of life and customary practices within slavery were often recognized and actually articulated as entitlements by social actors, and not just by the historian in the present. Although this local story is also cast in the "resistance" historiographical genre, the approach here is based on a notion of praxis (that is, of meaning-laden and directed practice) rather than on the use of a sweeping concept of resistance often yoked to a simple and reductionistic notion of "survival." As I point out in this study, political contentions over identity and social meaning took place not only through the more obvious kinds of mobilization such as uprisings and *cimarronaje* (flight), but also in and through the less investigated processes of litigation, as well as in the praxis of everyday life that constitutes the core of what I have repeatedly referred to in this book as microevents.

The royal slaves of El Cobre often made use of hegemonic ideologies such as those related to the figures of the Virgin and king in the popular social imaginary of the time to legitimize their reformulations of identity as far as possible. They spoke publicly in the royalist discourse of the colonial political culture of the day and invoked some fundamental aspects of a "global" popular Christianity. The cobreros cast the figure of the king—the ultimate arbiter of justice—as a benefactor, and that of the Virgin as their supernatural protectress and divine intercessor. These were the powers in the social imaginary of the time that could best deal with the most difficult entanglements of life.

One of the most important aspects of this study is to show that the cobreros actively contended entitlements and prerogatives (if not yet in the modern political language of "rights"). They did so from shifting and overlapping positions or identities: as slaves, as king's slaves, as Christians, as members of a pueblo, and to some extent, as a particular sort of Creole. The king's slaves of El Cobre, for instance, appealed to the right to subsistence that masters owed both legally and morally to their slaves. Through some precedent, this principle then turned into a sense of entitlement to self-pro-vision, in fact, one extended to the provisioning of their families. The right of subsistence, or self-and-family subsistence, was also stretched and linked to another form of entitlement, namely, entitlement to the *means* of pro-ducing those forms of subsistence; and from there on to other aspects of what may be regarded as a moral economy. Generally speaking, another principle to which slaves could appeal—and to which royal slaves of El Cobre did appeal—was to the entitlement to "good treatment." The actual practical meaning of this vague principle was conditioned by legal, moral, and customary arrangements that could vary greatly by region and time. A good part of this story concerns the concrete and practical definitions of "good treatment" negotiated by these royal slaves.

The enslaved people of El Cobre also invoked their status as the king's slaves to claim special status and prerogatives, such as access to copper tail-ings and land. As Christians they invoked rights to the preservation of mar-riage and the family, and even a special status in the eyes of the Virgin that entitled them to life as a community. As a pueblo, they acquired a corporate persona over and above their status as slaves with which they claimed land, some political representation and a measure of autonomous authority through a *cabildo* (local government), and even some legal representation before the state. As Creoles, they expected recognition of their right to a local homeland in the New World as Native Americans did.

One or two examples should suffice to recapitulate and illustrate in a more specific way some of these issues. Among the king's slaves, for instance, the entitlement to the means of producing subsistence was specif-ically linked early on to the appropriation of the copper tailings of the for-mer mining settlement. The precedent to what became a customary entitle-ment to engage in surface mining in El Cobre was established in the first years of the transition into Crown rule. Furthermore, this entitlement became socially imagined in a gendered way as the means available to females to produce subsistence while their spouses and male kin were away working for the state. The cobreros' position as the king's slaves was also linked to the contended right to exemption from a mining tax. Although the royal slaves may have been subject to limits on how far they could benefit materially from mining, and from their other economic activities as slaves, the significance of self-and-family provisioning and the customary arrangements related to it lay more in the social and symbolic aspects of the activity. The relative autonomy involved and the ability to control their own rhythm of production with no master to oversee them constituted forms of practical freedom, particularly in relation to the more usual forced labor practices that were associated with slavery.

Furthermore, the cobreros sometimes upheld with more or less success another entitlement in relation to their mining activities: the principle that they may trade freely with their copper in the domestic market. They articulated this when they protested the *repartimiento* deals or the local monopolies of royal officials and friends, and they did so in practice when they smuggled their copper out of the village. The commodity production and exchange of copper on one's own account was also related, in the social imaginary of the time, with forms of freedom. The royal slaves were portrayed as having the means to exchange goods in the market "as free people" and thus to select more or less freely what to buy in return for their productive activities. In fact, as I have argued, through their access to the market, the cobreros also contested the sartorial practices and sumptuary codes of the time.

Other enslaved peoples in the Americas had access to provision grounds. Most striking here, however, is the degree to which the cobreros reformulated the right to subsistence—and to the means of producing subsistence—into an entitlement to land as the king's slaves and as a community. The deprivatization of the mining jurisdiction provided the political occasion to redefine the status of the land in the mining jurisdiction as *realenga* (public land) and to place claims over it. Although the royal slaves in principle imagined their entitlement to be over the complete jurisdiction of their master—the king—their most important battle, particularly during the first half-century of Crown rule, focused on the enormous tract of pasture lands known as Barajagua. The royal slaves argued for this land both under a claim to their rights to the means of producing their subsistence and as an actual grant from the king to them as royal slaves. Moreover, the entitlement to land was socially imagined as access to land that could provide for what were customarily regarded as the staples for subsistence in the moral economy of the time: cassava and meat, or arable land for yucca and pasturing land for livestock—or at the very least, access to hunting territory for wild game.

But the cobreros' sense of entitlement to land went even farther, acquiring yet another dimension of meaning, one, in principle, incompatible with their status as slaves. As the High Court of Santo Domingo gave the king's slaves access and rights to a surrounding league of territory for their self-pro-visioning—in some ways reinforcing or confirming the royal slaves' previous and subsequent claims to it as a grant from the king—this land also became socially imagined as corporate land. As such, both royal slaves and freemen—as cobreros—came to have a claim over it as members of a com-munity. Indeed, the cobreros' sense of entitlement over land often rested on overlapping claims as royal slaves and as a corporate community. While no sense of private property in land seems to have been contested by the cobreros (although it was by other sectors of society with regard to village territory), there was a strong sense of corporate usufruct rights that was man-ifested in the cobreros' repeated use of the courts. This use of the courts as a corporate persona itself constituted an important form of praxis that was indicative of political rights, and of the recognized possibility of battling opponents, even powerful opponents, in this sphere.

The most radical customary entitlement that the royal slaves were able to negotiate with the king/state was the possibility of turning El Cobre into a corporate community. This particular kind of public identity was opposed to enslavement because of the natal territorial, social, and political bonds inde-pendent of the master-slave relation such status implied in the Spanish world. I have shown that the making and recognition of a corporate com-munity entailed some collective political rights and institutions—such as a *cabildo*, a parish, and militias—whose existence and significance was often also subject to contestation, especially in the case of these royal slaves. Moreover, constituting a corporate village was particularly significant, not only because most cobreros were royal slaves but also because in Spanish colonial society even free people of African descent were not often granted the status and sovereignty implied in the constitution of a (racially based) imagined local community or homeland.

Stories of the past such as that of the three cacique Indian brothers artic-ulated in a popular way these (and other) formulations of entitlements among the cobreros. Such rights to land also became associated with Creoleness, and more specifically, with a sense of local homeland (or pueblo as *patria chica*). Such an identity was bound up with the notion of the right not to be removed or "exiled" from the land, their local home-land—certainly a prerogative that could clash with these villagers' enslaved status. The story of Our Lady of Charity encoded some of these social and political significations as well and constituted an important attempt to legit-imize them through divine will.

Overall, I have shown in this study how the king's slaves made use of dominant discourses to formulate and push their entitlements to the limits possible in a slave society. They publicly negotiated—amid multiple restrictions—entitlements such as access to the mining and marketing of copper; to usufruct rights to land; to a corporate persona; to a *pater familias* role; to bear arms; to litigate; to improved treatment in the forced labor sphere; to property (and the rights to bequeath and inherit it); to buy and sell in the market; to representative political rights through a *cabildo* and *apoderados* (legal spokesman and proxies); to nonremoval from their village; and eventually to collective freedom, and not just individual liberty by means of *coartación* (self-manumission).

Yet, the fact that they could not transcend their juridical status as slaves or their forced labor obligations to the state (particularly in the fortification projects) ultimately shows the prevalent force of colonial strictures in this slave society and the limits with which reformulations of status and identity through customary practice were faced. The cobreros were not able to define themselves as "free" people, not even given their military defense services and burdens. Even after their final years of litigation in Spain, the formal freedom they obtained remained constrained.

It is important to compare the customary practices developed by the cobreros to those of other ethnic and class sectors of the population in order to determine what was shared and what was distinct among them. Hopefully this study will contribute to a collective effort to produce a more global and ample social history of Cuba—and of the Americas—from below.

Considerations of Context

In this study I also consider the role that the historical context of early modern Cuba played in the cobreros' political maneuvering. The location of this pueblo in a frontier region with Jamaica and Saint Domingue, for instance, played a significant role. The possibility of a military attack on Cuba and the cobreros' complicitness with the enemy in such an emergency were considerations that lurked in the background for colonial authorities throughout the period. Even the possibility of a public "disorder" among people armed to defend the Spanish Empire could constitute a restraining factor on authorities that provided further negotiating political power to this community of royal slaves. Furthermore, the pervasiveness of contraband trade in the region—an illegal trade always persecuted by the Crown—also provided political opportunities for the cobreros to denounce colonial authorities' involvement in smuggling activities and in other actions against the king's law and the community.

The frontier location and military role of the Oriente region, however, could also have negative repercussions for the king's slaves. Given the labor requirements for the construction and maintenance of its fortification projects, the colonial state made use of its power to coerce labor from this community: the power of the state and its traditional legal formulation of slavery made its force felt and placed limits upon what was negotiable.

Contention also took place through tactical alliances with other sectors of society and not just in terms of simple dichotomies of slaves versus masters, or colonizers versus colonized. The cobreros filed complaints against governors and other royal officials, yet they also used hierarchical superiors as patrons and sponsors. The cobreros also sought support from a relatively strong church in early colonial Cuba and from its network of ecclesiastics—from parish priests to bishops—while denouncing clergy to secular colonial authorities when the situation called for it. I argued that these were all important forms of political mobilization that in themselves should command as much attention as the results they yielded.

In general, the picture of late-seventeenth- and eighteenth-century society in this "hinterland" corner of the Spanish Empire that emerges from this study is one in which, notwithstanding Oriente's distance from direct control of the Crown and of Havana, colonial power in its discursive and institutional forms was pervasive. The sheer amount of documentation generated through the years speaks for this control at different levels of power. The intensive use of the court system—at all levels of appeal—evidences, too, the vitality of this royal institution, one engaged in this region even by peasants and lower sectors of the population such as the cobreros or the Indians of Jiguaní and El Caney. The presence of the church was also strong, particularly in urban areas, but also in El Cobre, given the high profile of the pueblo's Marian sanctuary. The high profile of this Marian cult itself is testimony of the diffusion of these colonial (and "global") popular traditions. The presence of similar, if more modest, local shrines throughout other population centers in the island further shows how widespread these popular religious traditions were.

The case of El Cobre suggests that peasant villages in this region were by no means isolated, peripheral entities. Not only did the cobreros share the ability of subordinate groups elsewhere to move at different levels of appeal in the colonial court system, but they also mobilized throughout a wide geographical area that took them to Havana, Santo Domingo, and at least twice in the eighteenth century to the Council of the Indies in Madrid. Furthermore, while most cobreros resided in their village and in nearby Santiago de Cuba, some were also found residing in other population centers in the Oriente region as well as in Havana, thereby evidencing the degree of mobility and interaction sustained by people at the lower levels of society in this early, and small, colonial world. Finally, I also want to give a sense of the sometimes labyrinthine aspects of social and political life even in this hinterland were popular sectors and elites at times joined in what I have termed (hierarchically based) *tactical alliances*. Overall, in this study I have focused more on how subordinate sectors faced constraints and mobilized to negotiate identities and entitlements in a hinterland slave society than on the better-known exploitative aspects of that world.

A Simpler Story

In the final analysis, this is a story of the past that attempts to narrate several dimensions of a local subordinate group's practical life and imaginary. If it gives a sense of the tenor of life in this settler society, at a time and place outside the world of sugar, it has accomplished part of what it set out to do. If it shows how important history and memory was for these Creole peasant-miners in this forgotten corner of the Americas, it has accomplished more. If it demonstrates how vividly they imagined identity and entitlements, how actively and tenaciously they mobilized, despite innumerable restrictions and limits, it has achieved still more. Finally, if it comes close to bringing to life the multiple social, political, cultural, and affective meanings that permeated everyday practices and ordinary microevents among the cobreros in the past, it has done its work.

This is a history of people particularly constrained in their slavery, as they imagined and remade colonial spaces and turned them into a new homeland; as they produced social memory and traditions; as they reinvented their past and their present as a new people. For better or worse, it is a story of deep transformation, loss, and oppression, but also one of resistance, creativity, creolization, and regeneration.

Epilogue

The story of El Cobre is very uncertain, not to say
fantastic, as it was populated exclusively by Indians
[*sic*] and men of color until recently when the
riches of its mines attracted more illustrious settlers
and even foreign enterprises.
　　—Report of Governor Don Cayetano de Urbina,
February, 1846

From King's Slaves to Private Slaves to Freedom, 1780–1800

A hundred years after the mines of El Cobre had passed into royal jurisdiction and the slaves had become the king's slaves, the mining territory was
once more privatized. This privatization took place in the late eighteenth
century, during the period of Bourbon reforms in the Spanish colonial
world and during the transition into "modernity" and "progress" in Cuba.
Ironically, privatization of the mining jurisdiction at this point represented
in some ways a return to the past, as well.

In 1778, the island was in the midst of change. After the British occupation of Havana in 1762–1763 and the loss of Florida to the British, the
Spanish Crown undertook a reform of its military defense system on the
island, so as to reinforce Cuba's old imperial role as the "Key to the New
World." At the same time, historians have regarded the British invasion as
central to the opening up of external trade, particularly the slave trade, and
to the unleashing of major productive forces on the island. It is as if the
brush with the British had opened a door to "modernity" in Cuba. The classic story about the dawn of that period is, of course, one about the dramatic
growth of sugar production and the transformations it brought about. It was
a world envisioned and imagined, but also ushered in politically, economically, and culturally, by the likes of Francisco Arango y Parreño, whom Manuel Moreno Fraginals etched caustically in his book *El ingenio* as an "icon"
of the enlightened, developmentalist, modernizing "vanguard" of a new

Cuban generation and class. In any case, the liberalization of Spanish monopolistic trade regulations and provisions for an expanding and increasingly unrestricted slave trade (thriving precisely at the time when that trade began to be challenged in England) were major policy interventions that helped pave the way for that new world. In this context, the descendants of the seventeenth-century private contractors of the mines, Don Joseph de Eguiluz and his son-in-law Don Francisco de Salazar, petitioned the Crown in 1778. They manifested interest in reactivating the production of mines that they claimed belonged to their family and argued that in the century since confiscation the Crown had paid to itself any debts that may have justified the confiscation initially. The Crown saw the occasion to develop this sector of industry and approved the restitution.

Two years later, in 1780, the privatization of the mines took place. The king's slaves of El Cobre then became the privately owned slaves of the purported heirs to the mines. The descendants of the major players in the local history of the previous century faced each other once more as masters and slaves. Instead of reactivating the mines, however, the so-called heirs removed their repossessed slaves from El Cobre, partitioned them among their own extended families, and sold them all over the island and even elsewhere "as if they were *negros de Guinea*," African slaves. The sale of some eight hundred slaves on favorable terms in the island's opening markets at the time constituted a highly profitable transaction.

But a century of local transformations had not gone by in vain, nor was the hegemonic hold of the new order sufficiently strong. Empowered by the certainty that they were not slaves, at least not regular slaves, confident of their special relation to the king and the Virgin, and intent on preserving their customary entitlements and communal identity, the cobreros were able to strike back with some of the old tools. For the next twenty years they mobilized continuously through flight (*cimarronaje*), acts of violence, and, particularly in the case of the five hundred or so freemen and -women left behind in the pueblo, through litigation to contest the heirs' presumed rights over the former royal slaves and over the land and territory of El Cobre. If, after the Crown's confiscation of the mines (1670), the cobreros had struggled to define in practice the meaning of their identity as the king's slaves and as a pueblo, once their representative Gregorio Cosme Osorio went to Spain in 1784, that struggle became one to redefine their legal status and identity as free villagers. A complex drama involving different "tactical alliances," including the long-standing one with the church, and an increasingly threatening situation in Saint Domingue as well as the war with the French and the British during the 1790s eventually resulted in the cobreros' emancipation. On April 7, 1800, the king signed a royal edict declaring the community collectively free.[1] With juridical freedom came also an official upgrading of the pueblo of El Cobre to the status of *villa* (town). The formal recognition of a group of free people of color as constituents of a corporate *villa* was analogous (if in principle less radical) to the constitution of royal slaves as a pueblo in the previous century. A few decades later in the nineteenth century, the memory of an earlier pueblo or *villa* of free people of color would seem, as Governor Urbina put it, "uncertain" and "fantastic" (see epigraph). However, such an entity (even if it had strings attached) was still imaginable and possible in Cuba at the turn of the nineteenth century.

From Vision to Practice Once More

Because of the symbolic meaning of Our Lady of Charity in this community, the edict of freedom was read publicly from the porch of the Marian sanctuary. The cobreros' collective liberation from slavery, and the juridical recognition of their freedom, however, do not constitute a neat ending to this story. For one thing, it remained unclear who would be accountable for the bills occasioned by their successful litigation. Furthermore, the Crown's definition of the cobreros' newfound freedom seemed more restricted than what Cosme Osorio and his constituents had expected. Indeed, from the Crown's perspective there was to be change but no change at all.

The royal edict of 1800 ordered, for instance, that all cobreros be returned to the *villa* of El Cobre where they would be organized as a corporate community, but it restricted the cobreros' mobility by ordering that all should return to their community of origin. The Crown upheld the cobreros' right to hold land as a corporate community, and ordered a measurement of boundaries and the distribution of plots to heads of families, but the cobreros were apparently charged with the costs of the survey. Finally, the royal edict made the cobreros as a community subject to *mita* (labor requisitions) as needed by governors. The latter was a major constraint on their freedom since during the days of Crown rule, freemen and -women of El Cobre had been, at least in principle, free from such labor exactions.[2]

The freedom that the Crown had in mind did not stray too far from the negotiated customary entitlements and constraints that the cobreros had known in the past as the slaves of the king. In fact, the edict of 1800 merely suggested a return to the status quo ante, with a juridical ratification designed to presumably protect the community from future reenslavement. The new legal identity as freemen and -women, however, did not imply a fixed status—any more than did the old identity as king's slaves. Indeed, if the local history narrated in this book was that of the cobreros' struggle to define in practice what it meant to be king's slaves, the story that remains to be written is that of how the cobreros defined and contested, through collective and everyday social practice, the actual and customary meaning of their new legal "freedom." This story about the negotiation of the meaning of freedom would be repeated in different ways all over the Americas after the abolition of slavery.

In the end, it is not known how many cobreros—from that whole "lost" generation that was obliged to spend much of its life in private servitude— were actually restored to their village. For that matter, it is not known how many even wanted to return to the new *villa* of Santiago del Prado. It is highly unlikely, for instance, that the few who were supposedly shipped in slavery to other countries ever made it back to El Cobre, or even out of slavery. Moreover, some of those who returned may have resisted doing so, given the forced labor restrictions imposed on the community or their possible accommodation to the localities in which they had lived for almost twenty years. Indeed, some of these cobreros may have chosen to join the ranks of freedmen of color in other regions of the island, thereby exercising the free person's right to mobility despite the Crown's explicit orders of relocation in El Cobre. In effect, it is not known what the meaning of reconcentration and relocation in their *villa* may have represented for many cobreros—a welcomed opportunity to reconstitute themselves as a (free) community, or a bitter memory of royal slavery and restriction on their present freedom. Furthermore, it remains unknown to what extent these villagers were later able to resist the kinds of labor requisitions that in fact blurred lines between freedom and slavery.

With respect to the distribution of lands to the community ordered by the Crown, in 1814 the cobreros were still petitioning for the enforcement of the royal edict of 1800;[3] it was not until the 1840s that the official distribution of lands was actually carried out.[4] By then the distribution took place within a policy context permeated by new ideas of "modernity." Concretely, this meant the de-corporativation of community land and the distribution of titles and full private property rights to individual landholders in El Cobre—the same process, particularly with regard to Indian land, that was unleashed by the triumph of liberalism elsewhere in the independent countries of Latin America during the mid- and late nineteenth century. The conflict was also reenacted at about the same time among the corporatively organized Indian communities of El Caney and Jiguaní, in the Oriente region of Cuba.

By the time this land was actually distributed to the cobreros, a considerable portion of El Cobre's land had gone to new white *colonos* (settlers) in a rapidly changing mining town.[5] Thus, one of the most important concessions made to the cobreros in 1800 seems to have become an issue of contention at the local level, one that would not find a resolution for decades and that was ultimately put to rest in a way that must have been entirely unsatisfactory to the cobreros. The conflict over other entitlements during those decades must have also been a fierce one.

A New Modern Order Based on Mining and Not Sugar: The Post-1830s

The full force of modernity, however, did not fall upon El Cobre until the 1830s. The beginning of the end for El Cobre's existence as a black pueblo, and for the cobreros' limited control over their own community affairs came with the arrival of "more illustrious settlers and even foreign enterprises" lured by "the riches of its mines."[6] British and Cuban mining consortiums with superior technology and capital obtained concessions from the Spanish Crown to reactivate the copper-mining industry. The policy of granting extraction and export rights to British firms is itself illustrative of the extent of the policy changes that were taking place at that time.[7] Although by then the possibility of reenslavement no longer loomed large for the old-time cobreros, the implementation of this new mining policy further undermined the social and political control they could exercise in what was no longer their own community.

The arrival of the mining consortiums spelled a demographic "revolution" with respect to the overall population and racial composition of the town — a social transformation that undoubtedly brought cultural change as well.[8] With the mining corporations there arrived more than one thousand slaves to work in the mines, as well as hundreds of new free people of color and a few hundred white merchants and clerical personnel to staff the mining companies.[9] By the mid-nineteenth-century Chinese "coolies," or indentured workers, were also found toiling in the mines, thereby adding further complexity to the ethnic makeup of the mining *villa*'s population.[10] It may have been around that time that a white fisherman appeared symbolically in the canoe alongside the Indian and the Black figures representative of the local community to whom Our Lady of Charity had first appeared in the Bay of Nipe; a Chinese Juan, however, never made it to the legendary canoe. Despite official bans on the slave trade by that time, mining companies, including British ones, imported hundreds of African slave operators. The newly arrived African slaves may have played a large role in "Africanizing" some cultural practices in El Cobre—adding, perhaps precisely at this time, neo-African layers to the cult of the Virgin of Charity.

Drastic changes not only occurred in the social environment of El Cobre, but they also took place in its landscape. Camels, for instance, were introduced into this tropical corner of the hemisphere to transport to the coast the massive amounts of ore now being produced for export; and the railroad lines were constructed in the 1840s, among the first on the island. If sugar introduced the railroad elsewhere in Cuba, copper mining did so in this eastern region.

Politically the cobreros also lost influence. Although in 1841 four of the town's *regidores* (aldermen) were still cobreros, by then the two *alcaldes* (local government officials), the notary and the *síndico procurador* (attorney of El Cobre) were whites—a fact that shows how the power of the cobreros in this institution had been eroded.[11] In 1838 a royal official had gone as far as to recommend the elimination of the town's *ayuntamiento* (municipal government), protesting that it was unnatural to have blacks dictating the fortunes of whites in any community.[12] Thus, if a century before the royal officials had complained about the irregularity of having slaves presiding over a *cabildo* (local government), now the issue was entirely racial: free blacks were not to compete with whites for social or political standing. Eventually, however, the *cabildo* was abrogated altogether and a military government put in place, a process that echoed the wider militarization of the island in the 1840s.

Not only the cobreros faced the new forces of modernity in the *villa* of El Cobre: in a metaphoric clash between the forces of the old order and the new in El Cobre, even the church was drawn into conflict and litigation with the new mining companies. The conflict erupted over rights to coveted holy ground on which the Virgin's sanctuary stood atop of what were believed to be rich copper deposits.[13]

In short, the new age of progress, modernity, and a devouring export economy that was unleashed by the sugar revolution elsewhere in the island eventually arrived in El Cobre in the guise of the new copper-mining consortiums of the 1830s.[14] The cobreros' relation to their past, and to the new hegemonic discourse and forces of modernity, can only be imagined beyond this point. This holds true as well for their relation to the Virgin and to the king in the changing world of the nineteenth century, a new world that would break into an anticolonial war in a matter of decades.

While "the King" of this study's title was brought down with the end of Spanish colonialism, "the Virgin" survived. Moreover, she acquired a new meaning and stature in the island's imaginary. Early in the twentieth century the Virgin of Charity became the mother of the emergent Cuban nation, the official patroness of the new republic, and as some still have it, the "queen" of Cuba.[15] Despite the protested bridge to the past that a "tradition" purports to be, there is, however, little memory among Cubans today of the remarkable historical community in which the Virgin of Charity's legend and tradition first flourished. While the history told in this book uncovers some one hundred years of a rich and startling history, the stories of the nineteenth and twentieth centuries have not yet been recounted. Major events in the island's history resonated in El Cobre and left their imprint there. One wonders how the global, the national, and the local came together in this corner of Oriente and the Caribbean in more recent history. Perhaps when all is told, El Cobre will become the island's own "historical" version of Macondo, with broad touches of Chaimoiseau's Texaco: a new source of "archival fictions" for Cuban, Caribbean, and Latin American master narratives. Or perhaps it will become yet another poetic matrix for the Caribbean archipelago's "repeating island."[16]

Reference Matter

Chronology

1530s	Initial efforts to exploit copper mining by private prospectors.
1599–1620	Captain Don Francisco Sánchez de Moya is royal administrator of the mining jurisdiction of Santiago del Prado. Peak years of mining production in El Cobre.
1616	Don Juan de Eguiluz wins bid to private exploitation of the mines. Agrees to sell an annual quota of copper to the Crown.
1620	Don Juan de Eguiluz becomes private contractor of the mines. Mines and slaves in mining jurisdiction are transferred to him.
mid-1620s to 1630s	Failures to produce agreed quotas. Eguiluz goes to Spain to settle conflicts and accusations over his administration of mines. Dies on return in 1638. Other administrators appointed by governor.
1640s	Don Francisco de Salazar, one of Eguiluz's sons-in-law, claims the mines on behalf of the family. Takes over the administration of the mines in 1648. Dramatic decline in mining production.
1660s	Intra-family conflicts over administration of the mines. Salazar's neglect of mining production is denounced to the Crown by brother-in-law Don Antonio Matta y Haro in hopes of taking over the administration of the mines.
1670	The Crown takes over the mining jurisdiction from the Eguiluz family for neglecting production and for failure to comply with contract. Governor Don

	Andrés de Magaña oversees the royal takeover of the mining jurisdiction. Private slaves become the king's slaves. Land within the mining jurisdiction begins to be distributed by the *cabildo* (local government) of Santiago de Cuba. Reconstruction of hermitage to the Virgin of Charity begins.
1673–1674	Royal edicts order the *coartación* (self-purchase), sale, or transference of royal slaves to work in Havana. No compliance.
1677	Judge Don Antonio Ortiz de Matienzo adjudicates the civil case of mining jurisdiction. Royal slaves flee to the mountains to resist the ordered removal of male slaves to work in the fortifications of Havana. Royal slaves are allowed to remain in El Cobre.
1683	Father Onofre Fonseca de la Caridad takes over as chaplain of the hermitage to the Virgin. Institution-alization and growth of Marian cult accelerates. Ecclesiastic penetration of the mining jurisdiction.
1687	Notarized deposition of Captain Juan Moreno regarding the miraculous finding of the Virgin's effigy in the Bay of Nipe.
1690	Governor Don Juan de Villalobos tries to recruit royal slaves to work in fortification projects and meets strong resistance.
1692	Conflict between Governor Villalobos and visiting judge, Don Francisco Manuel de Roa. Participation of royal slaves and Indians of El Caney in the con-flict and deposition of governor.
1700	New efforts of the Crown to reactivate the mines through private contractors fail.
1700–1708	Governor Don Juan Barón de Chávez in power. Sends expeditions to Providence Island to expel the British. War of Succession rages in Spain.
1703	Chaplain Fonseca finishes his manuscript about the miracles of the Our Lady of Charity.

1708–1709	Conflicts between Governor Don Joseph Canales and the community of royal slaves mainly over extraction of copper, labor requisitions, and disarmament of cobreros.
1709	Diego de Rosas goes to Madrid to denounce Governor Canales's transgressions against the community, possible contraband deals, and suspicious dealings with the British.
1709–1711	Investigation of Judge Don Nicholás Chirino from the High Court of Santo Domingo. Canales is deposed and found guilty by Chirino but is eventually acquitted in Spain. Cobreros believe Chirino left a royal provision on their behalf.
c. 1713	Governor rents pasture lands of Barajagua. Royal slaves lose access to this land.
1720–1721	New efforts to reactivate the mines through a private contractor fail.
1723–1728	Governor Don Carlos Sucre in power. Deposed by former Governor Don Juan Hoyos y Solórzano and imprisoned for four years in cells of El Morro.
1728–1729	Matías Moreno and another cobrero go to the High Court of Santo Domingo to claim back pasture lands of Barajagua.
1729	Governor Hoyos y Solórzano deposed during a tumult in the town of Puerto Príncipe.
1729–1738	Colonel Don Pedro Ignacio Ximénez becomes Governor of Santiago de Cuba. Ongoing conflict with cobreros throughout the 1730s.
1731	Cobreros flee armed to the mountains with militia banner. Dean Don Pedro Agustín Morell de Santa Cruz and *cabildo* of Santiago de Cuba mediate conflict. Governor Ximénez is reprimanded.
1733	Another round of conflict resumes when Barajagua lands are not forthcoming. Internal tensions in the village. Cobreros refuse to return to work in the fortification projects.

c. 1734	Matías Moreno and a group of cobreros go to litigate in Havana.
1737	Factionalism gives way to a tumult in the village. Strong repression by Governor Ximénez ensues. Interrogation, confiscation of property, and exile of many arrested cobreros.
1739	Governor Don Francisco Antonio Cagigal de la Vega takes over the administration and prepares for war with the British.
1741	Four-month British occupation of Guantánamo in the northeast region of Oriente led by Admiral Vernon. Occupation of Santiago de Cuba is averted.
1756–1757	Dean Morell de Santa Cruz becomes bishop and makes detailed pastoral visit of the island.
1762	British invasion of Havana.
1766	Official survey of El Cobre's land boundaries made. Litigation and conflict over village's arable land ensues throughout the 1770s.
1778	The heirs of the Eguiluz family reclaim their mining property.
1780	Royal edict orders return of mining jurisdiction to the heirs of Eguiluz. Reprivatization of the mines and slaves of El Cobre. Many cobreros reenslaved and removed from the village by alleged owners. Beginning of protracted conflict.
1784	Cobreros send freedman Gregorio Cosme Osorio to Madrid to appeal the reprivatization orders and litigate on behalf of the cobreros' collective freedom and rights to land.
1800	Royal edict orders the collective freedom of the cobreros and the Eguiluz's heirs' dispossession of the mining jurisdiction.
1830s	British and Spanish mining consortiums arrive to revive mining industry. Beginning of major transformation of El Cobre.

Governors of the Oriente Region: 1670–1799

Sargento Mayor D. Andrés de Magaña	1670
D. Francisco de la Vega y de la Guerra	1677
Sargento Mayor D. Gil Correoso Catalán	1683
D. Tomás Pizarro Cortés	1683
D. García Perea, Gobernador Político, y Sargento Mayor D. Alvaro Romero Venegas, Gobernador Militar, interinos	1686
Capitán D. Juan de Villalobos	1690
D. Diego de Baños, interino	1691
Capitán D. Sebastián de Arencibia e Isasi	1692
Capitán D. Mateo de Palacios Saldurtum	1699
D. Julián Herrera y D. Marcos Larrea, alcaldes, respectivamente, gobernadores políticos, y D. Mateo Hechevarría, Gobernador Militar: interinos	1699
Capitán D. Juan de Chávez, Barón de Chávez	1700
Coronel D. José Canales	1708
Sargento Mayor D. Pedro Ferrer, interino	1710
Capitán D. Luis Sañudo de Anaya	1713
D. Manuel Castañeda y D. Francisco Ramos, alcaldes, gobernadores políticos, y D. Pedro Ferrer, Gobernador Militar, interinos	1713
Coronel D. Mateo López de Cangas	1713
Teniente coronel D. Juan del Hoyo Solórzano	1718
Coronel D. Carlos Sucre	[1723]

SOURCE: Emilio Bacardí y Moreau, *Crónicas de Santiago de Cuba*, 2d ed., 1973, pp. 18–19. Years given are those in which governors took office; corrections to original listing are enclosed in brackets.

[Teniente coronel D. Juan del Hoyo Solórzano (brief second term)   1728]

Coronel D. Pedro Ignacio Jiménez   1729

Coronel D. Francisco Antonio Cagigal del la Vega   1738

Brigadier primero, Mariscal de Campo después, D. Alonso
de Arcos y Moreno   1746

Coronel D. Lorenzo de Madariaga   1754

Brigadier D. Fernando Cagigal de la Vega, Marqués
de Casa-Cagigal   1765

Coronel D. Miguel de Muesas, interino   1766

Teniente coronel C. Esteban de Oloris, interino   1769

Brigadier D. Juan Daban, interino   1771

Brigadier D. Juan Antonio Ayanz de Ureta   1771

Coronel D. José Tentor   1776

Teniente coronel D. Antonio de Salas y Sotomayor, interino   1777

Coronel D. Vicente Manuel de Céspedes, interino   1780

Brigadier D. Nicolás de Arredondo Pelegrín Alvarado y Venero   1782

Teniente coronel D. Antonio de Salas y Sotomayor, interino   1785

Coronel D. Isidro José de Limonta, interino   1787

El propietario Sr. Arredondo   1788

Coronel, después Brigadier, D. Juan Bautista Vaillant Berthier   1788

Coronel D. Isidro José de Limonta, interino   1796

Coronel D. Juan Nepomuceno de Quintana   1796

Bigadier, después Mariscal de Campo, D. Isidro José de
Limonta, interino   1798

Coronel, después Brigadier, D. Sebastián Kindelan y O'Regan   1799

Petition of Captain Juan Moreno
Mines of Santiago del Prado, July 13, 1677
Fols.454–55v, AGI-SD 1631

El Capitan Juan Moreno negro criollo y natural de las minas de Santiago del Prado del Cobre desta ciudad de Cuba por si y en nombre de los demas nengros criollos naturales de dichas minas esclavos que somos de su Mag[esta]d que Dios guarde y Particularmente los que fueramos nombraos en la divicion y alcance que hara a nuestro amo el Capitan Don Francisco Salazar y Acuña q[u]e del presente hasse por V[uestrs] me[rce]d antte quien paresemos en la mejor via y forma que aya lugar En d[e]r[ech]o y desimos que por quanto todos los mas negros y mulatos criollos de dichas minas somos cassados y thenemos mas familias que siempre hemos sustentado quieta y pacificamente estando ocupados quando se a ofrecido en el trabajo de d[ic]has minas fabrica de la Santa Yglesia y leales vasallos de su mag[esta]d emos acudido con toda prontitud a n[ues]tra costa y mencion guardando y obedeciendo todas la hordenes de los superiores y demas justicias de d[ic]ha Ciudad de Cuba en que nos an ocupado asien esto como en rancherias y Palenques de negros esclavos fugitivos de los vecinos de toda esta ysla q[ue] emos apressado deseando siempre mayores ocasiones del R[ea]l Servicio q[u]e nos ocuparan pa[ra] conseguir acciones grandes que aunque no se nos premiaran solo quedaramos contentos de haverlas consegido y siendo como es esto tanta verdad que sse hallara entre nosotros estar con grande prevencion para la ocassion y defenssas de la plassa de Cuba a ottro qualquier lugar q[ue] aunq[ue] es verdad que ttodos sus becinos lo estan tambien y que conseguiran qualquiera accion con todo q[uan]do sea ofrecido ocasion Alguna novedad los S[eñor]es Governadores nos an ocupado hasiendo memoria de nosotros aunque negros humildes esclavos de n[uest]ro Rey y S[eñ]or por haber reconocido quissa ntro buen deseo y a venido a n[ues]tra noticia q[ue] los que llegaremos a quedar con el alcansse que dissen hara n[uest]ro Rey y S[eñ]or a n[uest]ro amo Don francisco en muchos Esclalvos y q[ue] sean de sacar por V[uestra] m[erce]d para llevarnos a la ciudad de la havana y por que paresse elamor de n[ues]tra patria y n[ues]tro travajos nos mueben a suplicar como por la presente suplicamos a V[uestra] m[erce]d que ssi posible Señor conseda de m[erce]d que quedemos en n[ues]tro pueblo pagando tributo conforme el estilo que se dispusiere mientras buscamos Para n[ues]tra libertad o lo que mas bien se dice Pusiere por d[e]r[ech]o en que de equidad y piedad por V[uestra] m[erce]d devemos ser amparados en nombre de Ntro Rey y S[eñ]or haviendo lugar para ello por tanto [illegible] a V[uestra] m[erce]d pedimos y suplicamos nos aya Por pressentados mandando considerarnoslo assi que sera justicia y m[e]r[ce]d que pedimos y lo mas nessessario, Juan Moreno.

Juan Moreno's Account
of the Virgin's Apparition
Excerpt of Captain Juan Moreno's notarized
deposition, Investigation of the Virgin's
Apparition, Mines of Santiago del Prado,
April 1, 1687, Fols. 12v–18v, AGI-SD 363

En el lugar de las minas de Santiago del Prado en primero dia del mes de
abrill de mill seiscientos ochenta y siette años... para que conste de la
Aparizion y milagros de la Santisima Virgen Maria Madre de Dios y Señora
Nuestra de la Charidad y Remedios hiso pareser al Capittan Juan Moreno
del qual fue rresevido juramento por Dios y una Cruz que hiso segun forma
derecho prometio desir verdad de lo que supiera y le fue preguntado se le
pregunto lo siguiente:

Fuele preguntado como se llama de donde es natural que edad estado y ofi-
cio tiene. Dijo, que se llama Juan Moreno negro esclavo nattural deste dicho
lugar y que fue Capitan deste dicho lugar y que es de ochentta y cinco años.

Preguntado declare lo que save en rrason de la aparizion de Nuestra
Señora de la Charidad y Remedios.

Dijo que save este declarantte que siendo de dies años de edad fue por
ranchero a la Bahia de Nipe que es en la vanda del nortte desta Ysla de
Cuba en compañia de Rodrigo de Joyos y de Juan de Joyos que los dos eran
hermanos y yndios naturales los quales yban a coger sal y haviendo rancha-
do en cayo franzes que esta en medio de dicha Bahia de Nipe para con
buen tiempo yr a la Salina estando una mañana la mar en calma salieron
de dicho caio Franzes anttes de salir el sol los dichos Juan y Rodrigo de
Joyos y este declarante embarcados en una canoa para la dicha Salina y
aprattados de dicho Cayo Franses vieron una cossa blanca sobre la espuma
del agua que no distinguieron lo que podria ser y asercandose mas les pare-
cio pajaro y a mas serca dijeron dichos yndios parese una niña y en estos dis-
cursos llegados reconosieron y vieron la Ymagen de Nuestra Señora de la
Virgen Santisima con un Niño Jesus en los brazos sobre una tablita
pequeña y en dicha tablita unas letras grandes las quales leyo dicho Rodrigo
de Joyos y desian yo soy la Virgen de la Charidad y siendo sus vestiduras de
rropaje se admiraron que no estavan mojadas y en esto llenos de goso y ale-
gria cojiendo solo tres tercios de sal se vinieron para el jatto de Varajagua

donde estava Miguel Galan Mayoral de dicho jatto y le dijeron lo que pasava de haver hallado a Nuestra Señora de la Charidad y dicho mayoral mui
contentto y sin dilazion embio luego a Anttonio Angola con la noticia de
dicha Señora al Capitan Don Francisco Sanchez de Moya que administra-
va las minas de dicho lugar para que dispusiese lo que havia de haser y
mientras llegava la noticia pusieron en la cassa de vivienda de dicho jatto un
altar de tablas y en el a la Virgen Santissima con luz ensendida y con la
rreferida noticia el dicho Capitan Don Francisco Sanchez de Moya embio
orden al disho Maioral Miguel Galan que viese una casa en dicho hatto, y
que allai pusiese la ymagen de Nuestra Señora de la Charidad y que siempre la tubiese con luz y para ello le embio una lampara de cobre y se hiso la
cassa cubiertta de Guano zercada de tablas de palma y puesta en su altar
esta Divina Señora dicho yndio Rodrigo de Joyos cuydava de ensender la
lampara yendo de noche a rreformar dicha lampara no hallava a esta Divina
Señora en su altar y dando vozes dicho Rodrigo de Joyos al mayoral y demas
personas que serian hasta veinte y una las personas que estavan en dicho
hato de barajagua les desia que la Virgen Santissima no estava en su altar y
hasiendo todas las diligencias no la hallavan en su cassa y al ottro dia por la
mañana volviendo a la cassa la hallavan en su altar los bestidos mojados y
esto se vio por dos vezes de cuios milagros el mayoral Miguel Galan dio
aviso al Capitan Don Franzisco Sanchez de Moya el qual luego que tubo la
notticia dispuso que fuese al dicho Jato de Varajagua el Padre Bonilla reli-
giosso de San Francisco y no se acuerda de su nombre si lo save y se acuerda que estava administrando el curato deste lugar de las minas del cobre y
con ttoda prevencion de sera le despacho acompañado de toda la Ynfanteria
del Real destas minas y mucha gente de su poblacion para que tragese a la
Virgem Santissima como lo hiso en unas andas en prosecion y la pusieron
en un altar en la yglesia Parroquial destte lugar donde tenian a esta Divina
Señora de la Charidad mientras le hasian una hermita y deseando fuese en
parte de su Santissimo agrado le encomendaron al Espiritu Santo y para
ello le hisieron una fiesta de misa canttada y sermon y discurriendo haser la
santta hermitta en una loma que llaman la cantera se vieron tres luzes arriba del zerro de la mina en derecho de la fuentte y dichas luzes se apare-
sieron y vieron por tres noches continuas con admiracion de ttodos y luego
se desaparesian y por este milagro eligieron el lugar donde se vian las luzes
para la hermitta y Santta Cassa desta Divina Señora de la Charidad que oy
esta es dicho zerro hasiendo muchos milagros con los devottos que le llaman y muchos frequentan esta santta cassa viniendo a nobenas de la ziudad
de Cuba que dista cinco leguas poco mas o menos y de la villa de San
Salvador del Vayamo que dista mas de treinta leguas.

Two letters by cobreros to Governor
Don Pedro Ignacio Ximénez
El Cobre, ca. July–Aug. 1731.
In untitled cuaderno that came with letter of
Governor Ximénez, Santiago de Cuba, Dec. 6, 1731,
AGI-SD 493

LETTER 1 (fols. 31v–32)
Sr Governador Pedro Ximenez, Lo que nos motiva a hacer esta detenencia
es la gran necesidad y rigor con q[ue] Ud nos trata y por esa cedula q[ue]
vera Ud como el Rey nuestro Amo nos hace conbeniencia y nos da descan-
so en ellos y q[ue] se nos de buen trato lo cual Ud no nos ha dado por
infortuna nuestra por q[ue] otros Sres Governadores antecesores de Ud no
nos lo han dado asi y con saber tantos años ha q[ue] sabemos q[ue] el Rey
n[ues]tro Amo nos ha hecho [merced?] hemos estado sirviendo y trabajando y pudieramos haverle hecho antes alguna fuga pero ya la misma nesesidad nos ha obligado y siempre q[ue] Ud no nos diere lo q[ue] nuestro amo
nos ha dado como Su Alteza mando siempre estamos detenidos como es el
original de este en el auto y el hatto [...?]. [Transcription of spelling from
document not exact.]

LETTER 2 (fols. 38v–39v)
Repondemosle a V[uestra] S[eñoria] como estamos en nuestro lugar
esperando q[ue] Ud nos de lo q[ue] el Rey nuestro Amo nos ha dado por
en cuanto nos queremos caer de nesesidad nosotros siempre hemos estado
en todos los goviernos muy obedientes al servicio de N[ues]tro Amo y particularmente en el G[o]vierno de VS en la Ciud[ad] de Cuba paran dos
cedulas del Rey n[ues]tro Sr queremos gozar de lo q[ue] nuestro amo nos
ha dado. Estamos todos prontos y muy obedientes a lo q[ue] la cedula
mandare. De parecido estas cedulas estamos obligados y nos obligamos y
nos reglamos a lo q[ue] estas cedulas rezaren aqui nos ha metido Ud

teniente adonde no era nesesario por q[ue] siempre le hemos dado
cumplimiento a Ud con nuestros alcaldes, en el Govierno de VS nos estamos mirando q[ue] adonde quiera q[ue] vamos nos traen amarrados y si
Ud en esto no pone remedio nos pasaremos a dar cuenta al Rey nuestro
amo porq[ue] pasamos a pedir misericordia a una Real Audiencia de Santo
Domingo en el govierno de [?] y no hemos visto nada y Ud perdone nuestros enfados q[ue] no tenemos a quien quejarnos sino a VS pues esta en
lugar de nuestro Amo el Rey. Nos esclavos de S[u] Magestad.
[Transcription of spelling from document not exact.]

Petition of the Cobreros to Captain General Güemes y Horcacitas

Petition of cobreros to Captain General Don
Juan Francisco Güemes y Horcacitas [ca.
1734], "Autos Año de 1735. Sobre lo acaecido
con los negros esclavos de S.M. que residen en
el pueblo de Santiago del Prado Minas del
Cobre remitidos por el Gobernador de la
Habana Don Juan Francisco Güemes y
Horcacitas"
Fols. 658–65/3–9v, AGI-SD 451

A El S[eñ]or D[o]n Juan Fran[cis]co de Guemez y Horcacitas Mariscal de
Campo de los Exer[cito]s de S[u] M[a]g[esta]d Su Gov[ernad]or y
Cap[ita]n G[ene]ral de esta ysla y Ci[uda]d de la Havana
  Los esclavos de las Minas de Santiago del prado y Vesinos de dho Pueblo
nos presentamos ante Vssa en la mejor forma que halla lugar en d[e]r[ech]o
[SPACE]
  Y es a saver q[u]el añ[o] de treinta y dos [sic] hisimos fuga todos los
esclavos de d[ic]ho pueblo a los campos con una bandera de S Mgd reti-
randonos de el mucho rigor conque el Señor Dn Pedro Ynasio Gimenes
Governador desta plasa y Su Judirision pensionandonos Con graves penas
con que nos molestava como ya lo tendra V[ue]s[tra]s[eñori]a por notisia pr
una que remitimos a esa Capitania con fha de beynte y nuebe de Junio
deste presente año de mil setesientos y treinta y quatro a[ño]s en cuya copia
espresaba dhos procedim[ien]tos que pasamos con dho Señor Governador[.] Hisimos dha sulevasion a Compañados de n[uest]ra ynorancia y
seguedad en que estabamos metidos de que el rein[uest]ro amo señor nos
havia hecho mersed de livertad aviendo sido causante el Señor
Gov[ernad]or Dn Jo[se]ph Canales q[ue] lo fue en esta dha plasa y en
medio de Su Gover[naci]on determino su Señoria el pasar a este lugar yn
flugiendo varias materias con que nos hiso cargo de [e]llas quitandonos
nuestras armas y Jieros de nuestros ofisios que mando las fraguas en que
benefisiamos el Granillo de Cobre que percanciamos para sursir n[uest]ras

nesesidades y viendo el mucho daño que se nos segia nos determinanos el
poner en notisia de nro amo y Señor lo que pornosotros pasava siguiendo a
dha diligensia Diego de Rosas Hijo natural de este dho Pueblo persona tal
q[ue] con la probidencia divina puso en notia de nro amo y Señor
n[uest]ros Clamores segun las notisias q[ue] nos dio el Señor Dn Nicolas
Chirino quien bino en reconosimiento de dhos Yn formorme y de aver lle-
gado dho Señor Dn Nicolas Chirino a la siudad de S[an]tiago de Cuba hiso
llamar los Regidores que estaban per firiendo antes de la resolusion de dho
Sor Gov[ernad]or y viendo Su orden y recaudo pasamos sintener dilasion
alguna y estando en su presensia ordeno su Señoria se sentassen en los van-
col de Cavildo de dha Ciu[da]d con nombramiento de Regidores hechos
En bos de anbas magestades y en vista de tales onras se escusaban el ocupar
dho asiento que se les ofresia por ser pobres y de color quebrado dandole las
grasias a el dho Sr y Su Señoria le ysto o cupasen los dhos asientos que hera
orden de nuestro amo y Señor que Su benida avia sido p[ar]a dos diligensias
y que la una hera el bolver lo quitado que sesarian ya nuestras eniquidades
que el nos mostraria como nro amo y Señor no nos tenia sino hera para el
resguardo de esta plasa y su rial Corona que lo dexaramos tomar mansion
que todo se conpondria: quedo como lo dispuso su señoria esperandolo nos
bolviese allamar no lo hiso y teniendo notisia nosotros de como los
Capitulares de dha Ciu[da]d hasian m[ucho]s empeños para que no nos
diese y mostrara lo prometido Con Cuyas notisias pasamos asu casa y le preguntamos nos dixiesse en la disposicion que nos hallabamos y nos respondio
que todavia no hera tarde que tubiessemos pasiensia. Con su respuesta nos
pasamos a nuestro lugar hasta el ynterin su señoria disponia lo mas con-
biniente quedando asu cuy[da]do nuestro disinio se pasaron mas de quatro
meses que fue el tiempo en que dispuso su viaje y estando sercana la parti-
da pasamos de segunda asu casa y le preguntamos en que disposicion nos
dexaba y nos respondio que en la Contaduria de dha Ciu[da]d quedava
n[uest]ro vien q[ue] hera q[uan]to podia haser y aver echo por nosotros
sigio su Viaje dexando nos segun estabamos de antes aun con mas nesesidades[.] Continuandose la dha fabrica De n[uest]ro Amo y Señor a la qual
a sistimos con toda prontitud en la Governacion de el Señor Dn Luis
Sañado ya nalla que fue p[o]r dos años y medio nos atendio con toda piedad
y sus prosedimientos pretendio el hasernos algun vien y lo estorbaron lo
dhos Señores Capitulares sertificandolo la Señora su esposa que aviendose
ofresido la fatalidad q[ue] se ofresio vino a este n[uest]ro lugar a despedirse
de la Reyna de la Caridad y nos dixo que en dha Contaduria estaba lo que
deseabamos que su esposo lo avia de aver mostrado, no lo avia echo no sien-

do el culpado, que nos quexasemos a los vesinos de Cuba queran quien lo avian estorvado. Entro el Señor Dn Matheo Lopez de Cangas su su sesor del Señor Dn Luis Sañudo llamando ala fabrica ocurimos como de antes lo hasiamos y estando en su segimiento vino el Señor Dn Fran[cis]co delgado y Castilla vesino de dha Ciu[da]d con fa cultad y nombramiento de Comisario R[ea]l de Minas p[or] voluntad de n[uest]ro amo y Señor con una Real Sedula que le vino a dho Señor Gov[ernado]r en la qual ordena y manda lo q[ue] Vssa vera por hese testimonio sacado de dha real sedula quien ha sido cavelillo de nuestra mayor seguedad por puntos que en el declara en que se satisfara V[uestr]a s[eñori]a del modo con que S Mgd nos favorese y manda nos atiendan a si en hesa como las otras. a de mas la esperiensia q[ue] p[or] nuestro antecesores hemos tenido como se les a tendia quando ocurian a el dho trabajo q[ue] a unque no se les dava mas q[ue] era un rial para la comida tenian p[or] suyas todas las tierras que tiene n[uest]ro amo y Señor rn que tenian sus labransas y criansas de geneados bacunos y serda con que sursian la cortedad de dha rasion. se les a tendia como esclavos de quien somos estando siempre unibles[?] y confor[mes] a cudir a dhas fabrica con toda prontitud no siendo menos nosotros en las o casiones que nos han ocupado en dhas fabricas con n[ues]tra continuada nesesidad hemos sido fieles en cunplir nuestra obligacion como lo sertificaremos con los vesinos de dha Ciu[da]d y Justicias della ante quien hemos representado nra nesesidad con sitados pedimentos que ansido continuos desde q[ue] nos han hido quitando las dhas tierras hasta que nos han dexado con una legua en contorno en donde puede Vssa ver si sera cosa posible de mantenerse tantas familias como tiene n[uest]ro amo y Señor sin tener mas de mi soria q[ue] es el dho rial y heso los que estan trabajando en dhas fabricas que los demas los mantiene la reyna de la Caridad que a no ser por us a usilio murieramos sin mas. Ver p[or] q[ue] el q[ue] es casado con esclava de nuestro amo y Señor se emplea en dcha fabrica el tiempo en que le toca y en dho tiempo queda su muger y yjos dispuestos apereser en las cala midades de la cortedad de dho Pueblo hemosla representado en nuestros pedimento a lso Gov[ernador]es y demas Justisias de dha Ciu[da]d y nos dan de respuesta que le pidamos a nro amo y Señor q[ue] hellos no nos pueden delantar rasion ni darnos tierras por tenerlas a rendadas. Hemos hecho las mas vibas diligencias p[ar]a ver sise nos podia remediar en algun modo. como es notorio pasamos asan to Domingo con dho pedimento y el Sr presidente de sirvio de probeer una rial probision en nro favor con la qual nos presentamos ante el Señor Gov[ernado]or y lo que con hella obro fue y hasido hechar bando en este lugar que pena de la vida el que comprase bas-

timentos de todo lo espresado hemos dado cuenta y en distintos pedimentos
como lo hisimos el dia veynte Del corriente mes de Nobriembre deste presente mes y año de mil setesiento y t[r]eynta y quatro que vino el Señor
Tesorero Dn Mig[ue]l Serrano vesino de dha Ciu[da]d a compañado de el
Señor escribano Manuel Gonz[ale]s a leer una rial sedula en q[ue] nos
ordena y manda ocuramos a el continuado trabajo q[ue] se nos mirara y
atendera segun nra miseria obedientes nos resolvimos a obedeser como
esclavos q[ue] somos preguntado que mandava S Mgd nos diesse. Dixeron
sus [title illegible] que un rial de hario para los que fueran a dho trabajo
preguntamos de segunda ves sino manda otra cosa alguna con que se pud-
iesen remediar los demas vesinos y dixeron que no ordenaba mas que lo
espresado q[ue] viesemos nosotros lo que respondiamos para ynformar a el
rial Consejo de S Mgd, dimos de respuesta q[ue] si sus m[e]r[ce]des siendo
oficiales de la R[ea]l asienda de nro a mo y Señor no podian disponer los
mejores medios sobre el buen tratamiento de sus maravedises que viesen la
nesesidad q[u]e padeciamos q[ue] hera colmada que remediassen q[uan]do
no del todo en algun modo para poder en trar en el seguimiento de dho trabajo que estamos prontos como llevamos declarado.

Y nos dan de respuesta que ellos en q[uan]to lo que pediamos no podian
disponer cosa alguna mas que hera lo que ordenaba dha rial sedula q[ue] en
lo demas su Mag[esta]d hera quien podia dar tierras como suyas q[ue] hellos en q[uan]to las que tenia no posian disponer cosa alguna p[or] estar
arendadas de algunos vesinos de dha Ciu[da]d.

Y nosotros en vista de tales respuestas hemos determinado el que fuesen
treynta compañeros a essa Capitaneria como lo hemos executado escusando qualesquiera Perturbasion de las que se ofresen en este nro pueblo siendo el motivo los vesinos de dha Ciud[a]d q[ue] de continuo andan buscan-
do brecha para poder hasernos capito en nuestra contra. Y escusando tal se
ofresca nos de terminamos el partirnos como de [illegible] parados buscan-
do el patrosinio de Vssa que como Juez reto y benino lial vasallo de nuestro
amo y señor determine el ocuparnos en hesa ciudad en cosas del servisio de
nro amo y Señor y agrado de Vssa que nuestra mucho obediensia esta siempre prosima a executar las ordenes de Vssa con todo Cuy[da]do hasta el
ynterin el amable pecho de Vssa se sirve de ynformar a nuestro amo y señor
las penalidades que p[or] sus maravedises pasa. Suplicamos todos a Vssa se
sirva p[or] medio de Su buen obrar poner en notisia de nuestro amo y Señor
como ha amas de sien años que nos exersitamos en cosas de su rial Servisio
como es notorio que hemos sidos continuos en la dha fabrica en asistir a un

rebato y a otras cosas nesesarias como lo sertificaremos en todos tiempos con los dhos vesinos de dha Ciud[dad] que declararan si hemos sido fieles en n[uest]ro cumplimiento en qualesquiera tiempo y hora que se nos ha llamado y ocupado sei hemos estado prontos selosos y vigilantes en todo lo que hasido en serivisio de nuestro amo y Señor en cuya notisia pondra Vssa por amor de [illegible] como estamos en este lugar mil y mas personas pasando las nesesidades declaradas y rodos pedimos p[or] medio de el a usilio de Vssa un resqate p[or] un tiempo que no hallamos en disposicion de mercarnos mediandosu rial persona un presio regular en que podamos redimirnos trayendo a su real memoria nuestra notificada probesa resiviendo nos dinero tabaco trigo cobre y demas frutos que da la tierra q[ue] otorgandonos surial persona nuestro pedimento p[or] medio de Vssa entre el dho tiempo q[ue] llevamos pedido seremos fieles en cumplir lo prometido sin que sea nesesario tome su Magd otra resolusion alguna en que seamos pensionados que los executaremos con toda prontitud como llebamos declarado no apartandonos de servir a su rial persona en todo lo que sea de su rial agrado a un con mas vigilansa que la que hemos gastado en lo antepasado no siendo menos nuestro agradecimiento p[ar]a con Vssa hasiendonos la caridad de poner por su parte en notisia de nuestro amo y Señor nuestros clamores doliendose de nuestra miseria que no hemos hallado otro medio y persona mas ynportante ante quien poner nuestro [illegible] que salga a lus sino es a la afabilidad de Vssa como piadoso y lial vasallo de S Mgd en quien tiene la rial persona recargado el mayor peso de su Corona assi recargamos nosotros como en persona tal en quien esperamos se servira de probeer y manda lo que mas convenga en este nuestro pedimento.

Jurando lo nesesario los esclavos de las riales minas de Santiago del prado por S Mgd.

Archives

Archivo General de Indias. Seville, Spain.
Archivo Histórico Nacional. Madrid, Spain.
Collection of Leví Marrero's Papers, Florida International
    University, Miami, U.S.A.
Santuario de la Virgen de la Caridad del Cobre. Parish Records.
    El Cobre, Cuba.

ABBREVIATIONS USED

Archivo Histórico Nacional (AHN)
Archivo General de Indias (AGI)
Sections of AGI:
Escribanía (ESC)
Audiencia de Santo Domingo (SD)
Cuaderno (C)
Expediente (expte.)
Folio(s) (fol.[s.])
Verso (v)

Notes

PREAMBLE

1. Hernández 1993, 101–2.

INTRODUCTION

1. For Spain, see Pike 1983; Cortés López 1989, 64–65, 110–13. There were also royal slaves in modern Portugal; however, according to Saunders (1982, 80–84), they seem to have been few and scantily employed. Despite Roman templates found in Iberian law and institutions, slavery to the king does not seem to have followed the model of Rome's imperial slaves (i.e., the Familia Caesaris) studied by Weaver 1972.

2. Macías Domínguez 1978; Marrero vol. 3:144–63; Pérez Guzmán 1990; Pike 1983, 136–39. Voelz (1993, 68–69) mentions the use of Crown slaves for public works and fortification projects by the Spanish, the French, and in some cases by the British in Jamaica.

3. Of these 163 royal slaves, however, 40 were too old to work in the fortification projects and 32 were female slaves occupied in domestic services (Macías Domínguez 1978, 280–85). The Crown also made use of royal slaves in the royal tobacco factory of Havana (Marrero vol. 11:18).

4. The 2,000 includes slaves and *forzados* in the projects of El Morro, La Cabaña, and Atarés (Pérez Guzmán 1990, 245). Pike (1983, 136–39), however, found that between 1763 and 1765, the highest peak of employment of royal slaves in the fortification projects of Havana, there were some 795 slaves. In Puerto Rico, the Crown apparently relied more heavily on penal labor.

5. The only single study about labor among royal slaves is Pérez Guzmán 1990. This study, however, is institutionally oriented and does not deal with questions of representation and ideology.

6. Family Census of 1773, Archivo General de Indias, Santo Domingo (hereafter AGI-SD) 1628. The majority (61 percent) of the free people of color in this village were males.

7. There were also some Afro-American pueblos that resulted from negotiations between colonial authorities and former maroon communities. For references to Afro-American pueblos in the Caribbean and circum-Caribbean region: on Gracia Real de Santa Teresa de Mose, see Lander 1990, 9–30; on San Lorenzo de las Minas, see Deive 1980, 532–43. On pueblos elsewhere in Spanish America, see Palmer 1976; Taylor 1970, 442–46; Love 1967, 89–103; and Granda 1983, 229–64. There may be many other formal and informal colonial Afro-American pueblos awaiting "rediscovery" from the archives and oral social memory.

8. In Jamaica the movement toward reconstituted peasant villages after emanci-

pation was spearheaded by Baptist clergy (Mintz 1974, 157–79; Besson 1984; Paget 1964).

9. I use the term "cultural" here in its wider definition as the underlying premises, meanings, and values informing different aspects of life in a given society (including political and economic life, as in a political culture, or, for instance, in a "moral economy"). In this sense its more narrow and conventional sense as a series of expressive practices in a sphere of social life ("Culture/[folk] culture") is subsumed under the larger concept of culture. For programmatical statements about anthropology and history, and culture and practice, and for examples in the Caribbean region, see Bourdieu 1997; Cohen 1981; Comaroff 1985; J. and J. Comaroff 1991; Dening 1991; Clifford and Marcus 1986; and Rosaldo 1986. For the Caribbean region, see Mintz 1960; McCarthy Brown 1994; and Horowitz 1971. In the discipline of history, there is also the particularly important tradition of Native American ethno-history.

10. Moreno Fraginals 1977, 1978. Many of the gaps in social and cultural history in the historiography of slavery, particularly in Cuba, but also elsewhere in Latin America, may be also implicitly related to an ongoing backlash against Frank Tannenbaum's (1947) old cultural reductionistic thesis on Iberian slavery, or even to orthodox Marxist-oriented approaches to the peculiar institution that tend to be dismissive of "superstructural" epiphenomena.

11. A recent book on Cuban slavery entitled *The Cuban Slave Market, 1790–1880*, by Bergad et al. (1995), is a meticulous compilation of a long series of slave prices in Cuba for almost a century. It is intended to address once more the question of whether slavery was indeed profitable right until the eve of abolition or at least perceived as such by planters willing to pay high prices for slaves.

12. In 1774, the free population of color in the Oriente region constituted 33 percent of the population; in 1846, they still constituted a high 31.5 percent, see Kiple 1976. On free people of color in Cuba in general, see Knight 1972; Deschamps-Chapeaux 1971; Paquette 1988; and Martínez Alier 1974. For a closer look at the Oriente region during the late nineteenth century, see Pérez 1989. For studies on Brazil that recognize the importance of the "continuum" and that encompass the activities of free and enslaved people, see Schwartz 1985, 252–53; and Lauderdale-Graham 1992.

13. For classic studies of slavery and Cuban plantation society, see Moreno Fraginals 1978; Knight 1970; Guerra y Sánchez 1976 [1944]; Bergad 1990; Bergad et al. 1995; Corwin 1967; and R. Scott 1985.

14. Report of Don Juan Francisco de Cerquera, Havana, July 15, 1728, AGI-SD 380.

15. Kagan 1981; Taylor 1972; Borah 1983; Stern 1982; Cutter 1986, 1995; Hunefeldt 1994; R. Scott 1985; Helg 1995.

16. At least two other peasant subordinate communities, the Indian pueblos of Jiguaní and El Caney, mobilized actively through the courts like the cobreros. See Chapter 11 in this volume.

17. Pastoral Visit of Bishop Don Pedro Agustín Morell de Santa Cruz to El Cobre, Santiago de Cuba, Dec. 8, 1756, AGI-SD 534. I have also referenced the document in its published version by García del Pino 1985.

18. A leading figure in this interwar intellectual cultural movement was Fernando Ortiz, known as the "father" of modern Afro-Cuban studies and founder of institutions such as the Sociedad de Estudios Afrocubanos and its journal in the 1930s, *Estudios Folklóricos Cubanos*. Aside from his important scholarship on Afro-Cuban expressive practices and religion per se, Ortiz reconceptualized and legitimized these traditions as Cuban folklore. He was also an important promoter of the notion of *cubanía* and of "creolization" as a merging of transcultural ethnic traditions. On Fernando Ortiz himself as an emblematic figure of "Cubanness," see Pérez Firmat 1989. In literature and literary studies there were modernist figures such as Alejo Carpentier, Nicolás Guillén, José Arrom, and others incorporating African strands into canonic "Cuban" culture. See Barreda 1979.

19. J. Arrom 1959.

20. Fernando Ortiz's notes are reproduced in Portuondo Zúñiga's (1995) Appendix 1.

21. Benítez Rojo 1989, xvi–xxii.

22. For a study of the Marian shrine in Miami, see Tweed 1997.

23. Of the forty-four figures depicted in the mural, two are female secular "stand-ins" for the Marian symbol. They are Bernarda Gómez Toro and Mariana Grajales. Both were the wives and/or mothers of heroes of Cuba's Independence War. They both gave up male sons in sacrifice for the *patria* (homeland). Furthermore, nineteen of the forty-four figures constitute well-known and little-known ecclesiastics that emphasize the Catholic conception of Cuban history in the mural.

24. Miracles as contested events are a fascinating topic in religious studies and popular culture. Indeed, there was no cultural consensus regarding what may be regarded as a miracle even among otherwise staunch religious believers in former (or modern) times.

25. Bakhtin 1981. The Bakhtinian theoretical "fad" took hold mostly in sociolinguistic, anthropological, and literary studies.

26. More specifically in the case of Cuba, see the nineteenth-century text of Juan Manzano's autobiography, *Autobiography of a Slave* (Shulman 1995), and the more complex case of Barnet's *Biografía de un cimarrón* (1968), translated into the English version as *Autobiography of a Runaway Slave*.

CHAPTER 1

Epigraph. Inventory of the Mines, May 9, 1677, fols. 377v–79v, AGI-SD 1631.

1. Between 1610 and 1620 the annual average of copper produced for the Crown was 1,850 quintals; by the 1640s annual production had been drastically reduced to an average of 202 quintals per year (Marrero vol. 3:253–85). For the king's slaves' copper production after the 1670s, see Table 6 in Chapter 8 in this volume.

2. Don Antonio Matta y Haro to the Crown, Havana, Feb. 10, 1665, AGI-SD 104.

3. Inventory of the Mines, Jan. 29, 1620, fols. 221v–43, AGI-SD 1631.

4. Inventory of the Mines, Sept. 2, 1670, fols. 137–44, AGI-SD 1631.

5. Inventory of the Mines, May 9, 1677, fols. 377v–79v, AGI-SD 1631.

6. Inventory of the Mines, Sept. 2, 1670, fols. 137–44; and 1677, fols. 377–79v, both in AGI-SD 1631.

7. Assessment of Slaves and Land, July 12, 1677, Inventory of the Mines, fols. 453–54, AGI-SD 1631.

8. Inventory of the Mines, May 9, 1677, fols. 377–79v, AGI-SD 1631.

9. Ibid.

10. Inventory of the Mines, May 9, 1677, AGI-SD 1631; and Jan. 29, 1620, fol. 228, AGI-SD 1631. See also Chapter 5 in this volume.

11. Inventory of the Mines, May 9, 1677, fol. 377v, AGI-SD 1631. Most cobreros came to have both a residence in the pueblo and another in their farms. In 1756 Bishop Morell de Santa Cruz registered 140 houses (20 made of tile) and 104 farms in El Cobre (García del Pino 1985, 110–14). The family census of 1750 (AGI-SD 1630) registers the separation of neighborhoods by the river. The family censuses of 1773 and 1775 (both in AGI-SD 1628) detail the street layout and list those families that did not possess a residence in the village.

12. Research for subsequent sections in this chapter was based on the following slave inventories. Hereafter in this chapter I will only cite the particular inventories on which data is based in the text but will not cite again their archival sources. Inventories of Slaves: Report of Captain Francisco Sánchez de Moya, Santiago del Prado, Nov. 30, 1608, AGI-SD 451; Feb. 18, 1620, fols. 240–46v/205–10, AGI-SD 1631; [ca. Dec. 3], 1647, fols. 7–14, AGI-SD 104; Dec. 28, 1665, AGI-SD 104; [ca. Sept. 22], 1670, fols. 126–34/201–9, AGI-SD 1631; [ca. May 9], 1677, fols. 363v–75v, AGI-SD 1631. Hereafter in this book abbreviated references to these inventories of slaves will only include year and archival *legajo* (bundle of documents).

13. The figures provided throughout this chapter are only rough estimates, barely sufficient to make approximations, establish general trends, raise suggestive questions, and make speculations.

14. On the contrary, some 9 slaves were sold before 1680, while another 6 were granted to the family of the former contractor of the mines in the 1690s (Court Relator's Judicial Report [Apuntamiento del relator] [hereafter Judicial Report], [Madrid, ca. 1799], cuaderno [hereafter C] 2, fols. 9v, 11–11v, AGI-SD 1627). In fact, there may have been an additional sale of some 30 to 63 royal slaves before 1683 that was recalled some five decades later in the midst of a major conflict: see Cobreros to Governor Don Carlos Sucre, [El Cobre, ca. Aug. 1731], [untitled cuaderno with documents related to Governor Sucre's case (includes fols. 1–23)] (hereafter [C 1, Autos Sucre]), fols. 5v–7, AGI-SD 493; Testimony of Don Gerónimo de Valenzuela, Santiago de Cuba, Oct. 16, 1731, Investigation of Governor Ximénez, [untitled cuaderno; came with letter of Governor Ximénez, Santiago de Cuba, Dec. 6, 1731 (includes fols. 1–150)] (hereafter [C 2, Autos 1731]), fol. 140, AGI-SD 493.

15. No ages were recorded in the Inventory of Slaves of 1608, but *negritos criollos* (Creole slave children) were listed separately, and their ages were recorded. They were all under 8 years old.

16. Report of Don Francisco Sánchez de Moya, Santiago del Prado, Nov. 30, 1608, AGI-SD 451.

17. No ages were recorded in the Inventory of Slaves of 1620, but slave couples and families were recorded as units, from whence the 75 sons and daughters recorded as living with parents. Not until 1677 does another inventory record again the slaves in their family units as had been done in 1620.

18. Craton 1978, 96; B. Bush 1989, 130–31; Higman 1976, 154.

19. From 1670 to 1677, there was also an increase from 60 to 81 females of child-bearing age.

20. The questions of the relation between slavery and low fertility have been the subject of some debate and much speculation. See among others B. Bush 1989, 120–50; and Craton 1978.

21. Craton (1978, 61, 72) refers to these classic plantation populations as having a "lobbed Christmas tree" shape.

22. See Table 9 in Chapter 9 in this volume, for self-manumission trends.

23. From subsequent years (1667–1697), for instance, while most royal slaves legally married other natives of El Cobre—some 10.7 percent (9 total) married personal slaves outside the community, and another 10.7 percent (another 9) married freemen and -women from outside the village who would have settled with their royal slave spouses in El Cobre. Since only about one-fifth of royal slaves' marriages involved outsiders, El Cobre can be considered a relatively endogamic community, at least during these last decades of the seventeenth century (Marriage Records, Book 1, 1667–1697, Sanctuary of the Virgin of Charity, El Cobre, Cuba).

24. Ages were recorded in the Inventory of Slaves of 1647, but they are unreliable because they were rounded off by decades. As a result, there seems to be an improbably high number of slaves in very aged cohorts.

25. For the contrasting shapes of a "lobbed Christmas tree" and a "pyramid," see Craton 1978, 61,72.

26. There were 20 soldiers residing in the settlement in 1608 (Report of Captain Don Francisco Sánchez de Moya, Santiago del Prado, Nov. 30, 1608, AGI-SD 451). The Inventory of Slaves of 1620 notes the housing provided for soldiers, but it gives no specific figures.

27. Family Census of 1773, AGI-SD 1628.

28. Inventory of Slaves, 1677; Assessment of Slaves, July 12, 1677, fols. 446v–53v, both in AGI-SD 1631.

29. The distinction between the two meanings is based on the opposition of the term *criollo* to *natural* ("Creole" to "native"). The generic term "Creole" was applied to second-generation Spaniards born in the Indies as well as to second-generation Africans, but never to Indians who were referred to by the equally generic term "natives." The term "native," however, could also acquire a more specific meaning when linked to a region or town wherein it would apply to anyone born in that particular locality: a "native" of Seville, of Havana, of the Congo, or of El Cobre.

30. In a couple of cases, Creole or New World-born status in El Cobre was also indicated through a city, as in the case of Francisco Camaguey (Inventory of Slaves, 1647) and Juan de Santiago (Inventory of Slaves, 1665).

31. The colonial valuation was reflected in the higher market prices that Creole slaves fetched at least in the nineteenth century and in the occupations they tended to hold (Bergad et al. 1995). For a still-too-general view of Creole societies in the West Indies, see Brathwaite 1971.

32. For the study of naming practices among slaves elsewhere, see Craton 1978, 156–59 for Jamaica; and Gutman 1976 for the U.S. South. For Christian naming

conventions among elites in the sixteenth- and seventeenth-century Congo, see Hilton 1985, 89–90; and Thornton 1998, 17–19.

33. The number in 1608 was probably much higher. African males were usually given an ethnic "surname" (or any surname) more consistently than females: 103 (74.6 percent) of the 138 male slaves had an African "ethnic" name, while 20 (41.6 percent) of the 48 adult females had an African "ethnic" name.

34. In a report to the Crown made in 1608, the administrator of the mines, Captain Don Francisco Sánchez de Moya, referred to the slave population in the settlement collectively as "Angolans" (Santiago del Prado, Nov. 30, 1608, AGI-SD 451).

35. Phonetic distortions in the transcription of names may account for much of the apparent variety. The following is a list of solo African names in the inventory of 1608: Cabagasa; Cabanga; Caculo; Cangunba; Capiche; Carabalí; Catunes; [Camacho?]; Embote; Enbax; Enchico; Farenbule; Manga; Mayala; Mayuca; Mondonguero; Mosungo; Natu; Oloferno; and Quesincle. I have systematically capitalized these ethnic African names in my text.

36. Although the number of slaves with a "Congo" "ethnic" name also declined, proportionally speaking the decline was not as dramatic as in the case of "Angolas": 10 males and 4 females were recorded as "Congos" in 1608, while 6 males and 1 female were in 1620.

37. I want to thank Professor John Thornton for suggesting these meanings and locations in a vast and unidentifiable set of names.

38. By 1647, African-named slaves were mostly confined to elderly men and women in age groups over 50 years.

39. In 1608, there was a range of twenty-nine African names and twenty-five Christian first names among the 152 male slaves of Santiago del Prado. For 1620, the numbers were fifty-one African and forty Christian names among 220 males; and for 1647 there were fifty-nine different African names and forty-five Christian first names for a total of 177 males.

40. In 1608, there was a range of nine African last names and twenty-seven Christian first ones among 57 females; in 1620, there were five African names and thirty-five Christian ones for 112 females; and in 1647, there were twenty-six different African names and fifty-six Christian ones among 132 females in the settlement. The range of Christian names for males was narrower than for females, particularly if measured against population figures (see note 39, above).

41. In 1647, there were only 12 slaves explicitly listed as "Angolans" in the slave inventory.

42. See Chapter 7 in this volume for discussion of personal slaves of African origin held by royal slaves and free villagers in El Cobre.

43. Afro-Cuban cabildos (ethnic associations) were often organized along African "nation" or ethnicity lines. They were headed by slaves with the title of capitán (captain) or rey (king) (F. Ortiz 1984a). Although there is no record of these kinds of cabildos in the seventeenth century, Bishop Morell de Santa Cruz tried to Christianize some of them in the mid-eighteenth century by providing them with Marian effigies with different advocacies (Marrero vol. 8:157–61; see also Howard 1998).

44. For copper mining in Africa, including Angola and Congo, see Herbert 1984.

45. Crosby 1972; Hilton 1985, 78–79.

46. Matías de Olivera—a former Spanish soldier—was charged by Captain Sánchez de Moya, and with the bishop's approval, to evangelize the slaves sometime before 1608. Years later this function may have been taken up by the parish priest (Report of Captain Francisco Sánchez de Moya, Santiago del Prado, Nov. 30, 1608, AGI-SD 451). See also Chapter 5 in this volume.

47. Christian 1981b, 108–12; Rubial García 1993.

48. Inventory of Slaves, 1620, AGI-SD 1631.

49. There were 2 old slaves, Blas and Lorenzo, aged 60 and 80, respectively, and 4 younger ones—Juan de Salas, Pedro, Juan Manuel, and Lorenzo—all termed *criollos* who were *maestros de chirimía* (master players of a wind instrument) in 1647. In addition there were 2 other young men, Juan Sabio (age 25) and Pedro, son of Baltasar (age 17), who were listed as "musician of the church" and "musician" in the Inventory of Slaves of 1647. In the Inventory of Slaves of 1677, one of the young *chirimías* of 1647, Juan de Salas, was a *ministril* (a string or wind instrument player), and Lorenzo, now de Arroyo, was still *maestro de chirimía*. It is not clear if women's voices were used as a chorus in the seventeenth century, but in the eighteenth century, women were singers in the Sanctuary of the Virgin (Memorial of Don Joseph Espinoza de los Monteros, Gregorio Cosme Osorio, and Carlos Ramos, Madrid, Apr. 4, 1784, C 5/83, fols. 654–75, AGI-SD 1629). Testimony of Vicente de la Caridad, fols. 9v–10, from a series of hearings regarding the judicial status of cobreros (hereafter entitled "Testimonios") "Testimonio Vicente de la Caridad," 1788, C 67/59/24, AGI-SD 1628. There is no record of any African music performed in the settlement during those years, but in the early eighteenth century, a royal slave complained that the governor made them dance "indecent dances" during festivities to the Virgin (Petition of Colonel Joseph Canales, [Santiago de Cuba, ca. Jan. 1711], "Cargos y descargos del Coronel Joseph Canales" [hereafter "Cargos"], C 8, fols. 61–61v, AGI-Escribanía [hereafter AGI-ESC] 92C).

50. See Thornton 1993.

51. In the Inventory of Slaves of 1647, there was a Cosme, a Moreno, a Salas, and an Arroyo. By 1665, there were additional Hispanic surnames, including Márquez, García, González, Vicente, Agua. Finally, by 1677, there were Reyes, Cruz, Rodríguez, Muñoz, Pérez, and Ortíz. Some of these more conventional surnames became lineages, while others like the Arroyo, García, Muñoz, and Márquez disappeared. Some of these surnames may have started out as first names such as "Vicente" (marking a filial relation as Juan "de Vicente" [son of Vicente] and eventually took on the role of surnames).

52. This is not to say that kinship relations were not otherwise noted. Filiation to mother or father, for instance, was oftentimes indicated in slave censuses even before the widespread use of "surnames"—and particularly in the case of small children—through the addition of "de," or "child of [father or mother's first name]." In these cases it is surprising to see the number of father-son filiation cases indicated and recognized by inventory takers. For instance, of approximately 55 cases of filiation indicated in the inventory of 1647, 18 were "children of father" and 37 "children of mother." Of the 18 cases of the identification of filiation to father, 16 constituted

cases of son of father, while only 2 were daughter of father. And of the 37 cases of filiation to mother identified in the inventory, 10 consisted of son of mother and 27
daughter of mother. Interestingly, as many as 15 cases seem to constitute identification of wives to husbands, while there were none of husbands to wives.

53. There is evidence that sometimes freed and enslaved people also used the
mother's family name. Thus, a son of Juan Moreno named Faustino in 1677 was
recorded in the census of 1709 with his mother's surname as Faustino de los Reyes
(Family Census of 1709, C 23, "Demanda," fols. 26–29v, AGI-ESC 93A).

54. The last appearance of a Matamba surname in the records was that of Clara
Matamba in the baptism register of a child of hers in 1719 (Baptism Records of Royal
Slaves, 1680–1769, fols. 92v–170/77v–155, AGI-SD 1630).

CHAPTER 2

Epigraph. Father Don Pedro de Cerquera to Don Antonio Matta y Haro, Santiago del Prado, June 10, 1672, AGI-SD 104.

1. Notary's Note, Havana, Dec. 7, 1672, AGI-SD 104.

2. Inventory of Slaves, 1670, AGI-SD 1631.

3. Notary's Note, Havana, Dec. 7, 1672, AGI-SD 104.

4. Testimony of Captain Juan de Santiago, Investigation of the Virgin's
Apparition, Santiago del Prado, Apr. 1, 1687, fols. 21v–22, AGI-SD 363. Captain Juan
de Santiago was able to sign his deposition, while Juan Moreno could not sign (fols.
18v, 24). See also Chapter 4 in this volume.

5. Assessment of Slaves, July 12, 1677, fols. 446v–53v, AGI-SD 1631.

6. Although not all slave officials in El Cobre were literate, in 1709 the *alcalde*
(bailiff) Félix Cosme apparently could also read and write, as attested to by some of
the written orders sent to him by the governor and written by him to the community. In the 1730s, at least one other villager who was not an officer was also literate. By
the 1780s, Gregorio Cosme Osorio, an educated mulatto freedman, went to Madrid
to litigate for the freedom of his fellow royal slaves. Cosme Osorio kept steady correspondence particularly with one other literate freedman in the village, Justo
Cruzata. See Chapter 11 in this volume.

7. During Bishop Morell de Santa Cruz's pastoral visit of 1756–1757, he established schools for girls and boys (catechism, reading, writing, and good manners) in
every village and town in the island (including the Indian pueblo of El Caney), but
not in El Cobre (García del Pino 1985). An occupational entry stating "school
[*escuela*]," however, appeared next to a freewoman's name in the Family Census of
1773, AGI-SD 1628. In a letter to the freedman Gregorio Cosme Osorio, the community's legal representative in Madrid, Salvador Quiala, wrote in 1784, "The
teacher Gervasio wants you to see if you can [also] get the school," thereby suggesting that there was already a teacher in the village and that he was seeking royal funding for a school (Salvador Quiala to Gregorio Cosme Osorio, El Cobre, Aug. 19,
1784, fol. 48, AGI-SD 1627).

8. Father Don Pedro de Cerquera to Don Antonio Matta y Haro, Santiago del
Prado, June 10, 1672, AGI-SD 104.

9. Ibid.
10. Ibid.
11. Ibid.
12. Petition of Cobreros to Captain General Don Juan Francisco Güemes y Horcacitas, [ca. 1734], "Autos Año de 1735. Sobre lo acaecido con los negros esclavos de S.M. que residen en el pueblo de Santiago del Prado Minas del Cobre remitidos por el Gobernador de la Habana Don Juan Francisco Güemes y Horcacitas" (cuaderno includes fols. 655–802) (hereafter "Autos 1735"), fols. 658–65/3–9v, AGI-SD 451.
13. Report of Captain Don Francisco Sánchez de Moya, Santiago del Prado, Nov. 30, 1608, AGI-SD 451. See also Chapter 6 in this volume.
14. Father Don Pedro de Cerquera to Don Antonio Matta y Haro, Santiago del Prado, Apr. 16, 1672, AGI-SD 104. Don Blas de Tamayo, the *alférez* (lieutenant) of Santiago de Cuba and a member of the city's *cabildo* was in an especially favorable position to obtain land. He received at least one other piece of land for a sugar mill and another to grow cacao. There were at least three other land grants for the development of sugar mills, thus bringing to four total major concessions given to citizens interested in sugar production. Other minor concessions of land for small farms were granted to other citizens of Santiago de Cuba. The uses to which the allocated lands were to be put reflected the growing economic activity in the region. See also Declaration of Captain Francisco Salazar, Inventory of the Mines, May 9, 1677, fols. 377–77v, AGI-SD 1631.
15. Testimony of Captain Francisco Salazar, Inventory of the Mines, May 9, 1677, fols. 376v–77, AGI-SD 1631.
16. Inventory of the Mines, Jan. 29, 1620, fols. 251–54v, AGI-SD 1631. See also Chapter 6 in this volume.
17. Father Don Pedro de Cerquera to Don Antonio Matta y Haro, Santiago del Prado, Apr. 16, 1672, AGI-SD 104.
18. Nicholás Montenegro to Doña Paula de Eguiluz y Montenegro, Santiago del Prado, July 7, 1672, AGI-SD 104.
19. For a more detailed account of the loss and struggle over Barajagua, see Chapters 6 and 11 in this volume.
20. Nicholás Montenegro to Doña Paula de Eguiluz y Montenegro, Santiago del Prado, July 7, 1672, AGI-SD 104.
21. Ibid.
22. Ibid.
23. See Chapter 8 in this volume.
24. Nicholás Montenegro to Doña Paula de Eguiluz y Montenegro, Santiago del Prado, July 7, 1672, AGI-SD 104.
25. Hispanic sumptuary laws attempted to prescribe and regulate symbolic distinctions between status groups (Slave Code of 1680, examined in Knight 1970, 124).
26. There are some references to women in El Cobre during the eighteenth century who owned gold rings and silver rosaries. Martín de Salazar to Gregorio Cosme Osorio, El Cobre, Aug. 21, 1792, AGI-SD 1627; Testimony of Marcelina Antonia de los Reyes, [ca. Mar. 1789], fol. 100, "Testimonio Marcelina Antonia de los Reyes," 1797, no. 35/43, AGI-SD 1628. The royal slave Luis Cosme who was living as a free-

man and working as a muleteer in a hacienda near Havana earned 50 annual pesos in the 1780s. With this income level Cosme was able to own a relatively ample wardrobe that attested to the care he placed in apparel. It included a silver buckle, a new cloak, three shirts of fine linen [*de bretaña*], one with frills, two pairs of silk socks, embroidered handkerchiefs, and other items (Inventory of Luis Cosme's Property, "Testimonio Luis Cosme," 1783, no. 29/73/65, AGI-SD 1628).

27. Nicholás Montenegro to Doña Paula de Eguiluz y Montenegro, Santiago del Prado, July 7, 1672, AGI-SD 104.

28. Don Antonio Matta y Haro to the Crown, Havana, Mar. 15, 1672, AGI-SD 104.

29. Ibid.

30. Gibson 1964, 183–85; see also Haskett 1991, 200.

31. Inventory of Slaves, 1608, AGI-SD 451.

32. Inventory of Slaves, 1647, AGI-SD 104.

33. Nicholás Montenegro to Doña Paula de Eguiluz y Montenegro, Santiago del Prado, July 7, 1672, AGI-SD 104.

34. Don Antonio Matta y Haro to the Crown, Havana, Mar. 15, 1672, AGI-SD 104.

35. See Chapter 11 in this volume, for a sustained discussion of this point.

36. Testimony of Francisco Xavier Quiala, fol. 38v, "Testimonio Teresa Ramos alias Coba," 1793, no. 42/34, AGI-SD 1628.

37. Ibid., Testimony of Pedro Antonio Moreno, fol. 39.

38. Ibid., Testimony of José Basilio Maestre, fol. 52.

39. Francisco Capitango in 1620 was probably Francisco Capitán in 1647, a broken (*quebrado*) man aged sixty. Eighteen years later, in 1665, Captain Francisco was still the only slave holding that title although he was labeled as a physically disabled man. Less is known of the position of *capitán* that he held in the early days of the mining enterprise (Inventories of Slaves: 1620, AGI-SD 1631; 1647, AGI-SD 104; 1665, AGI-SD 104).

40. Inventory of Slaves, 1647, AGI-SD 104.

41. F. Ortiz 1984a. At least one direct reference to the appointment of a head of a *cabildo de nación* (African ethnic association) with the title of *capitán* is found in the petition of Captain Joseph Antonio Ramos of the *cabildo de negros carabalíes nombrados Asicuato*, Havana, Feb. 20, 1772, AGI-Cuba 1197. Another document evincing a *cabildo* with first and second captains and subordinates with the titles analogous to a military hierarchy (with *oficiales* [officers] and *soldados* [soldiers]) is the Report of Captain Joseph Carmelita of the *morenos de nación ungua* in the *cabildo* named San Agustín, Havana, Sept. 19, 1769, AGI-Cuba 1197.

42. See Chapter 4 in this volume.

43. This mediating role of Captain Juan Moreno in 1677 may have also overlapped with that of *alcaldes* in the early 1670s. See Chapter 3 in this volume.

44. See Chapters 3 and 10 in this volume.

45. Nicholás Montenegro to Doña Paula de Eguiluz y Montenegro, Santiago del Prado, July 7, 1672, AGI-SD 104.

46. Marriage Records, Book 1, 1667–1697, Sanctuary of the Virgin of Charity, El Cobre, Cuba.

47. Family Census, 1709, AGI-ESC 93A.

48. Ibid.

49. Ibid.

50. The kind of rights that the private contractor Don Juan de Eguiluz and his heirs allegedly possessed was a matter of some controversy in the history of this juris-diction. The legal controversy hinged around whether the contract of 1620 between Eguiluz and the Crown stipulated private property rights or only private usufruct rights over the mines, lands, and slaves of Santiago del Prado (Marqués de Bajamar, Francisco Gutiérrez de Piñeres, [?] de Posada y Soto, Junta's Report and Recom-mendations to the Crown [hereafter Junta's Report], Madrid, Oct. 31, 1799, AGI-SD 1146; Judicial Report, [Madrid, ca. 1799], C 2, fols. 7–8, AGI-SD 1627; Díaz 1992, 30–33).

51. In the mid-1690s and again in 1720–1721, there were some concrete attempts to privately contract the mines, but the agreements fell through at some point of the negotiation (Judicial Report, [Madrid, ca. 1799], C 2, fols. 12–21, AGI-SD 1627; Díaz 1992, 38–45). In 1778, the heirs of the Eguiluz family claimed their alleged property back (Judicial Report, C 2, fols. 26–31, AGI-SD 1627).

CHAPTER 3

Epigraph. Petition of Captain Juan Moreno, Santiago del Prado, July 13, 1677, fols. 454–55v, AGI-SD 1631.

1. Royal Edict, Madrid, Apr. 18, 1673, AGI-SD 1631.

2. Klein 1989 [1967], 196–200; Bergad et al. 1995, 122–42. The term *coartado* was formally introduced in Spain for the first time in 1712, in the ninth version of the Law of the Indies. The institution as such was supposedly founded in Cuba, and it is there that the practice became more extended. It remained active in nineteenth-century Cuban plantation society. The use of the term in a royal edict of 1673 shows that it was already officially recognized at that early date.

3. Royal Edict, Madrid, Apr. 18, 1673; Royal Edict, Madrid, Sept. 9, 1674, both in "Testimonio de varias copias de cédulas certificadas," no. 14/23, AGI-SD 1627; also in AGI-SD 1631.

4. Petition of Captain Juan Moreno, Santiago del Prado, July, 13, 1677, fols. 454–55v, AGI-SD 1631.

5. Ibid. The inventory of the mines and its slaves made during the visit and investigation of Judge Ortiz de Matienzo was dated May 9, 1677 (fols. 363v–75v), but the actual appraisal of the value of the slaves was dated on July 12, 1677 (fols. 446v–53v), a day before the judge recorded having received Captain Moreno's peti-tion (fols. 454–55v), all in Inventory of the Mines, 1677, AGI-SD 1631.

6. An exception would be the lay brotherhoods and the *cabildos de nación* among African slaves. These were also drawn up as collective documents through official channels.

7. On Antonio Salazar's letter, see Testimonies of Bartolomé Rodríguez (fol. 239), Juan Diego González (fols. 286–87), Claudio Alcántara (fols. 275–76v), Santiago de Cuba, [ca. Feb.–Mar. 1737], Investigation of Governor Ximénez regard-ing sublevation of 1737 [untitled cuaderno that begins with Petition of Salvador

Borzaga, Santiago de Cuba, Feb. 26, 1737] (hereafter [Autos 1737]), AGI-SD 451. The cuaderno includes fols. 2–367v/829–1195v; I will use the 2–367v folio notation sequence. For a series of five letters by cobreros to Governor Ximénez, [ca. July–Aug. 1731], see fols. 24–39v, [C 2, Autos 1731], AGI-SD 493. See also Cobreros to Governor Sucre, [ca. Aug. 1731], fols. 1–2v, 5v–7, [C 1, Autos Sucre], AGI-SD 493; Cobreros to Dean Morell de Santa Cruz, [ca. Oct. 21–26, 1735], "Diligencias e Instrumentos recibidos últimamente del Gobernador de la Cdad de Cuba sobre lo acaecido con los negros esclavos de S.M. que habitan en el Pueblo de Santiago del Prado Minas del Cobre. Año 1735" [cuaderno includes fols. 803–28] (hereafter "Diligencias 1735"), fols. 817v–18v, AGI-SD 451. For other references to letters written, circulated, and read among cobreros, see the Testimonies of Juan Diego González (fols. 288v–90v) and Captain Thomás Rodríguez (fol. 121), Santiago de Cuba, [ca. Feb.–Mar. 1737], [Autos 1737], AGI-SD 451. See also Chapter 11 in this volume.

8. Letter of Father Don Juan Antonio Pérez, Santiago del Prado, Apr. 14, 1709, C 3, "Demanda de los vecinos del Pueblo de Santiago del Prado Minas de Cobre" (hereafter "Demanda"), fols. 7–11, AGI-ESC 93A.

9. The meaning of "paying tribute" here is unclear. The most conventional reading would be its reference to a down payment or to an installment fee for *coartación* (self-manumission). Another more onerous possibility is that it referred to the payment of actual tribute (as Native Americans and free people of color made) in addition to the *coartación* installment fees. Tribute in the literal sense was never paid, however.

10. The first *coartaciones* among the royal slaves did not take place until 1689. Overall, relatively few slaves purchased their freedom until the 1740s. See Table 9 in Chapter 9 for self-manumission trends.

11. The rights of *coartados* included, for example, a fixed price on their freedom regardless of sale or any change in owners as well as a percentage on capital earned correlative to the investment already made in his or her freedom; also the right to change masters as long as the new master was willing to buy him or her in his or her *coartado* status. Overall, *coartados* had a greater degree of freedom than regular slaves (Klein 1989 [1967], 196–200; Bergad et al. 1995, 122–42).

12. On the position of the slave according to Spanish law, see Klein 1989 [1967], 57–68. For a discussion of the socially and politically "dead" status of a slave, see Patterson 1982.

13. In Spanish law a distinction was made between civil (individual) and political (corporate) liberty. While civil liberty included vassalage to the Crown, political liberty protected subjects as a body, and thus was considered more encompassing and important than civil freedom. These legal formulations were set down by the *letrado* (university graduate) Don Simón Echenique in 1793 to argue that by living as a pueblo the cobreros had even reached the highest form of freedom possible, one indeed higher than personal freedom as individuals (Representation of Don Simón Echenique, Madrid, Mar. 12, 1793, AGI-SD 1630).

14. For a more detailed account of the process, see Chapter 5 in this volume.

15. By the 1690s, official reports and letters quoted in the court relator's report systematically referred to El Cobre as a "pueblo" (Judicial Report, [Madrid, ca.

1799], C 2, fols. 10–18v, AGI-SD 1627). In the Family Census of 1709 (AGI-ESC 93A) the village was referred to as the "Pueblo de las Minas de Santiago del Prado," thus its association to a mining settlement was not really completely shed. In his letter of 1709, Father Pérez already referred to the "pueblo of the Mines of Santiago del Prado" (Letter of Father Don Juan Antonio Pérez, Santiago del Prado, Apr. 14, 1709, C 23, "Demanda," fols. 7–11, AGI-ESC 93A). Later inscriptions reflected other variations. In the 1730s, for example, the village was formally registered in the local family censuses as the "Pueblo de Santiago del Prado Minas de Cobre" (1731, AGI-SD 493; 1735, "Autos 1735," fols. 761–66/104–9, AGI-SD 451); or as "Pueblo de Santiago del Prado Real de Minas del Cobre" (Apr. 12, 1739, fols. 22–43v, AGI-SD 385). At times, however, it was inscribed only as "Pueblo del Cobre" (Family Census of 1773, AGI-SD 1628).

16. Letter of Father Juan Antonio Pérez, Santiago del Prado, Apr. 14, 1709, C 23, "Demanda," fols. 7–11, AGI-ESC 93A. It is unclear, however, if a proper adjudication of land had been made by the High Court of Santo Domingo. See ibid., Auto of Judge Nicholás Chirino, Santiago de Cuba, Nov. 21, 1711, fol. 156. For the 1-surrounding league of land recognized at least by custom, see ibid., Representation of Don Bernardo Antonio Castillo, [ca. 1710], fols. 33–36v.

17. The overwhelming importance of local community and identity in Spain until recently has been discussed by Christian 1989, 18–28. In France, too, a similar local identity (the *pays*) was still strong throughout the nineteenth century (Weber 1976, 45–49). In Cuba, Bishop Morell de Santa Cruz made repeated use of the term *patria* (homeland) in the mid-eighteenth century when referring to the local birthplace of clergymen in the city of Bayamo (García del Pino 1985, 100–3).

18. On the creolization of the mining settlement's slaves, see Chapter 1 in this volume.

19. The colonial term "Creole" is one of the most widely used and taken-for-granted terms in the historical literature on the colonial period. Very little is known about what this Creole identification may have actually entailed and what prerogatives—if any—custom conferred upon this kind of slave in different places and points in time. Did that identity entail special prerogatives, particularly in relation to African slaves? And if so, were these customary prerogatives extensive throughout the Spanish Empire, or how did they vary through differing regions and time? Without further research into the question, it cannot even be assumed that "Creoleness" formed the basis of any assumed identity among slaves in colonial society, or what kind of claims they may have pushed on the basis of this identity. In the case of eighteenth-century Cuba, there may have been some vaguely recognized customary (but not legal) prerogatives—such as perhaps some kind of proscription of sale—underlying expressions of disapproval such as being sold "as if they were *bozales* [African born]."

20. Written histories were often expressions of identities and of patriotic identification; in the colonial period, they took the form of local histories too. The first historical text considered to reflect a patriotic Creole identity in the island was José Martín Félix de Arrate y Acosta's *Llave del Nuevo Mundo antemural de las Indias occidentales*, written in 1761 but first published in 1830. This patriotic work, however, is nothing but a local history of the author's native city of Havana. Thus, as late as

the 1760s, and even by the 1830s, the term *patria* was still synonymous in this colonial setting with local place of origin. Similarly, another early historical work from Cuba also focused on the history of Havana (Urrutia y Montoya 1963 [1791]). In his dedication the author wrote, "As a good son I was always pained to see my beloved *patria* without its particular history . . . ," identifying his "beloved *patria*" as the capital of the island, Havana.

21. The specific reference here is to Benedict Anderson's work *Imagined Communities*, where the historicity and constructed character of the nation-state and of national identities is examined. Anderson tends to counterpose the (imagined) community of the nation, where more abstract solidarities are forged and consolidated through invented traditions and identities, to the (given and not "imagined"?) local community based on the immediacy of face-to-face relations and kin-based bonds. In doing so, Anderson tends to forgo the anthropological insight that local communities are historically construed and "imagined" too. I have also used the termed "imagined" throughout the pages of this book to indicate a wide range of culturally and historically constructed practices constitutive of other forms of social identity beyond local community or the nation. For the invention of traditions, see Hobsbawn 1984.

22. Patterson 1982, 6–7. For another important theoretical/phenomenological reflection on what enslavement entailed with a similar thrust, see Meillassoux 1991.

23. The general historiography on slavery since the 1970s has been, to a large extent, directed at demonstrating that slaves indeed enjoyed "social life," at least outside the master/slave relation. Blassingame's (1972) work on the "slave community" constitutes a turning point on this line of thinking and writing slavery. Other revisionist works followed opening up different debates in the literature regarding the slave family, the internal economy, and cultural traditions. Most of this work, however, relies on a vague use of the term "community."

24. "Diligencias 1735," Santiago del Prado, Apr. 23, 1735, fols. 806–7, AGI-SD 451.

25. Salvador Quiala to Gregorio Cosme Osorio, El Cobre, Aug. 19, 1784, fol. 48, AGI-SD 1627. Cosme Osorio, by contrast, sometimes referred to his fellow villagers as his children (*hijos mios*), Madrid, Oct. 6, 1795, C 75, fols. 217v–19, AGI-SD 1629.

26. "Diligencias 1735," Santiago del Prado, fols. 806–7, AGI-SD 451. For other such references during an interrogation of some royal slaves, see Testimony of Lorenzo González, fol. 195v, [Autos 1737], AGI-SD 451.

27. Series of letters by cobreros to Governor Ximénez, [ca. July–Aug. 1731], [C 2, Autos 1731], fols. 24–27v, 31v–34, 38v–39v, AGI-SD 493; Cobreros to Dean Morell de Santa Cruz, [ca. Oct. 21–26, 1735], "Diligencias 1735," fols. 817v–18v, AGI-SD 451.

28. Representation of Justo Cruzata, Villa de Santiago del Cobre, Feb. 28, 1798, AGI-SD 1630.

29. The term *cobreros* was invoked by a royal official in making reference to a copy "de la carta de los cobreros" (of the cobreros' official letter), Santiago de Cuba [ca. Aug. 17, 1731], expte. sublevación 1731–1732, [1st]C, fol. 15v, AGI-SD 493.

30. Martín Salazar to Gregorio Cosme Osorio, El Cobre, Aug. 21, 1792, fol. 209, AGI-SD 1627.

31. Testimony of Don Lorenzo de Vergueyferos, Investigation of Governor Ximénez, [Autos 1737], [ca. fols. 5–15], AGI-SD 451.

32. Ibid., Testimony of Juan, [ca. fols. 28–37].

33. Christian (1989, 21) made a similar point with regard to contemporary Spain when he noted, "Because each village keeps to itself and forms a social world apart, each takes on a different accent in its speech, which even a relative novice can distinguish in time."

34. Representation of Don Francisco Mancebo y Quiroga, [ca. Aug. 14, 1792], "Escritos presentados en causa sobre graves heridas dadas a mi hermano D. Fernando Mancebo" (hereafter "Escritos graves heridas"), fol. 93, AGI-SD 1627.

35. For the cobreros' mobilization through the courts, see Chapter 11 in this volume.

36. Klein 1989 [1967], 62, 94–95.

37. Judicial Report, [Madrid, ca. 1799], C 2, fol. 9v, AGI-SD 1627.

38. Report of Governor Don Joseph Correoso, Santiago de Cuba, Sept. 4, 1700, C 70, AGI-SD 451.

39. Crown Attorney's Report, Madrid, July 24, 1737, fols. 1475–76v, AGI-SD 1630.

40. Captain Juan Moreno to Judge Ortiz de Matienzo, Santiago del Prado, Nov. 7, 1677, AGI-SD 1631.

41. See Chapter 6 in this volume.

42. Petition of Captain Juan Moreno, Santiago del Prado, July 13, 1677, fols. 454–55v, AGI-SD 1631.

43. Ibid.

44. Captain Juan Moreno to Judge Don Antonio Ortiz de Matienzo, Santiago del Prado, Nov. 7, 1677, AGI-SD 1631.

45. An account by the parish priest Father Don Juan Antonio Pérez in 1709 also stated that the cobreros had been called by the governors of the city for some sixty years to defend some ports when threatened by an enemy attack. Pérez had been priest in the village since 1701 so his account was based on oral history (Father Don Juan Antonio Pérez, Santiago del Prado, Apr. 14, 1709, C 23, "Demanda," fols. 7–11, AGI-ESC 93A). On the 1662 English invasion of Santiago de Cuba and its aftermath, see Bacardí y Moreau 1973, 106–8.

46. Klein 1989 [1967], 63. See also Chapter 11 in this volume.

47. Captain Juan Moreno to Judge Don Antonio Ortiz de Matienzo, Santiago del Prado, Nov. 7, 1677, AGI-SD 1631. The letter also referred to other services such as the persecution of runaway slaves.

48. For an excellent anthropological-historical analysis of the discourse of military service entailed in the presidios of northern New Spain, see Alonso 1995.

49. Klein 1966. For militias of free people of color elsewhere in Spanish America, see Kuethe 1971; McAlister 1957; and Lander 1990. Freemen of color were also organized into militias elsewhere in the Caribbean, particularly in the French colonies but at times also in the British ones, see Hall 1972, 173–75; Hall 1992; Goveia 1965, 297; and Voelz 1993, 111–16; for emergency recruitment even of slaves, see Gaspar 1985, 118–24. For Brazil, see Voelz 1993, 121–22; and Russell-Wood 1972, 118–22.

50. Pastoral Visit of Bishop Morell de Santa Cruz to Jiguaní, Sept. 2, 1756, and to El Caney, Dec. 10, 1756, both published in García del Pino 1985, 107–9, 115–16. There were some exceptions elsewhere too. In Florida, Indians were also employed in military defense (Lander 1990, 21). For Peru, see Spalding 1984, 231.

51. Marrero vol. 3:22, 225.

52. Crown Attorney's Summary, Madrid, June 3, 1732, AGI-SD 493. See also Royal Edict, Madrid, Sept. 3, 1733, "Autos 1735," fols. 670–72v, AGI-SD 451.

53. Cobreros to Dean Morell de Santa Cruz, [El Cobre, ca. Oct. 21–26, 1735], "Diligencias 1735," fols. 817v–18v, AGI-SD 451.

54. Judge Don Antonio Ortiz de Matienzo, Santiago de Cuba, Nov. 8, 1677, [ca. fol. 456], AGI-SD 1631. See also Judicial Report, [Madrid, ca. 1799], C 2, fols. 9–9v, AGI-SD 1627.

55. The outcome may have been more problematic. It is not clear if repression followed the act of flight. For instance, some five decades later, in the midst of another conflict that resulted in flight to the mountains, references can be found in the record to the sale or removal of thirty to sixty-three royal slaves from El Cobre during the administration of Governor Don Francisco de la Guerra (1677–1683) (Cobreros to Governor Don Carlos Sucre, [ca. Aug. 1731], [C 1, Autos Sucre], fols. 1–2v, 5v–7, AGI-SD 493; Testimony of Don Gerónimo de Valenzuela, Santiago de Cuba, Oct. 16, 1731, [C 2, Autos 1731], fols. 140–41v, AGI-SD 493).

56. Judge Don Antonio Ortiz de Matienzo, Santiago de Cuba, Nov. 8, 1677, AGI-SD 1631; see also Judicial Report, [Madrid, ca. 1799], fols. 9–9v, C 2, AGI-SD 1627. When Ortiz de Matienzo eventually adjudicated the civil case over rights to the mines, he ruled that mines and slaves remained the property of the Eguiluz family. The property, however, remained under royal embargo until debts incurred by the failure to comply with the contract were paid to the Crown. This ruling may have reinforced the decision to retain the slaves in the mining settlement. In fact, it may have worked in favor of the slaves since the "rightful" owners could not touch their "property" while in debt to the Crown. The issue over rights, however, was not settled in favor of the Crown until 1700—and then again not definitively. In 1778, Eguiluz's descendants reclaimed their property rights over the mines and slaves. The Crown's decision to reinstitute to the heirs their alleged property led to the reprivatization of the mining jurisdiction and to a major conflict among the Crown, heirs, and cobreros. The cobreros appealed the case to the Council of the Indies in 1784 and obtained a final revocation of the Eguiluz family's property rights over the mines, as well as the community's legal freedom in 1800 (Judicial Report, [Madrid, ca. 1799], C 2 fols. 13, 26–39v, AGI-SD 1627; Resolution of the Royal Council, Madrid, Oct. 31, 1799, AGI-SD 1146).

57. Royal Edict, Madrid, Sept. 3, 1733, AGI-SD 451; Reserved letter of Governor Céspedes to Don Diego J. Navarro, Santiago de Cuba, Dec. 8, 1780, "Autos 1735," fols. 670–72v, AGI-Cuba 1231; Junta's Report, Madrid, Oct. 31, 1799, AGI-SD 1146.

CHAPTER 4

Epigraph. Report of Don Joseph de Losada and Don Joseph Echevarría to the *cabildo* of Santiago de Cuba, [C 2, Autos 1731], [ca. Aug, 11, 1731], fol. 55v, AGI-SD

493. Salvador Quiala to Gregorio Cosme Osorio, El Cobre, Aug. 19, 1784, fol. 48, AGI-SD 1627.

1. Testimony of Captain Juan Moreno, Investigation of the Virgin's Apparition, Santiago del Prado, Apr. 1, 1687, fols. 12v–18v, AGI-SD 363. A transcription of the full document can be found in the Collection of Leví Marrero's Papers at Florida International University. See excerpt on which the present chapter is based in Appendix 4.

2. Warner 1976; Christian 1981b; Stevens-Arroyo 1998.

3. MacCormack 1984; Dean 1993; Gutiérrez 1991; Gruzinski 1993; Vargas Ugarte 1956; Portuondo Zúñiga 1995, 40–45.

4. Vargas Ugarte's (1956) two-volume work thoroughly surveys the major Marian shrines and their founding histories and legends on a country-by-country basis from an avowed Marian devotee's perspective. A closer look into other local or minor regional shrines could uncover more apparition accounts in which blacks played an important role. Notwithstanding the existence of other such stories, the shrines did not attain the regional or national "fame and recognition" to make it into Vargas Ugarte's rather thorough (if perhaps official) compilation.

5. Popular Memory Group 1982.

6. The following analysis is based on Juan Moreno's notarized testimony given in Santiago del Prado on Apr. 1, 1687, fols. 12v–18v, AGI-SD 363.

7. See Chapter 2 in this volume.

8. In his *Apparitions* (1981a, 16–20), William Christian points out that the theme of an apparition or the finding of a statue in Marian shrines usually takes place in the "wilderness." He sees it as a theme of popular devotion against the established church represented by the parish church in the village.

9. Pastoral Visit of Bishop Morell de Santa Cruz to El Cobre, Santiago de Cuba, Dec. 8, 1756, AGI-SD 534, published in García del Pino 1985, 112.

10. For a fuller account of these events, see the Epilogue in this volume.

11. Memorial of Don Joseph de Espinoza, Carlos Ramos, and Gregorio Cosme Osorio, Havana, Dec. 10, 1783, "Pieza formada de las instancias hechas por Gregorio Cosme Osorio sobre libertad esclavos," no. 9 (hereafter "Pieza 9"), fols. 8–23, AGI-SD 1627.

12. By the 1780s, for instance, several cobreros in the village were literate. The free cobrero Gregorio Cosme Osorio, one of the cosigners of the document, was a highly literate man.

13. Memorial of Don Joseph Espinoza de los Monteros, Gregorio Cosme Osorio, and Carlos Ramos, Havana, Dec. 10, 1783, "Pieza 9," fols. 8–23, AGI-SD 1627.

14. Inventory of the Mines, 1608, AGI-SD 451.

15. Memorial of Don Joseph Espinoza de los Monteros, Gregorio Cosme Osorio, and Carlos Ramos, Havana, Dec. 10, 1783, "Pieza 9," fols. 8–23, AGI-SD 1627.

16. Ibid.

17. Ibid.

18. Representation of Don Francisco Mancebo y Quiroga, Santiago de Cuba, [ca. Aug. 14, 1792], "Escritos graves heridas," fols. 91v–92, AGI-SD 1627.

19. Petition of Cobreros to Captain General Güemes y Horcacitas, [ca. 1734], "Autos 1735," fols. 658–65/3–9v, AGI-SD 451.

20. Cobreros to Governor Don Carlos Sucre, [ca. Aug. 1731], [C 1, Autos Sucre], fols. 5v–7, AGI-SD 493.

21. Cobreros to Governor Ximénez, [ca. July–Aug. 1731], [C 2, Autos 1731], fols. 24–25, AGI-SD 493.

22. Report of Don Luis Nieto de Villalobos, Aug. 16, 1731, [C 2, Autos 1731], fols. 86–87v, AGI-SD 493.

23. Report of Don Joseph de Losada and Don Joseph Echevarría to the *cabildo* of Santiago de Cuba, [ca. Aug, 11, 1731], [C 2, Autos 1731], fol. 55v, AGI-SD 493.

24. Father Don Juan Jacintho de Silva, El Cobre, Aug. 17, 1731, AGI-SD 493.

25. Crown Attorney's Summary, Madrid, June 3, 1732, AGI-SD 493.

26. Salvador Quiala to Gregorio Cosme Osorio, [El Cobre], Aug. 19, 1784, fol. 48, AGI-SD 1627.

27. Ibid.

28. Gregorio Cosme Osorio to the Cobreros, Madrid, Oct. 6, 1795, C 75, [ca. fols. 212–17], AGI-SD 1629.

29. Chaplain Fonseca, who inserted this episode in his history, had a sister named Apolonia, a fact which may speak to his own recasting of the story with a personal detail, Portuondo Zúñiga 1995, 146.

30. The case in question involved the placing of a "bundle" in a cross as a threat to drive away an outsider who had settled without the community's authorization in what the cobreros regarded as village land (Testimony of Lorenzo de los Reyes, Santiago de Cuba, [ca. Feb.–Mar. 1737], [Autos 1737], fol. 29, AGI-SD 451). During the unrest of the 1730s in El Cobre, the only accusatory story that was recorded about "witchcraft" (*hechicería*) practices went back a whole century, to the 1620s, a period when the then-private mining slaves were for the most part still African slaves. At that time two slaves had been deported to Cartagena for allegedly practicing witchcraft (Inventory of the Mines, Jan. 29, 1620, fols. 248–49, AGI-1631).

31. Cabrera 1980; Millet 1993; Sánchez Lussón 1996; Lago Vieito 1996; Corbea Calzado 1996.

32. See Chapter 1 in this volume.

33. For a highly speculative discussion of the Native American elements allegedly contained in Paz y Ascanio / Fonseca's account of the Apparition and other miracles, see J. Arrom 1959; Portuondo Zúñiga 1993, 63; and Portuondo Zúñiga 1995, 53–80. Fernando Ortiz also speculated on the "aboriginal elements" found in the Virgin of Charity's figure. Other than archetypal generalities applicable to innumerable cases, he was unable to find concrete motifs with which to ground her in a Native American tradition (Portuondo Zúñiga 1995, 28, 77, 291–92). For a similarly contrived interpretation of the Virgin of Charity's identification with the creolized Yoruban deity Ochún in Santería, see a recently (1993) republished article by Rómulo Lachatañeré, originally published in 1936. The author, however, indicates that this identification first took place in the western region of Cuba and was mainly a nineteenth-century phenomenon.

34. In an extremely suggestive piece about the significance of the Virgin of Charity in El Cobre's contemporary popular culture, the cobrero historian Julio

Corbea Calzado points out that even though other religious cults with Afro-Cuban elements are actively practiced locally today, Santería is not widely practiced in El Cobre. In fact, Corbea points out that the only fully practicing devotee of Santería in the town was an outsider who was initiated in Havana only two years before. More importantly, Corbea found that most people in El Cobre did not even seem to be aware that the Virgin of Charity was Ochún. Paradoxically, the little that is known about this allegedly prevalent syncretism seems to be derived from the media (Corbea Calzado 1996, 6–7; see also Hernández 1993).

35. The *lucumís* arrived in great quantities to the island in the nineteenth century and concentrated in the sugar belt of the island's western region. In Oriente, however, *lucumís* were only third in importance. Instead, slaves from the Congo region had a more preponderant presence in this eastern region. Thus, the mainly Bantu character of the African population in Oriente suggests a different form of syncretism than that found in the Yoruba tradition. On the ethnic typology of the island's enslaved population by regions, see Lachatañeré 1939.

CHAPTER 5

Epigraph. Inventory of the Mines, 1608, AGI-SD 451. Pastoral Visit of Bishop Morell de Santa Cruz to El Cobre, Santiago de Cuba, Dec. 8, 1756, AGI-SD 534, published in García del Pino 1985, 113.

1. These Marian traditions and shrines are by no means an exclusive phenomenon of the past. The twentieth century has seen its share of cases, if with their own specificities of time and space. Our Lady of Fatima in Portugal in 1917; the apparition of the Virgin of Ezquioga in 1931 in the Basque region of Spain; and the Madonna of 115th St. in New York in the 1920s and 1930s constitute but a few examples (see Zimdars-Swartz 1991; Christian 1987, 1996; Orsi 1985).

2. Christian 1981b. For an excellent discussion of the main issues in Mexican colonial historiography regarding local or popular religion, see Taylor's (1996, 47–73) more extended discussion.

3. Inventory of the Mines, 1608, AGI-SD 451.

4. Report of Captain Don Francisco Sánchez de Moya, Santiago del Prado, Nov. 30, 1608, AGI-SD 451. See also Inventory of the Mines, 1608, AGI-SD 451.

5. Inventory of the Mines, Jan. 29, 1620, fol. 228, AGI-SD 1631.

6. Ibid., fols. 221v–27.

7. Ibid. On the widespread devotions to the Virgin of the Rosary in the New World, see Vargas Ugarte 1956.

8. On black *cofradías* (lay brotherhoods) of Our Lady of the Rosary—and others—in Brazil, where they have been best studied, see Mulvey 1976; Russell-Wood 1974, 1982; Nishida 1998; and Karash 1998.

9. Inventory of the Mines, 1647, AGI-SD 104.

10. Although the inventory of the mines of 1647 (AGI-SD 104) refers to the three effigies as Our Ladies of Charity, based on a later document Portuondo Zúñiga (1995, 103) has noted that one was a Virgen de la Candelaria, the other a Virgen de la Concepción, and the third a Virgen de la Caridad.

11. *Historia de la aparición milagrosa de Nuestra Señora de la Caridad del Cobre*

sacada de un manuscrito que el primer Capellán que fue de ella Presbítero D. Onofre de Fonseca, compuesta por el año de 1703 i sacada de los autos que en el de 1688 se formaron ante juez competente, los cuales se hallan en el archivo de la santa casa. The manuscript was revised and published by Don Alejandro Paz y Ascanio, in 1829. A later edition (the one consulted here) was published in 1853. Hereafter I will shorten the reference to the 1853 text by referring to its indeterminate author(s) as Paz y Ascanio / Fonseca, 34.

12. The issue of the origin (and "authenticity") of the image has received much attention in the still small historiographical tradition on Our Lady of Charity of El Cobre. See Wright 1922; J. Arrom 1959; Portuondo Zúñiga 1993, 63; and Portuondo Zúñiga 1995, 43–46, 96–99; and the debate as recounted by Tweed 1997, 19–23. Rather than acknowledge the constructed or reinvented character and indeterminate origins of the Virgin of Charity's tradition, most of this debate is cast in positivistic terms. At its worst the debate addressed highly speculative questions such as how did the figure "really" get to the Bay of Nipe's waters. For the most part, however, the debate turned around the issue of whether the present effigy of the Virgin of Charity is a direct descendant, a "true copy" or clone, of that of Illescas in Spain or if it is a local (read "authentic," "Creole," "Cuban") production. The apparently positivistic debate has a strongly charged culturalist and political subtext that I see as part of the Virgin's twentieth-century reinvented (secular) tradition.

13. Both alternatives—the reinvention of memory and tradition or its casting at the moment of events and its recall later—were possible. William Christian's work (1981a, 1981b, 1989) has shown how these village traditions can be recast in social memory with the years, and he has also discussed (1987, 1996) a case in the 1930s where the supernatural character was disputed at the time of the occurrence as events were being fixed into a "coherent" account. For another study of an even more recent case in the "development of an apparition narrative," see Zimdars-Swartz 1991. See Kleinberg 1992, for a similar process in the negotiation of saintly reputations in the later Middle Ages. For other kinds of reinvented traditions, see Hobsbawn 1984.

14. Paz y Ascanio / Fonseca 1853, 30–31.

15. Testimony of Juan Moreno, Santiago del Prado, Apr. 1, 1687, fols. 17–17v, AGI-SD 363. A typical motif in apparition narratives is the disappearance of statues in the night to the place where they were found—in this case the sea (Christian 1981a, 16–20). This classic motif has been held by José Arrom (1959) to constitute a precolonial Indian cultural motif. According to Arrom, *cemíes* (Taino idols) disappeared, and thus this part of the story constituted an instance of syncretism. For a more recent reiteration of this interpretation, see Portuondo Zúñiga 1995, 71–73.

16. Inventory of the Mines, May 9, 1677, AGI-SD 1631.

17. Pastoral Visit of Bishop Morell de Santa Cruz, Regla, Aug. 20, 1756, AGI-SD 534, published in García del Pino 1985, 38–39. A parish census recorded one hermit in El Cobre as late as 1810, "Moradores que comprende el Beneficio curado del Real de Minas del Cobre, Año 1810," AGI-SD 1689.

18. Christian 1981b, 169–70, 108–12.

19. A popular hermit in Mexico during the seventeenth century, however, was a mestizo. Fray Bartolomé de Jesús María, the mestizo hermit of Chalma, even

became a possible candidate for sainthood around the 1680s (Rubial García 1993, 81–90).

20. Paz y Ascanio / Fonseca 1853, 13.

21. Ibid, 41–42.

22. Family Census of 1735, AGI-SD 451; and 1739, AGI-SD 385. For *beatas* in Spain, see Perry 1990, 97–117; Christian 1981b, 16–17.

23. License from the bishop became a requirement after the Council of Trent and constituted part of the reforms directed at greater control by the church over the orthodoxy of popular religion (Christian 1981a, 169–70).

24. Paz y Ascanio / Fonseca 1853, 32–35.

25. Ibid. See also the notarized testimony of Captain Juan Moreno, Santiago del Prado, Apr. 1, 1687, fol. 18, AGI-SD 363.

26. Paz y Ascanio / Fonseca 1853, 24.

27. Christian 1981a; Rubial García 1993, 75.

28. Christian 1981b, 147–48, 152–53, 178–80. In his history of the colonial Cuban village of Remedios, Fernando Ortiz (1975) makes a similar case for demonology, if in more critical and acerbic terms.

29. Pastoral Visit of Bishop Morell de Santa Cruz, 1756, published in García del Pino 1985, 70, 105, 116, 120.

30. The possible association here with the already popular Our Lady of Guadalupe who appeared to the Indian Juan Diego in Mexico should not be dismissed. See Taylor 1996, 283–85.

31. Christian 1981b, 23–69.

32. Bacardí y Moreau 1973, 228.

33. Portuondo Zúñiga 1995, 114–16.

34. Bacardí y Moreau 1973, 145.

35. Ibid., 190.

36. Ibid., 117–18.

37. Ibid., 182.

38. Ibid., 188, 203–4.

39. Salvador Quiala to Gregorio Cosme Osorio, El Cobre, Aug. 19, 1784, fol. 48, AGI-SD 1627.

40. Bacardí y Moreau 1973, 230.

41. The hermitage to Our Lady of Regla became the equivalent of that of Our Lady of Charity in the western part of the island. This hermitage was made in the 1690s, and by 1714 the Virgin was patroness of the Bay of Regla. Although the protagonist in the founding miracle story of this shrine was a Spaniard, the effigy was a black Madonna. According to Bishop Morell de Santa Cruz, the Virgin's "color is quite black," and what distinguished this image as a prodigious effigy was that she had never accepted touch ups with white color. Thus, here was a Marian story with strands of racial meanings and identities in Havana (Pastoral Visit of Bishop Morell de Santa Cruz, 1756, published in García del Pino 1985, 38–39; see also Vargas Ugarte 1956).

42. Letter of Bishop Juan [Lasso de la Vega], Havana, Apr. 9, 1738, AGI-SD 363.

43. Pastoral Visit of Bishop Morell de Santa Cruz, Santiago de Cuba, Dec. 8, 1756, AGI-SD 534, published in García del Pino 1985, 112.

44. Inventory of the Mines, 1620, AGI-SD 1631.

45. Eventually, by the 1730s and perhaps before, slave (*cabildo*) officials in the village seemed to have had occasion to sit upon benches in the front of the church, thereby recreating the hierarchies and protocols of colonial society in general. For a

fuller discussion of what became a controversial issue in the early 1730s, see Chapter 10 in this volume.

46. In 1756, Bishop Morell de Santa Cruz's pastoral report (García del Pino 1985, 112) described the parish church as of "decent modesty"—a not unflattering depiction that reflected more its active care and upkeep than a wealthy constituency. Its walls and ceiling were well painted, but, like in many other parish churches of the time, its floor was still a dirt one. There were five altars furnished with paintings and painted *frontales*, rather than the more expensive effigies of former times. The church even had an organ (broken) as well as three bells in its front door.

47. By the time of the Crown's confiscation of the mines, most of the religious furnishings and paraphernalia of the parish church were gone along with the better-off parishioners and personnel of the mining settlement. For instance, the former altars to the Virgin of the Rosary and to Saint Barbara with their religious parapher-nalia had disappeared, as well as the *cofradías* that sustained their devotions and the effigy of the patron Saint James. A crucifix was the only icon left in an austere church that had taken on an almost un-Catholic-like appearance. Only the indis-pensable paraphernalia to perform religious cult rites remained (Inventory of the Mines, Sept. 2, 1670, fols. 137–44, and May 9, 1677, fol. 337v, AGI-SD 1631).

48. By the 1730s, the parish was at least partly sustained through the tithes, first fruits, and sacramental fees that the cobreros—free *and* slave—paid to their priest (Cobreros to Dean Morell de Santa Cruz, [El Cobre, ca. Oct. 21–26, 1735], "Diligencias 1735," fols. 817v–18v, AGI-SD 451; Petition of Cobreros to the Captain General, [ca. 1735], "Autos 1735," fols. 710–17v/54–61v, AGI-SD 451).

49. Inventory of the Mines, 1677, AGI-SD 1631; and 1670, AGI-SD 1631.

50. Paz y Ascanio / Fonseca 1853, 45–46.

51. Report of Governor Don Juan de Villalobos, 1693, published in Marrero vol. 5:50.

52. Pastoral Visit of Bishop Morell de Santa Cruz to El Cobre, Dec. 8, 1756, published in García del Pino 1985, 112–13.

53. By 1750, however, the number of the Virgin's slaves in the sanctuary had gone down to five. Private slaves employed in a sanctuary were presumably an inno-vation of New World shrines. By contrast, the parish church itself did not have its own private slaves, but the parish priests held a few of their own (Family Censuses of 1735, AGI-SD 451; 1739, AGI-SD 385; and 1750, AGI-SD 1630).

54. See epigraph to this chapter. Pastoral Visit of Bishop Morell de Santa Cruz to El Cobre, Dec. 8, 1756, AGI-SD 534.

55. Paz y Ascanio / Fonseca 1853, 45–58.

56. For the institution of *faginas* or of local "forced" labor for community proj-ects, see Chapter 9 in this volume.

57. Memorial of Don Joseph Espinoza de los Monteros, Gregorio Cosme Osorio, and Carlos Ramos, Madrid, Apr. 4, 1784, C 5/83, fols. 654–75, AGI-SD 1629. Other documents did not single out the community's contributions, but instead pointed out that the gifts and donations proceeded from devotees to the Virgin in general (Paz y Ascanio / Fonseca 1853; Letter of Bishop Juan [Lasso de la Vega], Havana, Apr. 9, 1738, AGI-SD 363).

58. Representation of Don Simón Echenique, Madrid, Mar. 12, 1793, AGI-SD 1630.

59. Ibid.

60. Christian 1981b.

61. Memorial of Don Joseph Espinoza de los Monteros, Gregorio Cosme Osorio, and Carlos Ramos, Madrid, Apr. 4, 1784, C 5/83, fols. 654–75, AGI-SD 1629. See also Testimony of José Valentín Saavedra, "Testimonio Teresa Ramos alias Coba," Feb. 14, 1793, C 42/34, fol. 36v, AGI-SD 1628; and Testimony of Vicente de la Caridad, "Testimonio Vicente de la Caridad," 1788, C 67/59/24, fols. 9v–10, AGI-SD 1628.

62. The Family Censuses of 1735, AGI-SD 451; 1739, AGI-SD 385; and 1750, AGI-SD 1630 registered hermits in the chaplain's household usually as "under care of [the chaplain]."

63. Portuondo Zúñiga 1995, 116–18.

64. Certification of Don Pedro Ignacio de Torres y Ayala, Santiago de Cuba, July 15, 1738, AGI-SD 363; Title of the Foundation of a Chaplaincy in the Sanctuary of Our Lady of Charity, Don Manuel Cabral de Melo and Don Baltasar Moreno Girón, Santiago de Cuba, Aug. 5, 1705, AGI-SD 363.

65. Private funding and sustenance is sometimes used as a criterion of the popular (versus institutionally controlled) character of a shrine.

66. Letter of Bishop Juan [Lasso de la Vega], Havana, Apr. 9, 1738, AGI-SD 363.

67. Family Census of 1750, AGI-SD 1630.

68. Pastoral visit of Bishop Morell de Santa Cruz to El Cobre, Santiago de Cuba, Dec. 8, 1756, AGI-SD 534.

69. In 1756, the Indian villages of El Caney and Jiguaní had two and one clergymen, respectively, serving in their parishes. So did the larger, if somewhat isolated city of Baracoa. More dynamic cities with larger populations like Santiago de Cuba and Bayamo, however, had greater concentrations of clergymen (if perhaps not all employed in the church). Santiago de Cuba had approximately forty *presbíteros* (ordained priests) (not including some twenty-one friars in its Franciscan convent) and Bayamo some thirty-four (and forty friars in its two convents).

It is notable that by the mid-eighteenth century, the Oriente region seems to have been producing its own Creole clergy. In Santiago de Cuba, for instance, there were only two Spanish priests in 1756 and thirty-six clergymen born in that city. Of the thirty-four clergymen in Bayamo whose name and place of birth Bishop Morell de Santa Cruz recorded during his pastoral visit to that city, one was from Santiago de Cuba and thirty-three were natives of Bayamo (Bayamo was their "patria [chica]" noted the Bishop). In El Cobre, three were natives of Santiago de Cuba; another was from Havana; only one (the newly appointed organist) was from Oviedo, Spain (Pastoral Visit of Bishop Morell de Santa Cruz, 1756, published in García del Pino 1985, 100–104, 114, 162–66).

70. Yet, Father Bravo finished a manuscript on the history of the sanctuary in 1766.

71. Paz y Ascanio / Fonseca 1853, 36; Pastoral Visit of Bishop Morell de Santa Cruz to El Cobre, 1756, in García del Pino 1985, 114; Bravo 1766; Legacy of Father

Don Alejandro Paz y Ascanio, Mar. 3, 1836, Archivo Histórico Nacional (hereafter AHN-Ultramar 702(472)).

72. The parish priest Silva had two personal slaves in 1739, but by 1750 he had seven. Father Julián Joseph Bravo owned one personal slave in 1739 and three by 1750. The sacristan of the parish church, Father López Macaya, owned three personal slaves in 1750. Father Francisco Suárez Calderín, by contrast, owned as many as five personal slaves in 1735. Family Censuses of 1735, AGI-SD 451; 1739, AGI-SD 385; and 1750, AGI-SD 1630.

73. See Chapter 6 in this volume.

74. Family Census of 1773, AGI-SD 1628; and explanation to the "plano de las tierras delineadas al Cobre y lo que en ellas se introducen sus colindantes," Don Josef de Zayas, [ca. 1780], AGI-Mapas y Planos SD 468.

75. Legacy of Father Don Alejandro Paz y Ascanio, Santiago de Cuba, Mar. 3, 1836, AHN-Ultramar 702(472).

76. Family Censuses of 1735, AGI-SD 451; 1739, AGI-SD 385; and 1750, AGI-SD 1630.

77. Family Censuses of 1739, fols. 22–43v, AGI-SD 385; and 1750, fols. 27v–56, AGI-SD 1630.

78. Cobreros to Dean Morell de Santa Cruz, [El Cobre, ca. Oct. 21–26, 1735], "Diligencias 1735," fols. 817v–18v, AGI-SD 451; Petition of Cobreros to the Captain General, [ca. 1735], "Autos 1735," fols. 710–17v/54–61v, AGI-SD 451.

79. For a thorough account of these types of issues, see Taylor 1996.

80. Father Juan Jacintho de Silva, "Testimonio de un memorial del cura del Cobre en que noticia haberse ausentado muchos esclavos de S.M." (hereafter "Memorial cura esclavos ausentados"), [ca. Aug. 9, 1756], C 102, fols. 1–3v, AGI-SD 1630.

81. For a discussion of the village's internal labor system or *faginas*, see Chapter 9 in this volume.

82. Letter of Father Juan Antonio Pérez, Santiago del Prado, Apr. 14, 1709, "Demanda," C 23, fols. 7–11, AGI-ESC 93A.

83. Father Juan Jacintho de Silva, "Memorial cura esclavos ausentados," Santiago de Cuba [ca. Aug. 9, 1756], C 102, fols. 1–3v, AGI-SD 1630; the King to Father Juan Jacintho de Silva, [Royal Edict], Madrid, Sept. 13, 1733, AGI-SD 1627.

84. Testimony of Captain Simón Mascarreñas, Santiago de Cuba, Aug. 20, 1731, [C 21, Autos Sucre], fols. 20–22v, AGI-SD 493. See also Chapter 11 in this volume.

85. Auto of Governor Vaillant, Santiago de Cuba, Dec. 7, 1795, C 12, 1796, fols. 142–42v; and Petition of Cobreros to Bishop Osés y Alzúa, El Cobre, Dec. 5, 1795, fols. 138–40, all in AGI-SD 1631.

86. Justo Cruzata to Gregorio Cosme Osorio, El Cobre, Dec. 27, 1795, C 135, AGI-SD 1627.

87. Cobreros to Dean Morell de Santa Cruz, [El Cobre, ca. Oct. 21–26, 1735], "Diligencias 1735," fols. 817v–18v, AGI-SD 451; "Expediente sobre disposición Obispo sobre que los alcaldes del Pueblo del Cobre esclavos de V.M. metiesen asientos en la Iglesia y se les diese paz" (hereafter "Expte. asientos Iglesia"), fols. 640–54, AGI-SD 451; Dean Morell de Santa Cruz to the King, Santiago de Cuba, Aug. 26, 1731, AGI-SD 493; Crown Attorney's Summary, Madrid, June 3, 1732, AGI-

SD 493; Memorial of Don Joseph Espinoza de los Monteros, Gregorio Cosme Osorio, and Carlos Ramos, Madrid, Apr. 4, 1784, C 5/83, fols. 654–75, AGI-SD 1629; Bishop Don Joaquín Osés y Alzúa to Captain General Las Casas, Santiago de Cuba, May 13, 1796, C 12, 1796, fols. 161–68v, AGI-SD 1631. For further discussion of these alliances with ecclesiastics and other state officials, see Chapter 11 in this volume.

88. The manuscript of the notarized account of 1687 was lost at some point. The closest remaining account for many years was that of Fonseca's treatise transcribed and first published by Paz y Ascanio in 1829. The historian Leví Marrero unexpectedly found the notarized document sent by the bishop in the Archive of the Indies some years ago. (From a devotee's discursive ground, this "discovery" would undoubtedly be regarded as a "miracle.") See Marrero vol. 5:92–94.

89. By papal decree of 1625, the publication of miracle books and other hagiographical literature required the approval of ecclesiastic authorities (Rubial García 1993, 76). Father Bravo, however, suggested that manuscripts of miracle books about the Virgin of Charity nevertheless circulated in Santiago de Cuba (Bravo 1766).

90. Chaplain Don Julián Joseph Bravo, "Aparición prodigiosa de la Ynclita Ymagen de la Caridad que se venera en Santiago del Prado y Real de Minas de Cobre," 1766. Olga Portuondo Zúñiga kindly provided me with a copy of this manuscript for consultation.

91. J. Arrom 1959, 185; Paz y Ascanio / Fonseca 1853, 4–6.

92. At about this time, the Sociedad de Amigos del País began to promote secular "patriotic" histories of Cuba (usually of Havana). Perhaps the most important one was José Martín Félix de Arrate y Acosta's *Llave del Nuevo Mundo* published in 1830.

93. J. Arrom 1959, 185. Significantly, these publications took place in the midst of a wave of changes in El Cobre as British and Cuban mining companies arrived between the late 1820s and 1830s to reactivate the mines. Eventually, mining interests would clash with ecclesiastical ones over drilling near the sanctuary (see Epilogue in this volume).

94. Paz y Ascanio / Fonseca 1853. This is the version I was able to consult.

95. Father Paz y Ascanio (1853) explicitly stated in his edition of the *Historia* that it was based on Fonseca's 1703 manuscript. He may have glossed over what may have been a straightforward miracle book or history, but he did not actualize it. All the miracles cited are from the seventeenth century, thus suggesting that he faithfully followed Fonseca's text. Similarly, a good part of Chaplain Bravo's miracles were those cited by Paz y Ascanio, further pointing to his use of Fonseca's manuscript. Father Bravo's text (1766), however, also listed some current miracles, such as one related to the great earthquake of 1766.

96. The first press in Santiago de Cuba was established by Don Matías Alqueza in 1790. The first work it published was a religious sermon (Bacardí y Moreau 1973, 262). For a discussion of publication protocols and the Creoles' desire to have their hagiographic literature published, see Rubial García 1993:77–81.

97. Paz y Ascanio / Fonseca 1853, 5–10. The revised narrative became so prevalent—even in oral tradition—that a century later the scholar José Arrom (1959) saw the need to make a "positivist" informed refutation of the claim regarding the (historical) "origins" of the effigy. That Arrom took the exercise so seriously may speak

more about the *mentalité* of the period and of his own literal reading of the ecclesiastical text than about the (obviously construed) events of the narrative. For another eighteenth-century reference to this early Conquest Marian episode in a context not related to the Virgin of Charity's story, see Bishop Morell de Santa Cruz's Pastoral Visit to Bayamo, June 22, 1756, published in García del Pino 1985:92–94.

98. Our Lady of Guadalupe was declared patroness of the Viceroyalty of New Spain in 1746, a title confirmed by the Pope in 1754. In 1756, widespread celebrations to promote the devotion ensued (Taylor 1996, 283–85). These events had taken place one or two decades before Father Bravo finished his manuscript in which he conferred the name of Juan Diego to one of the seers of El Cobre.

99. Aside from prophetic powers, Bravo (1766) invoked a common miracle motif found in claims to saintly status for the hermit of El Cobre, namely, the beatitude of his expression at death and the fragrant odor expelled by the alleged saint's body. Rubial García (1993, 77–79) points out that since the seventeenth century, Creoles in Mexico, and generally in the Americas, had hoped (with few results) that Rome would canonize saints who had either been born or had lived in the New World. Father Bravo's account may have reflected such a trend.

100. On the search for Creole consciousness, identities, or even patriotism in colonial religious texts, see Brading 1985; Lafaye 1976; Rubial García 1993; among others. Oftentimes these studies are linked to the search for the "origins" of nationalism in problematic ways.

101. Bravo 1766.

102. The only other miracle story in which Father Bravo (1766) made reference to sorcery practices and beliefs in his treatise is one where a black woman in Santiago de Cuba caressed the daughter of the *alférez* Laureano Pérez del Castillo and cast a *mal de ojo* (evil eye) upon the girl by touching her. The girl almost died and her legs became paralyzed. The girl was taken to the sanctuary and the Virgin healed her. His way of reporting the event—even in writing—shows that Bravo believed in the black woman's powers of sorcery as did the family of the girl. The reported episode constitutes another example of an ecclesiastic's partaking of a wider popular culture of witchcraft beliefs.

103. Oettinger 1997, 94–105; Medina San Román 1997, 106–24.

104. This tradition was also alive in the Sanctuary of Regla by the mid-eighteenth century. Bishop Morell de Santa Cruz reported paintings hung from the walls and multiple silver charms (ex-votos) during his pastoral visitation to Regla on Aug. 20, 1756, published in García del Pino 1985, 38–39.

105. Paz y Ascanio / Fonseca 1853, 43–45, 66–67.

106. Family Census of 1773, AGI-SD 1628. These popular paintings of miracles were common in sanctuaries throughout Spain, Mexico, and elsewhere in the New World (Oettinger 1997). For a passing reference to paintings, see Paz y Ascanio / Fonseca 1853, 26.

107. Interview with cobrero (name withheld) by author, El Cobre, Sept. 1996. This older man was unable to specify when the story had taken place, but he did say that it was long before the Revolution.

108. Hernández 1993, 95–98. For some present-day anecdotes of miracles among cobreros, see Corbea Calzado 1993a, 86–87.

109. For a brief account of the public revival of these festivities, see the Preamble to this volume.

110. Paz y Ascanio / Fonseca 1853, 25.

111. Bravo 1766; Family Census of 1773, AGI-SD 1628.

112. Portuondo Zúñiga 1995, 212–23; and Hernández 1993, 99.

113. The cautious new rapprochement between state and church in Cuba, as well as the new interest in fomenting a tourist industry on the island, permitted the revival of festivities. The post–1992 state policies that opened the way to limited individual business outside the sponsorship of the state also contributed to the reemergence of booths and small-time vendors during the festivities.

114. Interrogation of Colonel Joseph Canales, Santiago de Cuba, Dec. 14–17, 1710, "Cargos" (Cargo no. 23), C 8, fols. 1–31, AGI-ESC 92C.

115. Father Labat described a "lascivious" dance or rhythm, which he called *calenda*, in the French Caribbean and stated that it was danced in churches and Catholic processions. In the eighteenth century, Moreau de Saint-Méry described a similar dance that he called *kalenda* (Benítez Rojo 1989, 54–62). On tango, *chuchumbé*, and other kinds of popular dances in Cuba and the Americas during the seventeenth and eighteenth centuries, see Carpentier 1972, 58–70. Benítez Rojo has suggested that common African-based rhythms and performative styles throughout the Caribbean constitute the "matrix" of a common Caribbean Creole culture since at least the seventeenth century (Benítez Rojo 1989). I am more interested in the point that people across different sectors of society moved their bodies to popularized African-based poly-rhythms and dance conventions that the church often saw as improper but could not abolish. This is indeed an important aspect of creolization, but given its performative character and the fact that it constitutes expressive oral and popular culture in motion, the historian today does not have much access to these cultural manifestations in the past except perhaps in very impressionistic ways.

116. Petition of Colonel Joseph Canales, [Santiago de Cuba, ca. Jan. 1711], "Cargos," C 8, fols. 61–61v, AGI-ESC 92C.

117. Father Labat quoted in Benítez Rojo 1989, 54–62.

118. Representation of Don Francisco Mancebo y Quiroga, Santiago de Cuba, [ca. Oct. 16, 1792], "Escritos graves heridas," fols. 107v–8, AGI-SD 1627.

119. For a fuller discussion of this clash of protocol, see Chapter 10 in this volume.

CHAPTER 6

Epigraph. Testimony of Francisco Sánchez, El Cobre, [ca. Apr. 8, 1790], C 6 AGI-SD 1629. Testimony of Cipriano Rodríguez, Santiago de Cuba, Investigation of Governor Ximénez, Santiago de Cuba, [Autos 1737], fol. 315v, AGI-SD 451.

1. See Chapter 2 in this volume.

2. Inventory of the Mines, May 9, 1677, fols. 376–76v, AGI-SD 1631.

3. Letter of Father Juan Joseph Antonio Pérez, Santiago del Prado, Apr. 14, 1709, "Demanda," C 23, fols. 7–11, AGI-ESC 93A. Although Pérez stated that the High Court of Santo Domingo had made the land grant to the pueblo, it is unclear if the adjudication was properly made or if it was contested by the *cabildo* of Santiago de

Cuba, see Auto of Judge Nicholás Chirino, Santiago de Cuba, Nov. 21, 1711, "Demanda," C 23, fols. 155–57, AGI-ESC 93A.

4. By 1677, Juan Moreno was referring to the royal slaves' plots as *estancias* (farms) (Captain Juan Moreno to Don Antonio Ortiz de Matienzo, Santiago del Prado, Nov. 7, 1677, AGI-SD 1631).

5. The term "reconstituted peasantry" was coined by Mintz to refer to the paradoxical historically "new" (or recent) character of peasantries in the Caribbean particularly during the postemancipation period. He also coined the term "proto-peasantries" to refer to the small-farming productive activities of slaves in their provision grounds before emancipation, especially in the case of Jamaica (Mintz 1974, 131–45, 151–52).

6. Testimony of Francisco Sánchez, El Cobre, [ca. Apr. 8, 1790], C 6 AGI-SD 1629.

7. For references to pre-Columbian Indian traditions in (ethnic Spanish) Creoles' writings understood as early strategies to signify an American identity, see among others, Brading 1985; Lafaye 1976. These studies, however, focus on elite and literate manifestations of a presumed (Spanish) Creole identity. The case of the "three cacique brothers" story and other such lore may constitute a similar strategy for the manifestation of Creole identity at a popular level.

8. The similarities included a corporate land grant, usufruct rights to land, militia companies, and a *cabildo*.

9. Bishop Morell de Santa Cruz recounted these oral stories of Bayamo in his pastoral visit of the region, published in García del Pino 1985, 92–96.

10. For land boundaries of El Cobre in 1710, see Representation of Don Bernardo Antonio Castillo, Santiago de Cuba, [ca. Nov. 1710–Mar. 1711], "Demanda," C 23, fols. 33–36v, AGI-ESC 93A.

11. Cobreros to Dean Morell de Santa Cruz, [El Cobre, ca. Oct. 21–26, 1735], "Diligencias 1735," fols. 817v–18v, AGI-SD 451.

12. Ibid.

13. Petition of Cobreros to Captain General Don Juan Francisco Güemes y Horcacitas, [ca. 1734], "Autos 1735," fols. 658–65, AGI-SD 451.

14. Owners were required by law to sustain their slaves. Failure to do so would allow slaves to change owners. With the establishment in 1880 of the *patrocinado* system in Cuba (R. Scott 1985), failure to provide for slaves could free a slave—precisely the implicit claim made by the cobreros a century and a half earlier. For slaves' prevalent use of the courts to present claims against masters that led to change of owners in nineteenth-century Lima, see Hunefeldt 1994.

15. Tomich 1993, 221–23; Tomich 1990, 259–80; Marshall 1993, 203–20; McDonald 1993, 279–80, 290–91.

16. Marrero vol. 8:80–81; Pérez Guzmán 1990, 6–11.

17. See Chapter 11 in this volume.

18. The city of Santiago de Cuba had come to depend on the cattle ranchers of the Bayamo district to supply them with livestock—a burden that the latter evaded or fought to be rid of as they found better outlets for their products in an extensive contraband trade with Jamaica and Saint Domingue (Marrero vol. 6:212–13).

19. Although the cobreros continued hunting for wild game as a source of meat and also had small corrals with a few hogs in their houses, the result of these transformations was an increasing reliance on the market for their supply of meat. The cobreros supplied themselves from cattle transported from Bayamo to Santiago de Cuba via routes near the village. Reliance on that market, however, could be a problem, for there was strong competition for these quotas of cattle. Governors, like the harsh Ximénez, intervened at times to prohibit the sale of cattle in El Cobre, particularly during periods of drought affecting the region. Events such as this further underscored the urgency of having pasture land available to directly provision themselves (Bacardí y Moreau 1973, 142, 156; Crown Attorney's Summary, Madrid, June 3, 1732, AGI-SD 493).

20. Report of the *cabildo* of Santiago de Cuba, Apr. 25, 1735, "Autos 1735," fol. 750, AGI-SD 451. Regarding the concession to make use of the pasture lands of El Ramón and Guarinao negotiated during the sublevation of 1731, see the Report of Don Joseph Losada, Aug. 14, 1731, [C 2, Autos 1731], fol. 109, AGI-SD 493.

21. For the demarcation and sale of El Ramón in 1757, see document reproduced in Marrero vol. 6:166–67.

22. For *composición*, see Marrero vol. 6:151–74; Le Riverend 1967, 13–15; Lockhart and Schwartz 1983, 137.

23. Marrero vol. 6:152–53. The same land reform efforts were extended to Puerto Rico (A. Ortiz 1983, 76–78). For earlier trends elsewhere in the Spanish Empire, see Stern 1982, 116, 134.

24. Le Riverend 1967, 14.

25. A rationalization of the land tenure system through the standardization of types of landholdings, areas, uses, and arrangements was also part of this broader land reform process (Marrero vol. 6:169–71).

26. Petition of Cobreros to Captain General Don Juan Francisco Güemes y Horcacitas, [ca. 1734], "Autos 1735," fols. 658–65; see also Petition of Cobreros to Captain General Güemes y Horcacitas, [ca. 1735], "Autos 1735," fols. 710–17v, both in AGI-SD 451. For confirmation of the surrounding league in place, see Certification of Dean Morell de Santa Cruz, Santiago de Cuba, May 7, 1735, "Autos 1735," fol. 784, AGI-SD 451.

27. "Informe arreglado a los autos pendientes entre los naturales del Pueblo del Cobre y colindantes sobre la propiedad y medida de los terrenos que ocupan" (hereafter "Informe propiedad y medida terrenos"), Dec. 6, 1780, fols. 741–43v, AGI-Cuba 1231. See also Governor Céspedes to Captain General Diego J. Navarro, Santiago de Cuba, Jan. 13, 1781, fols. 799–802, AGI-Cuba 1231.

28. "Testimonio de las diligencias del Deslinde de las tierras del Cobre y su plano" (hereafter "Deslinde tierras"), 1775, C 14/102, fols. 665–73, AGI-SD 1630. See also "Testimonio de los Autos obrados sobre el reseñalamiento de las tierras de la circunferencia del Pueblo del Cobre" (hereafter "Autos reseñalamiento"), [ca. Oct. 2, 1767], AGI-SD 1512; Governor Marqués de Casa Cagigal to Captain General Antonio Bucareli, Santiago de Cuba, Oct. 27, 1767, AGI-SD 1512.

29. Annotations in "Mapa del Real de Minas del Cobre," Josef de Zayas, Aug. 7, 1780, AGI-Mapas y Planos SD 467. The value of land had gone up considerably

since the last appraisal in 1677. At that time, the whole 5 by 6 leagues jurisdiction (excluding Barajagua) had been appraised at 5,000 pesos (Inventory of the Mines, May 9, 1677, fol. 453v, AGI-SD 1631). The present appraisal valued the encompassed land at 9,699 pesos and 2 reales.

30. The heirs of the original contractor Don Juan de Eguiluz ordered another survey when they claimed back in 1780 the territory of the mines as their property. They alleged that some thirty-five properties had usurped part of the original mining jurisdiction, including nine more in the neighboring *hato* (cattle ranch) of Puerto Pelado. They also ordered a survey and the return of Barajagua—thus echoing (albeit opposing) the cobreros' claims (Land Survey of El Cobre, Jan. 27, 1783, AGI-SD 1628).

31. "Informe propiedad y medida terrenos," Dec. 6, 1780, fols. 741–43v, AGI-Cuba 1231; "Deslinde tierras," 1775, C 14/102, fols. 665–73, AGI-SD 1630.

32. "Representación de los comisionados del Pueblo del Cobre" (hereafter "Representación comisionados"), [ca. Dec. 23, 1775], fols. 666–66v, AGI-SD 1630.

33. "Deslinde tierras," 1775, C 14/102, fols. 667–70v, AGI-SD 1630.

34. "Representación de los vecinos y moradores del Cobre," in "Informe propiedad y medida terrenos," Dec. 6, 1780, fols. 744–45, AGI-Cuba 1231. See also Captain General Diego J. Navarro to Governor Céspedes, [Havana], Oct. 9, 1780, fols. 746–49, AGI-Cuba 1231; Governor Céspedes to Captain General Diego J. Navarro, Santiago de Cuba, Jan. 13, 1781, fols. 799–802, AGI-Cuba 1231.

35. Ibid., "Representación de los vecinos y moradores del Cobre."

36. For the 1746 orders that *composición* include ecclesiastics, see Marrero vol. 6:172.

37. The reprivatization of the mining jurisdiction in 1780 implied the privatization of the land and the new alleged owners demanded rent for the farmland that the cobreros considered theirs by corporate right and by previous royal grant. Part of the conflict of those years turned around the fundamental issue of landholding rights. The cobreros consistently resisted the payment of rents to the heirs of the mines.

38. Governor Alonso de Arcos Moreno, Mar. 30, 1752, cited in Marrero vol. 6:168.

39. Marrero vol. 6:149–50, 168; Dossier of Land Claims of the Village of Jiguaní, AGI-SD 1617.

40. Representation of Father Don Juan Rivero de Arauz, May 20, 1731, AGI-SD 520. These cases may have had to do with the rentals in which the villages had engaged and also perhaps with their classification as *realengos* (royal or public land). On the other side of the island, the Indian village of Guanabacoa also undertook a long litigation process in defense of territory that was being denounced as *realengo* under current trends. That process ended successfully for the Indian village in 1748 when its boundaries were legally ratified (Marrero vol. 6:148–49).

41. To be sure, the size of these farms may have varied from whence the different ratios in Santiago de Cuba and El Cobre. But, again, if compared to Bayamo, the proportion of farms in Santiago de Cuba's district was also much smaller than in the former's.

42. Pastoral Visit of Bishop Morell de Santa Cruz to El Cobre, Dec. 8, 1756,

published in García del Pino 1985, 110–14. The bishop was ambiguous regarding the status of these landholdings. He portrayed them as small farms engaged as well in the production of sugar, tobacco, and swine.

43. Ibid., 112.

44. Crosby 1972, 173–75, 186–88. Crosby reports that in some part of the Bas Congo, manioc is reported to yield 5 tons per hectare of land too infertile for maize.

45. Inventory of Confiscated *Estancias*, [Autos 1737], fols. 142v–46v, AGI-SD 451.

46. The estimate is based on ongoing wage rates in the 1730s for unskilled labor in the fortification projects. More importantly, if 100 pesos was the ongoing cost of a young male cobrero's *coartación* (see Table 8 in Chapter 9), it would have taken an average farmer nine and a half years to buy his freedom if he commercialized all his produce and did not use any for subsistence purposes. Indeed, manioc farming in El Cobre was not important in a commercial sense.

47. Le Riverend 1967, 35–39; Marrero vol. 7:41–90.

48. Family Census of 1773, AGI-SD 1628.

49. F. Ortiz 1995, 27.

50. Ibid.

51. The following analysis is based on "Jazmia de los tabacos sembrados en los Partidos de esta factoria de Santiago de Cuba" (hereafter "Tabacos"), expte. 270, Santiago de Cuba, May 17, 1776, AGI-Cuba 1184. The Tobacco Factory was reestablished in 1763 (it had first operated between 1717 and 1727) and was not abolished until 1817. Ironically, just when Bourbon reforms began to open up trade restrictions (late 1760s) in its Spanish Empire, the Crown monopoly over the island's tobacco production became stricter. As a result, between 1764 and 1773 tobacco production increased by 313 percent. See Marrero vol. 11:1–46.

52. While the average number of tobacco plants cultivated per operator in individually or privately owned *vegas* (tobacco farms) was 11,000, that in sharecropped ones was only about 2,000 plants per peon. The considerably lower productivity of these farms probably reflected their part-time character. At times the Royal Tobacco Factory's document referred to these farms as *conucos*, but more often than not it listed them more vaguely as "the peons of [the above listed individual owner]." Ibid., "Tabacos," expte. 270.

53. Ibid., "Tabacos," expte. 270.

54. A significant 26 percent of the total number of *vegas* in the Cauto region were worked by peons (perhaps slaves) on their own account. Production in these units, however, was roughly one-fourth that in an individually-held farm. Ibid.

55. Their importance may have been greater: there were many other *vegueros* (tobacco farmers) in the pueblo who did not appear in the Royal Tobacco Factory's listing (perhaps they were peons in other farmers'); and some were simply listed in the village census of 1773 as *labradores*, but they were recorded in the Royal Factory's list as tobacco farmers. Ibid.

56. Although women, particularly widows, were landholders in Cuba and they also worked in *vegas*, it is significant that there is not one female listed among the hundreds of tobacco farm owners in the records of Santiago de Cuba's Royal Tobacco Factory. Ibid.

57. Family Censuses of 1767, AGI-SD 1630; and 1773, AGI-SD 1628; "Tabacos," expte. 270, Santiago de Cuba, May 17, 1776, AGI-Cuba 1184.

58. These two Cosme brothers were registered in the Family Census of 1773 (AGI-SD 1628) as owning two slaves each, which they may have employed as operators in their *vegas*.

59. Family Censuses of 1773 and 1775, both in AGI-SD 1628. In the census of 1773, these same cobreros were listed as *labradores*, and females' occupations were not listed. Because the census of 1773 included both free and royal slaves, it is possible that there were other free cobreros who, although cattle ranchers, were simply recorded as *labradores*.

60. Martín Salazar to Gregorio Cosme Osorio, El Cobre, Aug. 21, 1792, fol. 209, AGI-SD 1627.

61. Bacardí y Moreau 1973, 233.

62. Don Gaspar de Silva's sugar mill is listed (#5) in the explanation to the map entitled "Plano de las Tierras Delineadas al Cobre y lo que en ellas se introducen sus colindantes," Don Josef de Zayas, [ca. 1780], AGI-Mapas y Planos SD 468. Gaspar's brother, the deceased Father Juan Jacintho de Silva, had seven personal slaves in 1750, an indication that he was engaged in some commercial farming, perhaps in this very same family estate (Family Census of 1750, AGI-SD 1630).

63. Testimony of Cayetano, [Autos 1737], fols. 15–16, AGI-SD 451; Martín Salazar to Gregorio Cosme Osorio, El Cobre, Aug. 21, 1792, fol. 209, AGI-SD 1627. In the 1775 census (AGI-SD 1628), the only cobreros recorded as working or owning a sugar mill were two young González brothers, Francisco and Juan. The Gonzálezes, like the Cosmes, were also a slave-owning lineage in the village (see Chapter 7 in this volume).

64. The scarcity of research or of available information is not restricted to the case of Cuba. Even in an important anthology that examines in some depth "slave economies" in the Americas, little material on the social aspects of provision grounds can be found (Berlin and Morgan 1993).

65. Family Census of 1773, AGI-SD 1628.

66. Ibid. The term *labrador* seems to have been used in a generic sense in this census. The category in Spain was also imprecise and could acquire different meanings in different places, without carrying the connotation of proprietorship (Vassberg 1984, 137–47; Herr 1989, 29–30).

67. Occupations for females were only registered in the Family Census of 1775 (AGI-SD 1628), but this document excluded free people in El Cobre.

68. Family Censuses of 1773 and 1775, both in AGI-SD 1628.

69. The *labradores* of the 1773 census were defined as *estancieros* (farmers) in the census of 1775.

70. In many parts of Africa, and for our purposes particularly in Angola, females did much of the agricultural labor (Manning 1990, 115).

71. Inventory of the Slaves, 1647, AGI-SD 104.

72. In Spain, eighteenth-century *padrones* (hearth censuses) that noted occupations seem by convention to only record that of males (Vassberg 1984, 137–47; Herr 1989, 29–30).

73. The distribution of occupations among free cobrera females may have been

similar to that of royal slave ones. In the case of free and royal slave cobrero males, the occupational distribution of agricultural activities was similar, but not the artisanal one.

74. Family Census of 1775, AGI-SD 1628.

75. Testimony of Claudio Alcántara, [Autos 1737], fols. 277–78v; see also fol. 18, AGI-SD 451.

76. The methodology used in this section is based on the "linkages" of individuals and their families through different family censuses and other documents to reconstruct landholding practices. Rather than repeatedly cite archival references, I list here the whole set of family censuses utilized for the reconstruction and thereafter \ just refer to the document by its date in the text. Family Censuses: 1709, "Demanda," C 23, fols. 26–29v, AGI-ESC 93A; 1731, AGI-SD 493; 1735, "Autos 1735," fols. 761–66/104–9, AGI-SD 451; Apr. 12, 1739, fols. 22–43v, AGI-SD 385; 1750, fols. 27v–52, AGI-SD 1630; 1767, fols. 52–77v, AGI-SD 1630; 1773, C 30, fols. 1–25, AGI-SD 1628; Slave Family Census 1775, C 32/24/15, fols. 1–29v, AGI-SD 1628. Hereafter in this volume abbreviated references to these family censuses will only include year and archival *legajo*.

77. Testimony of Cipriano Rodríguez, [Autos 1737], fol. 315v, AGI-SD 451.

78. The mapping out of the *estancias* in Río Abajo is based on the testimonies of Pedro Parada, Claudio Alcántara, and Carlos Vicente, [Autos 1737], fols. 16–25, AGI-SD 451.

79. It is not clear from the records if the sons and sons-in-law who shared a house in the village in 1773 also worked in her farm, or if they had their own *estancias*.

80. [Autos 1737], fols. 16–25, AGI-SD 451; Family Census of 1735, AGI-SD 451.

81. A bilateral transmission system is prescribed by Spanish law, but it is also operative in customary law among peasants elsewhere in the Caribbean, even in places that were under British colonial law (which calls for primogeniture and patrilineal rules of inheritance) (see Chapter 7 in this volume).

82. Report of Nicholás Velasco Calderín, [Autos 1737], fols. 151–52v, AGI-SD 451.

83. Ibid.

84. One man, Alejandro Moreno, did have his house confiscated (ibid., fol. 146).

85. Inventory of Confiscated Property, [Autos 1737], fols. 144–45, AGI-SD 451.

86. Report of Governor Cayetano de Urbina, Santiago de Cuba, Feb. 1846, AHN-Ultramar 4638(2).

87. Indeed, female-headed households constituted a range of 26 to 32 percent of households in El Cobre throughout the eighteenth century (Family Censuses of 1709, AGI-ESC 93A; 1735, AGI-SD 451; 1750, AGI-SD 1630; 1773, AGI-SD 1628).

88. For the accusations brought against them by local *alcaldes* and colonial authorities, see Chapter 10 in this volume.

89. Interrogation of cobrera women, [Autos 1737], fols. 350–64, AGI-SD 451.

90. Ibid., Testimony of María de la Rosa, fol. 250v.

91. Ibid., Inventory of Confiscated Property, fol. 145v.

92. Ibid., Testimony of María Magdalena Quiala, fol. 364.

93. Oral interviews and visit by author, El Cobre, Sept. 1996. See also Hernández 1993, 96, 99–101.

94. Report of Don José de Aguilés, Santiago de Cuba, Mining Division, Aug. 31, 1838, AHN-Ultramar 6(1).

CHAPTER 7

1. Family Censuses of 1709, AGI-ESC 93A; 1731, AGI-SD 493; and 1735, AGI-SD 451.

2. Lieutenant Velasco Calderín to Governor Ximénez, El Cobre, [ca. Feb.–Mar. 1737], [Autos 1737], fol. 160, AGI-SD 451.

3. Family Censuses of 1735, AGI-SD 451; and 1739, AGI-SD 385.

4. Klein 1989 [1967], 196–97.

5. The "linkage" of individuals to reconstruct family histories and slaveholding patterns is made through the following set of documents: Family Censuses of 1709, AGI-ESC 93A; 1731, AGI-SD 493; 1735, AGI-SD 451; 1739, AGI-SD 385; 1750, AGI-SD 1630; 1767 AGI-SD 1630; 1773 and 1775 AGI-SD 1628. Also used are the Baptism Records of the King's Slaves, El Cobre, 1680–1769, fols. 92v–170/77v–155, AGI-SD 1630; and "Certificación libros contaduría: corte y libertades" (hereafter "Corte y libertades"), Santiago de Cuba, Aug. 20, 1689 to Sept. 28, 1734, "Autos 1735," fols. 755–58, AGI-SD 451. Hereafter, reference will only be made to their dates in the case of family censuses and to the type of document in other cases.

6. For the 1774 islandwide average of slaves, see Knight 1970, 22.

7. Figures for 1780 are based on the Census of Santiago de Cuba and its Jurisdiction, Santiago de Cuba, Feb. 24, 1780, AGI-Cuba 1272.

8. Figures are for the region of Jaguaripe in the Reconçavo in Brazil, cited in Schwartz 1974, 60–61. Areas with a more mixed economy had higher numbers of slaves per owner. In the mining region of Minas Gerais (Brazil) the mean size of a slaveholding varied from 3.7 slaves to 6.5 during the eighteenth century, but slave owners with 1 to 4 slaves predominated. Of the slaveholders in this mining region, however, only from 3.3 to 14.6 percent were free people of color (Schwartz 1974, 66, 75).

9. The highest mean of 3.7 per clergy for El Cobre in 1750 is still lower than that of Brazil where clergy held a mean of 4.5 slaves each (Schwartz 1974, 66).

10. Slaves under fifteen years of age were counted as minors, and their sex distribution was equal in the village. There was no correlation between masters' sex and slaves' sex in the records of El Cobre.

11. Testimonies of Lorenzo González (fol. 192v) and Jacintho Rodríguez (fol. 260v), Santiago de Cuba, 1737; and Inventory of Confiscations (fols. 142v–46v), all in Investigation of Governor Ximénez, [Autos 1737], AGI-SD 451.

12. Inventory of Slaves, 1677, AGI-SD 1631; Baptism Records of the King's Slaves, El Cobre, 1680–1769, AGI-SD 1630.

13. "Corte y libertades," Aug. 20, 1689 to Sept. 28, 1734, AGI-SD 451.

14. See Table 9 in Chapter 9, for general self-manumission trends in the village.

15. In these kin-based complex households or even residential blocs, there may well have been echoes of the Caribbean institution of "houseyards." (Houseyards are living quarters of members of a same family partaking of a yard space.) They were a pervasive institution among reconstituted peasants all over the English-speaking

Caribbean, but they have not been documented or noted in the Spanish-speaking Caribbean. It is believed that the origin of this modern residential institution goes back to the time of slavery (Besson 1984; Mihelic 1993; Mintz 1974, 225–50). Yet, however extensive this institution may be, there still exist strong local differences in the residential patterns throughout the Caribbean. In Jamaica, for instance, kin set their huts separately upon family land or inhabit contiguous households around a houseyard, while in Guyana residential spaces are neolocal and kin avoid clustering in households or blocs (R. T. Smith 1971).

16. On males' higher rate of self-manumission, particularly after the 1740s, see Table 9 in Chapter 9.

17. Although in this particular case it is clear that Joseph Cosme received the slave from his mother, his wife's siblings had also inherited a family slave. Perhaps this case also illustrates a local practice of marriages between slave-owning families.

18. For increased self-manumission rates after the 1740s, see Table 9 in Chapter 9.

19. For bilateral inheritance rules in Spanish law, see S. Arrom 1985, 63–68. For a particularly clear description and glossing of Roman-based Iberian (in particular, Portuguese) inheritance law, see Metcalfe 1992, 95–100.

20. Edith Clarke (1957, 1971) noted the bilateral inheritance patterns that informed the customary institution of "family land" in postemancipation Jamaican society. "Family land" constitutes jointly held land to which "all children" in both sides have a right; for Guyana cases, see R. T. Smith 1971. The best overview of the varying arguments regarding the European or African source of this "family land" tradition and its related inheritance patterns is found in Besson 1984. Besson argues that the widespread institution should be approached as a pan-Caribbean tradition that grew out of a common resistance to plantation conditions and not as an African tradition per se. A deeper study of property-holding and transmission practices in El Cobre in relation to traditions of other groups in Cuba and in the wider Caribbean would throw much light on the question of the origins and "reinvention" of this tradition among Afro-Caribbean people.

21. Metcalfe's study of Brazil (1992, 102–6) shows planters manipulating the possibilities (and loopholes) inherent in Iberian inheritance laws to create customary practice or tradition. Interestingly, these elite families tended to favor daughters and their spouses in the transmission of property. In this sense, family fortunes traveled by custom preferably through females in the family line.

22. On equal partitioning legal prescriptions, see S. Arrom 1985:63. For the case of Brazil and the local strategies used to resist fragmentation of property through partitioning, see Metcalfe 1992, 95–102.

23. On Spanish law regarding conjugal property rights, see S. Arrom 1985, 67–68, 73–79.

24. The case is confusing. Bernardino and Clara owned two slaves as far back as 1709. Interestingly, at that time the census taker noted that these were "Bernardino's slaves." Yet, of the only six households that owned slaves at that time, two of them were headed by the Matamba sisters—Clara and Manuela—and their husbands. Whether the sisters inherited slaves from their own families or coincidentally married the few men who owned them is unclear.

25. Lieutenant Velasco Calderín to Governor Ximénez, El Cobre, [ca. Feb.–Mar. 1737], fol. 153; and Testimony of Jacintho Rodríguez, fol. 260v, both in Investigation of Governor Ximénez, [Autos 1737], AGI-SD 451.

26. Family Census of 1750, AGI-SD 1630.

27. On conjugal property rules, see S. Arrom 1985, 67–68, 73–79.

28. Lieutenant Velasco Calderín to Governor Ximénez, El Cobre, [ca. Feb.–Mar. 1737], Investigation of Governor Ximénez, [Autos 1737], fol. 157, AGI-SD 451.

29. Inventory of Confiscated Property, El Cobre, [Autos 1737], fols. 142v–46v, AGI-SD 451. Although Norate supposedly owned two farms, his mother had a *conuco* (garden plot). Norate's father was absent from the village in the 1730s. There is thus a possibility that the second *estancia* may have belonged to Hilario Norate's father and that Hilario stood as its trustee or custodian.

30. Illegitimates could not legally inherit according to Spanish law, but they could be served by one-fifth of the estate that could be willed freely. Although a father had no legal obligations whatsoever toward an illegitimate child, he was required to support and rear natural children (i.e., children born to an unmarried couple). Nevertheless, he did not have to leave those children inheritance. S. Arrom 1985, 69–70; for Brazil, see Metcalfe 1992, 101. In Jamaica, customary law allowed for the inheritance of illegitimates (although in a somewhat more restricted way than for legitimates), but British law did not (Clarke 1957, 1971).

31. Inventory of Confiscated Property, El Cobre, [Autos 1737], fols. 142v–46v, AGI-SD 451. At this time the house was shared by four sisters and two brothers. Only the youngest brother was married, and in this case, his wife lived with him in the parental house (Family Census of 1735, AGI-SD 451).

32. Interestingly, extended and joint family households are also widespread in contemporary Cuba, if for altogether different reasons. Shortage of housing has led to a pervasive trend evinced by the fact that in 1973 three-fourths of couples under the age of twenty-four lived with relatives or someone else (Smith and Padula 1996, 157). Although housing is one of the main problems in El Cobre today, no disaggregated local figures (or patterns) are available for this case (Hernández 1993, 96).

33. There are no studies of residential patterns for the Spanish-speaking Caribbean. Although in principle the rule is neolocal and nuclear-family based, an uxorilocal tendency, for instance, has been registered in an anthropological study of a Puerto Rican white peasant community in the 1950s. The prevalence of this practice, however, has not been assessed (Mintz 1960, 91). For mother-centered or matrifocal trends in the English-speaking Caribbean, see R. T. Smith 1996, 39–57.

34. No clear pattern of gender-based transmission of slaves is apparent either. Females inherited male and female slaves just as males did.

35. It is difficult to identify the origin of slaves in the 1730s, because in some cases their ethnic names were dropped. The personal slave Antonio was registered in the hearth listing of 1731 as "Antonio Congo," but in the family censuses of 1735 and 1739, he was inscribed as "Antonio." So it was with "Pedro Arará" and "Antonia Arará." Thus there may have been other cases in the 1730s as well. By 1750 few slaves (four out of twenty-one) bore African names; by 1767, however, five of Joseph Cosme's twelve slaves (and of a total of twenty-three slaves) in El Cobre were identi-

fied aggregately as *bozales* but not individually by ethnic names. By 1773 almost all slaves were recorded with their masters' family name.

36. Marrero vol. 6:30–31.

37. There is no record of royal slave men married to female personal slaves.

CHAPTER 8

Epigraph. Report of Don Joseph Palacios de Saldustum, Santiago de Cuba, July 31, 1739, fols. 13–15v, AGI-SD 385. Report of Don José de Aguilés, Santiago de Cuba, Reino de Minería, Aug. 31, 1838, AHN-Ultramar 6(1).

1. Mintz and Hall 1970.

2. Nicholás Montenegro to Doña Paula de Eguiluz y Montenegro, El Cobre, July 7, 1672, AGI-SD 104. Montenegro did not mark the reported activity in gender terms.

3. These observations are echoed in other accounts and formal reports. Testimonies of Francisco Farán (fols. 36–37), Alonzo Vicente (fols. 36–38v), and Silvestre Vicente (fols. 37–38v), Santiago de Cuba, [ca. Aug.–Dec. 1731], [C 2, Autos 1731], AGI-SD 493. Report of Don Joseph Palacios de Saldustum, July 31, 1739, fols. 13–15v, AGI-SD 385.

4. Father Don Pedro de Cerquera to Don Antonio Matta y Haro, El Cobre, June 10, 1672, AGI-SD 104.

5. Nicholás Montenegro to Doña Paula de Eguiluz y Montenegro, El Cobre, July 7, 1672, AGI-SD 104.

6. See also Montenegro's observations about changes in sartorial practices in Chapter 2 in this volume.

7. Letter of Father Juan Antonio Pérez, Santiago del Prado, Apr. 14, 1709, "Demanda," C 23, fols. 7–11, AGI-ESC 93A.

8. The estimate is based on the ratio of smelted ore to metal reported by the cobreros to a royal official. According to them, a *carga* (weight) of 10 arrobas yielded 2 (and sometimes 3) arrobas of liquid metal. Report of Don Nicholás Velasco Calderín, Santiago de Cuba, July 31, 1739, fols. 19–20v, AGI-SD 385. Other estimates provided at other points in time, however, were much lower. Earlier in the century, around 1710, 8 arrobas of crushed and smelted ore reportedly yielded 1 arroba of metal, so that the metal content of the ore was roughly 12.5 percent. In 1779 a report was made of the metal content in the branches of veins of the mines. In the best mine, "La Lechuza," 14 arrobas of ore yielded 47 pounds (almost 2 arrobas) of copper metal (or a metal content of almost 14 percent). Overall, 300 arrobas of ore extracted from several mines yielded 37 arrobas of copper metal (a general average of 12.3 percent of metal content). For the 1710 estimate, see Representation of Don Bernardo Antonio Castillo, [Santiago de Cuba, ca. Nov. 1710–Mar. 1711], "Demanda," C 23, fols. 33–36v, AGI-ESC 93A. For the 1779 estimates, see Report of Don Isidro Limonta to Captain General Diego J. Navarro, Santiago de Cuba, Oct. 4, 1779, fols. 1111–13, AGI-Cuba 1231.

9. Report of Mines to Captain General Diego J. Navarro, Santiago de Cuba, Nov. 20, 1777, AGI-Cuba 1230.

10. Ibid.

11. Report of Don Isidro Limonta to Captain General Diego J. Navarro, Santiago de Cuba, Oct. 4, 1779, fols. 1111–13, AGI-Cuba 1231. For similar observations years earlier, see Report of Don Joseph Palacios de Saldustum, Santiago de Cuba, July 31, 1739, fols. 13–15v, AGI-SD 385.

12. Report of Don Nicholás Velasco Calderín, Santiago de Cuba, July 31, 1739, fols. 19–20v, AGI-SD 385; Report of Don Joseph Palacios de Saldustum, July 31, 1739, fols. 13–15v, AGI-SD 385.

13. Testimony of Father Don Diego Duque de Estrada, Santiago de Cuba, Apr. 24, 1711, "Demanda," C 23, fols. 77–79v, AGI-ESC 93A.

14. Testimony of Alonzo Vicente, Santiago de Cuba, [ca. Aug.–Dec. 1731], Investigation of Governor Ximénez, [C 2, Autos 1731], fols. 36–38v, AGI-SD 493. For similar references, see Testimony of Father Don Diego Duque de Estrada, Santiago de Cuba, Apr. 24, 1711, "Demanda," C 23, fols. 77–79v, AGI-ESC 93A; Report of Don Nicholás Velasco Calderín, Santiago de Cuba, July 31, 1739, fols. 19–20v, AGI-SD 385; Report of Don Isidro Limonta to Captain General Diego J. Navarro, Santiago de Cuba, Oct. 4, 1779, fols. 1111–13, AGI-Cuba 1231.

15. Report of Don Joseph Palacios de Saldustum, Santiago de Cuba, July 31, 1739, fols. 13–15v, AGI-SD 385.

16. Inventory of Slaves, 1647, AGI-SD 104.

17. Herbert 1984, 36, 44–45. For copper mining in the Angola and Congo regions, see Herbert 1984, 19–23. It should be noted that there is little memory today in El Cobre of women working in the copper mines, even as surface miners. Cobreros remember one such woman and her children (one of these children is a mature woman today), but the fact that she is seen as an extraordinary case in El Cobre suggests the extent to which the industry has been de-feminized during this century, if not before.

18. Crown Attorney's Summary, Madrid, June 3, 1732, AGI-SD 493.

19. Testimony of Father Don Diego Duque de Estrada, Santiago de Cuba, Apr. 24, 1711, "Demanda," C 23, fols. 77–79v, AGI-ESC 93A.

20. Marrero vol. 6:192–213. Estimate is based on 1 real of income, which, as will be discussed later, was reported by a royal official in the 1730s.

21. Nicholás Montenegro to Doña Paula de Eguiluz y Montenegro, El Cobre, July 7, 1672, AGI-SD 104; Inventory of Confiscated Property, [Autos 1737], fols. 142v–46v, AGI-SD 451; Martín de Salazar to Gregorio Cosme Osorio, El Cobre, Aug. 21, 1792, fol. 209, AGI-SD 1627. As will be discussed further on, copper, for better or worse, also gave them access to contraband goods, particularly clothes.

22. Interrogation of cobrera women, Santiago de Cuba, 1737, [Autos 1737], fols. 350–64, AGI-SD 451.

23. Family Census of 1775, AGI-SD 1628.

24. Sewing was perhaps the lowest-paid female occupation, at least in nineteenth-century Cuban colonial society (Marrero vol. 13:152). For the importance of this occupation in the female labor sphere in nineteenth-century Brazil, see Lauderdale-Graham 1992.

25. For further echoes of this issue, see Testimony of Father Don Diego Duque de Estrada, Santiago de Cuba, Apr. 24, 1711, "Demanda," C 23, fols. 77–79v, AGI-ESC 93A.

26. Cobreros to Governor Ximénez, [El Cobre, ca. Aug.–Dec. 1731], [C 2, Autos 1731], fols. 33v–34, AGI-SD 493.

27. This was a trend contrary to that found in the agricultural sector elsewhere in the Caribbean where slave women seemed to control the marketing of the agricultural products that they and their families produced (Mintz 1974, 216; Beckles 1989, 84–87).

28. In some parts of Africa copper working was not only a male activity, but also it was a hereditary occupation and the preserve of some families (Herbert 1984, 33, 46–47). These occupational transmission practices have not been studied among Native Americans in New Spain or for that matter among Spaniards. Furthermore, in places such as the Congo, master smelters also possess supernatural powers and secret knowledge passed on from generation to generation, a characteristic not readily apparent in the cobreros' case (Herbert 1984, 32–42).

29. Pedro Deschamps Chapeaux (1976, 52–56) points out that artisans avidly sought military office in the free militias of color to consolidate their petty bourgeois elite status in colonial society and at times were able to buy honorary military ranks. But the white Creole elite also sought the status of military rank in the Havana militias where the close ties between officer corps, titled nobility, and leaders in the growing sugar industry were strong. After 1780 the Crown was also selling military offices to white Creoles (Kuethe 1986, 55–60, 149–52).

30. Nicholás Montenegro to Doña Paula de Eguiluz y Montenegro, El Cobre, July 7, 1672, AGI-SD 104.

31. Ibid.

32. Appraisal of Slaves, July 12, 1677, fols. 446v–53v, AGI-SD 1631; Family Census of 1709, AGI-ESC 93A.

33. Inventory of Slaves, 1677, AGI-SD 1631.

34. "Memoria de armas y herramientas," [Santiago de Cuba, ca. Nov. 1710–Mar. 1711], "Demanda," C 23, fols. 38–39v, AGI-ESC 93A.

35. Family Census, 1709, AGI-ESC 93A.

36. Testimony of Silvestre Vicente, Santiago de Cuba, [ca. Aug.–Dec. 1731], [C 2, Autos 1731], fols. 37–38, AGI-SD 493; Family Census of 1709, AGI-ESC 93A.

37. Family Censuses of 1709, AGI-ESC 93A; and 1773, AGI-SD 1628.

38. It was independent from the state insofar as the local apprenticeship went. During the earlier private mining days, however, there had also been at least one case of occupational transmission along a slave family line: the occupation of iron smith was passed down from father to son among three generations in the Viojo family (Inventories of the Mines: 1620, AGI-SD 1631; 1647, AGI-SD 104; 1677, AGI-SD 1631). For such practices among iron smiths in Africa too, see Herbert 1984, 32–34.

39. Letter of Father Juan Antonio Pérez, Santiago del Prado, Apr. 14, 1709, "Demanda," C 23, fols. 7–11, AGI-ESC 93A.

40. "Memoria de armas y herramientas," [Santiago de Cuba, ca. Nov. 1710–Mar. 1711], "Demanda," C 23, fols. 38–39v, AGI-ESC 93A. Another assessor estimated the cost of 17 arrobas (or 425 pounds) at 4 reales per pound for a total of 215 pesos and 5 reales. "Tazación," Santiago de Cuba, Jan. 5, 1712, "Demanda," C 23, fols. 168–68v, AGI-ESC 93A.

41. The vat was embargoed pending the cobreros' payment of litigation costs esti-

mated at 123 pesos and 7 reales. A royal fifth (*quinto*) (approximately 42.4 pesos) was to be deducted from the total estimated value of the vat (some 212.5 pesos); and from the remaining amount the litigation costs were to be deducted. The difference (some 46 pesos) was to be returned to Juan de Ojeda. It is not known if the community was able to pay the litigation costs, in which case the full amount (less the royal fifth) would have been reinstated to Ojeda (Jan. 5, 1712, "Demanda," C 23, fols. 168–71v, AGI-ESC 93A).

42. Family Census, 1731, AGI-SD 493.

43. "Corte y libertades," Santiago de Cuba, Aug. 1689–Sept. 28, 1734, "Autos 1735," fols. 755–58, AGI-SD 451. The list of forty-two cobrero slaves self-manumitted during this period may not be complete, however.

44. Family Census, 1709, AGI-ESC 93A.

45. Cabildo of Santiago de Cuba, Aug. 5, 1731, [C 2, Autos 1731], fols. 1–1v, AGI-SD 493.

46. Testimony of Francisco Farán, Santiago de Cuba, [ca. Aug.–Dec. 1731], [C 2, Autos 1731], fols. 36v–37, AGI-SD 493.

47. "Corte y libertades," Santiago de Cuba, Aug. 1689–Sept. 28, 1734, "Autos 1735," fols. 755–58, AGI-SD 451; Family Census of 1709, AGI-ESC 93A.

48. Testimony of Andrés González, Santiago de Cuba, Feb. 26, 1737, [Autos 1737], fol. 225v, AGI-SD 451.

49. The precedent of not taxing the surface-mining activities in El Cobre was set down in the early 1670s. In 1731, however, Governor Ximénez imposed the *quinto* (a 20-percent levy), but later claimed he did so on smelters and buyers, and not on the surface miners. Apparently the tax prevailed at least until 1755. In principle the *quinto* was a tax applicable to the mining of metals (usually silver and gold), but given the low prices of copper, the application of the tax was debatable. In New Spain, for example, copper miners were never charged more than a 2-percent levy, until 1780 when it was raised to 8 percent, so the levy in El Cobre was quite out of order. Crown Attorney's Summary, Madrid, June 3, 1732, AGI-SD 493; Bacardí y Moreau 1973, 133; Marrero vol. 7:33; Barrett 1987, 57.

50. Family Censuses of 1773 and 1775, both in AGI-SD 1628.

51. A minimal annual production of 40 quintals of copper in the village would have required a total of four to six or seven small smelting operations each month. The estimate is based on the time frame for an operation reported by a royal official and the ratio of smelted ore to metal reported by the cobreros (Report of Don Nicholás Velasco Calderín, Santiago de Cuba, July 31, 1739, fols. 19–20v, AGI-SD 385).

52. Ibid.

53. Report of Don Diego Peñalver Angulo, Havana, Apr. 15, 1734, fols. 1471–74, AGI-SD 1630.

54. Ibid.

55. Ibid.

56. Julio Le Riverend (1967, 69) makes a passing reference to copper mines in the jurisdiction of Santa Clara that were "apparently" operating after 1700.

57. Report of Don Isidro Limonta to Captain General Diego J. Navarro, Oct. 4, 1779, fols. 1111–13, AGI-SD 1231. For similar assessments made earlier, see Reports of

Don Joseph Palacios Saldustum and of Don Nicholás Velasco Calderín, both in Santiago de Cuba, July 31, 1739, fols. 19–20v, AGI-SD 385.

58. In 1741, Governor Cagigal de la Vega bought 81 arrobas of copper and minted more than 30,000 pesos worth in copper coins as an emergency measure during Admiral Vernon's British invasion. The governor apparently bought the copper from Don Manuel Palacios who must have been an intermediary of the copper produced in El Cobre. He sold at 12 pesos and 5 reales per quintal of copper, while he may have bought it at 2 pesos per quintal (Marrero vol. 8:72–73; see also Table 7 in this chapter).

59. Report of Don Joseph Palacios Saldustum, Santiago de Cuba, July 31, 1739, fols. 13–15v, AGI-SD 385; Report of Don Francisco Sánchez de Castel, [Santiago de Cuba, ca. 1739], fols. 17–17v, AGI-SD 385.

60. Le Riverend 1967, 58.

61. Moreno Fraginals 1978, vol. 1:98; Barrett 1987, 45, 49. In New Spain itself, demand for copper for the sugar industry tripled between 1786 and 1801, reaching a high average of 500 quintals per year in 1798–1799 (Barrett 1987, 44). The proportional increase of the demand in Cuba is not known, but if one considers the sheer increase in the volume of sugar production between the mid- and late eighteenth century, a rough sense of the parallel expansion that must have taken place in the demand for copper can be gauged. In 1746, the Cuban sugar harvest totaled 726 metric tons; by 1766, it had increased to 6,350 metric tons; and by 1791, it had reached 16,731 metric tons (Marrero vol. 9:135; Moreno Fraginals 1978, 62–71). The greatest expansion, however, would take place in the nineteenth century.

62. In 1759, for example, at a time when the sugar industry was barely beginning to expand, Havana produced as much as 75 percent (3,856 metric tons) of the island's sugar (Marrero vol. 9:135).

63. Report of Don Francisco Sánchez de Castel, [ca. 1739], fols. 17–17v, AGI-SD 385.

64. Ibid.

65. Nicholás Montenegro to Doña Paula de Eguiluz y Montenegro, El Cobre, July 7, 1672, AGI-SD 104.

66. Marrero vol. 7:33.

67. Petition of the Pueblo of El Cobre to the King, Santiago del Prado, Nov. 19, 1738, AGI-SD 426.

68. Testimony of Francisco Farán, Santiago de Cuba, [ca. Aug.–Dec. 1731], [C 2, Autos 1731], fols. 36–37, AGI-SD 493.

69. Assayer's Report, [ca. 1733], quoted in Marrero vol. 8:71.

70. Marrero vol. 8:71.

71. Report of Don Joseph Palacios de Saldustum, Santiago de Cuba, July 31, 1739, fols. 13–15v, AGI-SD 385.

72. See Chapter 9 in this volume.

73. The *repartimiento* of merchandise consisted of the legal privilege of commercial monopoly given to royal officials in charge of Indians. Under cover of this concession the *corregidor de Indios* introduced merchandise double or triple the amount allowed by law. Working through the internal connection of the Indian cacique, he also pushed commodities for sale in the community for which the

Indians had no need. The system was not abolished until the last quarter of the eighteenth century (Haring 1947, 67, 133; Spalding 1984, 188–90).

74. Petition of the Pueblo of El Cobre to the King, Santiago del Prado, Nov. 19, 1738, AGI-SD 426.

75. Report of Don Isidro Limonta to Captain General Diego J. Navarro, Santiago de Cuba, Oct. 4, 1779, fols. 1111–13, AGI-Cuba 1231.

76. Report of Don Juan Francisco de Sequeira, Havana, July 15, 1728, AGI-SD 380.

77. Report of Don Juan García de Palacios and Don Juan Francisco de Sequeira, Havana, July 13, 1728; and Report of Sequeira, Havana, July 15, 1728, both in AGI-SD 380. The possibilities for graft implicit in this deal should not be overlooked either. Furthermore, the deal may have entailed the Crown's activation of the mines and a greater regimentation of labor for the cobreros. Governor Canales may have had a similar monopoly in mind in 1709, which the cobreros protested. See Representation of Don Bernardo Antonio Castillo, [Santiago de Cuba, ca. 1710], "Demanda," C 23, fols. 33–36v, AGI-ESC 93A.

78. Crown Attorney's Summary, Madrid, June 3, 1732, AGI-SD 493.

79. See Chapter 11 in this volume.

CHAPTER 9

Epigraph. Cobreros to Governor Ximénez, [El Cobre, ca. July–Aug. 1731], [C 2, Autos 1731], fols. 31v–32, AGI-SD 493. See letter 1 in Appendix 5.

1. From July 1 to July 15, 1777, for instance, there were fifteen cobreros and seven penal convicts, skilled laborers, and several peons working in the fortification projects of the San Francisco garrison in Santiago de Cuba ("Cuentas de obras reales," July 1 to Dec. 31, 1777, AGI-Cuba 1230).

2. Testimonies of Pedro Mártir de Salazar (fols. 2–4) and Juan Alexo Sánchez (fols. 4–6), Santiago de Cuba, Apr. 14, 1791, "Cuaderno sobre el modo en que corrían las cosas" (hereafter "Modo corrían cosas"), Pieza 13, AGI-SD 1627.

3. Exceptions include the works of Macías Domínguez 1978; and Pérez Guzmán 1990 in Spain. For Santiago de Cuba in particular, see Marrero vol. 3:157–64. For a very brief recent account, see Blanes Martín 1987.

4. For a general debate on the legal character and actual conditions of slavery in the Americas with particular reference to Cuba, see Klein 1989 [1967]; Knight 1970; and Moreno Fraginals 1978; and for royal slavery in Havana, see Pérez Guzmán 1990.

5. For a work that begins to compile studies about slaves' negotiating strategies within a wider context of labor bargaining, see Turner 1995. See also Tomich 1990, 216–17; and Mintz 1995.

6. Construction of San Pedro de la Roca (El Morro) started in the early 1640s. Private slaves of El Cobre, and from elsewhere in the region, may have been rented out to work in the fortification projects then. On the belated construction of El Morro in Santiago de Cuba, see Marrero vol. 3:158–62.

7. Representation of Captain Francisco Salazar, Santiago de Cuba, Sept. 28, 1673, fols. 177–80v, AGI-SD 1631.

8. Royal slaves may have been employed sporadically in the fortification projects during the 1680s, however, but no mention can be found in the record.

9. Petition of Captain Juan Moreno, Santiago del Prado, July 13, 1677, fols. 454–55v, AGI-SD 1631; Judicial Report, [Madrid, ca. 1799], C 2, fol. 10, AGI-SD 1627.

10. Ibid., Judicial Report; Don Antonio Matta y Haro to the Crown, Havana, Mar. 5, 1672, AGI-SD 104.

11. Don Antonio Matta y Haro to the Crown, Havana, Mar. 5, 1672, AGI-SD 104.

12. Ibid.

13. Pastoral visit of Bishop Morell de Santa Cruz, Santiago de Cuba, Oct. 28, 1756, AGI-SD 534; see also Marrero vol. 5:48–53.

14. Since the mines were impounded, the slaves were still formally the property of the heirs. Governor Villalobos's deal consisted of the right to use the slaves of El Cobre for construction projects, while he reimbursed the heirs for the amount of money that had entered the royal treasury for the *coartación* of seven cobreros. In addition, Villalobos allowed the heirs to remove four slaves from El Cobre for their own personal use. In 1700, the Crown ordered the heirs to either pay their debts or definitely give up their rights of possession to the mines (Judicial Report, [Madrid, ca. 1799], C 2, fols. 10–19, AGI-SD 1627).

15. Bacardí y Moreau 1973, 121.

16. See Chapter 11 in this volume, for a fuller discussion of the practice of denunciations.

17. Bacardí y Moreau 1973, 120.

18. Report of Governor Don Juan de Villalobos, 1693, cited in Marrero vol. 5:50.

19. Ibid.

20. Pastoral Visit of Bishop Morell de Santa Cruz, Santiago de Cuba, Oct. 28, 1756, AGI-SD 534.

21. Eventually the episode ended badly for both men: Roa was charged with sedition and died in exile; and the governor was deposed and died before the end of the investigation in which he was found guilty of embezzlement (Marrero vol. 5:50; Bacardí y Moreau 1973, 120).

22. Judicial Report, [Madrid, ca. 1799], C 2, AGI-SD 1627.

23. Report of Don Diego Oviedo y Baños, 1693, cited in Judicial Report, [Madrid, ca. 1799], C 2, fols. 14v–15, AGI-SD 1627.

24. Judicial Report, [Madrid, ca. 1799], C 2, fols. 12–18, AGI-SD 1627.

25. Report of Don Juan de Villalobos, 1693, cited in Marrero vol. 5:50. Similarly, during the revolt of 1731 against Governor Ximénez, royal slaves articulated among their many grievances the suspicion that they may really be free, but this claim was not associated to the Roa episode.

26. Letter of Father Juan Antonio Pérez, Santiago del Prado, Apr. 14, 1709, "Demanda," C 23, fols. 7–11, AGI-ESC 93A.

27. According to Spanish legal codes, slaves were entitled to Sundays and holidays without work (Klein 1989 [1967]). During the eighteenth century, the royal slaves in the fortification projects of Havana worked 283 days and rested for 82—that is, they worked 77.5 percent of the year (Pérez Guzmán 1990).

28. Governor Sebastian Arancibia, 1696, cited in Judicial Report, [Madrid, ca. 1799], C 2, fols. 12–12v, AGI-SD 1627.

29. Petition of Captain Juan Moreno, Santiago del Prado, July 13, 1677, fols. 454–55v, AGI-SD 1631.

30. Crown Attorney's Summary, Madrid, June 3, 1732, AGI-SD 493.

31. Report of Governor Ximénez to Captain General Güemes y Horcacitas, Santiago de Cuba, June 5, 1735, "Autos 1735," fols. 776–76v, AGI-SD 451.

32. Ibid.

33. Royal Edict, Madrid, Sept. 3, 1733, "Autos 1735," fols. 670–72v, AGI-SD 451.

34. Ibid.

35. Bacardí y Moreau 1973, 133.

36. Petition of the Cobreros to the Captain General, [ca. 1735], "Autos 1735," fols. 710–17v/54–61v, AGI-SD 451.

37. On the ideal (but unsuccessful) claim to freedom from forced labor requisitions, or to freedom altogether, see Chapter 11 in this volume.

38. In Spanish, the term *escuadra* refers primarily to a unit of soldiers under a *cabo* and to other similarly related military meanings. The term *cabo*, however, although primarily a military title, can also refer to a foreman. *Diccionario de la Real Academia Española*. The equivalent work units in the fortifications of Havana were called brigades (Pérez Guzmán 1990, 245).

39. There were four *escuadras* of sixteen to twenty men each in 1731 (Testimony of Don Manuel Bernardo Limonta, Aug. 14, 1731, [C 2, Autos 1731], fol. 61v, AGI-SD 493). See also Reserved Letter of Governor Vicente Manuel de Céspedes to Captain General Diego J. Navarro, Santiago de Cuba, Dec. 8, 1780, AGI-Cuba 1231.

40. Testimony of Juan Alexo Sánchez, Santiago de Cuba, Apr. 14, 1791, "Modo corrían cosas," Pieza 13, fols. 4–6, AGI-SD 1627.

41. Investigation of Governor Ximénez, Santiago de Cuba, Apr. 23, 1735, AGI-SD 451. "Revista de esclavos del Cobre sexos y edades," 1774, C 20/28, AGI-SD 1628.

42. Family Census of 1735, AGI-SD 451.

43. Family Census of 1773, AGI-SD 1628; "Listas de escuadras," 1775, AGI-SD 1628; and see also "Revista de esclavos del Cobre sexos y edades," 1774, C 20/28, AGI-SD 1628.

44. In 1709, there were a total of one hundred ten royal slave males between the ages of sixteen and sixty. Of these, however, eighteen were absent or away from the village (Family Census of 1709, AGI-ESC 93A).

45. The number of absent royal slave males of working age in 1735 seems unusually high (forty-four). This was due to the fact that during those turbulent years a brigade of twenty to thirty men from El Cobre went to litigate in Havana (Family Census of 1735, AGI-SD 451).

46. One explanation for the discrepancy could lay in the way the squadrons were constituted and counted. It could have been, for instance, that only adult males were actually regarded as properly forming part of a work squadron and only they were counted among the fifteen to twenty men composing each brigade. That muchachos who were called to work at age fifteen were considered peripheral to the squadron may be suggested by the fact that these youths received half the ration allotted to adult men, and they were required to perform lighter tasks such as transporting water and wood. Another reason for the gap in the counts—but only a partial one—was the fact that there was a category of royal slaves who were exempt from

compulsory labor. Royal slaves with positions of rank such as *alcaldes* or *regidores* or officials in the militia, for example, were exempted from *escuadra* work—but these officials would not have constituted more than eight or twelve men in the 1730s. Thus, by themselves, these privileged slaves cannot fully account for the relative short numbers of recruited men in the squadrons, either. Nor could the handicapped of the village have been so many as to subtract full squadrons of laborers from the system.

47. Family Census of 1709, AGI-ESC 93A.

48. Family Census of 1735, AGI-SD 451.

49. Some of these absent royal slaves may have also been employed elsewhere in the service of the Crown, however.

50. "Testimonio Juana María Bayesteros y sus hijos," Santiago de Cuba, Nov. 17, 1788, C 30/38, fols. 34–45, AGI-SD 1628.

51. The following reconstruction is based on the "Noticia de los cobreros esclavos de Su Magestad que se hayan ausentes de la revista pasada en dicho Pueblo por el Sr. Gobernador de esta Plaza" (hereafter "Noticia ausentes de la revista"), Apr. 15, 1758, fols. 1–11v, AGI-SD 1630.

52. The data for this section is also based on the "Noticia ausentes de la revista," ibid.

53. The cobreros were also assigned watches from the Port of Guaicabón, just as the Indians of El Caney were from the Port of Juragúa. It is not known how these militia-related services were coordinated. Perhaps these other routine defense-related services (cleaning artillery, rowing in the *Piragua*) were part of the lower-level duties assigned to the slave militia company.

54. Records of the San Francisco castle in 1777 demonstrate that only one squadron was at work in any given week at this site, thus confirming the depiction of this report as well ("Cuentas de obras reales," Santiago de Cuba, July 1 to Dec. 31, 1777, AGI-Cuba 1230).

55. Pedro Sánchez Griñán, Santiago de Cuba, "Noticia ausentes de la revista," Apr. 15, 1758, fols. 3v–4, AGI-SD 1630.

56. Petition of Don Joseph Espinoza de los Monteros, Joseph Antonio Vicente, Cristóbal Francisco de Salas, and Juan Joseph González, Havana, July 30, 1795, AGI-SD 1629.

57. Family Census of 1750, AGI-SD 1630.

58. Required labor periods varied throughout the Spanish territories. C. H. Haring (1947, 59) cited legal work periods of one to two weeks and in some mining regions of four to five weeks at a time, generally three or four times a year. On Peru, in contrast, Spalding (1984, 185) cites an official six-month period of *mita* labor every six or seven years, or an average of one month per year. In practice, however, particularly with the population decline, the yearly load could increase. Spalding calculates that the average Indian in the eighteenth century worked a six-month turn every four to six years—thus, less than one and a half months per year. Farriss (1984, 47–56) indicates that in Yucatan the formal labor of Indians at the end of the sixteenth century was one week per year, but in practice the period extended to two or three weeks.

59. Pérez Guzmán 1990, 245; Klein 1989 [1967]. For calculations of time off for

provision grounds the literature has become extensive, see especially Berlin and Morgan 1993.

60. Certification of Don Miguel Serrano, Santiago de Cuba, Dec. 9, 1734, Investigation of Governor Ximénez, [Autos 1735], fols. 687–87v, AGI-SD 451.

61. Testimony of José Basilio Maestre, "Testimonio Teresa Ramos alias Coba," 1793, C 42/34, fol. 35v, AGI-SD 1628.

62. Records indicated that in 1777 it was 2 reales a day ("Cuentas obras reales," Santiago de Cuba, July 1–Dec. 31, 1777, AGI-Cuba 1230). Witnesses questioned in 1791, however, stated that the royal slaves received 1 real for a ration. Testimonies of Pedro Mártir de Salazar (fols. 1–3) and Juan Alexo Sánchez (fols. 4–6), Santiago de Cuba, Apr. 14, 1791, "Modo corrían cosas," Pieza 13, AGI-SD 1627.

63. The price of meat in cattle-raising societies like Cuba could be quite low. In 1743, for example, in the midst of a food supply crisis that followed a drought, the *cabildo* of Santiago de Cuba gave orders that beef could be sold at 5 to 6 pounds for 1 real. The reports on the diets of royal slaves and *forzados* (penal convicts) in the fortification projects of Havana in the late eighteenth century included daily rations of a half pound of jerked meat, 2 pounds of yams or other root vegetables, a half pound of rice and another half pound of cassava, half a *galleta* (cracker), and half a cup of *aguardiente* with other variations that could include corn meal or honey (Pérez Guzmán 1990, 6–11).

64. Testimony of Captain Ignacio de los Reyes, Santiago de Cuba, Sept. 1, 1731, [C 2, Autos 1731], fol. 55, AGI-SD 493; "Cuentas obras reales," Santiago de Cuba, July 1 to Dec. 31, 1777, AGI-Cuba 1230.

65. On July 1, 1777, for instance, there were fifteen cobreros and seven penal convicts working in the fortification projects of the San Francisco garrison in Santiago de Cuba. Accounts indicate that both groups received 2 reales per diem for their rations, while peons were paid 4 reales. The salaries of skilled workers fluctuated between 7 and 10 reales ("Cuentas obras reales," Santiago de Cuba, July 1 to Dec. 31, 1777, AGI-Cuba 1230).

66. Farriss 1984, 48; Spalding 1984, 191.

67. "Cuenta de paga," Don Manuel Bernardo Limonta, Santiago de Cuba, 1729–1731, fols. 59v–63, AGI-SD 493. The accounts of payments made to the men from El Caney refer to six men for six days of work, and twelve men working on *fagina* during two days at two reales per day. The *fagina* points to a system of compulsory labor but with lighter requisitions and usually of a more local character.

68. Ibid., fols. 61–61v.

69. The structural similarity between Indians and cobreros in other aspects of colonial life as depicted in popular stories of the time has been discussed elsewhere, but El Cobre was often confused for a village of Indians—or of Indians and blacks— in some outsiders' accounts. The Supreme Council in Madrid, for example, referred to the (forced) labor system in El Cobre as a *mita* in 1799 (Junta's Report, Madrid, Oct. 31, 1799, AGI-SD 1146). Similarly, the title pages in *legajos* AGI-SD 1628 and 1629 read, "Expediente de los Indios del Pueblo del Cobre." Moreover, many years later a nineteenth-century governor in Santiago de Cuba referred to El Cobre as a village which had been "populated exclusively by Indians and men of color until

recently" (Report of Governor Cayetano de Urbina, Santiago de Cuba, 1846, AHN-Ultramar 4638[2]).

70. Testimony of Alcalde Joseph Moreno, Santiago de Cuba, Sept. 1, 1731, fols. 58–59, and of Don Manuel Bernardo Limonta, Aug. 14, 1731, fols. 61v–63, both in [C 2, Autos 1731], AGI-SD 493; "Listas de escuadras," C 94, 1772, AGI-SD 1630.

71. "Listas de escuadras," C 94, 1772 and 1774, AGI-SD 1630.

72. Testimony of Captain Ignacio de los Reyes, Santiago de Cuba, Sept. 1731, [C 2, Autos 1731], fol. 55, AGI-SD 493.

73. Ibid., fols. 56–56v.

74. Ibid., Testimony of Captain Fernando de Rosas, fol. 58.

75. Félix Cosme, El Cobre, Mar. 30, 1709, "Demandas," C 23, fol. 95, AGI-ESC 93A. See also Chapter 10 in this volume.

76. Cobreros to Governor Sucre, [ca. July–Aug., 1731], [C 1, Autos Sucre], fols. 5v–7, AGI-SD 493.

77. Testimonies of Captain Ignacio de los Reyes (fols. 54v–56v), and of Captain Fernando de Rosas (fols. 57–58), Santiago de Cuba, Sept. 1, 1731, [C 2, Autos 1731], AGI-SD 493; "Razón firmada por Alférez Don Manuel Bernardo Limonta," Santiago de Cuba, Nov. 13, 1731, [C 2, Autos 1731], fols. 59–63, AGI-SD 493.

78. Testimony of Lieutenant Don Pedro Arando (fol. 64), Santiago de Cuba, Aug. 14, 1731, and of Don Manuel Bernardo Limonta (fol. 132), Oct. 15, 1731, [C 2, Autos 1731], AGI-SD 493.

79. Representation of the Heirs of Don Juan de Eguiluz, Santiago de Cuba, [ca. 1786–1789], C 4, AGI-SD 1629.

80. Representation of Don Miguel de Mueses to Captain General Antonio Bucareli, Santiago de Cuba, Sept. 14, 1768, AGI-Cuba 1084.

81. See Chapter 2 in this volume.

82. For the politics of accusations through the judicial system and of vertical tactical alliances at all levels of colonial society, but particularly those involving the cobreros, see Chapter 11 in this volume.

83. Testimony of Juan Alexo Sánchez, Santiago de Cuba, Apr. 14, 1791, "Modo corrían cosas," Pieza 13, fols. 4v–5, AGI-SD 1627.

84. Inventory of Slaves: 1608, AGI-SD 451; 1620, AGI-SD 1631; and 1647, AGI-SD 104. Paz y Ascanio / Fonseca 1853, 46. See also Chapter 8 in this volume, for female mining activities.

85. For women's healing role and work in hospitals in Seville, for instance, see Perry 1990, 20–32.

86. In 1736, the hospital of Santiago de Cuba had only twelve beds, Hospital de Cuba, AGI-SD 363. During his pastoral visit in 1756, Bishop Morell de Santa Cruz proposed the foundation of a hospital for men and women in El Cobre as well as in other villages and towns, but nothing came of it (García del Pino 1985, 113). Today the Ambrosio Grillo Hospital, a 600-bed provincial hospital that was founded in the 1940s as an antituberculosis clinic, stands in El Cobre (Hernández 1993, 96, 101). In Miami, the Virgin of Charity's hermitage stands next to the (Catholic) Mercy Hospital.

87. "Testimonio Juana María Bayesteros y sus hijos," Santiago de Cuba, Nov. 17, 1788, C 30/38, fols. 34–45, AGI-SD 1628.

88. "Testimonio María Manuela Borrero," 1786, C 37/45, fols. 1v–2, AGI-SD 1628.

89. "Testimonio Manuel de Jesús," 1786, C 15/50/58, fol. 3, AGI-SD 1628.

90. "Testimonio Antonio Vicente Norate," 1786, C 20/63/55, fols. 4–5, AGI-SD 1628.

91. Petition of the Pueblo of El Cobre to the King, Nov. 19, 1738, AGI-SD 426.

92. For a general account of the conflict during the 1730s and for other denunciations filed by the cobreros, see Chapter 11 in this volume.

93. Certification Don Miguel Serrano, Santiago de Cuba, Dec. 9, 1734, "Autos 1735," fols. 687–87v, AGI-SD 451; see also Reserved Letter of Governor Vicente Manuel de Céspedes to Captain General Diego J. Navarro, Santiago de Cuba, Dec. 8, 1780, AGI-Cuba 1231; and Testimonies of Pedro Mártir de Salazar (fol. 3) and Juan Alexo Sánchez (fols. 4v–5), "Modo corrían cosas," Pieza 13, AGI-SD 1627. Testimony of José Basilio Maestre, "Testimonio Teresa Ramos alias Coba," Feb. 14, 1793, C 42/34, fol. 35v, AGI-SD 1628.

94. Report of Don Pedro Sánchez Griñán to Governor Don Lorenzo de Madariaga, Santiago de Cuba, 1761, AGI-Cuba 1237.

95. Ibid.

96. Ibid.

97. B. Bush 1989, 33, 44–46; Morrissey 1989, 18, 31, 117.

98. In Barbados, for example, new mothers received only two weeks before expected childbirth and two weeks after off from fieldwork. Pregnant and nursing slave women in the French Caribbean enjoyed more liberal terms as they were employed in lighter tasks during this time. In Martinique, they even stopped working after the seventh month of pregnancy and did not return to work until forty days after childbirth (Morrissey 1989, 126). In Cuba, during the nineteenth century, slave women returned to work forty-five days after childbirth and the children were placed under the care of an older slave woman, while mothers worked in the fields (Knight 1970, 76). Moreno Fraginals (1978, 2:46, 56–57), however, states that women returned to work two or three days after childbirth, and children were placed in charge of the *criollera* (an older woman caring for children or breeding Creole slaves).

99. Governor Don Sebastián de Arancibia, Santiago de Cuba, 1696, cited in Judicial Report, [Madrid, ca. 1799], C 2, AGI-SD 1627.

100. By the 1820s, for example, slave women in the British West Indies were allowed relief from work three months before childbirth and two months after; nursing women were placed in second field gangs where labor was lighter; and in Jamaica, women who had six or more children were exempted from hard work altogether (Morrissey 1989, 127; B. Bush 1989, 29).

101. It is worthwhile to make an aside at this point to note that if encouraging procreation was indeed a goal informing the policy of exempting married slave women from compulsory labor since the end of the seventeenth century, then it appears to have proved effective. Contrary to slave populations in Cuba and elsewhere, the population of (royal) slaves in El Cobre increased naturally, particularly after the Crown took over the mining jurisdiction (see Chapter 1 in this volume). It

is difficult to determine in any precise way just what the causes of this demographic increase were, but low female labor requisitions (and probably low male ones as well) could have very well played a direct or indirect role in this trend.

102. Representation of the Heirs of Don Juan de Eguiluz, Santiago de Cuba, [ca. 1786–1789], C 4, AGI-SD 1629.

103. Ibid.

104. "Testimonio de la lista del Bejuco y Majagua que saca cada familia de los cobreros" (hereafter "Lista del Bejuco y Majagua"), 1772, C 18/26, AGI-SD 1628. For communal requisitions in Indian pueblos Farriss (1984, 47–48), for instance, has shown that in Yucatan Indians were subject to labor exactions for the state such as construction and repair of public works like roads, forts, cathedrals, and other public buildings—the equivalents to the squadron work in the fortifications by the royal slaves. But communities were also supposed to provide other services such as a postal service of relay runners from town to town (also in El Caney), the maintenance of hostels in each town for travelers, and the transport of people and goods connected to official business. In addition Indians were subject to local *tequias*—a community tax equivalent to one day's labor per week for local projects such as the construction and repair of local churches and even the service of native leaders. The cobreros' *faginas* may have been the analogues of the Native American *tequias* elsewhere.

105. "Lista del Bejuco y Majagua," 1772, C 18/26, AGI-SD 1628.

106. Justo Cruzata to Gregorio Cosme Osorio, El Cobre, Dec. 27, 1795, AGI-SD 1627.

107. Representation of Don Joseph Espinoza de los Monteros, Gregorio Cosme Osorio, and Carlos Ramos, Havana, Dec. 10, 1783, Pieza 9, fols. 8–23, AGI-SD 1627.

108. "Lista del Bejuco y Majagua," 1772, C 18/26, AGI-SD 1628; "Listas de escuadras," C 94, 1772, AGI-SD 1630.

109. "Lista del Bejuco y Majagua," 1772, C 18/26, 1628.

110. Testimonies of Captain Ignacio de los Reyes (fols. 54–56v), and of Captain Fernando de Rosas (fols. 57–58), Santiago de Cuba, Sept. 1, 1731, [C 2, Autos 1731], AGI-SD 493.

111. Generally speaking, females consistently made up a higher proportion of the free population of color throughout the slave societies of the Americas (Cohen and Greene 1972). Specifically in Cuba, females constituted 54 percent of the free people of color in Santiago de Cuba and 58 percent in Havana in 1778 (General Census of the Island of Cuba, Havana, Dec. 31, 1778, AGI-Indiferente 1527). Studies of actual comparative *coartación* patterns are more difficult to come by, however.

112. Petition of Cobreros to Captain General Güemes y Horcacitas, [ca. 1734], "Autos 1735," fols. 664–65/8v–9v, AGI-SD 451.

113. See Chapter 11 in this volume, for a discussion of military service as a basis for a claim to freedom or at the very least to *coartación* on easy terms. Although there was a big jump in the number of *coartaciones* in the decades following British military invasions (1740s and 1760s), the dates for these paid manumissions do not cluster around these events, but are instead relatively evenly spread out ("Certificación corte y libertades," 1743 to Dec. 1775, fols. 63–68v, AGI-SD 1627; and

"Corte y libertades," Dec. 1740 to Oct. 26, 1742, in "Testimonio de autos que varios naturales del Cobre siguieron en Cuba sobre su libertad," 1780, C 29/37, fols. 34–35, AGI-SD 1628).

CHAPTER 10

Epigraph. Petition of Cobreros to Captain General Don Juan Francisco Güemes y Horcacitas, [ca. 1734], "Autos 1735," fols. 658–65/3–9v, AGI-SD 451. See Appendix 6. Governor Ximénez, "Expediente sobre disposición del Obispo sobre que los Alcaldes del Pueblo del Cobre esclavos V.M. metiesen asientos en la Iglesia y se les diese la Paz" (hereafter "Expte. bancos iglesia"), Dec. 24, 1732, fols. 640–43, AGI-SD 451.

1. Testimony of Captain Francisco X[aisme] de Loreto (fols. 66–66v); see also that of Don Manuel Bernardo Limonta (fols. 62v–63), Santiago de Cuba, [ca. Aug. 14, 1731], Investigation of Governor Ximénez, [C 2, Autos 1731], AGI-SD 493.

2. Representation of Don Joseph Espinoza de los Monteros, Gregorio Cosme Osorio, and Carlos Ramos, Havana, Dec. 10, 1783, Pieza 9, fols. 8–23, AGI-SD 1627.

3. Captain General Gerónimo de Valdés to the Secretary of State and Government of Ultramar, Havana, Sept. 28, 1841, AHN-Ultramar 4613. After the captain general abolished the cobreros' *ayuntamiento* in 1841, he installed a military government. That local policy echoed the larger militarization of Cuban colonial society, the new forms of capitalist development (in this case, through mining), the "need" to control a menacing "Africanization" of the island's population, and the racism developing in the island. See Epilogue in this volume.

4. Petition of Colonel Canales, [Santiago de Cuba, ca. Jan. 1711], "Cargos," C 8, fols. 68–68v, AGI-ESC 92C. See Chapter 2 in this volume.

5. Representation of Don Simón de Echenique, Madrid, Mar. 12, 1793, AGI-SD 1630.

6. Ots y Capolequi 1969, 143–46; Haring 1947, 163–65.

7. Le Riverend 1967, 14.

8. These functions are reflected in the acts of the city's *cabildo* (Bacardí y Moreau 1973).

9. Bacardí y Moreau 1973, 189–90.

10. Haring 1947, 161–62; Lockhart and Schwartz 1983, 114–17, 170–73; Haskett 1991.

11. See Chapter 11 in this volume, for a more detailed account of this event.

12. Petition of Cobreros to Captain General Güemes y Horcacitas, [ca. 1734], "Autos 1735," fol. 659, AGI-SD 451.

13. Although not explicitly stated in the story, Diego de Rosas was a royal slave (Family Census of 1709, AGI-ESC 93A).

14. In Santiago de Cuba, for instance, the civil body represented by the *cabildo* officials sat on a special bench on one side of the altar and the military sat facing them. There were also continuous conflicts of protocol in this city. For some examples, see Bacardí y Moreau (1973, 189, 199, 211) among others throughout the eighteenth century.

15. Testimony of Don Manuel Bernardo Limonta, Santiago de Cuba, [C 2, Autos 1731], fols. 133v–34, AGI-SD 493.

16. Governor Ximénez, Santiago de Cuba, Dec. 24, 1732, "Expte. bancos iglesia," fols. 642–42v, AGI-SD 451.

17. Testimony of Claudio Alcántara (fols. 276v–77); see also those of Juan Diego González (fols. 287–87v) and Jacintho Rodríguez (fol. 264), all in Investigation of Governor Ximénez, [Autos 1737], AGI-SD 451.

18. Family Census of 1709, AGI-ESC 93A; Pastoral Visit of Bishop Morell de Santa Cruz to El Cobre, Dec. 8, 1756, published in García del Pino 1985, 111. Similarly elders of the community reported in 1791 that before 1780 there had been four perpetual regidores and four alcaldes. Testimonies of Pedro Mártir de Salazar (fols. 2–3) and of Juan Alexo Sánchez (fols. 4–6), Santiago de Cuba, Apr. 14, 1791, "Modo corrían cosas," Pieza 13, AGI-SD 1627.

19. Pastoral Visit of Bishop Morell de Santa Cruz (1756) to El Caney, published in García del Pino 1985, 115; Jiguaní, ibid., 108; and Baracoa, ibid., 120.

20. The only free cobrero recorded in a list of some twenty-eight names compiled from different sources for the decade of the 1730s was Captain Ignacio de los Reyes. It is not clear if Joseph Cosme, for instance, had already manumitted himself by the time he was alcalde in the late 1730s.

21. Of the twenty-eight names registered with a title at some point in the 1730s, ten were recorded as regidores; thirteen as alcaldes; three or four had been alcaldes and regidores; and only one had appeared with the title of alférez (Investigations of Governor Ximénez: [C 2 Autos 1731], fols. 105–6v, 115–19, AGI-SD 493; "Autos 1735," fols. 673v–75v, AGI-SD 451; see also Family Census of 1735, AGI-SD 451; and of 1739, AGI-SD 385). For 1709 the list was smaller, but there are fewer sources, too: one alcalde, one regidor, and one alférez; Family Census of 1709, AGI-ESC 93A; Governor Joseph Canales to Félix Cosme, Santiago de Cuba, May 11, 1709, "Demanda," C 23, fol. 96, AGI-ESC 93A.

22. Governor Ximénez, Santiago de Cuba, Dec. 24, 1732, "Expte. bancos iglesia," fol. 642v, AGI-SD 451.

23. It is not clear who appointed the regidores. A recorded mention of the cabildo officials selected at the time, however, refers to "the appointed Regidores" but to "elected alcaldes ordinarios" (Report of Don Joseph Losada, [ca. Aug. 14, 1731], fols. 105–6v; and Report of Luis Nieto de Villalobos, fols. 115–19, AGI-SD 493).

24. Ibid., Report of Don Joseph Losada, fols. 106v–7. For the governor's required approval of elected alcaldes in the cabildos of the colonial Spanish republics, see Harring 1947, 155; for the case of Indian republics, see Haskett 1991.

25. Report of Don Miguel Serrano, Santiago del Prado, Dec. 9, 1734, "Autos 1735," fol. 688v, AGI-SD 451.

26. Testimony of Bartolomé Rodríguez, Santiago de Cuba, [ca. 1737], [Autos 1737], fol. 239, AGI-SD 451.

27. Governor Ximénez, Santiago de Cuba, Dec. 24, 1732, "Expte. bancos iglesia," fols. 642–42v, AGI-SD 451.

28. Ibid.

29. See Chapter 9 in this volume.

30. Governor Canales, Santiago de Cuba, May 17, 1708, "Demanda," C 23, fol. 89, AGI-ESC 93A.

31. Ibid., Governor Canales, Santiago de Cuba, July 7, 1708, fol. 93.

32. [Félix Cosme], Minas de Santiago del Prado, Mar. 30, 1709, "Demanda," C 23, fol. 95, AGI-ESC 93A. The fine seems to refer to the possibility of hiring a substitute (see Chapter 9 in this volume). The note may have been written in the first person by someone on behalf of the *alcalde* Félix Cosme, however.

33. By the 1730s, however, the fining/replacement system had become customary among the royal slaves and no longer among free cobreros, and it constituted an ambiguous mechanism of control over their own labor power (see Chapter 9 in this volume).

34. Governor Canales to Félix Cosme, Santiago de Cuba, May 11, 1709, "Demanda," C 23, fol. 96, AGI-ESC 93A.

35. Governor Don Juan de Hoyos y Solórzano complained that the *alcaldes* of El Cobre did not properly perform their duties regarding the drafting of royal slaves for work as called for, claiming that the labor squadrons were sent with insufficient numbers of men. He dissolved the *cabildo* during his administration of 1728–1729 and militarized the labor system by placing the captains of the militias in charge of it (Testimony of Don Pedro de Aranda, Santiago de Cuba, Aug. 14, 1731, [C 2, Autos 1731], fols. 64v–65, AGI-SD 493).

36. Testimony of Félix Gerónimo Hernández, Santiago de Cuba, Dec. 18, 1735, "Autos 1735," fols. 723–23v, AGI-SD 451.

37. Testimony of Alcalde Marcelo González, Santiago de Cuba, Jan. 3, 1735, "Autos 1735," fol. 728, AGI-SD 451.

38. Testimony of Juan Diego González, Santiago de Cuba, [Autos 1737], fols. 286v–87, AGI-SD 451.

39. Ibid. See also Testimony of Claudio Alcántara, fols. 275–76.

40. After the attempted reprivatization of the mines in 1781, the *alcaldes* of El Cobre would all be freemen because most of the enslaved cobreros were removed from El Cobre.

41. Matías Quiala signed the power of attorney given to the village's *apoderado* to Madrid (Representation of Don Francisco Mancebo y Quiroga, Aug. 14, 1792, AGI-SD 1627). Quiala's signature also appeared on a petition in support of the parish priest, Santiago del Prado, Dec. 5, 1795, C 12, fols. 138–40, AGI-SD 1631.

42. Testimony of Matías Quiala to Governor Juan Nepomuceno, Santiago de Cuba, Oct. 17, 1796, AGI-SD 1631. Similarly, the *alcalde* Nicholás de Ojeda declared, "It is true that [Governor Vaillant] had once threatened to punish him in a vault but that it was if he did not comply with his obligation as an *alcalde pedáneo*" (Testimony of Nicholás de Ojeda to Governor Juan Nepomuceno, Santiago de Cuba, Oct. 17, 1796, AGI-SD 1631).

43. Governor Don Juan Nepomuceno to the Captain General Don Luis de las Casas, Santiago de Cuba, Aug. 15, 1796, AGI-SD 1631.

44. Petition of Cobreros to Bishop Joaquín Osés y Alzúa, Santiago de Cuba, Dec. 5, 1795, C 12, 1796, fols. 138–40, AGI-SD 1631.

45. Representation of Don Joseph Espinoza de los Monteros, Carlos Ramos,

and Gregorio Cosme Osorio, Havana, Dec. 10, 1783, Pieza 9, fols. 8–23, AGI-SD 1627.

46. [Félix Cosme], Minas de Santiago del Prado, Mar. 30, 1709, "Demanda," C 23, fol. 95, AGI-ESC 93A. Although the end of the document is missing so that it is not explicitly clear who actually signed it, this was the year when Félix Cosme was *alcalde*. The reference to "the king, *mi amo*" [my master] suggests that the order was issued by a royal slave.

47. Ibid. Such restrictions of mobility impeded, among other things, hunting and were strongly protested by the cobreros (Memorial of Diego de Rosas, [Madrid, 1709], "Demanda," C 23, fols. 3–5, AGI-ESC 93A).

48. Governor Joseph Canales, Santiago de Cuba, July 2, 1708, "Demanda," C 23, fol. 92, AGI-ESC 93A. Similarly, a month before, the governor had sent an order to the *alcalde* of El Cobre to be on the lookout for any unknown foreigners—white or of color—who may come by the village because of an "intended death" [*muerte alevosa*] that had taken place in Santiago de Cuba (Santiago de Cuba, June 9, 1708, "Demanda," C 23, fol. 90, AGI-ESC 93A).

49. Testimonies of Alcalde Patricio Cosme (fols. 94–102), of Gaspar de los Reyes (fol. 115), of Francisco Xavier Quiala (fol. 217), and of Alcalde Joseph Cosme (fols. 127v–28), [Autos 1737], AGI-SD 451.

50. Ibid., Testimony of Alcalde Patricio Cosme, fol. 98.

51. Ibid., fol. 97.

52. Justo Cruzata to Gregorio Cosme Osorio, El Cobre, Dec. 27, 1795, C 135, AGI-SD 1627.

53. Ibid.

54. Testimony of Alcalde Juan Manuel Quiala, Santiago de Cuba, Dec. 2, 1734, "Autos 1735," fols. 579v–680v, AGI-SD 451.

55. Testimony of Lorenzo González, Santiago de Cuba, Feb. 26, 1737, [Autos 1737], fol. 194v, AGI-SD 451.

56. Testimony of Phelipe Gutiérrez, Santiago de Cuba, Nov. 17, 1731, [C 2, Autos 1731], fols. 50v–52v, AGI-SD 493. Another cobrero, Xtóbal Vicente, stated that Phelipe Vicente, who was married and lived in Sancti Espíritu, was going to Spain (ibid., fols. 209v–10).

57. Report of Josef Emigio Maldonado, Santiago de Cuba, July 11, 1796, C 73, fols. 204–11, AGI-SD 1629.

58. Testimony of Juan Ravelo, [Autos 1737], fol. 186, AGI-SD 451.

59. For a discussion of the *fagina* system, see Chapter 9 in this volume.

60. Testimony of Lorenzo de los Reyes, [Autos 1737], fol. 27, AGI-SD 451.

61. Ibid.

62. Testimony of Sergeant Matías Maynan, [Santiago de Cuba, ca. Dec. 1, 1795], C 12, fols. 83–84, AGI-SD 1631.

63. "Representación comisionados," [ca. Dec. 23, 1775], AGI-SD 1630.

64. Five cobrero *cabildo* officials granted power of attorney to Don Bernardo Antonio Castillo to represent them legally in their case against Governor Canales. Santiago de Cuba, [ca. Nov. 1710], "Demanda," C 23, fols. 15–15v. By February 25, 1711, the cobreros' first attorney had died and four of the former *alcaldes* and *regi-*

dores granted power of attorney to a new one, Don Diego Calderín. The legal transfer of power took place in front of three witnesses, *vecinos* of Santiago de Cuba, who were backing the community against a common enemy, former Governor Canales ("Demanda," C 23, fols. 63–63v, AGI-ESC 93A).

65. Testimony of the Alcalde Patricio Cosme, [Autos 1737], fols. 100v–1, AGI-SD 451.

66. Ibid., Testimony of the Regidor Félix Gerónimo Hernández, fols. 107v–8.

67. Ibid., Testimony of Alcalde Joseph Cosme, fols. 133–33v. See also ibid., Testimony of Joseph Rodríguez, fol. 137v.

68. Ibid., Testimony of Tiburcio de Rosas, fol. 141v.

69. Similarly royal officials in 1731 declared that village women provoked sedition and were shameless and arrogant. Testimonies of the Alférez Don Manuel Bernardo Limonta (fol. 132v), and of Don Gerónimo Valenzuela, (fols. 140–41v), Santiago de Cuba, Oct. 15, 1731, [C 2, Autos 1731], AGI-SD 493.

70. Report of Lieutenant Nicholás Velasco Calderín, El Cobre, [Autos 1737], fol. 163, AGI-SD 451.

71. Ibid.

72. Ibid., fol. 162v; see also fol. 177v.

73. Ibid., Testimony of Lieutenant Nicholás Velasco Calderín, fol. 177. See also ibid., "Cargos," fols. 162v–63.

74. Ibid., "Cargos," fols. 163–63v.

75. Ibid., Testimony of Lieutenant Nicholás Velasco Calderín, fol. 177.

76. Report of Don Josef Emigdio Maldonado, Santiago de Cuba, July 11, 1796, C 73, fols. 204–11, AGI-SD 1629.

77. Ibid.

78. Petition of Cobreros to Bishop Osés y Alzúa, El Cobre, Dec. 5, 1795, C 12, 1796, fols. 138–40, all in AGI-SD 1631.

79. Representation of Don Domingo García, (fol. 101v), "Testimonio Marcelina Antonia de los Reyes," 1797, C 43/35, AGI-SD 1628.

80. Ibid., Representation of Doña Ana de Rocha, fols. 105–11v.

81. "Testimonio Juana María Bayesteros y sus hijos," C 30/38, Santiago de Cuba, Nov. 17, 1788, AGI-SD 1628.

CHAPTER 11

Epigraph. Petition of Colonel Joseph Canales, [Santiago de Cuba, ca. Jan. 1711], "Cargos," C 8, fols. 70–70v, AGI-ESC 92C. Cobreros to Governor Ximénez, [ca. July–Aug. 1731], [C 2, Autos 1731], fol. 39, AGI-SD 493. See letter 2 in Appendix 5.

1. More studies beyond Borah's (1983) Indian-level court are needed. We know that some Native Americans engaged the Spanish judicial system individually at the highest level, as exhibited by Guaman Poma (Adorno 1988) with his famous *relación* to the king. But we know next to nothing about those who may have actually traveled to represent their cases in Spain.

2. Contemporaries for the most part referred to these forms of resistance among the cobreros as flight (*fuga*), sublevation (*sublevación*), or even as revolutions (*rev-*

olución), but not usually as *cimarronaje*. There were some exceptions, however, particularly after the 1780s when many cobreros did run away and had to live as runaways to prevent reenslavement. A group of them accused of a crime settled in the Loma de la Cruz (Justo Cruzata to Gregorio Cosme Osorio, El Cobre, Dec. 27, 1795, C 135, AGI-SD 1627; Report of Josef Emigdio Maldonado, Santiago de Cuba, July 11, 1796, C 73, fols. 204–11, AGI-SD 1629; "Testimonio Marcelina Antonia de los Reyes," 1797, C 35/43, fols. 95–96, AGI-SD 1628). In these cases the term *cimarrón* was sometimes applied to them, although the cobreros themselves rarely used it. The term may have been in colonial discourse too full of negative connotations related to slavery and "wildness" for the cobreros to apply it to themselves and their actions. For the quintessential story of *cimarronaje* in Cuba, see Barnet 1968. See also Price 1979 and 1990.

3. Pérez de la Riva (1979, 54–55) erroneously portrayed El Cobre as a maroon community (as a *palenque*) that lasted from 1731 to 1781. In the early 1970s little research existed on El Cobre so that Pérez de la Riva's short account of this important community (first published in English in 1972) was based on fragments of information and some factual errors. These problems of documentation led him to premature and unfounded generalizations. A more sustained (albeit still factually problematical) reconstruction of the cobreros' struggles that focuses on conflict during the 1780s and 1790s is Franco 1975. Franco's account does not make the error of referring to El Cobre as a maroon community, but he refers to events of rebellion and flight among the cobreros as acts of *cimarronaje* and often builds up possible links with maroon slaves in the region. These accounts have been instrumental in forging a new sense of El Cobre's local history and origins. In fact, they inform to a considerable extent the recent monument in homage to the maroon (or rebel) slave that was unveiled in the mountains of El Cobre in 1998 (Figarola 1998, 80–82).

4. Bacardí y Moreau 1973, 119–26.

5. Klein 1989 [1967], 60–65. Slave codes sometimes regulated hours of work and food rations as well as *coartación* provisions (Knight 1970, 126–31). See Chapter 9 in this volume, for denunciations of "bad treatment" in labor matters.

6. Klein 1989 [1967], 65.

7. For early law-oriented studies, see Tannenbaum 1947; Meiklejohn 1974, 1971; and for Cuba, see Klein 1989 [1967]. For more materialist-oriented revisionist studies, see Knight 1970; and Moreno Fraginals 1978.

8. Significantly, at about this time the use of the judicial system by Native Americans in Spanish colonial society began to receive more attention (Taylor 1972; Borah 1983; Stern 1982). Early colonial studies, however, had also been strongly grounded in analysis of the law. For more recent approaches to the law in anthropology and in colonial studies elsewhere, particularly Africa, see J. and J. Comaroff 1997; and particularly the review article by Sally E. Merry 1991.

9. Lockhart and Schwartz 1983, 127–28.

10. Hunefeldt 1994; R. Scott 1985; Klein 1989 [1967]. For engagements of the courts, such as those described by Hunefeldt, slaves needed sponsors and must have engaged in the personal politics of *apadrinamiento* typical of subordinate groups in hierarchical societies.

11. After 1780, once the mines were reprivatized and the royal slaves became so-called private slaves, the litigation pattern changed as the *apoderados* became free cobreros.

12. Reserved Letter of Governor Vicente Manuel de Céspedes to Captain General Diego J. Navarro, Santiago de Cuba, Dec. 8, 1780, AGI-Cuba 1231.

13. Klein 1989 [1967], 63.

14. Silvestre de Balboa's epic poem *Espejo de paciencia* written in 1608 — aesthetically a mediocre work but with the canonic distinction of being considered the earliest known Cuban "Creole" literary text — depicts one such historical act of service by a slave (appropriately) "named Salvador" who was a "son of Golomón, a prudent old man." The poem deals with the ransoming and rescuing of Bishop Juan de las Cabeza y Altamirano who had been apprehended by the pirate Gilberto Girón during one of the frequent pirate and corsair raids of the time. Salvador killed the pirate and saved the bishop. Salvador Golomón not only obtained manumission for his act of service but also attained the honor of having the service recognized and inscribed in the poem as a heroic act. The inclusion of slaves and Indians in the text and the type of New World drama that it depicts are some of the themes that inform the creolization of the text and perhaps its reflection of an incipient Creole mentality. See Cintio Vitier's critical commentary in Balboa 1962; and López Segrera 1968, 34–44.

15. Representation of Don Joseph Espinoza de los Monteros and Carlos Ramos, Madrid, Nov. 17, 1784, C 5/83, fols. 654–75, AGI-SD 1629; Gregorio Cosme Osorio, Madrid, Jan. 14, 1785, "Pieza formada de las instancias hechas por Gregorio Cosme Osorio sobre libertad esclavos" (hereafter "Instancias Cosme Osorio"), C 9, AGI-SD 1627.

16. Memorial of Diego de Rosas, [Madrid, ca. 1709], "Demanda," C 23, fols. 3–5, AGI-ESC 93A.

17. Governor Barón de Chávez first stopped in Cartagena de Indias where he collected incriminating evidence against Governor Canales. Diego de Rosas may have made his trip to Madrid via Cartagena in the company of the governor. Canales, for instance, protested to the Crown that the Barón de Chávez had "instigated men of the lower life [*de mala vida*] to declare against me [in Cartagena] . . ." (Petition of Colonel Joseph Canales, [Santiago de Cuba, Jan. 1711], "Cargos," C 8, fols. 70–70v, AGI-ESC 92C).

18. The cobrero freedmen Gregorio Cosme Osorio and Carlos Ramos traveled in 1784 with false passports as employees or servants of their sponsor, a Spanish merchant from Havana (Representation of Don Joseph Espinoza de los Monteros and Carlos Ramos, Madrid, Nov. 17, 1784, "Pieza formada por instancias hechas por Joseph Espinoza sobre libertad esclavos" [hereafter "Instancias Espinoza"], AGI-SD 1627; Gregorio Cosme Osorio, Madrid, Jan. 14, 1785, "Instancias Cosme Osorio," C 9, fols. 53–54v; see also fols. 34–34v, AGI-SD 1627).

19. Letter of Father Juan Antonio Pérez, Santiago del Prado, Apr. 14, 1709, "Demanda," C 23, fols. 7–11, AGI-ESC 93A.

20. Justo Cruzata to Gregorio Cosme Osorio, Madrid, Dec. 27, 1795, C 135, AGI-SD 1627; Gregorio Cosme Osorio to Cobreros, Madrid, Oct. 6, 1795, AGI-SD 1631.

21. Gregorio Cosme Osorio to Cobreros, Madrid, [ca. Mar. 16, 1795], C 2/75/67, fol. 17, AGI-SD 1628.

22. Memorial of Diego de Rosas, [Madrid, ca. 1709], "Demanda," C 23, fols. 3–5, AGI-ESC 93A; Letter of Father Juan Antonio Pérez, Santiago del Prado, Apr. 14, 1709, "Demanda," C 23, fols. 7–11, AGI-ESC 93A.

23. Specifically other major charges included the prohibition of surface-mining activities, leaving the village's area to hunt, requisitions of cassava to supply El Morro garrison, the construction of a house for the governor in the pueblo and another for an *alférez* of Santiago de Cuba, see Representation of Don Bernardo Antonio Castillo, [ca. Nov. 1710–Mar. 1711], "Demanda," C 23, fols. 33–36v, AGI-ESC 93A. Governor Canales, in turn, defended himself of these charges by claiming that the cobreros defrauded the royal treasury with their small mining operations; that they left the village to hunt for long periods of time and were thus not available to work in the fortification projects; that the royal slaves had to be recruited to work by force; and that he had taken away their weapons "in order to punish them." As to the burning of the village houses, Canales stated that he had only burned one with a copper-smelting workshop. Interrogation of Colonel Joseph Canales, Santiago de Cuba, Dec. 17, 1710, "Cargos," C 8, fols. 28–30, AGI-ESC 92C.

24. With the exception of a few firearms, most of the cobreros' weapons consisted of *espadines*, machetes, and knives. A careful inventory was made of all the weapons and possessions confiscated. The total value claimed for the dispossessed goods amounted to the significant figure of 993 pesos ("Memoria de armas y herramientas," [ca. Nov. 1710–Mar. 1711], "Demanda," C 23, fols. 38–39v, AGI-ESC 93A). See also ibid., Representation of Don Bernardo Antonio Castillo, fols. 33–36v; and Auto Governor Luis Sañudo y Anaya, Santiago de Cuba, Mar. 6, 1711, "Demanda," C 23, fols. 50–51, AGI-ESC 93A.

25. Memorial of Diego de Rosas, [Madrid, ca. 1709], "Demanda," C 23, fols. 3–5, AGI-ESC 93A.

26. Ibid.

27. In her penetrating study of the peasant military colonies of the northern Mexican frontier, and particularly of Namiquipa, Alonso (1995, 35, 54–55) has remarked that individual as well as corporate rights were contingent on fighting against the Apache enemy and in defense of the state.

28. Petition of Colonel Canales, [Santiago de Cuba, ca. Jan. 1711], "Cargos," C 8, fols. 70–70v, AGI-ESC 92C.

29. Memorial of Diego de Rosas, [Madrid, ca. 1709], "Demanda," C 23, fols. 3–5, AGI-ESC 93A.

30. During Spain's War of Succession (1700–1713), the English backed the Austrian Archduke Charles III against the Bourbon Philip V. The Spanish conflict also had its political resonances in the colonial world. British propaganda circulated in Cuba throughout the war. In Havana the divisions penetrated the city's *cabildo*, and the partisans of Charles III had contacts with Jamaicans. In Havana and Santiago de Cuba there were manifestations of unrest supported by emissaries of the government of Jamaica (Marrero vol. 6:72–76). Former Governor Barón de Chávez was a supporter of the French Bourbons. Thus, at stake may have been political

accusations against Governor Canales for sympathies with Charles III and with the British.

31. Parry 1948, 35–39.

32. For the prevalence of contraband trade throughout the island, see Marrero vol. 7:170–96. Pérez (1988, 55) has suggested that as much as 45 percent of Cuban products left the island as contraband trade.

33. "Auto de cargos," Santiago de Cuba, Jan. 7, 1711, "Cargos," C 8, fols. 32–45v, AGI-ESC 92C.

34. Ibid.

35. Bacardí y Moreau 1973, 122. Former Governor Barón de Chávez had sponsored a major Franco-Spanish expedition to the Bahamas, particularly to the Providence Key (Marrero vol. 6:72).

36. Marrero vol. 7:173–74.

37. "Auto de cargos," Santiago de Cuba, Jan. 7, 1711, "Cargos," C 8, fols. 32–45v, AGI-ESC 92C.

38. On Governor Canales's acquittal in Spain, see Bacardí y Moreau 1973, 123. Denunciations of illicit trade with the French may have been unfounded or they may have fallen within an ambiguous category given the fact of the Franco-Spanish alliance during the Spanish War of Succession as Philip V had authorized limited commercial exchanges between the French and ports in the Indies (Marrero vol. 6:74 and vol. 7:174). For the different categories of contraband crimes and the ineffectual judicial processes against them, see Marrero vol. 7:171–74.

39. For an account of the "terrible ordeal" that these inquiries could become, particularly if the governor had offended powerful interests in his district, see Parry 1948, 74.

40. Bacardí y Moreau 1973, 123.

41. Petition of Cobreros to Captain General Don Juan Francisco Güemes y Horcacitas, [ca. 1734], "Autos 1735," fols. 658–65, AGI-SD 451.

42. Judge Chirino ordered the restitution of the cobreros' property and that Colonel Canales pay from his goods whatever was missing. He also determined, however, that Sergeant Ojeda's copper vat be embargoed pending the pueblo's payment of the litigation costs which amounted to 123 pesos and 7 reales. Chirino gave the cobreros four months to pay in order to recover the copper vat (assessed at 221 pesos and 5 reales). He also ordered the imposition of the *quinto* on the value of the vat. The amount remaining after these deductions should be returned to the vat's owner, Sergeant Ojeda. Chirino ordered the *cabildo* of Santiago de Cuba to make a demarcation of the pueblo's land (Provision of Judge Chirino, Santiago de Cuba, Nov. 21, 1711, fols. 155–57; and Assessment of Costs, "Demanda," C 23, fols. 168v–71v, both in AGI-ESC 93A).

43. Bacardí y Moreau 1973, 125–26. Governor Hoyos y Solórzano was deposed in a tumult in Puerto Príncipe while making an investigation in that town. He was imprisoned in El Morro in Havana for other accusations from the High Court of Santo Domingo, while awaiting orders from the Crown (Marrero vol. 7:179–81).

44. The King to Royal Officials of Santiago de Cuba; to Judge Juan García Chicano; and to Captain General [Güemes y Horcacitas], [Royal Edict], Madrid, Sept. 13, 1733, "Testimonio de varias copias de cédulas certificadas," AGI-SD 1627.

45. Cited in ibid., the King to Judge Juan García Chicano, [Royal Edict], Madrid, Sept. 13, 1733.

46. Cited in ibid., the King to Captain General [Güemes y Horcacitas], [Royal Edict], Madrid, Sept. 13, 1733.

47. Stern (1982, 119–21) has noted the significance of cleavages in the state and among elite sectors of colonial society for Indians in Huamanga, Peru.

48. Haring 1975, 131.

49. In 1702, the lieutenant of the Indian militia company of Jiguaní went in representation of the community to litigate community boundaries; in 1727, the community sent two representatives, Francisco Rodríguez and Ignacio Dieguez. In 1782, a Fonseca was turned back in Baracoa but apparently managed to embark in 1784 or 1785 (Dossier of Land Claims of Jiguaní, AGI-SD 1617; see also Marrero vol. 6:149–50, 168).

50. It is difficult to trace, through existing records, any direct line of descent for Matías Moreno from Captain Juan Moreno. The two leaders, however, may have been related because they carried the same surname and were probably part of the same local lineage.

51. The cited descriptions of the paths from Santiago de Cuba to Baracoa were made by Bishop Morell de Santa Cruz in his pastoral visit to that city in 1756 (published in García del Pino 1985, 119, 124).

52. Testimony of Captain Simón Mascarreñas, Santiago de Cuba, Aug. 20, 1731, [C 1, Autos Sucre], fols. 20–22v, AGI-SD 493.

53. Ibid.

54. Ibid.

55. Bacardí y Moreau 1973, 125–26; Marrero vol. 7:179–81.

56. Cobreros to Governor Ximénez, [ca. July–Aug. 1731], [C 2, Autos 1731], fols. 33v–34, AGI-SD 493.

57. The transgressions included disruption of the established corvée labor regime, the refusal to recognize the community's *cabildo*, the taxation of copper mining, and the prohibition to buy meat, among others (Crown Attorney's Summary, Madrid, June 3, 1732, AGI-SD 493; see also Chapters 8 and 9 in this volume).

58. These relations have been studied in particular in the fields of Latin American studies and anthropology (Strickton and Greenfield 1979; Forman, Shepard, and Riegelhaupt 1979). For a historical approach to the study of patronage in nineteenth-century Brazil, see Graham 1990. For a political scientist's approach to patron-client relations in Southeast Asia, see J. Scott 1972.

59. Letter to Governor Sucre, [El Cobre, ca. 1731], AGI-SD 493. Given Sucre's incommunicado state in the vaults of the Morro Castle, is not clear how the cobreros were able to give him the note. The only mention made is to a slave boy delivering the note. Perhaps the boy brought the note along with food or goods that the imprisoned governor could receive as gifts to sustain himself in prison (Investigation of Governor Ximénez, Santiago de Cuba, Oct. 15, 1731, AGI-SD 493). For further references to royal edicts, see documents in Appendixes 5 and 6.

60. During his four years of imprisonment, Sucre allegedly "had to feed himself from the charity of the Captains of the Garrison," so that gifts from former "clients" or protégés may have been expected and welcomed (The King to Royal Officials of

Santiago de Cuba, [Royal Edict], Madrid, Sept. 13, 1733, "Testimonio de varias copias de cédulas certificadas," AGI-SD 1627).

61. The provision of 1721 referred to another episode of conflict that had occurred in the early 1720s and of which little is known. The conflict was related to the Crown's attempt to subcontract the mines to Don Joseph Delgado, a *vecino* of Santiago de Cuba and a royal official. The adjusted provisions of the contract eventually led Delgado to retreat (Díaz 1992).

62. Letters from the parish priest, Dean Morell de Santa Cruz, and the captain general of Havana were sent to Madrid blaming the governor for the revolt in the face of his abuses or breaches of custom. These letters also included denunciations against the imprisonment and treatment of former Governor Sucre, thereby linking these events as manifestations of Ximénez's excesses (Crown Attorney's Summary, Madrid, June 3, 1732, AGI-SD 493).

63. Royal Edict of Sept. 3, 1733, Madrid, "Autos 1735," fols. 670–72v, AGI-SD 451.

64. Cobreros to Dean Morell de Santa Cruz, [ca. Oct. 21–26, 1735], "Diligencias 1735," fols. 817v–18v, AGI-SD 451.

65. Cobreros to Governor Ximénez, [ca. July–Aug. 1731], [C 2, Autos 1731], fol. 39, AGI-SD 493. See letter 2 in Appendix 5.

66. Petition of Cobreros to the Captain General, [ca. 1735], "Autos 1735," fols. 710–17v/54–61v, AGI-SD 451.

67. Report of Governor Ximénez, Aug. 18, 1734, cited in Marrero vol. 6:41–42.

68. There is some indication that they were prepared to send the cobrero Phelipe Vicente as their emissary to Spain. Although Vicente was absent from the village and living in Sancti Espíritu, his ties to the pueblo (or to his *local patria*) presumably obligated him to make this difficult trip on their behalf (Testimony of Phelipe Gutiérrez, [ca. Nov. 17, 1731], [C 2, Autos 1731], fols. 50v–52v, AGI-SD 493).

69. Ibid. See also Chapter 10 in this volume. Litigation costs to the pueblo during Judge Chirino's investigation ran into 123 pesos and 7 reales. The cobreros were given four months to pay ("Demanda," C 23, fols. 171–71v, AGI-ESC 93A).

70. Petition of Cobreros to the Captain General, [ca. 1735], "Autos 1735," fols. 710–17v/54–61v, AGI-SD 451. The cobreros listed as cases of harassment the closing of the road to Santiago de Cuba and prohibitions to travel to that city to buy and sell provisions and to seek medical help. They also denounced the governor's arrest of several cobreros living both in that city and on their farms.

71. Ibid.

72. Bacardí y Moreau 1973, 131, 133. Ximénez was strongly reprimanded, partly because of the imprisonment of Sucre and the other denunciations related to his policies toward the cobreros (Crown Attorney's Summary, Madrid, June 3, 1732, AGI-SD 493).

73. On the cobreros' refusal to return to work until they got the land they needed, see Chapter 9 in this volume, which deals with labor conflict. See also letter 1 in Appendix 5.

74. Testimony of Alcalde Patricio Cosme, [Autos 1737], fol. 97, AGI-SD 451. For a further discussion of community conflict with *cabildo* officials, and their alliance to local bad government, see Chapter 10 in this volume.

75. Correspondence between Lieutenant Nicholás Velasco Calderín and Governor Ximénez, Apr. 25–28, 1737, [Autos 1737], fols. 79–92, AGI-SD 451; see particularly fol. 87v.

76. Captain General Güemes y Horcacitas, Havana, Nov. 4, 1737, AGI-SD 451. For a listing of the convicted cobreros exiled to Cartagena and Mexico, see the Family Census of 1739, AGI-SD 385.

77. Petition of the Pueblo del Cobre to the King, Nov. 19, 1738, AGI-SD 426.

78. Stationed soldiers in the village were demanding the payment of 1 real from those who could not comply. During their revolt in 1731, the cobreros denounced this abuse against males in the labor squadrons (see Chapter 9 in this volume).

79. Petition of the Pueblo del Cobre to the King, Nov. 19, 1738, AGI-SD 426. See Chapter 8 in this volume, for another important excerpt of this document and for further discussion of the relation of these practices to the forced trade of copper.

80. The cobreros petitioned easy terms for their *coartación* in case they were not to receive the grant of Barajagua that they were requesting (Petition of Cobreros to Captain General Güemes y Horcacitas, [ca. 1734], "Autos 1735," fols. 658–65/3–9v, AGI-SD 451). See Appendix 6.

81. See Table 9 in Chapter 9 in this volume.

82. Governor Cagigal de la Vega, Aug. 17, 1739, cited in Marrero vol. 7:31. A belated royal edict of Dec. 20, 1740, approved the repression against the cobreros, including the exile and deportation of thirty-six to Peru and New Spain (Franco 1975, 48–49).

83. For the inscription of many of these same convicted men in the village census living with their families, see Family Census of 1750, AGI-SD 1630. A few were marked *ausentes*; others whose names could not be found in the family census may have either died or may have remained in exile.

84. For another case in which (elite white) participants in a tumult were punished by exile (in this case, to the North African presidio of Ceuta, to Spain, and elsewhere in Cuba), but years later were allowed to return to their hometown of Puerto Príncipe, see Marrero vol. 7:181–84.

85. Gregorio Cosme Osorio to the Cobreros, Madrid, Oct. 6, 1795, C 75, fol. 217, AGI-SD 1629.

86. Gregorio Cosme Osorio to the Cobreros, Madrid, Mar. 16, 1795, C 2/75/67, fol. 16v, AGI-SD 1628.

EPILOGUE

Epigraph. Report of Governor Cayetano de Urbina, Santiago de Cuba, Feb. 1846, AHN-Ultramar 4638(2).

1. Royal Edict, Aranjuez, Apr. 7, 1800, reproduced in Franco 1975, 133–45. See also Royal Council's Resolution, Madrid, Dec. 21, 1799, Doc. 3, AGI-SD 1627.

2. Ibid.

3. Report of Don Mateo Echevarría, Madrid, Oct. 13, 1818, AGI-SD 1158.

4. Report of Governor Cayetano Urbina, Santiago de Cuba, Feb. 1846, AHN-Ultramar 4638(2).

5. Several British and Spanish companies established themselves in El Cobre in the 1830s. The British Compañía Consolidada de Minas del Cobre (1835) and the Real de Santiago (1836) employed more than 800 and 500 people, respectively; the Spanish firm San José (1836) employed 450 operators (Report of Cayetano de Urbina, Santiago de Cuba, Feb. 1846, AHN-Ultramar 4638[2]).

6. See epigraph to this chapter (Report of Governor Urbina, Santiago de Cuba, Feb. 1846, AHN-Ultramar 4638[2]).

7. North American mining companies did not arrive in El Cobre until the turn of the twentieth century, during the U.S. occupation of Cuba (Portuondo Zúñiga 1995, 241–44).

8. By 1843, the population of El Cobre totaled 4,636 souls: 881 whites (19 percent); 2,134 freemen of color (46 percent); and 1,621 slaves (35 percent) (Report of the Intendancy of Santiago de Cuba, Jan. 26, 1843, AHN-Ultramar 6[2]). Another report made in 1846 stated that there were more than 5,400 souls in the villa of El Cobre of which 3,000 were employed in the mines (Report of Governor Cayetano de Urbina, Santiago de Cuba, Feb. 1846, AHN-Ultramar 4638[2]).

9. González Loscertales and Roldán de Montaud 1980, 294–95.

10. Abdala Pupo 1993.

11. Representation of Vecinos of El Cobre, El Cobre, May 4, 1841, AHN-Ultramar 4613.

12. Report of Joaquín Gasene, Feb. 30, 1838, AHN-Ultramar 4613.

13. González Loscertales and Roldán de Montaud 1980, 293–99; Portuondo Zúñiga 1995, 220. In the early twentieth century, a new round of conflict erupted with the forces of modernity embodied by North American mining companies (Portuondo Zúñiga 1995, 241–44).

14. The story of the profound transformations brought about on the island with the sugar revolution has been poignantly recounted by Knight 1970; Cepero Bonilla 1948; Moreno Fraginals 1978; and R. Scott 1985, among others.

15. In his recent visit to Cuba, the Pope crowned the image of the Virgin "Queen of all Cubans." The Virgin of Charity had already been declared official patroness of the Cuban nation in 1916 (Portuondo Zúñiga 1995, 245). For the extension of that symbolism into the Cuban exile community in Miami, see Tweed 1997.

16. References in these closing lines are to García Márquez 1967; Chaimoiseau 1997; González Echevarría 1990; and Benítez Rojo 1989.

Works Cited

Abdala Pupo, Oscar Luis. 1993. "Los primeros culíes chinos en Santiago de Cuba." *Del Caribe* 21: 88–94.

Adorno, Rolena. 1988. *Guaman Poma: Writing and Resistance in Colonial Peru.* Austin: University of Texas Press.

Alonso, Ana María. 1995. *Thread of Blood: Colonialism, Revolution, and Gender on Mexico's Northern Frontier.* Tucson: University of Arizona Press.

Anderson, Benedict R. 1983. *Imagined Communities: Reflections on the Origin and Spread of Nationalism.* London: Verso.

Arrate y Acosta, José Martín Félix de. [1830] 1964. *Llave del Nuevo Mundo, antemural de las Indias Occidentales.* 4th ed. Havana: Comisión Nacional Cubana de la UNESCO.

Arrom, Juan J. [1959] 1971. "La Virgen del Cobre: historia, leyenda y símbolo sincrético." In *Certidumbre de América: estudios de letras, folklore y cultura,* 184–214. Madrid: Editorial Gredos, S.A.

Arrom, Silvia M. 1985. *The Women of Mexico City.* Stanford, Calif.: Stanford University Press.

Bacardí y Moreau, Emilio. 1973. *Crónicas de Santiago de Cuba.* 2d ed. Madrid: Breogán, I.G. S.A.

Bakhtin, Michael. 1981. *The Dialogic Imagination.* Austin: University of Texas Press.

Balboa Troya y Quesada, Silvestre de. [1608] 1962. *Espejo de Paciencia.* Facsimile and Critical Commentary by Cintio Vitier. Havana: Comisión Nacional Cubana de la UNESCO.

Barnet, Miguel. 1968. *Biografía de un cimarrón.* Barcelona: Ediciones Ariel. (Published in English as *Autobiography of a Runaway Slave.*)

Barreda, Pedro. 1979. *The Black Protagonist in the Cuban Novel.* Amherst: University of Massachusetts Press.

Barrett, Elinore M. 1987. *The Mexican Colonial Copper Industry.* Albuquerque: University of New Mexico Press.

Beckles, Hilary McD. 1989. *Natural Rebels: A Social History of Enslaved Black Women in Barbados.* New Brunswick, N.J.: Rutgers University Press.

Benítez Rojo, Antonio. 1989. *La isla que se repite: El Caribe y la perspectiva posmoderna.* Hanover, N.H.: Ediciones del Norte.

Bergad, Leird. 1990. *Cuban Rural Society in the Nineteenth Century: The Social and Economic History of Monoculture in Matanzas.* Princeton, N.J.: Princeton University Press.

Works Cited

————, Fé Iglesias García, and María del Carmen Barcia. 1995. *The Cuban Slave Market, 1790–1880*. London: Cambridge University Press.

Berlin, Ira, and Philip D. Morgan, eds. 1993. *Cultivation and Culture: Labor and the Shaping of Slave Life in the Americas*. Charlottesville: University Press of Virginia.

Besson, Jean. 1984. "Family Land and Caribbean Society: Toward an Ethnography of Afro-Caribbean Peasantries." In E. M. Thomas-Hope, ed., *Perspectives on Caribbean Regional Identity*. Liverpool, Eng.: University of Liverpool Centre for Latin American Studies.

Blanes Martín, Tamara. 1987. "Estudio comparativo de tres Castillos del Morro en el Caribe." *Del Caribe* 7: 64–74.

Blassingame, John W. 1972. *The Slave Community: Plantation Life in the Antebellum South*. Oxford: Oxford University Press.

Borah, Woodrow W. 1983. *Justice by Insurance: The General Indian Court of Colonial Mexico and the Legal Aides of the Half-real*. Berkeley and Los Angeles: University of California Press.

Bourdieu, Pierre. 1997. *Outline of a Theory of Practice*. Cambridge: Cambridge University Press.

Brading, David. 1985. *Los orígenes del nacionalismo mexicano*. 3d ed. Mexico: Ediciones Era.

Brathwaite, Edward. 1971. *Creole Society*. Oxford, Eng.: Clarendon Press.

Bravo, Julián Joseph. 1766. "Aparición prodigiosa de la Ynclita Ymagen de la Caridad que se venera en Santiago del Prado y Real de Minas de Cobre." Unpublished manuscript.

Bush, Barbara. 1989. *Slave Women in British Caribbean Society: 1650–1832*. London: Currey.

Bush, M. L., ed. 1996. *Serfdom and Slavery: Studies in Legal Bondage*. New York: London and Longman.

Cabrera, Lydia. 1980. *Yemayá y Ochún Kariochas, Iyalorichas, y Olorichas*. New York: Colección del Chicheruká en el Exilio.

Calhoun, Craig, Edward Lipuma, and Moishe Postone, eds. 1993. *Bourdieu: Critical Perspectives*. Chicago: University of Chicago Press.

Canny, Nicholas, and Anthony Pagden, eds. 1987. *Colonial Identity in the Atlantic World, 1500–1800*. Princeton, N.J.: Princeton University Press.

Carpentier, Alejo. [1946] 1972. *La música en Cuba*. 2d ed. Mexico: Fondo de Cultura Económica, Colección Popular.

Cepero Bonilla, Raúl. 1948. *Azúcar y abolición: Apuntes para una historia crítica del abolicionismo*. Havana: Editorial Cenit.

Chaimoiseau, Patrick. 1997. *Texaco*. New York: Pantheon.

Christian, William A., Jr. 1981a. *Apparitions in Late Medieval and Renaissance Spain*. Princeton, N.J.: Princeton University Press.

————. 1981b. *Local Religion in Sixteenth Century Spain*. Princeton, N.J.: Princeton University Press.

————. 1987. "Tapping and Defining New Power: The First Month of the Visions at Ezquioga, July 1931." *American Ethnologist* 14: 140–66.

————. 1989. *Person and God in a Spanish Valley*. 2d ed. New York: Seminar Press.

———. 1996. *Visionaries: The Spanish Republic and the Reign of Christ*. Berkeley and Los Angeles: University of California Press.

Clarke, Edith. [1953] 1971. "Land Tenure and the Family in Four Selected Communities in Jamaica." In Michael M. Horowitz, ed., *Peoples and Cultures of the Caribbean*, 201–42. Garden City, N.Y.: Natural History Press.

———. 1957. *My Mother Who Fathered Me*. London: George Allen and Unwin Ltd.

Clifford, James, and George Marcus, eds. 1986. *Writing Culture: The Poetics and Politics of Ethnography*. Berkeley and Los Angeles: University of California Press.

Cohen, Bernard S. 1981. "Anthropology and History in the 1980s." *Journal of Interdisciplinary History* 12: 227–52.

Cohen, David W., and Jack P. Greene, eds. 1972. *Neither Slave Nor Free: The Freedmen of African Descent in the Slave Societies of the New World*. Baltimore, Md.: Johns Hopkins University Press.

Comaroff, Jean. 1985. *Body of Power, Spirit of Resistance*. Chicago: University of Chicago Press.

Comaroff, Jean, and John Comaroff. 1991. *Of Revelation and Revolution: Christianity, Colonialism, and Consciousness in South Africa*. Vol. 1. Chicago: University of Chicago Press.

———. 1997. *Of Revelation and Revolution: The Dialectics of Modernity on a South African Frontier*. Vol. 2. Chicago: University of Chicago Press.

Corbea Calzado, Julio. 1993a. ed. 1993. "Anécdotas sobre la Virgen de la Caridad del Cobre." *Del Caribe* 21: 86–87.

———. 1996. "La Virgen de la Caridad del Cobre: construcción simbólica y cultura popular." *Del Caribe* 25: 4–11.

Cortés López, José Luis. 1989. *La esclavitud negra en la España peninsular del siglo XVI*. Salamanca: Ediciones Universidad de Salamanca.

Corwin, Arthur F. 1967. *Spain and the Abolition of Slavery in Cuba 1817–1886*. Austin: University of Texas Press.

Craton, Michael. 1978. *Searching for the Invisible Man: Slaves and Plantation Life in Jamaica*. Cambridge, Mass.: Harvard University Press.

Crosby, Alfred. 1972. *The Columbian Exchange: Biological and Cultural Consequences of 1492*. Westport, Conn.: Greenwood Publishing Co.

Cutter, Charles R. 1986. *The Protector of Indios in Colonial New Mexico, 1659–1821*. Albuquerque: University of New Mexico Press.

———. 1995. *The Legal Culture of Northern New Spain, 1700–1810*. Albuquerque: University of New Mexico Press.

Dean, Caroline S. 1993. "The Renewal of Old World Images and the Creation of Colonial Peruvian Visual Culture." Essay for exhibition "Creating the New World: Spanish Colonial Art in the Americas." The Brooklyn Museum, New York.

Deive, Carlos Esteban. 1980. *La esclavitud del negro en Santo Domingo, 1492–1844*. Santo Domingo: Museo del Hombre Dominicano.

Dening, Greg. 1991. "A Poetic for Histories: Transformations that Present the Past." In A. Biersack, ed., *Clio in Oceania: Toward a Historical Anthropology*, 347–80. Washington, D.C.: Smithsonian Institution Press.

Deschamps-Chapeaux, Pedro. 1971. *El negro en la economía habanera del siglo XIX.* Havana: Instituto Cubano del Libro.

———. 1976. *Los batallones de pardos y morenos libres.* Havana: Editorial Arte y Literatura.

Díaz, María Elena. 1992. "Constituting Identity: Sociocultural Changes in a Black Colonial Village (El Cobre, Cuba, 1670–1800). Ph.D. diss. University of Texas at Austin.

Domínguez Ortiz, Antonio. 1952. "La esclavitud en Castilla durante la edad moderna." *Estudios de historia social de España.*

Duharte Jiménez, Rafael. 1993. "El Cobre: historia, mito y leyenda." *Del Caribe* 21: 76–78.

Farriss, Nancy M. 1984. *Maya Society Under Colonial Rule: The Collective Enterprise of Survival.* Princeton, N.J.: Princeton University Press.

Figarola, Joel James. 1997. "Impedir el olvido es una necesidad de todos los oprimidos: palabras pronunciadas en la inaguración del Monumento al Cimarrón." *Del Caribe* 27: 80–82.

Forman, Shepard, and Joyce F. Riegelhaupt. 1979. "The Political Economy of Patron-Clientship: Brazil and Portugal Compared." In Maxine Margolis and William E. Carter, eds., *Brazil: Anthropological Perspectives*, 379–400. New York: Columbia University Press.

Franco, Luciano. 1975. *Las minas de Santiago del Prado y la rebelión de los cobreros, 1530–1800.* Havana: Editorial de Ciencias Sociales.

García del Pino, César, ed. 1985. *La visita eclesiástica.* Havana: Editorial Ciencias Sociales.

García Márquez, Gabriel. 1967. *Cien Años de Soledad.* Buenos Aires: Editorial Sudamericana, S.A.

Gaspar, David Barry. 1985. *Bondmen and Rebels: A Case Study of Master-Slave Relations in Antigua, with Implications for Colonial British America.* Baltimore, Md.: Johns Hopkins University Press.

Gibson, Charles. 1964. *The Aztecs Under Spanish Rule: A History of the Indians of the Valley of Mexico.* Stanford, Calif.: Stanford University Press.

González Echevarría, Roberto. 1990. *Myth and Archive: A Theory of Latin American Narrative.* Cambridge: Cambridge University Press.

González Loscertales, Vicente, and Inés Roldán de Montaud. 1980. "La minería del cobre en Cuba. Su organización, problemas administrativos y repercusiones sociales (1828–1849)." *Revista de Indias* no. 159–62 (Jan.): 255–99.

Goveia, Elsa. 1965. *Slave Society in the British Islands at the End of the Eighteenth Century.* New Haven, Conn.: Yale University Press.

Graham, Richard. 1990. *Patronage and Politics in Nineteenth-Century Brazil.* Stanford, Calif.: Stanford University Press.

Granda, Germán de. 1983. "Orígen, función y estructura de un pueblo de negros y mulatos libres en el Paraguay del siglo XVIII (San Agustín de la Emboscada)." *Revista de Indias* no. 43: 229–64.

Gruzinski, Serge. 1993. *The Conquest of Mexico: The Incorporation of Indian Societies into the Western World, 16th to 18th Centuries.* Cambridge, Eng.: Polity Press.

————. 1989. *Man-Gods in the Mexican Highlands: Indian Power and Colonial Society, 1520–1800*. Stanford, Calif.: Stanford University Press.

Guerra y Sánchez, Ramiro. [1944] 1976. *Azácar y población en las Antillas*. Havana: Editorial de Ciencias Sociales.

————, ed. 1952. *Historia de la nación cubana*. 10 vols. Havana: Editorial Historia de la Nación Cubana.

Gutiérrez, Ramón A. 1991. *When Jesus Came the Corn Mothers Went Away: Marriage, Sexuality, and Power in New Mexico, 1500–1846*. Stanford, Calif.: Stanford University Press.

Gutman, Herbert G. 1976. *The Black Family in Slavery and Freedom, 1750–1925*. New York: Vintage Books.

Hall, Gwendolyn M. 1972. "Saint Domingue." In David W. Cohen and Jack P. Greene, eds., *Neither Slave Nor Free*, 172–92. Baltimore: Johns Hopkins University Press.

————. 1992. *Africans in Colonial Louisiana: The Development of Afro-Creole Culture in the 18th Century*. Baton Rouge: Louisiana State University.

Haring, C. H. 1947. *The Spanish Empire in America*. New York: Oxford University Press.

Haskett, Robert S. 1987. "Indian Town Government in Colonial Cuernavaca: Persistence, Adaptation, and Change." *Hispanic American Historical Review* 67: 203–31.

————. 1991. *Indigenous Rulers: An Ethnohistory of Town Government in Colonial Cuernavaca*. Albuquerque: University of New Mexico Press.

Helg, Aline. 1995. *Our Rightful Share: The Afro-Cuban Struggle for Equality, 1886–1912*. Chapel Hill: University of North Carolina Press.

Herbert, Eugenia W. 1984. *Red Gold of Africa: Copper in Pre-Colonial History and Culture*. Madison: University of Wisconsin Press.

Hernández, Jorge Luis. 1993. "Una visita a El Cobre en marzo de 1993." *Del Caribe* 21: 95–109.

Herr, Richard. 1989. *Rural Change and Royal Finances in Spain at the End of the Old Regime*. Berkeley and Los Angeles: University of California Press.

Higman, Barry W. 1976. *Slave Population and Economy in Jamaica 1807–1834*. Cambridge: Cambridge University Press.

Hilton, Anne. 1985. *The Kingdom of Congo*. Oxford, Eng.: Clarendon Press.

Hobsbawm, Eric J., and Terence Ranger, eds. 1984. *The Invention of Tradition*. Cambridge: Cambridge University Press.

Horowitz, Michael M., ed. 1971. *Peoples and Cultures of the Caribbean*. Garden City, N.Y.: Natural History Press.

Howard, Philip A. 1998. *Changing History: Afro-Cuban Cabildos and Societies of Color in the Nineteenth Century*. Baton Rouge: Louisiana State University Press.

Hunefeldt, Christine. 1994. *Paying the Price of Freedom: Family and Labor Among Lima's Slaves, 1800–1854*. Berkeley and Los Angeles: University of California Press.

Inglis, Gordon Douglas. 1979. "Historical Demography of Colonial Cuba, 1492–1780." Ph.D. diss. Texas Christian University.

Kagan, Richard L. 1981. *Lawsuits and Litigants in Castile, 1500–1700.* Chapel Hill: University of North Carolina Press.

Karash, Mary C. 1987. *Slave Life in Rio de Janeiro, 1808–1850.* Princeton, N.J.: Princeton University Press.

———. 1998. "Queens and Judges: Afro-Brazilian Women in the Lay Brotherhoods of Central Brazil." Unpublished paper delivered at the 1998 meeting of the Latin American Association, Chicago.

Kiple, Kenneth F. 1976. *Blacks in Colonial Cuba, 1774–1899.* Gainesville: University Presses of Florida.

Klein, Herbert S. 1966. "The Colored Militia of Cuba: 1568–1868." *Caribbean Studies* 6, no. 2: 17–27.

———. [1967] 1989. *Slavery in the Americas: A Comparative Study of Virginia and Cuba.* Chicago: Elephant Paperbacks, Ivan R. Dee, Inc.

Kleinberg, Aviad M. 1992. *Prophets in their Own Country: Living Saints and the Making of Sainthood in the Later Middle Ages.* Chicago: University of Chicago Press.

Knight, Franklin W. 1970. *Slave Society in Nineteenth Century Cuba.* Madison: University of Wisconsin Press.

———. 1972. "Cuba." In David W. Cohen and Jack P. Greene, eds., *Neither Slave Nor Free: The Freedmen of African Descent in the Slave Societies of the New World.* Baltimore, Md.: Johns Hopkins University Press.

Kuethe, Allan J. 1971. "The Status of the Free Pardo in the Disciplined Militia of New Granada." *Journal of Negro History* 56 (Apr.): 105–15.

———. 1986. *Cuba: 1753–1815: Crown, Military, and Society.* Knoxville: University of Tennessee Press.

Lachatañeré, Rómulo. 1939. "El sistema religioso de los lucumís y otras influencias africanas en Cuba." *Estudios afrocubanos.* Vol. 3. Havana.

———. [1936] 1993. "La religión santera y el milagro de la Caridad del Cobre." *Del Caribe* 21: 79–81.

Lafaye, Jacques. 1976. *Quetzalcoatl and Guadalupe: The Formation of Mexican National Consciousness, 1531–1813.* Chicago: University of Chicago Press.

Lago Vieito, Angel. 1996. "El espiritismo de cordón en el Bayamo colonial." *Del Caribe* 25: 16–19.

Lander, Jane. 1990. "Gracia Real de Santa Teresa de Mose: A Free Black Town in Spanish Colonial Florida." *American Historical Review* 95: 9–30.

Lauderdale-Graham, Sandra. [1988] 1992. *House and Street: The Domestic World of Servants and Masters in Nineteenth-Century Rio de Janeiro.* Austin: University of Texas Press.

Le Riverend, Julio. 1967. *Historia económica de Cuba.* Havana: Instituto del Libro.

———. 1992. *La Habana. Espacio y vida.* Madrid: Editorial Maptre.

Lockhart, James, and Stuart B. Schwartz. 1983. *Early Latin America: A History of Colonial Spanish America and Brazil.* New York: Cambridge University Press.

Lopéz, Segrera, Francisco. 1968. *Los orígenes de la cultura cubana, 1510–1790.* Havana: Unión de Escritores y Artistas de Cuba.

Love, Edgar F. 1967. "Negro Resistance to Spanish Rule." *Journal of Negro History* 52: 89–103.

MacCormack, Sabine. 1984. "From the Sun of the Incas to the Virgin of Copacabana." *Representations* (Fall) 8: 30–59.

Macías Domínguez, Isabelo. 1978. *Cuba en la primera mitad del siglo XVII*. Seville: Escuela de Estudios Hispano-Americanos.

Manning, Patrick. 1990. *Slavery and African Life: Occidental, Oriental, and African Slave Trades*. New York: Cambridge University Press.

Manzano, Juan Francisco. [1840; 1937] 1995. *Autobiography of a Slave/Autobiografía de un esclavo*. Bilingual edition by Ivan A. Schulman. Detroit, Mich.: Wayne State University Press.

Marrero, Leví. 1972–1988. *Cuba: economía y sociedad*. 14 vols. Río Piedras: Editorial San Juan.

———. 1980. Los esclavos y la Virgen del Cobre: dos siglos de lucha por la libertad de Cuba. Miami: Ediciones Universal.

Marshall, Woodville K. 1993. "Provision Ground and Plantation Labor in Four Windward Islands." In Ira Berlin and Philip D. Morgan, eds., *Cultivation and Culture: Labor and the Shaping of Slave Life in the Americas*, 203–20. Charlottesville: University Press of Virginia.

Martínez Alier, Verena. 1974. *Marriage, Class and Colour in Nineteenth Century Cuba*. Cambridge: Cambridge University Press.

Marzahl, Peter. 1978. *Town in the Empire: Government, Politics, and Society in Seventeenth Century Popayán*. Austin, Tx.: Institute of Latin American Studies.

McAlister, Lyle N. 1957. *The "Fuero Militar" in New Spain, 1764–1800*. Gainesville, Fla.: University of Florida Press.

McCarthy Brown, Karen. 1994. *Mama Lola: A Vodou Priestess in Brooklyn*. Berkeley and Los Angeles: University of California Press.

McDonald, Roderick A. 1993. "Independent Economic Production by Slaves in Antebellum Louisiana Sugar Plantations." In Ira Berlin and Philip D. Morgan, eds., *Cultivation and Culture: Labor and the Shaping of Slave Life in the Americas*, 275–99. Charlottesville: University Press of Virginia.

Medina San Román, María del Carmen. 1997. "Votive Art: Miracles of Two Thousand Years." In Marion Oettinger Jr., ed., *Folk Art of the Americas*. San Antonio, Tx.: San Antonio Museum of Art.

Meiklejohn, Norman A. 1974. "The Implementation of Slave Legislation in Eighteenth-Century New Granada." In Robert B. Toplin, ed., *Slavery and Race Relations in Latin America*, 176–203. Westport, Conn.: Greenwood Press.

———. 1971. "The Observance of Negro Slave Legislation in Colonial Nueva Granada." Ph.D. diss. Columbia University.

Meillassoux, Claude. 1991. *The Anthropology of Slavery: The Womb of Iron and Gold*. Chicago: University of Chicago Press.

Merry, Sally Engle. 1991. "Law and Colonialism: Review Essay." *Law and Society Review* 25:889–992.

Metcalfe, Alida C. 1992. *Family and Frontier in Colonial Brazil: Santana de Parnaíba, 1580–1822*. Berkeley and Los Angeles: University of California Press.

Mihelic Pulsipher, Lydia. 1993. "Changing Roles in the Life Cycles of Women in Traditional West Indian Houseyards." In J. H. Momsen, ed., *Women and Change in the Caribbean*, 50–64. Bloomington: Indiana University Press.

Miller, Joseph C. 1988. *Way of Death: Merchant Capitalism and the Angolan Slave Trade, 1730–1830*. Madison: University of Wisconsin Press.

Millet, José. 1993. "La virgen de la Caridad y el espiritismo." *Del Caribe* 21: 82–85.

Mintz, Sidney W. 1960. *Worker in the Cane*. New Haven, Conn.: Yale University Press.

———. 1974. *Caribbean Transformations*. Chicago: Aldine Publishing Co.

———. 1995. "Slave Life on Caribbean Plantations: Some Unanswered Questions." In Stephen Palmié, ed., *Slave Cultures and the Cultures of Slavery*, 12–22. Knoxville: University of Tennessee Press.

———, and Douglas Hall. 1960. "The Origins of the Jamaican Internal Market System." In *Papers in Caribbean Anthropology*, 57: 3–26. New Haven, Conn.: Yale University Press.

Momsen, Janet H., ed. 1992. *Women and Change in the Caribbean*. Bloomington: Indiana University Press.

Moreno Fraginals, Manuel. 1977 "Aportes culturales y deculturación." In Manuel Moreno Fraginals, ed., *Africa en América Latina*, 13–33. UNESCO Series "El Mundo en América Latina." Mexico: Siglo Veintiuno Editores, S.A.

———. 1978. *El ingenio: el complejo económico social cubano del azúcar*. 3 vols. Havana: Editorial de Ciencias Sociales.

Morrissey, Marietta. 1989. *Slave Women in the New World: Gender Stratification in the Caribbean*. Lawrence: University Press of Kansas.

Mulvey, Patricia A. 1976. "The Black Lay Brotherhoods of Colonial Brazil: A History." Ph.D. diss. City University of New York.

Nishida, Mioko. 1998. "From Ethnicity to Race and Gender: Transformations of Black Lay Sodalities in Salvador, Brazil." *Journal of Social History* 32:329–48.

Oettinger, Marion Jr., ed. 1997. *Folk Art of the Americas*. San Antonio, Tx.: San Antonio Museum of Art.

Orsi, Robert A. 1985. *The Madonna of 115th Street: Faith and Community in Italian Harlem, 1880–1950*. New Haven, Conn.: Yale University Press.

Ortiz, Altagracia. 1983. *Eighteenth-Century Reforms in the Caribbean: Miguel de Muesas, Governor of Puerto Rico, 1769–76*. Rutherford, N.J.: Fairleigh Dickinson University Press.

Ortiz, Fernando. [1940] 1963. *Contrapunteo cubano del tabaco y el azúcar*. Las Villas, Cuba: Universidad Central de las Villas.

———. [1947] 1995. *Cuban Counterpoint of Tobacco and Sugar*. Durham, N.C.: Duke University Press.

———. [1921] 1984a. "Los cabildos afrocubanos." In *Ensayos etnográficos: Fernando Ortiz*, 11–40. Havana: Editorial de Ciencias Sociales.

———. [1920] 1984b. "La antigua fiesta afrocubana del Día de Reyes." In *Ensayos etnográficos: Fernando Ortiz*, 41–84. Havana: Editorial de Ciencias Sociales.

———. 1975. *Historia de una pelea cubana contra los demonios*. Havana: Editorial Ciencias Sociales.

Ots y Capolequi, José María. 1969. *Historia del Derecho español en América y del Derecho indiano*. Madrid: Editorial Aguilar.

Palmer, Colin A. 1976. *Slaves of the White God: Blacks in Mexico, 1570–1650*. Cambridge, Mass.: Harvard University Press.

Paquette, Robert L. 1988. *Sugar Is Made with Blood: The Conspiracy of La Escalera and Conflict Between Empires over Slavery in Cuba*. Middletown, Conn.: Wesleyan University Press.

Parry, J. H. 1948. *The Audiencia of New Galicia in the Sixteenth Century: A Study in Spanish Colonial Government*. Cambridge: Cambridge University Press.

Patterson, Orlando. 1982. *Slavery and Social Death: A Comparative Study*. Cambridge, Mass.: Harvard University Press.

Paz y Ascanio, Chaplain Alejandro de. [1829] 1853. *Historia de la aparición milagrosa de Nuestra Señora de la Caridad del Cobre*. Santiago de Cuba: Imprenta de la Viuda e Hijos de Espinal.

Pérez, Louis A. 1988. *Cuba: Between Reform and Revolution*. New York: Oxford University Press.

———. 1989. *Lords of the Mountain: Social Banditry and Peasant Protest in Cuba, 1878– 1918*. Pittsburgh, Pa.: University of Pittsburgh Press.

Pérez de la Riva, Francisco. [1952] 1979. "Cuban Palenques." In Richard Price, ed., *Maroon Societies: Rebel Slave Communities in the Americas*, 49–59. Baltimore, Md.: Johns Hopkins University Press.

Pérez Firmat, Gustavo. 1989. *The Cuban Condition: Translation and Identity in Modern Cuban Literature*. New York: Cambridge University Press.

Pérez Guzmán, Francisco. 1990. "Modo de vida de esclavos y forzados en las fortificaciones de Cuba: siglo XVIII." *Anuario de Estudios Americanos*, vol. XLVII, 241–57.

Perry, Mary Elizabeth. 1990. *Gender and Disorder in Early Modern Seville*. Princeton, N.J.: Princeton University Press.

Pike, Ruth. 1983. *Penal Servitude in Early Modern Spain*. Madison: University of Wisconsin Press.

Popular Memory Group. 1982. "Popular Memory: Theory, Politics, Method." In Richard Johnson et al., eds., *Making Histories: Studies in History Writing and Politics*. London: Hutchinson in assoc. with the Centre for Contemporary Studies, University of Birmingham.

Portuondo Zúñiga, Olga. 1993. "La Virgen de la Caridad: mito, historia y cultura nacional." *Del Caribe* 21: 62–66.

———. 1995. *La Virgen de la Caridad: símbolo de cubanía*. Santiago de Cuba: Editorial Oriente.

Price, Richard, ed. [1973] 1979. *Maroon Societies: Rebel Slave Communities in the Americas*. Baltimore, Md.: Johns Hopkins University Press.

———. 1990. *Alabi's World*. Baltimore, Md.: Johns Hopkins University Press.

Rosaldo, Renato. 1986. "From the Door of His Tent: The Fieldworker and the Inquisitor." In James Clifford and George E. Marcus, eds., *Writing Culture*, 77–97. Berkeley and Los Angeles: University of California Press.

Rubial García, Antonio. 1993. "Los santos milagreros y malogrados de la Nueva España." In Clara García Ayluardo and Manuel Ramos Medina, eds., *Manifestaciones religiosas en el mundo colonial americano*, vol. 1:71–105. Mexico: UIA Dept. of Historia; INAH, Dirección de Estudios Históricos; CONDUMEX, Centro de Estudios de Historia de Mexico.

Russell-Wood, A. J. R. 1972. "Colonial Brazil." In David W. Cohen and Jack P.

Greene, eds., *Neither Slave Nor Free*, 84–133. Baltimore: Johns Hopkins University Press.

———. 1973. "Black and Mulatto Brotherhoods in Colonial Brazil: A Study of Collective Behavior." *Hispanic American Historical Review* 54: 567–602.

———. 1982. *The Black Man in Slavery and Freedom in Colonial Brazil*. New York: St. Martin's Press.

Saunders, A. C. de C. M. 1982. *A Social History of Black Slavery and Freedmen in Portugal, 1441–1555*. New York: Cambridge University Press.

Sánchez Lussón, José. 1996. "Los cordoneros de orilé: presencia histórica y alcance cultural en Manzanillo." *Del Caribe* 25: 20–22.

Scott, James C. 1972. "Patron-Client Politics and Political Change in Southeast Asia." *American Political Science Review* 66: 91–113.

———. 1985. *Weapons of the Weak*. New Haven, Conn.: Yale University Press.

Scott, Rebecca J. 1985. *Slave Emancipation in Cuba: The Transition to Free Labor, 1860–1899*. Princeton, N.J.: Princeton University Press.

Sharp, William F. 1976. *Slavery on the Spanish Frontier: The Colombian Chocó, 1680–1810*. Norman: University of Oklahoma Press.

Schwartz, Stuart B. 1974. "Patterns of Slaveholding in the Americas: New Evidence from Brazil." *American Historical Review* 54: 603–35.

———. 1985. *Sugar Plantations in the Formation of Brazilian Society*. Cambridge Latin American Series, no. 52. Cambridge: Cambridge University Press.

———. 1992. *Slaves, Peasants, and Rebels: Reconsidering Brazilian Slavery*. Chicago: University of Illinois Press.

Smith, Lois, and Alfred Padula. 1996. *Sex and Revolution: Women in Socialist Cuba*. Oxford: Oxford University Press.

Smith, Raymond T. [1955] 1971. "Land Tenure in Three Negro Villages in British Guiana." In Michael M. Horowitz, ed., *Peoples and Cultures of the Caribbean*, 243–66. Garden City, N.Y.: The Natural History Press.

———. 1996. *The Matrifocal Family: Power, Pluralism, and Politics*. New Brunswick, N.J.: Rutgers University Press.

Spalding, Karen. 1984. *Huarochirí: An Andean Society Under Inca and Spanish Rule*. Stanford, Calif.: Stanford University Press.

Stern, Steve J. 1982. *Peru's Indian Peoples and the Challenge of Spanish Conquest: Huamanga to 1640*. Madison: University of Wisconsin Press.

Stevens-Arroyo, Anthony M. 1998. "The Evolution of Marian Devotionalism within Christianity and the Ibero-Mediterranean Polity." *Journal for the Scientific Study of Religion* 37: 50–73.

Strickton, Arnold, and Sidney M. Greenfield, eds. 1979. *Structure and Process in Latin America: Patronage, Clientage, and Power Systems*. Albuquerque: University of New Mexico Press.

Stubbs, Jean. 1985. *Tobacco in the Periphery: A Case Study in Cuban Labour History, 1860–1958*. Cambridge: Cambridge University Press.

Tannenbaum, Frank. 1947. *Slave and Citizen: The Negro in the Americas*. New York: Alfred A. Knopf.

Taylor, William B. 1970. "The Foundation of Nuestra Señora de Guadalupe de los Morenos de Ampa." *The Americas* 26: 442–46.

———. 1972. *Landlord and Peasant in Colonial Oaxaca*. Stanford, Calif.: Stanford University Press.

———. 1996. *Magistrates of the Sacred: Priests and Parishioners in Eighteenth-Century Mexico*. Stanford, Calif.: Stanford University Press.

Thornton, John K. 1983. *The Kingdom of Kongo: Civil War and Transition, 1641–1718*. Madison: University of Wisconsin Press.

———. 1993. "Central African Names and African-American Naming Patterns." *The William and Mary Quarterly* L, no. 4: 727–42.

———. 1998. *The Kongolese Saint Anthony: Dona Beatriz Kimpa Vita and the Antonian Movement, 1684–1706*. Cambridge: Cambridge University Press.

Tomich, Dale W. 1990. *Slavery in the Circuit of Sugar: Martinique and the World Economy, 1830–1848*. Baltimore, Md.: Johns Hopkins University Press.

———. 1993. "Une Petite Guinée: Provision Ground and Plantation in Martinique, 1830–1860." In Ira Berlin and Philip D. Morgan, eds., *Cultivation and Culture: Labor and the Shaping of Slave Life in the Americas*, 221–42. Charlottesville: University Press of Virginia.

Turner, Mary, ed. 1995. *From Chattel Slaves to Wage Slaves: The Dynamics of Labor and Bargaining in the Americas*. Bloomington: Indiana University Press.

Tweed, Thomas A. 1997. *Our Lady of the Exile: Diasporic Religion at a Cuban Catholic Shrine in Miami*. New York: Oxford University Press.

Urrutia y Montoya de, Ignacio. [1791] 1963. *Teatro histórico, jurídico y político militar de la isla de Fernandina de Cuba y principalmente de su capital*. Havana: Comisión Nacional Cubana de la UNESCO.

Vargas Ugarte, Rubén. 1956. *Historia del culto de María en Ibero-América y de sus imágenes y santuarios más celebrados*. 3d ed. Madrid: Talleres Gráficos Jura.

Vassberg, David E. 1984. *Land and Society in Golden Age Castile*. Cambridge: Cambridge University Press.

Voelz, Peter M. 1993. *Slave and Soldier: The Military Impact of Blacks in the Colonial Americas*. New York: Garland Publishing Inc.

Warner, Marina. 1976. *Alone in All Her Sex: The Myth and the Cult of the Virgin of Mary*. New York: Alfred A. Knopf.

Weaver, P. R. C. 1972. *Familia Caesaris: A Social Study of the Emperor's Freedmen and Slaves*. Cambridge: Cambridge University Press.

Weber, Eugen. 1976. *Peasants into Frenchmen: The Modernization of Rural France, 1870–1914*. Stanford, Calif.: Stanford University Press.

Wood, Betty. 1995. *Women's Work, Men's Work: The Informal Slave Economies of Low Country Georgia*. Athens: University of Georgia Press.

Wright, Irene A. 1916. *The Early History of Cuba, 1492–1586*. New York: Macmillan.

———. 1922. "Our Lady of Charity: Nuestra Señora de la Caridad de Cobre (Santiago de Cuba), Nuestra Señora de la Caridad de Illescas (Castilla, Spain)." *Hispanic American Historical Review* 5: 709–17.

Zimdars-Swartz, Sandra. 1991. *Encountering Mary: From La Salette to Madjugorje*. Princeton, N.J.: Princeton University Press.

Index

Index

Index